Management and Restoration of Fluvi
Broad Historical Changes and Hun

edited by

L. Allan James
Geography Department
University of South Carolina
Columbia, South Carolina 29208
USA

Sara L. Rathburn
Department of Geosciences
Colorado State University
Fort Collins, Colorado 80523
USA

G. Richard Whittecar
Old Dominion University
Norfolk, Virginia 23529
USA

THE
GEOLOGICAL
SOCIETY
OF AMERICA®

Special Paper 451

3300 Penrose Place, P.O. Box 9140 ▪ Boulder, Colorado 80301-9140, USA

2009

Published by The Geological Society of America, Inc.
3300 Penrose Place, P.O. Box 9140, Boulder, Colorado 80301-9140, USA
www.geosociety.org

Printed in U.S.A.

GSA Books Science Editors: Marion E. Bickford and Donald I. Siegel

Library of Congress Cataloging-in-Publication Data

Management and restoration of fluvial systems with broad historical changes and human impacts /
    edited by L. Allan James, Sara L. Rathburn, G. Richard Whittecar.
        p. cm. — (Special paper ; 451)
    Includes bibliographical references and index.
    ISBN 978-0-8137-2451-5 (pbk.)
        1. River engineering—United States—History. 2. Soil erosion—United States—History.
    3. Nature—Effect of human beings on—United States—History. 4. Rivers—United States—
    Regulation—Environmental aspects—History. 5. Fluvial geomorphology—United States—History.
    I. James, L. Allan. II. Rathburn, Sara L., 1962–. III. Whittecar, George Richard, 1952–.
    TC423.M28 2009
    627'.12—dc22

                                                                          2008046779

Cover, front: Infrared aerial photo of Po River, Italy, in 1977. This reach (upstream from Torino) has experienced mining activity and a recent meander cutoff. Flow is to top of image. Photo provided by Ornella Turitto. Photo used with permission from CNR-IRPI (Consiglio Nazionale delle Ricerche–Istituto di Recerca per la Protezione Idrogeologica) of Turin, Italy. **Back cover, above:** Redwood Creek, California, USA: Looking upstream at eroding fine-grained flood deposits dating from 1964, with coarsened bar in foreground at cross section 23 of Madej and Ozaki paper (Chapter 3). For scale, survey rod is 7.6 m (25 ft) tall. Photo by Vicki Ozaki. **Back cover, below:** Stream gauging on Redwood Creek, California. Photo by Robert Belous, National Park Service.

10 9 8 7 6 5 4 3 2 1

Contents

Introduction: Managing rivers with broad historical changes and human impacts

L. Allan James

Geography Department, University of South Carolina, Columbia, South Carolina 29208, USA

Sara L. Rathburn

Department of Geosciences, Colorado State University, Fort Collins, Colorado 80523, USA

G. Richard Whittecar

Old Dominion University, Norfolk, Virginia 23529, USA

Growing concerns over global environmental change, water resources, river restoration, and sustainable river management are focusing attention on the human dimension of fluvial systems. This Geological Society of America (GSA) Special Paper presents a set of studies and interpretations of river-channel change that reflect modern viewpoints of river management in the twenty-first century. It seeks to bridge a rich body of literature borne of late-twentieth-century river studies based in classic concepts of fluvial geomorphology with modern studies of river management and restoration, integrated watershed science, modern fluvial geomorphology, and historical channel-change reconstructions. Collectively, the papers document or recognize extensive changes to fluvial systems over a prolonged period, present analytical methods that can be used to examine and understand fluvial systems, and examine or recommend policies for river management and restoration.

BACKGROUND

The papers in this Special Paper were drawn from presentations in Topical Session 17 at the GSA Annual Meeting in Denver, 28–31 October 2007. The title of the topical session was the same as this volume: *Management and Restoration of Fluvial Systems with Broad Historical Changes and Human Impacts*. In addition to inviting selected authors and keynote speakers, the themes and structure of the session were listed by the GSA prior to the meeting, and many authors volunteered papers through this open forum. The favorable response and high level of commitment received from senior scientists and scholars, and the wide range of topics covered, indicate a strong, diverse interest in long-term anthropogenic changes to watersheds and river responses, and rapid growth in the field of river management and restoration. The session drew 34 presentations, including 8 posters and 2 oral paper sessions consisting of 26 papers. The oral papers concluded with a spirited panel discussion.

PANEL DISCUSSION

A panel consisting of Peter Downs, Faith Fitzpatrick, Will Graf, Jim Pizzuto, Ellen Wohl, and Bill Renwick made several important points and raised just as many questions concerning long-term human impacts on rivers and the implications for river management. The discussion began with comments by Bill Renwick, Faith Fitzpatrick, Greg Pasternack, Cliff Hupp, Jim Pizzuto, Peter Downs, and others about the importance of impoundments and legacy sediment to sediment regimes and how this factor has changed through time and space. The question of scale is an important aspect of this issue. The importance of large reservoirs to downstream sediment loadings on large rivers has long been recognized. More recently, however, the extensive nature of small headwater impoundments such as farm ponds and mill dams on intermediate-order drainages has come to be recognized. To many environmental scientists—such as those concerned with total maximum daily loads (TMDLs)—all sediment is treated as a pollutant. This perspective is in conflict with the need to introduce sediment to sediment-starved reaches below impoundments or where coarse sediment needs to be recruited to replenish spawning gravels on riffles and bars. This conflicting view toward sediment illustrates the need to recognize unique situations; attempts to prescribe a universal approach (e.g., sediment reduction) to river management may fail to restore needed ecological functions if they do not match specific local or regional geomorphic situations.

The panel discussion next turned to a stimulating dialogue about river-management policy. Robb Jacobson noted how the "democratization" of resource management raises issues of decision making based on limited scientific understanding and may result in policies that treat all rivers alike. Will Graf described a case in which scientists and stakeholders met in two separate groups, then later met together to develop solutions. This procedure took 6 yr to complete, but the result was successful.

James, L.A., Rathburn, S.L., and Whittecar, G.R., 2009, Introduction: Managing rivers with broad historical changes and human impacts, *in* James, L.A., Rathburn, S.L., and Whittecar, G.R., eds., Management and Restoration of Fluvial Systems with Broad Historical Changes and Human Impacts: Geological Society of America Special Paper 451, p. v–x, doi: 10.1130/2009.2451(00).

When discussion shifted to the diversity of goals and philosophies of river restoration, Jack Schmidt pointed out that biologists may regard channel geomorphic features merely as a substrate to support species, whereas geomorphologists see them as a product of dynamic river processes that should be allowed to operate. Pat McDowell indicated that reach-scale restoration projects may not be resilient and are vulnerable to failure over the long term. Much could be learned from the history of ecosystem management, which has long embraced landscape-scale approaches to natural systems. Thus, the conversation turned back again to issues of scale, as Will Graf pointed out how projects of larger extent have a greater difficulty of surviving the budgetary appraisal process. These concepts of developing flexible policy guidelines based on sound science to integrate human impacts over watershed spatial scales and centennial temporal scales formed an appropriate summation of the sessions and a springboard for this volume.

OBJECTIVES OF THIS SPECIAL PAPER

Recognition of the complexity, potential anthropogenic contributions, and dynamics of fluvial system change at time scales up to a few centuries is essential to the proper management of river systems. This recognition, along with methods and strategies for managing rivers in this context, is the primary theme of this volume. In many watersheds, long-term anthropogenic changes—such as deforestation, cultivation, fires, urbanization, road construction, and mining—initially resulted in widespread increases in runoff generation, flood magnitudes, erosion, and sedimentation. These changes to watersheds indirectly affect river channels. In addition, direct alterations to channels include dams, levees, channelization, bank protection, instream mining, and removal of vegetation or large woody debris. In many basins, subsequent changes may have initiated relaxation from an earlier period of disruption. For example, reforestation in many regions has reversed the trend away from increased runoff and erosion. In a different sense, dam construction has locally or regionally reversed some effects of increased sediment production by trapping sediment in upstream reaches. In addition to the perturbations and subsequent relaxation from changes, the effects of climate change should be factored into an understanding of watershed processes that drive channel changes.

Several of the studies in this volume are concerned with long-term fluvial changes that recognize the cumulative impacts of human activities over periods that span several generations and up to multiple centuries. Most of the studies are broad in scope and adopt a modern watershed perspective that is both spatially and process integrated. Many also recognize that long-term land-use and land-cover changes, as well as legacy sediment, can be strongly related to modern river processes. These studies provide examples of why attempts to manage or rehabilitate rivers should seek to identify linkages between broad watershed processes and river behavior. Understanding geomorphic and hydrologic changes to surface-water and sediment systems is an essential prerequisite to devising viable management strategies for maintaining stable but dynamic and diverse channels, floodplains, and aquatic ecosys-

tems in a pseudo-natural state, and for anticipating and mitigating further changes. The papers in this volume are divided into three sections related to the implications of historical changes to managing and restoring river systems:

    I. Large-Scale, Long-Term Sediment and Geomorphic Changes
    II. Hydrologic Considerations for River Restoration
    III. River Management and Restoration

The first section emphasizes changes in sediment loadings through time and historical geomorphic changes in rivers. It purveys the extensive nature of changes that characterize many river systems, and how these changes continue to determine modern river processes. The second section is concerned with hydrologic changes and how they may drive river processes, or methods of evaluating them. The final section presents papers that evaluate the success or examine the feasibility of stream restoration. Throughout the volume a recurrent theme of the papers is the pervasive nature of human impacts on river systems and how river management should be keenly sensitive to this legacy.

Divisions between these sections are not absolute, and several of the papers overlap the categories. Although all such classifications have limitations, this structure provides the basis and context from which broader implications can be derived from the papers. The sequence of the sections establishes the background of pervasive change to fluvial systems, followed by examples of hydrologic factors that often drive changes in sediment and geomorphology. Finally, examples of the effectiveness or feasibility of stream restoration provide a reality check for river managers who seek to adopt restoration practices. The brevity of this volume constrains the ability to address all of the topics in detail, and the intent is not to provide a comprehensive treatment of these subjects but a sampling only. The remainder of this introduction briefly describes these three sections of the volume and the papers that are included in them.

LARGE-SCALE, LONG-TERM SEDIMENT AND GEOMORPHIC CHANGES

The first section presents examples of long-term or broadly extensive changes to watersheds—often human-induced—that drive channel changes in streams and rivers. The emphasis on sediment loads in most of the papers reflects the importance of sediment to geomorphic form, which in turn drives other river functions such as habitat diversity. Sediment dynamics are difficult to measure but have often changed substantially over time and can be critical to proper river management and robust restoration strategies. These papers demonstrate the importance of changing sediment regimes over time, and the need to understand the history of these changes in order to anticipate responses to management policies. The perspective that change is the rule, rather than the exception, is important to most river restoration or management planning. The assumptions that changes in sediment loadings and channel morphology have been minor, and that pristine reference reaches exist that can be emulated to design stable yet "natural" reengineered reaches, should both be critically evaluated on a case-by-case basis.

These papers also demonstrate the importance of a watershed-scale analysis sensitive to historical legacies. A disconnection often exists between river management or restoration efforts performed at the river-reach scale and the processes governing fluvial systems that operate at a broader basin scale. Without an understanding of the spatially distributed nature of hydro-geomorphic processes operating over a centennial time scale, local restoration efforts may be prone to failure. The eight papers in this section impart an appreciation for this spatially and temporally broad-scale perspective of substantial change. The importance of interactions between present and historical sediment budgets, channel morphology, and engineering works is made clear in the first paper.

Jacobson et al. (this volume) note the influence of dams and bank protection on spatial patterns of sedimentation, suspended sediment loads, and channel morphology in the Lower Missouri River. The history of channel engineering in the Lower Missouri River includes construction of the largest reservoir storage system in North America and bank stabilization and channelization projects between 1930 and 1960. Altered sediment regimes below dams impose constraints on river restoration and management options, and the ability to manage dam releases to compensate for those altered regimes is severely limited. The reservoir system has reduced downstream flow variability and sediment loads, and reservoir operation policies aimed at managing sediment must contend with uncertainty in how channels will respond. This uncertainty calls for a better understanding of present and historical sediment fluxes.

Using observed fluxes on the mainstem of the Lower Missouri River, Jacobson et al. compute suspended sediment budgets that reveal distinct temporal and spatial changes. At Yankton, South Dakota, below Gavins Point Dam, post-dam suspended sediment loads (1994–2006) were only 0.2% of pre-dam values. This proportion increased downstream to 11% at Omaha, Nebraska, and 17% at Hermann, Missouri. Tributaries are key contributors to mainstem sediment loads below the dams. The amount of sediment contributed by tributaries decreased between 1948 and 1952 and 1994 and 2006 owing largely to improved land-conservation practices in tributary watersheds. Bank stabilization (1930–1960) reduced channel top widths by two-thirds, the sequestering of sediment preferentially removed sand from the suspended load, and commercial channel mining continues to remove much sand. Textures of the active load, therefore, have fined downstream and through time. Most channels responded to reduced sediment loads with bed incision, which decreased lateral connectivity between channels and floodplains. Aquatic habitat restoration—active since 1984—was stimulated in 2003 by mandates to restore and increase shallow-water habitats (SWH) and emergent sandbars. Naturalized reservoir releases with periodic high flows will be used to laterally connect channels with floodplains, build emergent sandbars, and increase SWH. Pulsed reservoir releases are constrained by flood risks in low-lying lands below Omaha where channels have not incised. Sandy sediment derived from excavations and placed in the channel to improve SWH will contribute ~34×10^6 Mg yr^{-1} to the main channel over the next 15 yr; i.e., ~62% of the 1994–2006 suspended sediment budget. This planned project raises questions of the capac-

ity of the river to carry the increased load. Given the complexities and constraints of the Lower Missouri system, the authors recommend concentrating restoration efforts in zones where they will be most effective with regard to costs and sustainable benefits.

Fitzpatrick et al. (this volume) demonstrate the pervasive nature of change to fluvial and wetland systems brought about by sedimentation derived from agricultural forest clearance and engineering works in an upper Midwestern watershed over the past 160 yr. The study was initiated to identify restoration alternatives. It demonstrates the need to understand the history and geomorphic evolution of a system rather than simply basing restoration strategies on channel morphology that was fundamentally changed from low to high banks by human-induced sedimentation. They cite sediment cores, geochemical dating, historical aerial photographs, and other evidence to constrain sedimentation rates and locations. Peak volumetric overbank sedimentation rates to the marsh occurred from 1919 to 1936, owing primarily to agricultural practices. These rates were seven times greater than modern rates (1994–2006), which are, in turn, more than four times rates during the early settlement period from 1846 to 1885. A full understanding of sedimentation and channel morphologic change requires knowledge of the history of levees, railroad embankments, dams, and channelization in the area.

Madej and Ozaki (this volume) emphasize the longevity of geomorphic impacts of massive sedimentation events in the gravel-bed Redwood Creek, California, caused by a series of ~25-yr flood events in the 1950s through 1975. Based on a data set collected over the past 30 yr, they examine the effects of a 1997 10-yr flood event on channels recovering from the earlier sedimentation. Comprehensive field measurements are used to document protracted sediment reworking after three decades. Over the long term, channel incision is characterized by decelerating rates of bed lowering that define an exponential decay rate from progressive bed armoring. Spatial patterns of recovery are nonuniform in the basin; sediment evacuation in the upper basin has been relatively rapid compared with that downstream. Pool depths and frequencies increased through time until they were partially refilled by the 1997 flood. Little is known about how quickly gravel-bed rivers in mountainous forested basins recover from episodic sedimentation. The observed pattern of punctuated recovery of the channel system is important, therefore, to river managers and restoration scientists, who should consider the feasibility of passive restoration; i.e., letting nature do the work.

James et al. (this volume) contrast styles of channel change and recovery between two rivers that were managed by distinctly different policies beginning in the late nineteenth century. Historical reconstructions of the lower Yuba and Feather Rivers—severely impacted by hydraulic mining sedimentation—are based on evaluations of a large number of historical maps and aerial photographs and high-resolution 1999 LiDAR-sonar composite topographic data. Both the timing and styles of geomorphic responses were markedly dissimilar in the two rivers owing to contrasting engineering strategies practiced from the 1880s through the mid-twentieth century. These watersheds represent the earliest example of federally sponsored river-basin management west of the Mississippi River, so this post-project evaluation documents the consequences of one of the longest-running river-engineering experiments in the western United States.

Surian et al. (this volume) present a European perspective of long-term anthropogenic channel morphological changes in the context of Italian rivers. They use historical maps, aerial photographs, and field survey data to examine changes in dimensionless channel width (W/W_{max}) and bed elevation over the past 200 yr in 12 rivers, seven heading in the Alps and five in the Apennines. Changing sediment loads were the primary causes of channel change, but this relationship was driven by factors that varied within and between watersheds and through time. Most channels underwent a long period of incision and narrowing that began in the late nineteenth century and lasted well into the twentieth century. This incision was driven largely by human activities, beginning with levees, followed by bank protection and reforestation. Incision intensified from 1950 to the 1980s with dam construction and gravel mining. The incision processes have reversed or stabilized over the past 15 to 20 yr in most rivers. In light of the extreme changes to these rivers, the authors do not recommend trying to use channel conditions prior to human disturbances as a reference for restoration. They call for a focus on sediment management in severely impacted fluvial systems such as these.

Hupp et al. (this volume) present measurements of modern bank erosion and floodplain sedimentation rates in the Roanoke River, on the Coastal Plain of North Carolina, USA. They use erosion pins, repeated transects, clay pads, and other techniques to evaluate bank stability and floodplain deposition, and for development of a sediment budget for 153 km of the river downstream of two dams built in 1953 and 1963. Channel widening (net bank erosion) occurred on 90 transects, whereas only 12 transects display narrowing (net deposition). The zone of most rapid overall bank retreat has apparently progressed downstream through the upper reaches near the dams. Bank retreat is now greatest in the middle reaches of the study area, where mean annual rates on transects were found to be 63 mm yr^{-1} compared with 44 mm yr^{-1} upstream near the dams, and 24 mm yr^{-1} farther downstream (not including mass wasting events). High low-flow river stages after dam construction have concentrated fluvial bank erosion on the lower banks. This bank undercutting has encouraged mass wasting of mid- and upper banks composed largely of historical alluvium. Bank mass wasting, which was not well represented in the sediment budget, is suggested as an explanation for a large sediment surplus—deposition on lower Roanoke floodplains in excess of bank erosion—of approximately 2.8 10^6 m^3 yr^{-1}.

Güneralp and Rhoads (this volume) demonstrate a multi-methodological approach, including the use of a variety of geospatial methods, to compute stream powers, map lateral migration locations, estimate migration rates, and evaluate bank stabilization and stream restoration potential. They analyze channel planform changes over a 60-yr period in seven 5- to 10-km stream reaches in the Kishwaukee River watershed in northern Illinois, using a geographic information systems (GIS)-based channel-change detection with historical aerial photographs. Cross-sectional stream power (total power per unit flow width) correlates with lateral migration rates. None of the reaches had mean bankfull stream powers as high as 35 W m^{-2}, the threshold for meander recovery often noted in the literature. Local stream powers were also less than the threshold except in one steep headwater watershed, where they were as high as 63 W m^{-2}. In spite of stream powers below the threshold for meander recovery, most reaches underwent substantial lateral planation, and spatial patterns of channel migration were strongly related to stream power. The authors conclude that historical evaluations of channel change and computations of stream power provide important river-management tools.

Gran et al. (this volume) examine sediment loads in the Le Sueur River, an agriculture-dominated tributary to the Minnesota River, in the upper Midwest, USA. They take a long-term perspective by comparing mean Holocene production rates of suspended sediment in the watershed with modern low-turbidity management goals. Sediment production in the Le Sueur River is strongly influenced by the geomorphic history of the basin. Deep knickpoints were initiated by regional post-glacial base-level lowering associated with the catastrophic drainage of glacial Lake Agassiz. These knickpoints have eroded headward 30 to 35 km over ~11,500 yr and are now located in the lower reaches of all three main tributaries of the Le Sueur. Calculations of Holocene sediment production rates, based on topographic analyses of post–glacial valley formation using high-resolution LiDAR data, indicate that modern sediment loads are 1.3 to 3.4 times higher than the average load over the past 11,500 yr BP. These modern rates compare with a tenfold increase in regional post–European-settlement production rates based on sedimentation in Lake Pepin. The watershed can be divided into agricultural uplands above the knickpoints, and a lower incised zone dominated by steep bluffs and ravines that contributes from 61% to 74% of the total basin sediment. The watershed now contributes a disproportionate amount of sediment to the Minnesota River and Lake Pepin largely from sediment produced in the deeply incised channels. Total suspended solid (TSS) loads are an order of magnitude greater than regulatory standards, so this spatial knowledge is important for targeting remedial measures.

HYDROLOGIC CONSIDERATIONS FOR RIVER RESTORATION

The three studies in this section provide examples of the importance of hydrology to river systems. Hydrologic influences are key to many watershed problems, and methods of analyzing hydrologic inputs and outputs are welcome additions to most river managers' tool boxes. Hydrology may drive biogeomorphic factors through flow frequencies or connectivity and may govern sediment loads, channel morphology, water quality, and aquatic ecology. The first paper begins with a broad consideration of channel changes in semiarid streams that are largely influenced by flow regulation and diversions. It includes a case study of refuge pools in headwater streams that can be linked to groundwater during low-flow periods. The second paper proposes a method for determining appropriate flow releases from reservoirs. The third paper utilizes a method of analyzing annual maximum flow data to detect spatial and temporal change. The first two papers are concerned with providing guidance for management of river environments, whereas the third paper is more concerned with demonstrating hydrologic change and a method for quantifying this change.

Wohl et al. (this volume) review historical fluvial changes in the Great Plains. They demonstrate the need to study rivers as spatially heterogeneous systems rather than as disjunct reaches. The paper considers a broad array of management factors and implications of low flows, such as water allocation, water-table fluctuations, biology, and riparian vegetation composition. The authors place emphasis on the seasonal lack of longitudinal connectivity on small intermittent headwater streams that have received less attention than larger, perennial Great Plains rivers. These pools are essential to the fragile ecosystems of small ephemeral rivers. Regionally, intensive groundwater withdrawals have reduced the volume and longitudinal connectivity of refuge pools that provide important habitat for native aquatic species. A case study within Pawnee National Grasslands illustrates the challenges of preserving refuge pools as an integral part of the riverscape of the western Great Plains. A lack of statistical correlations between biological activity and most physical pool characteristics or location within the drainage network leads the authors to recommend that programs aimed at sustaining ecological systems should concentrate on pool size. They suggest that management strategies should focus on protecting larger pools from consumptive water use.

Rathburn et al. (this volume) develop a four-step method for identifying appropriate environmental flows needed to control sediment transport and vegetation. The method is aimed at integrating dam-operating policies with river management to ensure environmental flows that meet conservation targets. Flows along the North Fork Cache La Poudre River in north-central Colorado are characterized using a method that links sediment-transporting events and riparian vegetation composition and structure to specific flow recurrence intervals. Results of a hydrologic analysis, coupled with the sediment and riparian vegetation data, quantify the in-channel and overbank flows necessary to maintain channel processes and ecologically healthy riparian areas. Developing rational dam-operating policies that ensure appropriate environmental flows is an example of the emerging science of active river management for restoration purposes. Environmental flow standards developed by interdisciplinary teams of scientists can quantify the complex system processes responsible for maintaining ecological health within fluvial systems. These efforts to quantitatively link river flow to conservation priorities as a means of managing riverine ecosystems represent a turning point in how societies view and value regulated rivers.

Galster (this volume) uses extensive U.S. Geological Survey (USGS) gauging data from U.S. rivers to evaluate the rate at which peak annual discharge increases downstream with drainage area. Most of the studied rivers flow out of the Appalachian Mountains in the eastern USA. The discharge-area relationship is often assumed to be linear; i.e., a log-log (power function) relationship in which the exponent is approximately equal to 1.0. Results of this study, however, indicate a nonlinear or secular trend in time with most of the basins.

Many rivers had exponents <0.75, indicating greater runoff generation and conveyance in tributaries than in larger rivers downstream. Many other rivers demonstrated substantial changes in discharge-area relationships through time primarily from dams, urbanization, and other land-use changes. Documenting linkages between the instrumental hydrologic record and channel morphology has been a prominent enterprise in fluvial geomorphology for several generations. These findings and the method of analysis have important implications for river management and policy, particularly given the limited flow data for most watersheds. Drainage area is often used as a proxy for discharge in hydrologic models, flood-hazard analyses, channel-stability computations, ecological-habitat evaluations, and other planning tools, but assuming a linear relationship between discharge and drainage area should be done with caution.

RIVER MANAGEMENT AND RESTORATION

The papers in this section provide scientific findings relevant to river management and restoration policy. Few post-project studies have been conducted of restored river reaches, so much is to be learned about which restoration methods are most appropriate, and which river reaches are most likely to be geomorphically durable or ecologically viable. The first two papers in this section provide detailed examinations of restored river reaches that should be a welcomed addition to the restoration literature. The third paper provides clear insights into the reasoning involved in selecting reference reaches and viable sites for restoration. Collectively, these three papers provide much-needed information about the relatively young science of river restoration.

Elliot and Capesius (this volume) analyze geomorphic changes along high-gradient rivers at sites on three "reclaimed" reaches in Colorado monitored for the USGS Reconfigured-Channel Monitoring and Assessment Program (RCMAP). Repeated cross-section surveys in these gravel-bed rivers document changes to banks, bars, and channels and constructed boulder and log structures following 4- and 6-yr floods at two of the sites. The authors provide quantitative hydraulic information about flow environments and grain size. Boundary shear stresses for floods are computed using the Hydrologic Engineering Centers River Analysis System (HEC-RAS) model, and critical shear stresses for median sediment size are computed using Shield's criteria. The ratio of these values (τ_o/τ_c) is used to estimate the sediment-entrainment potential for a given cross section. Use of this ratio and recognition of areas with excessive flood boundary shear stress, relative to the resistive force of the sediment, often explain the spatial patterns of bank erosion and streambed deposition and scour observed at the monitored sites. The quantitative approach, coupled with abundant field data and thorough documentation, makes this paper a valuable contribution to stream restoration science.

Chin et al. (this volume) examine two small step-pool stream channels in California as unique case studies evaluating the ecological potential of step-pool restoration. The two streams, restored in 1996 and 2003, were examined for geomorphic stability of the step-pool systems and characteristics of benthic macro-invertebrates present. Geomorphic stability has been maintained through storms exceeding 14- to 20-yr recurrence intervals. The biological effectiveness of restoration by artificially manipulating step-pool systems was assessed through monitoring percentages of sensitive taxa to determine if ecologically viable environments were created. Comparisons were made across habitat types, to identify the most beneficial habitat, and across watersheds including a reference reach. Five to 12 yr after restoration the reference reach was found to have healthier ecological conditions and biological indicators than in the restored reaches, which were not significantly different than in unrestored reaches above or below the restored reaches.

Smith et al. (this volume) evaluate the effects on low-gradient rivers of extensive watershed disturbance in western Tennessee. Excessive sedimentation generated by deforestation and agricultural erosion on sandy uplands has induced complex channel and valley-bottom responses, including formation and growth of valley plugs, upstream migration of the zone of aggradation, and widespread flooding. Reformation of meanders owing to avulsions around plugs—sometimes reoccupying former channels—is identified as a form of passive self-restoration. Long-standing policies that promote extensive channelization and canal maintenance conflict with mandates to protect wetlands and restore streams. The authors' descriptions of river restoration efforts in this highly altered hydrologic setting, and the role of beaver and unmanaged channel avulsions in restoring natural conditions, provide lessons that should lead to more sustainable management programs.

CONCLUDING REMARKS

From the breadth of papers included in this volume, it is evident that many scientists are working on diverse fluvial systems to address timely questions relevant to river management and restoration. These studies reflect growing interests in environmental resources, ecological sustainability, and anthropogenic change that are driving modern movements in aquatic restoration and sustainable river management. The papers in this volume provide a repository of information that demonstrates the complexities of managing river systems that are responding to legacy conditions and that may have been highly altered by human activities. We hope this body of knowledge will benefit others by elucidating the historical and spatial dimensions of watershed processes that should be understood for decision making to be well informed. The challenge to river scientists is the need for continuing assessment of the broad historical changes to fluvial systems brought on by human and nonhuman factors in order to develop practical solutions and policies for sound management of river resources.

REFERENCES CITED

Chin, A., Purcell, A.H., Quan, J.W.Y., and Resh, V.H., 2009, this volume, Assessing geomorphological and ecological responses in restored step-pool systems, *in* James, L.A., Rathburn, S.L., and Whittecar, G.R., eds., Management and Restoration of Fluvial Systems with Broad Historical Changes and Human Impacts: Geological Society of America Special Paper 451, doi: 10.1130/2009.2451(13).

Elliott, J.G., and Capesius, J.P., 2009, this volume, Geomorphic changes resulting from floods in reconfigured gravel-bed river channels in Colorado, USA, *in*

James, L.A., Rathburn, S.L., and Whittecar, G.R., eds., Management and Restoration of Fluvial Systems with Broad Historical Changes and Human Impacts: Geological Society of America Special Paper 451, doi: 10.1130/2009.2451(12).

Fitzpatrick, F.A., Knox, J.C., and Schubauer-Berigan, J.P., 2009, this volume, Channel, floodplain, and wetland responses to floods and overbank sedimentation, 1846–2006, Halfway Creek Marsh, Upper Mississippi Valley, Wisconsin, *in* James, L.A., Rathburn, S.L., and Whittecar, G.R., eds., Management and Restoration of Fluvial Systems with Broad Historical Changes and Human Impacts: Geological Society of America Special Paper 451, doi: 10.1130/2009.2451(02).

Galster, J.C., 2009, this volume, Testing the linear relationship between peak annual river discharge and drainage area using long-term USGS river gauging records, *in* James, L.A., Rathburn, S.L., and Whittecar, G.R., eds., Management and Restoration of Fluvial Systems with Broad Historical Changes and Human Impacts: Geological Society of America Special Paper 451, doi: 10.1130/2009.2451(11).

Gran, K.B., Belmont, P., Day, S.S., Jennings, C., Johnson, A., Perg, L., and Wilcock, P.R., 2009, this volume, Geomorphic evolution of the Le Sueur River, Minnesota, USA, and implications for current sediment loading, *in* James, L.A., Rathburn, S.L., and Whittecar, G.R., eds., Management and Restoration of Fluvial Systems with Broad Historical Changes and Human Impacts: Geological Society of America Special Paper 451, doi: 10.1130/2009.2451(08).

Güneralp, İ., and Rhoads, B.L., 2009, this volume, Planform change and stream power in the Kishwaukee River watershed, Illinois: Geomorphic assessment for environmental management, *in* James, L.A., Rathburn, S.L., and Whittecar, G.R., eds., Management and Restoration of Fluvial Systems with Broad Historical Changes and Human Impacts: Geological Society of America Special Paper 451, doi: 10.1130/2009.2451(07).

Hupp, C.R., Schenk, E.R., Richter, J.M., Peet, R.K., and Townsend, P.A., 2009, this volume, Bank erosion along the dam-regulated lower Roanoke River, North Carolina, *in* James, L.A., Rathburn, S.L., and Whittecar, G.R., eds., Management and Restoration of Fluvial Systems with Broad Historical Changes and Human Impacts: Geological Society of America Special Paper 451, doi: 10.1130/2009.2451(06).

Jacobson, R.B., Blevins, D.W., and Bitner, C.J., 2009, this volume, Sediment regime constraints on river restoration—An example from the Lower Missouri River, *in* James, L.A., Rathburn, S.L., and Whittecar, G.R., eds., Management and Restoration of Fluvial Systems with Broad Historical Changes and Human Impacts: Geological Society of America Special Paper 451, doi: 10.1130/2009.2451(01).

James, L.A., Singer, M.B., Ghoshal, S., and Megison, M., 2009, this volume, Historical channel changes in the lower Yuba and Feather Rivers, California: Long-term effects of contrasting river-management strategies, *in* James, L.A., Rathburn, S.L., and Whittecar, G.R., eds., Management and Restoration of Fluvial Systems with Broad Historical Changes and Human Impacts: Geological Society of America Special Paper 451, doi: 10.1130/2009.2451(04).

Madej, M.A., and Ozaki, V., 2009, this volume, Persistence of effects of high sediment loading in a salmon-bearing river, northern California, *in* James, L.A., Rathburn, S.L., and Whittecar, G.R., eds., Management and Restoration of Fluvial Systems with Broad Historical Changes and Human Impacts: Geological Society of America Special Paper 451, doi: 10.1130/2009.2451(03).

Rathburn, S.L., Merritt, D.M., Wohl, E.E., Sanderson, J.S., and Knight, H.A.L., 2009, this volume, Characterizing environmental flows for maintenance of river ecosystems: North Fork Cache la Poudre River, Colorado, *in* James, L.A., Rathburn, S.L., and Whittecar, G.R., eds., Management and Restoration of Fluvial Systems with Broad Historical Changes and Human Impacts: Geological Society of America Special Paper 451, doi: 10.1130/2009.2451(10).

Smith, D.P., Diehl, T.H., Turrini-Smith, L.A., Maas-Baldwin, J., and Croyle, Z., 2009, this volume, River restoration strategies in channelized, low-gradient landscapes of West Tennessee, USA, *in* James, L.A., Rathburn, S.L., and Whittecar, G.R., eds., Management and Restoration of Fluvial Systems with Broad Historical Changes and Human Impacts: Geological Society of America Special Paper 451, doi: 10.1130/2009.2451(14).

Surian, N., Rinaldi, M., Pellegrini, L., Audisio, C., Maraga, F., Teruggi, L., Turitto, O., and Ziliani, L., 2009, this volume, Channel adjustments in northern and central Italy over the last 200 years, *in* James, L.A., Rathburn, S.L., and Whittecar, G.R., eds., Management and Restoration of Fluvial Systems with Broad Historical Changes and Human Impacts: Geological Society of America Special Paper 451, doi: 10.1130/2009.2451(05).

Wohl, E., Egenhoff, D., and Larkin, K., 2009, this volume, Vanishing riverscapes: A review of historical channel change on the western Great Plains, *in* James, L.A., Rathburn, S.L., and Whittecar, G.R., eds., Management and Restoration of Fluvial Systems with Broad Historical Changes and Human Impacts: Geological Society of America Special Paper 451, doi: 10.1130/2009.2451(09).

MANUSCRIPT ACCEPTED BY THE SOCIETY 15 SEPTEMBER 2008

The Geological Society of America
Special Paper 451
2009

Sediment regime constraints on river restoration—
An example from the Lower Missouri River

Robert B. Jacobson
U.S. Geological Survey, 4200 New Haven Road, Columbia, Missouri 65201, USA

Dale W. Blevins
U.S. Geological Survey, 401 NW Capital Drive, Lees Summit, Missouri 64086, USA

Chance J. Bitner
Kansas City District Corps of Engineers, 601 E. 12th Street, Kansas City, Missouri 64106, USA

ABSTRACT

Dammed rivers are subject to changes in their flow, water-quality, and sediment regimes. Each of these changes may contribute to diminished aquatic habitat quality and quantity. Of the three factors, an altered sediment regime is a particularly unyielding challenge on many dammed rivers. The magnitude of the challenge is illustrated on the Lower Missouri River, where the largest water storage system in North America has decreased the downriver suspended-sediment load to 0.2%–17% of pre-dam loads. In response to the altered sediment regime, the Lower Missouri River channel has incised as much as 3.5 m just downstream of Gavins Point Dam, although the bed has been stable to slightly aggrading at other locations farther downstream. Effects of channel engineering and commercial dredging are superimposed on the broad-scale adjustments to the altered sediment regime.

The altered sediment regime and geomorphic adjustments constrain restoration and management opportunities. Incision and aggradation limit some objectives of flow-regime management: In incising river segments, ecologically desirable reconnection of the floodplain requires discharges that are beyond operational limits, whereas in aggrading river segments, small spring pulses may inundate or saturate low-lying farmlands. Lack of sediment in the incising river segment downstream of Gavins Point Dam also limits sustainable restoration of sand-bar habitat for bird species listed under the Endangered Species Act. Creation of new shallow-water habitat for native fishes involves taking sediment out of floodplain storage and reintroducing most or all of it to the river, raising concerns about increased sediment, nutrient, and contaminant loads. Calculations indicate that effects of individual restoration projects are small relative to background loads, but cumulative effects may depend on sequence and locations of projects. An understanding of current and historical sediment fluxes, and how they vary along the river, provides a quantitative basis for defining management constraints and identifying opportunities.

Jacobson, R.B., Blevins, D.W., and Bitner, C.J., 2009, Sediment regime constraints on river restoration—An example from the Lower Missouri River, *in* James, L.A., Rathburn, S.L., and Whittecar, G.R., eds., Management and Restoration of Fluvial Systems with Broad Historical Changes and Human Impacts: Geological Society of America Special Paper 451, p. 1–22, doi: 10.1130/2009.2451(01). For permission to copy, contact editing@geosociety.org. ©2009 The Geological Society of America. All rights reserved.

INTRODUCTION

Dams profoundly affect flow regime, water-temperature regime, and fluxes of materials in river systems (Petts, 1989). Effects of dams on flow regime has attracted substantial analysis (Poff et al., 1997; Richter et al., 1997), and recent work has addressed designs of flow regimes to mitigate the effects of dams (Richter et al., 2006; Jacobson and Galat, 2008). Engineered solutions have been proposed to mitigate temperature effects (Rounds, 2007), water-quality effects (Bednarek and Hart, 2005; Sullivan and Rounds, 2006), and fish passage (Schilt, 2007).

Managing dams and the rivers downstream from dams, to mitigate for alterations of sediment fluxes, is considerably more challenging. This results in part from the difficulty of predicting channel responses to complex interactions among flow regime, sediment supply, and riparian vegetation (Williams and Wolman, 1984; Collier et al., 1996; Brandt, 2000; Schmidt and Wilcock, 2008). Difficulties also arise because many dams were not designed to permit sediment bypass (Yang, 2006).

Depending on the strength of interactions among flow regime, sediment regime, bank materials, channel slope, and riparian vegetation, channels downstream of dams may incise, aggrade, widen, narrow, stabilize, or increase rates of lateral erosion (Brandt, 2000; Grams and Schmidt, 2005; Schmidt and Wilcock, 2008). These changes may engender subsequent changes in economic or ecological values, such as increased or decreased inundation of valley-bottom lands, alterations of in-channel habitat quality and quantity, and erosional threats to property and infrastructure. For these reasons, dam-related changes to sediment fluxes are of concern to river managers and can be a substantive constraint to river restoration.

The Lower Missouri River (Fig. 1) presents a typical example of restoration and management challenges imposed by a profoundly altered sediment regime. This case study illustrates

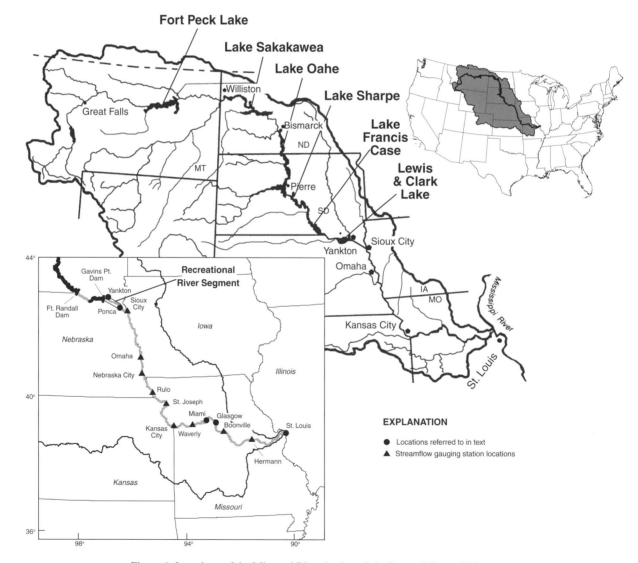

Figure 1. Locations of the Missouri River basin and the Lower Missouri River.

a set of issues common to management of many large, dammed rivers, including geomorphic responses to altered flow and sediment regimes, and how those responses constrain opportunities for restoration. We start with background on engineering of the Lower Missouri River and an assessment of pre-engineering and modern suspended-sediment fluxes. Restoration objectives are discussed in the context of the suspended-sediment flux and ongoing geomorphic adjustments of the channel to altered flow and sediment regimes.

ENGINEERING OF THE MISSOURI RIVER

The mainstem of the Missouri River is host to the largest reservoir system in North America, consisting of six reservoirs constructed between 1937 and 1963. The combined total storage is nearly 91 km³ (Galat et al., 2005b). The upstream-most reservoir in the system, Fort Peck, was closed first in 1937, followed by Fort Randall Dam (Lake Francis Case) in 1952, Garrison Dam (Lake Sakakawea) in 1953, Gavins Point Dam (Lewis and Clark Lake) in 1955, Oahe Dam (Lake Oahe) in 1958, and Big Bend Dam

(Lake Sharpe) in 1963. The system is managed for multiple purposes, including maintenance of navigation flows, flood control, hydropower, public water supply, recreation, and fish and wildlife resources (U.S. Army Corps of Engineers, 2004b). Regulation has resulted in substantial alteration to the flow regime downstream of the reservoirs, including reduced intra-annual flow variability with generally decreased spring pulses and increased summer low flows along the 1,300 km downstream of Gavins Point Dam (Galat and Lipkin, 2000). Hydrologic alteration diminishes downstream from the dams as less-regulated tributaries enter the Missouri River (Fig. 2). From Gavins Point Dam to the Platte River, annual variability is suppressed as spring pulsed flows are diminished and summer-fall flows are increased to support navigation (Sioux City and Nebraska City gauges; Fig. 2). The 590 km downstream of the Kansas River confluence (at Kansas City, Missouri) has increased summer low flows relative to natural levels but retains substantial intra-annual variability, including spring-summer flow pulses (Kansas City and Hermann gauges; Fig. 2).

Engineering of the Lower Missouri River channel began in the 1830s with clearing of large woody debris and some bank

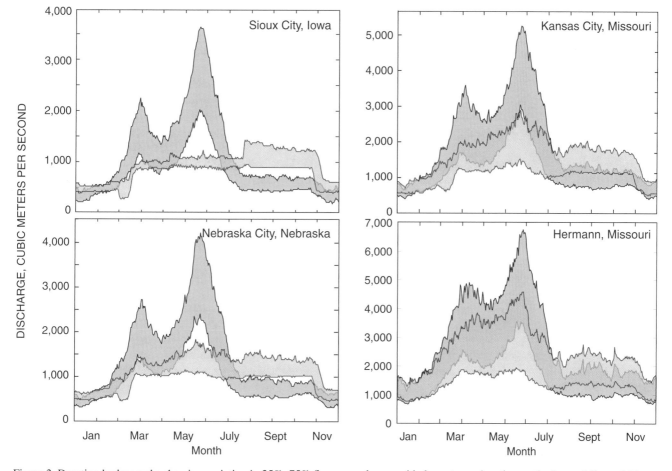

Figure 2. Duration hydrographs showing variation in 25%–75% flow exceedances with downstream location on the Lower Missouri River. Gray bands are modeled daily flows of the reference (run of the river) flow regime. Blue bands are modeled daily flows of the current water control plan (2004). Data from the U.S. Army Corps of Engineers Daily Routing Model (U.S. Army Corps of Engineers, 1998).

stabilization to improve conditions for steamboat navigation. However, most of the river's engineering structures date from the Missouri River Bank Stabilization and Navigation Project (BSNP), first authorized in the Rivers and Harbors Act of 1912, followed by an additional six acts of Congress through 1945 (Ferrell, 1996). A primary engineering goal was to develop a self-maintaining 9-ft-deep, 300-ft-wide navigation channel. This was mostly accomplished between 1930 and 1965 by narrowing the active channel with pile dikes and willow mats to trap sediments. Accretion of marginal land decreased the active channel-top width by about two-thirds, resulting in loss of ~404 km^2 of active channel area (Funk and Robinson, 1974; Hesse and Sheets, 1993; National Research Council, 2002; Galat et al., 2005b). After the land was accreted, the banks were stabilized with revetments and wing dikes to narrow and focus the thalweg to maintain a navigation channel from Sioux City, Iowa, 1200 km downstream to St. Louis, Missouri. In addition, ~120 km of river length, ~10%, has been lost between St. Louis and Sioux City since 1890 because of engineered and natural bend cutoffs (U.S. Army Corps of Engineers, 2004a).

In addition to altering the flow regime, the reservoirs trapped sediment, resulting in a profoundly altered sediment regime downstream of Gavins Point Dam. Decreases in sediment load have been associated with channel incision (Williams and Wolman, 1984; U.S. Army Corps of Engineers, 2007a) and with decreases in turbidity that might directly and indirectly affect native fish fauna (Galat et al., 2005a; Blevins, 2006).

APPROACH AND METHODS

Sediment-Load Data

Sediment budgets—an accounting of sediment transport, erosion, and deposition—are fundamental to understanding geomorphic evolution of altered river systems. In a dammed river system, the sediment budget quantifies the flux of materials available for maintaining or creating habitat, therefore strongly constraining the potential for management or restoration.

In this section we describe changes to the major components of the sediment budget estimated from suspended-sediment fluxes at locations along the Lower Missouri River, downstream of Gavins Point Dam (Fig. 1). Detailed data on bed load, sediment fluxes from tributaries, and background exchanges of sediment with floodplains are lacking. However, mainstem suspended-sediment fluxes are generally proportional to total sediment loads, and suspended-sediment fluxes provide an indicator of trends and broad-scale changes in the sediment budget.

Sediment-transport data for the Lower Missouri River are limited to measures of suspended sediment. Suspended sediment is defined operationally as the sediment that is captured in a suspended-sediment sampler and consists of sediment in suspension within the water column. Bed-load sediment is defined as that component of total sediment load that is transported by rolling and saltating along the bed and is not captured

in a suspended-sediment sampler. Depending on the transport conditions, some sediment size fractions might be transported as either bed load or in suspension. Sand-size sediment that is captured by a suspended-sediment sampler is typically referred to as bed-material load, whereas silt- and clay-size sediment is referred to as wash load. Depending on hydraulic conditions within a river reach, it is possible for sand-size sediment to be transported mostly in suspension (and measured as part of the suspended load) or to move mostly as bed load (Nittrouer et al., 2008). In general, bed load is thought to be <10% of the total average annual sediment load in large, lowland rivers like the Missouri (Allen, 1997; Inman and Jenkins, 1999). One estimate for instantaneous bed-load transport of the Lower Missouri River calculated bed-load transport at 8% of total sediment load (Gaeuman and Jacobson, 2007). In another example, computed bed load (assuming no supply limitation) for the 1993 flood on the Mississippi River was <5% of the measured suspended-sediment load (Holmes, 1996). Although some approaches to measuring bed load on large, sand-bed rivers show promise (Gaeuman and Jacobson, 2007), no systematic data sets currently exist for bed-load sediment fluxes on the Missouri River. The remainder of this article addresses only suspended-sediment load as an indicator of the bulk of sediment flux in the Lower Missouri River. Total sediment fluxes may be as much as 10% greater than reported, and the proportion of sediment transported as bed load may vary spatially and over time.

We analyzed historic and modern suspended-sediment loads using two approaches. In the first approach we determined average suspended-sediment transport loads for four time intervals using statistical models of suspended-sediment concentrations and flow measurements. Suspended-sediment-concentration data were obtained from published and unpublished files maintained by the U.S. Geological Survey (USGS) and the U.S. Army Corps of Engineers (USACE) and as online water-quality data sets (U.S. Geological Survey, 2001) (http://nwis.waterdata.usgs.gov/usa/nwis/qw). Because sample-collection methods and agency requirements have varied over time, some of these suspended-sediment concentrations were recorded as point samples, some as vertically depth-integrated samples, and some as values that were mathematically composited to cross-section average concentrations. For the purposes of this study, cross-section average concentrations were calculated from the primary concentration data to provide as much consistency as possible over the Lower Missouri River (Table 1A). We used daily mean discharges to develop transport models because instantaneous discharges were not available for all suspended-sediment samples. Moreover, within-day variation of discharge on a large river like the Missouri is probably small relative to other sources of error like within-flood or within-season concentration hysteresis (Holmes, 1996).

Particle-size data were available for many suspended-sediment samples. Where available, we used particle-size data to calculate suspended-sand concentrations and loads separately from the total flux, which includes clay and silt.

TABLE 1. ANNUAL SUSPENDED SEDIMENT LOADS CALCULATED FOR LOCATIONS AND TIME PERIODS INDICATED

A. CALCULATED FROM CONCENTRATION DATA FOR THIS REPORT

| Gauge | 1994–2006* | | | | | 1981–1993* | | | | 1968–1980* | | | | 1949–1952*† | |
| | Suspended load (Mg × 10⁶/yr) | | Sand load (Mg × 10⁶/yr) | | Sand percentage | Suspended load (Mg × 10⁶/yr) | | Sand load (Mg × 10⁶/yr) | | Suspended load (Mg × 10⁶/yr) | | Sand load (Mg × 10⁶/yr) | | Suspended load (Mg × 10⁶/yr) | |
	Load	S.E.§	Load	S.E.		Load	S.E.	Load	S.E.	Load	S.E.	Load	S.E.	Load	S.E.
Yankton	0.24	0.03	0.01	0.002	3%	N.A.#	N.A.	N.A.	N.A.	N.A.	N.A.	N.A.	N.A.	N.A.	N.A.
Sioux City	7.3	0.1	N.A.	N.A.	N.A.	9.9	0.9	4.0	0.6	15.6	0.7	13.2	1.7	N.A.	N.A.
Omaha	18.6	2.2	6.5	0.4	35%	16.4	1.1	6.4	0.4	18.9	1.0	11.6	0.6	N.A.	N.A.
Nebraska City	20.6	0.3	N.A.	N.A.	N.A.	41.1	13.7	8.4	0.7	29.4	1.2	16.3	0.9	N.A.	N.A.
St. Joseph	27.6	1.9	10.0	0.7	36%	77.6	32.1	16.6	3.4	63.6	4.6	N.A.	N.A.	270.2	12.0
Kansas City	41.9	3.0	13.2	1.1	32%	53.0	8.4	16.7	4.5	61.0	2.8	N.A.	N.A.	280.2	39.7
Hermann	55.2	4.4	13.6	1.3	25%	72.9	4.8	42.8	3.3	77.0	121.2	23.2	4.0	326.4	11.6

B. COMPILED FROM OTHER REPORTS

| Gauge | Suspended load (Mg × 10⁶/yr) | | | |
	1940–1952 (USACE, 1951, 1957)**	1948–1952 (USACE, 1957)**	1929–1931 (Secretary of War, 1934)††	Pre-dams (MBIC, 1971)§§
Yankton	125.0	121.0	N.A.	120.7
Sioux City	N.A.	N.A.	64.0	N.A.
Omaha	148.6	233.4	71.3	148.8
Nebraska City	N.A.	N.A.	N.A.	N.A.
St. Joseph	N.A.	233.4	N.A.	233.1
Kansas City	N.A.	299.8	118.8	297.6
Hermann	N.A.	289.1	N.A.	295.7

Note: USACE—U.S. Army Corps of Engineers; MBIC—Missouri Basin Inter-Agency Committee.
*Loads calculated using rating curve models in LOADEST; details in text.
†Loads calculated from unpublished concentration data, U.S. Geological Survey.
§S.E.—standard estimate of prediction.
#N.A.—not available.
**Calculated from daily loads; methods are documented in reference.
††Calculated from daily loads; methods are documented in reference; samplers may not be comparable to later samplers.
Average 1 July 1929 to 30 June 1931.
§§Annual loads given 1940–1952, 1949–1952; method of calculation unspecified.

Total suspended-sediment and sand-sized suspended-sediment loads were calculated using the LOADEST program (Runkel et al., 2004). This program explores a variety of regression models for transported constituent concentrations as a function of discharge and other variables. Explanatory variables can include measures of date and season to address trends and seasonal variation. We selected one of the nine pre-loaded model structures based on the Akaike Information Criterion. Given a time series of discharge, the model then calculates the mean daily suspended-sediment load, plus a standard error of prediction, for the time period.

In order to address changes in suspended-sediment loads over time, we divided the record into pre-dam (up to 1952), and three 12 yr intervals after the Missouri River dams had completely filled with water and reservoir management had stabilized in 1967: 1968–1980, 1981–1993, and 1994–2006 (Table 1A). The intervals were defined to separate post-dam periods before and after the 1993 flood and to address post-dam trends. Horowitz (2003) noted that sediment transport for equivalent discharges was substantially diminished at Mississippi River sediment stations after the 1993 flood, a persistent phenomenon that he attributed to sediment evacuation by the flood. Suspended-sediment concentration samples were not collected with uniform frequency at all stream-gauging stations through these four time intervals. We used the best concentration data available for each time interval and daily discharges for the entire interval as input to the LOADEST procedure.

In the second approach we used pre-calculated daily suspended-sediment loads that were available for some gauges and some time intervals. These came from U.S. Army Corps of Engineers reports (U.S. Army Corps of Engineers, 1951, 1957, 1965, 1970, 1972, 1976) and U.S. Geological Survey online daily data (U.S. Geological Survey, 2001). Some samples were collected originally on a daily basis, or were used to calculate daily suspended-sediment loads (Table 1B); we used these data to verify suspended-sediment fluxes calculated from the transport models and to illustrate annual variability (Table 1B; Fig. 3). In addition, pre-dam annual suspended-sediment loads from an unspecified period of record are provided from another historical source for reference (Missouri Basin Inter-Agency Committee, 1969).

SEDIMENT FLUXES OF THE LOWER MISSOURI RIVER

The mainstem reservoir system of the Missouri River impounds the upstream 53% of the 1.3-million-square-kilometer (km²) basin upstream of St. Louis, Missouri. Most of the impounded drainage area is in the Great Plains, an area characterized by naturally high sediment yields (Langbein and Schumm, 1958). Downstream of Gavins Point Dam, tributaries like the Platte, Kansas, and Grand Rivers also contribute sediment from areas that have high sediment-yield potential as well (Simon et al., 2004). This geography results in a complex spatial and temporal response to sediment loads diminished by the mainstem dams.

Pre-Dam Period

Closure of mainstem reservoirs on the Missouri River started in 1937, the last of the six mainstem reservoirs was closed in 1963, and storage was considered full in 1966 (U.S. Army Corps of Engineers, 2006b). For the purposes of this report we use available data before 1952 as indicative of pre-dam suspended-sediment loads. Pre-dam suspended-sediment loads were calculated from concentration data for 1949–1952 (Table 1A; unpublished U.S. Geological Survey data) and were available as calculated daily loads for 1940–1952 (U.S. Army Corps of Engineers, 1951, 1957), as calculated annual loads for 1929–1931 (Secretary of War, 1934), and as annual loads for an unspecified pre-dam interval (Table 1B) (Missouri Basin Inter-Agency Committee, 1971).

Pre-dam annual loads indicate a great deal of scatter, some of which is associated with variation in mean annual discharge (Fig. 3). Notably, high pre-dam suspended-sediment loads calculated for St. Joseph, Kansas City, and Hermann, Missouri, occurred during a 4 yr period of increased mean annual discharge, 1948–1952. The 1930–1931 data (for Sioux City, Omaha, and Kansas City) and 1940–1952 data (averaged and annual, for Omaha and Yankton) may be more representative of average, pre-dam flow and sediment conditions. Interpretation of the pre-dam suspended-sediment loads is complicated in part by potential differences in sampling methodology.

Based on calculations from daily suspended-sediment loads averaged over 1940–1952, the annual suspended-sediment load at Yankton, South Dakota, just downstream of Gavins Point Dam, was approximately of 125×10^6 megagrams per year (Mg*yr^{-1}, or metric tons per year; Table 1B). Based on similar data, although over a shorter time interval, the load increased downstream at Hermann, Missouri to ~289×10^6 Mg*yr^{-1}, or ~326×10^6 Mg*yr^{-1}, based on calculations from transport models (Tables 1A, 1B; Fig. 3). The increase of $164–201 \times 10^6$ Mg*yr^{-1} may be attributable to suspended sediment input from tributaries, including large rivers like the Platte, Kansas, Grand, and Osage (Fig. 1), or from sediment released from floodplain storage. As this was a period during which engineering activities resulted in accretion of floodplain lands, the latter is probably negligible. Particle-size data were not available to allow calculation of the pre-dam suspended sand load.

Post-Dam Period

Annual suspended-sediment loads were substantially lower than pre-dam loads during 1952–1956 and were highly variable through 1968 (Fig. 3A). Post-dam suspended-sediment loads (after 1968) are considerably smaller than pre-dam loads (Tables 1A, 1B). During 1994–2006 the sediment load at Yankton, South Dakota, was only 0.2% of the pre-dam value. The percentage increases in the downstream direction to 11.3% at Omaha, Nebraska, and 17.0% at Hermann, Missouri. The 1994–2006 sediment load at Hermann was 55.2×10^6 Mg*yr^{-1}. The

1994–2006 average suspended-sediment loads at Nebraska City, St. Joseph, Kansas City, and Hermann were all less than those calculated for the 1968–1993 intervals. This decrease over time may be attributable to depletion of readily transportable sediment owing to the high flow in 1993 (Horowitz, 2003), or it could be interpreted as a continuation of long-term decreases in sediment transport resulting from deposition behind the dams or land-use changes in tributary basins.

At Sioux City, Iowa, 100 km downstream from Gavins Point Dam, suspended-sediment load decreased during the three post-dam intervals (1968–1980, 1981–1993, and 1994–2006; Fig. 3), presumably reflecting ongoing equilibration of channel morphology and bank-erosion rates to diminished sediment load at the dam and a consequent decrease in streambank erosion contributions to the sediment load (Williams and Wolman, 1984; Biedenharn et al., 2001; Elliott and Jacobson, 2006). Biedenharn et al. (2001) calculated a total annual sediment load exported from the river segment upstream of Sioux City of ~4.6 × 10⁶ m³*yr⁻¹ for 1974–1986. With a typical bulk density of 1.6 megagrams per cubic meter (Mg*m⁻³), this equates to 7.4 × 10⁶ Mg*yr⁻¹,

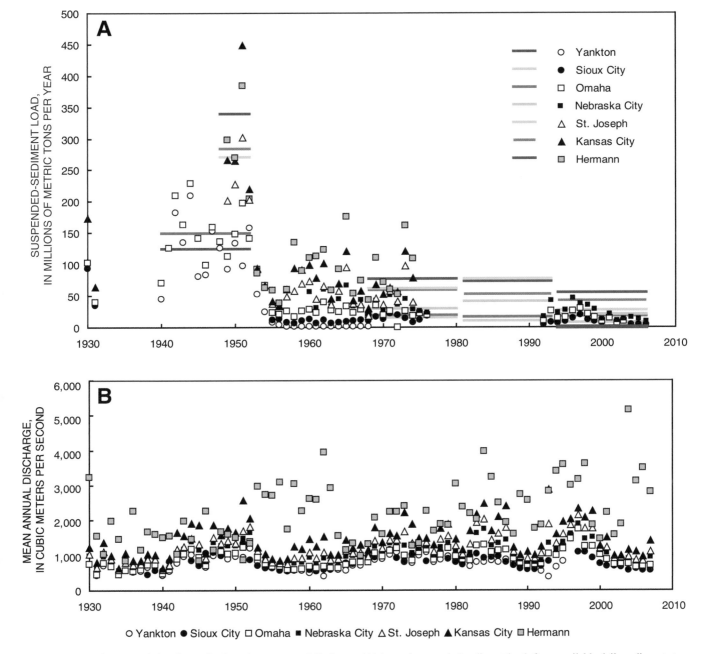

Figure 3. Trends in suspended-sediment loads and mean annual discharge. (A) Annual suspended-sediment loads from available daily sediment stations (markers), and loads calculated over multi-year periods (colored lines). (B) Mean annual discharges at indicated streamflow-gauging stations.

in agreement with our 1981–2006 suspended-sediment load at Sioux City of 7.3×10^6 Mg*yr^{-1} calculated from suspended-sediment concentrations.

Current suspended-sand load (as a percentage of total suspended-sediment load) initially increases from 3% at Yankton, South Dakota, to 26% at Omaha, Nebraska, and remains near 25% downstream at Hermann, Missouri. The decrease in suspended-sand load may be attributable to dilution of the suspended load with fine sediments contributed from downstream tributaries.

CHANGES IN THE SEDIMENT BUDGET

In addition to closure of the dams, four major structural changes have taken place on the Missouri River. Each of these has had the potential to alter the sediment budget by increasing storage of sediment in the floodplain, increasing erosion of sediment from the floodplain, altering tributary inputs, or extracting sediment from the sediment flux.

Bank Stabilization and Navigation Project

Floodplain accretion during the BSNP narrowed the Lower Missouri River active channel and decreased its area by ~404 km² (U.S. Army Corps of Engineers, 2004b). The depth of this accreted sediment varies along the river, but based on excavations for most restoration projects, we estimate the average depth at 5 m. Using this depth, the total accreted land is estimated at 2.0×10^9 m³, equivalent to 3.2×10^9 Mg using a bulk density of 1.6 Mg*m^{-3} (Table 2). Land accretion occurred from 1910 to 1981 (Ferrell, 1996), yielding an average deposition rate over these 71 yr of $~45.5 \times 10^6$ Mg*yr^{-1}, equivalent to ~14% of the pre-dam (1948–1952) annual suspended-sediment load at Hermann, Missouri. Land-accretion activity was more concentrated from the early 1930s to the mid-1960s, so deposition rates may have been as high as 107×10^6 Mg*yr^{-1}, equivalent to almost one-third of the pre-dam annual suspended-sediment load at Hermann.

Accreted land preferentially sequestered coarse sediment sizes from the total suspended load, whereas finer sediments were washed downstream. At Jameson Island, Missouri, for example (Fig. 1), 24 6–9-m-deep soil borings through accreted land produced an average sand-gravel concentration of 78%, with finer materials being only 22% (Ghimire et al., 2007; U.S. Army Corps of Engineers, 2007c). For comparison, the average modern (1994–2006) suspended load at Hermann, Missouri is 25% sand and 75% fines.

Tributary Inputs

Suspended-sediment-load data for tributaries to the Lower Missouri River are fragmentary, and compilation of the available records is beyond the scope of this article. Generally, sediment loads of Missouri River tributaries in the pre-dam era

TABLE 2. CALCULATIONS OF VOLUMES, MASSES, AND LOADING RATES OF SEDIMENT AND SAND FROM ACCRETED LAND AND AQUATIC HABITAT RESTORATION ACTIVITIES

Accreted land or lost aquatic habitat (km²)	Average bank height (m)	Total sediment volume (m³ x 10⁶)	Average sediment bulk density (Mg/m³)	Mass of sediment (Mg x 10⁶)	Mass of sand, assuming 78% (Mg x 10⁶)	Time period (yr)	Sediment loading rate, deposited or released (Mg x 10⁶/yr)	Sand loading rate, deposited or released (Mg x 10⁶/yr)
404	5.0	2,020	1.6	3,232	2,521	71	45.5	35.5
64	5.0	320	1.6	512	399	15	34.1	26.6

may have been higher than natural background rates because of agricultural and other land uses, similar to other North American landscapes (Trimble, 1974; Trimble and Lund, 1982; Jacobson and Coleman, 1986; Kesel, 1988). More recently, decreasing sediment yields to streams have been attributed to soil-erosion-control practices. On average in the Missouri River basin, soil erosion on cropland has been estimated to have diminished from 17.7 Mg/hectare to 11.0 Mg/hectare from 1982 to 2003 (Natural Resources Conservation Service, 2003). The fact that the Missouri River suspended-sediment load increased by $\sim$160–200 $\times$ 10^6 Mg*yr^{-1} between Yankton City, South Dakota, and Hermann, Missouri, during 1948–1952, but increased by only 55 $\times$ 10^6 Mg*yr^{-1} under 1994–2006 conditions, attests to substantial decreases in tributary inputs, or the existence of an extreme disequilibrium in either the 1948–1952 or 1994–2006 sediment budgets. Possibly, large amounts of sediment transport during the flood of 1951 resulted in a larger-than-average increase in estimated sediment load at Hermann in the pre-dam period. Without more detailed sediment data from tributaries it is not possible to separate tributary effects from ongoing adjustment of the Missouri River to the BSNP and diminished sediment load. Once the BSNP was completed in 1981, however, it is reasonable to assume that little exchange of sediment between the channel and the floodplain took place because the channel was engineered to maximize sediment conveyance. Hence, the increase in the average suspended-sediment load of 55 $\times$ 10^6 Mg*yr^{-1} from Sioux City to Hermann during 1994–2006 is probably all due to tributary inputs.

Commercial Dredging for Aggregate

Although the Lower Missouri River is engineered to be a self-scouring navigation channel that does not generally require maintenance dredging, the channel is mined commercially for sand and fine-gravel aggregate. Commercial aggregate mining is concentrated near large metropolitan areas along the river, principally Kansas City, Jefferson City, and St. Charles, Missouri. During 2003–2005, annual commercial dredging was estimated at 7.6 $\times$ 10^6 Mg*yr^{-1} (U.S. Army Corps of Engineers, 2007c). If all of this came from the sand portion of the suspended-sediment load, it would amount to nearly 56% of the suspended-sand load passing Hermann, Missouri. To the extent that dredging extracts unmeasured bed load (as much as 10% of the total sediment load) or underlying sediments that are not presently part of the Missouri River sediment flux, the actual proportion of total sediment load extracted would be <56%. For example, if bed load is 10% of the total load (11% of suspended load), total sand load at Hermann, Missouri would be $\sim$19.7 $\times$ 10^6 Mg*yr^{-1}. Total annual commercial dredging then would be $\sim$40% of the sand load at Hermann.

Habitat Restoration

From 1984 to 2006, over $133 million was expended on habitat-restoration activities on the Lower Missouri River (U.S.

Army Corps of Engineers, 2006a). Initially, efforts focused on mitigating effects of the BSNP by restoring a variety of aquatic and terrestrial habitats. To comply with a Biological Opinion that found that the USACE management of the river put the survival of the pallid sturgeon in jeopardy (U.S. Fish and Wildlife Service, 2003), restoration activities began to emphasize creation of shallow-water aquatic habitat beginning in 2004. *Shallow-water habitat* (SWH) has been defined on the Lower Missouri River as 0–1.5 m depth and 0–0.6 m*s^{-1} current velocity, and is thought to be important for rearing of larval and juvenile pallid sturgeon (U.S. Fish and Wildlife Service, 2003; U.S. Army Corps of Engineers, 2004b).

The 2003 Biological Opinion mandates restoration of 4800–7900 ha of lost aquatic habitat (assumed to be SWH) by the year 2020. The midpoint of this range, 64 km^2, is used in subsequent calculations and in Table 2. Shallow-water habitat is being created by a variety of mechanisms, including excavation of side-channel chutes (Jacobson et al., 2001; Jacobson et al., 2004) and bank notches. Designs have stipulated that most sediment excavated to create SWH will be placed directly in the river or will be sidecast to be eventually delivered to the river as banks erode. Using the same bank height and bulk-density estimates used in the calculations for sediment mass deposited in the accreted lands, excavation of the 64 km^2 would release 34 $\times$ 10^6 Mg*yr^{-1} as an annual average over the projected 15 yr of construction, assuming that all the sediment was delivered to the channel during the construction phase (Table 2). This additional sediment flux would be only 14% of the 1949–1952 average annual suspended-sediment load at Hermann, Missouri, but equal to 62% of the 1994–2006 value. Because the sediment released to the river from the floodplain is on the order of 78% sand, the additional sand flux would be estimated at 196% of the present-day annual suspended-sand flux at Hermann. Although it can be assumed that most of this sand was originally deposited from suspension, when reintroduced to the river it may be transported in part as bed load. The 27 $\times$ 10^6 Mg*yr^{-1} of sand added to the river through habitat restoration would be $\sim$135% of the estimated annual total (suspended plus bed-load) sand load at Hermann, Missouri (20 $\times$ 10^6 Mg*yr^{-1}).

Major changes to the Lower Missouri River sediment budget are shown diagrammatically in Figure 4. This diagram is intended to illustrate the generalized relative magnitudes and timing of large changes to the Lower Missouri River sediment budget, including deposition into flood-plain storage as land was accreted during the BSNP, projected release from storage in creating SWH, and decrease of sand storage by commercial dredging. The diagram assumes that deposition of accreted lands owing to the BSNP was dominantly from suspended-sediment load and was distributed through 71 yr (1910–1981), although as indicated above, the bulk of the accretion was probably concentrated during the mid-1930s to mid-1960s. The diagram also assumes that the earliest measured suspended-sediment loads were already affected by deposition in accreted lands; therefore, the resultant sediment flux was decreased by the estimated annual BSNP

Jacobson et al.

deposition rate (that is, the total imposed suspended-sediment load at Hermann would have been ~372×10^6 Mg*yr^{-1}, instead of the measured 326×10^6 Mg*yr^{-1}, because of the 46×10^6 Mg*yr^{-1} that was being sequestered in accreted land). The extractions from storage by commercial dredging assume that dredged material comes from sediment in transit, although it is not known how it would be partitioned between bed load and bed material in the suspended load. Suspended-sediment fluxes and annual dredging amounts during 1994–2006 were extrapolated through 2040 to illustrate the effect of delivery of a sediment pulse from restoration projects during 2004–2020.

Although considerable uncertainties are associated with the suspended-sediment loads and volumes of sediment added and subtracted from floodplain storage, this analysis illustrates the magnitudes of possible sediment storage and sediment release by comparing them with suspended-sediment loads at Hermann, Missouri. In particular, it illustrates the additive effect of sediment impoundment by dams and land accretion under the BSNP in diminishing suspended-sediment load and the relative magnitude of sediment that may be reintroduced to the river through habitat restoration. The observation of downstream decreases in suspended-sediment concentrations during 1929–1932 supports

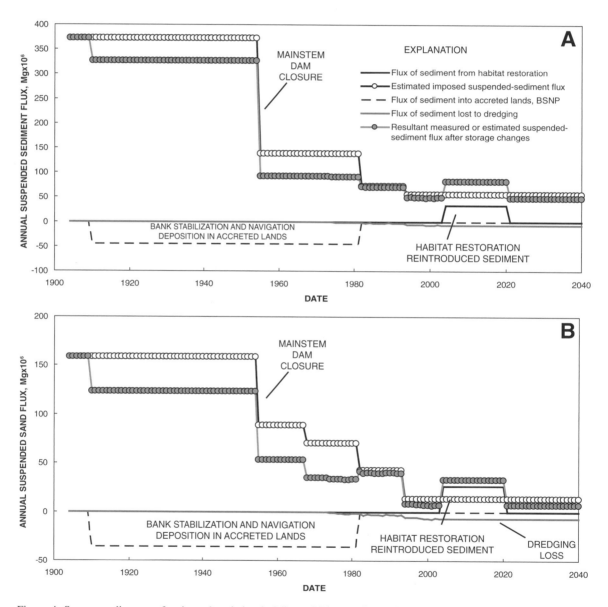

Figure 4. Summary diagram of estimated variation in Missouri River sediment flux through time at Hermann, Missouri, showing effects of deposition in accreted lands of the Bank Stabilization and Navigation Project (BSNP), reintroduction of sediment to the river from aquatic-habitat-restoration projects, and loss of sediment from commercial aggregate dredging. (A) Calculations based on total suspended-sediment loads. (B) Calculations based on suspended-sand loads.

the idea that deposition of suspended sediment in BSNP accretion lands significantly diminished suspended-sediment loads (Secretary of War, 1934).

GEOMORPHIC ADJUSTMENTS OF THE LOWER MISSOURI RIVER TO AN ALTERED SEDIMENT REGIME

Mean streambed elevations at streamflow-gauging stations along the Lower Missouri River indicate general trends in channel responses to changes in flow regime, sediment regime, and channel engineering (Fig. 5). Measurements at streamflow-gauging stations are a unique source of information on long-term channel changes; however, because gauges are preferentially located in stable cross sections associated with bridges,

care must be taken in extrapolating interpretations upstream and downstream (Jacobson, 1995; Smelser and Schmidt, 1998). All gauges indicate channel incision during this time period, but incision is greatest and most persistent at Sioux City and Kansas City. Incision at Sioux City has been ~6 m since 1920 and appears to have accelerated after dam closure. From 1960 to 2007 mean streambed elevation at Sioux City has decreased by ~4 m. Incision at Kansas City has been more gradual, amounting to ~5 m since 1940, and 4 m since 1960. Mean streambed elevations at Omaha, St. Joseph, and Hermann have declined as much as 2 m since dam closure. Streambed elevation at St. Joseph initially declined rapidly during 1960 to 1980, but has since stabilized.

Incision of the Lower Missouri River channel has been accompanied by narrowing by navigation structures, revetments,

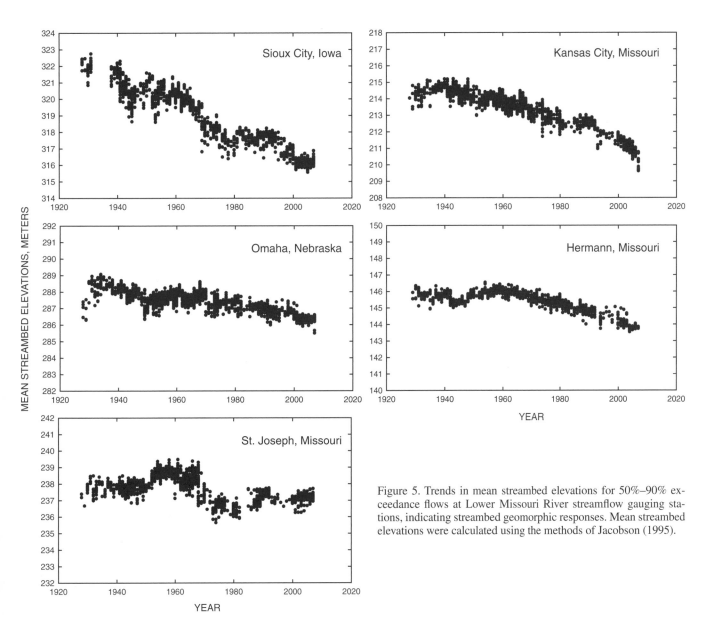

Figure 5. Trends in mean streambed elevations for 50%–90% exceedance flows at Lower Missouri River streamflow gauging stations, indicating streambed geomorphic responses. Mean streambed elevations were calculated using the methods of Jacobson (1995).

and levees. The net effect of these morphological changes has been to alter stage-discharge relations at gauges; the stage-discharge relations are indicative of morphological responses and illustrate the net effects of how morphology has changed the frequency of flooding of lands adjacent to the channel (Fig. 6) (Pinter and Heine, 2005; U.S. Army Corps of Engineers, 2007a). For example, during 1955–2006, water-surface elevations of high-frequency flows decreased 3–3.5 m from Gavins Point Dam to Sioux City, Iowa. Near Omaha and Nebraska City, water-surface elevations of these same flows have changed little since dam closure, although higher-magnitude discharges attain water-surface elevations as much as 1.5 m higher than those attained in 1955. Water-surface-elevation declines of >2 m are apparent in the Kansas City area bed incision and stage declines and may require as much as $60 million for retrofitting infrastructure such as water intakes for municipal and industrial water supplies (Graham, 2007). Downstream of Kansas City, water-surface elevations for low-moderate frequency discharges are near 1955 values or slightly lower, whereas higher-magnitude discharges are increased, presumably because overbank flows are constricted by levees (Pinter and Heine, 2005).

More recently, the USACE has conducted a more spatially detailed analysis based on sequential surveys of the flow-adjusted Construction Reference Plane (CRP), a continuous water-surface datum, defined as the water-surface altitude of the flow that is equaled or exceeded 75% of the time during the navigation season. CRP elevations were updated on the Lower Missouri River downstream of Sioux City, Iowa, in 1990, 2002, and 2005 at an average spacing of 5.3 km (Fig. 7) (U.S. Army Corps of Engineers, 2007b). These data complement the streamflow-gauging-station data by providing greater spatial detail of water-surface elevation changes and inferred bed changes, although for a shorter time interval. These measurements are consistent with the trends at streamflow-gauging stations and indicate recent stream-bed lowering from Sioux City, Iowa (river mile 753), to river mile 645, and bed aggradation of as much as 0.44 m from river miles 645–500. As much as 1.4 m of recent bed incision can be inferred from river miles 500–378 (near Kansas City, Missouri). Downstream of Kansas City, changes in water-surface elevation have been variable. Maxima of streambed incision can be inferred at river miles 260 (near Miami, Missouri), 147 (near Jefferson City, Missouri), and 40 (near St. Charles, Missouri).

There is a strong correspondence between peaks of commercial dredging production and locations of water-surface-elevation declines (Fig. 7); however, other sources of geomorphic disturbance, such as changes in tributary sediment loads and channel engineering modifications, have not been eliminated as potential causes of the inferred bed incision. No commercial dredging has taken place upstream of river mile 500.

Ongoing channel incision downstream from Gavins Point Dam is consistent with models of bed responses downstream of dams (Williams and Wolman, 1984; Schmidt and Wilcock, 2008), where the ratio of transport capacity to sediment supply has been increased. The recovery of the bed and minor aggradation

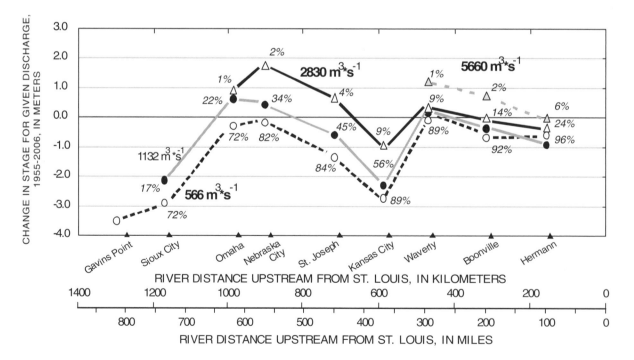

Figure 6. General degradation trends, Lower Missouri River, shown as stage changes from 1955 to 2006 for given discharges; daily flow exceedances for the discharge are indicated in italics as percentages. Figure modified from Jacobson and Galat (2006).

downstream of Omaha can be interpreted in two different ways. First, the Lower Missouri River may have reached an equilibrium adjustment to the altered sediment supply, channel engineering, and flow regime. The stable to aggrading reaches between Omaha and Nebraska City could be the result of adjustment to sediment load provided by the Platte River. In contrast, the channel profile may not be in equilibrium, in which case the incision and aggradation are transient responses that will continue to change as the bed evolves.

An equilibrium explanation is supported by results of a computational hydraulic channel-evolution model (Karim and Holly, 1986). This model replicated the general pattern of channel adjustment during 1960 to 1980; most of the bed adjustment occurred during the first 6–10 yr, and little additional adjustment occurred when the model was run through 2000. The authors concluded that coarsening of the bed through armoring was a controlling variable in adjustment to the diminished sediment supply.

A nonequilibrium explanation is supported by Schmidt and Wilcock's (2008) calculations that predict that the Lower Missouri River response should be dominated by sediment deficit and therefore should be incising downstream at least to Kansas City. Lack of equilibrium is also supported by the continued incision at Sioux City, and the pattern of rise and gentle fall of the bed at Omaha and St. Joseph (Fig. 5). The channel profile could also be out of equilibrium with sediment load at locations of commercial

sand dredging, potentially explaining some of the localized areas of sharp decline in water-surface elevations (Fig. 6). The long-term bed responses to these spatially limited, but volumetrically significant, extractions of bed material are unknown.

IMPLICATIONS FOR RIVER RESTORATION AND MANAGEMENT

Changes in sediment regimes, combined with changes in the flow regime and geomorphic adjustments of the channel, have profound implications for restoration and management of the Missouri River. Similar to many regulated rivers, the Lower Missouri River is expected to produce more ecological benefits while maintaining traditional socioeconomic services like hydropower generation, navigation, flood control, and water supply. Whereas flow regime and channel morphology are amenable to a broad range of restoration actions—within socioeconomic constraints—altered sediment regimes challenge river managers with persistent and unpredictably evolving conditions for which engineering solutions are elusive.

Management Objectives

The immediate restoration objective on the Lower Missouri River is to recover endangered species, with restoration of ecological functions as a secondary objective. The listed species on the

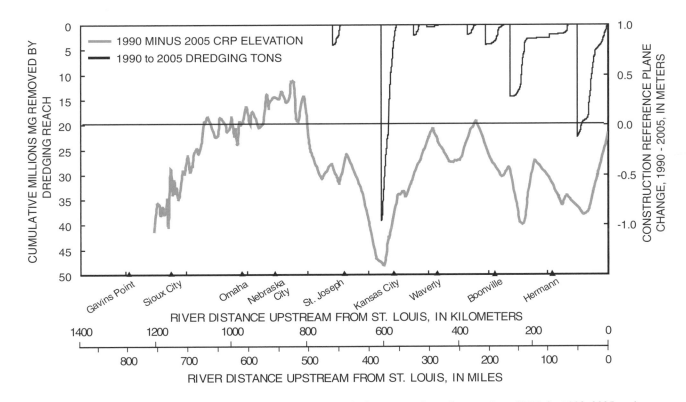

Figure 7. Detailed streambed elevation changes indicated by change in the construction reference plane (CRP) for 1990–2005, and comparison with commercial dredging production. See text for definition of construction reference plane.

Lower Missouri River are two shore birds (interior least tern and piping plover) and a large benthic fish, the pallid sturgeon. The 2003 amended Biological Opinion (U.S. Fish and Wildlife Service, 2003) stipulates that to remove or preclude jeopardy status for these species, an increase in emergent sandbar habitat (ESH) for bird nesting is required, particularly in the segment from Gavins Point Dam to near Sioux City, Iowa. In addition, the river needs to have an increase in SWH from Sioux City to St. Louis to provide adequate larval and juvenile rearing habitat for the pallid sturgeon (U.S. Fish and Wildlife Service, 2003). The Biological Opinion also stipulated that the flow regime from Gavins Point Dam should be naturalized to (1) periodically connect the channel with the floodplain to allow for nutrient exchange and fish access, (2) allow sediment transport to build ESH, (3) increase SWH during summer by providing a low-flow period, and (4) provide an environmental spawning cue for the pallid sturgeon. As is commonly the case, meeting multiple objectives is not straightforward in river management. In particular, the USACE argued in response that the first two of these objectives were inconsistent with their flood-control authorization, and the third would require low flows that would severely compromise navigation (U.S. Army Corps of Engineers, 2003). The proposed solution was to create ESH and SWH by reengineering the channel, and to provide modest pulsed flows for spawning cues (Jacobson and Galat, 2008).

Additional restoration objectives for the Missouri River were articulated by the National Research Council (NRC) (2002), although their focus was on the entire river, not just the Lower Missouri River. In addition to the previous objectives, the NRC report emphasized the need to restore dynamic geomorphic processes of channel migration, erosion, and deposition ("cut and fill alluviation") to restore critical ecological functions. The following sections discuss these management objectives in terms of constraints imposed by the altered Lower Missouri River sediment regime.

Floodplain Connectivity

Although a linkage between floodplain-connecting flows and survival of the listed Lower Missouri River species has not been identified, periodic flooding of low-lying lands is generally considered an important attribute of lowland river ecosystems (Junk et al., 1989; Sparks, 1995; Poff et al., 1997; Sparks et al., 1998; Jacobson and Galat, 2008). The geomorphic adjustment of the Lower Missouri River to the altered sediment regime poses both challenges and opportunities for achieving floodplain connectivity. Incision downstream of Gavins Point Dam has lowered the channel so that the former floodplain is no longer reached by moderate floods. Figure 8 shows 2 yr flood elevations intersected with land-surface elevations as an indicator of potential to flood valley-bottom lands (U.S. Army Corps of Engineers, 2004c; Jacobson et al., 2007). Much of the former floodplain from Gavins Point Dam to Omaha is no longer reachable by floods of this magnitude. New floodplain is being

formed at a lower elevation in the Recreational River segment of the river (Gavins Point Dam to Ponca, Nebraska, Fig. 1) as the channel adjusts to the diminished sediment supply, but the area of this connectable floodplain is relatively small (Elliott and Jacobson, 2006).

Conversely, low-lying lands adjacent to the river in the stable-to-aggrading reach between Omaha and St. Joseph are more sensitive to flooding (Fig. 8). Flooding along this segment of the river was perceived as a strong constraint on design of a pulsed flow regime because of concerns that even modest flow pulses would restrict drainage through levee flap gates draining agricultural lands (Jacobson and Galat, 2008). Because the bed has not incised, this segment of the river offers opportunities to restore connectivity to large areas of low-lying floodplain with only modest or no changes to the flow regime.

Emergent Sandbar Habitat

Emergent sandbars are considered necessary for nesting and rearing of listed shorebirds (National Research Council, 2002; U.S. Fish and Wildlife Service, 2003). ESH is most effective where no vegetation is present to provide cover to predators, and abundant areas are available at elevations that do not get flooded out during natural or managed spring pulsed flows. Because of the total trapping of sand-size sediment by the reservoir system, declining rates of bank erosion, and limited input of sediment from tributaries, sand load is small upstream of Sioux City in the Recreational River segment (Table 1A; Fig. 1). To maintain this scarce resource requires management actions that minimize sand transport to the channelized segments downstream while maximizing habitat values such as elevation and lack of vegetation in the non-channelized segment. Under current management approaches, mechanical construction techniques are being used to build sandbars, and mechanical and chemical means are being used to control vegetation (Latka, 2006; Price and Martz, 2007).

Ultimately, the sediment deficit limits the extent of ESH possible in the Recreation River segment. Under a simple, first-order assumption that a sustainable area of ESH is directly related to available suspended-sediment load, the ratio of the present-day sediment load at Sioux City (7.3×10^6 Mg*yr^{-1}) to the estimated historical value ($125–148 \times 10^6$ Mg*yr^{-1}) indicates that only ~5% of the historical ESH area may be achievable in the long term.

Shallow-Water Habitat

The 2003 Biological Opinion sets quantitative goals for areas of SWH that must be attained every five years from 2005 to 2020 to mitigate for habitat lost from the BSNP. Most of the habitat lost as the river was channelized was shallow areas adjacent to the main channel, side-channel chutes, and backwaters. These habitats are thought to be important for various ecological functions, including primary and secondary productivity, forage fish production, and providing rearing habitat for larval and juvenile pallid sturgeon (Funk and Robinson, 1974; U.S. Fish and Wildlife Service, 2003; Galat et al., 2005a; Jacobson and Galat, 2006).

As noted earlier, restoration of 64 km² (16%) of the 404 km² lost to the BSNP would require excavating large areas of the accreted land, as much as 320 × 10⁶ m³ of floodplain sediment (Table 2). Because the goal of habitat creation is to accommodate more water in the channel margin and floodplain, the standard design has been to return the excavated sediment to the river. This was justified under the assumption that a river ecosystem already in sediment deficit can accommodate the additional sediment without causing significant socioeconomic or ecological problems. Moreover, some ecological benefits would likely accrue to native fish, like the pallid sturgeon, shovelnose sturgeon, flathead catfish, and channel catfish, which have evolved to live in turbid water with high sediment loads (Hesse and Sheets, 1993; Galat et al., 2005a; Galat et al., 2005b). The decrease in turbidity is thought to have diminished the ability of these species to compete

with sight-feeding predators (National Research Council, 2002; U.S. Fish and Wildlife Service, 2003). Moreover, decreased turbidity may be responsible for increased primary production of phytoplankton, a disturbance to the food web with possible far-reaching consequences (Blevins, 2006).

Calculations of the volume and tonnage of sediment potentially added to the river, however, are substantial. The addition of 34×10^6 Mg*yr⁻¹ as an average over the projected 15 yr of SWH restoration is ~62% of the annual post-dam suspended-sediment flux at Hermann, Missouri, although it would be on the order of 10% of the pre-dam suspended sediment load. Moreover, most of the sediment released from floodplain storage as a result of SWH construction is sand size. Therefore, the contribution to the sand load is proportionally greater, as much as 196% in comparison with the post-dam suspended sand load at Hermann, Missouri. Whereas the modern sediment-transport capacity of the Missouri River at Hermann has been calculated to be sufficient to transport

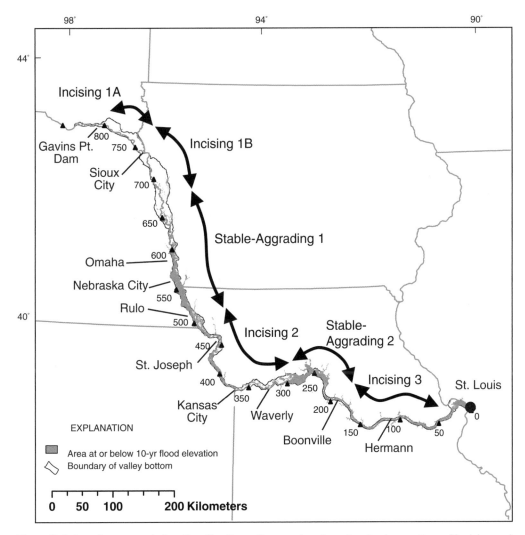

Figure 8. Index of area at or below 2-yr flooding reference elevation, showing how pattern of incision and aggradation affects potential for restoring floodplain connectivity on the Lower Missouri River. Zones are described in Table 4. From Jacobson et al. (2007).

modern loads (U.S. Army Corps of Engineers, 2007d), large changes in sand supply indicated by these calculations might be expected to locally or periodically exceed transport capacity.

The response of the channel to sediment reintroduced to the river depends on many interacting and poorly predictable factors, including timing and sequence of sediment-transporting events, distance of sand transport per event, and residence time of sand in transit. It is notable that the volume of sediment that may be reintroduced to the river through restoration activities is substantially greater than that being extracted by commercial dredging (Fig. 4). If areas of recent channel incision of the Lower Missouri River are related to commercial dredging of relatively small proportion of the sediment load (Fig. 7), reintroduction of equivalent volumes of sand could be expected to have similarly substantial effects on the bed profile, although presumably through deposition rather than erosion. Restoration projects that are designed to use sand released from floodplain storage to create additional habitat within the channel margins, and to maximize the residence time of that sand, would optimize the habitat value of the sediment.

Sediment Quality

Sediment quality is another potential concern in restoration, as sediments returned to the river or re-suspended from the riverbed could introduce contaminants and excess nutrients to the river. Recent studies have documented some limited sediment contamination on the Lower Missouri River. A study of fine sediment (silt and clay size) deposited by an extreme flood in 1993 detected small amounts of common agricultural pesticides in most of the sampled areas of the Lower Missouri River floodplain (Schalk et al., 1997). Chapman et al. (2001) detected limited areas of lead contamination in sediment near Omaha, Nebraska, whereas another study detected "hot spots" of some pesticides, polyaromatic hydrocarbons, polychlorinated biphenyls, and metals near Kansas City, Missouri (Echols et al., 2008). The Chapman et al. (2001) study sampled sediments within the Missouri River channel adjacent to and downstream from an abandoned lead refinery, and the Echols et al. study sampled fine sediment in depositional environments downstream of wing dikes from

upstream of Omaha, Nebraska (river mile 615), to just downstream of Jefferson City, Missouri. In the latter study, sediment-affinitive constituents were uniformly low and probably below biological-effect levels, except for isolated high concentrations near Kansas City (river mile 367), and just downstream of the Blue River confluence (river mile 357). These studies establish that the potential for sediment contamination exists on the Lower Missouri River, but the documented extent of potentially harmful concentrations is limited.

An additional suite of studies was conducted during 2007 at five Lower Missouri River habitat restoration sites (river miles 209–550) to characterize potential for excavated sediments to deliver contaminants and nutrients to the Missouri River (CDM Federal Programs Corporation, 2007). One of these sites (Jameson Island, river miles 209–213) was selected for construction of a 3000-m-long, 6-m-wide side-channel chute that would contribute ~18 ha of SWH. Excavation would remove ~6.7 m of floodplain sediment, most of which was accreted as a result of BSNP channel engineering (Ghimire et al., 2007). Typical of most of the Lower Missouri River floodplain, sediments at this site consist of 1–2 m of a loamy-sand to silty-clay top stratum over 10 m or more of fine to medium sand with scattered gravel layers (Schalk and Jacobson, 1997; Holbrook et al., 2006). Geotechnical boreholes established that the topmost 6–9 m of sediment at Jameson Island consisted of 78% sand-size or coarser sediment (U.S. Army Corps of Engineers, 2007c).

The upper 1.5–2.5 m of the floodplain sediments was sampled for nutrients, available metals, polychlorinated biphenyls (PCBs), pesticides, total organic carbon, total petroleum hydrocarbon–diesel range organics (TPH-DRO) and benzene, toluene, ethylbenzene, and xylene (BTEX) (CDM Federal Programs Corporation, 2007). Metals, PCBs, pesticides, TPH-DRO, and BTEX were all either below detection limits or below probable biological-effects limits. Nutrients in these samples were not elevated in comparison with reference Missouri soils. Under the assumption that all chute sediments would be delivered to the river during one year, increases in total nitrogen and total phosphorus loads were calculated to be 0.23% and 2.6% of the annual loads at Hermann, Missouri (Table 3). These are likely high estimates because sampling of sediments was concentrated in the

TABLE 3. ANNUAL SUSPENDED SEDIMENT, SUSPENDED SAND, TOTAL NITROGEN, AND TOTAL PHOSPHORUS LOADS, MISSOURI RIVER AND CONTRIBUTED BY A RESTORATION PROJECT

	Total suspended sediment (Mg × 10⁶/yr)	Suspended sand (Mg × 10⁶/yr)	Total nitrogen (Mg/yr)	Total phosphorus (Mg/yr)
Annual loads, Hermann, 1994–2006	55.2	13.6	209,975	32,292
Jameson Island excavation	1.95	1.52	473	831
Jameson Island excavation as percentage of river load	3.5%	11.2%	0.23%	2.6%

Note: Calculations of constituents contributed by excavation at Jameson Island restoration project, assuming all sediment is delivered to the river in one year, and compared with annual constituent loads at Hermann, Missouri. Hermann total nitrogen and total phosphorus from Aulenbach et al. (2007); Jameson Island data from CDM Federal Programs Corporation (2007).

finer, upper two-thirds of the excavation, and the design actually called for sediment to be introduced to the river over multiple years. Similarly, if sediment from this one restoration site was re-introduced to the river during one year, it would contribute ~3.5% to total suspended-sediment load and 11.2% to suspended-sand load (Table 3). These percentages would be decreased to the extent that excavated sediment is transported as bed load and to the extent that delivery of sediment would be protracted over multiple years.

These studies indicate that floodplain sediments are generally unlikely to contribute contaminated sediment to the Lower Missouri River, although local concentrations of contaminants are possible. Also, individual restoration sites are generally unlikely to contribute significantly to existing sediment and nutrient loads. Cumulative loads from multiple restoration sites needed to achieve SWH goals, however, could add up to a significant proportion of the post-dam sediment and total phosphorus loads (Tables 2, 3), depending on sequencing and location along the river. Restoration sites located upstream of channel incision or dredging operations may even mitigate local sediment and turbidity deficits, at least during the lifetime of restoration construction.

FUTURE PROSPECTS

In the short term (years to decades), Lower Missouri River managers will be challenged to restore some degree of ecological functioning by moving sediment from the channel to sandbars to create ESH, and by moving sediment from the floodplain to the channel to create SWH, and possibly replacing some of the sediment lost from bed incision. Understanding the spatial distribution of sediment fluxes and geomorphic adjustments should help in planning effective, systemic restoration within the constraints of a persistent sediment deficit. Alternatively, more holistic restoration, such as that envisioned by the National Research Council (2002), would require substantive relaxing of constraints by providing more sediment. Such long-term solutions may involve altering the budget through sediment replenishment (Pasternack et al., 2004) or reservoir bypass or flushing (Yang, 2006).

Restoration Zonation

Recognition of the spatial patterns of sediment fluxes and geomorphic adjustments of a regulated river can help focus restoration techniques where they are most feasible and sustainable. The longitudinal variation in channel incision and aggradation of the Lower Missouri River illustrates zones of the river that present—at least for the short term—inherent challenges or opportunities for restoration (Table 4; Fig. 8). These zones delineate where engineering of specific ecological functions may be most cost effective and sustainable. For example, restoration of flood-plain wetlands is more feasible in aggrading reaches than in incising reaches. Moreover, land acquisition for restoration purposes in aggrading reaches could mitigate ongoing costs of flood control and land drainage in these areas. Similarly, sand delivered to the river from SWH sites upstream of incising reaches could, at least temporarily, mitigate channel incision.

TABLE 4. GEOMORPHIC AND RESTORATION MANAGEMENT ZONES ALONG LOWER MISSOURI RIVER

Zone	Approximate river miles	Features	Management factors
Incising 1A	811–750	Complex channel morphology Severely altered flow regime Severe sediment deficit Degraded channel	Conserve sediment Enhance, maintain in-channel complexity
Incising 1B	750–675	Simple channel morphology Severely altered flow regime Severe sediment deficit Degraded channel	Conserve sediment Develop in-channel complexity
Stable-aggrading 1	675–500	Simple channel morphology Moderately altered flow regime Sediment surplus Aggraded channel	Develop in-channel complexity Develop floodplain connections
Incising 2	500–300	Simple channel morphology Moderately altered flow regime Sediment deficit Severely degraded channel	Conserve sediment Develop in-channel complexity
Stable-aggrading 2	300–210	Simple channel morphology Slightly altered flow regime Sediment balance	Develop in-channel complexity Develop floodplain connections
Incising 3	210–0	Simple channel morphology Slightly altered flow regime Sediment deficit Degraded channel	Conserve sediment Develop in-channel complexity

Optimal engineering feasibility, however, does not necessarily equate to optimal ecological functioning. ESH, for example, needs to occur in areas that will be useful for migrating shorebirds during the nesting season. SWH, if intended for rearing of larval and juvenile sturgeon, needs to occur downstream of spawning habitats within typical drift distances needed for larval fish to reach the stage for exogenous feeding (Wildhaber et al., 2007). Hence, optimization of restoration activities within an altered sediment regime also depends on detailed and comprehensive understanding of the ecological processes of interest.

Reservoir Sediment Management

Long-term solutions to altered sediment regimes on regulated rivers often include approaches to bypassing or evacuating sediment from reservoirs (White, 2001; Yang, 2006). The Missouri River reservoir system was designed before sustainable life-cycle management approaches to reservoir design were generally accepted (Ferrell, 1993; Engineering and Hydrosystems Inc., 2002) and therefore lack physical infrastructure to bypass sediment. The large reservoirs in the system have lost very little storage as a percentage of total storage (U.S. Army Corps of Engineers, 1994), but Lewis and Clark Lake—the most downstream reservoir—is estimated to fill by 2175 (Engineering and Hydrosystems Inc., 2002). Recent feasibility studies have addressed the extent to which sediment could be managed by bypassing or evacuating sediment from Lewis and Clark Lake. Although Lewis and Clark Lake impounds only ~6% more drainage area than the area impounded by the next upstream reservoir, the drainage includes the Niobrara River, which carries a high sediment load and has developed a large delta into Lewis and Clark Lake. The annual total sediment load into Lewis and Clark Lake, measured as subaqueous accumulation in the delta, has been estimated as 4.7×10^6 Mg*yr^{-1} (Engineering and Hydrosystems Inc., 2002). Evacuation of the annual sediment load to the river downstream of Gavins Point Dam would extend the useful life of the lake, and it would help mitigate the downstream sediment deficits. The annual load to the lake is only 3.5% of the pre-dam annual suspended-sediment load at Yankton; however, in comparison with present-day suspended-sediment loads, it is 19 times the load at Yankton and 64% of the load at Sioux City. Hence, bypassing of the annual sediment load around Gavins Point Dam would not be expected to reproduce sediment loads of the pre-dam reference condition but could nevertheless substantially increase sediment availability in the modern channel and riverine habitats of the Recreational River segment.

Sediment management scenarios for Gavins Point Dam also have potential liabilities, including cost, detrimental effects of sudden sediment inputs to benthic habitats downstream of the dam, detrimental effects of associated sudden water-quality shifts in parameters like dissolved oxygen and temperature, and effects of flooding. Hydraulic flushing of sediment during a reservoir drawdown was identified as an attractive approach in one study, but preliminary calculations indicated that without structural modifications to Gavins Point Dam, flows >14,100 m^3 per second (m^3*s^{-1}) for a duration of one day (or >4800 m^3*s^{-1} for 8 d) would be required annually to sustain reservoir storage capacity (Engineering and Hydrosystems Inc., 2002). For comparison, the peak post-dam discharge at Sioux City was 2900 m^3*s^{-1} in 1984, flows >1700 m^3*s^{-1} are considered to increase flooding downstream of Gavins Point Dam (Engineering and Hydrosystems Inc., 2002), and power-plant capacity is ~1000 m^3*s^{-1}. Hence, long-term sediment management on the Lower Missouri River faces substantive challenges to achieving even fairly modest restoration of the sediment regime.

CRITICAL UNCERTAINTIES

Key uncertainties in predictions of how the Lower Missouri River sediment regime will constrain management and restoration in the future include (1) uncertainty in suspended- and bed-load-sediment fluxes of the mainstem and tributaries; (2) the state of long-term geomorphic adjustment of the river channel; (3) how restoration activities will affect transport capacity and the sediment budget at the reach scale; (4) how reach-scale adjustments may cumulatively affect the entire Lower Missouri River; and (5) social, economic, and ecological demand for Missouri River sediment from downstream. These uncertainties are typical of restoration projects on large rivers.

• Sediment-flux data are the foundation for understanding the magnitude and spatial distributions of sediment-regime constraints on management and restoration of regulated rivers. Presently, available data on the Lower Missouri River are limited to suspended-sediment data that have been collected using different sampling protocols at different stations and frequencies. Lack of uniform sediment data collection along the river and for major tributaries, and gaps in the sediment record, make it difficult to assess trends and components of the sediment budget. Perhaps more important is the inability to quantify bed-load sediment transport, resulting in inherent potential errors of 5%–10% or more for individual total sediment-load calculations (Inman and Jenkins, 1999). Because of the critical role of bed material in creating aquatic habitat and maintaining channel grade, these potential errors are particularly significant. Moreover, bed-load sediment-flux data are critical for assessing sustainable amounts of commercial dredging.

• Understanding of long-term geomorphic adjustment of the Lower Missouri River channel long profile is essential for determining how and where to invest in sustainable restoration activities. Whether the present-day channel profile is in a state approaching dynamic equilibrium is a key question. If the present-day longitudinal profile is in a transient state, continuing to evolve toward a new equilibrium with the sediment regime, restoration projects designed for present-day conditions are unlikely to function sustainably in the future. Predictive understanding of long-term changes would be improved by integrating monitoring of a suite of system characteristics (channel incision–aggradation, trends in bed-material size, channel morphology, sediment transport) with predictive modeling of bed evolution (Holly and Karim, 1986).

• At the reach scale, ongoing restoration activities will change how sediment moves into and out of storage. Direct transfer of floodplain sediments to the main channel creates new accommodation space that may continue to erode, become refilled with sediment, or be maintained, depending on complex interaction of sediment transport, geomorphic evolution of the sites, and vegetation dynamics. This interaction is only broadly predictable but is likely to have an ongoing effect on ecological functioning of restored areas as well as on production of ecosystem services such as flood-peak mitigation and nutrient processing.

• Effects of individual restoration projects of tens or hundreds of hectares will be superimposed on the regional, long-term geomorphic adjustment. When, where, and how projects are constructed will determine how they interact with the sediment regime and how cumulative effects are propagated through the river. Prediction of these cumulative effects is confounded by lack of information on sediment fluxes and how geomorphic adjustments propagate through the mainstem.

• Finally, optimization of management and restoration of the Lower Missouri River takes place within the broader context of the Mississippi River drainage basin. Even if socioeconomic and ecological conflicts are resolved within the Lower Missouri River, management actions also may be limited by how these actions influence navigation on the Mississippi River, transport of sediment to replenish Mississippi Delta wetlands, and potential transport of sediment-hosted nutrients to the Gulf of Mexico.

Although the data and calculations presented in this article serve to illustrate the general scope of issues associated with managing and restoring the Lower Missouri River, the key uncertainties listed above limit predictive understanding of how sources and sinks of sediment will interact along the river and through time. Increased predictive understanding would require increased investment in strategic suspended-sediment monitoring, deployment of innovative bed-load measurements, and comprehensive monitoring of ongoing geomorphic adjustments.

SUMMARY AND CONCLUSIONS

The Lower Missouri River has much in common with other large, regulated and intensively engineered river systems in which a balance is being sought between traditional socioeconomic and newer ecological objectives. Sustainable achievement of all these objectives can be limited or complicated by profound alterations of the sediment regimes because of sediment entrapment in upstream reservoirs.

Regional geomorphic responses to the dam-related sediment deficit on the Lower Missouri River have resulted in zones of channel incision and moderate aggradation. Additional zones of acute channel incision related to commercial dredging or channel engineering are superimposed on the regional trends. Incision and aggradation limit what flow-regime management can accomplish in some reaches to restore ecosystem functions. In incising river segments, ecologically desirable reconnection of the floodplain has become an almost impossible goal. In stable-aggrading river segments, small spring pulses intended to provide spawning cues for endangered sturgeon threaten to inundate or saturate farm lands. However, these low-lying alluvial lands in aggrading river reaches may also provide the greatest opportunity to restore seasonally connected wetlands owing to more frequent flooding and higher groundwater levels.

Lack of sediment in incising river segments of the Lower Missouri River limits sustainable restoration of sandbar habitat for listed bird species. Management practices that minimize downstream transport of sand would help optimize ESH availability in the short term. In the long term, however, without implementation of costly artificial sediment replenishment, the sand supply will limit ESH in the Recreational River segment of the Lower Missouri River.

Creation of new shallow-water habitat introduces potential problems of putting too much sediment in the river. Creation of SWH involves taking sediment out of floodplain storage and delivering it to the main channel, a process that produces concerns about how long it might take the river to transport large quantities of additional sediment, and whether sediment-hosted nutrients and contaminants could harm the aquatic ecosystem. Whereas typical individual restoration projects may deliver amounts of sediment that are small relative to background suspended-sediment fluxes, sand delivery and cumulative effects are a concern. For example, the Jameson Island project in central Missouri would deliver a maximum of 3.5% of the background total suspended-sediment load of the river, but because sediment excavated from the floodplain is 78% sand, it could add as much as 11.2% to the post-dam annual suspended-sand load, as measured at Hermann, Missouri. At rates presently projected to meet restoration goals, a cumulative 34×10^6 Mg*yr^{-1} (or, for comparison, ~62% of the annual post-dam suspended-sediment load passing Hermann, Missouri) would potentially be delivered to the river until 2020, and suspended-sand load would be as much as 196% of the present rate. Nevertheless, the increased suspended-sediment load will still be <30% of the pre-dam load. The effects of this extra sediment load on the socioeconomic and ecological functions of the Lower Missouri River and the greater Mississippi River depend in large part on the locations and timing of the restoration projects. Strategic placement of restoration projects may help to mitigate local problems with channel incision.

Effective restoration strategies on dammed rivers like the Lower Missouri River require integrated, predictive understanding of ongoing geomorphic adjustments to altered sediment and flow regimes, and how these adjustments relate to restoration objectives. Because sediment-augmentation approaches (for example, sediment bypasses for reservoirs or flushing flows) may be costly or involve substantial environmental risk, restoration goals may need to accommodate a future with a permanently altered sediment regime.

ACKNOWLEDGMENTS

This manuscript benefited from thoughtful reviews by Paul Boyd, Jim Fairchild, Allen Gellis, Jim O'Connor, Dan Pridal, and John Remus.

REFERENCES CITED

Allen, P.A., 1997, Earth Surface Processes: Cambridge, Massachusetts, Blackwell Publishing, 404 p.

Aulenbach, B.T., Buxton, H.T., Battaglin, W.A., and Coupe, R.H., 2007, Streamflow and Nutrient Fluxes of the Mississippi-Atchafalaya River Basin and Subbasins for the Period of Record through 2005: U.S. Geological Survey Open-File Report 2007-1080, http://toxics.usgs.gov/pubs/of-2007-1080/index.html.

Bednarek, A.T., and Hart, D.D., 2005, Modifying dam operations to restore rivers: Ecological responses to Tennessee River dam mitigation: Ecological Applications, v. 15, p. 997–1008, doi: 10.1890/04-0586.

Biedenharn, D.S., Soileau, R.S., Hubbard, L.C., Hoffman, P.H., Thorne, C.R., Bromley, C.C., and Watson, C.C., 2001, Missouri River—Fort Peck Dam to Ponca State Park geomorphological assessment related to bank stabilization: Unpublished report to U.S. Army Corps of Engineers, 151 p.

Blevins, D.W., 2006, The Response of Suspended Sediment, Turbidity, and Velocity to Historical Alterations of the Missouri River: U.S. Geological Survey Circular 1301, 8 p., http://pubs.usgs.gov/circ/2006/1301/.

Brandt, S.A., 2000, Classification of geomorphological effects downstream of dams: CATENA, v. 40, p. 375–401, http://www.sciencedirect.com/science/article/B6VCG-40K9V4B-3/2/57f979121de22c250403c20ad2393005, doi: 10.1016/S0341-8162(00)00093-X.

CDM Federal Programs Corporation, 2007, Miscellaneous military and civil hazardous waste investigation projects for the U.S. Army Corps of Engineers, Kansas City District: Kansas City, Missouri, unpublished file reports.

Chapman, D.C., Allert, A.L., Fairchild, J.F., May, T.W., Schmitt, C.J., and Callahan, E.V., 2001, Toxicity and Bioavailability of Metals in the Missouri River Adjacent to a Lead Refinery: U.S. Geological Survey Biological Science Report USGS/BRD/BSR—2001-0004, 27 p.

Collier, M., Webb, R.H., and Schmidt, J.C., 1996, Dams and Rivers: A Primer on the Downstream Effects of Dams: U.S. Geological Survey Circular 1126: Tucson, Arizona, U.S. Geological Survey, 94 p.

Echols, K.R., Brumbaugh, W.G., Orazio, C.E., May, T.W., Poulton, B.C., and Peterman, P.H., 2008, Distribution of pesticides, PAHs, PCBs and bioavailable metals in depositional sediments of the Lower Missouri River, USA: Archives of Environmental Contamination and Toxicology, v. 55, p. 161–172.

Elliott, C.M., and Jacobson, R.B., 2006, Geomorphic Classification and Assessment of Channel Dynamics in the Missouri National Recreational River, South Dakota and Nebraska: U.S. Geological Survey Scientific Investigations Report 2006-5313, 66 p., http://pubs.er.usgs.gov/usgspubs/sir/sir20065313.

Engineering and Hydrosystems Inc., 2002, Conceptual Analysis of Sedimentation Issues on the Niobrara and Missouri Rivers, South Dakota and Nebraska: Omaha, Nebraska, U.S. Army Corps of Engineers, 19 p.

Ferrell, J., 1993, Big Dam Era—A Legislative History of the Pick-Sloan Missouri River Basin Program: Omaha, Nebraska, U.S. Army Corps of Engineers, 228 p.

Ferrell, J., 1996, Soundings—100 Years of the Missouri River Navigation Project: Omaha, Nebraska, U.S. Army Corps of Engineers, 171 p.

Funk, J.L., and Robinson, J.W., 1974, Changes in the Channel of the Lower Missouri River and Effects on Fish and Wildlife: Jefferson City, Missouri, Missouri Department of Conservation, 52 p.

Gaeuman, D., and Jacobson, R.B., 2007, Field assessment of alternative bedload transport estimators: Journal of Hydraulic Engineering, v. 133, p. 1319–1328, doi: 10.1061/(ASCE)0733-9429(2007)133:12(1319).

Galat, D.L., and Lipkin, R., 2000, Restoring ecological integrity of great rivers: Historical hydrographs aid in defining reference conditions for the Missouri River: Hydrobiologia, v. 422–423, p. 29–48, doi: 10.1023/A:1017052319056.

Galat, D.L., Berry, C.R., Gardner, W.M., Hendrickson, J.C., Mestl, G.E., Power, G.J., Stone, C., and Winston, M.R., 2005a, Spatiotemporal patterns and changes in Missouri River fishes, in Rinne, J.N., et al., eds., Historical Changes in Large River Fish Assemblages of the Americas: Bethesda, Maryland, American Fisheries Society, Symposium 45, p. 249–291.

Galat, D.L., Berry, C.R., Jr., Peters, E.J., and White, R.G., 2005b, Missouri River Basin, in Benke, A.C., and Cushing, C.E., eds., Rivers of North America: Oxford, UK, Elsevier, p. 427–480.

Ghimire, M.K., Bondy, A.K., Cordova, A.J., Noah, D., and Holbrook, J., 2007, Surficial material geologic map of the Arrow Rock 7.5' quadrangle: Rolla, Missouri, Missouri Department of Natural Resources, Division of Geology and Land Survey, Geological Survey Program, OFM-05-XXX-GS, scale 1:24,000, 1 sheet.

Graham, B., 2007, Costs mount as river erodes—Experts say expensive measures are needed to offset the effects of channel cutting on the Missouri: Kansas City Star, 16 January 2007, p. B1.

Grams, P.E., and Schmidt, J.C., 2005, Equilibrium or indeterminate? Where sediment budgets fail: Sediment mass balance and adjustment of channel form, Green River downstream from Flaming Gorge Dam, Utah and Colorado: Geomorphology, v. 71, p. 156–181, http://www.sciencedirect.com/science/article/B6V93-4G1R3G6-4/2/12d5c369569697fb9f2ad610b5b4bb30.

Hesse, L.W., and Sheets, W., 1993, The Missouri River hydrosystem: Fisheries, v. 18, p. 5–14, doi: 10.1577/1548-8446(1993)018<0005:TMRH>2.0.CO;2.

Holbrook, J., Kliem, G., Nzewunwah, C., Jobe, Z., and Goble, R., 2006, Surficial alluvium and topography of the Overton Bottom North Unit, Big Muddy National Fish and Wildlife Refuge in the Missouri River valley and its potential influence on environmental management, in Jacobson, R.B., ed., Science to Support Adaptive Habitat Management, Overton Bottoms North Unit, Big Muddy National Fish and Wildlife Refuge, Missouri: U.S. Geological Survey Scientific Investigations Report 2006-5086, p. 17–32.

Holly, F.M., and Karim, F., 1986, Simulation of Missouri River bed degradation: Journal of Hydraulic Engineering, v. 112, p. 497–517.

Holmes, J.R.R., 1996, Sediment Transport in the Lower Missouri and the Central Mississippi Rivers, June 26 through September 14, 1993: U.S. Geological Survey Circular 1120-L, 23 p.

Horowitz, A.J., 2003, An evaluation of sediment rating curves for estimating suspended sediment concentrations for subsequent flux calculations: Hydrological Processes, v. 17, p. 3387–3409, doi: 10.1002/hyp.1299.

Inman, D.L., and Jenkins, S.A., 1999, Climate change and the episodicity of sediment flux of small California rivers: Journal of Geology, v. 107, p. 251–270, doi: 10.1086/314346.

Jacobson, R.B., 1995, Spatial controls on patterns of land-use induced stream disturbance at the drainage-basin scale—An example from gravel-bed streams of the Ozark Plateaus, Missouri, in Costa, J.E., Miller, A.J., Potter, K.W., and Wilcock, P.R., eds., Natural and Anthropogenic Influences in Fluvial Geomorphology: AGU Geophysical Monograph 89, The Wolman Volume, p. 219–239.

Jacobson, R.B., and Coleman, D.J., 1986, Stratigraphy and recent evolution of Maryland Piedmont flood plains: American Journal of Science, v. 286, p. 617–637.

Jacobson, R.B., and Galat, D.L., 2006, Flow and form in rehabilitation of large-river ecosystems: An example from the Lower Missouri River: Geomorphology, v. 77, p. 249–269.

Jacobson, R.B., and Galat, D.L., 2008, Design of a naturalized flow regime on the Lower Missouri River: Ecohydrology, v. 1, no. 2, p. 81–104.

Jacobson, R.B., Laustrup, M.S., and Chapman, M.D., 2001, Fluvial processes and passive rehabilitation of the Lisbon Bottom side-channel chute, Lower Missouri River, in Dorava, J.M., et al., eds., Fluvial Processes and Physical Habitat: American Geophysical Union, Water Science and Application Series, v. 4, p. 199–216.

Jacobson, R.B., Laustrup, M.S., D'Urso, G.J., and Reuter, J.M., 2004, Physical Habitat Dynamics in Four Side-Channel Chutes, Lower Missouri River: U.S. Geological Survey Open-File Report 2004-1071, 60 p., http://infolink.cr.usgs.gov/RSB/USGS_OFR_2004-1071/index.htm.

Jacobson, R.B., Chojnacki, K.A., and Reuter, J.M., 2007, Land Capability Potential Index (LCPI) for the Lower Missouri River Valley: U.S. Geological Survey Scientific Investigations Report 2007-5256, 19 p., http://pubs.usgs.gov/sir/2007/5256/.

Junk, W.J., Bayley, P.B., and Sparks, R.E., 1989, The flood pulse concept in river-floodplain systems: Canadian Special Publication of Fisheries and Aquatic Sciences, v. 106, p. 110–127.

Karim, M.F., and Holly, F.M., 1986, Simulation of Missouri River bed degradation: Journal of Hydraulic Engineering, v. 112, p. 497–517.

Kesel, R.H., 1988, The decline in the suspended load of the Lower Mississippi River and its influence on adjacent wetlands: Environmental Geology and Water Sciences, v. 11, p. 271–281, doi: 10.1007/BF02574816.

Langbein, W.B., and Schumm, S.A., 1958, Yield of sediment in relation to mean annual precipitation: American Geophysical Union Transactions, v. 39, p. 1076–1084.

Latka, B., 2006, Fact Sheet—Programmatic Environmental Impact Statement for the Maintenance and Creation of Emergent Sandbar Habitat on the Upper Missouri River: Omaha, Nebraska, U.S. Army Corps of Engineers, 2 p.

Missouri Basin Inter-Agency Committee, 1969, The Missouri River Basin Comprehensive Framework Study: Washington, D.C., v. 6, 143 p.

Missouri Basin Inter-Agency Committee, 1971, The Missouri River Basin Comprehensive Framework Study: Washington, D.C., U.S. Government Printing Office, v. 6, 143 p.

National Research Council, 2002, The Missouri River Ecosystem, Exploring the Prospects for Recovery: Washington, D.C., National Academy Press, 176 p.

Natural Resources Conservation Service, 2003, National Resources Inventory 2003 Annual NRI Soil Erosion: U.S. Department of Agriculture, Natural Resources Conservation Service, available online at http://www.nrcs .usda.gov/technical/land/nri03/nri03eros-mrb.html, 22 p.

Nittrouer, J.A., Allison, M.A., and Campanella, R., 2008, Bedform transform rates for the lowermost Mississippi River: Journal of Geophysical Research, v. 113, doi: 10.1029/2007JF000795.

Pasternack, G.B., Wang, C.L., and Merz, J.E., 2004, Application of a 2d hydrodynamic model to design of reach-scale spawning gravel replenishment on the Mokelumne River, California: River Research and Applications, v. 20, p. 205–225, doi: 10.1002/rra.748.

Petts, G.E., 1989, Perspectives for ecological management of regulated rivers, *in* Gore, J.A., and Petts, G.E., eds., Alternatives in Regulated River Management: Boca Raton, Florida, CRC Press, p. 3–24.

Pinter, N., and Heine, R.A., 2005, Hydrodynamic and morphodynamic response to river engineering documented by fixed-discharge analysis, Lower Missouri River, U.S.A: Journal of Hydrology, v. 302, p. 70–91, doi: 10.1016/j .jhydrol.2004.06.039.

Poff, N.L., Allan, J.D., Bain, M.B., Karr, J.R., Prestegaard, K.L., Richter, B.D., Sparks, R.E., and Stromberg, J.C., 1997, The natural flow regime: Bioscience, v. 47, p. 769–784, doi: 10.2307/1313099.

Price, K.H., and Martz, M., 2007, Evaluating constructed backwater habitat and sandbar islands on the Missouri River, *in* World Environmental and Water Resources Congress, 2000: Tampa, Florida, Restoring Our Natural Habitat, American Society of Civil Engineering, p. 1–10.

Richter, B.D., Baumgartner, J.V., Wiginton, R., and Braun, D.P., 1997, How much water does a river need?: Freshwater Biology, v. 37, p. 231–249, doi: 10.1046/j.1365-2427.1997.00153.x.

Richter, B.D., Warner, A.T., Meyer, J.L., and Lutz, K., 2006, A collaborative and adaptive process for developing environmental flow recommendations: River Research and Applications, v. 22, p. 297–318, doi: 10.1002/ rra.892, http://dx.doi.org/.

Rounds, S.A., 2007, Temperature Effects of Point Sources, Riparian Shading, and Dam Operations on the Willamette River, Oregon: U.S. Geological Survey Scientific Investigations Report 2007-5185, 34 p.

Runkel, R.L., Crawford, C.G., and Cohn, T.A., 2004, Load Estimator (LOADEST): A FORTRAN Program for Estimating Constituent Loads in Streams and Rivers: U.S. Geological Survey Techniques and Methods Book 4, Chapter A5, 69 p.

Schalk, G.K., and Jacobson, R.B., 1997, Scour, Sedimentation, and Sediment Characteristics at Six Levee-Break Sites in Missouri from the 1993 Missouri River Flood: U.S. Geological Survey Water-Resources Investigations Report 97-4110, 72 p.

Schalk, G.K., Holmes, R.R., and Johnson, G.P., 1997, Physical and Chemical Data on Sediments Deposited in the Missouri and Mississippi River Flood Plains during the July through August 1993 Flood: U.S. Geological Survey Circular 1120-L, 62 p.

Schilt, C.R., 2007, Developing fish passage and protection at hydropower dams: Applied Animal Behaviour Science, v. 104, p. 295–325, http://www.sciencedirect.com/science/article/B6T48-4MBC4T8

-1/2/7264029674694e756a3c2d8dd3bf9d58, doi: 10.1016/j.applanim.2006 .09.004.

Schmidt, J.C., and Wilcock, P.R., 2008, Metrics for assessing the downstream effects of dams: Water Resources Research, v. 44, doi: 10.1029/2006WR005092.

Secretary of War, 1934, Missouri River: House Document 238: Washington, D.C., Government Printing Office.

Simon, A., Dickerson, W., and Heins, A., 2004, Suspended-sediment transport rates at the 1.5-year recurrence interval for ecoregions of the United States: Transport condition at the bankfull and effective discharge?: Geomorphology, v. 58, p. 243–262, doi: 10.1016/j.geomorph.2003.07.003.

Smelser, M.E., and Schmidt, J.C., 1998, An assessment methodology for determining historical changes in mountain streams: U.S. Forest Service General Technical Report RMRS-GTR-6, 29 p.

Sparks, R.E., 1995, Need for ecosystem management of large rivers and their floodplains: Bioscience, v. 45, no. 3, p. 168–182.

Sparks, R.E., Nelson, J.C., and Yin, Y., 1998, Naturalization of the flood regime in regulated rivers: Bioscience, v. 48, p. 706–720, doi: 10.2307/1313334.

Sullivan, A.B., and Rounds, S.A., 2006, Modeling Water Quality Effects of Structural and Operational Changes to Scoggins Dam and Henry Hagg Lake, Oregon: U.S. Geological Survey Scientific Investigations Report 2006-5060, 36 p.

Trimble, S.W., 1974, Man-Induced Soil Erosion on the Southern Piedmont, 1700–1970: Ankeny, Iowa, Soil Conservation Society of America, 180 p.

Trimble, S.W., and Lund, S.W., 1982, Soil Conservation and Reduction of Erosion and Sedimentation in the Coon Creek Basin, Wisconsin: U.S. Geological Survey Professional Paper 1234, 35 p.

U.S. Army Corps of Engineers, 1951, Suspended Sediment in the Missouri River—Daily Record for Water Years 1937–1948: Omaha, Nebraska, U.S. Army Corps of Engineers, Missouri River Division, 219 p.

U.S. Army Corps of Engineers, 1957, Suspended Sediment in the Missouri River—Daily Record for Water Years 1949–1954: Omaha, Nebraska, U.S. Army Corps of Engineers, Missouri River Division, 210 p.

U.S. Army Corps of Engineers, 1965, Suspended Sediment in the Missouri River—Daily Record for Water Years 1955–1959: Omaha, Nebraska, U.S. Army Corps of Engineers, Missouri River Division, 118 p.

U.S. Army Corps of Engineers, 1970, Suspended Sediment in the Missouri River—Daily Record for Water Years 1960–1964: Omaha, Nebraska, U.S. Army Corps of Engineers, Missouri River Division, 190 p.

U.S. Army Corps of Engineers, 1972, Suspended Sediment in the Missouri River—Daily Record for Water Years 1965–1969: Omaha, Nebraska, U.S. Army Corps of Engineers, Missouri River Division, 248 p.

U.S. Army Corps of Engineers, 1976, Suspended Sediment in the Missouri River—Daily Record for Water Years 1970–1974: Kansas City, Missouri, U.S. Army Corps of Engineers, Missouri River Division, 201 p.

U.S. Army Corps of Engineers, 1994, Missouri River Master Water Control Manual Review and Update Study: Volume 5: Aggradation, Degradation, and Water Quality Conditions: Omaha, Nebraska, U.S. Army Corps of Engineers, Missouri River Division, 52 p.

U.S. Army Corps of Engineers, 1998, Reservoir regulation studies—Daily routing model studies, master water control manual Missouri River review and update study: Omaha, Nebraska, U.S. Army Corps of Engineers, Northwest Division, v. 2A, 137 p.

U.S. Army Corps of Engineers, 2003, Final Biological Assessment on the Operation of the Missouri River Mainstem Reservoir System, the Operation and Maintenance of the Bank Stabilization and Navigation Project, and the Operation of the Kansas River Reservoir System: Omaha, Nebraska, U.S. Army Corps of Engineers, Northwestern Division, Missouri River Basin Water Management Division, 29 p.

U.S. Army Corps of Engineers, 2004a, Missouri River Stage Trends: Omaha, Nebraska, U.S. Army Corps of Engineers, Northwestern Division, Reservoir Control Center Technical Report A04, 43 p.

U.S. Army Corps of Engineers, 2004b, Summary Missouri River Final Environmental Impact Statement—Master Water Control Manual Review and Update: Omaha, Nebraska, U.S. Army Corps of Engineers, Northwest Division, 28 p.

U.S. Army Corps of Engineers, 2004c, Upper Mississippi River System Flow Frequency Study: Rock Island, Illinois, U.S. Army Corps of Engineers, 33 p.

U.S. Army Corps of Engineers, 2006a, Missouri River Bank Stabilization and Navigation Project, Fish and Wildlife Mitigation Project—Annual

Implementation Report: Kansas City, Missouri; Omaha, Nebraska; U.S. Army Corps of Engineers, 35 p. plus appendices.

U.S. Army Corps of Engineers, 2006b, Missouri River Mainstem Reservoir System—Master Water Control Manual, Missouri River Basin: Omaha, Nebraska, Northwestern Division, Missouri River Basin, Water Management Division, 431 p., http://www.nwd-mr.usace.army.mil/rcc/reports/mmanual/MasterManual.pdf.

U.S. Army Corps of Engineers, 2007a, Missouri River Stage Trends: Omaha, Nebraska, U.S. Army Corps of Engineers, Northwestern Division, Reservoir Control Center Technical Report Ja-07, 43 p., http://www.nwd-mr.usace.army.mil/rcc/reports/pdfs/Ja07MRStageTrends.pdf.

U.S. Army Corps of Engineers, 2007b, Results of Ongoing Study of Missouri River Bed Degradation: CRP Water Surface and Commercial Dredging Volume Comparisons, 1990 vs. 2002 and 2005: U.S. Army Corps of Engineers File Report, 11 p.

U.S. Army Corps of Engineers, 2007c, unpublished data, Subsurface exploration data at Jameson Island, 43 p.

U.S. Army Corps of Engineers, 2007d, unpublished report, Missouri River sediment changes and aquatic habitat construction activities: Kansas City District, U.S. Army Corps of Engineers file memorandum, 30 p.

U.S. Fish and Wildlife Service, 2003, Amendment to the 2000 Biological Opinion on the Operation of the Missouri River Main Stem Reservoir System, Operation and Maintenance of the Missouri River Bank Stabilization and Navigation Project, and Operation of the Kansas River Reservoir System: U.S. Fish and Wildlife Service, 308 p., http://www.nwd-mr.usace.army.mil/mmanual/FinalBO2003.pdf.

U.S. Geological Survey (USGS), 2001, National Water Information System (NWISWeb) data: http://waterdata.usgs.gov/nwis/ (accessed June 2007).

White, R., 2001, Evacuation of Sediments from Reservoirs: London, Thomas Telford Services, 280 p.

Wildhaber, M.L., DeLonay, A.J., Papoulias, D.M., Galat, D.L., Jacobson, R.B., Simpkins, D.G., Braaten, P.J., Korschgen, C.E., and Mac, M.J., 2007, A Conceptual Life-History Model for Pallid and Shovelnose Sturgeon: U.S. Geological Survey Circular 1315, 19 p.

Williams, G.P., and Wolman, M.G., 1984, Downstream Effects of Dams on Alluvial Rivers: U.S. Geological Survey Professional Paper 1286, 83 p.

Yang, C.T., 2006, Erosion and Sedimentation Manual: Denver, U.S. Department of Interior, Bureau of Reclamation, Technical Service Center, various pagings.

MANUSCRIPT ACCEPTED BY THE SOCIETY 15 SEPTEMBER 2008

The Geological Society of America
Special Paper 451
2009

Channel, floodplain, and wetland responses to floods and overbank sedimentation, 1846–2006, Halfway Creek Marsh, Upper Mississippi Valley, Wisconsin

Faith A. Fitzpatrick
U.S. Geological Survey, 8505 Research Way, Middleton, Wisconsin 53562, USA

James C. Knox
University of Wisconsin–Madison, Department of Geography, 550 North Park Street, Madison, Wisconsin 53706-1491, USA

Joseph P. Schubauer-Berigan
U.S. Environmental Protection Agency, Office of Research and Development, 26 W. Martin Luther King Drive, Cincinnati, Ohio 45268, USA

ABSTRACT

Conversion of upland forest and prairie vegetation to agricultural land uses, following Euro-American settlement in the Upper Mississippi River System, led to accelerated runoff and soil erosion that subsequently transformed channels, floodplains, and wetlands on bottomlands. Halfway Creek Marsh, at the junction of Halfway Creek and the Mississippi River on Wisconsin's western border, is representative of such historical transformation. This marsh became the focus of a 2005–2006 investigation by scientists from the U.S. Geological Survey, the University of Wisconsin–Madison, and the U.S. Environmental Protection Agency, who used an understanding of the historical transformation to help managers identify possible restoration alternatives for Halfway Creek Marsh. Field-scale topographic surveys and sediment cores provided data for reconstructing patterns and rates of historical overbank sedimentation in the marsh. Information culled from historical maps, aerial photographs, General Land Office Survey notes, and other historical documents helped establish the timing of anthropogenic disturbances and document changes in channel patterns. Major human disturbances, in addition to agricultural land uses, included railroad and road building, construction of artificial levees, drainage alterations, and repeated dam failures associated with large floods. A volume of approximately 1,400,000 m³, involving up to 2 m of sandy historical overbank deposition, is stored through the upper and lower marshes and along the adjacent margins of Halfway Creek and its principal tributary, Sand Lake Coulee. The estimated overbank sedimentation rate for the entire marsh is ~3,000 m³ yr⁻¹ for the recent period 1994–2006. In spite of reduced surface runoff and soil erosion in recent years, this recent sedimentation rate still exceeds by ~4 times the early settlement (1846–1885) rate of 700 m³ yr⁻¹,

Fitzpatrick, F.A., Knox, J.C., and Schubauer-Berigan, J.P., 2009, Channel, floodplain, and wetland responses to floods and overbank sedimentation, 1846–2006, Halfway Creek Marsh, Upper Mississippi Valley, Wisconsin, *in* James, L.A., Rathbun, S.L., and Whittecar, G.R., eds., Management and Restoration of Fluvial Systems with Broad Historical Changes and Human Impacts: Geological Society of America Special Paper 451, p. 23–42, doi: 10.1130/2009.2451(02). For permission to copy, contact editing@geosociety.org. ©2009 The Geological Society of America. All rights reserved.

when anthropogenic acceleration of upland surface runoff and soil erosion was beginning. The highest rate of historical bottomland sedimentation occurred from 1919 to 1936, when the estimated overbank sedimentation rate was 20,400 m³ yr⁻¹. This rate exceeded by nearly 30 times the 1846–1886 rate. Artificial levees were constructed along the upper reach of Halfway Creek in the marsh during the early twentieth century to restrict flooding on the adjacent bottomlands. Anomalously high overbank sedimentation rates subsequently occurred on the floodplain between the levees, which also facilitated more efficient transport of sediment into the lower marsh bottomland. Although overbank sedimentation rates dropped after 1936, corresponding to the widespread adoption of soil-conservation and agricultural best-management practices, the continuation of anomalously high overbank sedimentation between the levees led to increased bank heights and development of a relatively deep channel. The deep cross-section morphology is commonly mistaken as evidence of channel incision; however, this morphology actually resulted from excessive overbank sedimentation. The historical metamorphosis of the Halfway Creek channel and riparian wetlands underscores the importance of understanding the long-term history of channel and floodplain evolution when restoration of channels and riparian wetlands are under consideration. Sedimentation patterns and channel morphology for Halfway Creek Marsh probably are representative of other anthropogenically altered riparian wetlands in the Upper Mississippi River System and similar landscapes elsewhere.

INTRODUCTION

The present study examines channel, floodplain, and wetland responses to historical floods and overbank sedimentation accelerated by human-related environmental changes in a Mississippi River tributary following conversion of upland vegetation of prairie and forest to agricultural land. This conversion accelerated surface runoff and soil erosion. In turn, increased downstream flooding and sedimentation altered the morphology of stream channels, floodplains, and riparian wetlands. This metamorphosis of bottomlands is especially prominent where tributary streams enter the Mississippi River Valley.

In 2005–2006, the U.S. Geological Survey (USGS), University of Wisconsin–Madison, U.S. Environmental Protection Agency (USEPA), and U.S. Fish and Wildlife Service (USFWS) conducted a cooperative research study of the effects of historical overbank sedimentation and floods on channels, floodplains, and wetlands in and near Halfway Creek Marsh, a riparian wetland complex in the Upper Mississippi River System near Midway, Wisconsin (Fig. 1). The marsh is fed by floodwaters from two small agricultural watersheds, Halfway Creek and Sand Lake Coulee (total of 114 km²) and is influenced by backwaters during floods on the Mississippi River. The marsh is part of the Upper Mississippi River National Wildlife and Fish Refuge and is within the Wisconsin Driftless Area (Fig. 1), where steep topography and silty soils are highly susceptible to erosion and gullying.

Earlier investigations documented widespread accelerated soil erosion and sedimentation in valley bottomlands following clearing of woodlands and prairies for cropland and pasture of the Upper Mississippi River System and elsewhere in the United States (Happ et al., 1940, and references therein). Much of the sediment eroded during the eighteenth, nineteenth, and twentieth

centuries remains stored in floodplains, along channel margins, or in former millponds (Costa, 1975; Knox, 1977; Magilligan, 1985; Trimble, 1981; Fitzpatrick and Knox, 2000; Walling and Owens, 2002; Ross et al., 2004; Allmendinger et al., 2007; Walter and Merritts, 2008). Ross et al. (2004) reported that much of the historical overbank deposits of Chesapeake Bay tributaries are stored in lower main valleys, near entrances to larger water bodies (large rivers, lakes, estuaries, or ocean coasts) in environments represented by critical aquatic, wetland, and riparian habitats. Excess sediment in channels, natural levees, and floodplains increases flood hazards for downstream areas, obstructs drainages, reduces reservoir storage capacity in millponds, impairs navigation, and alters vegetation growth along riparian corridors (Happ et al., 1940; Magilligan, 1985; Wolfe and Diehl, 1993). Sediment episodically deposited in channels and on floodplains and wetlands during large historical floods also accelerates alluvial-fan formation, especially where tributaries enter valley bottoms of large rivers. Previous studies have shown that timing, rates, and magnitudes of overbank sedimentation vary systematically with position of a site within the larger stream network, and with local proximity to other valleys and sediment sources, valley constrictions or widening, and base-level controls (Magilligan, 1985; Fitzpatrick and Knox, 2000).

Accelerated erosion and sedimentation in the Upper Mississippi River System were especially prominent over ~100 yr from the mid-1800s through the mid-1900s (Knox, 2002). This acceleration is characteristic of the loess-covered, hilly Driftless Area of southwestern Wisconsin and northwestern Illinois and in similar topographic landscapes of northeastern Iowa and southeastern Minnesota (Adams, 1940, 1942; Beach, 1994; Faulkner, 1998; Happ, 1944; Happ et al., 1940; Knox, 1972, 1977, 1987, 2001, 2006; Lecce, 1997; Lecce and Pavlowsky, 2001; Magilligan,

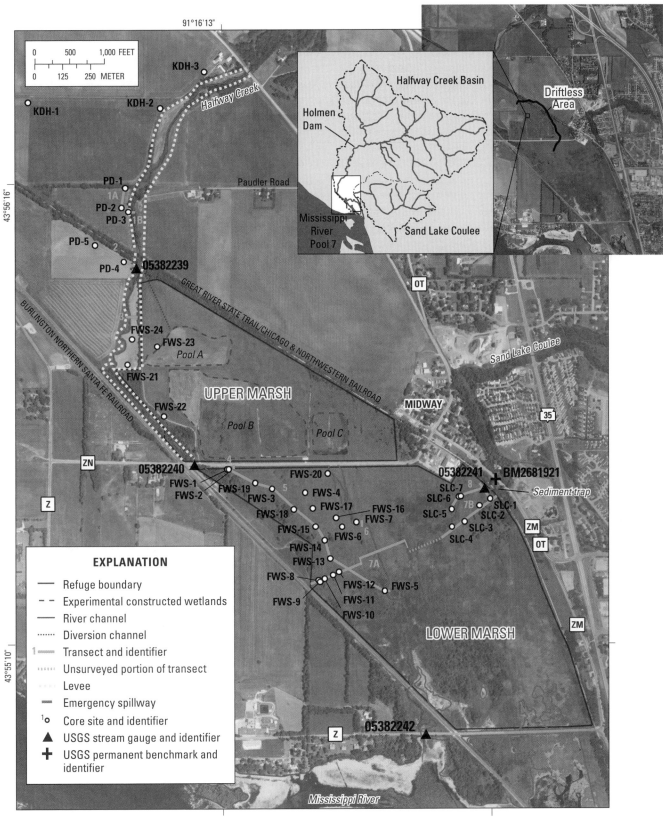

Figure 1. Study location, core locations, and U.S. Geological Survey stream gauges near the Upper Mississippi River National Wildlife and Fish Refuge Halfway Creek Marsh, Wisconsin.

1985, 1992; Trimble, 1983, 1993, 1999; Woltemade, 1994). Long-term average postsettlement floodplain sedimentation rates are about an order of magnitude or more higher than presettlement rates (Knox, 2006), but rates of sedimentation varied over the period of agricultural disturbance. For example, postsettlement overbank sedimentation rates for the Galena River in the southern Driftless Area were highest prior to 1940 (1.9 cm yr yr⁻¹) and decreased after 1940 (0.75 cm yr⁻¹) in response to widespread soil conservation efforts and implementation of agricultural best-management practices (Magilligan, 1985). A sediment budget constructed for Coon Creek in the Wisconsin Driftless Area by Trimble (1981) indicated that prior to implementation of conservation management practices in the 1940s and 1950s, >50% of the historical sediment load was deposited in valleys, especially the lower main valleys. Construction of the lock and dam system along the Upper Mississippi River in the 1930s raised the base level of tributary valley mouths by up to 2 m and contributed to accelerated sedimentation along tributary lower reaches and at their mouths (Knox, 2006).

The present study uses various-age benchmarks to define six historic periods of channel, floodplain, and wetland responses to historical floods and accelerated overbank sedimentation. The six periods include 1846–1885, 1886–1918, 1919–1936, 1937–1969, 1970–1993, and 1994–2006. These six periods adequately capture evolving changes in upland land use and other human-related structural modifications (dams, roads, etc.) in the watershed. The six periods represent sufficient amounts of time to show that responses to upland environmental change involved rapid alteration of downstream flooding and sedimentation which, in turn, quickly impacted the morphology of channels, floodplains, and riparian wetlands. The results of the present investigation illustrate the importance of understanding long-term evolutionary geomorphic processes rather than relying mainly on morphologic evidence alone when channel restoration efforts are under consideration. In the study area, greatly accelerated overbank sedimentation produced a channel cross-section morphology that gives a false impression that stream incision is occurring, but the history of geomorphic change shows that the deep-channel cross-section morphology is a consequence of excessive sediment loading and extreme overbank deposition. This example illustrates that over-reliance on morphology can lead to misinterpretation of actual prevailing physical processes.

STUDY AREA

Halfway Creek Marsh is located in the Mississippi River Valley, along the western edge of the unglaciated Driftless Area in west-central Wisconsin (Fig. 1). The marsh is part of the Upper Mississippi River National Wildlife and Fish Refuge, which was established in 1924 to preserve habitat for plants, fish, migratory birds, and other wildlife in a 420-km corridor between Rock Island, Illinois, and Wabasha, Minnesota.

The marsh is fed by Halfway Creek, which drains a watershed of 93 km², and by Sand Lake Coulee, which drains a watershed of 21 km². The watersheds of these streams are characterized by moderate to steep, forested slopes separated by relatively flat, narrow agricultural uplands. Land cover in the combined watersheds is dominated by forest (49%) and row crops with some hay (32%). Other types of land cover and land use include pasture (10%), urban areas (6%), barren land (2%), and wetland (1%) (Reese et al., 2002). An impounded marsh wetland was designed and constructed by Ducks Unlimited for the USFWS in 1999–2000 in the upper Halfway Creek Marsh. The marsh was designed to (1) capture stormwater and associated sediment and nutrients during high-water events before they enter the lower marsh, and (2) to restore, enhance, and preserve wetland habitat, especially for migratory birds (Fig. 1; U.S. Fish and Wildlife Service, 2000).

The geologic setting of the watersheds of Halfway Creek and Sand Lake Coulee is influenced by Paleozoic bedrock, Pleistocene loess (windblown silt), and sand and gravel deposited by former meltwaters of late Pleistocene glaciers in the Mississippi River headwaters. Bedrock is mainly Ordovician dolomite underlying upland drainage divides, and Cambrian sandstone underlying hillslopes (Evans, 2003). Lower hillslopes contain thick deposits of late Pleistocene colluvium.

The longitudinal profile of Halfway Creek can be divided into three contrasting segments that include (1) a headwater reach in the Driftless Area uplands where the stream flows on either bedrock or shallow alluvial fills of sand and gravel; (2) a middle reach entrenched into a terminal Pleistocene terrace, which is underlain by sand and gravel and capped by loess and dune sand; and (3) a downstream reach associated with Holocene alluvial-fan deposition along a large relict channel that was incised by terminal Pleistocene meltwaters (Fig. 2) (Knox, 1999; Fitzpatrick et al., 2008). This study mainly is focused on the downstream reach (Figs. 1, 2). Halfway Creek deposited sediment across the alluvial fan beginning ~16,000 yr ago, and ending in the late nineteenth and early twentieth centuries, when human activities began to restrict its course (Fig. 2; Knox, 1999). The sand and gravel deposits underlying the entrenched terrace and the alluvial fan are sources of coarse-grained substrate and bed load for present-day Halfway Creek. Easily eroded, the silt-dominated loess, which is the principal soil parent material of agricultural fields, is the major source of fine-grained sediment and suspended load for Halfway Creek.

METHODS

The locations of historical stream channels on archival notes and maps were digitized and overlaid on 2005 aerial photographs (U.S. Department of Agriculture, 2005) in a geographic information system (GIS) to help identify areas in the marsh with overbank sedimentation. Field notes and maps used in the GIS overlays included the 1846 General Land Office notes and maps (http://digicoll.library.wisc.edu/SurveyNotes/SurveyInfo. html), an 1866 map from the G.K. Warren surveys of the Mississippi River (Warren, 1867), and an 1878 plat map (Snyder, Van Vechten & Co., 1878). Twentieth-century channel locations

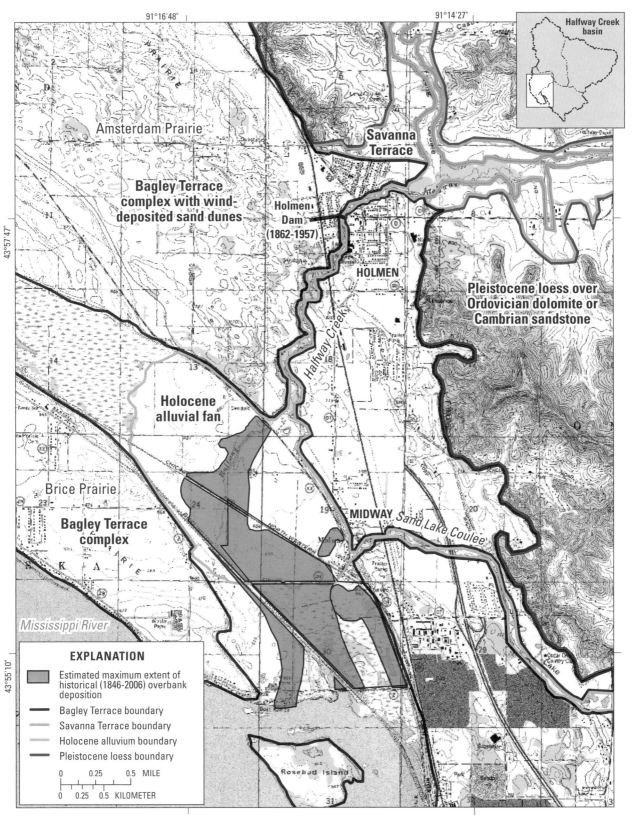

Figure 2. Generalized geologic map of Halfway Creek Marsh, Wisconsin, and surrounding area (modified from Evans, 2003).

were obtained from a 1906 plat map (Ogle, 1906), land economic inventory maps (Bordner Surveys) for La Crosse County from 1937 to 1938 (Wisconsin Department of Agriculture and Wisconsin Geological and Natural History Survey, 1938), 1973 USGS 7.5-min topographic quadrangle maps, and 2005 aerial photographs (U.S. Department of Agriculture, 2005). The resolution of channel locations improved over time as mapping resolution improved. U.S. Department of Agriculture aerial photographs from 1938 to 1940, 1956, 1997, and 2002 also were used to provide additional temporal controls for historical positions of lower Halfway Creek.

The complete flood history for Halfway Creek was impossible to reconstruct because there are no long-term streamflow gauges on or near Halfway Creek. However, large floods were documented in historical accounts such as those summarized by Olson (1962), recorded in safety check notes for the dam at Holmen (Wisconsin Department of Natural Resources Dam Field File no. 32.02, Madison, Wisconsin), and from interpretation of county rainfall records (Renggly et al., 1881).

Estimates of the thicknesses and extents of historical overbank deposits were determined with traditional coring, transect surveying, and floodplain stratigraphic techniques (Happ et al., 1940; Knox, 1987; Fitzpatrick et al., 1999; and Vanoni, 2006). A detailed description of the methods is provided in Fitzpatrick et al. (2008). Coring transects were undertaken and surveyed across modern and historic channels, alluvial fans, floodplains, and levee splays. Cores were collected mainly from September 2005 to March 2006 using either a 2.5-cm-diameter hand-held soil probe or a 5-cm-diameter hydraulic geoprobe. Cores KDH-1 through KDH-3 were previously collected in 1996 using the Wisconsin Geological and Natural History Survey's drill rig with a 7.5-cm-diameter "split-spoon" core barrel (Fig. 1; Fitzpatrick et al., 2008). Cores were generally 3.5–4.5 m deep and penetrated into the glacial outwash that underlies Holocene alluvium. Historical overbank deposits in the study area (post-1846) were distinguished from alluvium deposited prior to Euro-American settlement by their sandy texture, lack of pedogenic development, light color, prominent stratified bedding, and lack of compaction (Knox, 1987). A dark, well-developed soil below the historical overbank deposits was assigned the year 1860, which approximates the beginning of significant Euro-American settlement in the watershed of Halfway Creek Marsh (Butterfield, 1881; Wingate, 1975).

Three cores from the upper and lower marsh were selected for further quantification of particle size and historical depositional rates through radiometric dating. Subsamples from cores FWS-18 and FWS-21 were submitted to the Wisconsin State Laboratory of Hygiene, Madison, for ^{137}Cs analysis. Concentrations of ^{137}Cs were determined by direct gamma counting (Schelske et al., 1994). The isotope ^{137}Cs was first detected in 1945, and 1952 represents the first significant increase in atmospheric fallout in the Northern Hemisphere, corresponding to increased atmospheric testing of nuclear weapons (Krishnaswami and Lal, 1978; Anderson et al., 1987). Atmospheric fallout of ^{137}Cs underwent a relative minimum in 1960 but increased to a large

maximum in 1963. With the signing of the Nuclear Test Ban Treaty in 1963, atmospheric fallout of ^{137}Cs thereafter dropped substantially. The bonding of ^{137}Cs fallout with surficial sediment particles that subsequently were buried by sediment deposition provides a basis for estimating long-term differences in average overbank sedimentation rates for the historical periods before and after the prominent 1963 ^{137}Cs spike (McHenry et al., 1973; Callender and Robbins, 1993; Stokes and Walling, 2003; Fitzpatrick, 2005). Average sedimentation rates were calculated for the periods 1860–1963 and 1964–2006.

Subsamples of cores FWS-15 and FWS-21 were analyzed for particle size (sand and silt-clay composition) at the USGS Kentucky Water Science Center Sediment Laboratory in Louisville. There was insufficient sediment for particle-size analyses remaining in core FWS-18 after subsampling for ^{137}Cs, but a nearby core, FWS-15, with a similar depositional history, provided a surrogate particle-size profile for FWS-18.

Data for the degree of soil development and textural variations determined from sediment cores from the upper and lower marsh, in combination with radiometric results, were used to identify historical channel locations. Known dates for human activities, such as artificial levee construction, were used to characterize overbank sediment patterns and thickness for specific time frames. Overbank sediment thicknesses from individual cores were averaged for cores within similar depositional settings and age. Similar methods have been used for other Upper Mississippi River area historical sedimentation studies (Happ, 1944; Knox, 1987, 2001; Knox and Daniels, 2002; Theis and Knox, 2003) and elsewhere (Brakenridge, 1988; Demissie et al., 1992; Wolfe and Diehl, 1993; Gomez et al., 1998; Rumsby, 2000; Paine et al., 2002).

Sedimentation volumes were estimated by multiplying average sediment thicknesses in cores with areas of overbank deposition, derived from aerial photos and GIS for six historical periods: 1846–1885, 1886–1918, 1919–1936, 1937–1969, 1970–1993, and 1994–2006 (Fitzpatrick et al., 2008). Areal distribution of overbank sediment was mapped in a GIS by combining data from cores and features from historical maps and aerial photographs. Period breaks were dictated by the available archival record of temporal benchmarks represented by maps and aerial photographs. The temporal benchmarks also reflected dates of major changes in the rate and spatial extent of overbank sedimentation associated with human activities and changes in channel location. Estimated rates for the six periods were computed for three riparian areas along Halfway Creek (the upper floodplain, the upper marsh, and the lower marsh) and for two riparian areas along Sand Lake Coulee (upper marsh and lower marsh).

HUMAN ACTIVITIES, LARGE FLOODS, AND CHANNEL CHANGES

Human activities and large floods over the past 150 yr influenced the patterns and rates of overbank sedimentation, which in turn caused the historical transformation of channels, floodplains, and wetlands in Halfway Creek Marsh. In addition to agricultural practices in the Halfway Creek watershed, other local human activities that affected channel locations and overbank sedimentation patterns and rates were the construction of a dam at Holmen in 1862, railroad building in 1868 and 1886, artificial levee construction in 1919, and alterations in the drainage patterns through the marsh throughout the twentieth century (Figs. 1, 3, 4).

Euro-American settlement in the Halfway Creek Marsh area and replacement of prairie and forest with cropland and pasture occurred from the 1850s to 1870s (Olson, 1962; Wingate, 1975). In the late 1800s, wheat was the principal crop, with minor amounts of corn and oats (Butterfield, 1881, p. 253, 261). Farming practices associated with wheat production made the soils especially prone to degradation and sheet erosion and promoted accelerated runoff and gully erosion (Johnson, 1991). Sheet and gully erosion remained high during the early twentieth century after corn replaced wheat as the principal crop (Enlow and Musgrave, 1938; Zeasman and Hembre, 1963; Knox, 2001). Gully stabilization efforts began in the 1920s and 1930s by farmers, the Civilian Conservation Corps; and later the U.S. Soil Conservation Service expanded efforts in the 1940s to include contour plowing, strip cropping, terracing, and installation of grassed waterways (Zeasman and Hembre, 1963; Johnson, 1991). The usage of herbicides and fertilizers, which had become common by the 1950s, permitted corn to be planted more

closely and eliminated the need for two-directional (grid-like) cultivation. This resulted in less bare ground in summer and greater dominance of land cultivation along slope contours, which together further helped reduce runoff and soil erosion (Knox, 2001).

Corn remained the dominant row crop through the rest of the twentieth century. However, acreage planted in soybeans increased in the mid-1990s, and the most recent agricultural data for La Crosse County (the county in which the watersheds of Halfway Creek and Sand Lake Coulee are located) show that soybean cropland in the early 2000s was ~42% of the cropland historically devoted to corn (http://www.nass.usda.gov/QuickStats/). Soybean cropland is known to be associated with accelerated runoff and soil erosion (Karlen et al., 2006). Perhaps because of the recent introduction of soybeans, the effects of increased soybean cropland are not yet detectable in the alluvial stratigraphy of Halfway Creek Marsh.

Construction of railroad grades through Halfway Creek Marsh in the mid- to late 1800s changed the channel location of Halfway Creek and constricted floodplain areas (Figs. 1, 4). The first railroad grade was constructed across the upper marsh in 1867, and the second was constructed along the western edge of the lower marsh in 1886 (Renggly et al., 1881, p. 586–590; Railway and Locomotive Historical Society, 1937) (Fig. 3). The 1886 railroad construction

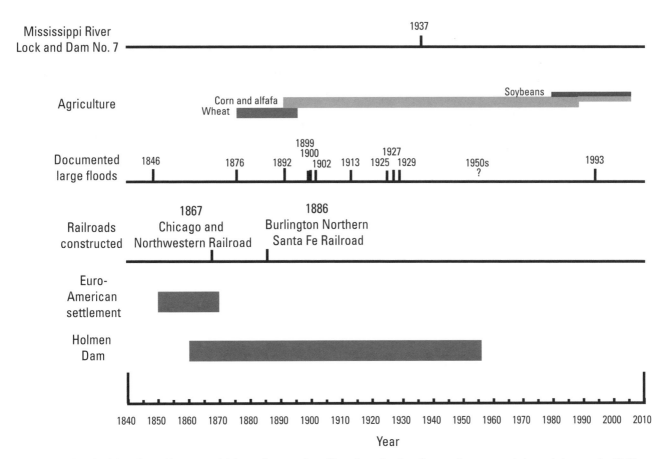

Figure 3. Historical time line of human activities and events that affected overbank sedimentation rates and channel changes for Halfway Creek Marsh, Wisconsin.

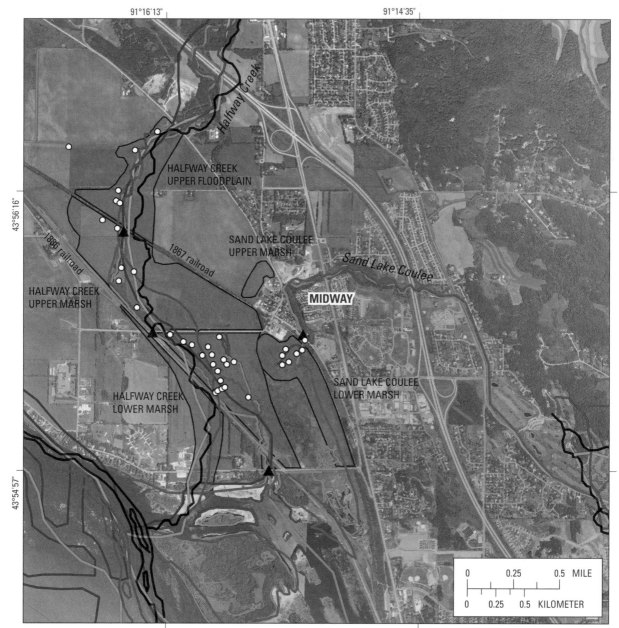

EXPLANATION

Estimated maximum extent of historical (1846-2006) overbank deposition

Historical channels

— 1846 General Land Office Survey

— 1866 (Warren, 1867)

— 1878 (Snyder, Van Vechten & Co., 1878)

— 1906 (Ogle, 1906)

— 1937–38 (Wisconsin Land Economic Inventory, 1938)

— 1973 (U.S. Geological Survey, 1978)

— 2005 (U.S. Department of Agriculture, 2005)

▲ U.S. Geological Survey stream gauge

○ Core site location

Figure 4. Historical channel location changes in Halfway Creek and Sand Lake Coulee, Halfway Creek Marsh, Wisconsin. Five subareas of the estimated maximum extent of historical (1846–2006) overbank deposition are highlighted in purple shading.

appears to have moved the location of the mouth of Halfway Creek 0.5 km to the east of its presettlement location.

Large floods played a key role in the historical evolution of Halfway Creek and its riparian marshland. Large floods are not unique to the agricultural period, as illustrated by a large damaging flood in the 1840s on the nearby Black River and its tributaries (Renggly et al., 1881, p. 372). Nevertheless, large floods in response to heavy rainfalls during the agricultural period had greater importance for the channel, floodplain, and marsh of Halfway Creek because these floods carried extreme sediment loads associated with cropland soil erosion, channel bank erosion, and repeated failures of the Holmen Dam. For example, large floods in 1876 and 1899 caused the Holmen Dam to fail, and caused extensive damage to roads and farms downstream (Olson, 1962). It also is likely that a large flood occurred on Halfway Creek in the fall of 1900, because nearby weather station data indicate that 18 cm of rain fell in a period of 22 h. Other large daily rainfalls of 10 to >12.5 cm occurred in 1896, 1902, 1909, and 1913—all before land conservation practices were implemented in the watershed (Renggly et al., 1881, p. 372). Widespread heavy spring rains in the early growing season before establishment of adequate ground cover were common in southwestern Wisconsin in 1892 and 1902, and these rains contributed to tributary gully expansion in that area (Knox, 2001).

The occurrence of large floods, multiple dam failures at Holmen, and sedimentation problems along the lower course of Halfway Creek in the early 1900s caused controversy between the dam operators and riparian landowners (Wisconsin Department of Natural Resources Dam Field File no. 32.02). Levees were constructed by the local riparian landowners in ~1919 along the reach of Halfway Creek where it flows over its Holocene alluvial fan (Figs. 1, 2). The constructed levees were washed out by large floods in the 1920s and occasionally thereafter. By 1929 the millpond upstream of Holmen Dam was nearly filled with sediment when a flood washed out the dam's gates and flushed large quantities of sediment to the downstream riparian environment (Wisconsin Department of Natural Resources Dam Field File no. 32.02, Madison). The Holmen Dam washed out for the last time in 1957 and was not replaced thereafter (Wisconsin Department of Natural Resources Dam Field File no. 32.02, Madison).

Prior to the twentieth century, surface-water drainage from Sand Lake Coulee infiltrated into the sand and sandy gravel of the Bagley Terrace and did not flow into Halfway Creek Marsh. However, in the early 1900s, Sand Lake Coulee drainage was artificially channelized to facilitate direct drainage into the lower eastern sector of Halfway Creek Marsh (Fig. 4). Until at least 1906, Sand Lake Coulee ended in sandy terrace deposits near the Mississippi Valley bluff ~2.5 km upstream of the lower marsh. Sometime between 1906 and 1937–1938, a straight channel for Sand Lake Coulee was dug through the terrace to Midway and then southward along the east side of the marsh. The 1938 aerial photos show that the dredged channel through the lower marsh had filled with sediment and that a new alluvial fan was forming in the northeast corner of the lower marsh (Fig. 5).

An additional cause of accelerated overbank sedimentation in the lower marsh was an artificial rise in base level. In 1937, Mississippi River Lock and Dam No. 7 were completed and caused the normal low-water stage of the Mississippi River to rise ~2 m at the mouth of Halfway Creek (Fig. 4). This rise significantly reduced the energy gradient of Halfway Creek through the marsh and favored more sedimentation.

From the 1960s through the 1990s, drainage through the marsh was repeatedly altered artificially to alleviate flooding and sedimentation problems, caused either by floods (some ice-jam related) coming from the watersheds of Halfway Creek and Sand Lake Coulee, or by high backwater from the Mississippi River. Sporadic ditching of Halfway Creek and Sand Lake Coulee through the marsh was done in the 1970s–1980s (Fig. 4). After the large 1993 Mississippi River flood, drainage was artificially modified again, and the roadbed elevation of County Highway ZN was raised.

From the 1990s through the early 2000s, management efforts by the USFWS were geared toward reducing the flow of sediment and related nutrients into the lower marsh. Within-channel sediment traps were added to Halfway Creek and Sand Lake Coulee in 1992–1993 to decrease sediment loading into the lower, more pristine marsh. Sand was removed annually or more often from these traps during 1994–2004 and from those of Sand Lake Coulee during 1994–2006. In 1999–2000, a diversion channel headed by a 0.9-m-diameter inlet structure was constructed to divert excess flood runoff into a new artificially designed wetland composed of a system of three connected impoundments (off-channel marsh cells or pools) covering ~31 ha. The design was structured to further reduce the flux of sediment and nutrients to the lower marsh, and to enhance wildlife habitat, especially for migrating waterfowl and shorebirds (Fig. 1; U.S. Fish and Wildlife Service, 2000).

HISTORICAL OVERBANK SEDIMENTATION AND CHANNEL MORPHOLOGICAL CHANGES

Sedimentation patterns and rates over the six historical periods (1846–1885, 1886–1918, 1919–1936, 1937–1969, 1970–1993, and 1994–2006) for Halfway Creek and Sand Lake Coulee varied in response to the combined effects of agricultural practices, large floods, railroad and road building, dam construction and repeated failures, artificial levee construction, and local drainage alterations (Table 1; Fig. 4). Variations in overbank sedimentation rates caused historical transformations of channels, floodplains, and wetlands in Halfway Creek Marsh. Over the entire historical period (1846–2006), ~1,400,000 m³ of overbank deposits were stored along the margins of Halfway Creek and Sand Lake Coulee represented by locations within the levee-restricted upper floodplain and the upper and lower marshes (Fig. 4). Historical overbank deposits are up to 2 m thick in places (Figs. 6–8). Historical overbank deposition along the relatively consistent location of Halfway Creek through the upper floodplain and marsh continued for >100 yr, resulting in anomalously high banks and development of a relatively deep channel (Fig. 9).

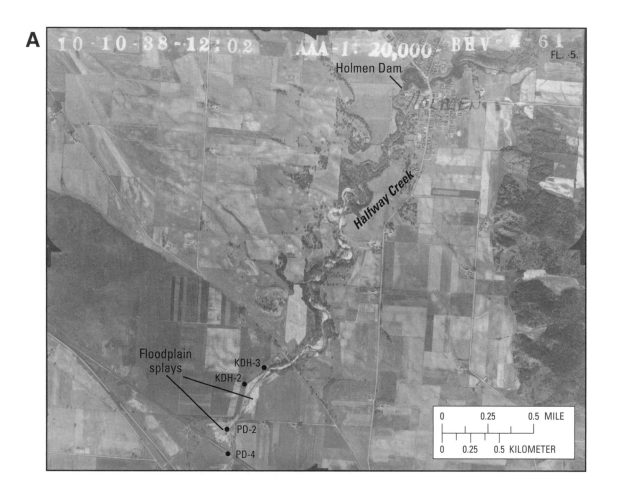

Figure 5. Aerial photographs of Halfway Creek (1938), showing floodplain splays following dam failure and levee breaks associated with a recent undocumented flood.

During the first historical period (1846–1885), overbank sedimentation along Halfway Creek was not substantially constricted by railroads and artificial levees, and the mouth of the creek was at the far western side of the lower marsh. The 1867 railroad construction across Halfway Creek in the upper marsh probably caused some small backwater effects during large floods. Such backwaters may have modestly accelerated overbank floodplain sedimentation directly upstream from the constriction where the stream passed under the railroad grade, but such effects were not detected in sediment cores. The estimated linear and volumetric rates of overbank sedimentation between 1846 and 1885 are 0.08 cm yr^{-1} and 700 m^3 yr^{-1}, respectively (Table 1). There were no sediment inputs from Sand Lake Coulee to the marsh during this period.

The second period of historical sedimentation started in 1886 with the construction of the railroad along the western lower marsh and ended in 1918, the year before levees were built and Sand Lake Coulee was connected to the marsh. The railroad construction in 1886 apparently was responsible for the relocation of Halfway Creek through the lower marsh (Fig. 4). Furthermore, the elevated railroad bed restricted the area of marsh available for overbank flows. Overbank sedimentation rates during the second period increased by an order of magnitude or more above that of the first period (1846–1885) (Table 1). The large increase reflects increased agricultural production in the watershed combined with several large floods and related dam failures. Estimated overbank sedimentation rates for the period 1886–1918 are 1.2 cm yr^{-1} for the riparian zone along Halfway Creek upstream of the 1867 railroad grade and the upper marsh and 0.5 cm yr^{-1} for the lower marsh (Table 1). These estimates are based on thickness of historical sediment in cores KDH-2 and FWS-22, both representing areas that, after 1919 levee construction, were cut off from Halfway Creek overbank sedimentation (Fig. 1; Fitzpatrick et al., 2008). A 1938 aerial photograph does

TABLE 1. OVERBANK SEDIMENTATION LINEAR AND VOLUMETRIC RATES FOR HALFWAY CREEK, SAND LAKE COULEE, AND HALFWAY CREEK MARSH, 1846–2006

Section	Overbank sedimentation linear rate (cm/yr)	Overbank sedimentation volumetric rate (m³/yr)
Period 1: 1846–1885		
Halfway Creek (all three areas)	0.1	700
Period 2: 1886–1918		
Halfway Creek (upper floodplain and upper marsh)	1.2	3500
Halfway Creek (lower marsh)	0.5	4800
Period 3: 1919–1936		
Halfway Creek (upper floodplain)	2.9	5600
Halfway Creek (upper marsh)	1.9	8800
Halfway Creek (lower marsh)	0.5	2200
Sand Lake Coulee (lower marsh)	2.9	3800
Period 4: 1937–1969		
Halfway Creek (upper floodplain)	1.6	3100
Halfway Creek (upper marsh)	1.0	3500
Halfway Creek (lower marsh)	1.4	6400
Sand Lake Coulee (upper marsh)	0.5	300
Sand Lake Coulee (lower marsh)	1.0	600
Period 5: 1970–1993		
Halfway Creek (upper floodplain)	0.3	700
Halfway Creek (upper marsh)	0.6	1800
Halfway Creek (lower marsh)	1.5	6800
Sand Lake Coulee (lower marsh)	1.3	800
Period 6: 1994–2006		
Halfway Creek (upper floodplain)	0.4	300
Halfway Creek (upper marsh)	0.3	400
Halfway Creek (lower marsh)	1.0	1400
Sand Lake Coulee (lower marsh)	3.8	900

Note: Affected area was divided into five potential areas of contribution: Halfway Creek upper floodplain upstream of the upper marsh, Halfway Creek upper marsh, Halfway Creek lower marsh, and Sand Lake Coulee upper and lower marshes (Fig. 1).

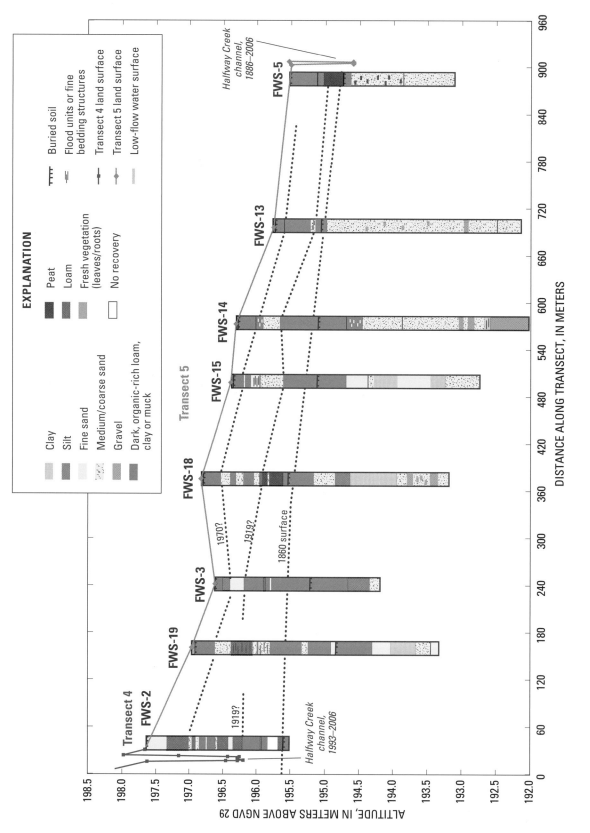

Figure 6. Longitudinal stratigraphic diagram of the Halfway Creek historical alluvial fan, lower Halfway Creek Marsh, Wisconsin, 2006. See Figure 1 for core and transect locations. NGVD 29—National Geodetic Vertical Datum of 1929.

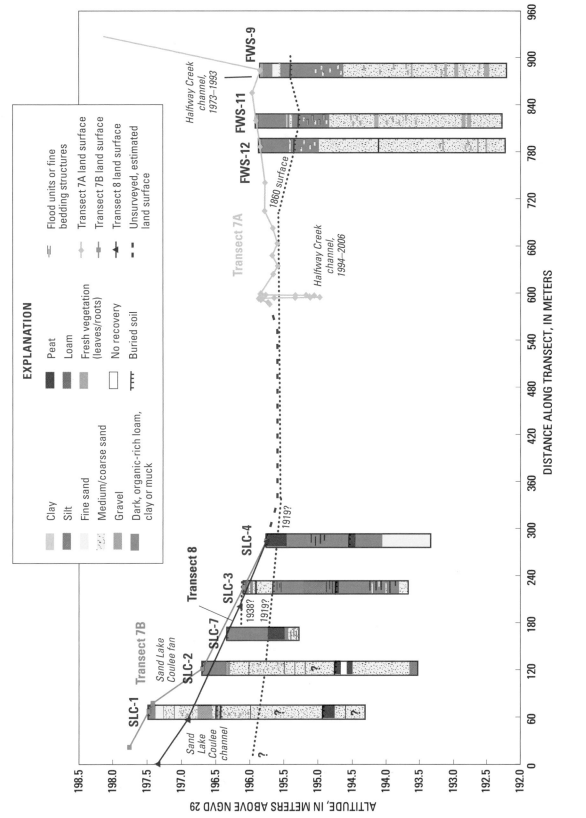

Figure 7. Stratigraphic diagram of historical overbank deposits across the lower Halfway Creek Marsh, Wisconsin, 2006. See Figure 1 for core and transect locations. NGVD 29—National Geodetic Vertical Datum of 1929.

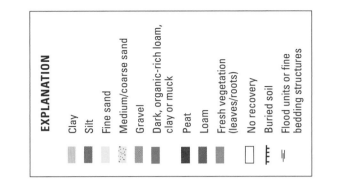

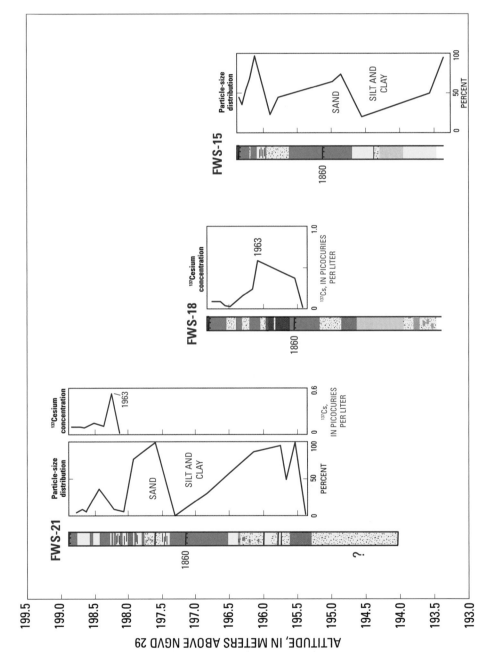

Figure 8. Graphs of particle size and ^{137}Cs concentrations from cores FWS-15, FWS-18, and FWS-21, with overlays of geologic descriptions and estimated dates, upper and lower Halfway Creek Marsh, Wisconsin, 2006. See Figure 1 for core locations. NGVD 29—National Geodetic Vertical Datum of 1929.

not show evidence of levee breaches and related floodplain splays along the west side of Halfway Creek near KDH-2 (Fig. 5). Volumetric rates of overbank sedimentation for Halfway Creek for 1886–1918 are 3500 m³ yr⁻¹ for the upper floodplain and marsh and 4800 m³ yr⁻¹ for the lower marsh, or 5–7 times 1846–1885 volumetric rates (Table 1).

The third sedimentation period began in 1919 with artificial levee construction and ended in 1936, the year before high-quality aerial photography became available for defining channel locations. The 1937–1938 photography shows large sediment splays (localized alluvial fans) on the floodplain near breaches or low spots in the artificial levees (Fig. 5). Splay sediments are represented in cores PD-1 through PD-5 as light-colored and stratified fine- to very coarse-grained sand (Fitzpatrick et al., 2008). Very fine to fine-grained sand that represents overbank sedimentation prior to levee construction underlies the splay deposits and overlies the preagriculture soil horizon. The stratified sand contrasts sharply with the underlying pre-1860 organic-rich, black silty soil. Splays are thickest near levee breaches, and they thin with distance from the breach. Average rates of overbank sedimentation from 1919 to 1936 along the upper floodplain and marsh of Halfway Creek were the highest of all the periods and were more than two times greater than rates before the levees were constructed. During this period an alluvial fan continued to build outward from where Halfway Creek entered the northwest corner of the lower marsh (Table 1; Fig. 6). The pre-1860 surface is represented by a dark, organic-rich soil 1–2 m below the modern (2006) surface on the alluvial fan (Fig. 6). This preagriculture soil or peat is, in turn, underlain by stratified medium- to coarse-grained sand and gravel

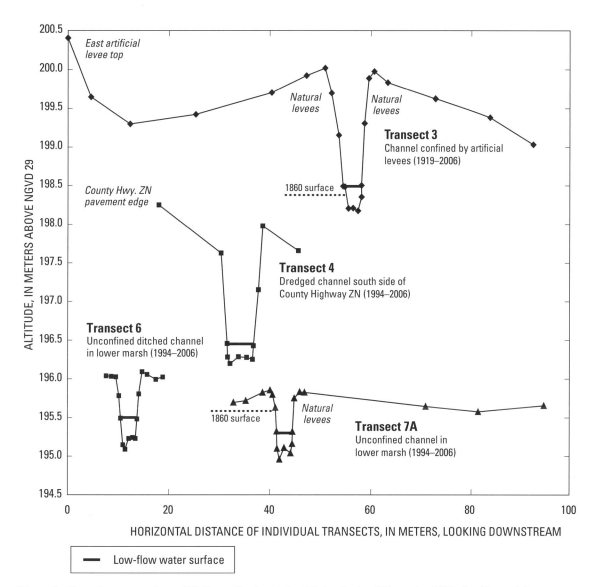

Figure 9. Channel cross sections of Halfway Creek and Sand Lake Coulee, Wisconsin, 2006. See Figure 1 for transect locations. NGVD 29—National Geodetic Vertical Datum of 1929.

associated with either late-glacial Mississippi River outwash or Holocene alluvial fan sediments.

After 1919, the east side of the lower marsh underwent high overbank sedimentation rates following the connection of Sand Lake Coulee drainage to the marsh (Figs. 4, 7). A constructed channel along the east side of the marsh soon filled with sediment (exact year unknown), resulting in formation of distributary channels and an alluvial fan due south of Midway village. The alluvial fan was well developed by 1937–1938 (Fig. 5). Cores SLC-1, -2, -3, and -4 descend the apex of the fan along transect 7. Core SLC-7 is near the 2006 channel location along transect 8 (Figs. 1, 7). Historical deposits underlying the fan are interlayered sand and organic-rich loams. Cores nearest the east side of the fan (SLC-1 and SLC-2) are missing a well-developed presettlement soil between elevations of 195 and 196 m, probably indicating removal by past erosion (Fig. 7). The buried soils in cores SLC-1 and SLC-2 between elevations of 194.5 and 195 m are likely of late Holocene age. Sedimentation derived from Sand Lake Coulee and delivered to the lower marsh involved linear and volumetric rates between 1919 and 1936 that approximate 2.9 cm yr^{-1} or 3800 m^3 yr^{-1}, respectively. These high magnitudes are consistent with erosive agricultural practices of the period and may also reflect active downcutting and channel-bank erosion associated with the newly constructed steep channel course across the terrace and into the Halfway Creek Marsh bottomland (Figs. 1, 4).

A fourth sedimentation period, 1937–1969, represents a time when land conservation practices were implemented to reduce surface runoff, peak flows, and upland soil erosion (Argabright et al., 1996). Dam failures were less common than during the previous period. Overbank sedimentation rates along Halfway Creek's upper floodplain and upper marsh dropped in comparison with the previous period (Table 1). In contrast, sedimentation rates in the lower marsh during the period 1937–1969 exceeded those of the previous period. The anomalous high-magnitude overbank sedimentation in the lower marsh occurred because an efficient "flume-like" upstream channel system evolved and promoted efficient transport of water and sediment downstream to the lower marsh. This efficient conveyance resulted from historical development of a meander plain with a large cross-section capacity. High-bank outer margins can contain most flood flows and relatively deep, high-energy flows of water and sediment. Constructed artificial levees set back a short distance from the channel banks along the reach of Halfway Creek in the upper marsh further accentuated the efficient transport of water and sediment. Together, these developments provided a system of flumelike channels that efficiently transported floodwaters and sediment downstream (Happ et al., 1940; Knox, 1987). Consequently, even though upland runoff and soil erosion decreased during this period, the channel and meander plain cross-section morphology produced confined, deep flows that were very effective in transporting lower marsh floodwaters and sediment that previously would have been attenuated or deposited on upstream floodplains. Anomalously high sedimentation rates in the lower marsh during this interval

also resulted in part from backwater effects caused by an average base-level rise of ~1.5–1.8 m following impoundment of Pool 7 on the Mississippi River in 1937.

Additional support for the difference in sedimentation between the upper and lower marsh for 1937–1969 is provided by ^{137}Cs profiles from a core in the upper marsh (FWS-21) and a core in the lower marsh (FWS-18) (Fig. 8). Average long-term sedimentation rates based on the ^{137}Cs dating at upper marsh core FWS-21 are 0.89 cm yr^{-1} for 1860–1963 and 1.31 cm yr^{-1} for 1963–2005. Rates for lower marsh core FWS-18 are 0.31 cm yr^{-1} for 1860–1963 and 2.59 cm yr^{-1} for 1963–2005. On the basis of all the cores, the upper marsh had an estimated 1919–1936 volumetric overbank sedimentation rate of 8800 m^3 yr^{-1} in comparison with an estimated 1937–1969 volumetric rate of 3500 m^3 yr^{-1} (Table 1). In contrast, volumetric rates for the lower marsh were 2200 m^3 yr^{-1} in 1919–1936 in comparison with an estimated 6400 m^3 yr^{-1} in 1937–1969. Rates of sedimentation from Sand Lake Coulee were substantially lower during the 1937–1969 period in comparison with the preceding period, probably in large part owing to anomalous high rates of erosion immediately following the newly constructed channel connecting Sand Lake Coulee to the lower marsh in the preceding period.

During the fifth period, 1970–1993, aggregate sedimentation rates for Halfway Creek dropped to 9300 m^3 yr^{-1} in comparison with 13,000 m^3 yr^{-1} in the previous period (Table 1). Implementation of agricultural best-management practices and an increase in forest cover are documented for this period in nearby watersheds 30–60 km south of Halfway Creek (Trimble and Lund, 1982; Franklin, 1997; Kent, 1999; Roldán, 2002). Similar changes probably occurred in the Halfway and Sand Lake Coulee watersheds. In Vernon County, ~20 km south of Halfway Creek, conservation practices increased by >23% from 1982 to 1992 and included conservation tillage, grassed waterways, contour cropping, and terraces (Kent, 1999). Nationally, land enrolled in the U.S. Department of Agriculture's Conservation Reserve Program, which was initiated in 1985, peaked in the mid-1990s (Kent, 1999). Juckem et al. (2008) identified base-flow increases and stormflow-volume decreases in a nearby watershed, the Kickapoo River, for the period 1971–2000, presumably from a combination of increased land conservation, agricultural best-management practices, and increased annual precipitation. The beginnings of soil development and accumulation of organic matter on the apex of the Halfway Creek alluvial fan indicate a decrease in overbank sedimentation rates (Fig. 6), and this trend supports the idea that improved land conservation practices are reducing surface runoff and soil erosion in the upstream area. The magnitude and distribution of ditching (channelization) between 1970 and 1993 in the upper and lower marsh is not documented, and it is not known how much sediment might have been removed by these activities.

During the 1970–1993 period, differences between volumetric sedimentation rates in the upper and lower marsh continued to increase. Upper marsh sedimentation rates dropped to below 1886–1919 rates, whereas lower marsh sedimentation rates remained similar to what they had been from 1937 to 1969. This differential reflects the efficient conveyance of water and sediment in the upstream channel system. The lower marsh accumulated an estimated volume of ~157,000 m³ of sediment over its northwestern half, and this volume represents ~70% of the total volume of sediment deposited along Halfway Creek between 1970 and 1993 (Fitzpatrick et al., 2008). The Sand Lake Coulee fan continued to build outward into the lower marsh from the east, just south of Midway during the 1970–1993 period (Figs. 1, 7).

The sixth period of sedimentation in the Halfway Creek Marsh is defined as 1994–2006. During this period, Halfway Creek channel was at its most eastern and central location through the lower marsh (Figs. 4, 7). Channels and floodplain areas accumulated sediment as a distributary channel network of Halfway Creek in the northwest corner of the lower marsh moved progressively eastward and southward. Estimated volumetric sedimentation rates decreased for all subareas of the marsh in comparison with the previous period. Although quantitative data on land use and land cover are limited for this period, conservation practices and the amount of forest cover continued to increase, along with an increase in soybean production at the expense of corn, pasture, and hay (Driftless Area Initiative, 2007). Furthermore, 12,200 m³ of sediment was removed from the Halfway Creek channel along the south side of County Highway ZN from 1994 to 2003. Sediment also was removed from the diversion channel and from the restored marsh constructed in 1999–2000 in the upper section of Halfway Creek Marsh (Fig. 1). Sand Lake Coulee floodplain volumetric sedimentation rates for 1994–2006 are similar to those of 1970–1993, even though 2400 m³ of sediment was removed from a sand trap at County Highway OT/ZM from 1994 to 2006 (Fig. 1; Table 1) (Fitzpatrick et al., 2008).

Comparison of data collected from cores with data representing sampled stream suspended-sediment loads indicates that the stratigraphic record of overbank sedimentation in the lower marsh provides a reasonable proxy of long-term suspended-sediment loads (Fitzpatrick et al., 2008). Estimates of annual suspended sediment loads at USGS stream gauges for 2004–2006 on Halfway Creek at County Highway ZN, the diversion channel, and Sand Lake Coulee (Fig. 1) indicate that 60%–66% of the suspended sediment load, ranging between 1900 and 8400 tonnes (t) yr⁻¹, was delivered to the lower marsh from 2004 to 2006. The stratigraphic record represented in sediment cores indicates that an average of 5500 t yr⁻¹ of sediment was stored in the lower marsh between 1994 and 2006.

Cross-section morphologies of the Halfway Creek channel through the levee-confined floodplain and marsh exhibit a wide range of dimensions that reflect the history of overbank sedimentation and human alterations discussed in the preceding sections (Fig. 9). For example, the channel and adjacent eastern floodplain area in the upper marsh are confined by artificial levees constructed in 1919 (Figs. 1, 9). Historical overbank sedimentation was accelerated within the narrow, confined floodplain between the levees. Cores FWS-21 (shown in Fig. 8) and

FWS-24 (not shown) indicate there has been ~1.5 m of historical floodplain sedimentation on the east side of the stream, and the top of the natural levee directly adjacent to the channel is now only ~30–40 cm lower than the top of the artificial levee to the east.

Although morphologic appearance and a large number of eroding banks give the impression that Halfway Creek is actively entrenching in the upper marsh, this is not the case; instead, Halfway Creek's deep channel is due almost entirely to the massive historical floodplain sedimentation, which has extended the heights of its banks above the bed. This development, in turn, has led to more frequent in-channel high-energy flows and increased rates of lateral channel migration and bank erosion. Confined deep flows generate sufficient shear stresses on the channel bed to move sand and gravel bed load and prevent extensive bed deposition. The small amount of aggradation of ~30 cm on the channel bed at transect 3 (Fig. 1) probably occurred after 1937 when the lock and dam system was constructed on the Mississippi River and base level was raised. Elsewhere, the entrenched appearance and large size of Halfway Creek along the south side of County Highway ZN (transect 4, Fig. 9) is the result of post–1993–1994 channel construction and periodic dredging of the constructed channel. The large capacity of the dredged channel is approximately double that of the cross-section capacity of the Halfway Creek channel in the lower marsh (transects 6 and 7A, Fig. 9). The relatively small capacity of the channel through the lower marsh reflects the absence of confining artificial levees there, relatively lower overbank sedimentation volumes downstream of the dredged reach, and the relatively young age of the channel in that area. Elsewhere in the upper marsh, where accelerated overbank sedimentation along Halfway Creek gives a false impression that active channel incision is occurring, stratigraphic data show that greatly accelerated rates of overbank sedimentation are responsible for the anomalous high banks and incised appearance of the Halfway Creek channels. Development of narrow, deep channels resulting from accelerated overbank deposition without channel incision is characteristic of many areas. The idea of convergence (similar results produced by different processes) was recognized by Schumm (1991) as a limitation of stream classification systems. The processes responsible for producing channel hydraulic geometries are often misunderstood during morphology-based geomorphic assessments or classifications (Juracek and Fitzpatrick, 2003). Rehabilitation techniques typically focus on channel hydraulic geometry and not on sediment-related processes that extend beyond the channel (Natural Resources Conservation Service, 2007). Erosion-control techniques for entrenched channels usually involve stabilizing banks and adding grade-control structures to reduce incision. Obviously, such applications would not be appropriate for channel morphologies that result from excessive overbank sedimentation. Reducing sediment loads and restoring floodplain connectivity to lower mainstem channels are challenges facing ecologists attempting to improve or restore critical aquatic and riparian habitats.

SUMMARY AND CONCLUSIONS

The overbank sedimentation history for Halfway Creek Marsh is representative of historical sedimentation rates and patterns in riparian marshes along many sectors of the Upper Mississippi River. The history of human activities, magnitudes of overbank sediment loading, and fluvial adjustments observed for Halfway Creek Marsh broadly approximate those of numerous other small tributaries that flow into critical backwater marsh habitats along the Upper Mississippi River National Wildlife and Fish Refuge of the Upper Mississippi River System. The extent and character of historical sand deposition in Halfway Creek marsh strongly depend on proximity of the deposits to historical channels, alluvial fans, and artificial levees. Historical overbank deposits up to 2 m thick occur along the banks of Halfway Creek through the upper marsh where the floodplain is confined by artificial levees. Floodplain splays in the upper marsh also are characteristic where breaches in artificial levees occurred during large floods. In the lower marsh, overbank sedimentation patterns correspond closely with locations of historical channels and alluvial fans. The northwest and northeast corners of the lower marsh, where Halfway Creek and Sand Lake Coulee, respectively, enter, have ~1.5 m of fine- to medium-textured sand that is interbedded with dark, organic-rich loam or silt-clay units associated with historical alluvial-fan deposition. The texture tends to become more fine grained and organic-rich in the downstream direction through the lower marsh. In general, the historical overbank deposits tend to be lighter in color, less compacted, more stratified and bedded, and have less soil development and organic content than underlying preagriculture deposits.

The estimated rate of overbank sedimentation on the entire marsh is ~3000 m³ yr⁻¹ for recent years (1994–2006), and in spite of noteworthy improvements in land-use conservation practices, this magnitude still exceeds by ~4 times the early settlement (1846–85) rate (700 m³ yr⁻¹). Nevertheless, the aggregate historical overbank sedimentation rate estimated for the period between 1919 and 1936 was 20,400 m³ yr⁻¹, a magnitude that exceeds by nearly 30 times the 1846–1886 estimated rate, and exceeds by more than 7 times the 1994–2006 estimated rate. The very high rate of overbank sedimentation between 1919 and 1936 was caused by watershed agricultural practices that promoted surface runoff and soil erosion. These factors contributed, in turn, to occurrences of several large floods and failures of the Holmen Dam, where related sediment flushing of millpond sediment and downstream bank erosion occurred. Further enhanced delivery of sediment to Halfway Creek Marsh resulted from an early twentieth-century channelization project that connected the drainage of Sand Lake Coulee to the lower marsh.

Overbank sedimentation rates for the lower marsh remain anomalously high because levees constructed earlier along the channel of Halfway Creek allow the remaining small floodplain and channel system to function as an efficient flume for transporting water and sediment into the lower marsh. In addition, construction of Lock and Dam No. 7 on the Mississippi River in 1937 raised the low-water base level ~2 m at the mouth of Halfway Creek, making the marsh more vulnerable to backwater flooding from the Mississippi River and sedimentation in a low-energy environment. Improved land conservation has reduced sediment inputs from the watershed uplands in recent years, but the flume-like function of the historical meander plains continues to contain floodwaters and effectively transport water and sediment downstream to Halfway Creek Marsh. Consequently, although channel changes and sedimentation rates in the lower marsh currently are less severe than a few decades ago, the channel in the lower marsh is, nevertheless, adjusting to efficient delivery of water and sediment from upstream, as indicated by the continued building of alluvial fans. Providing additional upstream floodplain storage for water and sediment during future floods would most likely reduce overbank sedimentation rates in the lower marsh.

Approximately 1,400,000 m³ of sandy historical overbank deposits are stored along the margins of Halfway Creek and Sand Lake Coulee through the upper and lower marsh. System-wide adjustments to historical sediment loading of this magnitude probably will continue for decades and centuries, manifested during extreme floods and moderate flows that episodically flush stored sediment from channel margins downstream into the lower marsh and eventually to the Mississippi River. Owing to a high probability for remobilization of stored historical sediment and associated nutrients, plus long-term effects on wetland vegetation and fish and wildlife habitat, it is important to improve understanding of how past human activities influenced patterns and rates of sedimentation in riparian environments and, in turn, how the legacy of past erosion and sedimentation will continue to influence current and future water quality, sediment loads, nutrient loads, and water-related resources. The results of this study further illustrate the importance of coupling an understanding of floodplain stratigraphy with channel morphology; over-reliance on channel morphology alone can lead to erroneous interpretation of ongoing fluvial processes, which can result in erroneous selection of channel-restoration designs.

ACKNOWLEDGMENTS

This study was made possible by the assistance of many people, who allowed land access, assisted with fieldwork, provided historical information, and reviewed and assisted with preparation of the manuscript. We are very grateful for permission to collect sediment cores on the property of John McHugh, Dale Emery (Stonehearth Kennels), Calvin Paudler, and Richard Knutson. Calvin Paudler and Ernest Knudson provided useful historical insights on dam history, channel location, and levee building. Field assistance was provided by Lindsay Theis Spigel (University of Wisconsin–Madison) for hand coring and surveying, and James Rauman (USGS) and Jason Smith (USGS) for geoprobe coring. James Nissen (U.S. Fish and Wildlife Service) assisted with access to the refuge, fieldwork, technical assistance, and historical information. Peter Hughes (USGS) provided technical assistance with the scope of the study as well as field assistance. Eleanor Lawry (Wisconsin Department of Natural Resources) helped to access the dam-inspection notes for the Holmen Dam. Marie Peppler (USGS) assisted with map overlays, cross-section layouts, and report illustrations. The authors are grateful for technical reviews by Randy Hines (USGS) and an anonymous reviewer. Research support was provided by an Interagency Agreement (DW14996301) between USEPA and USGS, and an Evjue-Bascom Professorship to J.C. Knox. The views expressed herein in no manner represent or reflect current or planned policy by the USEPA.

REFERENCES CITED

Adams, C., 1940, Modern sedimentation in the Galena River valley [M.S. thesis]: Iowa City, University of Iowa, 72 p.

Adams, C., 1942, Accelerated sedimentation in the Galena River valley [Ph.D. thesis]: Iowa City, University of Iowa, 67 p.

Allmendinger, N.E., Pizzuto, J.E., Moglen, G.E., and Lewicki, M., 2007, A sediment budget for an urbanizing watershed, 1951–1996, Montgomery County, Maryland, U.S.A.: Journal of the American Water Resources Association, v. 43, no. 6, p. 1483–1498.

Anderson, R.F., Schiff, S.L., and Hesslein, R.H., 1987, Determining sediment accumulations and mixing rates using ^{210}Pb, ^{137}Cs, and other tracers—Problems due to postdepositional mobility or coring artifacts: Canadian Journal of Fisheries and Aquatic Sciences, v. 44, Supplement 1, p. 231–240, doi: 10.1139/f87-298.

Argabright, M.S., Cronshey, R.G., Helms, J.D., Pavelis, G.A., and Sinclair, H.R., Jr., 1996, Historical changes in soil erosion 1930–1992—The northern Mississippi Valley loess hills: Washington, D.C., U.S. Department of Agriculture, Natural Resources and Conservation Service, Historical Notes no. 5, 92 p.

Beach, T., 1994, The fate of eroded soil: Sediment sinks and sediment budgets of agrarian landscapes in southern Minnesota, 1851–1988: Annals of the Association of American Geographers, v. 84, no. 1, p. 5–28, doi: 10.1111/j.1467-8306.1994.tb01726.x.

Brakenridge, G.R., 1988, River flood regime and floodplain stratigraphy, *in* Baker, V.R., Kochel, R.C., and Patton, P.C., eds., Flood Geomorphology: New York, John Wiley and Sons, p. 139–165.

Butterfield, C.W., 1881, History of Wisconsin, *in* History of La Crosse County, Wisconsin: Chicago, Western Historical Company, p. 19–308.

Callender, E., and Robbins, J.A., 1993, Transport and accumulation of radionuclides and stable elements in a Missouri River Reservoir: Water Resources Research, v. 29, no. 6, p. 1787–1804, doi: 10.1029/93WR00387.

Costa, J.E., 1975, Effects of agriculture on erosion and sedimentation in the piedmont province, Maryland: Geological Society of America Bulletin, v. 86, p. 1281–1286, doi: 10.1130/0016-7606(1975)86<1281:EOAOEA>2.0.CO;2.

Demissie, M., Fitzpatrick, W.P., and Cahill, R.A., 1992, Sedimentation in the Cache River Wetlands: Comparison of Two Methods: Illinois State Water Survey Miscellaneous Publication 129, 43 p.

Driftless Area Initiative, 2007, Major Land Resource Areas: Unpublished data: http://www.driftlessareainitiative.org/technical_resourc.html (accessed 28 May 2008).

Enlow, C.R., and Musgrave, G.W., 1938, Grass and other thick growing vegetation in erosion control, *in* Yearbook of Agriculture: 75th Congress, 2nd Session, House Document no. 398, p. 615–633.

Evans, T.J., 2003, Geology of La Crosse County, Wisconsin: Wisconsin Geological and Natural History Survey Bulletin 101, 33 p.

Faulkner, D.J., 1998, Spatially variable historical alluviation and channel incision in west-central Wisconsin: Annals of the Association of American Geographers, v. 88, no. 4, p. 666–685, doi: 10.1111/0004-5608.00117.

Fitzpatrick, F.A., 2005, Trends in Streamflow, Sedimentation, and Sediment Chemistry for the Wolf River, Menominee Indian Reservation, Wisconsin, 1850–1999: U.S. Geological Survey Scientific Investigations Report 2005-5030, 47 p.

Fitzpatrick, F.A., and Knox, J.C., 2000, Spatial and temporal sensitivity of hydrogeomorphic response and recovery to deforestation, agriculture, and floods: Physical Geography, v. 21, no. 2, p. 89–108.

Fitzpatrick, F.A., Knox, J.C., and Whitman, H.E., 1999, Effects of Historical Land-Cover Changes on Flooding and Sedimentation, North Fish Creek, Wisconsin: U.S. Geological Survey Water-Resources Investigations Report 99-4083, 12 p.

Fitzpatrick, F.A., Knox, J.C., and Schubauer-Berigan, J.P., 2008, Sedimentation History of Halfway Creek Marsh, Upper Mississippi River National Wildlife and Fish Refuge, Wisconsin, 1846–2006: U.S. Geological Survey Scientific Investigations Report 2007-5209, 40 p.

Franklin, N.M., 1997, Land use and water characteristics in the Middle Kickapoo River watershed [M.S. thesis]: University of Wisconsin–Madison, Institute of Environmental Studies, 189 p.

Gomez, B., Eden, D.N., Peacock, D.H., and Pinkney, E.J., 1998, Floodplain construction by recent, rapid vertical accretion: Waipaoa River, New Zealand: Earth Surface Processes and Landforms, v. 23, p. 405–413, doi: 10.1002/(SICI)1096-9837(199805)23:5<405::AID-ESP854>3.0.CO;2-X.

Happ, S.C., 1944, Effect of sedimentation on floods in the Kickapoo Valley, Wisconsin: Journal of Geology, v. 52, p. 53–68.

Happ, S.C., Rittenhouse, G., and Dobson, G.C., 1940, Some principles of accelerated stream and valley sedimentation: U.S. Department of Agriculture Technical Bulletin 695, 134 p.

Johnson, L.C., 1991, Soil Conservation in Wisconsin—Birth to Rebirth: Madison, University of Wisconsin, Department of Soil Science, 332 p.

Juckem, P.F., Hunt, R.J., Anderson, M.P., and Robertson, D.M., 2008, Effects of climate and land management change on streamflow in the Driftless Area of Wisconsin: Journal of Hydrology, v. 355, p. 123–130, doi: 10.1016/j.jhydrol.2008.03.010.

Juracek, K.E., and Fitzpatrick, F.A., 2003, Limitations and implications of stream classification: Journal of the American Water Resources Association, v. 39, no. 3, p. 659–670, doi: 10.1111/j.1752-1688.2003.tb03683.x.

Karlen, D.L., Hurley, E.G., Andrews, S.S., Cambardella, C.A., Meek, D.W., Duffy, M.D., and Mallarino, M.P., 2006, Crop rotation effects on soil quality at three Northern Corn/Soybean Belt locations: Agronomy Journal, v. 98, p. 484–495, doi: 10.2134/agronj2005.0098.

Kent, C.A., 1999, The influence of changes in land cover and agricultural land management practices on baseflow in southwest Wisconsin, 1969–1998 [Ph.D. thesis]: Madison, University of Wisconsin–Madison, 305 p.

Knox, J.C., 1972, Valley alluviation in southwestern Wisconsin: Annals of the Association of American Geographers, v. 62, no. 3, p. 401–410, doi: 10.1111/j.1467-8306.1972.tb00872.x.

Knox, J.C., 1977, Human impacts on Wisconsin stream channels: Annals of the Association of American Geographers, v. 67, p. 323–342, doi: 10.1111/j.1467-8306.1977.tb01145.x.

Knox, J.C., 1987, Historical valley floor sedimentation in the Upper Mississippi River Valley: Annals of the Association of American Geographers, v. 77, no. 2, p. 224–244, doi: 10.1111/j.1467-8306.1987.tb00155.x.

Knox, J.C., 1999, Long-term episodic changes in magnitudes and frequencies of floods in the Upper Mississippi River Valley, *in* Brown, A.G., and Quine, T.A., eds., Fluvial Processes and Environmental Change, Ch. 14: Chichester, UK, Wiley, p. 255–282.

Knox, J.C., 2001, Agricultural influence on landscape sensitivity in the Upper Mississippi River Valley: CATENA, v. 42, p. 193–224, doi: 10.1016/S0341-8162(00)00138-7.

Knox, J.C., 2002, Agriculture, erosion, and sediment yields, *in* Orme, A.R., ed., The Physical Geography of North America: Oxford, UK, Oxford University Press, p. 482–500.

Knox, J.C., 2006, Floodplain sedimentation in the Upper Mississippi Valley—Natural versus human accelerated: Geomorphology, v. 79, p. 286–310, doi: 10.1016/j.geomorph.2006.06.031.

Knox, J.C., and Daniels, M., 2002, Watershed scale and the stratigraphic record of large floods, *in* House, P.K., Levish, D.R., Webb, R.H., and Baker, V.R., eds., Ancient Floods, Modern Hazards: Principles and Applications of Paleoflood Hydrology: Washington, D.C., American Geophysical Union, p. 237–255.

Krishnaswami, S., and Lal, D., 1978, Radionuclide limnochronology, *in* Lerman, A., ed., Lakes—Chemistry, Geology, Physics: New York, Springer-Verlag, p. 153–177.

Lecce, S.A., 1997, Spatial patterns of historical overbank sedimentation and floodplain evolution, Blue River, Wisconsin: Geomorphology, v. 18, p. 265–277, doi: 10.1016/S0169-555X(96)00030-X.

Lecce, S.A., and Pavlowsky, R.T., 2001, Use of mining-contaminated sediment tracers to investigate the timing and rates of historical flood plain sedimentation: Geomorphology, v. 38, p. 85–108, doi: 10.1016/S0169-555X(00)00071-4.

Magilligan, F.J., 1985, Historical floodplain sedimentation in the Galena River Basin, Wisconsin and Illinois: Annals of the Association of American Geographers, v. 75, no. 4, p. 583–594, doi: 10.1111/j.1467-8306.1985.tb00095.x.

Magilligan, F.J., 1992, Sedimentology of a fine-grained aggrading floodplain: Geomorphology, v. 4, p. 393–408, doi: 10.1016/0169-555X(92)90034-L.

McHenry, J.R., Ritchie, J.C., and Gill, A.C., 1973, Accumulation of fallout cesium 137 in soils and sediments in selected watersheds: Water Resources Research, v. 9, no. 3, p. 676–686, doi: 10.1029/WR009i003p00676.

Natural Resources Conservation Service, 2007, Treatment technique design, Ch. 14, Stream restoration design: Washington, D.C., U.S. Department of Agriculture, National Engineering Handbook, Part 654, p. 14-1 to 14-9.

Ogle, G.A., 1906, Standard Atlas of La Crosse County, Wisconsin: Chicago, Geo. A. Ogle & Co., p. 7.

Olson, C., 1962, Holmen Area Centennial, 1862–1962: Holmen, Wisconsin, pamphlet.

Paine, J.L., Rowan, J.S., and Werritty, A., 2002, Reconstructing historic floods using sediments from embanked flood plains: A case study of the River Tay in Scotland: IAHS Publication 276, p. 211–218.

Railway and Locomotive Historical Society, 1937, The Railroads of Wisconsin, 1827–1937: Boston, Railway and Locomotive Historical Society, 73 p.

Reese, H.M., Lillesand, T., Nagel, D.E., Stewart, J.S., Goldmann, R.A., Simmons, T.E., Chipman, J.W., and Tessar, P.A., 2002, Statewide land cover derived from multiseasonal Landsat TM data—A retrospective of the WISCLAND project: Remote Sensing of Environment, v. 82, p. 224–237, doi: 10.1016/S0034-4257(02)00039-1.

Renggly, J.A., et al., 1881, History of La Crosse County, *in* History of La Crosse County, Wisconsin: Chicago, Western Historical Company, p. 309–731.

Roldán, K.M., 2002, Utilizing GIS for Mapping Reforestation of an Agricultural Landscape, 1939–1993, in Coon Creek Watershed, Wisconsin: Saint Mary's University of Minnesota, 15 p.: http://www.umbsn.org/private _lands/CoonCreekSuccess.pdf (accessed 27 May 2008).

Ross, K.M., Hupp, C.R., and Howard, A.D., 2004, Sedimentation in floodplains of selected tributaries of the Chesapeake Bay, *in* Bennett, S.J., and Simon, A., eds., Riparian Vegetation and Fluvial Geomorphology: American Geophysical Union, Water Science and Application 8, p. 187–208.

Rumsby, B., 2000, Vertical accretion rates in fluvial systems: A comparison of volumetric and depth-based estimates: Earth Surface Processes and Landforms, v. 25, p. 617–631, doi: 10.1002/1096-9837(200006)25:6<617::AID -ESP99>3.0.CO;2-Z.

Schelske, C.L., Peplow, A., Brenner, M., and Spencer, C.N., 1994, Low-background gamma counting—Applications for ^{210}Pb dating of sediments: Journal of Paleolimnology, v. 10, p. 115–128, doi: 10.1007/BF00682508.

Schumm, S.A., 1991, To Interpret the Earth: Ten Ways to Be Wrong: New York, Cambridge University Press, 121 p.

Snyder, Van Vechten & Co., 1878, Historical Atlas of Wisconsin: Milwaukee, Snyder, Van Vechten & Co., p. 64.

Stokes, S., and Walling, D.E., 2003, Radiogenic and isotopic methods for direct dating of fluvial sediments, *in* Kondolf, G.M., and Piegay, H., eds., Tools in Fluvial Geomorphology: New York, Wiley, p. 233–268.

Theis, L.J., and Knox, J.C., 2003, Spatial and temporal variability in floodplain backwater sedimentation, Pool Ten, Upper Mississippi River: Physical Geography, v. 24, p. 337–353, doi: 10.2747/0272-3646.24.4.337.

Trimble, S.W., 1981, Changes in sediment storage in the Coon Creek Basin, Driftless Area, Wisconsin, 1853 to 1975: Science, v. 214, p. 181–183, doi: 10.1126/science.214.4517.181.

Trimble, S.W., 1983, A sediment budget for Coon Creek basin in the Driftless Area, Wisconsin, 1853–1977: American Journal of Science, v. 283, p. 454–474.

Trimble, S.W., 1993, The distributed sediment budget model and watershed management in the Paleozoic Plateau of the upper Midwestern United States: Physical Geography, v. 14, p. 285–303.

Trimble, S.W., 1999, Decreased rates of alluvial sediment storage in the Coon Creek Basin, Wisconsin, 1975–1993: Science, v. 285, p. 1244–1246, doi: 10.1126/science.285.5431.1244.

Trimble, S.W., and Lund, S.W., 1982, Soil Conservation and the Reduction of Erosion and Sedimentation in the Coon Creek Basin, Wisconsin: U.S. Geological Survey Professional Paper 1234, 35 p.

U.S. Department of Agriculture, 2005, Wisconsin digital aerial photography, National Agriculture Imagery Program, 1-m pixel resolution: http://www.wisconsinview.org/documents/2005_NAIP_FAQs.pdf (accessed 5 March 2007).

U.S. Fish and Wildlife Service, 2000, Upper Halfway Creek Marsh Project, Final Report, December 2000: La Crosse, Wisconsin, U.S. Fish and Wildlife Service unpublished report, 19 p.

Vanoni, V.A., ed., 2006, Sedimentation Engineering—Chapter III, Sediment Measurement Techniques: American Society of Civil Engineers Manuals and Reports on Engineering Practice no. 54, p. 227–233.

Walling, D.E., and Owens, P.N., 2002, The role of flood plain sedimentation in catchment sediment and contaminant budgets: Proceedings from the International Symposium on Structure, Function, and Management Implications of Fluvial Sedimentary Systems, IAHS Publication 276, p. 407–416.

Walter, R.C., and Merritts, D.J., 2008, Natural streams and the legacy of water-powered mills: Science, v. 319, p. 299–304, doi: 10.1126/science .1151716.

Warren, G.K., 1867, Survey of the Upper Mississippi River: Washington, D.C., U.S. House of Representatives Executive Document 58, 39th Congress, 2nd Session, p. 5–38.

Wingate, R.G., 1975, Settlement patterns of La Crosse County, Wisconsin, 1850–1875 [Ph.D. thesis]: St. Paul, University of Minnesota, 212 p.

Wisconsin Department of Agriculture and Wisconsin Geological and Natural History Survey, 1938, Land Economic Inventory: La Crosse County, Wisconsin: scale 1:63,360: http://steenbock.library.wisc.edu/bordner/ (accessed 6 March 2007).

Wolfe, W.J., and Diehl, T.H., 1993, Recent Sedimentation and Surface-Water Flow Patterns on the Flood Plain of the North Fork Forked Deer River, Dyer County, Tennessee: U.S. Geological Survey Water-Resources Investigations Report 92-4082, 22 p.

Woltemade, C.J., 1994, Form and process: Fluvial geomorphology and flood-flow interaction, Grant River, Wisconsin: Annals of the Association of American Geographers, v. 84, no. 3, p. 462–479, doi: 10.1111/j.1467 -8306.1994.tb01870.x.

Zeasman, O.R., and Hembre, I.O., 1963, A Brief History of Soil Erosion Control in Wisconsin: Madison, Wisconsin State Soil and Water Conservation Committee and University of Wisconsin Extension Service, 49 p.

MANUSCRIPT ACCEPTED BY THE SOCIETY 15 SEPTEMBER 2008

The Geological Society of America
Special Paper 451
2009

Persistence of effects of high sediment loading in a salmon-bearing river, northern California

Mary Ann Madej

U.S. Geological Survey Western Ecological Research Center, 1655 Heindon Road, Arcata, California 95521, USA

Vicki Ozaki

Redwood National and State Parks, 1655 Heindon Road, Arcata, California 95521, USA

ABSTRACT

Regional high-magnitude rainstorms have produced several large floods in north coastal California during the last century, which resulted in extensive mass-movement activity and channel aggradation. Channel monitoring in Redwood Creek, through the use of cross-sectional surveys, thalweg profiles, and pebble counts, has documented the persistence and routing of channel-stored sediment following these large floods in the 1960s and 1970s. Channel response varied on the basis of timing of peak aggradation. Channel-stored sediment was evacuated rapidly from the upstream third of the Redwood Creek channel, and the channel bed stabilized by 1985 as the bed coarsened. Currently only narrow remnants of flood deposits remain and are well vegetated. In the downstream reach, channel aggradation peaked in the 1990s, and the channel is still incising. Channel-bed elevations throughout the watershed showed an approximate exponential decrease with time, but decay rates were highest in areas with the thickest flood deposits. Pool frequencies and depths generally increased from 1977 to 1995, as did median residual water depths, but a 10 yr flood in 1997 resulted in a moderate reversal of this trend. Channel aggradation generated during 25 yr return interval floods has persisted in Redwood Creek for more than 30 yr and has impacted many life cycles of salmon. Watershed restoration work is currently focused on correcting erosion problems on hillslopes to reduce future sediment supply to Redwood Creek instead of attempting in-channel manipulations.

INTRODUCTION

Many river channels have been disturbed by an increase in sediment loading from activities such as mining, grazing, agriculture, logging, and road construction. River restoration is an actively evolving field that seeks to improve channel conditions following disturbances. In order to effectively design river-restoration projects, however, it is important to understand the persistence of the problem that requires mitigation and the time required for the system to recover. The feasibility of *passive restoration,* whereby a river system is allowed to heal itself, can best be evaluated if rates of recovery are well understood. Unfortunately, in many cases the expected duration of anthropogenic effects is unknown. To fully understand the persistence of

Madej, M.A., and Ozaki, V., 2009, Persistence of effects of high sediment loading in a salmon-bearing river, northern California, *in* James, L.A., Rathburn, S.L., and Whittecar, G.R., eds., Management and Restoration of Fluvial Systems with Broad Historical Changes and Human Impacts: Geological Society of America Special Paper 451, p. 43–55, doi: 10.1130/2009.2451(03). For permission to copy, contact editing@geosociety.org. ©2009 The Geological Society of America. All rights reserved.

sediment effects, a watershed level analysis is needed to identify the location and timing of sediment input as well as to route sediment through the river network.

Channel recovery following disturbances can be defined in several ways. Wolman and Gerson (1978) characterize recovery in terms of reestablishing channel form, especially channel width, following large storms and climatic variations. Reconstruction of floodplains (Hack and Goodlett, 1960) or a return to former channel-bed elevation (Gilbert, 1917), to grade (James, 1999) or to a pre-aggradation hydraulic geometry (Lisle, 1982) have also been used. Planform can change from a braided system to a single-thread channel as a river recovers from elevated sediment loads (Harvey, 2007). Regulatory agencies commonly employ a return to low sediment yields as a recovery target; other regulatory targets include specific pool depths, frequencies, and substrate particle size (California Regional Water Quality Control Board, 1998).

Understanding how increased sediment volumes in a river network are evacuated through time and routed downstream is key to predicting the persistence of sediment effects on a river system. In his classic study, Gilbert (1917) described transport of hydraulic mining debris in the Sierra Nevada. Incorporating the influence of sediment storage on transport capacity expands upon his study of channel adjustments. Sediment transport-storage relations for degrading gravel-bed channels from flume experiments and field studies show a general exponential decline of stored sediment as gravel beds become more strongly armored, but a constant rate of decline when armoring did not occur (Lisle and Church, 2002). Consequently, characterizing the interaction between channel substrate and channel adjustment is essential in determining the duration of sediment impacts in a gravel-bed river and the length of time needed for channel recovery.

Channel cross-sectional and longitudinal surveys have been conducted in Redwood Creek, north coastal California, since the 1970s. The residence time of sediment in various sediment reservoirs in Redwood Creek was modeled on the basis of sediment-storage volumes estimated in the early 1980s (Kelsey et al., 1987). Trends in channel-bed elevations and pool development, based on surveys through the late 1990s, were summarized (Madej and Ozaki, 1996; Madej, 1999). At that time the downstream reach of Redwood Creek was actively aggrading. Since that time, patterns in channel response have shifted. In the present study, 30 yr of cross-sectional and longitudinal channel morphologic surveys and measurements of substrate particle-size distribution along most of the length of a river channel are used to detect temporal and spatial trends of channel changes following disturbances from high sediment supplies.

BACKGROUND

The Redwood Creek basin drains an area of 720 km² in north coastal California (Fig. 1A) and flows into the Pacific Ocean near the town of Orick. The main channel is 108 km long. Channel gradient decreases from 12% in the headwaters to 0.10% near the mouth (Fig. 1B). Total basin relief is 1615 m, and the average hillslope gradient is 26%. The basin receives ~200 cm of rainfall annually, most of which falls as rain between October and March.

The Redwood Creek watershed is underlain by the Franciscan Assemblage of Jurassic and Cretaceous age (Bailey et al., 1970) and is pervasively sheared and fractured. The basin is bisected by the Grogan Fault, which has juxtaposed different bedrock units on the east side (sandstones and siltstones) and west side (schist) of the watershed (Janda et al., 1975). Redwood Creek follows the trace of the Grogan Fault for most of its length. The combination of high precipitation, steep terrain, and fractured bedrock creates a landscape that is highly susceptible to mass movement and gullying. Annual suspended-sediment discharge of Redwood Creek (1000–2500 Mg km⁻¹ a⁻¹) is among the highest measured in the United States for basins of this size, apart from rivers draining active volcanoes or glaciers.

Aerial photographs show that prior to widespread commercial timber harvesting in Redwood Creek during the late twentieth century >80% of the basin was covered with old-growth redwood (*Sequoia sempervirens*) and Douglas fir (*Pseudotsuga menziesii*) forest, and the remaining areas were oak woodlands and prairie grasslands (Best, 1995). For much of its length, Redwood Creek was shaded by a thick canopy of large conifers, and the channel was narrow and sinuous in most reaches. The advent of large-scale timber harvesting began in the early 1950s, and by 1966, 55% of the coniferous forest had been logged. In 1968, Redwood National Park was established along lower Redwood Creek to preserve old-growth redwoods, and the park was subsequently expanded in 1978 to encompass the downstream one-third of the watershed. By 1978, 81% of the original conifer forests in the Redwood Creek basin had been logged (Best, 1995). Although timber harvesting ceased in the expanded park lands at that point, since 1978 about one-half of the land upstream of the park has been reentered for logging of second-growth trees and residual timber. During the last five decades, ~2000 km of logging roads and ~9000 km of skid roads were built throughout the watershed, with the vast majority having been built prior to forest-practice rules dealing with road standards (Best, 1995). A road removal program was initiated on park lands in 1978, and an erosion-control program on private lands in Redwood Creek began in the mid-1990s to correct the erosional problems associated with these roads. To date, ~350 km of road throughout the basin has been decommissioned.

Large floods occurred in 1953, 1955, 1964, 1972, and 1975 (Fig. 2). These floods, with peak discharges ranging from 1280 to 1420 m³s⁻¹, have a long-term recurrence interval of ~25 yr (Harden, 1995). Since 1975, annual peak flows measured on Redwood Creek near Orick have all been less than a 5 yr recurrence interval (895 m³s⁻¹), with the exception of a 10 yr flood in 1997. Floods in 1964, 1972, and 1975 initiated widespread road- and stream-crossing failures, gullying, and streamside landsliding throughout the basin. Hillslope disturbance from intensive logging and road building prior to these floods contributed to extensive geomorphic changes in

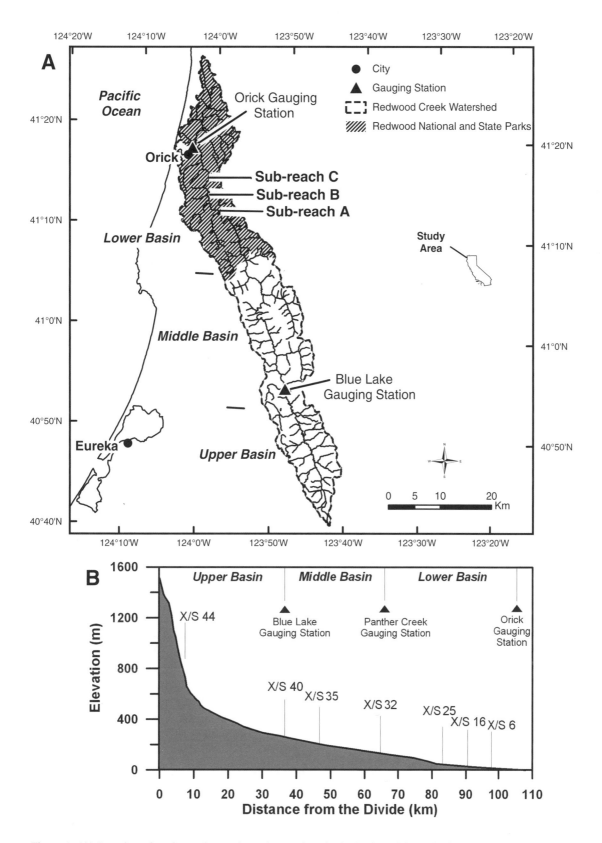

Figure 1. (A) Location of study reaches and gauging stations in the Redwood Creek basin. (B) Locations of cross-sectional transects (X/S) along longitudinal profile of Redwood Creek.

the basin. In comparison with a large flood of equal or greater magnitude in 1861, the 1964 flood caused much more widespread mass movement (Harden, 1995). Landslides delivered ~5.25 × 10⁶ m³ to Redwood Creek during the 1964 flood, and an additional 1.17 × 10⁶ m³ entered in 1972 and 1975 (Kelsey et al., 1995). Aerial photographs, field observations, and accounts by local residents documented that the channel widened, pools filled in, channel-bed material became finer, and the channel bed aggraded up to 9 m at some sites (Nolan and Marron, 1995; Madej, 1995). The 10 yr flood in 1997 initiated 250 landslides in the Redwood Creek basin and contributed an additional 0.42 × 10⁶ m³ of material to Redwood Creek (Curry, 2007). Although this volume was <10% of the 1964 landslide input, it did cause localized channel aggradation in parts of Redwood Creek.

Sedimentation of the mainstem channel from mid-twentieth-century floods impacted aquatic habitat in Redwood Creek as the stream channel aggraded, causing loss of pools, bank erosion, and loss of riparian trees. Redwood Creek is listed as both sediment- and temperature-impaired under Section 303 (d) of the federal Clean Water Act. Logging, roads, erosion and sedimentation, floods, and loss of riparian vegetation have been listed as having contributed to the impairment of Redwood Creek (California Regional Water Quality Control Board, 1998). Currently, three out of four salmonid fish populations (Chinook salmon, *Oncorhynchus tshawytscha*; coho salmon, *Oncorhynchus kisutch*; and steelhead trout, *Oncorhynchus mykiss*) have declined in Redwood Creek to the degree that they are currently listed as threatened under the Endangered Species Act.

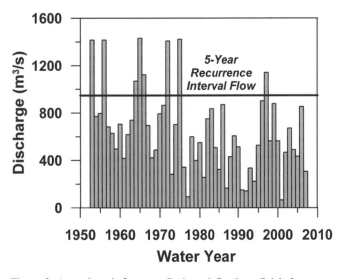

Figure 2. Annual peak flows on Redwood Creek at Orick from water years 1953–2007. A *water year,* WY, extends from 1 October to 30 September.

METHODS

Cross-Sectional Surveys

In 1973 the U.S. Geological Survey (USGS) established ~50 cross-sectional transects along the length of Redwood Creek (labeled XS in Fig. 1). Cross sections have been resurveyed by the USGS and Redwood National Park annually from 1973 to 1987, and periodically since then. Cross sections were monumented with steel rebars reinforced by concrete, and referenced to at least two other triangulation points. The cross sections were surveyed during the low-flow summer months with either an automatic level or an electronic total station. Changes in cross-sectional area from channel scour, fill, and bank erosion were calculated by comparing plots of successive cross-sectional surveys. The change in mean streambed elevation was calculated as the change in cross-sectional area, referenced to permanent endpoints, divided by bankfull width, which results in a stage-independent value. For each survey year, the cumulative change in mean streambed elevation was calculated to show trends at individual cross sections over time. Some transects have since been abandoned owing to lack of access or loss of monuments through bank erosion, but data from 23 cross sections span more than 30 yr and were used in the present analysis.

Thalweg Profiles

Thalweg profiles of lower Redwood Creek have been surveyed by the USGS and Redwood National Park since 1977. Subsequent profiles have been surveyed every 5 to 10 yr. Thalweg elevations and water depths were surveyed with an automatic level, or an electronic total station. All major morphologic features (i.e., top, middle, and base of pools, runs, and riffles) and breaks-in-slope were surveyed. Pools were characterized by slow-moving water with no surface disturbances. Runs had fast-moving water with a smooth surface and were typically ~1 m deep. Riffles had fast-moving, shallow water with surface disturbances. The average spacing of survey points was ~15 m in Redwood Creek, which is about one-fourth the bankfull channel width. The length of each surveyed profile was 20 to >30 channel widths, and survey distances were measured along the center line of the high-flow channel.

Residual pool depths were calculated for each thalweg profile. A *residual pool depth* is the difference in depth or bed elevation between the deepest part of a pool and the downstream riffle crest (Lisle, 1987). For this analysis, pools were defined as features that had residual depths of at least 1 m and a length or width of at least 10% of the bankfull channel width. Similar to the calculation of residual pool depths, the entire distribution of water depths below controlling riffle crests can be determined (Madej, 1999). In this case, thalweg elevations were interpolated between survey points to obtain bed-elevation values spaced 5 m apart. Consequently, each year's survey for a given reach had a similar sample size of bed elevations. Using the elevation of the downstream riffle crest, we determined a residual water depth for each bed-elevation point. Points on a riffle were assigned a value of zero. Because water depths were not normally distributed, we tested differences in the medians rather than in the means, using the nonparametric Mann-Whitney two-sample comparison test.

Substrate Particle-Size Distribution

The particle-size distribution of the channel bed at selected cross sections was determined using the Wolman pebble-count methodology (Wolman, 1954). Five transects perpendicular to the stream channel were measured, with the center transect located on the cross section. The length of streambed sampled equaled the active channel width, and transects were spaced a quarter-channel width apart. The B or intermediate axis was measured for 20 particles selected at regular intervals along each transect, for a total of 100 particles. This standard grid spacing assured that the same area of channel bed was sampled in each survey.

Class sizes ranged from <2 mm (sand) to >256 mm (boulders) and were classified into half-phi size intervals.

RESULTS

Channel-Bed Elevation

The trends in mean bed elevation at representative cross sections along Redwood Creek showed a general decrease, following channel aggradation in the 1960s and 1970s (Fig. 3). Cross sections in Redwood Creek were already aggraded by past floods by the time monitoring began in 1973. In general, cross-sectional surveys in the upper basin documented that the Redwood Creek channel downcut to a stable bed elevation by 1985. The channel bed at cross section 40 is now at the same elevation as in 1953, based on gauging-station records at this location. In the middle reach, the channel attained a more stable bed elevation at most cross sections by 1995. In lower Redwood Creek, the channel continues to downcut and evacuate sediment from the channel bed.

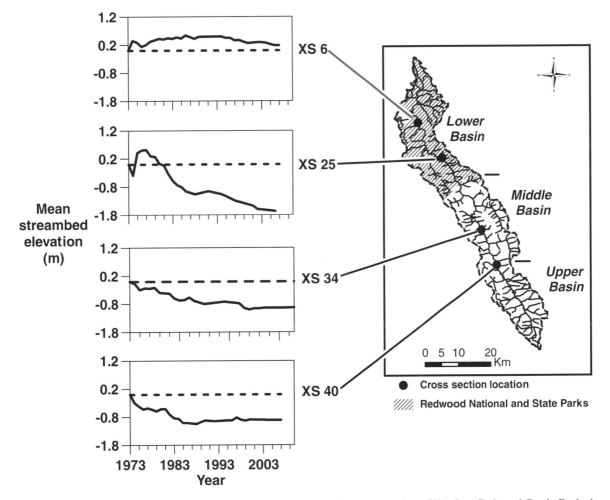

Figure 3. Change in E, mean streambed elevation, at four representative cross sections (XS) along Redwood Creek. Dashed line is zero; i.e., the bed elevation at the beginning of the surveys in 1973.

The most complete records of bed-elevation change were available for the downstream-most 26 km of Redwood Creek. Here, the timing of peak aggradation was delayed in a downstream direction. Channel aggradation at cross section 25, ~26 km upstream of the mouth, peaked in the early 1970s, whereas aggradation at cross section 6, 10 km upstream of the mouth, did not peak until the mid-1990s (Fig. 3). Following peak channel aggradation, the decrease in mean bed elevation ranged from 0.4 m near the mouth of Redwood Creek to 4 m at cross section 23, at km 25 (Fig. 4).

The decreases in mean channel-bed elevation as seen in Figure 3 were typical of most cross sections. These trends in channel incision were described by exponential decay functions in the form of:

$$E(t) = Ae^{-kt}, \qquad (1)$$

where E = mean streambed elevation relative to a cross-section datum; t = time since peak aggradation, in years; and A and k, the decay rate, are coefficients determined for individual cross sections through the least-squares technique. Exponential decay functions modeled decreases in channel-bed elevation at the cross sections reasonably well, with r^2 values generally >70% (Table 1). One exception (cross section 40) had a better fit with a power function ($r^2 = 0.77$). We also tested whether the magnitude of peak flows during a survey period influenced the rate of channel incision; however, when added to the exponential decay model, peak flow was not a significant variable for any of the cross sections ($p > 0.40$). There was no obvious trend between decay rates, k, and either channel width or distance along the channel (Table 1) ($p > 0.40$, through simple linear regression). Some of the highest decay rates, though, were associated with cross sections 19 through 25. This reach is just downstream of a steep canyon, where the channel gradient changes abruptly from 1.4% to 0.3%, which was the site of extensive flood deposits in the early to mid-1970s. Here, narrow remnants of flood deposits along the valley walls are 7 m high.

Particle Sizes of Channel Substrate

Pebble counts have been conducted at selected cross sections since 1979. In addition, we compared on-the-ground photographs of the channel taken in 1980 and in 2003 along the upstream-most 20 km of Redwood Creek to confirm trends in that reach, which does not have many cross sections. The dominant particle size, D_{84} (the 84th percentile of the surface-bed particle sizes) is important in controlling bed mobility, and as it increases, bed mobility decreases for a given flow. D_{84} increased at most cross sections during the past 27 yr (Fig. 5). At many cross sections D_{84} doubled during this period. Based on 2006 data, D_{84} decreased in a downstream direction, from 165 mm in the headwaters to 40–60 mm in the lower river. In general, the channel bed has coarsened as the channel has downcut (Fig. 6).

Thalweg Profiles

Pool frequencies and depths are important measures of aquatic habitat diversity. Comparisons of successive thalweg profiles showed that pool frequencies and depths on lower Redwood Creek have changed over time as the channel has responded to increases and decreases in coarse sediment supply. In general, pool frequency has increased in lower Redwood Creek since 1977. However, a comparison of three channel segments in lower Redwood Creek with differing lengths of time since peak aggradation showed different levels of pool development. Sub-reaches A and B (Fig. 1), the channel sub-reaches with the most recovery time (30 and 25 yr since peak aggradation, respectively) had a greater number of pools per channel length than sub-reach C, which had less recovery time (17 yr since peak aggradation) (Fig. 7). In sub-reach A the number of pools increased from 1977 to 1995, but following the 1997 flood the number of pools decreased by more than one-third (36%), and by 2007 there were still 14% fewer pools than prior to the flood. Pool frequency in sub-reach B has increased continually through time. In sub-reach C, the reach with the least recovery time, response was similar to that of sub-reach A, with a 50% decrease in pools following the 1997 flood. By 2006 the number of pools had not recovered to pre-flood frequency (25% fewer pools). In 2007 the average pool spacing for sub-reaches A and C was ~3.5 channel widths, and for sub-reach B the average pool spacing was 2.5 channel widths.

The dominant pool-forming mechanism in all three reaches was scour around bedrock outcrops or large boulders (59%, 54%, and 77% in sub-reaches A, B, and C, respectively). In addition, the deepest pools in each reach were associated with bedrock or boulders. As the channel has incised, bedrock blocks and boulders became exhumed, and pools were scoured around these obstructions. The size of the boulders decreased downstream. In sub-reaches A and B, several in-channel boulders were >10 m in diameter, whereas in sub-reach C, boulders were generally <2 m in diameter (Figs. 8A, 8B). About one-quarter of the pools were formed by scour around large woody debris. There were no channel-spanning logs in lower Redwood Creek, and pools were

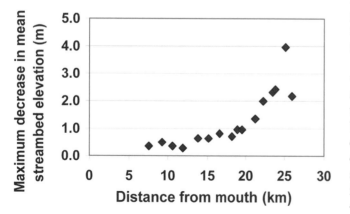

Figure 4. Maximum decrease in E, mean streambed elevation, since peak of aggradation in lower Redwood Creek.

TABLE 1. BANKFULL CHANNEL WIDTHS, DISTANCE DOWNSTREAM, AND EXPONENTIAL
DECAY RATES FOR MEAN STREAMBED ELEVATIONS MEASURED AT CROSS SECTIONS

Cross section	Distance from mouth (km)	Width of channel (m)	Number of surveys*	Decay rate, k	Correlation coefficient, r^2	Significance (p-value)
3	7.5	127	9	−0.01	92.84	<0.0001
5	9.2	114	14	−0.01	84.83	<0.0001
6	10.5	112	16	−0.05	79.94	<0.0001
10	11.8	99	7	−0.04	85.60	0.0028
11	13.8	71	18	−0.02	72.38	<0.0001
12	15.1	75	18	−0.03	69.50	0.0005
14	16.6	61	15	−0.01	78.19	<0.0001
15	18.2	62	15	−0.03	82.56	<0.0001
16	18.9	85	17	−0.04	77.49	<0.0001
17	19.5	87	15	−0.02	80.80	<0.0001
19	21.3	128	16	−0.07	95.39	<0.0001
20	22.2	58	18	−0.07	87.53	<0.0001
21a	23.4	71	16	−0.05	92.12	<0.0001
22	23.7	58	17	−0.12	64.04	0.0001
23	25.1	119	14	−0.09	93.96	<0.0001
25	25.9	49	18	−0.06	95.06	<0.0001
32	44.9	35	23	−0.02	77.64	<0.0001
32a	45.4	69	9	−0.01	65.29	0.0008
34	58.9	67	25	−0.02	89.26	<0.0001
34a	60.0	127	25	−0.02	80.16	<0.0001
35	62.7	51	23	−0.02	89.35	<0.0001
40	72.5	34	29	−0.01	52.64	<0.0001
44	102.4	15	16	−0.04	84.22	<0.0001

*Number of channel-bed surveys since peak of aggradation. Owing to access and crew
constraints, not all cross sections were surveyed each year.

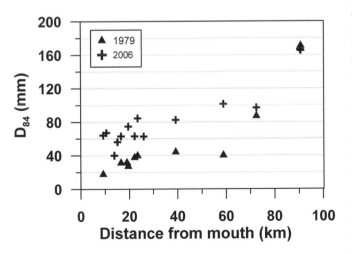

Figure 5. D_{84}, calculated from pebble counts conducted at cross sections in 1979 and 2006. See text for further explanation.

generally scoured around individual pieces of wood that were either anchored on the bank and dipped steeply into the river bed or around large (>2 m in diameter) redwood rootwads. Exhumation of in-channel wood also enhanced pool depths through time. The flow contribution from tributaries is small relative to the mainstem Redwood Creek, and confluence pools were small and few in number.

Pool frequency is only one aspect of aquatic habitat, and changes in pool depths were also analyzed. Channel recovery, if defined by greater pool depths, followed a similar trend as that for pool frequency. In 1977, following a series of large floods and massive landslide inputs to the channel, no pools were >0.6 m deep in lower Redwood Creek, and the channel lacked a well-defined pool-riffle morphology. By 1983 several pools had formed in sub-reaches A and B (Fig. 9), and from 1983 to 1995 pool depths increased in all sub-reaches. In the early 1980s, residual pool depths were skewed toward shallower pools, but by 1995 the number of deeper pools had increased. However, a moderate flood in 1997 (10 yr recurrence interval) and associated landslide activity filled in pools and set back pool recovery to pool depth distributions similar to those of the mid-1980s. Since 1997, it has taken more than a decade for pool depths to recover, and there are still fewer deep pools in sub-reaches A and B than prior to the flood. Sub-reach C, which was still actively aggrading in 1983 but is presently degrading, now has several deep pools.

Distribution of Residual Water Depths

An assessment of individual pools does not address other habitat units such as runs and riffles. To examine this aspect, we assessed the population of all residual water depths in a reach. For example, a reach with a greater length in riffles than in pools or runs will have a smaller value for median water depth. In the reach with the longest recovery time (sub-reach A), median residual water depth increased through time until 1997, when conditions after the flood reverted to those of 1983 (Table 2). By 2007, median water depth again increased and had almost doubled over the 1997 values. In contrast, sub-reach B did not show a large increase in median residual water depth through time, and conditions in 2006 were similar to those of the 1980s. Median water depths in sub-reach C increased greatly from 1983 to 1995 during a transition between peak aggradation in the channel and the initiation of channel incision. Here, water depths decreased by more than half following the 1997 flood, and the median of residual water depths in sub-reach C has not changed significantly since then.

DISCUSSION

Redwood Creek affords a unique opportunity to evaluate channel recovery from large floods and sediment input events. Since the last large flood in 1975, the stream has undergone only low to moderate peak flows. The monitoring data set covers >30 yr of channel adjustments without the influence of another major disturbance.

In the upstream two-thirds of Redwood Creek, where the average channel gradient ranges from 0.5% to 3%, the channel bed degraded rapidly following large sediment inputs and channel aggradation in the 1960s and 1970s. Subsequently, the rate of incision decreased as D_{84} increased, and presently the channel is strongly armored. Taking cross section 40 as representative of the upper basin, little change in mean streambed elevation has occurred since 1985, and a moderate flood in 1997, which initiated >100 landslides in this reach, only resulted in localized deposition.

In lower Redwood Creek, where the average channel gradient is 0.2%, cross-sectional surveys illustrated a somewhat different trend. The highest rates of sediment evacuation occurred 26 km upstream of the mouth of Redwood Creek in a channel reach that attained peak aggradation in the late 1970s. Similar to upstream reaches of Redwood Creek, the channel initially incised rapidly and then slowed as bed material coarsened through time. However, peak aggradation did not occur in the lower 10 km of Redwood Creek until the mid-1990s, and the channel bed is still incising in this area.

Exponential decay functions effectively modeled the rate of decrease in mean channel-bed elevations along the length of Redwood Creek. Such trends in sediment evacuation were consistent with other studies of geomorphic adjustment following disturbances (Graf, 1977; Gran, 2005) where channel response was rapid at first but slowed through time. In Redwood Creek the magnitude of channel-bed elevation decrease was not significantly related to peak flows, perhaps because the magnitude of

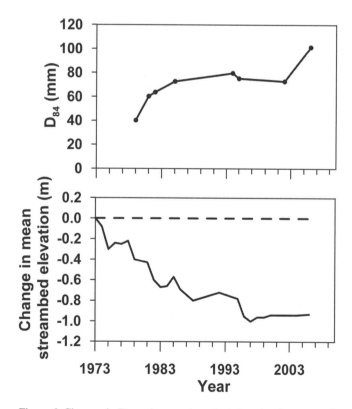

Figure 6. Changes in D_{84} and mean streambed elevation documented through field surveys at cross section 34.

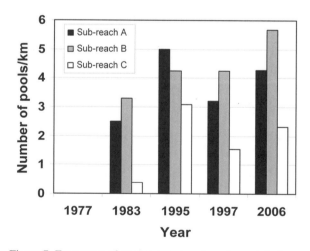

Figure 7. Frequency of pools >1 m deep by sub-reach in lower Redwood Creek, 1977–2007. Sub-reach A was surveyed in 2007; sub-reaches B and C were resurveyed in 2006.

Figure 8. (A) Large (16-m-diameter) boulder and associated pool in sub-reach A. Large wood is commonly trapped on such obstructions but is not the primary mechanism for pool scour. Flow is to the right. (Person on gravel bar on right, for scale.) (B) Channel in sub-reach C, showing relative lack of in-channel wood, bedrock outcrops, or large boulders. View is looking downstream.

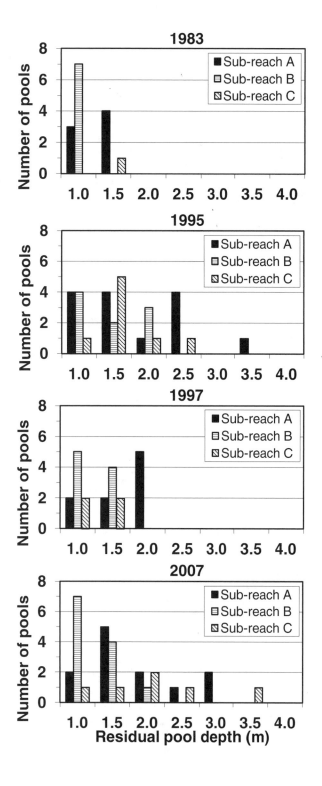

Figure 9. Distribution of pool depths through time in three sub-reaches of lower Redwood Creek. Class sizes represent the lower class boundaries.

TABLE 2. MEDIAN RESIDUAL WATER DEPTHS IN REDWOOD CREEK SUB-REACHES A, B, AND C

Survey date	Sub-reach A	Sub-reach B	Sub-reach C
1977	0	0	
1983	0.36 a	0.16 c	0.06
1986	0.46 b		
1995	0.51 b	0.24 d	0.30
1997	0.32 a	0.22 d	0.16 e
2006/2007	0.61	0.20 cd	0.15 e

Note: Median residual water depths in years not sharing a common letter were statistically different from one another (p < 0.05).

peak flows during the monitoring period was not high (all flows were less than a 12 yr return interval). This too is consistent with other studies, such as in Japan, where the exponential decay rate of channel-stored sediment removal was not strongly related to the magnitude of the peak flows (Maita, 1991). There, in the steep (~10% gradient) stream channel, sediment was evacuated quickly, and sediment storage returned to pre-flood levels within 3 years; however, the rate of decrease was somewhat slower in wide valley segments. In Redwood Creek, though, there was not a clear relationship between decay rates determined from cross-sectional data and channel width or distance along the channel. The highest decay rates were associated with a reach of river downstream of a canyon where flood deposits were at least 7 m thick, on the basis of the height of remnants of flood terraces. The thick deposits would have caused a local steepening of channel gradient, increasing sediment transport capacity and presumably sediment evacuation rates. A high transport capacity related to high storage volume is consistent with the concepts put forth by Lisle and Church (2002).

Net erosion between surveys at these cross-sectional transects indicates that as channel-stored sediment was evacuated from a reach, it was not completely replaced, owing to reduced sediment supply to the channel. Sediment supply was reduced over time through several mechanisms. Streamside landslides delivered much less material to the channel in the post-1980s than in the previous two decades. Channel-stored sediment in tributaries was evacuated rapidly after the 1970s floods, where 60%–100% of recent flood deposits was evacuated in 5 to 10 yr (Madej, 1987). Thus, the role of tributaries as a source of sediment diminished through time. The Redwood Creek channel bed became more strongly armored as the bed incised, which then required higher shear stresses to mobilize the bed particles over time. As the channel bed incised and flood deposits were eroded, the remaining deposits became more isolated from the main flow. Although not quantified in the present study, the establishment of woody vegetation at the base of flood deposits probably hindered erosion as well, as it has been shown to stabilize streambanks in other aggraded systems (Hupp, 1992). Since 1978, hillslope restoration activities, focused on the roads with the highest erosion risk, have removed about one-fifth of the road network in Redwood Creek, further reducing sediment contributions from hillslopes.

Pool frequencies varied among reaches with different lengths of time since peak aggradation. Pool spacing in lower Redwood

Creek was 2.5–3.5 channel widths apart. This is a closer spacing than the five to seven channel widths generally reported for pool-riffle rivers formed in alluvium (Leopold et al., 1964). In Redwood Creek, most of the stream length has streambanks composed of bedrock or coarse colluvium, however, and large in-channel wood also induces bed scour. Pool spacing reflects the importance of such obstructions in pool formation in this system (Lisle, 1986). Exhumation of buried boulders and, to a lesser extent, buried logs, has led to higher pool frequency through time and plays an important role in recovery of this habitat feature.

Considering that coastal redwood trees are the tallest trees in the world, one might expect that large woody debris would have a stronger influence on pool formation in this system. Nevertheless, the lower Redwood Creek channel is wide enough (60–130 m) so that no fallen trees span the channel. We have observed that even old-growth trees that fall into the channel have floated out of the system during average winter flows. Upstream, where the channel is narrower, streambanks have been logged, so presently there is not a source of large trees. Currently, only when wood becomes lodged against boulders or bedrock, or is firmly anchored on the streambank, is it effective in forming or enhancing pools.

Trends in pool depths and median residual water depths were not necessarily the same as trends in pool frequency. For example, over time sub-reach B developed more pools per channel length than sub-reach A (the reach with the longest time since peak aggradation), but pools were not as deep in sub-reach B, and the median residual water depth was less than that in sub-reach A.

In general, both pool frequencies and depths were sensitive to a 10 yr flood in that fewer deep pools occurred in lower Redwood Creek after the 1997 flood. In sub-reach A, median residual water depths have increased greatly from 1997 to 2007, although pool frequency and pool depths are still somewhat reduced from 1995 levels. This trend suggests that sediment persists in pools even as the runs are becoming deeper as the channel incises. In sub-reaches B and C, pool frequencies and pool depths have increased in the 10 yr following the flood, whereas median residual water depths in 2006 are about the same as they were immediately post-flood. This suggests that scour of pools is localized and that runs and riffles along most of the channel length have not become deeper. These are sub-reaches where mean bed elevations have not decreased nearly as much as in sub-reach A. These trends also illustrate both the need to consider more than just pool frequency when assessing channel response, and the susceptibility of pools to filling even in moderate-sized floods.

The biological linkage to these habitat changes is not yet well established, but biological monitoring is beginning to assess the effects of sediment on aquatic biota in Redwood Creek. Salmon and steelhead trout have about a 4-year life cycle, and juvenile steelhead can rear in the mainstem of Redwood Creek for several years before migrating out to the ocean. Sediment impacts in Redwood Creek have persisted for several decades and consequently have reduced the quality and availability of aquatic habitat for many generations of anadromous salmonids. Population estimates for 1- and 2-year-old steelhead in Redwood Creek

have decreased for the past 8 years, or ~50% since the beginning of biological monitoring in 2000 (California Department of Fish and Game, 2007). Although Redwood Creek has been incising and coarsening through time, there has not yet been a positive response in steelhead populations. Anadromous salmonids spend most of their life cycle outside the freshwater environment and are affected by ocean conditions. This highlights the difficulty of using salmonids as biological indicators of stream health.

Freshwater mussels also can be used as bioindicators of stream condition (Young et al., 2003). In 2007, western pearlshells *(Margaritifera falcata)* were discovered in lower Redwood Creek in sub-reach A. Young subadult mussels were found in the mussel beds, indicating reproductive success over the last decade (Benson, 2007). The last known sighting in Redwood Creek was >50 yr ago, prior to the 1955 and 1964 floods. Pearlshell mussels live up to 100 yr, and the population in Redwood Creek has survived decades of sedimentation >2 m deep since peak aggradation in the 1970s, and channel incision has exposed bedrock substrate along streambanks that are colonized by mussels.

In contrast to extensive channel widening documented in the nearby Eel River basin (Sloan et al., 2001), the Redwood Creek channel responded to large floods and sediment inputs primarily through channel aggradation and subsequent incision. Lateral erosion of flood deposits was limited to the few unconfined reaches of river with wide valleys and floodplains, which account for only ~15% of the length of Redwood Creek. Although remnants of flood deposits from the 1960s and 1970s remain plastered against the valley walls at a few localized sites, the toes of these deposits are well vegetated and seem to be stabilized.

The removal of channel-stored sediment influences interpretations of sediment-yield measurements from a basin. For example, the degree of channel incision measured in sub-reach C (0.5 m) was much less than the 2–4 m of incision in sub-reach A. Because sub-reach C has just recently begun to incise, it is likely that sediment evacuation will continue in this area for many more years and affect sediment-transport rates measured at the downstream Orick gauging station. Erosion of in-channel stored sediment accounted for ~25% of the total sediment load and 95% of the bed load exported from Redwood Creek from 1980 to 1990 (Madej and Ozaki, 1996). Since that time the channel bed in upper Redwood Creek has coarsened, and bed elevations have stabilized. As a result, removal of in-channel stored sediment will probably play a lesser role in bed-load transport at the upstream gauging station (Redwood Creek at Blue Lake). Nevertheless, sediment yields, which are used as a target to document watershed recovery by regulatory agencies, should be used with caution because of the time lag in routing channel-stored sediment through the river network.

Although the magnitudes of peak flows in floods of 1964 and the 1970s were not unusual, the geomorphic effectiveness of those floods was great because streamside landslides contributed large volumes of material to the river channel during the floods. Channel aggradation that resulted from those floods has persisted in lower Redwood Creek for >30 yr. If channel recovery is defined as a return to a former streambed elevation, a coarser bed substrate, more frequent and deeper pools, and greater median residual water depth, the Redwood Creek channel has been on a trajectory of recovery. However, if we assume that channel-bed elevations will continue to decrease exponentially by the decay rates listed in Table 1, it will take until the year 2016 for the bed in lower Redwood Creek to return to the elevation of the mid-1970s. Because the probability of a 25 yr flood occurring within a 40 yr period (1975–2015) is 80% (Dunne and Leopold, 1978), it is highly likely that another large flood will occur before the flood deposits in lower Redwood Creek are fully evacuated.

Whereas the recent discovery of fresh-water mussels is encouraging and may signal a shift to improved fresh-water aquatic conditions, and long-term monitoring indicates that Redwood Creek is currently on a recovery trajectory from past floods, the stream still lacks improvement in some fundamental stream-habitat and water-quality components necessary to support a healthy aquatic ecosystem. Stream temperatures, large woody debris in the stream, and large conifer trees in the riparian zone have not recovered to a functional level to support anadromous salmonids (Madej et al., 2006). Evacuation of channel-stored sediment probably affects the Redwood Creek estuary at the mouth of Redwood Creek, which is an important rearing habitat for salmonids. Future research will examine the magnitude, distribution, rate, and source of estuarine deposition, and evaluate possible management actions. Restoration of the Redwood Creek estuary will play a critical role in the recovery of threatened salmon and steelhead trout (Cannata et al., 2006).

The persistence of sediment impacts has implications for river restoration. Once sediment enters a channel it can take decades to be routed through the system. In steep, confined mountain channels, in-channel restoration opportunities are limited because hillslope and channel processes are closely linked. In the case of Redwood Creek, restoration work has focused on ameliorating hillslope-erosion problems rather than attempting to modify the channel by such actions as installing channel structures, dredging sediment, or reshaping the channel. The goal of hillslope erosion–control work is to reduce sediment supply to Redwood Creek in future storms, but the effectiveness of this work in preventing road failures, landslides, and gullying has not yet been tested by a large (25 yr) event.

CONCLUSIONS

A series of 25 yr floods in the 1960s and 1970s resulted in channel aggradation in Redwood Creek, northwestern California. The temporal histories of this newly deposited sediment differed between upstream and downstream reaches of the river. Aggradation was especially severe in the upper basin, but by the mid-1980s the channel had incised to pre-disturbance levels; the dominant particle size of the bed, D_{84}, had doubled in size; and remnants of flood deposits along valley walls were becoming well vegetated and stabilized. In this reach, recovery time was similar to the recurrence interval of the floods that caused aggra-

dation. In contrast, in lower Redwood Creek, channel aggradation continued through the 1980s as sediment was redistributed downstream and did not peak until the 1990s. Here, the channel bed is still in the process of downcutting, and D_{84} is increasing in size. The decline in channel-bed elevations was initially rapid but slowed as the channel became more strongly armored. The decline can be modeled by exponential decay functions, and the magnitude of peak flows was not significant in defining the decrease in bed elevation.

As the channel has incised, pool frequencies and depths have increased. The degree of pool development differs among reaches with different lengths of time since peak aggradation. Highest pool frequencies were found in reaches for which 25–30 yr has elapsed since peak aggradation, in contrast to a reach for which only 17 yr has elapsed since peak aggradation. From 1983 to 2007 the reach with the greatest amount of channel incision consistently had the highest number of deep pools and the highest median residual water depth. In 1997 a 10 yr flood, with associated streamside mass-wasting activity, resulted in the loss or partial filling of some pools but did not have a large effect on mean streambed elevation. By 2007, median residual water depth had again increased to pre-1997 levels in the reach with 30 yr since peak aggradation, but had not significantly increased in downstream reaches. Pool depths have not recovered to pre-1997-flood values in any of the surveyed reaches.

The duration of sediment impacts in Redwood Creek has affected multiple lifecycles of salmon and steelhead, and channel aggradation has persisted longer than the recurrence interval of the flood that originally emplaced the deposits. Nevertheless, a 10 yr flood somewhat reversed the trend of recovery, and it is likely that the Redwood Creek channel will be impacted by another large flood (25 yr recurrence interval) before it fully evacuates all the recent in-channel flood deposits.

ACKNOWLEDGMENTS

Over the last 30 years, many survey crews, too many to name individually, assisted us in the field to collect channel morphologic data. Carrie Jones has been especially diligent in compiling and plotting cross-sectional data during the last 17 years, and Nick Varnum was instrumental in preparing technical reports in 1984 and 1986 involving cross-sectional surveys. Julie Yee assisted with the statistical analyses.

REFERENCES CITED

Bailey, E.H., Blake, M.C., Jr., and Jones, D.L., 1970, On-land Mesozoic oceanic crust in California Coast Ranges, *in* U.S. Geological Survey Professional Paper 700-C, p. 70–81.
Benson, K., 2007, 2007 Mill Creek Western Pearlshell Freshwater Mussel Monitoring and Discovery of Western Pearlshell Freshwater Mussel Population in Redwood Creek: Orick, California, Redwood National and State Parks Annual Progress Report, 17 p.
Best, D., 1995, History of timber harvest in the Redwood Creek basin, northwestern California, *in* Nolan, K.M., Kelsey, H.M., and Marron, D.C., eds., Geomorphic Processes and Aquatic Habitat in the Redwood Creek Basin,

Northwestern California: U.S. Geological Survey Professional Paper 1454-C. p. C1–C7.

California Department of Fish and Game, 2007, unpublished data on biological monitoring.

California Regional Water Quality Control Board North Coast Region, 1998, Proposed Redwood Creek Water Quality Attainment Strategy for Sediment (Total Maximum Daily Loads and Implementation Plan): Santa Rosa, California, 71 p.

Cannata, S., Henly, R., Erler, J., Falls, J., McGuire, D., and Sunahara, J., 2006, Redwood Creek Watershed Assessment Report. Coastal Watershed Planning and Assessment Program and North Coast Watershed Assessment Program: Sacramento, California Resources Agency and California Environmental Protection Agency, 166 p.

Curry, T.L., 2007, A landslide study in the Redwood Creek basin, northwestern California: Effects of the 1997 storm [M.S. thesis]: Arcata, California, Humboldt State University, 107 p.

Dunne, T., and Leopold, L.B., 1978, Water in Environmental Planning: San Francisco, W.H. Freeman, 818 p.

Gilbert, G.K., 1917, Hydraulic-Mining Debris in the Sierra Nevada: U.S. Geological Survey Professional Paper 105, 154 p.

Graf, W.L., 1977, The rate law in fluvial geomorphology: American Journal of Science, v. 277, p. 178–191.

Gran, K.B., 2005, Fluvial recovery following basin-wide sediment loading at Mount Pinatubo, Philippines [Ph.D. thesis]: Seattle, University of Washington, 203 p.

Hack, J.T., and Goodlett, J.C., 1960, Geomorphology and Forest Ecology of a Mountain Region in the Central Appalachians: U.S. Geological Survey Professional Paper 347, 66 p.

Harden, D.H., 1995, A comparison of flood-producing storms and their impacts in northwestern, California, *in* Nolan, K.M., Kelsey, H.M., and Marron, D.C., eds., Geomorphic Processes and Aquatic Habitat in the Redwood Creek Basin, Northwestern California: U.S. Geological Survey Professional Paper 1454-D, p. D1–D9.

Harvey, A.M., 2007, Differential recovery from the effects of a 100-year storm: Significance of long-term hillslope-channel coupling; Howgill Fells, northwest England: Geomorphology, v. 84, p. 192–208, doi: 10.1016/j.geomorph.2006.03.009.

Hupp, C.R., 1992, Riparian vegetation recovery patterns following stream channelization: A geomorphic perspective: Ecology, v. 73, p. 1209–1226, doi: 10.2307/1940670.

James, A., 1999, Time and the persistence of alluvium: River engineering, fluvial geomorphology and mining sediment in California: Geomorphology, v. 31, p. 265–290, doi: 10.1016/S0169-555X(99)00084-7.

Janda, R.J., Nolan, K.M., Harden, D.R., and Colman, S.M., 1975, Watershed Conditions in the Drainage Basin of Redwood Creek, Humboldt County, California, as of 1973: U.S. Geological Survey Open-File Report 75-568, 266 p.

Kelsey, H.K., Coghlan, M., Pitlick, J., and Best, D., 1995, Geomorphic analysis of streamside landslides in the Redwood Creek basin, northwestern California, *in* Nolan, K.M., Kelsey, H.M., and Marron, D.C., eds., Geomorphic Processes and Aquatic Habitat in the Redwood Creek Basin, Northwestern California: U.S. Geological Survey Professional Paper 1454-J, p. J1–J12.

Kelsey, H.M., Lamberson, R., and Madej, M.A., 1987, Stochastic model for long-term transport of stored sediment in a river channel: Water Resources Research, v. 23, p. 1738–1750, doi: 10.1029/WR023i009p01738.

Leopold, L.B., Wolman, M.G., and Miller, J.P., 1964, Fluvial Processes in Geomorphology: San Francisco, W.H. Freeman, 522 p.

Lisle, T.E., 1982, Effects of aggradation and degradation on pool-riffle morphology in natural gravel channels, northwestern California: Water Resources Research, v. 18, p. 1643–1651, doi: 10.1029/WR018i006p01643.

Lisle, T.E., 1986, Stabilization of a gravel channel by large streamside obstructions and bedrock bends, Jacoby Creek, northwestern California: Geological Society of America Bulletin, v. 97, p. 999–1011, doi: 10.1130/0016-7606(1986)97<999:SOAGCB>2.0.CO;2.

Lisle, T.E., 1987, Using 'Residual Depths' to monitor pool depths independently of discharge: U.S. Department of Agriculture, Pacific Southwest Forest and Range Experiment Station Research Note PSW-394, 4 p.

Lisle, T.E., and Church, M., 2002, Sediment transport-storage relations for degrading, gravel-bed channels: Water Resources Research, v. 38, p. 1219, doi: 1210.1029/2001WR001086.

Madej, M.A., 1987, Residence times of channel-stored sediment in Redwood Creek, northwestern California, *in* Erosion and Sedimentation in the Pacific Rim: International Association of Hydrological Sciences Publication 165, p. 429–438.

Madej, M.A., 1995, Changes in channel-stored sediment, Redwood Creek, Northwestern California, 1947–1980, *in* Nolan, K.M., Kelsey, H.M., and Marron, D.C., eds., Geomorphic Processes and Aquatic Habitat in the Redwood Creek Basin, Northwestern California: U.S. Geological Survey Professional Paper 1454-O, p. O1–O27.

Madej, M.A., 1999, Temporal and spatial variability in thalweg profiles of a gravel bed river: Earth Surface Processes and Landforms, v. 24, p. 1153–1169, doi: 10.1002/(SICI)1096-9837(199911)24:12<1153::AID-ESP41>3.0.CO;2-8.

Madej, M.A., and Ozaki, V., 1996, Channel response to sediment wave propagation and movement, Redwood Creek, California, USA: Earth Surface Processes and Landforms, v. 21, p. 911–927, doi: 10.1002/(SICI)1096-9837(199610)21:10<911::AID-ESP621>3.0.CO;2-1.

Madej, M.A., Currens, C., Ozaki, V., and Yee, J., 2006, Assessing possible thermal rearing restrictions for juvenile coho salmon (*Onchorhynchus kisutch*) through thermal infrared imaging and in-stream monitoring, Redwood Creek, California: Canadian Journal of Fisheries and Aquatic Sciences, v. 63, p. 1384–1396, doi: 10.1139/F06-043.

Maita, H., 1991, Sediment dynamics of a high gradient stream in the Oi River basin of Japan: U.S. Department of Agriculture, Forest Service General Technical Report PSW-GTR-130, p. 56–64.

Nolan, K.M., and Marron, D.C., 1995, History, causes and significance of changes in the channel geometry of Redwood Creek, northwestern California, 1936–1982, *in* Nolan, K.M., Kelsey, H.M., and Marron, D.C., eds., Geomorphic Processes and Aquatic Habitat in the Redwood Creek Basin, Northwestern California: U.S. Geological Survey Professional Paper 1454-N, p. N1–N22.

Sloan, J., Miller, J.R., and Lancaster, N., 2001, Response and recovery of the Eel River, California, and its tributaries to floods in 1955, 1964 and 1997: Geomorphology, v. 36, p. 129–154, doi: 10.1016/S0169-555X(00)00037-4.

Wolman, M.G., 1954, A method of sampling coarse river-bed material: American Geophysical Union Transactions, v. 35, p. 951–956.

Wolman, M.G., and Gerson, R., 1978, Relative scales of time and effectiveness of climate in watershed geomorphology: Earth Surface Processes, v. 3, p. 189–208, doi: 10.1002/esp.3290030207.

Young, M.R., Hastie, L.C., and Cooksley, S.L., 2003, Monitoring the Freshwater Pearl Mussel, *Margaritifera margaritifera*: Conserving Natural Rivers Monitoring Series No. 2: Peterborough, UK, English Nature, 20 p.

MANUSCRIPT ACCEPTED BY THE SOCIETY 15 SEPTEMBER 2008

The Geological Society of America
Special Paper 451
2009

Historical channel changes in the lower Yuba and Feather Rivers, California: Long-term effects of contrasting river-management strategies

L. Allan James
Geography Department, University of South Carolina, Columbia, South Carolina 29208, USA

Michael B. Singer
School of Geography & Geosciences, University of St. Andrews, Scotland KY16 9AL, UK, and
Institute for Computational Earth System Science, University of California, Santa Barbara, California 93106-3060, USA

Subhajit Ghoshal
Mary Megison
Geography Department, University of South Carolina, Columbia, South Carolina 29208, USA

ABSTRACT

Hydraulic gold-mining tailings produced in the late nineteenth century in the Sierra Nevada foothills of California caused severe channel aggradation in the lower Feather and Yuba Rivers. Topographic and planimetric data from historical accounts, maps, topographic surveys, vertical sections, aerial photographs, and LiDAR (light detection and ranging) data reveal contrasting styles of channel change and floodplain evolution between these two rivers. For example, levee cross-channel spacings up to 4 km along the lower Yuba River contrast with spacings <2 km on the larger Feather River. More than a quarter billion cubic meters of hydraulic-mining sediment were stored along the lower Yuba River, and the wide levee spacing was intentionally maintained during design of the flood-control system to minimize delivery of sediment to navigable waters downstream. Consequently, the lower Yuba floodplain has a multithread high-water channel system with braiding indices >12 in some reaches. Some of the larger of these channels remain clearly visible on aerial photographs and LiDAR imagery in spite of intensive agricultural leveling. Narrow levee spacings on the Feather River were designed to encourage transport of mining sediment downstream and keep the channel clear for navigation. Levee spacings on the lower Feather River reached a minimum near the turn of the twentieth century, when floodplain widths were reduced at several constricted reaches to <250 m. Historical data indicate that the general channel location of the lower Yuba River had stabilized by the end of the nineteenth century, whereas substantial channel avulsions began later and continued into the twentieth century on the lower Feather River.

James, L.A., Singer, M.B., Ghoshal, S., and Megison, M., 2009, Historical channel changes in the lower Yuba and Feather Rivers, California: Long-term effects of contrasting river-management strategies, *in* James, L.A., Rathburn, S.L., and Whittecar, G.R., eds., Management and Restoration of Fluvial Systems with Broad Historical Changes and Human Impacts: Geological Society of America Special Paper 451, p. 57–81, doi: 10.1130/2009.2451(04). For permission to copy, contact editing@geosociety.org. ©2009 The Geological Society of America. All rights reserved.

The striking contrasts in channel change between the Yuba and Feather Rivers are due, at least in part, to different river-management strategies, although the Yuba River received much more sediment. Early river engineering of these channels represented the first efforts at integrated river-basin management west of the Mississippi, so the observed long-term effects are instructive. Modern river management should consider how the disturbance factors in these channels and the imprint of early river management affect the modern morphologic stability and sediment-production potential of the channel and floodplain.

INTRODUCTION

Human impacts have been pervasive on many rivers, and rivers with strong anthropogenic geomorphic imprints may be the rule rather than the exception. Several rivers that were highly influential to the foundations of modern fluvial geomorphology are recognized as vestiges of severe human alterations, including Brandywine River, Seneca Creek, Watts Branch, and Western Run in the mid-Atlantic Piedmont (Walter and Merritts, 2008), and the Yuba River of northern California (Gilbert, 1917). Reappraising the effectiveness of human impacts can undermine assumptions often made about reference reaches as stable design targets for restoration (Montgomery, 2008) and can contribute to answering the question of "what is natural" with regard to alluvial rivers (Graf, 1996).

Historical analyses can benefit river-restoration projects in several ways (Kondolf and Larson, 1995). Knowledge of past fluvial changes can be useful for designing, restoring, and maintaining a sustainable river (Gregory, 2006), because true restoration of a river to a previous condition requires knowledge of previous channel states. Knowledge of channel changes may also be crucial to anticipating future behavior. For example, the tendency for abandoned channels to be reoccupied during floods provides an additional incentive to recognize the recent history of alluvial floodplains (Petts, 1989; Kondolf and Larson, 1995).

Most instrumental and observational records of streams are limited in time and space, so historical records such as maps, vertical stratigraphic sections, and contemporary observations are valuable for reconstructing past channel conditions. Several reviews have been written about various methods of historical analysis that can be used to reconstruct changes in landform dimensions, erosion rates, and land use (Hooke and Kain, 1982; Trimble and Cooke, 1991), or more specifically, to reconstruct historical channel changes (Patrick et al., 1982; Gurnell et al., 2003) through the use of historical maps (Petts, 1989; Gilvear and Harrison, 1991; Kondolf and Larson, 1995) and aerial photography (Gilvear and Bryant, 2003; Hughes et al., 2006). With the development of geospatial processing tools for georeferencing digital maps and images—and their increasing ease of use—a greater degree of quantification and a higher level of precision can now be obtained by co-registering sets of historical maps and images made at different scales and projections. The success of these methods varies with the level of precision of the original maps or images and the availability of ground-control points or other reference points common to precise spatial data. Even where map registrations are insufficiently accurate for making measurements, much can be learned from qualitative assessments of historical cartographic or remotely sensed records.

Knowing the nature of channel morphologies on the lower Yuba and Feather Rivers prior to Anglo-European settlement, and the subsequent changes that occurred from hydraulic mining, is crucial to the recognition of how these channels were adjusted to former equilibrium conditions and how they now differ from those conditions. These reconstructions are not motivated by the desire to restore channels to presettlement channel forms because pre-mining water and sediment discharge regimes have been so drastically changed by dams, levees, and channelization that full restoration is not plausible—if full restoration is defined as a return to a pristine past condition (National Research Council, 1992). Knowledge of past channel forms and subsequent changes to these anthropogenically disturbed rivers serves several purposes, including an understanding of rates of passive recovery or the long-term consequences of structural changes. Also of immediate importance is knowledge of the locations of former positions of channels that may underlie modern levees and compromise their integrity by allowing underseepage or bank erosion during floods.

Much can be learned by assessing the results of early river-management policies in these rivers. A valid critique of the modern river-restoration movement has been the lack of postproject assessments (Kondolf and Micheli, 1995; Bernhardt et al., 2005). A substantial effort was made to control the Yuba and Feather Rivers during and after the mining period, but little study has been made of these changes from a river-management perspective. Beginning as early as the 1880s, flood-control efforts sought to maintain wide cross-channel levee spacings in the non-navigable Yuba River to encourage deposition of hydraulic-mining sediment, and to construct levees with narrow spacings along the navigable Feather River to encourage self-scouring of the channels. This manipulation of levee spacings to control sediment storage and transport is an early example of attempts to stabilize a large river system following human impacts, and it provides an opportunity to assess the outcome of diverse river rehabilitation methods.

This paper contrasts the resulting channel morphologies of the lower Yuba and Feather Rivers. Both systems underwent severe morphological changes and continue to store large volumes of hydraulic-mining sediment, but the spatial patterns and processes of sediment redistribution and morphologic change are distinctly different. These morphological and sedimentologic adjustments remain relevant to river management in the region. Ongoing engineering changes to these rivers, such as major levee setback projects on the Bear and Feather Rivers, represent modern river-management efforts to reduce flood risks as residential developments encroach on flood-prone lands. Moreover, mercury toxicity of the mining sediment has recently been recognized as an important issue with the mining sediment (May et al., 2000; Hunerlach et al., 2004). Most of the historic sediment stored in both rivers is between levees and may be available for reworking.

The lower Yuba and Feather Rivers were severely altered by the arrival of sediment produced in the mountains by hydraulic gold mining. In addition to the rapid aggradation of channels, drastic engineering measures were taken to protect these rivers during the late nineteenth and early twentieth centuries. The history of hydraulic gold mining from its advent in 1853 to its cessation following an injunction in 1884 is covered elsewhere (May, 1970; Kelley, 1954, 1959, 1989; Greenland, 2001), as are discussions of its impact on rivers and floodplains (Gilbert, 1917; James, 1989, 1994; James and Singer, 2008; Singer et al., 2008). This paper documents the nature and timing of channel changes in the lower Yuba and Feather Rivers from hydraulic-mining sedimentation and river engineering works. It provides documentary and field evidence of the changes and puts them into the context of river-management strategies. The results are part of an ongoing study of hydraulic-mining sediment stored along the lower Yuba and Feather Rivers.

STUDY AREA: HYDRAULIC-GOLD-MINING SEDIMENTATION

The Feather River Basin heads in the northern Sierra Nevada and flows out onto the Sacramento Valley (Fig. 1). The basin includes the Yuba River and the Bear River, which join the Feather above its confluence with the Sacramento River. The mining districts are located on high ridges in the foothills of the Sierra Nevada and consist of rugged terrain with deep, narrow canyons. This study is concerned with the lower Feather River below the Yuba confluence and the lower Yuba River from the mountain front to the Feather River. The Feather River has a drainage area of 10,300 km^2 (3974 mi^2) directly above the Yuba River confluence, and the Yuba River has a drainage area of 3470 km^2 (1340 mi^2) at the U.S. Geological Survey stream gauge above Marysville (no. 11421000).

Hydraulic gold mining in the northern Sierra Nevada foothills produced 1.1 billion cubic meters of sediment (Table 1). Approximately 38% (~400 10^6 m^3) of the total hydraulic-mining sediment produced was stored in piedmont deposits of the Yuba and Bear Rivers and the lower Feather River (Table 2). The immense deposit in the lower Yuba River alone represents 24% of the hydraulic-mining sediment produced from 1853 to 1884. These low-lying, unconsolidated deposits reside below all dams and reservoirs and are largely between modern levees. Thus, they are subject to erosion and transport down-valley to the flood bypasses and Sacramento–San Joaquin Delta, where flood hazards are great (Mount and Twiss, 2005; Singer, 2007; Singer et al., 2008).

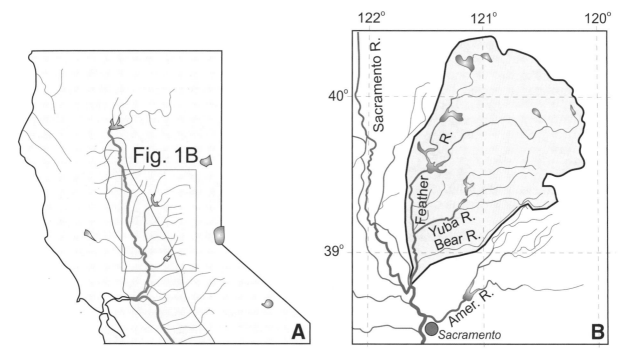

Figure 1. Map of Feather River Basin in northern California. (A) Region straddles the northwestern Sierra Nevada and southeastern Sacramento Valley. (B) Feather River Basin with Yuba and Bear sub-basins. Most hydraulic mines were near 121°W longitude in Yuba and Bear basins.

TABLE 1. SEDIMENT PRODUCTION BY HYDRAULIC GOLD
MINING IN SIERRA NEVADA, CALIFORNIA

River basin	Volume (10^6 m³)	Production (%)
Yuba River	523	49.0
Bear River	271	25.4
Feather River	76.5	7.2
Subtotal	871	81.6
American River	197	18.4
Total	1067	100

Note: Data from Gilbert (1917).

TABLE 2. HYDRAULIC-GOLD-MINING SEDIMENT STORAGE IN THE SIERRA NEVADA PIEDMONT

	1879–1880	1914	1985	Total production (%)
Lower Yuba River		253		24
Lower Feather River, Oroville to Yuba City	14.0	19.1		1.8
Lower Feather River below Yuba confluence	24.6			2.3
Bear River*	27.5		106	9.9
			Total:	38%

Note: Storage volume in lower Bear River was revised upward by coring (James, 1989). All values are in millions of cubic meters. Data from Gilbert (1917).

Most sediment produced in small watersheds is commonly stored close to the source of production, and its distant delivery is usually a small proportion of the sediment produced (Roehl, 1962; Walling, 1983; Novotny and Chesters, 1989). An exceptional feature of Feather River Basin sediment-delivery ratios is that initial sediment storage near the source did not dominate. Most storage occurred tens of kilometers downstream of the source, where gradients decrease along the margin of the Sacramento Valley. Most mines in the Yuba Basin dumped sediment into extremely steep, narrow canyons, where it was quickly and efficiently delivered downstream to alluvial fans and basins in the valley. (Exceptions include Shady, Spring, and Scotchman Creeks, where moderately large deposits remain near the mines.) The high sediment loads overwhelmed the transport capacity of valley channels and caused major geomorphic adjustments such as channel aggradation and avulsions. Engineering efforts to control sedimentation and flooding—including leveeing, channelization, and bank protection—contributed to morphological changes on these rivers and altered patterns of sedimentation. Construction of levees during the mining period was largely uncoordinated, and the history and characteristics of early levees is not well known. By the 1880s, river-management policies began to emerge that encouraged coordination of flood-control efforts (James and Singer, 2008). The strategies employed in the Feather and Yuba Rivers were strikingly different and encouraged contrasts between the floodplain geomorphology of the two rivers.

Methods

The evidence used in this paper to document channel changes over the past 150 yr consists of historical documents, recent maps and geospatial data, and field observations made in 2006 and 2007. The historical evidence is derived from field observations by contemporary experts and from historical maps and aerial photographs, which are compared with modern spatial data including digital orthophoto quarter quads (DOQQs) and LiDAR (light detection and ranging) and sonar topographic data. Numerous historical maps and aerial photographs of channels were visually inspected for channel features and conditions. Selected maps and images were georeferenced to 1999 DOQQs or to a modern geographic information system (GIS) map of section lines of the Public Land Survey System (PLSS, 2001) using ArcGIS 9.2 software. Most rectifications achieved reasonably small root mean square errors (RMSE) with 10 to 29 evenly spaced ground-control points using a second-order polynomial transformation (Table 3). The earliest of the rectified maps (Von Schmidt, 1859) is not sufficiently accurate to allow length or area measurements to be made of channel dimensions or planform changes, but it provides dates of pre-mining channel positions and islands shown on later, more accurate maps. It also allows first-order comparisons to be made of channels through time. Channel boundaries were digitized on-screen from the historic maps and were overlain on more recent maps and images to identify channel positions and features.

Field reconnaissance mapping of river-bank stratigraphy was conducted in the summers of 2006 and 2007 to identify the depths and locations of hydraulic-mining sediment and collect sediment samples. Generalized stratigraphic sections were measured using a total station or hand level to show the relative thickness of major alluvial units, especially contacts between historical sediment and the underlying presettlement alluvium. Stratigraphic and sedimentological evidence at four selected stream-bank exposures is used in this paper to demonstrate the magnitude and character of sedimentation associated with channel changes. Total mercury concentrations of the fine fraction (<63 µm) of sediment samples were determined via cold vapor

TABLE 3. MAP GEOREFERENCING STATISTICS

Map	Original scale	GCPs (N)	RMSE (m)	Transform
1859N Von Schmidt	1:63,400	29	43.7	2d order poly
1859S Von Schmidt	1:63,400	20	45.8	2d order poly
1881 Mendell	NA	23	27.5	2d order poly
1906 CDC map of Yuba	1:9,600	avg ~12	avg ~12	2d order poly
1909 CDC map of Feather*	1:9,600	NA	NA	NA

*Feather River map registration performed by California Department of Water Resources. GCPs—ground-control points; NA—not applicable; RMSE—root mean square errors; CDC—California Debris Commission; poly—polynomial.

atomic fluorescence spectroscopy to test field designations of historical and prehistorical alluvial units. Maps of historical deposits generated from digital soil maps were also consulted for evidence of former channel positions and alluviation.

CONTRASTING RIVER-MANAGEMENT STRATEGIES AND CHANNEL MORPHOLOGIES

Levees, dams, and channelization ultimately caused substantial channel changes in these rivers. Early policies of river management that sought to control mining sediment along the Yuba and Feather Rivers went through a period of evolution in which the emphasis shifted from small dams to levees and channelization. On the non-navigable Yuba and Bear Rivers, the goal was to sequester mining sediment and reduce sediment deliveries to the navigable waters of the Feather and Sacramento Rivers downstream. Initial attempts to detain sediment with dams in the piedmont failed. A brush and rock dam 1.8 m (6 ft) high on the Bear River failed within a year (Mendell, 1881) after impounding 735,000 m^3 of sediment from 1880 to 1881 (Mendell, 1882). A brush dam on the lower Yuba River built in 1880 failed the following year. Barrier No. 1, a gravel and stone dam, was constructed on the lower Yuba River in 1904, raised a total height of 4.2 m, and held 1,292,000 m^3 of sediment before failing in 1907 (Gilbert, 1917). The Daguerre Point Dam, built a few km below the Barrier Dam in 1910, persisted, but it provided too little sediment storage too late to encourage a policy of using dams to control sediment on these large rivers. Contemporary dam technology was simply not yet up to such a task.

Failure of the early dams led to an increased emphasis on channelization and levees to protect the Feather and Sacramento Rivers from flooding and sedimentation. This strategy included spacing levees widely in the lower Yuba River to encourage sediment retention and employing narrow levee spacings on the Feather River to encourage channel scour. By 1906, levee spacings in the Yuba River were as great as 4.1 km above Marysville but narrowed to a 640-m constriction at Marysville 1 km above the Yuba-Feather confluence (Fig. 2). No substantial change in the outer levee spacings has occurred along the Yuba River since 1906. To compensate for the widely spaced levees, main channel margins along the lower Yuba were armored with riprap to protect banks from erosion, and boulder wing dams to constrict flow widths within the main channel. Thus, the main Yuba chan-

nel was designed to convey water and scour sediment, but high lateral connectivity with a broad floodplain encouraged overbank deposition on floodplains and in high-water channels.

Levee spacings along the Feather River are much narrower than those along the Yuba River. By 1909, levee encroachment along much of the Feather River had reduced cross-channel spacings to dangerously small widths. At several points, levees

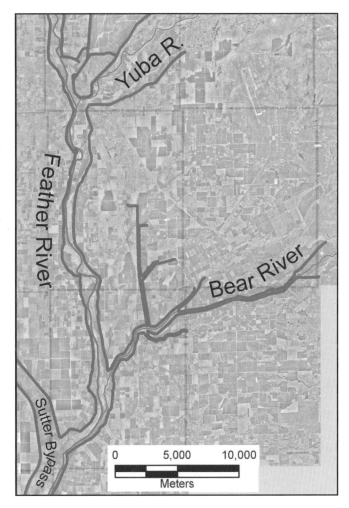

Figure 2. Levee cross-channel spacings with narrow Feather River floodway, wide Yuba River floodway, and narrow constriction at Yuba mouth. Digitized from 1999 digital orthophoto quarter quads (DOQQs).

constricted the width of the floodway to <2.5 times low-flow channel widths (Fig. 3). Levee spacings below Shanghai and Star Bends and at Star Bend in 1909 were on the order of only 240 m apart, not much wider than the low-flow channel (Fig. 4). These constrictions probably caused backwater effects during large floods, but they had been widened by 1999. Owing to frequent levee failures before the 1930s, the U.S. Army Corps of Engineers had set back many of the levees by 1940 (Eckbo, Dean and Williams, 2006). An extensive levee setback project was recently completed at the Feather-Bear River confluence, and another is currently under way in the reach above Star Bend. Downstream, near the confluence of the Feather and Sacramento Rivers, levee positions along the left bank did not change substantially between 1909 and 1999, but in 1909 a Southern Pacific Railroad embankment along the right bank constrained widths of moderate-magnitude floods to <250 m. High flood stages evidently flowed through the embankment into the Sutter Basin through a series of crevasses that are described later in this paper.

HISTORICAL CHANNEL TRANSFORMATIONS

Responses of the lower Feather and Yuba Rivers to the rapid influx of hydraulic-mining sediment varied owing to contrasts in water- and sediment-discharge regimes, geomorphology, and flood-control measures of the two rivers. Deep burial near the Yuba River fan apex graded downstream to broad, shallower deposits on the order of 5 m deep near Marysville (California Debris Commission [CDC], 1906). The lower Feather River deposits were constrained laterally by levees and—unlike in the Yuba River—two major post-1909 channel avulsions occurred. This section examines the historical record of channel changes. It begins with pre-mining conditions and then examines changes in

a geographic sequence progressing from the Yuba River fan area downstream to the mouth of the Feather River.

Pre-Mining Channel Conditions

Early descriptions of the Yuba and Feather Rivers prior to the onset of mining sediment are limited because of the fervor caused by the gold rush during pioneering settlement and the brief period from the late 1840s to 1861, before rapid sedimentation began to alter the rivers. Maps and descriptions by contemporaries allow some reconstructions of the nature of channel conditions at the time of settlement. For example, G.K. Gilbert interviewed an early resident on the Yuba River who remembered the presence of low terraces or banks ("bottom lands") up to the Barrier Dam but not on the Feather. He remembered bedrock outcrops in the Yuba channel bed above the Barrier Dam site (located ~3 km below Parks Bar):

Dr. C. E. Stone, 77, lived at Long Bar up the Yuba and 'practiced' in the region before the sixties. There were bottom lands along the Yuba, cultivated and dwelt on, up to above Daguire Point and nearly to site of dam. Half mile above dam first bedrock in river. A cascade at Narrows near Sucker Flat and considerable fall below. There were also high benches. Recalls no bottom land on the Feather. (Gilbert, 24 August 1905, Book no. 3499, p. 18)

Pre-mining channels in the Sacramento Valley were described as having high, steep banks with dark, fertile soils on low adjacent surfaces (Hall, 1880). Bottomlands were described by contemporaries as having dark soils, presumably representing floodplains in frequent lateral connectivity with the river.

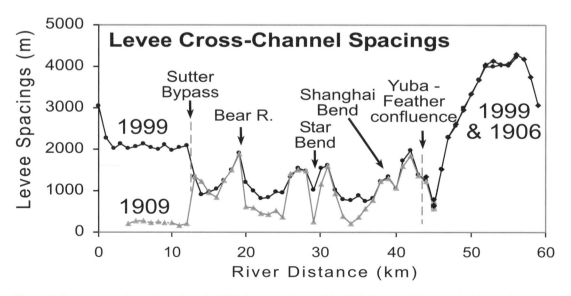

Figure 3. Levee cross-channel spacings in 1999 in comparison with 1909 (Feather River) and 1906 (Yuba River). Measured from 1999 DOQQs and California Debris Commission (CDC) 1906 and 1912 maps.

An early detailed (1:63,400) map produced from a survey by Von Schmidt (1859) is interpreted as representing the planimetry of pre-mining channels (Fig. 5), because hydraulic-mining sediment did not begin to be delivered to the valley in appreciable quantities until the 1861–1862 floods (Mendell, 1881). This and several other early maps (e.g., Gibbes, 1852) show the Yuba River joining the Feather River at an upstream, oblique angle, indicating that this unusual obliquity predated historical sedimentation influences. Likewise, downstream along the Feather River, the 1859 map shows the highly sinuous Elisa (aka Eliza) Bend near the present location of Shanghai Bend and an island upstream that persisted until the twentieth century. This large meander

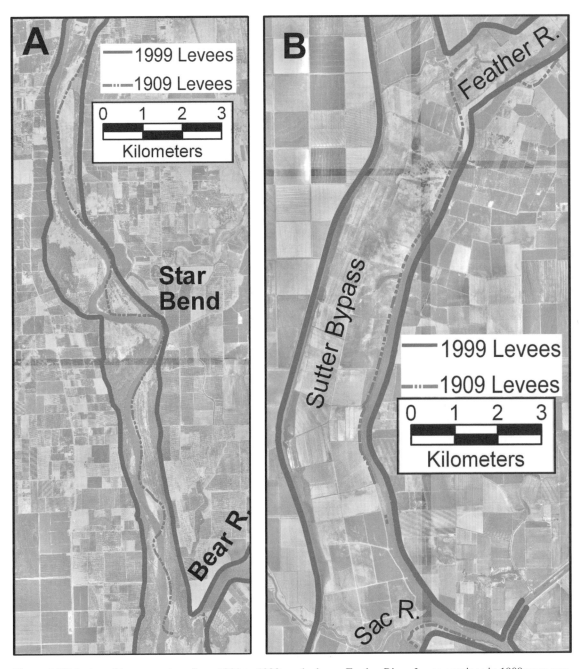

Figure 4. Widening of levee spacings from 1909 to 1999 on the lower Feather River. Levee spacings in 1909 were narrower as mapped from CDC (1912) maps. (A) On several reaches above Star Bend to Bear River, 1909 levees on the east bank constricted channels to little more than the width of the low-water channel. By 1999 these constrictions were gone. The 1909 west-bank levees were in essentially the same position as in 1999. (B) Below Bear River, levee positions on the east bank changed little from 1909 to 1999. A railroad embankment on the west bank constrained widths of moderate floods to <250 m. High floods flowed into Sutter Basin through crevasses. Sac R.—Sacramento River.

bend is shown prominently on other pre-mining maps (Gibbes, 1852; Wescoatt, 1861).

Mining Sediment and Channel Engineering

The rapid influx of hydraulic-mining sediment and human endeavors to control it caused extensive and prolonged channel changes to these Sacramento Valley rivers beginning in water year 1862. Owing to a lack of large floods in the late 1850s, little deposition of mining sediment in the Sacramento Valley had occurred previously:

The history of the impairment of these rivers is a gradual one. No one appears to have observed any considerable change in the bed or slopes of the streams until the great flood of 1862 had receded. Placer mining had been prosecuted by thousands of miners for thirteen years, and the gulches and water courses of the foot-hills had been receiving deposits of gravel and sand all these years, and particularly in the first five or six years succeeding the discovery of gold. In all these years there had been no great flood. The prolonged and excessively high water of 1862 brought down such masses of material that they could not escape observation. This flood was succeeded by others at intervals of six or seven years, and each of these had been observed to increase the evil. (Mendell, 1881, p. 6)

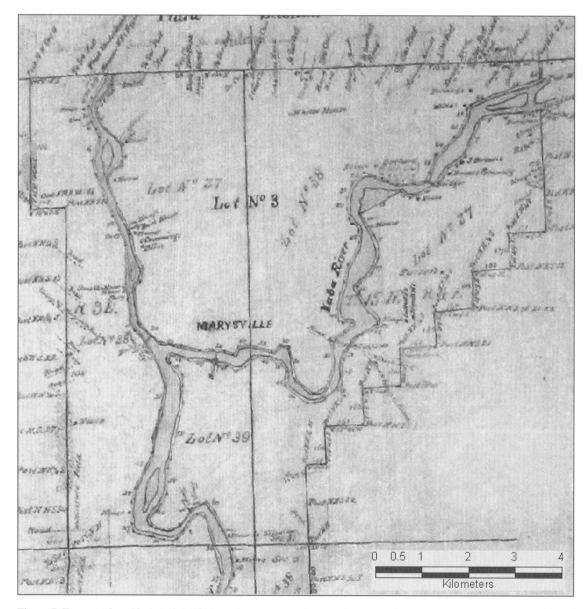

Figure 5. Excerpt of rectified north half of Von Schmidt (1859) map of lower Feather River (flowing north to south) and Yuba River (flowing from upper right). Scale added.

Some sedimentation may have occurred prior to 1862, although it is not well established:

> The effects of the mining debris first began to be seriously felt about 1860, and two years latter [*sic*] agriculture attained its maximum extent. The flood of 1862 left a sediment on Bear River about two feet thick, and created great alarm. (Chamberlain and Wells, 1879, Ch. 47)

Mining-sediment production rapidly decreased after an injunction on hydraulic mining in 1884. Channel aggradation and exacerbated flooding continued late into the nineteenth century, however, in spite of engineering works intended to control sedimentation and flooding (Hall, 1880; Mendell, 1881).

Channel avulsions on the lower Yuba River were rampant during the 1880s, but not on the lower Feather River. The early history of channel changes on the Feather has not been previously documented, but evidence presented in this paper indicates that nineteenth-century channel avulsions and lateral shifts were relatively minor there and increased in the early twentieth century after the main Yuba channel had begun to stabilize. Although the form and timing of change varied, the Yuba and Feather Rivers both changed substantially, as might be expected in fluvial systems so drastically altered. Levees, dikes, and other engineering works were constructed to stabilize the channel, and by the turn of the twentieth century, historical sediment deposits were largely bracketed by an extensive levee system (Figs. 2, 4). The

following sections present a series of historical observations from maps and aerial photographs at selected river reaches progressing downstream from the Yuba to the Feather Rivers.

Yuba River above the Yuba Gold Fields

Bed aggradation in the lower Yuba River ranged from 23 m in narrow canyons near the fan apex to ~5 m near Marysville (Fig. 6). The 1906 longitudinal profile shows Yuba channel-bed elevations near peak aggradation. Sediment storage is conspicuous behind Barrier No. 1 Dam, which was destroyed by the 1907 flood (Gilbert, 1917). The ~10 m break in slope at Barrier No. 1 is due to scour downstream in addition to deposition upstream of the dam. Elevations of the pre-mining channel were approximated by the CDC (1906) on the basis of numerous channel borings and other available information. Few boreholes reached the pre-mining surface, but they provided many minimum depths of hydraulic-mining sediment in an area where the deposit widens considerably. Depths to bedrock were interpolated by the CDC (1906) from four known depths at two boreholes and two exposures in the dredge fields. The longitudinal profile in Figure 6 shows increases in bed elevations but not floodplain elevations.

Degradation began high in the sediment fan of the Yuba River in the early twentieth century as documented by G.K. Gilbert. At Parks Bar, ~5 km downstream of the Narrows, where the Yuba River leaves the canyons at the east margin of the Sacramento Valley, Gilbert noted ongoing aggradation in 1905 and spreading of gravel onto the floodplain:

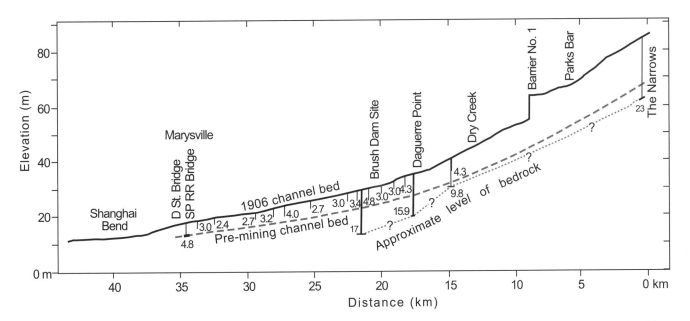

Figure 6. 1906 longitudinal profile of the lower Yuba River from The Narrows in the fan apex to Shanghai Bend below the Feather River confluence. Solid line is channel-bed elevation in 1906. Middle dashed and lower dotted lines are elevations of the pre-mining channel and bedrock, respectively. Numbers adjacent to thin vertical lines are depths of boreholes (meters) drilled in 1898–1899 that provide minimum depths of hydraulic-mining sediment. Two thick, vertical lines give depths to bedrock (17 and 15.9 m) on the basis of bedrock exposed by dredging. (Source: CDC [California Debris Commission], 1906.)

… at the Smartsville bridge the river bed is a waste of white gravel. The condition of the bank along my road of approach indicates aggradation of the river bed by the last flood. Oaks are being buried by gravel. (Gilbert, June 1905; Book no. 3497, p. 36)

At Parks Bar Bridge I found a bench or two. Found also the berm. … This bar is only two feet [0.6 m] above a gravel bar. … The filling of the channel here has made estuaries of side channels, and has caused spurs to be truncated. … (Gilbert, 7 August 1905; Book no. 3499, p. 13)

In 1907, and again in 1913, Gilbert revisited Parks Bar and noted no further aggradation of the floodplain by large 1907 or 1909 floods, but floodplain degradation had not begun:

At the Parks Bar Bridge I once photographed some small oaks half buried by gravel. Comparing the photos today I find practically no change. (Gilbert, 11 June 1907; Book no. 3504, p. 35)

An old photo near Parks bar bridge shows trees partly [buried] by gravel. This gravel is a few inches lower now, but the main bar outside looks like the foto [*sic*], and I can not say that degradation has begun. It is partly certain however that aggradation is checked. … (Gilbert, 4 August 1913; Book no. 3508, p. 29–30)

He recognized, however, that 3 m of channel degradation had occurred some time between 1905 and 1913:

On Bakers contour, 1905, the highest and lowest contours of the cross section are 10′ [3 m] apart, and the difference between low water level and the high gravel bar above the bridge must have been as small as 10′, more probably 9′ [2.7 m]. In 1913, we find it 19′ [5.8 m]. This, taken in connection with the foto record—where the lowering close to the shore is a few inches—indicates that the summer channel has been deepened about 10′ [3 m]. … (Gilbert, 6 August 1913; Book no. 3508, p. 34)

The pattern of channel incision often inferred from Gilbert's (1917) classic sediment-wave model differs from these observations. Channel incision did not progress from the Narrows downstream to Marysville between 1900 and 1905 but appears to have skipped over Parks Bar between 1900 and 1905. When incision began some time between 1905 and 1913 it was confined to the low-flow channel, leaving large amounts of floodplain gravels in storage. This topic will be revisited in the discussion of the Yuba-Feather confluence, where dredging suggests that channel degradation at Marysville may have resulted from local changes.

Approximately 5 km below Parks Bar, the Yuba River flows into a 12-km stretch dominated by extensive dredge spoils of the Yuba Gold Fields. The spoils are piled at the angle of repose in 7- to 20-m-high gravel ridges along both sides of the channel

as measured on 0.5-m contour lines derived from 1999 LiDAR data (Stonestreet and Lee, 2000; Towill, Inc., 2006). Dredging exploited modern channel alluvium, hydraulic-mining sediment, and Quaternary alluvium, so the spoils are likely to be of mixed composition that vary in space (Hunerlach et al., 2004). A GIS comparison between 1999 and 2006 DOQQs indicates that a 250 m section of the south ridge along the channel margin was eroded laterally up to 12 m during that period. The ridge in this area is ~10 m high, so ~30,000 m³ of dredge tailings may have been delivered directly to the channel from this short reach between 1999 and 2006.

Yuba River between the Yuba Gold Fields and Marysville

The floodplains above Marysville were the most extensively alluviated river reaches in the foothills or valley during the late nineteenth century. In the lower 12 km above the mouth of the Yuba River, gradients decrease, Holocene alluvium covers Quaternary outwash terraces, and floodplains widen. The 1859 map shows the pre-mining Yuba as a somewhat more sinuous, single-thread channel, although one large island is shown at the upper margin of the map (Fig. 5). A second master channel to the southeast was present in 1861 (Fig. 7), and probably earlier, even though it does not appear on the 1859 map.

Mining sediment ultimately spread out across the lower Yuba floodplain, causing multiple avulsions in the late nineteenth century. The first detailed survey of the Yuba floodplain was performed in 1879 by the Department of the State Engineer. The U.S. Army Corps of Engineers included this map in an annual report to Congress (Mendell, 1880). A revised version of the map, included in a later report to Congress (Mendell, 1882), shows undated paleochannels that match the 1859 channels (Von Schmidt, 1859) (Fig. 8). The 1859 channel passes under the south levee across from Marysville, which failed in 1997 and caused flooding in the

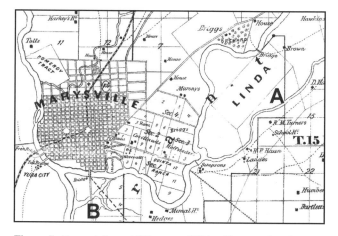

Figure 7. Excerpt from 1861 map of Yuba County, showing two features not shown on the 1859 map: (A) Channel southeast of the main channel around the area marked "Linda." (B) Western chute, cutting off confluence. These conditions should represent pre-mining channels. (Source: Wescoatt, 1861.)

town of Linda. Another channel scar, shown on the 1882 map almost 1 km north of the south levee, is labeled "pre-1876." This channel is interpreted as the same pre-mining channel shown on the Wescoatt (1861) map (Fig. 7) and indicates that the pre-mining Yuba River was a multithread channel system. The 1882 map also shows a channel system that hugs the south levee and is labeled "low-water channel in 1876." By the time of the 1879 Hall survey the low-water channel had apparently shifted 2 to 3 km to the northwest to its 1880 position. The 1880 report describes how the deposit at that time covered the lower banks:

The cross-section on the Yuba map shows the elevation of this mass of detritus to be here above the general level of the country. This general level is the second bench of the bank, the first being covered. The original bed of the stream is said to have been 10 or 12 feet below the lower bench. (Mendell, 1880, p. 3)

Several reliable observations or maps were made of this area during the first decade of the twentieth century, when the Yuba River was an unstable system of shifting sand and gravel channels:

For the lower 10 miles [16 km] of its course in the foothills the river is greatly clogged with debris from hydraulic-mining camps (estimated at many million cubic yards), and is between levees which have been raised from year to year to meet the overflow caused by the filling up of the area between them. ... The channels are irregular and change from winter to winter and sometimes during the summer. ... The changes in the bottom and in the position of the channel are so great that the gagings at the flood stages of the river would be unsatisfactory, and if undertaken from boats would be highly dangerous, if not impossible. (Manson, *in* Olmsted, 1901, p. 39–40)

Most of the main channel positions in Figure 8 are represented on a set of detailed topographic map sheets surveyed in 1906. They can also be seen on modern aerial photographs. This is particularly true of the 4-km-wide floodplain extending 5 km above the right-angle bend directly northeast of Marysville (Fig. 9). Shortly after Manson's description of the lower Yuba in 1901, channels evidently began to stabilize. The 2006 channel digitized from the low-water position on DOQQs (U.S. Department of Agriculture, 2006) corresponds closely in position with the 1906 low-water channel. The position of the upper 4 km of this reach corresponds with the approximate position of the

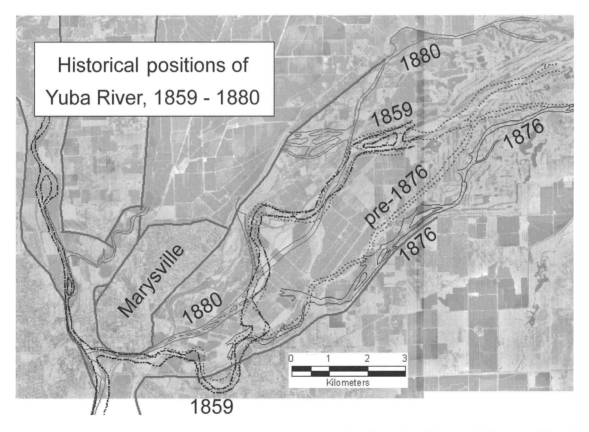

Figure 8. Early positions of lower Yuba River channels based on Mendell (1882) and Von Schmidt (1859) maps (cf. Fig. 5). North branch of pre-1876 paleochannels match 1859 channels. South branch of pre-1876 channel matches channel shown by Wescoatt (1861) and is interpreted as a branch of the 1859 channel. Channel along south levee was labeled "low-water channel in 1876" (Mendell, 1882). By 1880, much of the low-water Yuba channel had shifted 2 to 3 km northwest. (Source: Mendell, 1882, based on an 1879 survey by Hall, 1880.)

1859 channel. The main Yuba channel evidently had returned to its approximate pre-mining position in the area of Figure 9 by 1906, where it has remained to the present. Between 1861 and 1906, however, during the period of rapid aggradation, the channel occupied several positions away from this location, as shown in Figure 8. The 1880 channel position corresponded with only 1 km of the present channel at this location. Channel scars on the 1906 map represent pre-1906 channel positions and high-water channels some of which remain active during large floods. The braiding index of high-water channels on the 1906 Yuba floodplain in this area was between 8 and 19 channels, the maximum value for the Yuba and Feather Rivers. Recently, and at a local scale, comparison of 1999 and 2006 DOQQs reveals substantial channel lateral migration with gravel-bar erosion and deposition within the confines of the main channel.

On the basis of fieldwork in the summer of 2007, a generalized stratigraphy of the Yuba River south bank exposed at the U.S. Geological Survey stream gauge near Marysville was created, using a total station to measure relative elevations (Fig. 10). The elevation of the south terrace is the same beyond and within a short 2-m-high levee, indicating that the levee was constructed after most terrace deposition had occurred. This terrace elevation extends south beyond the plot for ~2.5 km and is now covered by orchards. A matching terrace on the north side extends 1.5 km to the levee. The pre-mining soil is a reddish alluvial silt that supported trees that were buried by historical sediment.

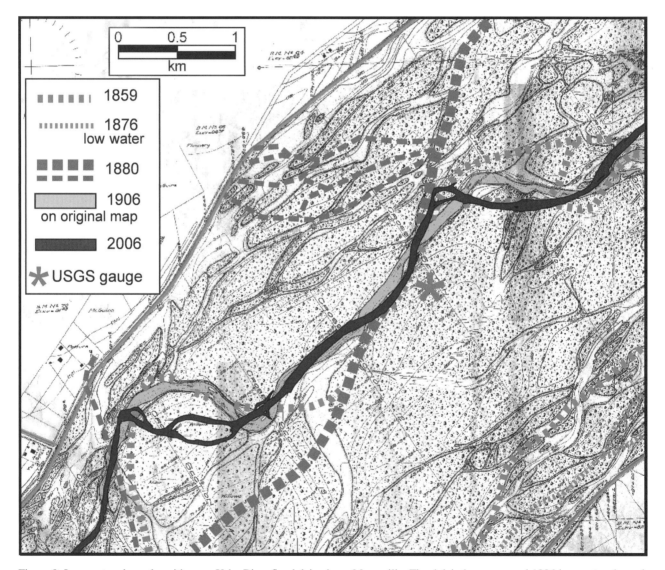

Figure 9. Low-water channel positions on Yuba River floodplain above Marysville. Floodplain base map and 1906 low-water channel are from CDC (1906, sheet 2). Northwest branch of 1859 channel is from Von Schmidt (1859). Southeast branch of 1859 channel, 1876 channel (in southeast corner), and 1880 channel are from Mendell (1882). Other channels on base map are 1906 high-water channels. Bordering lines along northwest and southeast floodplain margins are levees 4.1 km apart. U.S. Geological Survey stream gauge is site of stratigraphic section. Much of the modern channel has returned to its pre-mining (1859) position.

An abrupt wavy contact between the soil and the overlying historical alluvial sands and gravels suggests that scour occurred prior to deposition. The lowest unit of historical sediment is a well-sorted sand that appears to be associated with a scour hole around the roots of a stump (unit C). The overlying unit is a coarse, fining upward sequence that grades from gravel to fine sand with abundant white quartz pebbles (unit B). The upper bank is composed of quartzose sand with a distinctive white appearance and light-tan silts. A stump rooted in this exposure has two root crowns. The lower root crown corresponds with the level of the pre-mining soil, and the upper crown was rooted in

unit B. These relationships indicate that the tree survived the initial first meter of sedimentation and was growing for some time on a layer of mining sediment.

The mineralogic composition of the historical sediment is consistent with the distinctive lithology of mining sediment found in tailings fans near the mines (James, 1991). The interpretation that the upper strata are composed of mining sediment is corroborated by total mercury concentrations of the fine fraction (<63 μm). Concentrations in units A, B, and C of 0.17, 0.42, and 0.61 ppm, respectively, are high in comparison with a concentration of only 0.05 ppm in underlying unit D, which is

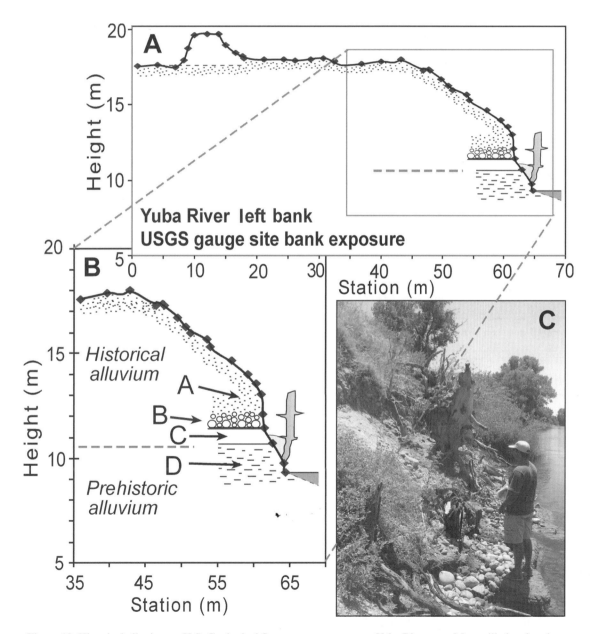

Figure 10. Historical alluvium at U.S. Geological Survey stream gauge on Yuba River near Marysville is >6 m deep. Stumps near base of section are rooted in prehistoric sediment. Center stump has two root crowns, indicating that tree survived initial burial.

typical of crustal abundance concentrations. Although dilution of mining sediment undoubtedly occurred as it was transported to the valley, these deposits are interpreted as dominantly mining sediment. Based on pebble lithologies, mining sediment dilution between the mountain mines and the Sacramento Valley in the Bear River was estimated at 22% (James, 1991).

The thickness of historical sediment from the lower contact to the high terrace surface ultimately reached ~7 m deep, but this may be close to the maximum thickness of mining sediment over the pre-mining floodplain level at this longitudinal position. The elevation of the pre-mining soil elsewhere on the pre-mining cross-valley profile is unknown. If the deposit thickness at this site was representative of the mean depth of mining sediment across the 4-km-wide Yuba floodplain, then the volume of the deposit in this vicinity would be ~28,000,000 m^3 per kilometer of valley length. At this depth a ~5-km-long reach of the Yuba floodplain in this vicinity would account for ~140 million m^3, or 55% of the 253 million m^3 of mining sediment estimated to have been stored in the lower Yuba (Gilbert, 1917). Realistically, the mean thickness of historical sediment at this position on the Yuba floodplain is likely to be <7 m.

Yuba and Feather Rivers near Marysville and Confluence

The pre-mining Yuba channel in the lower 8.9 km above Marysville was more sinuous (1.45) than the 2006 channel (1.22), owing to a broad meander bend southeast of Marysville (Figs. 5, 7, 8). Most of the 253 million m^3 of sedimentation in the Yuba River had occurred by the 1870s and was mapped in 1879 (Hall, 1880; Mendell, 1881, 1882). By 1865, distributary channels had formed, presumably in response to initial sedimentation, and as late as 1887 they carried floodwater and sediment from the south bend of the Yuba River to Elisa Bend on the Feather River near the present site of Shanghai Bend (Fig. 11). The broad Yuba meander was cut off at some time between 1861, when no cut-off channel is shown on historic maps, and 1880, when Mendell (1880) shows a new channel to the north. Mendell (1882) shows the southern channel as abandoned (Fig. 8). Although a map in 1873 (Hoffmann and Craven, 1873) shows no cutoff of the bend, a railroad survey map in 1865 (Fig. 11) shows both channels with an island between, suggesting that the cutoff had been initiated and was at least a high-water chute at that time. By 1880 the channel had avulsed to the northern cutoff near its present location along the north levee southeast of Marysville, and the southern meander bend was abandoned. Ultimately, a levee was built over the southern meander near where the levee failed in 1997 (Fig. 8).

At the turn of the twentieth century, floodplain sedimentation was continuing downstream in the lower Yuba near Marysville:

The Yuba at Marysville has a broad channel with many sloughs and sand bars. The higher sands are grown with willows and cotton woods, and among these are fruit trees, illustrating the encroachment of the river sands. (G.K. Gilbert, June 1905; Book no. 3497, p. 38)

Bed degradation had begun at the Marysville D-Street gauge by 1905 (Gilbert, 1917), although overbank sedimentation probably continued after 1905.

Channels were dredged at several locations near the Feather-Yuba confluence as a means of flood control at the turn of the twentieth century. A cutoff of the lower Yuba River mouth was dredged by 1905, which diverted the confluence to the south. Gilbert described this cutoff as "new" in 1905 and reported that it had created a fan that dammed the Feather River:

The Yuba has a new mouth, having been diverted by an artificial cutoff. At the mouth it is building a delta across the Feather, crowding the … channel close against the opposite bank. This has ponded the Feather above so that slack water extends for ½ mile. (Gilbert, 24 August 1905, Book no. 3499, p. 17)

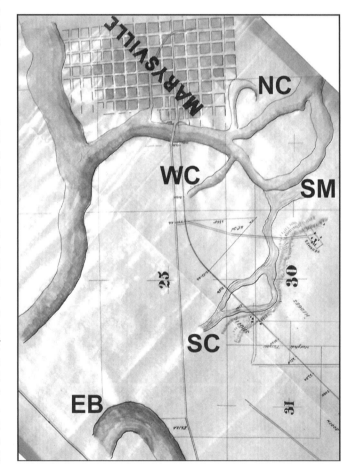

Figure 11. Excerpt from 1865 map of Yuba-Feather confluence, showing three cutoffs from the lower Yuba southern meander bend in early stages of channel aggradation. The *northern cutoff* (NC) became an avulsion, abandoning the *southern meander* (SM) over which the Linda levee was later built (Fig. 8). The *southern cutoff* (SC) apparently connected the Yuba River SM to the Feather River above *Elisa Bend* (EB), as shown on the Doyle (1887) map. The *western chute* (WC) may be the same high-water channel shown in 1861 (Fig. 7), which was later dredged. (Source: Pixley et al., 1865.)

The dam persisted and the impoundment behind it grew in length through at least 1913:

The pool in Feather above Yuba is said to be 4–5 miles long. It has recently received a fine deposit—partly because of clearing of flood-plain of brush. The Yuba channel now brings gravel to the mouth—so coarse as to include pebbles 1–2″ [2–5 cm] diameter. (Gilbert, 18 October 1913; Book no. 3508, p. 37)

The old confluence channel had become a high-water channel by 1909 (CDC, 1912), and by 1937 the abandoned channel scar was not easily distinguished on aerial photographs.

Two other substantial channel cutoffs were dredged near the Yuba confluence around the turn of the century and were mapped by the 1909 CDC survey. One ditch diverted flood flows from the Yuba River above the D Street Bridge opposite Marysville, ~3.5 km to the Feather River at Elisa Bend (CDC, 1912; Ellis, 1939). This cutoff began in a broad 160-m-wide high-water channel below the south end of the Southern Pacific Railroad bridge that passed under the D Street Bridge and fed into the Feather River (Fig. 12). The upper approach to the ditch apparently exploited the chute that existed between 1861 and 1865 (Figs. 7, 11). For 1909 a single ditch is shown connected to the high-water channel, beginning ~200 m below the D Street Bridge as a narrow, 30-m-wide channel, flowing southwest for 250 m and then directly south for 2.5 km to Elisa Bend. This ditch is not present on the CDC 1906 map. Ellis (1939) describes this ditch as a pair of parallel ditches that were dredged in two passes, one up toward Marysville, and a return trip to Elisa Bend. Vestiges of two ditches can be seen filled with sand ~1 km above Elisa Bend on aerial imagery (U.S. Department of Agriculture, 2006).

Another ditch was dredged from the mouth of the Yuba River 250 m above the Feather River confluence. This ditch was ~65 m wide with spoils on both banks. It flowed ~1.5 km to the southeast and joined the north-south ditch obliquely 1.3 km above Elisa Bend (CDC, 1912). None of this ditch remains, although the spoil piles can be seen in field patterns along the lower 800 m of its course. Both of the two ditches flowing into Elisa Bend are labeled "State Cutoff" on the 1909 map (CDC, 1912) and appear prominently on a later map (Crook, 1914). They are discussed further in the next section on Shanghai Bend.

A stratigraphic section was measured at a Yuba River north bank exposure near 2nd Avenue in Marysville (Fig. 13). The upper layers of sediment are interpreted as mining sediment as evidenced by stratification, coarse textures, quartz-rich mineralogies, and a relatively high total mercury concentration of 0.38 ppm in the fine fraction. The massive dark-brown silts at the base of the exposure are interpreted as pre-mining alluvium corroborated by a total Hg concentration of 0.02 ppm. The contact between historical sediment and the underlying pre-mining surface is interpreted at an abrupt wavy contact nearly 6 m in depth. This represents almost 6 m of floodplain sedimentation in

the lower Yuba near Marysville relative to previous estimates of 5 m of bed aggradation in this area (CDC, 1906).

Feather River Changes near Shanghai Bend

Elisa Bend, the precursor to Shanghai Bend, is shown on many early maps before and after the delivery of mining sediment began. The 1859 and 1861 maps show the original Elisa Bend, which is presumably a pre-mining feature of the river. On early maps (Von Schmidt, 1859; Wescoatt, 1861; Pennington, 1873; Hoffmann and Craven, 1873; Hall, ca. 1880a; Doyle, 1887) the upper approach to the bend was farther to the west. By 1895, however, the upper channel had been forced to the east by a new levee and flowed more directly south into the upper bend and then veered sharply eastward into Elisa Bend (Manson and Grunsky, 1895a). The eastward shift of the upper channel isolated an area of more than 3.5 km² of historical channel deposits from the Feather River to the west of the new levee. Along the modern west bank this surface is 3 m thick above the low-water line, and the bank is another 4 m above the thalweg, which is near the bank. A sample from a 1.2 m silt cap exposed in the bank had a total mercury concentration of 0.41 ppm, whereas the fine fraction isolated from the underlying sands had a concentration of 0.16 ppm Hg. Using 3 m as a minimum mean thickness of the deposit, the volume of mining sediment stored behind the levee in this reach is at least 10 million cubic meters.

After the turn of the twentieth century, channelization in the Shanghai Bend area was extensive. Surveys in 1906 and 1909 (CDC, 1906, 1912) show ditches above and below Elisa Bend, and later maps (Crook, 1914; Thomas, 1928) show two large ditches converging on Elisa Bend, as described earlier (Fig. 12). Another ditch was cut southward from above Elisa Bend and ran 4.8 km south along the west levee to where it rejoined the main channel. This straight channel was labeled "Dredged Canal" on the 1906 CDC map (Fig. 14A). By 1909, following major floods in 1907 and 1909, Elisa Bend had shifted southward and the upper entry to the ditch had been deflected eastward (Figs. 14A, 14B) and subsequently evolved into Shanghai Bend. Ultimately, the entire Feather River channel avulsed from Elisa Bend 1 km west into the ditch. The initial stages of the avulsion can be seen in 1909, although a secondary channel remained at Elisa Bend until at least 1999. By 1952, aerial photographs collected during low flows indicate that the eastern channel was heavily vegetated.

Topographic surfaces in 1999, derived from LiDAR bare-earth 3 m postings and bathymetric data from sonar (Stonestreet and Lee, 2000), reveal the modern configuration of Shanghai Bend (Fig. 14C). By 1999, Shanghai Bend had developed into a high-amplitude meander wave rotated 90° eastward from the orientation of Elisa Bend. Below Shanghai Bend, a shoal or knickpoint that drops 3 m and forms a barrier to river navigation developed across a cohesive soil unit. This break in the longitudinal profile may represent a headward limit to much of the vertical readjustment of the Feather River to pre-mining base levels. At present, the knickpoint is migrating upstream across

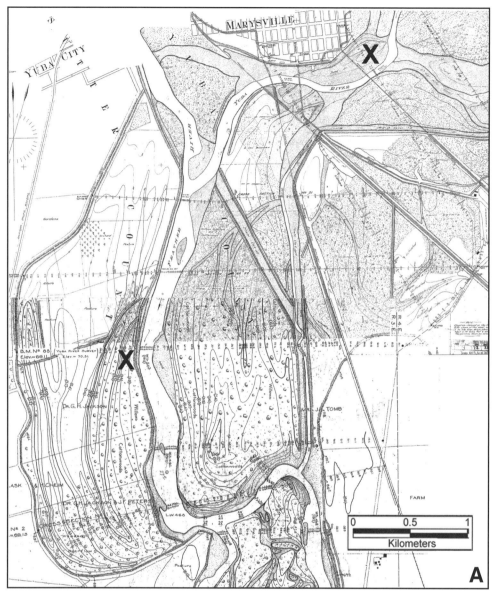

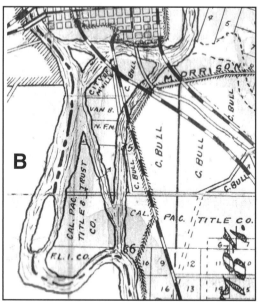

Figure 12. Channelization around Yuba-Feather confluence. Several ditches were dredged south of Marysville shortly before 1909. Two ditches connected with the Feather River at Elisa Bend, and another turned the confluence south. (A) Stratigraphic sections collected at Xs are shown in Figures 13 and 15A. (Source: CDC, 1912.) (B) Ditches are prominent (cartographically exaggerated) on 1914 map. (Source: Crook, 1914.)

the high paleosol surface toward the old channel position to the east. When it reaches the deeper former channel position, bed incision may accelerate, allowing the lower base level to rapidly propagate upstream.

A stratigraphic section on the west bank of the Feather River above Shanghai Bend indicates ~5.5 m of historical sediment accumulation in this area (Fig. 15A). The historical contact here is interpreted as the abrupt contact and color break between units C and D, with several tree stumps rooted in the lower layer. Total mercury concentrations in sediment samples at this site support this interpretation. The low concentration (0.05 ppm) in unit D is consistent with background levels of mercury in the pre-mining surface, whereas higher concentrations of 0.18, 0.47, and 0.35 are typical of mining sediment that has undergone some mixing with surrounding sediments. One of several exhumed stumps rooted in the soil at the base of the section was ^{14}C dated at ~1885 (65 ± 35 yr BP), clearly indicating a historic age (National Science Foundation [NSF] Arizona accelerator mass spectrometry [AMS] facility). All vertical sections were measured during low water, so the pre-mining soil surface at this site is low relative to the present water line. This is consistent with an interpretation that the bed of the Feather River near the Yuba confluence has not yet returned to pre-mining levels and continues to degrade (U.S. Army Corps of Engineers [USACE] and State of California Reclamation Board, 1998; Eckbo, Dean and Williams, 2006, Ch. 5).

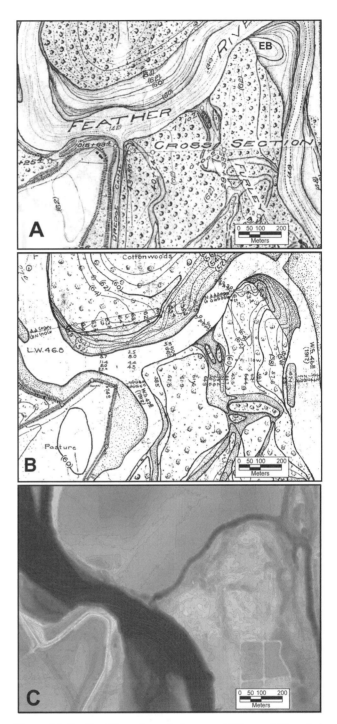

Figure 14. Feather River channel changes at Elisa and Shanghai Bends. (A) In 1906 the Feather River in this area was beginning to undergo changes in planform. Levees above the bend had shifted the channel eastward and altered the flow direction above the bend. The straight "Dredge Canal" to the south along the west levee initiated flows that bypassed Elisa Bend (EB) and ultimately resulted in an avulsion. (Source: CDC, 1912.) (B) By 1909, much of the flow was passing south through the dredged channel, which had begun a meander to the east. Elisa Bend was shifting south in a lower-amplitude wave. (C) The 1999 topography of upper Shanghai Bend and the channel scar that was Elisa Bend. Derived from 1999 LiDAR and sonar data.

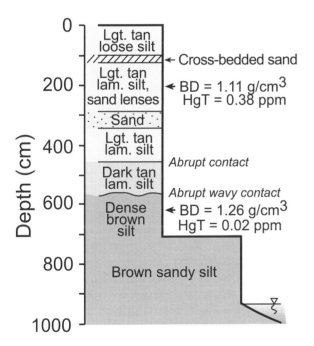

Figure 13. Stratigraphic section on north bank of lower Yuba River at Marysville. Dark, massive silts at base represent pre-mining alluvium. Historical sediment is highly stratified and 5.8 m thick down to an abrupt way contact. BD—bulk density; HgT—total elemental mercury concentration in sediment samples.

Low pre-mining surfaces and thick deposits of historical sediment extend along the right bank for a considerable distance above Shanghai Bend but not below the bend. Below the Shanghai Bend shoals a prominent soil can be seen on the west bank several meters above the low-water line. A stratigraphic section measured on the west bank below Shanghai Bend features a well-developed soil with a distinct A horizon and a reddish argillic B horizon (Fig. 15B). Total mercury concentrations corroborate the stratigraphic interpretations based on pedogenesis. Units A and B above the soil have relatively high total mercury concentrations of 0.10 and 0.14 ppm, respectively, whereas units C and D have low background levels of mercury of 0.04 ppm each. This soil is

continuous for hundreds of meters at mid-bank where dead trees are rooted in the A horizon. The higher level of the pre-mining soil below the shoals is due to deeper incision below the shoals and to the westward shift of the channel into the dredged channel at a higher position in the pre-mining landscape. The pre-mining soil surface increases downstream in height above the low-water surface. By Boyd Pump House Boat Ramp, a few km below Shanghai shoals, historical sediment is only ~1 m thick over a high pre-mining alluvial bank.

Feather River Changes near Star Bend

The earliest available historic maps indicate that Star Bend was largely stable throughout the period of mining and to the present. A large pre-mining island was mapped above Star Bend (Von Schmidt, 1859) that evolved into a broad meander bend through abandonment of the western channel. The west branch of the bifurcated channel was gone by 1909 (CDC, 1912). The east branch has not moved much and forms a large-amplitude meander above Star Bend that has remained horizontally stable (U.S. Department of Agriculture, 2006). The lower meander of Star Bend was largely stable from 1859 to the present, although the wavelength of the lower southern limb increased as the channel shifted ~500 m to the southeast by 1909 (CDC, 1912), leaving O'Connor Lake on the inside of the bend where the pre-mining channel had been.

Feather River Changes near Bear River Confluence

Large alternating point bars were present between Star Bend and the Bear River confluence in 1909 (CDC, 1912), in 1949 on an orthophotograph (U.S. Bureau of Reclamation [USBR], 1949), and on 6 May 1975 aerial photographs. The longitudinal bars were severely scoured by 3 November 1986 after a record flood, and the sinuosity of this reach has remained substantially less than it was in 1909. Farther downstream on the Feather River, two large islands were mapped in 1859, one above the present Bear River confluence, and another at the confluence. The upper island is shown on later maps (Doyle, 1887; Crook, 1914) but is shown on some maps as a large bar with a dominant eastern channel and a western channel remnant that is no longer connected on the upstream end (Hoffmann and Craven, 1873; Hall, ca. 1880a). The island is not shown on two 1895 maps (Manson and Grunsky, 1895a, 1895b), so its presence later (Crook, 1914) may be an artifact of cartographic replication of an older map, or it may indicate that the western channel was only a high-water channel. The lower island at the Bear River confluence persisted from 1859 through 1895 (Von Schmidt, 1859; Pennington, 1873; Hall, ca. 1880a; Doyle, 1887; Manson and Grunsky, 1895a, 1895b). By 1909 (CDC, 1912), however, this lower island had been converted to a point bar, with the eastern channel forming a high-amplitude meander bend, and the western channel reduced to a small lake (Rideout Lake) sealed off from the Feather River at the north and south ends. Both islands are missing on later

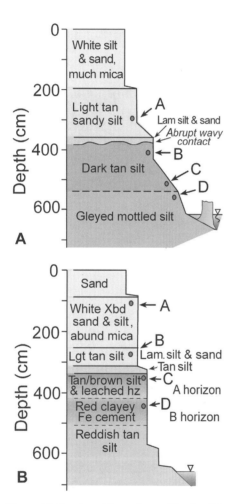

Figure 15. Stratigraphic sections of Feather River right-bank exposures. (A) Above Shanghai Bend, historical sediment is ~5.5 m thick. Total mercury concentrations in sediment samples A through D were 0.18, 0.47, 0.35, and 0.05 ppm, respectively. Stump rooted in unit D has a ^{14}C date of ~1885 (65 ± 35 yr BP). (B) Below Shanghai Bend a distinct soil marks a pre-mining surface ~3.3 m deep. Total mercury concentrations in units A and B were 0.10 and 0.14 ppm, respectively, signifying mining sediment, versus background values of 0.04 ppm in units C and D.

aerial photographs (USBR, 1949; California Transportation Agency, 1952), and the sinuosity of this area of the Feather River is now greatly reduced (U.S. Department of Agriculture, 2006).

Sedimentation, channelization, and channel shifting were pervasive at the Feather-Bear confluence during the mining period. The Feather River channel was obscured in this area in the late 1870s (Hall, 1880). Berry, a local resident, described ditches and levees in the area that diverted flows and described widespread sedimentation and channel filling in the area coming from both the Bear and Feather Rivers:

… the whole country outside of that levee is covered with deposit, and the channel filled in below; and what was formerly the mouth and lowland is all covered over, more or less … [with debris] from the Bear River and from the Feather [can't tell which]. Berry; testimony in 1876. (*Keyes v. Little York Gold Washing Co. et al.*, 1879)

The bed of the Feather River in this vicinity is now dominated by extensive sand sheets that are presumably dominated by reworked historical sediment (Fig. 16). During low water in June 2007, broad areas on the sand sheets were <12 cm deep.

Feather River Changes below Nicolaus

About 3 km downstream of the small town of Nicolaus, just before the Feather River enters Sutter Bypass, a large meander loop in the pre-mining channel had deflected flows to the north (Fig. 17). This bend, henceforth referred to as *Nelson Bend,* preceded the mining period and is shown on several early maps (Mileson and Adams, 1851; Von Schmidt, 1859; Pennington, 1873). The pre-mining Feather River was much more sinuous through this reach than at present. During the mining period, levees were constructed along the inside of the bend that forced flood flows through the circuitous meander (Pennington, 1873; Hall, ca. 1880a; Manson and Grunsky, 1895a). By 1909, the levee along the inner bend had been removed and a shallow "Overflow Channel" is mapped across the base of the bend (Fig. 17A). The

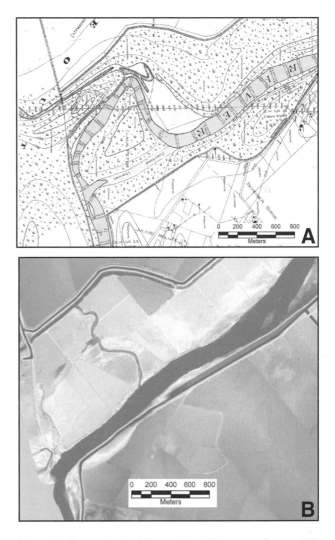

Figure 17. Lower Feather River at Sutter Bypass confluence. (A) 1909 CDC map: incipient cutoff of Nelson Bend. (B) Shaded-relief map with oxbow lake largely filled in 1999. Derived from LiDAR, a digital elevation model (DEM), and sonar channel bathymetry (Stonestreet and Lee, 2000; Towill, Inc., 2006).

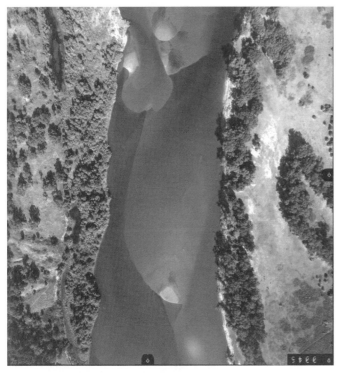

Figure 16. Sand sheets in bed of Feather River below the Feather-Bear confluence are composed largely of legacy sediment from the hydraulic-mining era. (Source: California Department of Water Resources, October 1998.)

bend is shown in the process of being cut off on a flood-control map (California Department of Public Works, 1925) where the bend is labeled "Nelson Bend" and the straight channel is labeled "Cutoff." It is not known if dredging was involved. By June 1952 the Feather River had completely shifted into the cutoff where it now flows, and Nelson Bend was largely filled with alluvium.

Channel aggradation by hydraulic mining sediment extended through the lower Feather River to the Sacramento River. By 1879 the bed of the Feather River near the Sacramento River confluence had risen between 0.9 and 1.2 m (3–4 ft) above its presettlement level (Hall, 1880). At this time, channel narrowing was noted in the Sacramento River between the mouth of the Feather River and the City of Sacramento, where channel deposits had been colonized by willows, and high pre-mining banks with riparian forest were set back from the contemporary channel margin (Mendell, 1882). Historic maps indicate that channel narrowing also occurred within the lower Feather River below Nelson Bend owing to development of alternating bars and a sinuous thalweg. Alternating longitudinal bars that cover approximately half a channel width were mapped by a topographic survey of the lower Sacramento River, which included the lower Feather River near the confluence (Hall, ca. 1880b). Alternating bars were also mapped in these reaches of the Feather River in 1909 (CDC, 1912) at a wavelength of ~12 low-flow channel widths. Alternating bars appear on a 1966 aerial photograph at a shorter wavelength of eight low-flow channel widths or four bankfull channel widths (Fig. 18). These post-mining bars indicate that channel narrowing was due to deposition of bed material in point bars. No bars are visible on aerial photographs flown 20 June 1958, 28 May 1964, 6 May 1975, and 10 November 1986 after a record flood, but they are present on 4 August 1966 aerial photographs (Fig. 18B). The disappearance and reappearance of bars indicate scouring and redeposition, and the transport of large volumes of sediment.

Below the zone of alternating bars, several crevasses were shown in the west bank railroad embankment in 1909 (Fig. 19). Crevasse splays of hydraulic mining sediment are likely to have been deposited through these crevasses during the late nineteenth century. Most of this railroad embankment had been removed by the time the Sutter Bypass was completed, although some rock and boulders remain. Levee spacings are now ~2 km wide in the lower Feather River along Sutter Bypass (Fig. 3).

DISCUSSION AND CONCLUSIONS

This paper uses historical and stratigraphic data to constrain the timing and location of major channel changes. Modern geospatial processing methods can be applied to historical maps and have ushered in a new era of historical cartometrics. Yet, simple examination of unrectified historical maps may provide crucial information about the dynamics of river-channel change over historical time periods. Historical analyses illustrate a variety of past and ongoing channel morphological changes that are relevant to management of these rivers. Channels in the Yuba and Feather Rivers appear to have been more similar in character in the

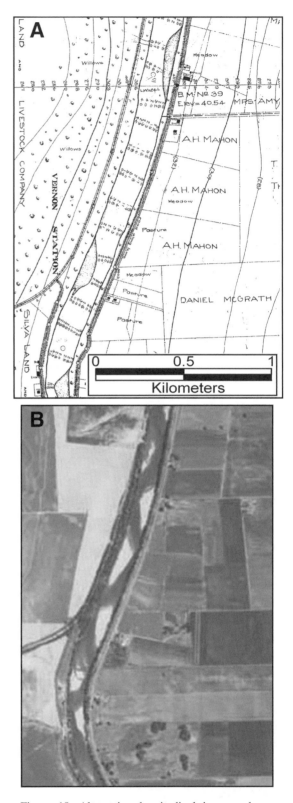

Figure 18. Alternating longitudinal bars on lower Feather River from the beginning of Sutter Bypass to the Sacramento confluence. (A) Long-wavelength bars on 1909 map (CDC, 1912). (B) Short-wavelength bars on 4 August 1966; aerial photograph (Earth Resources Observation System [EROS], 1966).

pre-mining period than after sedimentation commenced. Both channels were somewhat sinuous with occasional large, stable islands. The timing and style of channel changes in response to hydraulic mining differed greatly between the two rivers. The Yuba River underwent major morphologic changes early in the mining period, including deep and broad channel and flood-plain deposition that resulted in cutoffs of meander bends, channel avulsions, and development of distributary channels. Signs of morphologic change in the Yuba River had begun to appear by the mid-1860s and were in advanced stages by the time of topographic surveys in 1879 (Hall, 1880; Mendell, 1880, 1882). Channels continued to change through the turn of the twentieth century, when the Yuba floodplain was shown on large-scale (1:9,600) maps supporting a broad multithread high-water channel system. After 1906, planimetric changes on the Yuba River appear to have decreased in magnitude. Substantial amounts of local erosion and sedimentation can be documented by planimetric analysis of channel changes in recent years—e.g., lateral channel migration in the Yuba Gold Fields between 1999 and 2006—but large-scale channel avulsions were less common in the twentieth century, presumably owing to hardening of the flood-conveyance system with wing dams and riprap.

Morphologic changes in the Feather River were associated more with a single large channel shifting or avulsing, which occurred later than in the Yuba River. Some of the changes can be attributed to large-scale channelization and levee projects. Several large, pre-mining meander bends and islands on the Feather River persisted until the twentieth century. For example, Elisa Bend and Nelson Bend remained through 1909 (CDC, 1912), and Star Bend has remained largely unchanged to the present. In addition, large islands above Elisa and Star Bends persisted with minor changes until 1909. By 1909, however, the Feather River began showing signs of major morphologic change. Two large islands near the Bear River confluence were gone by 1909, probably because of hydraulic-mining sediment delivered by Bear River. Channel dredging is clearly associated with at least one of the changes—the westward avulsion of Elisa Bend and possibly the Nelson Bend cutoff. The Feather River continues to flow in most of the lower 4.8-km-long dredged channel below Shanghai Bend. The relatively cohesive older alluvium of this artificial channel helps to stabilize the channel and inhibits lateral migration. Abandonment of channels around islands may reflect increased sediment loads that encouraged construction of natural levees and longitudinal bars. This intereptation is supported by maps that show the upstream ends of channels being sealed before the downstream ends. Morphologic changes in the Feather River continued after the turn of the twentieth century. Comparison of detailed topographic maps surveyed in 1906 and 1909 at Shanghai Bend and the Feather-Yuba confluence reveal extensive changes caused by the 1907 flood (CDC, 1906, 1912).

A schematic diagram summarizing contrasts between the lower 10 km of the Yuba River and the lower Feather River below the Yuba confluence during three time periods is shown in Figure 20. In the late nineteenth century (ca. 1880; T1 in Fig. 20) the lower Yuba River was undergoing deep aggradation and channel instability. In the upper fan area above Parks Bar the channel had aggraded by ~18 m, and this thickness decreased downstream to 5 or 6 m near Marysville. Deposits increased in lateral extent downstream, reaching widths up to 4 km. Attempts to dam or constrict the channel with levees failed, so a system of widely spaced levees evolved that encouraged sediment deposition and channel shifting across a wide floodway. Multiple high-water channels, frequent avulsions, and local braiding characterized the lower Yuba River during this period. Changes to the lower Feather River in the late nineteenth century were quite different. Sediment deliveries were less and finer grained, overbank sedimentation was less extensive, stream powers were larger, and channels maintained lateral positions. Nevertheless, bed aggradation was severe near the Yuba and Bear River confluences. Low-flow channel-bed elevations rose throughout the lower Feather River below the Yuba confluence to the Sacramento River. Between the mouth of the Feather River and the City of Sacramento, the bed of the Sacramento River had risen ~1.5 m (5 ft) and narrowed (Mendell, 1882).

By the turn of the twentieth century (T2 in Fig. 20), the tendency for channel-bed aggradation in the Yuba had shifted to lower reaches. Channel beds in the upper reaches above Parks Bar had begun to incise, abandoning floodplains as terraces that continued to receive overbank deposits. Channel beds near

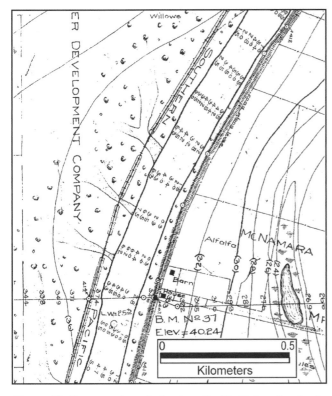

Figure 19. Crevasses through Southern Pacific Railroad embankment delivered water and sediment from lower Feather River to Sutter Basin. (Source: CDC, 1912.)

Marysville incised in response to extensive channel dredging and establishment of narrow levees near the Feather River confluence. By 1906 a long reach of the main lower Yuba channel, 5–10 km above Marysville, had returned to its pre-mining position. Multiple high-water channels remained active in the Yuba River, but main channel incision and enlargement lowered the frequency of flows in these channels. Hardening of the main Yuba channel, including revetment and wing dams, stabilized the banks, narrowed moderate-magnitude flows, and encouraged incision. Levee spacings remained wide, however, so large flows spread out and overbank deposition continued during large floods, such as in 1907 and 1909. In contrast, the lower Feather River during the period 1900–1910 began to undergo lateral channel changes. Some of this activity was caused by dredging and by levees in addition to responses to mining sediment. For example, the channel avulsion from Elisa Bend to Shanghai Bend was encouraged

by levee encroachment upstream that shifted the attack angle into the bend and a dredged channel that cut off flows above Elisa Bend. During this period, narrow levee cross-channel spacings along the lower Feather River severely constricted flood flows, reduced bed aggradation, and limited lateral channel adjustments. Some early mid-channel islands, which had been stable through the mining period, were converted to meander bends by sedimentation of one of the channels.

During the second half of the twentieth century, main channel erosion continued in the lower 10 km of the Yuba River, but lateral changes were relatively minor. Bank stabilization continued to limit the ability of the main channel to erode laterally while wide floodways continued to spread overflows across broad areas, reducing shear stresses that could have otherwise generated new channels or enlarged high-water channels. Stream regulation upstream also reduced sediment deliveries and

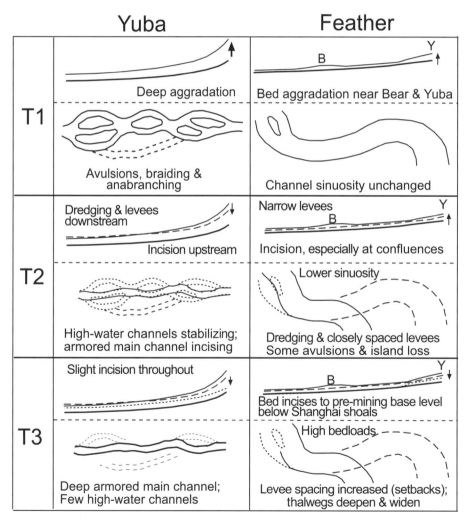

Figure 20. Schematic representation summarizing Yuba and Feather River morphologic changes for three periods (simplified and not to scale). Yuba River long profiles for each period extend from below bedrock canyon (below Narrows) to Marysville. Feather River profiles are from Yuba confluence to mouth at Sacramento. Map views are at a larger, reach scale. T1—1880; T2—1900–1910; T3—1950–1999.

magnitudes of peak flows. Several small high-water channels were abandoned—many leveled by agricultural activities—but a few remained active as flood bypass channels. In the Feather River, levee setbacks before 1950 reduced flow depths and increased flood conveyance. Levee spacings remained small relative to the smaller Yuba River, however, and this continued to encourage bed scour, although large amounts of bed material remain as vestiges of the mining era. Lateral migration can be seen in many channel reaches on modern aerial photographs, but the rates are less than those earlier in the twentieth century (T2 in Fig. 20), when lateral channel changes were substantial.

The strong differences in channel morphological change between the Yuba and Feather Rivers were due in part to contrasting styles of river management. In essence, an experiment in river engineering was initiated in the late nineteenth century, and the results reveal a lesson in how large rivers respond to such management in the long term. Explanations for slower, more subtle changes on the Feather than on the Yuba River include less mining sediment, finer sediment, later arrival, and the differences in large-scale river engineering efforts. The contrasting styles of river management between the lower Yuba and Feather Rivers amplified other differences between the two systems and are manifested in modern fluvial forms. An emphasis on navigation resulted in narrowly spaced levees on the Feather River, which constrained deposition and the ability of the river to change in planform. Levee cross-channel spacings appear to have been successful at promoting bed scour, although large sand sheets in the modern bed indicate that this is an ongoing process. Less extensive twentieth century changes to the Yuba River planform probably reflect structural bank-protection measures and may not have applied in areas such as the Yuba Gold Fields or upstream where these measures are lacking.

The geomorphic importance of legacy hydraulic-gold-mining sediments in the Yuba and Feather Rivers needs to be carefully considered by river managers in the region. For many years a conceptual model of regional sediment transport prevailed that led to an oversimplified view of the mining sediment either passing through piedmont rivers or being permanently stored there. Flaws with this viewpoint arise when sediment budgets are considered over longer time scales, when historical data are consulted at higher spatial and temporal resolutions, or when the importance of sediment remobilization is considered from the viewpoint of flood or toxic hazards.

Some theoretical lessons can be learned from the behavior of these rivers. Detailed historical information indicates that channel-bed incision on the Yuba River did not progressively translate downstream from the Narrows to Marysville as sediment-wave theory predicts. Based on an analysis of low-flow stage elevations at the two sites, Gilbert (1917, p. 30; cf. Gilbert's Fig. 4) concluded that peak elevations of aggraded channels passed through the Narrows upstream of Smartsville ~1900 and passed Marysville by 1905. By this model, little time separated the initiation of bed degradation in the upper debris fan from the fan toe at Marysville. Gilbert's field notes, however, show that

the spatial and temporal patterns of degradation above Marysville were more complex and slower, and that channel degradation did not simply progress downstream from the Narrows to Marysville. Degradation that began at the Marysville gauge in 1905 apparently preceded degradation upstream at Parks Bar, ~20 km above Marysville and 5 km below the Narrows. In fact, early channel incision at the Marysville D Street gauge may have been a response to two human alterations of the channel in that area. The channel had been constricted by levees spaced only 640 m apart at the gauge location, and dredging of a new confluence directly below the gauge took place shortly before 1905.

Field and historical evidence indicate that mine tailings have persisted in many locations along the Yuba and Feather River floodplains, and in most cases these deposits are not protected from erosion by levees or dams. Most of the storage is in high terraces that formed during the period of maximum aggradation, but much sediment is stored within the channels. The thickness of historical sediment in terraces varies in the longitudinal and lateral dimensions. On the Yuba River, historical sediment depths thin downstream from the fan apex to Marysville. Three recent topographic surveys measured the thickness of historical sediment in a sequence progressing downstream. The sections record a minimum thickness of 10.5 m above the low-water surface exposed in a historic terrace at Forbes Ranch ~6 km below the Narrows, a deposit 7 m thick in a south-bank exposure ~8 km above Marysville, and a 5.8-m-thick deposit in the north bank at Marysville.

On the Feather River, historical sediment in stream-bank exposures ranges from 1 to 5 m thick, depending on proximity to the Yuba and Bear River confluences and the history of lateral channel displacement. Thicknesses decrease abruptly below Shanghai Bend because an avulsion shifted the channel away from the deepest historical deposits. Knowledge of former channel positions is crucial to locating deep repositories of historical sediment. Approximately 10 million cubic meters of historical sediment is stored behind the west levee above Shanghai Bend, largely under a residential development. Total mercury concentrations (0.41 ppm) in a silt cap exposed in the bank along this deposit indicate toxicity and suggest that more testing is needed on the west side of the levee. Such storage that is isolated by levees and urbanized is not representative of most Yuba and Feather River deposits. Soil maps indicate that most of the historical sediment storage in these rivers is between the main levees, although many of the Yuba River floodplain deposits are stabilized by wing dams and riprap on channel banks. Large amounts of bed material are present along or within the main channels, including dredge spoils and gravel bars in the Yuba River and sand bars and sand sheets in the lower Feather River. Floodplain overbank deposition and abandoned channel filling are ongoing during floods except where lands are protected by levees or other structures (Eckbo, Dean and Williams, 2006; section 5.2, p. 7).

A recent study of the lower Feather River was conducted as part of an environmental impact assessment for a levee setback project (Eckbo, Dean and Williams, 2006; section 5.3, p. 27). The study conducted HEC-6 numerical sediment transport analyses for large floods and concluded that most channel degradation on the Feather River had been completed by the mid-1960s, that further degradation was unlikely within "an engineering time frame (50 years)," that channel base levels are controlled by sedimentation from the Yuba and Bear Rivers, and the channel is stable at these time scales. It concluded that the channels will remain relatively stable as long as hydraulic-mining debris stored in these channels continues to supply sediment. Ultimately ("hundreds to thousands of years in the future"), however, as sediment supplies decrease, the rivers will likely cut down to pre-mining elevations and begin migrating laterally. From an engineering perspective of evaluating channel hydraulic conditions, this interpretation may be largely correct with one important exception. The headward migration of the shoals below Shanghai Bend could lower base levels 3 m and initiate a major geomorphic response upstream. Comparison of 1999 sonar bathymetry with the DOQQs (U.S. Department of Agriculture, 2006) indicates that the shoals propagated 150 m upstream over that period. The 1999 bathymetry shows that <160 m separates the 2006 position of the shoals from a deep pool in the main channel upstream. Once the resistant bench is breached, an episode of channel incision generated by a 3-m base-level lowering could propagate up to the extensive historical deposits in the Yuba Gold Fields at DaGuerre Point Dam. The implications of this scenario are so far-reaching that a detailed hydraulic analysis should be conducted to test likely river responses to breaching of the shoals.

ACKNOWLEDGMENTS

This paper benefited from the insights and comments of Ellen Wohl and Rich Whittecar, who reviewed an early version of this paper and provided numerous thoughtful and constructive comments for which we are deeply grateful. Rolf Aalto provided substantial guidance and advice on this project, as well as funding for ^{14}C dating. Historical aerial photos and maps were made available for scanning by the University of California, Davis, Map Library (Dawn Collings and Kathleen Stroud), the California Department of Water Resources (Ruppert Grauberger), the California State Archives (Jessica Herrick), and the Sacramento Archives and Museum Collection Center (Patricia Johnson and Lisa Prince). The U.S. Army Corps of Engineers provided 1999 LiDAR and sonar data. Douglas Allen reconstructed the LiDAR data set. Field assistance was provided by Amanda Newbold, Joe Touzel, and John Wooten. Logistical help was provided by Catherine DeMauro and Steve James. The National Science Foundation provided funding via two awards: BCS 0520933 and BCS 0521663.

REFERENCES CITED

Bernhardt, E.S., Palmer, M.A., Allan, J.D., Alexander, G., Barnas, K., Brooks, S., Carr, J., Clayton, S., Dahm, C., Follstad-Shah, J., Galat, D., Gloss, S., Goodwin, P., Hart, D., Hassett, B., Jenkinson, R., Katz, S., Kondolf, G.M., Lake, P.S., Lave, R., Meyer, J.L., O'Donnell, T.K., Pagano, L., Powell, B.,

and Sudduth, E., 2005, Synthesizing U.S. river restoration efforts: Science, v. 308, p. 636–637, doi: 10.1126/science.1109769.

California Debris Commission (CDC), 1906, Map of the Yuba River, California from the Narrows to its mouth in the Feather River. Made under direction of Major Wm. W. Harts, U.S. Army Corps of Engineers, by G.G. McDaniel, Jr., August to Nov., 1906: scale 1:9,600.

California Debris Commission (CDC), 1912, Map of Feather River, California from Oroville to Southerly Limit of Gold Dredging Grounds. Surveyed under direction of Capt. Thos. H. Jackson, U.S. Army Corps of Engineers by Owen G. Stanley, Sept. to Oct., 1909: scale 1:9,600, 18 sheets.

California Department of Public Works (CDPW), 1925, Revised Sacramento Flood Control Project: Maps and Charts, sheet 1 of 7.

California Transportation Agency (CalTrans), 1952, Aerial photographs flown June 22, 1952. AAZ-1K-182-184: California State Archives, Box 9 of 9.

Chamberlain, W.H., and Wells, H.L., 1879, History of Yuba County, California: A Memorial and Biographical History of Northern California: Oakland, California, Thompson & West, 150 p.

Crook, L.B., 1914, Official map of Yuba County, California/Compiled from official records and surveys: San Francisco, Bashford Smith, University of California, Berkeley, Earth Science Library, scale 1:63,360, 1 sheet.

Doyle, J.M., 1887, Yuba County, State of California: University of California, Davis, Map Library, scale 1:125,000, 1 sheet.

Earth Resources Observation System (EROS), 1966, U.S. Geological Survey Historic Aerial Photograph Catalog System: http://edc.usgs.gov/products/aerial.html (July 2007).

Eckbo, Dean and Williams (EDAW), 2006, Final environmental impact report for the Feather River levee repair project: An element of the Yuba-Feather supplemental flood control project. Vol. I: Ch. 5. Report for Three Rivers Levee Improvement Authority: http://www.trlia.org (July 2007).

Ellis, W.T., 1939, Memories; My Seventy-Two Years in the Romantic County of Yuba, California; Introduction by Richard Belcher: Eugene, University of Oregon, 308 p.

Gibbes, C.D., 1852, A new map of California by Charles Dayton Gibbes from his own and other recent surveys and explorations: New York, Sherman & Smith, Sacramento, California State University, scale 1:1,330,560, 1 sheet.

Gilbert, G.K., 1905, 1907, 1913, Excerpts from unpublished field notes: Transcribed by L.A. James at National Archives, Washington, D.C.

Gilbert, G.K., 1917, Hydraulic-Mining Debris in the Sierra Nevada: U.S. Geological Survey Professional Paper 105, 154 p.

Gilvear, D.J., and Bryant, R., 2003, Analysis of aerial photography and other remotely sensed data, *in* Kondolf, G.M., and Piégay, H., eds., Tools in Fluvial Geomorphology: Hoboken, New Jersey, Wiley & Sons, p. 135–170.

Gilvear, D.J., and Harrison, D.J., 1991, Channel change and the significance of floodplain stratigraphy: 1990 flood event, Lower River Tay, Scotland: Earth Surface Processes and Landforms, v. 16, p. 753–761, doi: 10.1002/esp.3290160809.

Graf, W.L., 1996, Geomorphology and policy for restoration of impounded American rivers: What is "natural"? *in* Rhoads, B.L., and Thorn, C.E., eds., The Scientific Nature of Geomorphology, Proceedings of Binghamton Symposium, 27th, 27–29 September 1996: New York, Wiley & Sons, p. 443–473.

Greenland, P., 2001, Hydraulic Mining in California: A Tarnished Legacy: Spokane, Washington, Arthur H. Clarke, 320 p.

Gregory, K.J., 2006, The human role in changing river channels: Geomorphology, v. 79, p. 172–191, doi: 10.1016/j.geomorph.2006.06.018.

Gurnell, A.M., Peiry, J.L., and Petts, G.E., 2003, Using historical data in fluvial geomorphology, *in* Kondolf, G.M., and Piégay, H., eds., Tools in Fluvial Geomorphology: Hoboken, New Jersey, Wiley & Sons, p. 77–101.

Hall, W.H., 1880, Report of the State Engineer to the Legislature of California, Session of 1880: Sacramento, California Printing Office.

Hall, W.H., ca. 1880a, Part of Sutter County along Feather River showing property ownership. Hand-inked map on parchment with survey notes: Sacramento, California State Archives, item 5290-33.

Hall, W.H., ca. 1880b, Sacramento River from American River to Knights Landing. Survey line of river. Hand-inked map on parchment with survey notes: Sacramento, California State Archives, item 5290-52.

Hoffmann, C.F., and Craven, A., 1873, Map of the Tertiary auriferous gravel deposits lying between the middle fork of the American and the middle Yuba Rivers, *in* Memoirs of the Museum of Comparative Zoology, V. VI, Part I. J.D. Whitney: University of California, Davis, Map Library, scale 1:63,360, 1 sheet.

Hooke, J.M., and Kain, J.P., 1982, Historical Changes in the Physical Environment: A Guide to Sources and Techniques: London, Butterworth, 236 p.

Hughes, M.L., McDowell, P.F., and Marcus, W.A., 2006, Accuracy assessment of georectified aerial photos: Implications for measuring lateral channel movement in a GIS: Geomorphology, v. 74, p. 1–16, doi: 10.1016/j.geomorph.2005.07.001.

Hunerlach, M.P., Alpers, C.N., Marvin-DiPasquale, M., Taylor, H.E., and De Wild, J.F., 2004, Geochemistry of Mercury and Other Trace Elements in Fluvial Tailings Upstream of Daguerre Point Dam, Yuba River, California, August 2001: U.S. Geological Survey Scientific Investigations Report 2004-5165, 66 p.

James, L.A., 1989, Sustained storage and transport of hydraulic mining sediment in the Bear River, California: Annals of the Association of American Geographers, v. 79, p. 570–592, doi: 10.1111/j.1467-8306.1989.tb00277.x.

James, L.A., 1991, Quartz concentration as an index of alluvial mixing of hydraulic mine tailings with other sediment in the Bear River, California: Geomorphology, v. 4, p. 125–144, doi: 10.1016/0169-555X(91)90024-5.

James, L.A., 1994, Channel changes wrought by gold mining: Northern Sierra Nevada, California, *in* Marston, R., and Hasfurther, V., eds., Effects of Human-Induced Changes on Hydrologic Systems: American Water Resources Association, p. 629–638.

James, L.A., and Singer, M.B., 2008, Development of the lower Sacramento Valley flood-control system: An historical perspective: Natural Hazards Review, v. 9, no. 3, p. 125–135.

Kelley, R., 1954, Forgotten giant: The hydraulic gold mining industry in California: Pacific Historical Review, v. 23, p. 343–356.

Kelley, R., 1959, Gold vs. Grain: The Hydraulic Mining Controversy in California's Sacramento Valley: Glendale, California, Arthur H. Clarke, 327 p.

Kelley, R., 1989, Battling the Inland Sea: American Political Culture, Public Policy, and the Sacramento Valley, 1850–1986: Berkeley, University of California Press, 395 p.

Keyes v. Little York Gold Washing Co. et al., 1879, *53 Cal. 724, California Supreme Court.*

Kondolf, G.M., and Larson, M., 1995, Historical channel analysis and its application to riparian and aquatic habitat restoration: Aquatic Conservation, v. 5, p. 109–126, doi: 10.1002/aqc.3270050204.

Kondolf, G.M., and Micheli, E.R., 1995, Evaluating stream restoration projects: Environmental Management, v. 19, p. 1–15, doi: 10.1007/BF02471999.

Manson, M., and Grunsky, C.E., 1895a, Sutter Basin. Compiled from surveys made and data collected by the late State Engineer Dept. Commissioner of Public Works, Calif.: University of California, Davis, Map Library, 1 sheet.

Manson, M., and Grunsky, C.E., 1895b, Sacramento Valley from Iron Canon to Suisun Bay. From surveys made by the late State Engineer Dept. Commissioner of Public Works: University of California, Davis, Map Library, scale 1:126,720, 1 sheet.

May, J.T., Hothem, R.L., Alpers, C.N., and Law, M.A., 2000, Mercury Bioaccumulation in Fish in a Region Affected by Historic Gold Mining: The South Yuba River, Deer Creek, and Bear River Watersheds, California, 1999: U.S. Geological Survey Open-File Report 00-367, 30 p.

May, P., 1970, Origins of Hydraulic Mining in California: Oakland, California, Holmes Book Co., 88 p.

Mendell, Col. G.H., 1880, Mining debris in Sacramento River: *House Document 69, 46th Congress, 2nd Session:* 11.

Mendell, Col. G.H., 1881, Protection of the navigable waters of California from injury from the debris of mines: *House Document 76, 46th Congress, 3rd Session.*

Mendell, Col. G.H., 1882, Report upon a project to protect the navigable waters of California from the effects of hydraulic mining: *House Document 98, 47th Congress, 1st Session:* 110.

Mileson, M., and Adams, R., 1851, A complete map of the Feather & Yuba Rivers with towns, ranches, diggings, roads, distances: Marysville, California, R.A. Eddy, scale 1:475,200, 1 sheet. (Original at Berkeley is a negative.)

Montgomery, D.R., 2008, Dreams of natural streams: Science, v. 319, p. 291–292, doi: 10.1126/science.1153480.

Mount, J., and Twiss, R., 2005, Subsidence, sea level rise, and seismicity in the Sacramento–San Joaquin Delta: San Francisco Estuary and Watershed Science, v. 3, no. 1: http://repositories.cdlib.org/jmie/sfews/vol3/iss1/art5/ (December 2008).

National Research Council (NRC), 1992, Restoration of Aquatic Ecosystems. Committee on Restoration of Aquatic Ecosystems: Washington, D.C., National Academy Press, 552 p.

Novotny, V., and Chesters, G., 1989, Delivery of sediment and pollutants from nonpoint sources: A water quality perspective: Journal of Soil and Water Conservation, v. 44, no. 6, p. 568–576.

Olmsted, F.H., 1901, Physical characteristics of Kern River, California, by F.H. Olmsted, and Reconnaissance of Yuba River, California, by Marsden Manson: U.S. Geological Survey Water-Supply and Irrigation Paper 46, Washington Printing Office, 57 p.

Patrick, D.M., Smith, L.M., and Whitten, C.B., 1982, Methods for studying accelerated fluvial change, *in* Hey, R.D., Bathurst, J.C., and Thorne, C.E., eds., Gravel-Bed Rivers: Chichester, UK, Wiley & Sons, p. 783–815.

Pennington, J.T., 1873, Official map of Sutter County, California. Compiled and drawn from official surveys: Yuba County, California, Library scale 1:63,360.

Petts, G.E., 1989, Historical change in large European alluvial rivers, *in* Petts, G.E., and Muller, H., eds., Historical Change in Large European Alluvial Rivers: Chichester, UK, Wiley & Sons, p. 1–11.

Pixley, F.M., Smith, J.F., and Watson, N., 1865, Map of the location of the Yuba Railroad from Lincoln to Marysville: Sacramento, California State Archives scale 1:12,000. (Excerpt from Long scroll map [>8 ft long by ~14 in. tall].)

Public Land Survey System (PLSS), 2001, Downloaded from California Environmental Resources Evaluation System (CERES): http://www.ceres.ca.gov/ (December 2008).

Roehl, J.E., 1962, Sediment source areas, and delivery ratios influencing morphological factors: International Association of Hydrological Sciences, v. 59, p. 202–213.

Singer, M.B., 2007, The influence of major dams on hydrology through the drainage network of the Sacramento Valley, California: River Research and Applications, v. 23, p. 55–72, doi: 10.1002/rra.968.

Singer, M.B., Aalto, R., and James, L.A., 2008, Status of the lower Sacramento Valley flood-control system within the context of its natural geomorphic setting: Natural Hazards Review, v. 9, no. 3, p. 114–115.

Stonestreet, S.E., and Lee, A.S., 2000, Use of LIDAR mapping for floodplain studies, *in* Hotchkiss, R.H., and Glade, M., eds., Proceedings, Building Partnerships—2000 Joint Conference on Water Resource Engineering, Planning, and Management: Minneapolis, Minnesota, American Society of Civil Engineers, doi: 10.1061/40517(2000)58.

Thomas, G.C., 1928, Thomas Brothers map of Marysville and Yuba City: Sacramento, California State Archives.

Towill, Inc., 2006, Project Report for Topographic Surveys of the Lower Feather and Bear Rivers for the Sacramento and San Joaquin River Basins Comprehensive Study, California: Contract no. DACW05-99-D-0005 for U.S. Army Corps of Engineers, Sacramento District.

Trimble, S.W., and Cooke, R.U., 1991, Historical sources for geomorphological research in the United States: Professional Geographer, v. 43, p. 212–228, doi: 10.1111/j.0033-0124.1991.00212.x.

U.S. Army Corps of Engineers (USACE) and State of California Reclamation Board, 1998, Yuba River Basin Investigation, California: Draft Feasibility Report, Appendixes and Environmental Impact Statement/Environmental Impact Report: USACE Sacramento District.

U.S. Bureau of Reclamation (USBR), 1949, Controlled mosaic compiled at 1:19,200 by Fairchild Aerial Surveys from 1:20,000 photography dated March, April, and May 1949: Sacramento Archives.

U.S. Department of Agriculture (USDA), 2006, Digital Orthophoto Quarter Quad Mosaic. National Agriculture Imagery Program (NAIP), Aerial Photography Field Office: Salt Lake City, USDA FSAS APFO, acquired 8 September 2006.

Von Schmidt, A.M., 1859, Plat of the New Helvetia Rancho finally confirmed to John A. Sutter. Surveyed under instructions from the U.S. Surveyor General by A.M. Von Schmidt, Deputy Surveyor, September–October 1859: Sacramento Archives, scale 80 chains to an inch (1:63,360), 1 sheet.

Walling, D.E., 1983, The sediment delivery problem: Journal of Hydrology, v. 65, p. 209–237, doi: 10.1016/0022-1694(83)90217-2.

Walter, R.C., and Merritts, D.J., 2008, Natural streams and the legacy of water-powered mills: Science, v. 319, p. 299–304, doi: 10.1126/science.1151716.

Wescoatt, N., 1861, Official map of Yuba County, California: San Francisco, Lith. Britton & Co., University of California, Davis Map Library, scale ca. 1:63,360, 1 sheet.

MANUSCRIPT ACCEPTED BY THE SOCIETY 15 SEPTEMBER 2008

The Geological Society of America
Special Paper 451
2009

Channel adjustments in northern and central Italy over the last 200 years

Nicola Surian*

Department of Geography, University of Padova, Via del Santo, 26, Padova 35123, Italy

Massimo Rinaldi

Department of Civil and Environmental Engineering, University of Florence, Via S. Marta, 3, Florence, 50139, Italy

Luisa Pellegrini

Department of Earth Sciences, University of Pavia, Via Ferrata, 1, Pavia, 27100, Italy

Chiara Audisio
Franca Maraga

National Research Council, Institute for Geo-hydrological Protection, Strada delle Cacce, 73, Torino, 10135, Italy

Liliana Teruggi

Department of Civil and Environmental Engineering, University of Florence, Via S. Marta, 3, Florence, 50139, Italy

Ornella Turitto

National Research Council, Institute for Geo-hydrological Protection, Strada delle Cacce, 73, Torino, 10135, Italy

Luca Ziliani

Department of Geography, University of Padova, Via del Santo, 26, Padova 35123, Italy

ABSTRACT

This paper deals with channel evolution over the past 200 yr in 12 selected streams in northern and central Italy and aims at reconstructing the evolutionary trends (e.g., trends of channel width and bed elevation) and understanding the causes of channel adjustments. The selected streams have been studied using various sources and methods (historical maps, aerial photographs, topographic surveys, and geomorphological surveys). The selected rivers have undergone almost the same processes in terms of temporal trends; however, the magnitude of adjustments varies according to several factors, such as original channel morphology. Initially, river channels underwent a long phase of narrowing (up to 80%) and incision (up to 8–10 m), which started at the end of the nineteenth century and was intense from the 1950s to the 1980s. Then, over

*nicola.surian@unipd.it

Surian, N., Rinaldi, M., Pellegrini, L., Audisio, C., Maraga, F., Teruggi, L., Turitto, O., and Ziliani, L., 2009, Channel adjustments in northern and central Italy over the last 200 years, *in* James, L.A., Rathburn, S.L., and Whittecar, G.R., eds., Management and Restoration of Fluvial Systems with Broad Historical Changes and Human Impacts: Geological Society of America Special Paper 451, p. 83–95, doi: 10.1130/2009.2451(05). For permission to copy, contact editing@geosociety .org. ©2009 The Geological Society of America. All rights reserved.

the last 15–20 yr, channel widening and sedimentation, or bed-level stabilization, have become the dominant processes in most of the rivers.

Different human interventions have been identified as the causes of channel adjustments in Italian rivers (sediment mining, channelization, dams, reforestation, and torrent control works). Such interventions have caused a dramatic alteration of the sediment regime, whereas effects on channel-forming discharges have seldom been observed. Some notable implications for river management and restoration are (1) the state of rivers before major human disturbances and channel adjustments can rarely be taken as a reference, as at present rivers are far from their pristine condition; and (2) sediment management is and will be a key issue in such fluvial systems.

INTRODUCTION

During the last centuries, and particularly during the second half of the twentieth century, many fluvial systems have been significantly affected by human interventions. Such interventions involve both changes within drainage basins (e.g., land-use changes, torrent control works) and within river channels (e.g., channelization, dams, sediment mining), and may cause substantial alterations of flow and sediment regimes as well as boundary conditions of river channels. Several studies have analyzed the response of rivers to human impact, showing that different channel adjustments, such as incision, aggradation, and changes in channel width and pattern, generally take place (e.g., Leopold, 1973; Petts, 1979; Williams and Wolman, 1984; Knighton, 1991; Wyzga, 1993; Kondolf, 1997; Sear and Archer, 1998; Winterbottom, 2000; Liébault and Piégay, 2001; Marston et al., 2003; Gregory, 2006). These adjustments are generally much larger than those that could be expected from natural channel evolution, although some natural phenomena, such as large floods and volcanic eruptions, or short-term climatic fluctuations, may also have an important role in controlling channel instability and changes (Simon, 1992; Rumsby and Macklin, 1994; Macklin et al., 1998).

Most Italian rivers have undergone widespread channel adjustments, in particular incision and narrowing. Such adjustments have been analyzed in several studies since the 1960s (e.g., Roveri, 1965; Castiglioni and Pellegrini, 1981; Dutto and Maraga, 1994; Castaldini and Piacente, 1995; Capelli et al., 1997; Billi and Rinaldi, 1997; Rinaldi and Simon, 1998; Surian, 1999; Aucelli and Rosskopf, 2000; Rinaldi, 2003), but, as pointed out by a recent review (Surian and Rinaldi, 2003), most of the studies are largely descriptive and lack temporal reconstruction of key parameters such as channel width and bed level. The reconstruction of temporal trends of channel changes is fundamental in order to recognize relations between channel adjustments and their causes, define a channel-evolution model that could explain a sequence of processes regarding most Italian rivers, and understand recent river dynamics. Moreover, understanding evolutionary trends of river channels and their causes is a crucial issue for a sustainable management and restoration of streams that are largely affected by human impact (Downs and Gregory, 2004; Habersack and Piégay, 2008).

The research carried out in Italy during the last few years has focused on the following objectives: (1) reconstructing the channel changes (e.g., changes of channel width, bed elevation, braiding intensity, sinuosity) for several rivers, thereby increasing the relatively small number of case studies available; (2) understanding the relationship between channel adjustments and various human interventions; (3) improving existing conceptual models of channel evolution; and (4) analyzing the implications of channel adjustments in terms of river management and restoration. This paper deals with channel evolution over the past 200 yr in 12 selected streams in northern and central Italy, and it focuses on objectives 1 and 2, with a brief discussion of numbers 3 and 4. The selected streams have been studied using similar sources (historical maps, aerial photographs, topographic surveys, geomorphological surveys), and, most important, the same protocols for collecting, measuring, and processing data. Such an approach has allowed the creation of a homogeneous data set and, therefore, reliable comparisons among the studied rivers.

GENERAL SETTING

The selected streams are in northern and central Italy (Fig. 1): seven drain from the Alps (Stura di Lanzo, Orco, Brenta, Piave, Cellina, Tagliamento, and Torre) and five from the Apennines (Trebbia, Panaro, Magra, Vara, and Cecina). These rivers were selected in order to have a set of rivers representative of the study area, taking into account the following criteria: (1) a relatively wide range in terms of river size, and (2) fluvial systems with different degrees of human impact. The data availability was also important in the selection of the study cases.

The physiographic and hydrological characteristics of the 12 selected streams are reported in Table 1. The drainage-basin areas range from 446 to 3899 km^2, and the river length from 53 to 222 km. The basin relief is higher in the Alpine rivers than in those draining from the Apennines, being up to 3435 m and 2157 m, respectively. As for the discharge regime, there is a significant difference between low and high flows. This difference has been enhanced by stream regulation, which has significantly decreased low flows, but has not altered, in most cases (see next section), the high flows. The floods are relatively flashy and high in magnitude: the ratio between largest flood and mean annual discharge ranges between 34 (Brenta) and 129 (Cecina) (Table 1).

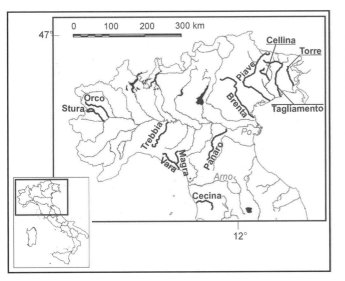

Figure 1. General setting of the selected rivers.

The study reaches, which range in length from 10 to 49 km, are those where major channel adjustments occurred over the past 200 yr and are located in the piedmont plain in most cases. In such reaches the river channels are generally very wide (some hundred meters) and are not confined or only slightly confined. Morphological and sedimentological characteristics of the selected reaches are reported in Table 2. There is a range of channel morphology at present, since several reaches exhibit a down-stream transition from braided to single-thread, but originally the braided configuration was dominant in the study reaches. Channel slope is generally in the range 0.002–0.006, but in three reaches it is ~0.01. River beds are composed of gravels, and banks are noncohesive or composite.

HUMAN IMPACT ON FLUVIAL SYSTEMS

A range of human impacts (channelization, sediment mining, dams, reforestation) has taken place in the selected streams during

TABLE 1. PHYSIOGRAPHIC AND HYDROLOGICAL CHARACTERISTICS OF THE SELECTED RIVERS

River	Drainage-basin area* (km²)	Length (km)	Basin relief (m)	Precipitation (mm yr⁻¹)	Mean annual discharge (m³ s⁻¹)	Largest flood (m³ s⁻¹)
Stura di Lanzo	928 (582)	80	3427	1107	20	2000
Orco	906 (630)	83	3435	1250	20	1650
Brenta	1567	174	3079	1390	71	2400
Piave	3899	222	3162	1330	132	5300
Cellina	446	58	2401	1770	N.A.	950
Tagliamento	2580	178	2696	2150	109	4650
Torre	1105 (168)	69	1679	2280	N.A.	730
Trebbia	1070	120	1406	1440	35	3500
Panaro	1783 (1036)	165	2157	1017	19	1400
Magra	1699 (932)	70	1639	1707	41	1440
Vara	572 (523)	65	1603	1770	23	820
Cecina	905 (634)	53	1018	944	8	1030

*Drainage-basin area—the area upstream of gauging stations, where discharges are measured, is in parentheses.
N.A.—not available.

TABLE 2. MORPHOLOGICAL AND SEDIMENTOLOGICAL CHARACTERISTICS OF THE SELECTED REACHES

River	Reach length (km)	Channel morphology*	Slope (%)	D₅₀ of bed sediments (mm)	Type of banks†
Stura di Lanzo	10	B/W	1.3	117	NC/CO
Orco	25	W	0.6	65–80	NC
Brenta	23	B/W/S	0.2–0.5	26–140	NC/CO
Piave (mountain reach)	32	B/W	0.3–0.6	20–48	NC
Piave (plain reach)	22	B/W/S	0.2–0.5	18–28	NC/CO
Cellina	10	B/W	1.2	N.A.	NC
Tagliamento	49	B/W/S	0.1–0.4	20–49	NC/CO
Torre	44	B/W/S	0.3–0.6	N.A.	NC/CO
Trebbia	32	B/W	0.2–0.4	33–80	NC
Panaro	38	W/S/M	0.05–0.4	27–90	CO/C
Magra (upper reach)	10	W	0.9	45–91	NC
Magra (lower reach)	11	W	0.15–0.4	21–40	CO
Vara	22	W/S	0.3–0.5	12–52	NC/CO
Cecina	40	W/S	0.2–0.5	12–34	NC/CO

*Channel morphology—braided (B), wandering (W), sinuous (S), meandering (M).
†Type of banks—noncohesive (NC), cohesive (C), composite (CO).
N.A.—not available.

the past centuries, particularly during the past 100 yr (Table 3). These interventions have both direct (e.g., levees and groins) and indirect (e.g., reforestation) effects on channel dynamics.

The chronology of human interventions is similar in the selected rivers, although some small differences exist (Table 3). In most cases, channelization started during the nineteenth century, initially with the construction of levees, and then, during the twentieth century, also with the construction of groins and other bank-protection structures. Reforestation and torrent control works are not well documented, but the available data suggest that both interventions generally started in the 1920s–1930s. Reforestation occurred after several centuries of intense deforestation, and it is still ongoing (Lamedica et al., 2007). Dams were constructed in 9 out of the 12 streams selected. Some were closed in the 1930s, but most of the dams were built during the 1950s. Since then, several millions of cubic meters of sediment have been trapped in reservoirs, especially in those river systems with a large impounded drainage area (e.g., Brenta, Piave, Cellina, and Vara). Gravel mining was intense between the 1950s and the 1980s. During relatively short periods of time (20–30 yr) large volumes of sediments were removed from the channels, e.g., 8.6×10^6 m^3 in the Brenta from 1953 to 1977, 24×10^6 m^3 in the Tagliamento from 1970 to 1991, 15×10^6 m^3 in the Torre from the 1950s to the 1970s, 24×10^6 m^3 in the Magra and Vara from 1958 to 1973, and 5.9×10^6 m^3 in the Panaro from 1962 to 1980 (such values are underestimates, because they come from official data, which commonly do not correspond to the real volumes extracted).

Such interventions have dramatically altered the sediment regime, although by different magnitudes and timing. A major effect has been produced by gravel mining, which has significantly decreased or ceased in the past 20 yr or so. Although several difficulties exist for obtaining reliable bed-load-transport

calculations, as well as the volume of the sediment extracted, we estimated that when mining was most intense the extraction rates exceeded replenishment rates by 10 or more times (e.g., Surian and Cisotto, 2007). The other interventions (e.g., dams, reforestation) likely have a lower, but more extended, effect on sediment regime.

Dams and diversions have markedly reduced low flows, but no reductions have occurred in channel-forming discharges of the selected rivers, according to previous works (Maraga, 1983; Surian, 2006; Surian and Cisotto, 2007). Historical trends of maximum annual discharges are available for six rivers (Fig. 2). These trends show that no significant changes occurred in four rivers (Brenta, Piave, Tagliamento, and Magra), whereas some changes occurred in the Cellina and Cecina. With regard to the Cellina, the decrease of maximum annual discharge is due to the construction of a dam in 1954, whereas the decrease in the Cecina could be due to climate changes, since there is no notable regulation along this river.

METHODS AND DATA SOURCES

Historical Maps and Aerial Photographs

The analysis of historical maps and aerial photographs, carried out using geographical information systems (GIS), has allowed us to examine channel changes over the past 200 yr. The maps are at scales ranging between 1:25,000 and 1:86,400 and refer to the nineteenth century and the first half of the twentieth century. The aerial photographs are at scales ranging from 1:7,000 to 1:33,000 and cover the period from the 1950s to the present. The historical maps are available from the beginning of the nineteenth century in 7 streams out of 12, whereas in the other cases from the 1870s or the 1880s. For each river reach, 9 dates

TABLE 3. HUMAN IMPACT IN THE SELECTED RIVERS

River	Drainage area upstream from dams (%)	Dates of dam closure	Dates of intense sediment mining	Construction of levees and other bank protection structures	Reforestation in the drainage basin
Stura di Lanzo	31	1931–1933	1960s–1980s	Since end of 19th century	N.A.
Orco	13	1927–1959	1960s–1980s	19th–20th century	20th century
Brenta	40	1954	1950s–1980s	19th–20th century	Since 1920s–1930s
Piave	54	1930s–1950s	1960s–1980s	15th–20th century	Since 1920s–1930s
Cellina	87	1954	1970s–1980s	19th–20th century	N.A.
Tagliamento	3	1950s	1970s–1980s	19th–20th century	20th century (?)*
Torre	8	1900	1960s–1970s	19th–20th century	N.A.
Trebbia	24	1950s–1970s	1960s–1980s	19th–20th century	Since 1940s
Panaro	3	1950s	1960s–1990s	1920s–1960s	Since 1920s–1930s
Magra	4	1950s	1960s–1970s	Since 1920s	Since 1920s–1930s
Vara	43	1930s	1960s–1970s	Since 1920s	Since 1920s–1930s
Cecina	0	–	1970s	Since 1920s–1930s	Since 1920s–1930s

*(?)—data with a higher degree of uncertainty.
N.A.—not available.

were analyzed on average, from a minimum of 6 (Stura di Lanzo) to a maximum of 12 (Vara and Tagliamento).

The digital maps and aerial photographs were co-registered using maps at 1:5,000 or 1:10,000 scale as base layers. Then, channel features were digitized in order to analyze planform characteristics (channel width, braiding index, sinuosity). As for channel width, both the "total channel width," that is, including islands, and the "active channel width," that is, the width of the single low-flow channels plus that of unvegetated or sparsely vegetated bars, were measured. It is worth noting that the measured width is affected by some errors owing to georectification and digitization. According to some preliminary assessment and to previous works (e.g., Gurnell, 1997; Winterbottom, 2000; Hughes et al., 2006), maximum errors of 15–20 m and 5–6 m were estimated, respectively, for measurements on maps and aerial photographs.

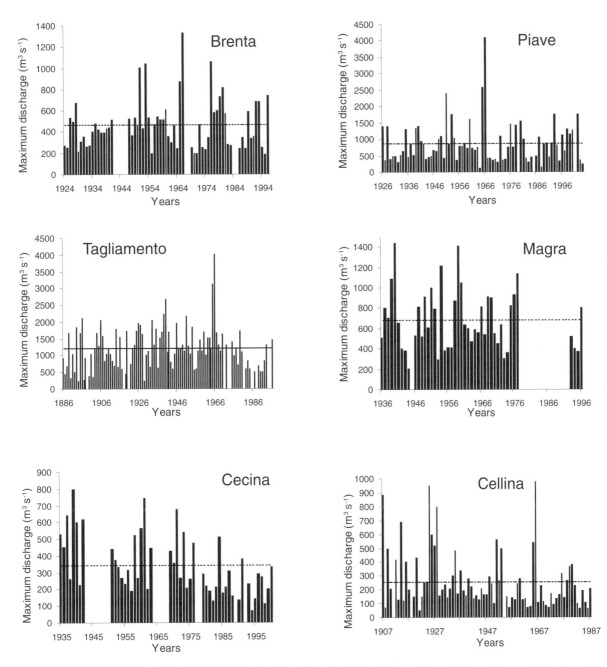

Figure 2. Historical trends of maximum annual discharge for six of the selected rivers (Brenta, Piave, Tagliamento, Magra, Cecina, and Cellina). Dashed line represents the average maximum discharge for the examined period. Some gaps do exist, in particular for Magra and Cecina, because data were not available.

Topographic Data

Longitudinal profiles and cross sections were available for all the selected streams, but they did not allow as detailed reconstructions of bed-level changes as was possible for planform characteristics. Several surveys are available only for the Magra and Brenta Rivers: six for the Magra, from 1914 to 2006, and seven for the Brenta, from 1932 to 1997. Besides the fact that few surveys are available for most of the study reaches, such topographic data refer to a limited period of time. The first surveys date back to the first decades of the twentieth century in 3 cases out of 12 (Brenta, Piave, and Magra), whereas for the other streams they date back to the 1950s–1970s.

Geomorphological Survey

Geomorphological surveys were carried out using standardized forms specifically designed to record measurements and observations of channel changes (Rinaldi, 2007). Data col-lected through such surveys should integrate those coming from the other sources (maps, aerial photographs, and topographic data) and are crucial in quantifying bed-level changes. In particular, the geomorphological surveys have allowed us to infer short-term channel changes, according to a number of morphological and sedimentological features (e.g., differences in elevation between bars and floodplain, presence-absence of sediment lobes, presence-absence of armoring, etc.).

RESULTS

Channel-Width Changes

The use of historical maps and aerial photographs has allowed a detailed analysis of channel-width change during the last 100–200 yr (Fig. 3; Tables 4, 5). Because the study reaches are relatively long and not homogeneous in terms of channel morphology, most of the reaches were divided into two or three sub-reaches. This division led to a total of 27 sub-reaches, which

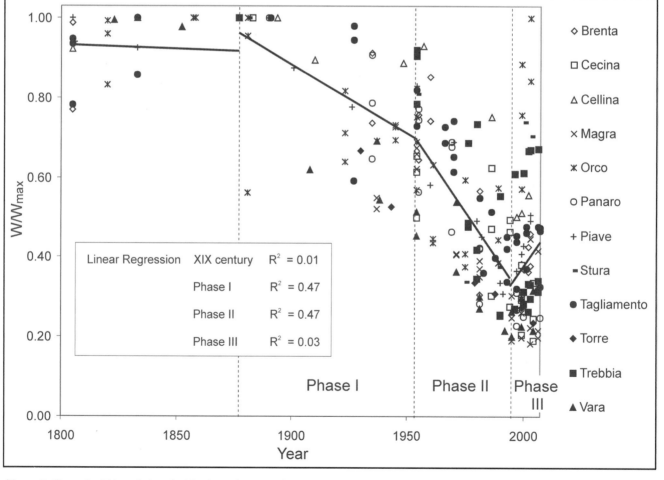

Figure 3. Channel width variations in 27 sub-reaches over the past 200 yr. In order to compare the 12 selected rivers a dimensionless width "W/W$_{max}$" is used, in which W is the width measured on the different dates, and W$_{max}$ the maximum width, for each sub-reach, for the study period. The three phases of channel adjustment that have occurred from the end of the nineteenth century to the present are pointed out.

TABLE 4. WIDTH CHANGES FROM THE BEGINNING OF THE NINETEENTH CENTURY TO THE 1980s/1990s

River	Reach	Width change in the 19th century			Width change in the 1st phase of adjustment (1880s–1950s)			Width change in the 2nd phase of adjustment (1950s–1980s/1990s)			Total width change (since the beginning of 19th century)	
		(m)	(%)*	(m yr^{-1})†	(m)	(%)	(m yr^{-1})	(m)	(%)	(m yr^{-1})	(m)	(%)
Stura di Lanzo		N.A.	N.A.	N.A.	−54	−19	−0.7	−134	−47	−6.4	−188	−66
Orco	Upper	−22	−9	−0.4	−58	−25	−0.8	−26	−11	−0.7	−105	−46
	Middle	−38	−17	−0.6	62	28	0.9	−120	−54	−3.4	−96	−43
	Lower	−57	−16	−0.9	−134	−36	−1.8	−60	−16	−2.9	−251	−68
Brenta	Upper	47	10	0.5	−122	−27	−1.9	−200	−44	−7.7	−275	−60
	Lower	n.c.			−82	−20	−1.3	−193	−46	−4.4	−275	−69
Piave	Mountain	40	7	0.5	−272	−45	−3.9	−160	−26	−5.3	−392	−64
	Plain	−120	−12	−1.2	−143	−15	−2.7	−437	−46	−11.8	−699	−73
Cellina		−89	−11	−1.0	−51	−6	−0.8	−310	−38	−7.8	−450	−55
Tagliamento	Upper	−224	−12	−2.6	−295	−16	−4.7	−606	−32	−15.5	−1125	−60
	Middle	273	28	3.2	−341	−35	−5.4	−415	−42	−12.2	−483	−49
	Lower	29	7	0.3	−41	−10	−0.6	−264	−63	−6.1	−275	−66
Torre		N.A.	N.A.	N.A.	−267	−47	−2.4	−142	−25	−2.5	−409	−73
Trebbia	Upper	N.A.	N.A.	N.A.	−23	−8	−0.3	−105	−37	−2.9	−127	−45
	Middle	N.A.	N.A.	N.A.	−197	−22	−2.6	−482	−53	−13.4	−679	−75
	Lower	N.A.	N.A.	N.A.	−54	−10	−0.7	−363	−65	−10.1	−417	−75
Panaro	Upper	N.A.	N.A.	N.A.	−66	−25	−1.0	−113	−44	−2.7	−179	−69
	Middle	N.A.	N.A.	N.A.	−87	−23	−1.3	−192	−50	−4.6	−278	−73
	Lower	N.A.	N.A.	N.A.	−112	−44	−1.7	−86	−34	−2.1	−198	−77
Magra	Upper	N.A.	N.A.	N.A.	−106	−33	−1.4	−120	−37	−2.9	−226	−70
	Middle	N.A.	N.A.	N.A.	−247	−38	−3.2	−279	−43	−6.8	−526	−81
	Lower	N.A.	N.A.	N.A.	−268	−34	−3.5	−324	−41	−7.9	−593	−75
Vara	Upper	N.A.	N.A.	N.A.	−125	−49	−1.6	−65	−25	−1.6	−189	−74
	Lower	n.c.			−301	−55	−3.9	−140	−26	−3.4	−441	−80
Cecina	Upper	N.A.	N.A.	N.A.	−63	−35	−0.9	−30	−16	−0.7	−93	−51
	Middle	N.A.	N.A.	N.A.	−72	−50	−1.0	n.c.			−72	−54
	Lower	N.A.	N.A.	N.A.	−62	−39	−0.9	−55	−34	−1.4	−117	−72

N.A.—not available; n.c.—no change; the width change is lower than the measurement error.
*(%)—calculated referring to the original width in the early nineteenth century or in the 1880s.
†(m yr^{-1})—average rate of change estimated over the different time periods, considering initial and final channel widths.

exhibit a distinct morphology (i.e., braided, wandering, or single-thread). Then, in order to compare such sub-reaches, whose average width ranges from 31 m (Cecina in 2004) to 1975 m (Tagliamento in 1833), a dimensionless width, "W/W$_{max}$," was defined, where W is the width measured on the different dates, and W$_{max}$ is the maximum width for each sub-reach for the study period. The data from the 27 sub-reaches clearly show that channel narrowing has been the dominant process, but also that changes have occurred at similar times because data are not randomly distributed (Fig. 3). Such a data distribution suggests that intervals characterized by different width changes can be defined. In taking the overall set of data, but also considering width change of the single sub-reaches, four intervals were defined.

During the first period, corresponding approximately to the nineteenth century, narrowing occurred in 6 sub-reaches out of 12 (for that period only a smaller data set was available), varying from 9% (upper reach of the Orco) to 17% (middle reach of the Orco); 4 sub-reaches underwent some widening, varying from 7% (mountain reach of the Piave and lower reach of the Tagliamento) to 28% (middle reach of the Tagliamento); and 2 sub-reaches show no change (Table 4). According to the limited data set, that period was characterized by small width changes in terms of magnitude and by the absence of a dominant process (i.e., channel widening or narrowing). Narrowing

became the dominant process in the following two phases. In the second period, from the end of the nineteenth century to the 1950s (first phase of adjustment in Fig. 3), narrowing occurred in 26 sub-reaches out of 27, the average being 29%, varying from 6% (Cellina) to 55% (lower reach of the Vara). In the third period, from the 1950s to the 1980s–1990s (second phase of adjustment), 26 sub-reaches underwent narrowing, and 1 sub-reach had no change. Narrowing varied from 11% (upper reach of the Orco) to 65% (lower reach of the Trebbia), the average being 37%. Narrowing was more intense in the third period than in the second, as evidenced by the rate of narrowing, which was 5.5 m yr^{-1} and 2.0 m yr^{-1} on average, respectively, in the two periods (Table 4). Maximum width reduction was reached in the 1980s–1990s in several of the selected rivers. At that time, width reduction was 65% on average, varying from 43% (middle reach of the Orco) to 81% (middle reach of the Magra). As for the most recent period, about the last 15–20 yr, a different phase of evolution is clearly shown by the data set (Table 5), but in contrast with the two previous phases when all the rivers showed a similar behavior, significant differences existed among the selected rivers. In fact, widening (varying from 1% to 91%) has occurred in 18 out of 27 sub-reaches, and narrowing in 6 sub-reaches (varying from 2% to 26%), whereas 3 sub-reaches show no change.

TABLE 5. WIDTH CHANGES DURING THE THIRD PHASE OF CHANNEL ADJUSTMENTS

River	Reach	Time period	Width change in the 3rd phase (1980s/1990s–2000/2007)			
			(m)	(%)*	(%)†	(myr⁻¹)
Stura di Lanzo		1975–2003	104	37	108	3.7
Orco	Upper	1989–2003	94	41	75	6.7
	Middle	1989–2003	201	91	160	14.3
	Lower	1975–2003	145	39	124	5.2
Brenta	Upper	1981–2003	90	20	49	4.1
	Lower	1999–2003	32	8	25	8.0
Piave	Mountain	1990–2003	111	18	51	8.5
	Plain	1991–2003	153	16	59	12.7
Cellina		1997–2002	39	5	11	7.8
Tagliamento	Upper	1993–2007	26	1	3	1.9
	Middle	1988–2007	96	10	19	5.0
	Lower	1997–2007	n.c.			
Torre		1999–2004	−22	−4	−14	−4.3
Trebbia	Upper	1990–2006	34	12	22	2.1
	Middle	1990–2006	79	9	34	5.0
	Lower	1990–2006	33	6	23	2.1
Panaro	Upper	1997–2000	n.c.			
	Middle	1997–2007	−8	−2	−8	−0.8
	Lower	1997–2000	n.c.			
Magra	Upper	1995–2006	37	12	38	3.4
	Middle	1995–2006	15	3	12	1.4
	Lower	1995–2006	−41	−6	−21	−3.7
Vara	Upper	1995–2004	13	6	20	1.5
	Lower	1995–2004	9	2	9	1.0
Cecina	Upper	1994–2004	−45	−26	−50	−4.5
	Middle	1994–2004	−18	−13	−27	−1.8
	Lower	1994–2004	−14	−9	−31	−1.4

Note: n.c.—no change; the width change is lower than the measurement error.
*(%)—calculated referring to the original width in the early 19th century or in the 1880s.
†(%)—calculated referring to the width at the beginning of the 3rd phase of adjustment.

Bed-Level Changes

In terms of bed-level changes, the available topographic data and the geomorphological surveys have allowed (1) a definition of the magnitude of changes over the medium term, (2) a qualitative assessment of short-term trends, and (3) a few detailed temporal reconstructions (Table 6; Fig. 4). Incision has been the dominant process in the medium term (about the past 100 yr), even if a few short sub-reaches (e.g., in the Stura di Lanzo, Brenta, and Torre) can be considered in equilibrium during that period. Bed-level lowering has been commonly moderate (1–2 m) or intense (2–4 m) in the upper reaches, and even very intense—that is, up to 8–10 m (e.g., in the Brenta, Panaro, and Magra)—in the downstream and middle reaches, which are characterized by single-thread morphology (Table 6). For the short term (about the last 10–15 yr), very few reaches in the selected streams have incised, and most of the reaches exhibit equilibrium or sedimentation. Temporal changes of bed level could be reconstructed for the Brenta, Magra, and Tagliamento. The representative bed-level trends reported in Figure 4 show that initially a more or less intense phase of incision took place, and that recently some reaches are in or are getting close to a state of equilibrium (e.g., upper reach of the Brenta; middle reach of the Tagliamento), whereas in oth-ers some sedimentation has occurred (e.g., lower reach of the Brenta or middle reach of the Magra).

Some Examples of Channel Adjustments: Brenta, Orco, and Cecina Rivers

Three rivers were selected to add some details to the over-all channel evolution described above. The Brenta River was selected because it is representative of many other rivers in terms of both channel adjustments and human impact. In contrast, channel adjustments in the Orco and Cecina Rivers differ in some way from the most common evolutionary trends.

The Brenta River, which drains from the Eastern Alps, shows a typical evolution in terms of channel-width changes; that is, a major phase of narrowing was followed by a recent chan-nel widening (Fig. 5). It is worth noting that the widening did not occur simultaneously along the study reach but took place first in the upper sub-reach and later in the lower sub-reach. Similar bed-level changes were consistent in the medium term but differed in the short term. Incision has been intense, up to 8.5 m, in the medium term, whereas bed level has been relatively stable and aggrading in the upper and lower sub-reaches during the last phase of the adjustment (Figs. 4, 5). The construction

TABLE 6. BED-LEVEL CHANGES IN THE MEDIUM AND SHORT TERM

River	Reach	Changes in the medium term (about last 100 yr)* (m)	Changes in the short term (about last 10–15 yr)[†]
Stura di Lanzo		–5 to 0	E and I
Orco		–3 to –1	E/S
Brenta	Upper	–5 to 0	E
	Lower	–8 to –4	S
Piave	Upper	–2 to –1	E/S
	Lower	–3 to –1	E/S
Cellina		N.A.[§]	N.A.
Tagliamento	Upper	N.A.	E
	Middle	–2 to –1	E
	Lower	–4 to –2	E
Torre		–5 to 0	I
Trebbia		–4 to –2	S
Panaro	Upper	–6 to –4	E
	Middle	–10 to –6	E
	Lower	–6 to –4	E
Magra	Upper	–4 to –2	E/S
	Lower	–8 to –5	E/S
Vara	Upper	–3 to –1	E/S
	Lower	–4 to –2	E/S
Cecina	Upper	–2 to –1	E
	Lower	–3 to –2	E

*A range of values is indicated for each river reach; for instance, "–3 to –1" (Orco River) means that incision varies from 3 m to 1 m within the reach.
[†]I—incision; E—equilibrium; E/S—equilibrium/sedimentation; S—sedimentation.
[§]N.A.—not available.

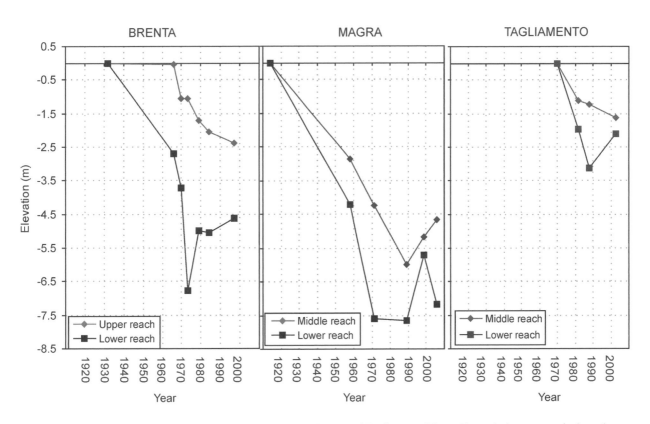

Figure 4. Temporal trends of bed-level changes in the Brenta, Magra, and Tagliamento Rivers. For each river, two typical trends are shown, e.g., one trend for the upper reach, and another for the lower reach in the case of the Brenta River.

of a sediment budget for the more recent period (1984–1997) points out that the sediments are supplied mainly by bank erosion and that little is supplied from upstream (Surian and Cisotto, 2007). This suggests that in the near future, once channel widening slows or ceases, bed-load supply could be very low, possibly causing a new phase of incision.

The evolution of the Orco River is unique, because after considerable channel narrowing from the 1950s to the 1980s, similar to that of most of the other rivers, intense widening occurred in the period 1989–2003 (Fig. 6). The channel widening has been so intense that in 2003 the width was larger than at the beginning of the nineteenth century (326 m and 221 m, respectively). The reasons for such recent widening are likely (1) the occurrence of a very large flood (the largest recorded in the twentieth century) in October 2000, and (2) the cessation of gravel mining since the end of the 1980s, implying higher in-channel sediment supply.

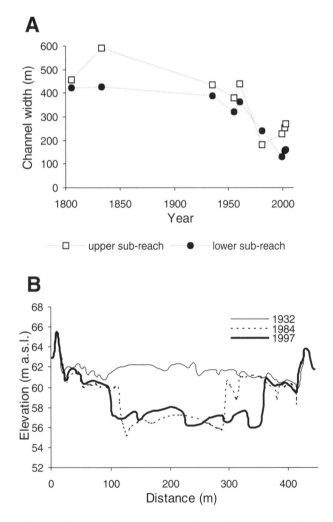

Figure 5. Channel adjustments in the Brenta River; a.s.l.—above sea level. (A) Temporal trends of channel width in the upper and lower sub-reaches. (B) Comparison of monumented cross sections, showing the major phase of incision and the recent phase of widening and sedimentation.

The Cecina River has been selected here because it is the smallest in size among the study cases, and it is representative of a geomorphological and climatic context distinct from the other cases, as it flows in the Apennines, with relatively low relief, and within an area of Mediterranean climate. In addition, there has been less human impact here than in other Italian rivers. Bed-level lowering has been generally moderate (1–3 m) during about the past 100 yr, whereas field evidence suggests that at present the dominant situation is of bed stability or, in some cases, of limited aggradation. The channel morphology of the Cecina in the 1950s can be described as wandering (locally braided), whereas in the following decades a significant narrowing occurred (Fig. 7), with a change in morphology to a sinuous, single-thread channel with alternate bars. A significant increase in sinuosity is observed, associated with channel narrowing, particularly during the last two decades (Fig. 7). The evolution of the Cecina River is, therefore, peculiar in some aspects and distinct from most of the other study cases, because (1) narrowing during the second phase of adjustment was less than in other rivers (Table 4), (2) narrowing is still going on (Table 5), and (3) increase in sinuosity appears to be an additional type of adjustment, with a partial shifting toward a single-thread, meandering morphology with gravel point bars.

DISCUSSION

The selected rivers underwent widespread channel adjustments over the past 100 yr. The dominant processes that have been observed are narrowing and incision: respectively the magnitude of such processes has been a decrease of as much as 81% in width (Magra River) and as much as 8–10 m of channel incision (Brenta, Panaro, and Magra Rivers). Narrowing and incision led to dramatic changes in channel configuration, becoming wandering or single-thread in several reaches that originally displayed a braided morphology. Subsequently, channel widening and sedimentation, or bed-level stabilization, have become dominant in most of the selected rivers over the last 15–20 yr, but the magnitude of such processes has generally been much lower in comparison with those of narrowing and incision. In fact, except for the Orco and Stura Rivers, which have undergone remarkable widening (up to 91% in the Orco River; see also Fig. 6), channel widening has been no more than 20%, and sedimentation on the order of 1–2 m (Fig. 4). It is worth noting that there are several examples outside of Italy where similar channel adjustments have been observed (e.g., in France, UK, USA, and China). Changes in channel width were often found to be comparable, whereas bed-level adjustments were generally less intense than in Italian rivers (e.g., Williams, 1978; Williams and Wolman, 1984; Simon, 1989; Xu Jiongxin, 1997; Sear and Archer, 1998; Winterbottom, 2000).

Although the same type of adjustments occurred in alluvial rivers of northern and central Italy, it is worth comparing the 27 sub-reaches in terms of both magnitude and time of channel adjustment. The fact that significant statistics ($R^2 = 0.47$ and P-values much lower than 0.05) exist for the first and second phase of adjustment is notable (Fig. 3), because it implies that

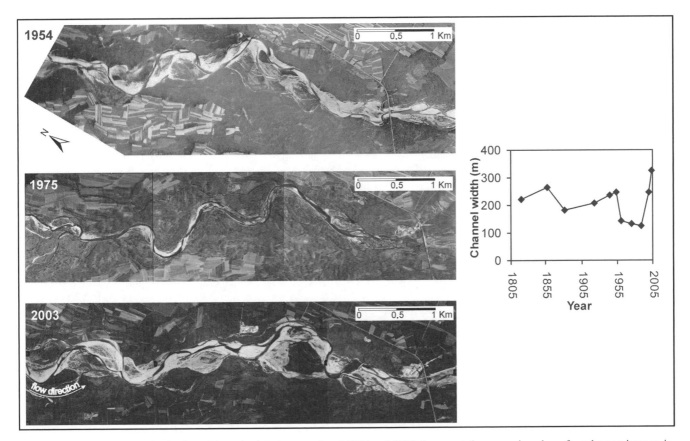

Figure 6. Channel changes in the Orco River: Aerial photographs of 1954 and 1975 document the narrowing phase from human impact, in particular gravel mining, whereas the 1975 and 2003 photographs show the remarkable widening that occurred in response to a number of floods, in particular the extreme flood of October 2000.

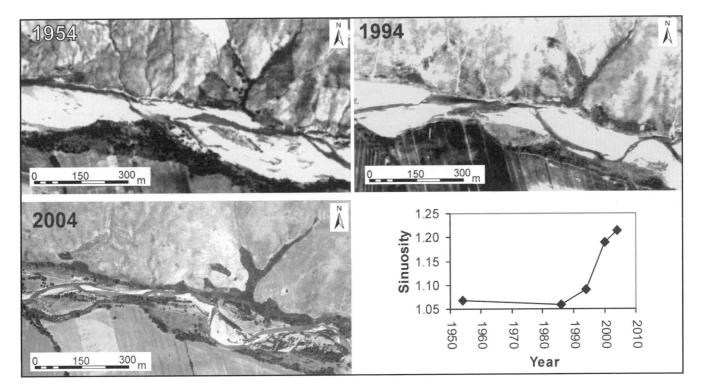

Figure 7. Channel adjustments in the Cecina River. This reach of the Cecina shows that channel narrowing instead of widening, as in most of the other rivers, has taken place from 1994 to 2004. A significant increase in sinuosity is observed, associated with channel narrowing.

those reaches not only underwent similar width changes but also that such changes took place at the same times. On the other hand, it is not surprising that the statistics are not significant for the third phase of adjustment ($R^2 = 0.03$, and $P = 0.42$). In fact, channel widening occurred only in 18 out of 27 sub-reaches, and four sub-reaches, those of the Stura and Orco, underwent an intense widening comparable to that of the other sub-reaches (Table 5). These results confirm that the existing models of channel evolution (Rinaldi, 2003; Surian and Rinaldi, 2003, 2004) are essentially correct, but they also give the opportunity for further development of such models. In particular, we improved the documentation of third phase of adjustment (the last 15–20 yr). This phase shows that channel widening and sedimentation, or bed-level stabilization, frequently occurred after narrowing and incision, but it also shows that the magnitude of processes can vary widely (see the case of the Orco). Besides, the fact that narrowing is still ongoing in some reaches will give the opportunity for investigating the reason why some reaches behave differently for certain periods of time.

The type, intensity, and chronology of various human actions described in a previous section suggest that the cause of channel adjustment is anthropogenic. That said, it is worth considering other possible causes, for instance, climate variability. Brunetti et al. (2006) found that precipitation in Italy over the past 200 yr has decreased (trends of total annual precipitation), but the decrease has been small and rarely significant. Similarly, no significant change of total annual precipitation was found for the Piave River (Surian, 1999). Though precipitation trends are not available for all the selected rivers, the data presented suggest that precipitation variability cannot be included among the major causes of channel adjustment. It is therefore reasonable to focus our attention on human actions. Besides the direct effect of channelization on channel morphology, what was the effect of human actions on flow and sediment regimes? Flow regulation has seldom affected maximum annual discharges (see Fig. 2), and consequently channel-forming discharges, whereas most human interventions (sediment mining, dams, reforestation, and torrent control works) have caused a dramatic alteration of sediment regime. Mining, usually intense between the 1950s and the 1980s, was likely the major cause of alteration because the extracted volumes largely exceeded replenishment rates. Gravel mining is not only a driving factor during the second phase of adjustment, but also during the most recent phase, which is characterized by widening and sedimentation, or bed-level stability, in several reaches. In fact, during this latter phase a significant reduction of mining has occurred, causing an increase of sediment availability. The effects of reforestation, torrent control, and dams on the sediment regime have been less intense than sediment mining but will be likely to persist for a longer period. Last, but not least, it is worth mentioning the role of large floods. It is well documented by the evolution of the Orco and Stura that large floods may have been the driving factor during the most recent phase of adjustment (Fig. 6). On the contrary, large floods seemed to have had less effectiveness during the second phase of

adjustment, as a very large flood that occurred in November 1966 (with a recurrence interval of 100 yr or more) had minor effects on the trends of channel evolution.

Knowledge of channel adjustments and their causes has important implications in river management and restoration (Downs and Gregory, 2004; Habersack and Piégay, 2008). First of all it is worth recognizing that most of the Italian rivers—those analyzed in this study as well as many others (Surian and Rinaldi, 2003)—have been strongly altered by human actions and at present are very far from their pristine condition. River management and restoration should take into account that several conditions, in particular sediment fluxes, have changed significantly in the fluvial systems. This implies that the state of rivers before major human disturbances and channel adjustments can rarely be taken as a reference.

A second important issue raised by this study is the key role of sediments in channel evolution. This is why sustainable management and restoration strategies should aim at promoting sediment supply in order to mitigate situations where bed-load deficit and incision have occurred with severe effects on hydraulic, ecological, environmental, and societal aspects (Bravard et al., 1999). Sustainable strategies may include both promotion of sediment input from tributaries and hillslopes and bank-erosion preservation or promotion (Piégay et al., 2005; Habersack and Piégay, 2008).

CONCLUSIONS

Alluvial rivers in northern and central Italy underwent similar channel adjustments over the past 200 yr: (1) narrowing and incision occurred in all 12 selected rivers from the end of the nineteenth century to the 1980s–1990s, and were intense from the 1950s to the 1980s–1990s; (2) widening and sedimentation, or bed-level stabilization, were the dominant processes in the last 15–20 yr, although channel narrowing is still ongoing in some reaches.

Channel adjustments were driven mainly by human actions, but the role of large floods was also notable in some cases. Besides the direct effect of channelization on channel morphology, the major effect of human actions was on sediment regime. A significant decrease of in-channel sediment supply was determined by gravel mining. On the other hand, channel-forming discharges did not undergo significant changes in most of the study streams.

Management and restoration should take into account the fact that these rivers are far from their pristine condition and that severe effects on hydraulic, ecological, and environmental aspects were caused by channel adjustments. Sustainable strategies should pay close attention to sediment fluxes, in particular to gravel transport, which were dramatically altered in the last decades.

ACKNOWLEDGMENTS

This research was supported by funds from MiUR (Ministero dell'Istruzione dell' Università e della Ricerca) PRIN 2005 Project "Present and recent dynamics of river channels in Northern and Central Italy: evolutionary trends, causes and management implications"). We thank the two anonymous reviewers for their helpful comments.

REFERENCES CITED

Aucelli, P.P.C., and Rosskopf, C., 2000, Last century valley floor modifications of the Trigno River (Southern Italy): A preliminary report: Geografia Fisica e Dinamica Quaternaria, v. 23, p. 105–115.

Billi, P., and Rinaldi, M., 1997, Human impact on sediment yield and channel dynamics in the Arno River basin (central Italy), *in* Walling, D.E., and Probst, J.L., eds., Human Impact on Erosion and Sedimentation: Rabat, Morocco, Proceedings of Rabat Symposium, IAHS Special Publication 245, p. 301–311.

Bravard, J.P., Kondolf, G.M., and Piegay, H., 1999, Environmental and societal effects of channel incision and remedial strategies, *in* Darby, S.E., and Simon, A., eds., Incised River Channels: Processes, Forms, Engineering and Management: New York, Wiley & Sons, p. 303–341.

Brunetti, M., Maugeri, M., Monti, F., and Nanni, T., 2006, Temperature and precipitation variability in Italy in the last two centuries from homogenised instrumental time series: International Journal of Climatology, v. 26, p. 345–381, doi: 10.1002/joc.1251.

Capelli, G., Miccadei, E., and Raffi, R., 1997, Fluvial dynamics in the Castel di Sangro plain: Morphological changes and human impact from 1875 to 1992: Catena, v. 30, p. 295–309, doi: 10.1016/S0341-8162(97)00008-8.

Castaldini, D., and Piacente, S., 1995, Channel changes on the Po River, Mantova Province, Northern Italy, *in* Hickin, E.J., ed., River Geomorphology: Chichester, New York, Wiley & Sons, p. 193–207.

Castiglioni, G.B., and Pellegrini, G.B., 1981, Two maps on the dynamics of a river bed: Erosion and sediment transport measurement: Florence, Proceedings of IAHS Symposium, v. 22–26, p. 223–228.

Downs, P.W., and Gregory, K.J., 2004, River Channel Management: Towards Sustainable Catchment Hydrosystems: London, Edward Arnold, 395 p.

Dutto, F., and Maraga, F., 1994, Variazioni idrografiche e condizionamento antropico. Esempi in pianura padana: Il Quaternario, v. 7, p. 381–390.

Gregory, K.J., 2006, The human role in changing river channels: Geomorphology, v. 79, p. 172–191, doi: 10.1016/j.geomorph.2006.06.018.

Gurnell, A.M., 1997, Channel change of the river Dee meanders, 1946–1992, from the analysis of air photographs: Regulated Rivers: Research and Management, v. 13, p. 13–26, doi: 10.1002/(SICI)1099-1646(199701)13:1<13::AID-RRR420>3.0.CO;2-W.

Habersack, H., and Piégay, H., 2008, River restoration in the Alps and their surroundings: Past experience and future challenges, *in* Habersack, H., Piégay, H., and Rinaldi, M., eds., Gravel-Bed Rivers VI—From Process Understanding to River Restoration, Developments in Earth Surface Processes: New York, Elsevier, p. 703–738.

Hughes, M.L., McDowell, P.F., and Marcus, W.A., 2006, Accuracy assessment of georectified aerial photographs: Implications for measuring lateral channel movement in a GIS: Geomorphology, v. 74, p. 1–16, doi: 10.1016/j.geomorph.2005.07.001.

Knighton, A.D., 1991, Channel bed adjustment along mine-affected rivers of northeast Tasmania: Geomorphology, v. 4, p. 205–219, doi: 10.1016/0169-555X(91)90004-T.

Kondolf, M.G., 1997, Hungry water: Effects of dams and gravel mining on river channels: Environmental Management, v. 21, p. 533–551, doi: 10.1007/s002679900048.

Lamedica, S., Dalla Valle, E., Pilli, R., and Anfodillo, T., 2007, Variazioni di superficie e fissazione di carbonio in foresta nel territorio montano della Regione Veneto in riferimento all'applicazione del Protocollo di Kyoto: Forest@, v. 4, p. 283–297, doi: 10.3832/efor0472-0040283.

Leopold, L.B., 1973, River channel change with time: An example: Geological Society of America Bulletin, v. 84, p. 1845–1860, doi: 10.1130/0016-7606(1973)84<1845:RCCWTA>2.0.CO;2.

Liébault, F., and Piégay, H., 2001, Assessment of channel changes due to long-term bedload supply decrease, Roubion River, France: Geomorphology, v. 36, p. 167–186, doi: 10.1016/S0169-555X(00)00044-1.

Macklin, M.G., Passmore, D.G., and Newson, M.D., 1998, Controls of short and long term river instability: Processes and patterns in gravel-bed rivers, the Tyne basin, Northern England, *in* Klingemann, P.E., Beschta, R.L., Bradley, J., and Komar, P.D., eds., Gravel Bed Rivers in the Environment: Highlands Ranch, Colorado, Water Resources Publications, p. 257–278.

Maraga, F., 1983, Morphologie fluviale et migration des cours d'eau dans la haute plaine du Po (Italie, partie nord-ouest): Geologisches Jahrbuch, v. 71, p. 219–236.

Marston, R.A., Bravard, J.P., and Green, T., 2003, Impacts of reforestation and gravel mining on the Malnant River, Haute-Savoie, French Alps: Geomorphology, v. 55, p. 65–74, doi: 10.1016/S0169-555X(03)00132-6.

Petts, G.E., 1979, Complex response of river channel morphology subsequent to reservoir construction: Progress in Physical Geography, v. 3, p. 329–362, doi: 10.1177/030913337900300302.

Piégay, H., Darby, S., Mosselman, E., and Surian, N., 2005, A review of techniques available for delimiting the erodible river corridor: A sustainable approach to managing bank erosion: River Research and Applications, v. 21, p. 773–789, doi: 10.1002/rra.881.

Rinaldi, M., 2003, Recent channel adjustments in alluvial rivers of Tuscany, Central Italy: Earth Surface Processes and Landforms, v. 28, p. 587–608, doi: 10.1002/esp.464.

Rinaldi, M., 2007, Geomorphological field survey for interpretation and classification of river channels adjustments: Epitome, v. 2, p. 362.

Rinaldi, M., and Simon, A., 1998, Bed-level adjustments in the Arno River, Central Italy: Geomorphology, v. 22, p. 57–71, doi: 10.1016/S0169-555X(97)00054-8.

Roveri, E., 1965, Sul ciclo d'erosione rinnovatosi lungo i corsi d'acqua dell'Appennino emiliano: Bollettino Società Geologica Italiana, v. 84, p. 290–309.

Rumsby, B.T., and Macklin, M.G., 1994, Channel and floodplain response to recent abrupt climate change, the Tyne basin, northern England: Earth Surface Processes and Landforms, v. 19, p. 499–515, doi: 10.1002/esp.3290190603.

Sear, D.A., and Archer, D., 1998, Effects of gravel extraction on stability of gravel-bed rivers: The Wooler Water, Northumberland, UK, *in* Klingeman, P.C., Beschta, R.L., Komar, P.D., and Bradley, J.B., eds., Gravel-Bed Rivers in the Environment: Highlands Ranch, Colorado, Water Resources Publications, p. 415–432.

Simon, A., 1989, A model of channel response in disturbed alluvial channels: Earth Surface Processes and Landforms, v. 14, p. 11–26, doi: 10.1002/esp.3290140103.

Simon, A., 1992, Energy, time, and channel evolution in catastrophically disturbed fluvial systems: Geomorphology, v. 5, p. 345–372, doi: 10.1016/0169-555X(92)90013-E.

Surian, N., 1999, Channel changes due to river regulation: The case of the Piave River, Italy: Earth Surface Processes and Landforms, v. 24, p. 1135–1151, doi: 10.1002/(SICI)1096-9837(199911)24:12<1135::AID-ESP40>3.0.CO;2-F.

Surian, N., 2006, Effects of human impact on braided river morphology: Examples from Northern Italy, *in* Sambrook Smith, G.H., Best, J.L., Bristow, C., and Petts, G.E., eds., Braided Rivers: Cambridge, Massachusetts, Blackwell Science, IAS Special Publication 36, p. 327–338.

Surian, N., and Cisotto, A., 2007, Channel adjustments, bedload transport and sediment sources in a gravel-bed river, Brenta River, Italy: Earth Surface Processes and Landforms, v. 32, p. 1641–1656, doi: 10.1002/esp.1591.

Surian, N., and Rinaldi, M., 2003, Morphological response to river engineering and management in alluvial channels in Italy: Geomorphology, v. 50, p. 307–326, doi: 10.1016/S0169-555X(02)00219-2.

Surian, N., and Rinaldi, M., 2004, Channel adjustments in response to human alteration of sediment fluxes: Examples from Italian rivers, *in* Golosov, V., Belyaev, V., and Walling, D.E., eds., Sediment Transfer through the Fluvial System: IAHS Press, Wallingford, UK, IAHS Special Publication 288, p. 276–282.

Williams, G.P., 1978, The Case of the Shrinking Channels—The North Platte and Platte Rivers in Nebraska: U.S. Geological Survey Circular 781, 48 p.

Williams, G.P., and Wolman, M.G., 1984, Downstream Effects of Dams on Alluvial Rivers: U.S. Geological Survey Professional Paper 1286, 83 p.

Winterbottom, S.J., 2000, Medium and short-term channel planform changes on the Rivers Tay and Tummel, Scotland: Geomorphology, v. 34, p. 195–208, doi: 10.1016/S0169-555X(00)00007-6.

Wyzga, B., 1993, River response to channel regulation: Case study of the Raba River, Carpathians, Poland: Earth Surface Processes and Landforms, v. 18, p. 541–556, doi: 10.1002/esp.3290180607.

Xu Jiongxin, 1997, Evolution of mid-channel bars in a braided river and complex response to reservoir construction: An example from the middle Hanjiang River, China: Earth Surface Processes and Landforms, v. 22, p. 953–965, doi: 10.1002/(SICI)1096-9837(199710)22:10<953::AID-ESP789>3.0.CO;2-S.

MANUSCRIPT ACCEPTED BY THE SOCIETY 15 SEPTEMBER 2008

The Geological Society of America
Special Paper 451
2009

Bank erosion along the dam-regulated lower Roanoke River, North Carolina

Cliff R. Hupp
Edward R. Schenk
U.S. Geological Survey, 12201 Sunrise Valley Drive, MS 430, Reston, Virginia 20192, USA

Jean M. Richter
U.S. Fish and Wildlife Service, 114 West Water Street, Windsor, North Carolina 27983, USA

Robert K. Peet
Department of Biology, University of North Carolina, Chapel Hill, North Carolina 27599, USA

Philip A. Townsend
Department of Forest Ecology and Management, University of Wisconsin, Madison, Wisconsin 53706, USA

ABSTRACT

Dam construction and its impact on downstream fluvial processes may substantially alter ambient bank stability and erosion. Three high dams (completed between 1953 and 1963) were built along the Piedmont portion of the Roanoke River, North Carolina; just downstream the lower part of the river flows across largely unconsolidated Coastal Plain deposits. To document bank erosion rates along the lower Roanoke River, >700 bank-erosion pins were installed along 66 bank transects. Additionally, discrete measurements of channel bathymetry, turbidity, and presence or absence of mass wasting were documented along the entire study reach (153 km). A bank-erosion–floodplain-deposition sediment budget was estimated for the lower river. Bank toe erosion related to consistently high low-flow stages may play a large role in increased mid- and upper-bank erosion. Present bank-erosion rates are relatively high and are greatest along the middle reaches (mean 63 mm/yr) and on lower parts of the bank on all reaches. Erosion rates were likely higher along upstream reaches than present erosion rates, such that erosion-rate maxima have since migrated downstream. Mass wasting and turbidity also peak along the middle reaches; floodplain sedimentation systematically increases downstream in the study reach. The lower Roanoke River is net depositional (on floodplain) with a surplus of ~2,800,000 m³/yr. Results suggest that unmeasured erosion, particularly mass wasting, may partly explain this surplus and should be part of sediment budgets downstream of dams.

Hupp, C.R., Schenk, E.R., Richter, J.M., Peet, R.K., and Townsend, P.A., 2009, Bank erosion along the dam-regulated lower Roanoke River, North Carolina, *in* James, L.A., Rathburn, S.L., and Whittecar, G.R., eds., Management and Restoration of Fluvial Systems with Broad Historical Changes and Human Impacts: Geological Society of America Special Paper 451, p. 97–108, doi: 10.1130/2009.2451(06). For permission to copy, contact editing@geosociety.org. ©2009 The Geological Society of America. All rights reserved.

INTRODUCTION

Over half of the world's largest river systems (172 of 292) have been moderately to strongly affected by dams (Nilsson et al., 2005). The downstream hydrogeomorphic effects of high dams have been documented for >80 yr (Lawson, 1925; Petts and Gurnell, 2005). More recently, the ecological effects of regulated flow below dams have been investigated (Ligon et al., 1995; Richter et al., 1996; Poff et al., 1997; Friedman et al., 1998). Flow regulation often dramatically alters the regime of alluvial rivers both through confined water-release scenarios and through substantial reductions in transported sediment below dams (Petts, 1979; Williams and Wolman, 1984; Church, 1995; Brandt, 2000). Channel beds and banks may undergo a wide range of adjustments to regulation (Williams and Wolman, 1984; Grant et al., 2003). Channel narrowing downstream of dams is a common response along several streams in the western United States (Allred and Schmidt, 1999; Grant et al., 2003). However, along single threaded alluvial rivers without bedrock control or relatively coarse bed sediment, a common effect is channel incision and subsequent widening through bank erosion (Williams and Wolman, 1984; Bravard et al., 1997; Friedman et al., 1998; Brandt, 2000). Williams and Wolman (1984) suggest that certain aspects of regulated flow may increase bank erosion, including (1) decreased sediment loads that enhance entrainment of bed and bank material, leading to channel incision; (2) a decrease of sediment delivered and stored on or near banks; (3) consistent wetting of lower bank surfaces through diurnal flow fluctuations associated with upstream power generation that promotes greater erodibility; and (4) channel degradation, which allows for flow impingement low on the banks that may remove stabilizing toe slopes and woody vegetation. There are few models that allow for prediction of the downstream effects of dams and even less that include the geological setting as a central factor (Grant et al., 2003). A model of channel change following dam construction that includes geology, climate, sediment supply, topography, and hydrologic regime was developed by Grant et al. (2003) and quantitatively extended in the development of physical metrics (drivers) to predict sediment balances below dams by Schmidt and Wilcock (2008).

Few studies have documented, in detail, bank erosion along regulated Coastal Plain rivers (Ligon et al., 1995), and none to our knowledge have linked erosion with equally detailed floodplain sediment-deposition information. Three high dams were completed along the Roanoke River, North Carolina, between 1953 and 1963. The largest of these forms the John H. Kerr Dam and Reservoir, which controls major water discharges downstream and is currently under evaluation through a Federal Section 216 study (authorized review of operations) conducted by the U.S. Army Corps of Engineers for flood-control effects. One of the principal objectives of this study is to assess environmental and economic impacts downstream. Two smaller hydroelectric dams located downstream of the Kerr Reservoir are the Gaston Dam, which has operated as a power station since 1963, and farther downstream the smaller Roanoke Rapids Dam, which has operated as a power station since 1955; both of these dams are regulated by the Dominion Power Company. The ecological effects of these dams were investigated by Richter et al. (1996) for which they developed a series of biologically relevant hydrologic attributes that characterize intra-annual variation in flow conditions and used the lower Roanoke River as a case study. Flood-control operations on the Roanoke River have had large hydrologic impacts, including the elimination of high-magnitude flooding and a greater frequency of both high and particularly low flow pulses; this impact has been implicated in various forms of ecosystem degradation (Richter et al., 1996).

Evidence of bank erosion along the lower Roanoke River is common where bank heights (above mean water levels) are substantial (>2 m), particularly along middle reaches between the Fall Line and the Albemarle Sound (Figs. 1A, 1B). Evidence may take the form of particle-by-particle erosion along straight banks and cutbanks, with concave-upward profiles often leaving overhanging (undercut rootwads) trees and shrubs on the top of the bank, or mass wasting through slab and rotational bank failures that may carry large amounts of soil and vegetation partly or completely down the bank slope (Hupp, 1999). The purposes of the present paper are, in general, to document, measure, and interpret bank erosion along the lower Roanoke River. Additional objectives include the quantitative description and interpretation of channel dynamics in relation to downstream trends in turbidity and floodplain trapping-storage of sediment. Specific research questions include: How do the current dam-flow releases affect bank-erosion patterns on the lower Roanoke River? Does sediment entrained from bank erosion affect downstream floodplain sediment deposition? Data used to complete these objectives and address these questions are derived, in part, from new specific analyses of bank erosion (the present study) and from previous studies by the U.S. Geological Survey (USGS) and others on floodplain sediment deposition.

Site Description

The lower Roanoke River is located on the northern Coastal Plain of North Carolina (southern part of the Mid-Atlantic Region), an area of broad, upland plains with low relief and broad, sometimes underfit bottomlands (Hupp, 2000). This region is characterized by humid temperate climatic conditions with a mean annual temperature of 15.8 °C and an average annual precipitation of 1267 mm as measured at Williamston, North Carolina, elev. 6.1 m (National Geodetic Vertical Datum [NGVD] 1929) above sea level (station 319440 Williamston 1E, 1971–2000 Climate Normals, State Climate Office of North Carolina). The average water discharge (1964–2007) is 228 m^3 per second (cms) as measured at Roanoke Rapids, North Carolina (USGS streamflow gauge 02080500) below the downstream-most dam; daily mean discharges range from 23 to 1008 cms over the period of record (43 yr). Prior to dam construction, annual peak flows regularly ranged from ~1400 cms to 2800 cms with extreme events >3400 cms (Fig. 2). Over the present gauging-station record (since 1964) the maximum peak flow was 1055 cms with normal peak-flow maxima ~980 cms. Conversely, low flows are sustained at higher discharges than before dam construction, annual flows rarely are <220 cms, and most peaks are held at ~560 cms (Fig. 2). Water-stage information is recorded at six streamflow gauges along the lower river from Roanoke Rapids (also the discharge-measurement station) near the dam, and in downstream order, at Halifax, Scotland Neck, Hamilton, Williamston, and Jamesville, North Carolina, nearest the Albemarle Sound (Figs. 1A, 1B).

The lower reach of the Roanoke River flows generally southeasterly from near the Fall Line to the Albemarle Sound as a largely single threaded, meandering stream (Fig. 1) across Miocene sedimentary material overlain by Quaternary alluvium (Brown et al., 1972). The material consists largely of unconsolidated fine sands, silt, and clay, although the clayey Miocene deposits may be indurated. Additionally, the floodplain along the lower river trapped a large volume of sediment associated with postcolonial agriculture

(Hupp, 1999). This legacy sediment may be between 4 and 6 m in depth along upstream reaches of the lower river (P. Townsend, 2006, written commun.), which thins downstream to near zero near the Albemarle Sound. The river is generally incised through the legacy sediment and other Coastal Plain sediments; although erosion on cutbanks and many straight reaches appears active, there is limited point-bar development. The floodplain along the lower river supports the largest contiguous Bottomland Hardwood Forest on the Atlantic Coastal Plain (Hupp, 2000).

METHODS

Techniques for monitoring bank erosion along the lower Roanoke River are described in detail in this section. However, this report uses some information gained from other, prior studies on floodplain deposition; pertinent techniques from these efforts are summarized here.

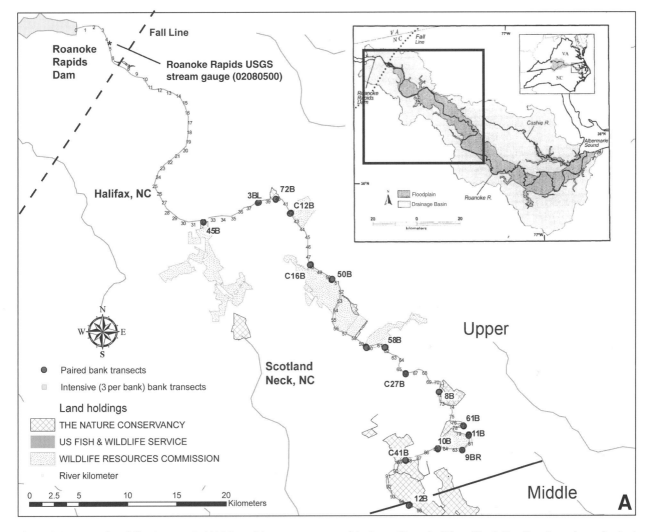

Figure 1 (*continued on following page*). (A) Map of the upstream part of the lower Roanoke River, North Carolina. Locations of paired transects, river kilometers below dam, and land holdings are indicated. Inset: maps of the entire lower Roanoke River reaches and the watershed in Virginia–North Carolina.

Transect Bank Erosion

Bank transects were established along a 153 km reach of the lower river, from upstream near the Fall Line to near the Albemarle Sound, where banks become <1 m high; ultimately the banks are nonexistent nearest the sound (Fig. 1). Site selection for transects was stratified to capture proportionate amounts of inside bends, outside bends, and straight reaches. Whenever possible, transects were located near existing floodplain sedimentation transects to facilitate interpretation of process linkage between bank erosion and downstream floodplain deposition. We (USGS in cooperation with the U.S. Fish and Wildlife Service, USFWS) instrumented 66 transects 32 of which are in pairs on opposite sides of the river. Further, 36 additional transects (in 6 pairs with triplicate transects), originally established by the USFWS, were incorporated into the present study for a total of 102 transects. These transects begin near the water surface (low-water stages) and extend 3–10 m past

the top of bank onto the generally flat natural levee surface, oriented normal to the channel. Transects vary in length according to bank height, angle, and profile. Each transect is referenced by the establishment of a steel spike driven into the base of a mature nearby tree, which also serves as a temporary vertical benchmark and monument for current and future studies; monuments were assigned an arbitrary elevation for relative measurements and later corrected to NGVD 1929 datum. Transect locations were recorded on maps documented using global positioning system (GPS) technology (horizontal accuracy ~3.5 m).

Erosion pins (~1 m long) were placed along transects (Fig. 3), beginning at or near the low-water surface and ending on the levee adjacent to the top of bank, during the fall of 2005. Pins were spaced to capture prominent breaks in the bank slope or erosion along long, straight bank sections. Long transects (>25 m, high banks) typically had 7–10 pins established, whereas short transects, a few meters, had at least three pins. The pins were driven into the soil normal to

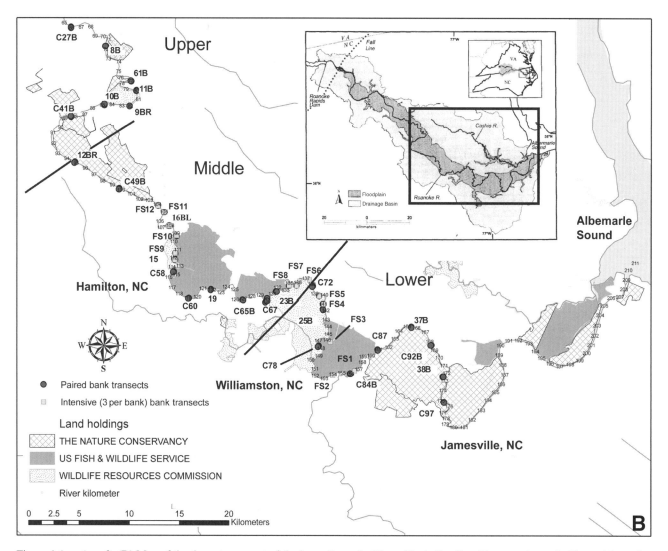

Figure 1 (*continued*). (B) Map of the downstream part of the lower Roanoke River, North Carolina. Features shown in Figure 1A are the same here, and the identification and delineation of upper, middle, and lower reaches/transects are shown.

the local bank slope, flush to the ground surface. In total, 706 pins were established for monitoring. The pins were revisited annually during the summers of 2006 and 2007; in selected cases, pins were revisited more frequently. During each visit the pins were measured for the amount of erosion (pin exposure) or amount of deposition (pin burial) that had taken place; buried pins were located using a metal detector. Measurements were taken along an axis normal to the local bank slope, parallel to the pin.

Each transect was differentially leveled in detail using a survey rod and optical level. Surveys were tied to the temporary benchmark, which had been assigned an arbitrary elevation. Every pin was specifically documented in the survey, and in addition to the temporary benchmark served to preserve horizontal stationing. All transects were leveled at the time of establishment (2005) and again during 2007 to document erosion-deposition over the intervening period. Erosion pins are highly accurate and allow for detailed measurement at specific locations. A comparison of differences between first and final surveys and mean pin measurements was used to infer erosion-deposition rates along the entire transect.

Paired transects, on opposite sides of the river, were tied to each other using bathymetric surveys (Fig. 3). Toe slopes were surveyed (from boat) using a tag line attached to the bank at the

water surface for horizontal station. A survey rod was used to determine elevation relative to the water surface (depth). This procedure was used for ~10 m of transect (cross section) length from the water's edge. The channel bed, along transect, was surveyed to capture the entire channel cross section between paired bank transects using a laser range finder for horizontal station and a narrow-beam depth finder to determine depth (elevation). Toe-slope and channel cross-section measurements were tied to the monumented bank surveys using a series of duplicate measurements, including rod and level, tag line and rod, and depth finder and range finder.

Channel Bathymetry, Turbidity, Mass Wasting

River surveys for channel bathymetry and bank-feature measurements were conducted as part of both the present study and the previous floodplain study. A series of observation points on the lower Roanoke River were established using GPS in 1998, mid-channel, from near the Fall Line downstream to and into the Albemarle Sound, covering a distance of ~200 river km (125 mi). Channel observation points are generally ~1.6 km (1 mi) apart. Depth, channel width, bank height, and bank angle were measured at each observation point using a laser range finder and a

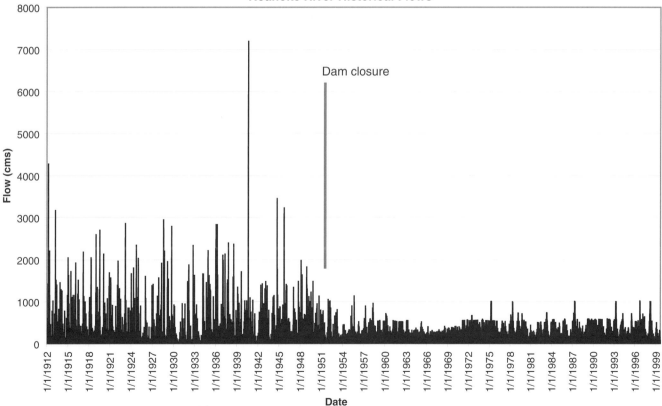

Figure 2. Daily flows in cubic meters per second (cms) (1912–1999) on the lower Roanoke River as measured at Roanoke Rapids, North Carolina, covering both pre- and post-dam operations. Date and effect of initial dam closure is shown.

sonic depth finder; a GPS unit was used to locate channel observation points. Each river survey was completed over a consecutive 2-day period. Water stage information was recorded for the observation period from the series of gauges on the lower river. Variation in water-surface elevation along the study reach was corrected by using the sum of the vertical distance from top of bank to mid-channel bed depth to estimate overall channel depth. The most recent survey was conducted in the summer of 2007. This survey also included measurements of turbidity, as determined from Secchi depth, and estimates of bank erosion using an index based on observation of bank erosion.

A Secchi disk is a simple device that is commonly used to quantitatively measure turbidity. It is a 20 cm (8 in.) disk with alternating black and white quadrants. It is lowered into the water until it can be no longer seen by the observer. The depth of disappearance is called the Secchi depth and may be affected by the color of the water, algae, and suspended sediments. Because the Roanoke River is a large alluvial (rather than blackwater) system with substantial velocity, even at low flow, an assumption was made that the preponderance of turbidity results from suspended sediment.

A bank-erosion index was developed to approximate the degree of primary mass wasting on both banks at the stations where bathymetric data were collected. The index ranges between zero and six, zero representing stable or depositional banks, and six representing active mass wasting on both banks. Field evaluations were performed independently by two USGS scientists, positioned in a boat mid-stream with at least 100 m of visible banks. The scientists agreed at more than 90% of the sites evaluated; this index is presented in Table 1.

Sediment Deposition on Floodplains

Floodplain deposition along the lower Roanoke River was intensively monitored between 2001 and 2004 as part of a larger multidisciplinary effort. The primary method for determining recent deposition rates and patterns was the installation of artificial markers. These markers (clay pads) are made by placing powderized white feldspar clay on the floodplain soil surface, which becomes a firm plastic layer that can be easily identified after coring the soil surface. These clay pads are revisited after inundation, and the depth of sedimentation above the marker surface is measured; deposition may be measured several times over clay pads. Details of the technique are provided in Kleiss (1996) and Hupp et al. (2008). Clay pads were positioned along the entire lower river in floodplain transects that extended, locally, from the levee surface near the bank well into the backswamp; transects ranged in length from a few hundred meters to >2 km. A total of 50 transects were established, comprising 335 pads; the number of pads per transect ranged from 2 to 13 with a mean of 7 pads per transect. Many of the bank transects in the present study are located at or near the natural levee terminus of the floodplain transects.

RESULTS AND DISCUSSION

The results and discussion presented in this section are preliminary, as this study is ongoing. These results cover a 2 yr period of bank-erosion monitoring. Nevertheless, the available point, transect, reach, and ancillary information allow worthwhile analyses. The scope of this paper is limited to bank erosion as determined by erosion pins monitored in transects, and channel morphology,

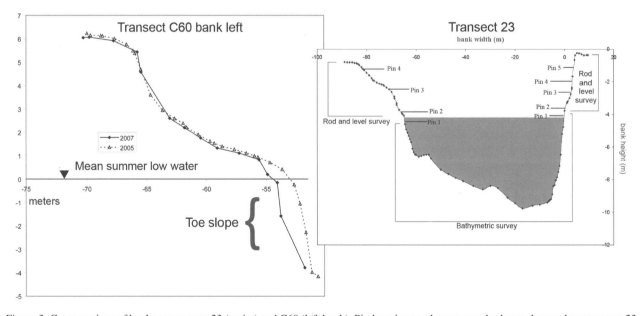

Figure 3. Cross sections of banks at transects 23 (entire) and C60 (left bank). Pin locations and survey methods are shown along transect 23; pins are driven into bank, flush to surface, typically at an oblique angle, normal to bank slope. Shaded part of cross section was surveyed below water surface using bathymetric techniques. Detail of differences in bank profile from 2005 to 2007 on C60 left bank; mean summer low-flow elevation is shown. Note that the >1 m difference between surveys is largely on the lowermost part of the bank and toe slope.

TABLE 1. BANK-EROSION INDEX, USED ON 2007 ROANOKE RIVER BATHYMETRIC RIVER SURVEY

Index	Description
0	No bank failure; banks are vegetated or composed of bedrock, and/or appear depositional.
1	Particle-by-particle erosion on one bank; evidence of erosion may include exposed tree roots, gully erosion, or unweathered soil surfaces. Erosion near the water surface caused by boat wakes is not included in the determination.
2	Particle-by-particle erosion on both banks.
3	Historical primary mass wasting (slump block includes top of bank; e.g., bank retreat) apparent on one bank, with weathered mass-wasting scars evident, extending to the top of bank. Slump blocks may contain vegetation exhibiting preferential growth (adapted to new aspect).
4	Historical primary mass wasting apparent on both banks.
5	Recent (<1 yr) primary mass wasting; vegetation within slump block is stressed or not exhibiting preferential growth, or slump scar appears fresh with an unweathered surface.
6	Recent primary mass wasting on both banks.

turbidity, and mass wasting measured from river bathymetric surveys. A preliminary bank-erosion–floodplain-deposition sediment budget (hereafter termed *sediment budget*) based on bank erosion and floodplain-sediment accretion (from a prior National Science Foundation [NSF] study) is also presented.

Bank Erosion

Net bank erosion (channel widening), by transect, was observed on 90 transects, while net deposition occurred on only 12 transects (Fig. 4). This erosion is greater than what would normally be expected on an equilibrated channel, and the literature is replete with examples of the destabilizing effects of dams on downstream reaches. In general, erosion rates increased from the upstream transects (mean 44 mm/yr) to those along the middle study reaches (mean 63 mm/yr), peaking in the vicinity of Hamilton (Fig. 1B), and then diminished (mean 24 mm/yr) toward the downstream transects (Table 2). Mean erosion by transect ranged from 520 mm/yr along a transect near Hamilton (Fig. 4) to nearly zero at many transects. To date, only one transect has captured a mass-wasting event; thus, these rates are conservative. Where there was net deposition, the transect was typically located on a point bar; the greatest mean deposition amount (99 mm/yr) occurred along the point bar directly opposite the cutbank with highest erosion (Fig. 4; near Hamilton). Bank-erosion rates were likely higher along upstream reaches (nearer the dam) immediately after dam closure. Total bank erosion tends to be greatest nearest the dam and attenuates downstream (Williams and Wolman, 1984). However, bank instability appears to migrate downstream (Fig. 4; Table 2), similar to upstream migrating instabilities associated with incised channels (Simon and Hupp, 1992). The upper bank slopes along the upper reaches of the study area are now relatively stable, but remnants of old slump failures are commonly visible. Bank-erosion rates on the Roanoke River (0.52 m/yr maximum) are similar to other published erosion rates (relatively rare in the literature) where human activities have affected natural channel processes. Madej et al. (1994) documented erosion rates of ~0.51 m/yr along a reach of the Merced River, California, that was

severely impacted by concentrated human recreational development including bank armoring. Maximum channel widening rates of 1.1 m/yr were documented below a dam on the Green River, Colorado (Merritt and Cooper, 2000). However, where mass wasting was explicitly included in channel-widening estimates, Simon and Hupp (1992) observed mean erosion rates from slightly above 0 m/yr on unaffected reaches to ~1.7 m/yr on actively eroding banks along West Tennessee streams following channelization. Simon and Rinaldi (2000) estimated mean maximum channel-widening rates of >2.1 m/yr along low-cohesion banks, affected by mass wasting in the loess area of the Midwestern United States. Other land uses such as mining may also stimulate channel widening; Kondolf et al. (2002) observed widening rates of 1.7 m/yr along a mine-affected stream in Idaho.

Variation in lower Roanoke River erosion rates occurs among straight and curved (inside and outside banks) reaches.

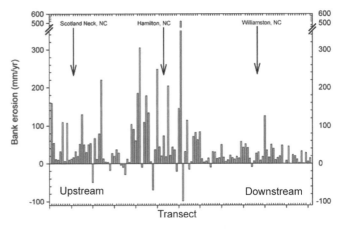

Figure 4. Mean bank-erosion rate on the lower Roanoke River from erosion-pin data from upstream (left) to downstream (right); left and right banks of each transect are shown separately. Observations-transects <0 are net depositional. Approximate locations of stream gauges near Scotland Neck, Hamilton, and Williamston, North Carolina, are shown.

TABLE 2. VARIATION BETWEEN UPPER AND LOWER BANK-EROSION RATES ALONG UPPER, MIDDLE, AND LOWER STUDY REACHES

River (km)	Mean bank-erosion rate (mm/yr)			Bank height (m)	Bank-erosion index	Mean channel width (m)
	Lower	Upper	Entire transect			
32–95	62.9	9.2	43.9	5.3	1	92.2
96–137	82.8	51.7	63.3	4.1	3	79.8
138–175	23.1	14.6	24.2	1.7	2	82.0

Note: Mean bank height, median bank-erosion index, and mean channel width for the three reaches are shown.

Mean erosion rates were greatest on the outside banks of curved reaches (~65 mm/yr), whereas straight and inside banks of curved reaches average ~40 mm/yr each. Considerable secondary bank failures of accreted material on inside bends (usually point bars) keep erosion rates relatively high. These rates do not reflect the impact associated with observed mass wasting. Simon and Hupp (1992) documented similar trends among reach types but with order-of-magnitude greater erosion rates when mass wasting was included.

Substantial variation in bank erosion may occur between upper and lower bank segments. Bank erosion, where divided into upper and lower parts (roughly half the pins in a given transect) of the bank, followed the same general trend of peaking in the middle reaches near Hamilton. Along all reaches, erosion tends to be greatest on the lower bank (Table 2). Further, erosion on the upper banks along the upper reaches is an order of magnitude less than that of the lower banks (Table 2), suggesting, again, that the highest erosion rates have migrated downstream from the upper reaches and now occur along the middle reaches. A subset of transect sites evaluated by the USFWS (FS transects, n = 10, FS 5 and 7 not included, Fig. 1B) was composed of three parallel transects spaced by 25 m and located so that the actively eroding middle reaches and part of the adjacent lower reaches were sampled. Along the unstable, actively eroding reach, the lower banks erode more rapidly than upper banks, whereas along the lower reaches this trend is reversed, albeit less pronounced (Fig. 5). Transect erosion-rate variation (at these intensely monitored sites, FS transects) is distinctly higher on the unstable middle reach than at sites on the lower, more stable reach (Fig. 5). This is perhaps expected, given the vagaries of thalweg impingement and the tendency for secondary bank failures to occur. Secondary bank failure is the collapse of previously failed material from high on the bank slope, which temporarily accumulates low on the bank slope (Simon and Hupp, 1992). Overall bank stability is strongly controlled by low bank erosion, including the toe slope, which is typically under water (Thorne and Abt, 1993; Simon et al., 2000); severely eroded toe slopes often lead to bank failure through mass wasting (Simon and Hupp, 1992). Pronounced erosion on the toe of banks occurs along the lower Roanoke River, documented partially in the pin measurements presented above and in rod and level surveys. An example of the predominant lower-bank and toe erosion is illustrated in Figure 3. Thus, the widespread observation of mass wasting in the form of slump blocks (yet to be significantly documented in erosion-pin transects) is expected particularly along the active middle study reaches (Figs. 4, 5).

Flow Duration, Mass Wasting, and Turbidity

It may be intuitively obvious that the elevation of flow and the duration of flow at various elevations are prime factors that affect most forms of bank erosion. Yet the development of quantitative causative linkage is difficult and not well documented, partly because the analytical and monitoring constraints during flow events are not normally conducive to real-time measurement (Simon et al., 2000). The stage-only gauge near Hamilton is located centrally in the middle study reaches where bank erosion is presently most active (Fig. 1B). The stage (elevation) and flow-duration relation, as measured by percentage of exceedance (percentage of time flow is at or above a specific elevation), is shown in Figure 6. The percentage of exceedance on most non-regulated streams for mid-bank elevations is in the range of 10%–20% (Osterkamp and Hedman, 1982). However, dam-regulated streams typically maintain abnormally high mid- and low-flow conditions (Williams and Wolman, 1984; Richter et al., 1996). Mid-bank locations along the Roanoke River in the vicinity of Hamilton (Fig. 1) have nearly 50% flow durations (Fig. 6), which are about double that which would be expected along nonregulated streams. Bank elevations distinctly above the low-flow elevation may be inundated 70% of the time or greater. Consistently

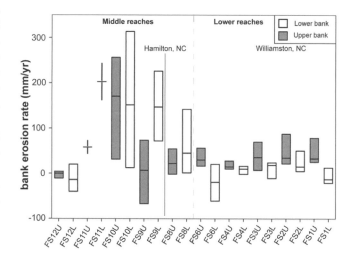

Figure 5. Mean bank erosion rate and variation at selected (triplicate) transect locations along middle and lower reaches of the lower Roanoke River. Location of separation between middle and lower reaches is shown in Figure 1B.

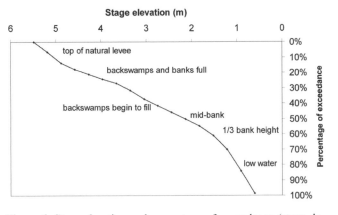

Figure 6. Stage elevation and percentage of exceedance (stage duration) for reaches near the Hamilton, North Carolina, stream-stage gauge (all data from post-dam period). Percentage of exceedance is the amount of time annually that water-surface elevation is at or above a specific location (elevation) on bank.

high low-flow elevations with associated long flow durations are cited as major contributors to channel widening through bank erosion on dam-regulated rivers (Williams and Wolman, 1984; Bravard et al., 1997; Friedman et al., 1998; Brandt, 2000).

Mass wasting, as measured by our bank-erosion index (Table 1), increased from the upper reaches to the middle reaches, where it peaked at 3 (Table 2) and decreased downstream to the lower reaches. Index values were estimated during the 2007 river survey, and when averaged over 8 km (approximate) river segments from ~30 to 175 km below the dam they also show the distinct trend of peaking along the middle reaches (Fig. 7). This trend is generally mirrored by mean transect-pin data plotted at

actual transect locations (Fig. 7). Both the bank-erosion index and pin data indicate a relatively stable reach in the vicinity of ~90 km below the dam (Fig. 7), which coincides with a reach where the channel is atypically incised into the indurated Miocene substrata. Median maximum bank-erosion-index values range between 4 and 5 (Fig. 7) over about a 24 km reach beginning just below Hamilton (river km 115, Fig. 1B), indicating that evidence of bank failure occurs along both banks and that many locations have recent (<1-yr-old) slumps. The channel-widening response to dams (Williams and Wolman, 1984) or stream channelization (Simon and Hupp, 1992) is accomplished most effectively through mass wasting. This instability migrates and attenuates, in the case of dam construction, downstream (Williams and Wolman, 1984), which from our data appears to be the case on the lower Roanoke River. Channel-width measurements, taken during river surveys, demonstrate that channel width decreases from upstream (near the dam) to the relatively narrow middle reaches and then increases toward the Albemarle Sound (Table 2). The increase in width near tidal water is typical for Coastal Plain streams (Hupp, 2000; Kroes et al., 2007). However, the downstream decrease in width, observed in the upper reaches of the lower Roanoke River, may be anomalous for alluvial systems. This trend in channel width supports the idea that channel widening was most active along the upper reaches fairly soon after dam closure and has since moved downstream, leaving a widened channel and high but relatively stable banks behind. Mass wasting eventually reduces bank angles so that relative stability may be attained (Simon and Hupp, 1992).

Turbidity, as measured by Secchi depths taken during the 2007 river survey, increased (low Secchi depth) from near the dam toward the actively eroding middle reaches (Fig. 7). Turbidity

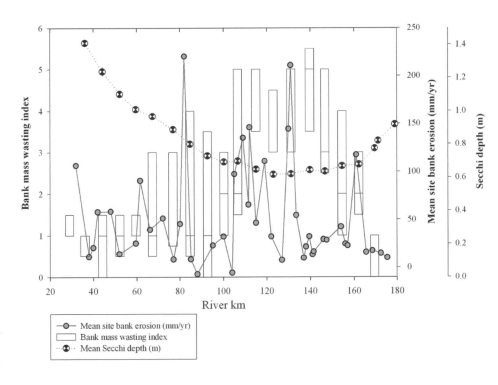

Figure 7. Trends in mean bank erosion, bank-erosion index, and turbidity (Secchi depth) from upstream to downstream by river kilometer. Mean bank erosion is obtained directly from transect-pin data; bank-erosion index and turbidity are averages over sequential river segments, ~8 km each.

decreased slightly in the lowest reaches near brackish tidal water (Fig. 7), as is typical along Coastal Plain rivers (Hupp, 2000). This trend in Secchi depth is expectedly and clearly inversely related to both bank erosion (pin measurements) and mass wasting (Fig. 7). The water released from high dams is notoriously clear; suspended sediment is normally low or nonexistent, as the reservoir is typically an effective sediment trap (Williams and Wolman, 1984). Thus, suspended sediment in the Roanoke River downstream of the dams must come from tributaries or from erosion and entrainment of bed and bank sediments. There are no substantial tributaries entering the Roanoke River between the dam and our downstream-most bank-erosion sites. It is reasonable to assume that a direct relation exists between turbidity and channel erosion (Fig. 7), most of which may be derived from the banks as noted in similar situations by Simon and Hupp (1992). Additionally, variation in flow velocity associated with power generation (peaking) may facilitate bank erosion, especially particle-by-particle entrainment, which also may lead to bank-toe removal and subsequent bank failure.

The early results of this study offer an example of channel widening that occurs in response to upstream dams. This response is different from the response demonstrated along several streams in the western United States where substantial channel narrowing has occurred (Allred and Schmidt, 1999; Grant et al., 2003). The Coastal Plain geologic setting may in large part explain these divergent results. The highly erodible beds and banks of these almost completely alluvial systems allow for rapid erosion following dam completion (Williams and Wolman, 1984; Ligon et al., 1995). The channel incision associated with this erosion increases effective bank heights, which lead to bank failure and ultimately channel widening (Simon and Hupp, 1992; Simon et al., 2000).

Sediment Budget

A sediment budget was estimated for the lower river by separating the study site into four 50-km-long river segments beginning just below the dam and continuing downstream. Bank-erosion rates were converted to volumes by assigning each transect a width of 1 m and multiplying the bank height by the erosion rate; 9, 22, 17, and 11 bank transects were used in each segment, respectively, downstream. Bank heights decrease from nearly 7 m near the upstream transects to <1 m in the vicinity of the downstream-most transects. Thus, the effective volume of eroded material decreases from upstream to downstream for any given erosion rate.

The floodplain-deposition volume (based on clay pads in transects and floodplain length from the NSF study) and bank-erosion approximations were made for each segment using mean clay-pad and erosion-pin rate data (Fig. 8); 8, 10, 17, and 13 floodplain transects were used in each segment, respectively, downstream. Floodplain areas were determined using USGS topographic maps (contour interval, 1.53 m, 5 ft), whereas bank heights were directly surveyed at transect sites. The conversion from erosion-deposition rates to volumes (m³/yr) more clearly illustrates the inverse downstream relation between bank erosion and, particularly, floodplain deposition (Fig. 8) and provides for a more realistic framework for establishing a sediment budget. From the forgoing discussions, it is assumed that upstream bank erosion on the mainstem largely provides the material for downstream floodplain deposition.

The sediment budget was developed using the mean bank-erosion and floodplain-deposition volumes (Fig. 8) and multiplied by the 50 km segment length. The organic proportion of deposited sediment was calculated using loss on ignition (LOI) methods on 72 samples collected in 2002. The organic portion of the deposition estimate (16.5%) was subtracted to allow the comparison between mineral soil loss on the bank and mineral soil accumulation on the floodplain; most bank material was derived from massive postcolonial deposition and presently contains little to no organic material (P. Townsend, 2007, written commun.). The lower Roanoke River system is net depositional. Deposition exceeds erosion increasingly from near the dam toward the Albemarle Sound (Fig. 9). The sediment budget predicts a surplus of 2,800,000 m³/yr, assuming that (1) measured floodplain-sedimentation rates can be applied equally across broad bottomlands, (2) sediment transport from upstream of the dam is negligible, and (3) bank pins and floodplain clay pads reflect all of the erosion and deposition within the system. The sediment surplus may be partly explained by the numerous mass-wasting events that have not been sufficiently documented by the bank-erosion pins. Some of this sediment may be transported out of the system, but many studies (e.g., Meade, 1982) have shown that as much 90% of suspended sediment is trapped within the system.

Only one transect of 106 in 2 yr of monitoring captured a primary mass-wasting event (T23BR), although many events were observed outside of our transects. A visual survey of mass-wasting events at 1.6 km intervals found 19 recent mass-wasting events, two each in river segments two and four (51–100 and 151–200 river km, respectively) and 15 in river segment three (101–150 km, the active middle reach). Mass wasting appears to play a substantial role in bank erosion along this regulated river, may account for the large floodplain-deposition volumes downstream, and should be taken into account for realistic sediment budget computation.

CONCLUSIONS

The lower Roanoke River has undergone dramatic alterations in hydrologic conditions since dam completion. The highly regulated dam-release patterns concentrate flow on middle and lower bank surfaces and facilitate bank erosion. Bank erosion along the lower Roanoke River is apparent in both particle-by-particle removal and mass wasting along most reaches, including cutbanks and straight and inside bend reaches, where 77% of transects (90) underwent erosion. Bank-erosion rates increased from the upstream transects to those along the middle study reaches and then diminished toward the downstream transects. Mean erosion by transect ranged from near zero to 520 mm/yr in the middle reaches. Both erosion by largely particle-by-particle removal and mass wasting presently peak in the middle reaches (95–137 river km below the dam). This middle part of the study area also demonstrates higher

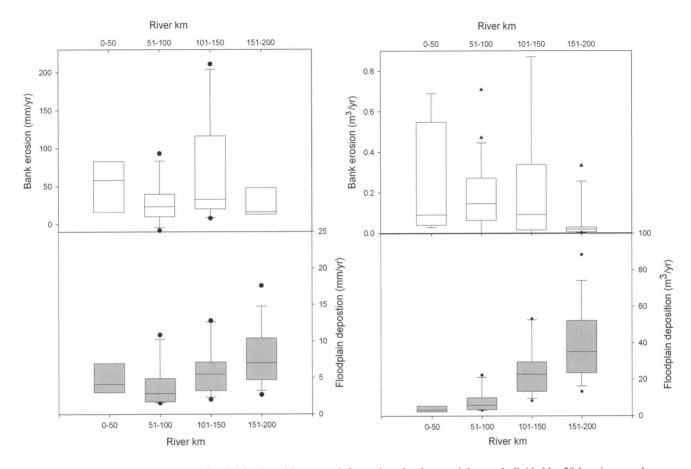

Figure 8. Trends in bank-erosion and floodplain-deposition rates, left panel, and volumes, right panel, divided by 50-km river-reach segments from upstream to downstream. Note the inverse relation between bank erosion and floodplain deposition, particularly as revealed in volume estimates.

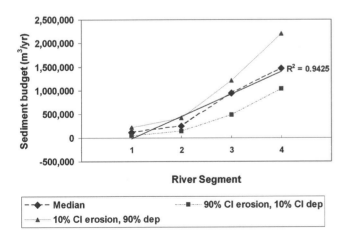

Figure 9. Bank-erosion–floodplain-deposition sediment budget by sequential 50-km river-reach segments, upstream to downstream (see Fig. 8), including calculations based on the erosion and deposition volumes of 10% and 90% confidence intervals (CI); dep—deposition.

flow elevations and durations for low-flow conditions than most nonregulated streams. Accordingly, bank erosion along the entire study reach is greatest on the lower half of the bank slopes, which is conducive to bank toe removal and, thus, bank failure. Rotational failures are common and indicative of deep-seated bank instability. These hydrologic conditions may, in part, affect the actively eroding nature of the middle reach. The upper reach has a wider channel (not the typical trend on alluvial rivers) and higher banks than downstream. The upper reach presumably began eroding soon after dam completion, and presently the impetus for erosion has lessened locally and migrated downstream to the middle reaches; old though relatively stable remnants of slump blocks are still evident on upper-reach banks.

Water released from high dams is typically nearly devoid of suspended sediment. This sediment-"starved" nature of dam releases is conducive to entrainment of sediment from channel beds and banks. The mid-channel water in the lower Roanoke River increases in turbidity from near the dam toward the Albemarle Sound downstream; no significant tributaries join the river along the study reach. Thus, this suspended sediment must come from the channel bed and banks; previous studies and our results indicate that bank erosion may provide the greatest share of the suspended-sediment load on the lower Roanoke River. The estimated sediment budget for the lower Roanoke River is net depositional (floodplain) with a surplus of ~2,800,000 m³/yr. Much of this surplus may be explained by the amount of sediment contributed by mass wasting on the banks, which, to date, is substantially under represented in the present transect monitoring effort. This suggests that mass wasting may play an important role here and elsewhere in sediment budgets below dams.

ACKNOWLEDGMENTS

The authors are grateful for the field and laboratory assistance provided by numerous individuals, including P. Mike Shackleford, Cody Hoehna, Russel Gray, and Katie Brutche. We especially appreciate the help of Dan Kroes, who was instrumental in the design and installation of the bank transects. This study was funded, in part, by the U.S. Army Corps of Engineers (USACE), the U.S. Fish and Wildlife Service (USFWS), and previous studies by the USGS and the Universities of North Carolina and Wisconsin, which were funded, in part, by the National Science Foundation (NSF) and The Nature Conservancy (TNC) on floodplain-sediment trapping, and also sediment-transport studies conducted by the USGS North Carolina Water Science Center. The manuscript benefited from critical reviews by Kyle Juracek, Phil Turnipseed, and two anonymous reviewers; their efforts are greatly appreciated.

REFERENCES CITED

Allred, T.M., and Schmidt, J.C., 1999, Channel narrowing by vertical accretion along the Green River, Utah: Geological Society of America Bulletin, v. 111, p. 1757–1772, doi: 10.1130/0016-7606(1999)111<1757:CNBVAA>2.3.CO;2.
Brandt, S.A., 2000, Classification of geomorphological effects downstream of dams: CATENA, v. 40, p. 375–401, doi: 10.1016/S0341-8162(00)00093-X.
Bravard, J.-P., Amoros, C., Pautou, G., Bornette, G., Bournaud, M., Creuze Des Chatelliers, M., Gibert, J., Piery, J.-L., Perrin, J.-F., and Tachet, H., 1997, River incision in south-east France: Morphological phenomena and ecological effects: Regulated Rivers: Research and Management, v. 13, p. 75–90, doi: 10.1002/(SICI)1099-1646(199701)13:1<75::AID-RRR444>3.0.CO;2-6.
Brown, P.M., Miller, J.A., and Swain, F.M., 1972, Structural and Stratigraphic Framework, and Spatial Distribution of Permeability of the Atlantic Coastal Plain, North Carolina to New York: U.S. Geological Survey Professional Paper 796, 79 p.
Church, M., 1995, Geomorphic response to river flow regulation: Case studies and time-scale: Regulated Rivers: Research and Management, v. 11, p. 3–22, doi: 10.1002/rrr.3450110103.
Friedman, J.M., Osterkamp, W.R., Scott, M.L., and Auble, G.T., 1998, Downstream effects of dams on channel geometry and bottomland vegetation: Regional patterns in the Great Plains: Wetlands, v. 18, p. 619–633.
Grant, G.E., Schmidt, J.C., and Lewis, S.L., 2003, A geological framework for interpreting downstream effects of dams on rivers, *in* O'Connor, J.E., and Grant, G.E., eds., A Peculiar River: American Geophysical Union, Water Science and Application 7, p. 209–225.
Hupp, C.R., 1999, Relations among riparian vegetation, channel incision processes and forms, and large woody debris, *in* Darby, S.E., and Simon, A., eds., Incised River Channels: Chichester, UK, Wiley & Sons, p. 219–245.
Hupp, C.R., 2000, Hydrology, geomorphology, and vegetation of Coastal Plain rivers in the southeastern United States: Hydrological Processes, v. 14,

p. 2991–3010, doi: 10.1002/1099-1085(200011/12)14:16/17<2991::AID-HYP131>3.0.CO;2-H.
Hupp, C.R., Demas, C.R., Kroes, D.E., Day, R.H., and Doyle, T.W., 2008, Recent sedimentation patterns within the central Atchafalaya Basin: Wetlands, v. 28, p. 125–140, doi: 10.1672/06-132.1.
Kleiss, B.A., 1996, Sediment retention in a bottomland hardwood wetland in eastern Arkansas: Wetlands, v. 16, p. 321–333.
Kondolf, G.M., Piegay, H., and Landon, N., 2002, Channel response to increased and decreased bedload supply from land use change: Contrasts between two catchments: Geomorphology, v. 45, p. 35–51.
Kroes, D.E., Hupp, C.R., and Noe, G.B., 2007, Sediment, nutrient, and vegetation trends along the tidal forested Pocomoke River, Maryland, *in* Conner, W.H., Doyle, T.W., and Krauss, K.W., eds., Ecology of Tidal Freshwater Forested Wetlands of the Southeastern United States: Netherlands, Springer, p. 113–137.
Lawson, J.M., 1925, Effect of Rio Grande storage on river erosion and deposition: Engineering News-Record, v. 95, p. 372–374.
Ligon, F.K., Dietrich, W.E., and Trush, W.J., 1995, Downstream ecological effects of dams: Bioscience, v. 45, p. 183–192, doi: 10.2307/1312557.
Madej, M.A., Weaver, W.E., and Hagans, D.K., 1994, Analysis of bank erosion on the Merced River, Yosemite Valley, Yosemite National Park, California, USA: Environmental Management, v. 18, p. 235–250, doi: 10.1007/BF02393764.
Meade, R.H., 1982, Sources, sinks, and storage of river sediments in the Atlantic drainage of the United States: Journal of Geology, v. 90, p. 235–252.
Merritt, D.M., and Cooper, D.J., 2000, Riparian vegetation and channel change in response to river regulation: A comparative study of regulated and unregulated streams in the Green River Basin, USA: Regulated Rivers: Research and Management, v. 16, p. 543–564, doi: 10.1002/1099-1646(200011/12)16:6<543::AID-RRR590>3.0.CO;2-N.
Nilsson, C., Reidy, C.A., Dynesius, M., and Revenga, C., 2005, Fragmentation and flow regulation of the world's large river systems: Science, v. 308, p. 405–408, doi: 10.1126/science.1107887.
Osterkamp, W.R., and Hedman, E.R., 1982, Perennial-Streamflow Characteristics Related to Channel Geometry and Sediment in the Missouri River Basin: U.S. Geological Survey Professional Paper 1242, 37 p.
Petts, G.E., 1979, Complex response of river channel morphology subsequent to reservoir construction: Progress in Physical Geography, v. 3, p. 329–362, doi: 10.1177/030913337900300302.
Petts, G.E., and Gurnell, A.M., 2005, Dams and geomorphology: Research progress and future directions: Geomorphology, v. 71, p. 27–47, doi: 10.1016/j.geomorph.2004.02.015.
Poff, N.L., Allan, J.D., Bain, M.B., Karr, J.R., Prestegaard, K.L., Richter, B.D., Sparks, R.E., and Stromberg, J.C., 1997, The natural flow regime: Bioscience, v. 47, p. 769–784, doi: 10.2307/1313099.
Richter, B.D., Baumgartner, J.V., Powell, J., and Braun, D.P., 1996, A method for assessing hydrologic alteration within ecosystems: Conservation Biology, v. 10, p. 1163–1174, doi: 10.1046/j.1523-1739.1996.10041163.x.
Schmidt, J.C., and Wilcock, P.R., 2008, Metrics for assessing the downstream effects of dams: Water Resources Research, v. 44, W04404, 19 p.
Simon, A., and Hupp, C.R., 1992, Geomorphic and Vegetative Recovery Processes along Modified Stream Channels of West Tennessee: U.S. Geological Survey Open-File Report 91-502, 142 p.
Simon, A., and Rinaldi, M., 2000, Channel instability in the loess area of the Midwestern United States: Journal of the American Water Resources Association, v. 36, p. 133–150, doi: 10.1111/j.1752-1688.2000.tb04255.x.
Simon, A., Curini, A., Darby, S.E., and Langendoen, E.J., 2000, Bank and near-bank processes in an incised channel: Geomorphology, v. 35, p. 193–217.
Thorne, C.R., and Abt, S.R., 1993, Analysis of riverbank instability due to toe scour and lateral erosion: Earth Surface Processes and Landforms, v. 18, p. 835–844, doi: 10.1002/esp.3290180908.
Williams, G.P., and Wolman, M.G., 1984, Downstream Effects of Dams on Alluvial Rivers: U.S. Geological Survey Professional Paper 1286, 83 p.

MANUSCRIPT ACCEPTED BY THE SOCIETY 15 SEPTEMBER 2008

The Geological Society of America
Special Paper 451
2009

Planform change and stream power in the Kishwaukee River watershed, Illinois: Geomorphic assessment for environmental management

İnci Güneralp*

Department of Geography, Texas A&M University, College Station, Texas 77843-3148, USA

Bruce L. Rhoads*

Department of Geography, University of Illinois, Urbana, Illinois 61801, USA

ABSTRACT

Effective watershed-scale environmental management and restoration require a sound understanding of the dynamics of fluvial systems at the watershed-scale and the impact of humans on these dynamics. In Illinois, concern has arisen about the need to implement bank stabilization along meandering rivers, where bank erosion associated with lateral migration is often viewed as a sign of channel instability. Also, many rivers in the state are low-energy fluvial systems that exhibit limited responses to direct human modification such as channel straightening. From an ecological perspective, the lack of response is problematic owing to its potential long-term alteration of aquatic habitat.

This study examines the spatial relationship between the planform dynamics of meandering rivers and stream power in the Kishwaukee River watershed in northern Illinois. The spatial extent of planform change at the scale of drainage network is quantified and related to spatial variations in the magnitude of stream power throughout the watershed. Historical channel change was determined using GIS-based analysis of aerial photography of several reaches scattered throughout the watershed. The results show that the amount of lateral migration per reach is greatest where stream power is highest, but that planform response to channelization is limited regardless of the magnitude of stream power. The findings from this historical analysis of channel change are useful for understanding both the fluvial dynamics of unmodified meandering rivers and the influence of human modification on these dynamics—knowledge that can help guide environmental decision making about the need to implement channel stabilization or restoration measures.

*E-mails: Güneralp: guneralp@geog.tamu.edu; Rhoads: brhoads@illinois.edu.

Güneralp, İ., and Rhoads, B.L., 2009, Planform change and stream power in the Kishwaukee River watershed, Illinois: Geomorphic assessment for environmental management, *in* James, L.A., Rathburn, S.L., and Whittecar, G.R., eds., Management and Restoration of Fluvial Systems with Broad Historical Changes and Human Impacts: Geological Society of America Special Paper 451, p. 109–118, doi: 10.1130/2009.2451(07). For permission to copy, contact editing@geosociety .org. ©2009 The Geological Society of America. All rights reserved.

INTRODUCTION

Effective environmental management can be defined as the management of human activities to protect, restore, or naturalize land, water, and associated ecological resources, while recognizing the need to accommodate economic growth and development. Effective environmental management of watersheds is a central concern of federal, state, and local agencies throughout the United States. An important aspect of effective management is the need to develop methods for evaluating the dynamics of environmental systems and the impact of humans on these dynamics.

In the state of Illinois, concern about effective watershed management has led to multiagency management initiatives involving collaborations between the Illinois Department of Natural Resources, the U.S. Army Corps of Engineers, and local community-based watershed groups. A common concern of these management agencies is stream-channel instability and its effect on sediment loads, water quality, and aquatic habitat. This concern raises the issue of what constitutes an unstable stream. From a geomorphological perspective, an unstable stream is one that exhibits abrupt, episodic, or progressive changes in location, geometry, gradient, or pattern owing to natural or human-induced changes that occur over a period of years or decades and that reflect local and catchment imbalances between the sediment inputs and outputs or the proximity of the system to a geomorphic threshold (Rhoads, 1995). However, bank erosion along meandering streams often is perceived as a sign of channel instability even when the erosion is associated with the natural fluvial process of lateral migration. To address this perceived problem, it is necessary to examine the dynamics of river channels in the context of historical analysis of channel change that considers spatial and temporal variability in the natural processes underlying system dynamics. Assessments of instability should consider how channel change is related to spatial variations in controlling factors, such as stream power. River dynamics may indeed simply be a function of spatial variation in erosional and depositional processes rather than human-induced changes in these processes.

In Illinois, many rivers have low values of stream power. In contrast to high-energy fluvial systems, where direct human modification results in channel instability (Brookes, 1988; Simon, 1989), the response of low-energy rivers in Illinois to human modifications is highly constrained (Rhoads and Urban, 1997; Urban and Rhoads, 2003). From an ecological perspective, the lack of response to the human-induced modifications is problematic because of its potential impact on aquatic habitat (Brookes, 1988; Frothingam et al., 2001, 2002; Rhoads et al., 2003). In fact, human-induced modification of the low-energy streams imposed by channelization may create more serious long-term threats to aquatic ecosystems than channelization of high-energy streams, because substantial recovery is unlikely to occur in low-energy streams over time-scales of human concern (Rhoads and Urban, 1997; Urban and Rhoads, 2003; Frothingam et al., 2001, 2002; Rhoads et al., 2003).

The magnitude of the stream power and its distribution within a watershed affect the dynamics of meandering rivers.

Past work has suggested a correlation between lateral migration rates and stream power (Hickin and Nanson, 1984; Nanson and Hickin, 1986). Moreover, in the case of artificially straightened lowland meander rivers, Brookes (1987, 1988, 1992) found that those with values of stream power per unit area for a bankfull discharge >35 W/m^2 exhibit short-term recovery of meandering characteristics, whereas those below this threshold value of stream power do not. These results provide some guidance in deciding whether a human-modified meandering river has the power to recover its original planform over the time scale of river management or whether some form of human intervention is necessary to restore morphology (Brookes, 1995). The connection between stream power and river dynamics suggests that evaluations of watershed-scale spatial variations in historical channel change and stream power are valuable for determining both the fluvial dynamics of unmodified rivers and the influence of human modification on these dynamics. Such information can usefully inform decision making about the need to implement channel stabilization or restoration measures.

The main goal of this paper is to explore the spatial relation between river planform dynamics and stream power in the Kishwaukee River watershed in northeastern Illinois. For this purpose, we quantify the spatial extent of planform change at the scale of drainage network, and then examine the relation of planform change to the magnitude and distribution of stream power throughout the watershed. The findings of the study provide insight into the fluvial dynamics of meandering rivers in the watershed, into the geomorphological consequences of human modifications induced by channelization, and into the implications of channel change for aquatic habitat—types of information that are important for environmental management of the watershed.

PHYSICAL SETTING

The Kishwaukee River watershed covers ~3,237 km^2 in northeastern Illinois, extending slightly into Wisconsin at its northern tip (Fig. 1). Major tributaries of the Kishwaukee River include Piscasaw Creek, Rush Creek, Beaver Creek, Killbuck Creek, the North Branch Kishwaukee, the South Branch, and the East South Branch (Fig. 1). Land cover in the watershed is much different than it was prior to settlement by European immigrants. Forests, wetlands, and prairies have been replaced by drained agricultural lands and scattered urban areas. Native vegetation in the watershed consisted mainly of prairie (26%) and forest (74%). Today, only 0.01% of high quality prairie and 5.1% of forest remain in the Kishwaukee River watershed. Agriculture is the dominant land use, with 63.5% of the watershed devoted to cropland and nearly 25% to pasture (grassland) (IDNR, 1998). Several low-head dams have been built on rivers and streams. The entire watershed lies within the region of Illinois influenced by Wisconsinan glaciation and is underlain by unconsolidated deposits of clay, sand, and silt associated with end moraines, ground moraine, lake beds, and glacial outwash. All of these deposits are overlain by 0.50–1.5 m of loess (Fehrenbacher et al., 1986). Valley bottoms and floodplains consist of alluvium (Cahokia alluvium) derived from reworking of glacial and eolian materials (Lineback, 1979). Although streams in the watershed are less channelized than those in some parts of Illinois, nearly 18% of the total length of the river network has been channelized, with the extent of channelization most prevalent in headwater portions of the network (Fig. 2).

The Kishwaukee River watershed is rated biologically as one of the three highest quality river systems in Illinois. Over 100 km of the streams in the Kishwaukee River watershed have been denoted by the Illinois Environmental Protection Agency as biologically significant. This evaluation is based on fish, aquatic macroinvertebrates, and mussel population data, biodiversity, and presence of listed species; the watershed as a whole has one of the highest Index of Biotic Integrity (IBI) values in northern Illinois (IEPA, 1988). The environmental quality of streams is threatened by the extent of human activity—a situation that has led to efforts to protect and manage environmental resources in the watershed.

METHODOLOGY

Assessment of Historical Channel Change Using GIS-Based Aerial Photography Analysis

Study Reach Selection

The river dynamics assessment of the Kishwaukee River watershed was performed using geographic information systems (GIS)–based historical aerial-photography analysis of the channel planform changes. A set of representative study reaches between 5 and 10 km in length was selected to characterize the fluvial system at the scale of drainage network. During the selection, considerable attention was given to the even distribution of the study reaches within the watershed. Other selection criteria included the location in the watershed (stream order and type), presence-absence of channelization, soil erodibility, and, the availability of historical aerial photography. Based on these criteria, seven reaches were selected for analysis of channel change (Tables 1, 2; Fig. 2). Five of the reaches represent relatively unmodified channels (reaches 1–5 and reach 6); however, reaches 1 and 4 include short sections that were channelized during the study period (Table 1). The reach in reach 7, which was completely channelized in the earliest photo, was selected as a representative reach for completely channelized reaches.

The dominant geologic parent material in the reaches is alluvium. Detailed geological mapping of the watershed at a scale sufficient to identify geological materials along each reach is not available. A map of surficial deposits of Illinois indicates that reaches 1–3 are entirely in Cahokia alluvium and that the other reaches traverse alluvium or small areas of loamy till, outwash sand and gravel, or lacustrine silt and clay (Lineback, 1979). However, the scale of this map is rather coarse (1:500,000), and aerial photographs indicate that all of the reaches are situated on

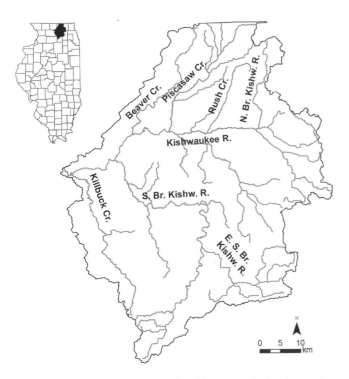

Figure 1. Location of the Kishwaukee River watershed and its main-channel streams (42° 09′ 36″ N, 88° 43′ 05″ W).

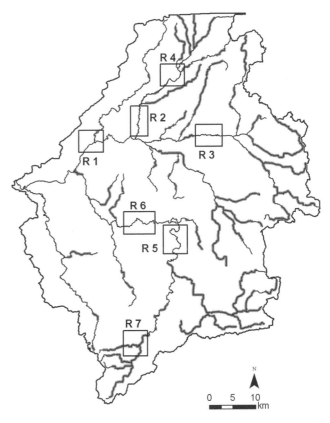

Figure 2. Extent of channelized streams (bold lines) and the study reaches (Rs) in the Kishwaukee River watershed.

TABLE 1. SUMMARY OF THE STUDY REACHES FOR THE ANALYSIS
OF SPATIAL EXTENT OF CHANNEL CHANGE

Reach	Branch	Meandering or channelized	Stream order	Approximate length (km)	Land cover
Reach 1	Beaver Creek	M & C	3–4	7	Forested & woodland
Reach 2	Piscasaw Creek	M	3	6	Woodland & marsh
Reach 3	Main branch	M	3	9	Forested
Reach 4	Piscasaw Creek	M & C	2	7	Cropland & woodland
Reach 5	South Branch	M	2	10	Cropland & woodland
Reach 6	South Branch	M	3	10	Cropland & woodland
Reach 7	South Branch	C	1–2	10	Cropland

TABLE 2. AERIAL PHOTO YEARS AVAILABLE FOR THE STUDY REACHES

Reach	Years
Reach 1	1941, 1954, 1988, 1998
Reach 2	1941, 1961, 1988, 1998
Reach 3	1939, 1961, 1967, 1988, 1998
Reach 4	1941, 1967, 1998
Reach 5	1939, 1954, 1964, 1970, 1979, 1998
Reach 6	1939, 1954, 1958, 1964, 1970, 1979, 1988, 1998
Reach 7	1939, 1954, 1964, 1970, 1979, 1988, 1998

modern floodplains composed of alluvium. Land use upstream from the reaches is dominated by agriculture, but riparian conditions vary somewhat and include forest, cropland, marsh, and woodland (Table 1).

Historical Analysis of Channel Change

Historical air photographs have been recognized as the best information source for detailed analysis of planform change, as the information available from aerial photography exceeds that available from topographic and other maps (Gurnell et al., 1994; Mossa and McLean, 1997; Rhoads and Urban, 1997; Leys and Werritty, 1999; Micheli and Kirchner, 2002; Urban and Rhoads, 2003). In addition, the frequency of repeat photography of a given area is generally higher than the production frequency of topographic maps (Wolf and DeWitt, 2000). For these reasons, this study made use of historical aerial photography as its main source of channel planform data. Aerial photography of the study reaches was obtained from the University of Illinois Map and Geography Library collection and the Illinois State Geological Survey (ISGS). Aerial-photography data on the planforms of the study reaches cover a period of ~60 yr from 1939–1941 to 1998, with intervals ranging from 4 to 34 yr (Table 2). All paper prints were scanned at 600 dpi using a large-format scanner to yield digital imagery that could be readily analyzed using computer-based, image-analysis software.

Because image distortions associated with topographic displacement are negligible for such a low-relief landscape (Wolf and DeWitt, 2000), orthorectification was deemed unneces-

sary, and two-dimensional (2D) rectification of each image was performed in ArcGIS® using 1998 digital orthophotos as base images. Rectification of each photo was based on a minimum 10–15 ground control points in Universal Transverse Mercator (UTM), North American Datum (NAD) 1983–Zone 16. Points were concentrated within the portion of the photo containing the river to minimize the error associated with the residual geometric distortion (i.e., root mean square error—rmse) (Hughes et al., 2006). The rectified photos had an average rmse of ~5 m.

Channel centerlines were digitized on-screen in ArcGIS® using a digitization interval corresponding to the average width of each channel. An interval less than the average width introduces excessive noise, whereas an interval larger cannot capture necessary detail (Ferguson, 1975; Hooke, 1984; Güneralp and Rhoads, 2008). Because of error associated with image registration, a digitized centerline may not exactly represent the true centerline of a channel. To account for this error, buffers (i.e., error bands) were generated around each centerline. The width of these buffers was equal to 2 times the rmse of each photograph. Locations where the buffers do not overlap are highly likely to reflect actual changes in channel–centerline position rather than image registration error (Fig. 3; Rhoads and Urban, 1997; Urban and Rhoads, 2003).

Buffered centerlines for successive intervals of photographic coverage for each reach were overlain onto one another, and conservative estimates of change in channel position were documented by identifying portions of the total reach length with nonoverlapping buffers (Fig. 3). Based on this analysis, four categories were defined for each time interval: no detectable change, lateral migration, channelization, and response to (recovery from) channelization (Rhoads and Urban, 1997; Urban and Rhoads, 2003). The total length of each channel was divided into segments corresponding to the four categories. The length of each segment was calculated in ArcGIS®. If the position of the channel centerline of a meandering segment of the reach changed from one photograph to the next, it was classified as lateral migration. If channelization (artificial straightening) was evident in a photograph, but the reach was meandering in the previous image, the change was defined as channelization. If the river was channelized in the earlier photograph but exhibits meandering in the later photograph, it was categorized as recovery from channelization.

Cases where the buffers overlap with one another over a photographic interval (i.e., do not fully separate) were classified as no detectable change (Fig. 3). To determine the extent of different types of change, changes in each category were expressed as a percentage of total reach length.

Spatial Distribution of Stream Power

To link planform change detected on historical aerial photography to fluvial processes in the watershed, the spatial variation of stream power was mapped throughout the drainage network. Cross-sectional stream power is defined as

$$\omega = \frac{\gamma Q S}{W} , \tag{1}$$

where ω denotes cross-sectional stream power (W/m²), γ represents specific weight of water (9800 N/m³), Q is discharge (m³/s), S is channel gradient, and W is width of the flow (m) (Rhoads, 1987).

The first step in calculating stream power throughout the network was to determine spatial variations in subwatershed gradients. The watershed was divided into 42 subwatersheds corresponding to the major tributaries of the Kishwaukee River system (Fig. 1). Drainage areas (A_d) and the length of the main channel in each subwatershed were determined using the ArcHydro module of ArcGIS®. The average gradient of the main channel in each subwatershed was derived from digital U.S. Geological Survey topographic maps by computing the difference between upstream and downstream channel elevations and dividing this value by channel length. The upstream and downstream channel elevations were determined by interpolating between contour lines bounding the mouths and upper ends of the subswatersheds.

Flow widths were estimated using the downstream hydraulic geometry relation for the Rock River basin, which includes the Kishwaukee River watershed (Stall and Fok, 1968):

$$W = 1.832 A_d^{0.405} Q^{0.229}, \tag{2}$$

where A_d is subwatershed drainage area (mi²) and Q is the discharge (m³/s). The values of flow width (W) from equation 2 were cross-checked against corresponding values of W measured directly on 1998 digital orthophotos. In general the two values were similar, although values of W from the photographs were ~25% less than those estimated from equation 2. This difference probably reflects the fact that the widths on the orthophotos correspond to flows that are less than bankfull stage.

A discharge with a recurrence interval on the partial duration series of 0.8 yr ($Q_{0.8}$), which approximates bankfull flow in rivers in this region of northern Illinois, was used as the value of Q in equations 1 and 2. Estimates of $Q_{0.8}$ for each subwatershed were provided by regression equations developed by Soong et al. (2004) for the hydrologic region of Illinois that includes the Kishwaukee River watershed.

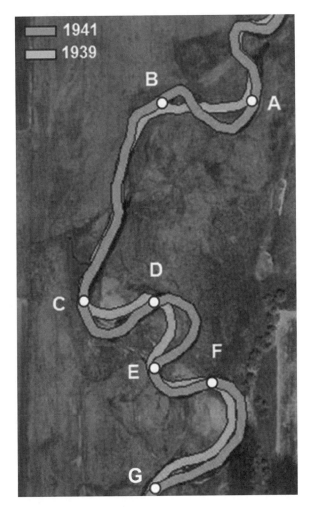

Figure 3. Buffer construction around the centerlines and the channel change classification: A–B, C–D, D–E, and F–G segments: *lateral migration;* E–F segment: *no detectable change;* B–C segment: *no recovery from channelization* (B–C segment appears channelized in the photo at the beginning of the photographic interval).

RESULTS AND DISCUSSION

River Dynamics

Table 3 summarizes the results of the planform-change analysis for five of the seven reaches over the entire period of record. For the sake of brevity, only results of channel change between the oldest and most recent photos are shown for reaches where there was only lateral migration or no change in channel location for individual photographic intervals. On the other hand, for the reaches where channelization or recovery from channelization occurred within individual photographic intervals, the results from each interval are included, because an analysis based only on change between the initial and the final photos would not reveal such information. Overall the results show that lateral migration dominates channel change at the study reaches (Tables 3, 4). At four of the reaches this category accounted for all of the change over the entire study period (1939–1941 to 1998). The percentages of the total length of the reaches affected by lateral migration ranged from 82% at reach 2 to 0% at reach 7. The most dynamic reaches in terms of channel change by lateral migration (reaches 1–4) are in the northern part of the watershed (Figs. 2, 4; Tables 3, 4), whereas the least dynamic ones are in the southern part of the basin (reaches 5–7) (Figs. 2, 5; Table 3). No detectable change was the second largest category. The channelized reach, reach 7, exhibited the least amount of change. Reach 2, the reach with the greatest

amount of lateral migration, had the smallest amount of undetectable change.

Channelization was evident at three of the reaches. A small part of reach 1 was channelized three times over the study period. Similarly, a small section of reach 4 was channelized twice over the same period. A very small section of reach 7, which was completely channelized at the beginning of the first interval of analysis (1939), was rechannelized over the study period (Table 3).

Almost all of the reaches that were channelized in the earliest photos or channelized during the study period exhibited little or no substantial recovery from the channelization, all of the recoveries being <3% of the reach length (Tables 3, 4). The 1% of the total length of reach 7 that was rechannelized over the study period did not exhibit detectable recovery from channelization after this modification (Fig. 5; Table 3). In contrast, between 1941 and 1954 a small part (4%) of reach 1 was straightened. In the following interval (1954–1988) most of the channelized section recovered to a meandering pattern (Table 4A). However, during this period, another section of the reach corresponding to 6% of the total reach length was channelized, but this section did not subsequently recover from this modification (Table 4A). Similarly, 9% of reach 4 was channelized at the beginning of the period, and only 22% of the channelized section recovered over 67 yr (Table 4B). These results suggest that at least some parts of the Kishwaukee River fluvial system are not dynamic enough to recover from the human-induced changes imposed by stream channelization, at least over periods of several years to several decades.

TABLE 3. SPATIAL EXTENT OF PLANFORM CHANGE AS A PERCENTAGE
OF THE REACH LENGTH FOR THE STUDY REACHES

Classification	Reach 2	Reach 3	Reach 5	Reach 6	Reach 7
	1941–1998	1939–1998	1939–1998	1939–1998	1939–1998
No change (%)	18	36	58	40	99
Lateral migration (%)	82	64	42	60	0
Channelization (%)	0	0	0	0	1
Recovery (%)	0	0	0	0	0

Note: The channelization (%) given in the table for reach 7 corresponds to additional modification of the channelized reach during the period.

TABLE 4. SPATIAL EXTENT OF PLANFORM CHANGE AS A PERCENTAGE OF THE REACH LENGTH
FOR REACH 1 AND REACH 4

Classification	A. Reach 1				B. Reach 4		
	1941–1954	1954–1988	1988–1998	1941–1998	1941–1967	1967–1998	1941–1998
No change (%)	80	42	22	20	58	39	19
Lateral migration (%)	16	49	78	65	33	61	74
Channelization (%)	4	6	0	14	9	0	5
Recovery (%)	0	3	0	3	0	2	2

Note: Percentage values of channelization class represent the channelization that occurred at the end of the photographic interval.

A

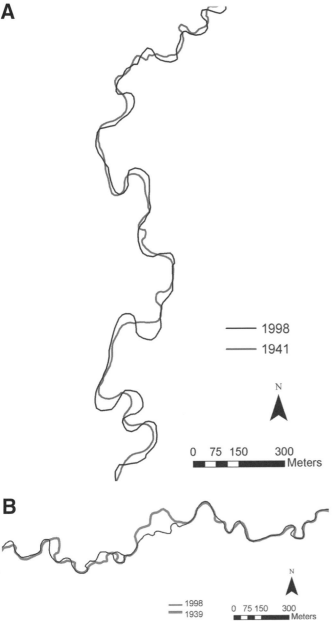

B

Figure 4. Examples from the sections of (A) *reach 2* and (B) *reach 3,* showing planform change associated with lateral migration of these meandering rivers (Fig. 2; Table 3).

A

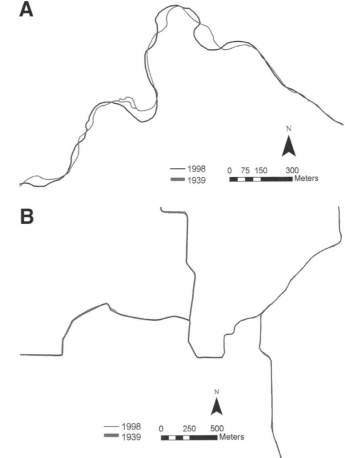

B

Figure 5. Examples from the sections of (A) *reach 6,* showing planform change associated with lateral migration, and (B) the completely channelized *reach 7,* showing no detectable change over a 59 yr period of photographic record (Fig. 2; Table 3).

Stream-Power Distribution and Historical Channel Change

To examine how historical channel change might be related to stream power in the Kishwaukee River watershed, the spatial distribution of stream power was mapped by subwatershed and compared with the results of channel change at the study reaches. Values of stream power in the subwatersheds range from 3.3 to 62.8 W/m² (Fig. 6). The highest values occur in the northern part of the watershed, and in headwater locations. The pattern of stream power generally reflects the spatial variation in the average slopes of the subwatersheds. A large part of the drainage network is characterized by values of stream power <35 W/m², the threshold below which lowland streams and rivers generally do not respond to human-induced morphological change (Brookes, 1987, 1988, 1992; Rhoads and Herricks, 1996; Urban and Rhoads, 2003).

The comparison of stream-power magnitudes in the study-reach subwatersheds, with the amount of channel change at the study reaches, reveals an important relation between stream power and channel change. When the study reaches are placed in order according to the amount of channel change associated with lateral migration and recovery from channelization, the two types of change that should be related to stream power, the rankings correspond to the rankings of stream-power magnitudes by subwatershed (Table 5). The most dynamic reaches (reaches 2 and 4) have the highest values of subwatershed stream power. These reaches are in the northern part of the watershed, where slopes, and therefore stream power, are greatest (Table 5; Fig. 6).

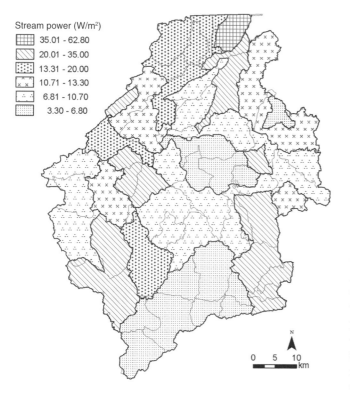

Stream power (W/m²)
- 35.01 - 62.80
- 20.01 - 35.00
- 13.31 - 20.00
- 10.71 - 13.30
- 6.81 - 10.70
- 3.30 - 6.80

0 5 10 km

Figure 6. Subwatersheds and stream-power distribution within the Kishwaukee River watershed.

The least dynamic reach, the channelized reach 7, has the lowest stream power of the reaches, which may also explain why it is channelized in the first place: this low-power reach is easily manipulated without its readjustment to that manipulation. Interestingly, however, none of the subwatersheds has an average stream power >35 W/m², the threshold for recovery from channelization. Reaches 4 and 1 did exhibit some response to channelization, but most of the total length of the channelized reaches remained straight, following human modification. These reaches, which exhibit lateral migration along a substantial part of the total reach length, apparently do not recover readily from artificial straightening. Moreover, the threshold of 35 W/m² below which there is generally a lack of channel change in channelized rivers certainly does not apply to lateral migration along unchannelized rivers. All of the reaches except reach 7, which has the lowest stream power and was completely channelized initially, exhibit substantial amounts of change by lateral migration over their total lengths.

Implications for Environmental Management

Overall the results of the assessment of historical channel change in the Kishwaukee River watershed indicate that the magnitude of channel change, expressed as a percentage of total channel length, is a function of stream power per unit area—an index of the capacity for channel change. Although factors such as land-use and geology can also influence channel change, the effects of these factors on the study reaches are probably minor, given the homogeneity of geological parent materials (glacially derived alluvium) and land-use (agriculture) throughout the watershed. Meandering reaches with high values of stream power exhibit more lateral migration than those with low values of stream power. This finding has important implications for river management. It indicates that bank erosion is more common where stream power is high than where it is low. Thus, efforts to "control" eroding banks in a part of the watershed where stream power is inherently high that are based on comparisons with the condition of channel banks where stream power is low may be fundamentally misguided. Over the past several years, structural controls intended to stabilize eroding streambanks have been implemented at hundreds of locations throughout Illinois through the Illinois Streambank Stabilization and Restoration program (Rhoads, 2003). Many of these reaches lie along meandering agricultural streams. In each case, judgments about the need for stabilization were based on visual observations of extant bank conditions or bank retreat over a few years. No effort was made to include historical analysis of river dynamics in the assessment process. The findings here show the value of assessment methodologies that emphasize historical evaluations of channel change (e.g., Rhoads, 2003; Simon et al., 2007) and the limitations of those that do not (e.g., Rosgen, 2006).

TABLE 5. COMPARISON OF RIVER CHARACTERISTICS AND DYNAMICS WITH STREAM-POWER-MAGNITUDE DISTRIBUTION IN THE KISHWAUKEE RIVER WATERSHED

Reaches	Lateral migration and recovery to channelization (%)	Ranking among reaches	Stream power (W/m²)	Ranking among subwatersheds
Reach 2	82	1	13.31–20.00	3
Reach 4	76	2	13.31–20.00	3
Reach 1	68	3	10.71–13.30	4
Reach 3	64	4	6.81–10.70	5
Reach 6	60	5	6.81–10.70	5
Reach 5	42	6	6.81–10.70	5
Reach 7	0	7	3.30–6.80	6

The results here also corroborate the findings of previous work that has indicated the lack of recovery potential of rivers with low stream power to channel straightening (Rhoads and Urban, 1997; Urban and Rhoads, 2003). Most of the total length of channels that were straightened in the case studies from the Kishwaukee River watershed remained straight for years or decades following human modification. The reach where the channels were completely channelized initially and had the lowest stream power of all the study reaches remained straight over the entire period of analysis (59 yr). These results emphasize the limited capacity for short-term restoration of instream physical habitat for aquatic organisms through passive recovery of geomorphological characteristics. As noted by Urban and Rhoads (2003) the channelization of a low-energy stream in essence represents a catastrophic event in the sense that the effects are long lasting and not readily changed by subsequent fluvial action within the modified system. These long-lasting effects, especially the degradation of physical habitat associated with elimination of geomorphological characteristics (e.g., pool-riffle sequences), can pose serious problems for instream ecosystems, such as reductions in species richness and the alteration of community structure and function (Frissell et al., 1986; Brookes, 1988; Swales, 1988; Gelwick, 1990; Osborne and Wiley, 1992; Aadland, 1993). Understanding the connections between the dynamics of fluvial systems and ecological impacts can help guide watershed-scale ecosystem-restoration practices. Thus, in the case of human-modified low-energy fluvial systems, active intervention may be needed to reshape channels into forms in which fluvial processes can effectively reestablish physical habitat if enhancing ecological diversity is a short-term goal of environmental management (Rhoads et al., 1999).

SUMMARY AND CONCLUSIONS

This study has explored the relationship between watershed-scale spatial variations in channel change and stream power in the Kishwaukee River watershed in northern Illinois. The channel-change analysis involved GIS-based determinations of historical channel change using aerial photography of several study reaches scattered throughout the watershed. The total length of channel change in each reach was assigned to four categories and compared with the spatial distribution of stream power. The main findings are as follows:

1. Meandering reaches with the highest values of stream power (13.31–20.00 W/m^2) exhibited the greatest amount of channel change through the process of lateral migration, whereas those with the lowest values of stream power (3.30–6.80 W/m^2) exhibit the least amount of change.

2. Reaches that were partially channelized (straightened) during the period of analysis exhibited limited capacity for recovery of a meandering planform following human modification. In fact, among the channelized reaches, the maximum recovery from channelization occurred in reach 4, where 22% of the channelized section of the river began to remeander over 67 yr.

3. The reach with the lowest stream power, which was entirely channelized in a 1939 aerial photo, remained unchanged over the 59 yr period of analysis.

The results of this study demonstrate the value of historical assessments of channel change for evaluations of channel "instability" and for determining the need to implement stream-bank-stabilization methods at the local or watershed scale. The findings also point out the limitations of assessment methods that do not consider historical channel change. Historical analysis can also reveal the extent and persistence of human impacts on river systems in the form of channelization. Such information is valuable for guiding decision making about the need for active as opposed to passive approaches to stream restoration and naturalization.

REFERENCES CITED

Aadland, L.P., 1993, Stream habitat types: Their fish assemblages and relationship to flow: North American Journal of Fisheries Management, v. 13, p. 790–806, doi: 10.1577/1548-8675(1993)013<0790:SHTTFA>2.3.CO;2.

Brookes, A., 1987, The distribution and management of channelized streams in Denmark: Regulated rivers: Research and Management, v. 1, p. 3–16, doi: 10.1002/rrr.3450010103.

Brookes, A., 1988, Channelized Rivers: Perspectives for Environmental Management: Chichester, UK, Wiley & Sons, 326 p.

Brookes, A., 1992, The recovery and restoration of some engineered British river channels, *in* Boon, P.J., Calow, P., and Petts, G.E., eds., River Conservation and Management: Chichester, UK, Wiley & Sons, p. 337–352.

Brookes, A., 1995, River channel restoration: Theory and practice, *in* Gurnell, A., and Petts, G.E., eds., Changing River Channels: Chichester, UK, Wiley & Sons, p. 369–388.

Fehrenbacher, J.B., Jansen, I.J., and Olson, K.R, 1986, Loess thickness and its effect on soils in Illinois: Urbana, Illinois, Agronomy Department, University of Illinois, Agricultural Experiment Station Bulletin 782, 14 p., 3 maps.

Ferguson, R.I., 1975, Meander irregularity and wavelength estimation: Journal of Hydrology, v. 26, p. 315–333, doi: 10.1016/0022-1694(75)90012-8.

Frissell, C.A., Liss, W.J., Warren, C.E., and Hurley, M.D., 1986, A hierarchical framework for stream habitat classification: Viewing streams in a watershed context: Environmental Management, v. 10, p. 199–214, doi: 10.1007/BF01867358.

Frothingham, K.M., Rhoads, B.L., and Herricks, E.E., 2001, Stream geomorphology and fish community structure in channelized and meandering reaches of an agricultural stream, *in* Dorava, J.M., Montgomery, D.A., Palcsak, B.B., and Fitzpatrick, F.A., eds., Geomorphic Processes and Riverine Habitat: Washington, D.C., American Geophysical Union, p. 105–117.

Frothingham, K.M., Rhoads, B.L., and Herricks, E.E., 2002, A multiscale conceptual framework for integrated eco-geomorphological research to support stream naturalization in the agricultural Midwest: Environmental Management, v. 29, p. 16–33, doi: 10.1007/s00267-001-0038-7.

Gelwick, F.P., 1990, Longitudinal and temporal comparisons of riffle and pool fish assemblages in a northeastern Oklahoma Ozark stream: Copeia, v. 4, p. 1072–1082, doi: 10.2307/1446491.

Güneralp, İ., and Rhoads, B.L., 2008, Continuous characterization of planform geometry and curvatures of meandering rivers: Geographical Analysis, v. 40, p. 1–25.

Gurnell, A.M., Downward, S.R., and Jones, R., 1994, Channel planform change on the River Dee meanders, 1876–1992: Regulated Rivers, Restoration and Management, v. 9, p. 187–204, doi: 10.1002/rrr.3450090402.

Hickin, E.J., and Nanson, G., 1984, Lateral migration rates of river bends: Journal of Hydraulic Engineering ASCE, v. 110, p. 1557–1567.

Hooke, J.M., 1984, Changes in river meanders: A review of techniques and results of analyses: Progress in Physical Geography, v. 8, p. 473–508, doi: 10.1177/030913338400800401.

Hughes, M.L., McDowell, P.F., and Marcus, W.A., 2006, Accuracy assessment of georectified aerial photographs: Implications for measuring lateral channel movement in GIS: Geomorphology, v. 74, p. 1–16, doi: 10.1016/j.geomorph.2005.07.001.

Illinois Department of Natural Resources (IDNR), 1998, The Kishwaukee River Area Assessment Volume 3: Living Resources: Champaign, Illinois, Illinois Department of Natural Resources, Office of Scientific Research and Analysis, Natural History Survey Division, 199 p.

Illinois Environmental Protection Agency (IEPA), 1988, An intensive survey of the Kishwaukee River and its tributaries, 1983: Springfield, Illinois, Division of Water Pollution Control, IEPA/WPC/88-009, 60 p.

Leys, K.F., and Werritty, A., 1999, River channel planform change: Software for historical analysis: Geomorphology, v. 29, p. 107–120, doi: 10.1016/S0169-555X(99)00009-4.

Lineback, J.A., compiler, 1979, Quaternary deposits of Illinois [map]: Urbana, Illinois State Geological Survey, scale 1:500,000, one sheet.

Micheli, E.R., and Kirchner, J.W., 2002, Effects of wet meadow riparian vegetation on streambank erosion: 1. Remote sensing measurements of streambank migration and erodibility: Earth Surface Processes and Landforms, v. 27, p. 627–639, doi: 10.1002/esp.338.

Mossa, J., and McLean, M., 1997, Channel planform and land cover changes on a mined river floodplain: Applied Geography (Sevenoaks, England), v. 17, p. 43–54, doi: 10.1016/S0143-6228(96)00026-4.

Nanson, G., and Hickin, E.J., 1986, A statistical analysis of bank erosion and channel migration in western Canada: Geological Society of America Bulletin, v. 97, p. 497–504, doi: 10.1130/0016-7606(1986)97<497:ASAOBE>2.0.CO;2.

Osborne, L.L., and Wiley, M.J., 1992, Influence of tributary spatial position on the structure of warmwater fish assemblages: Canadian Journal of Fisheries and Aquatic Sciences, v. 49, p. 671–681, doi: 10.1139/f92-076.

Rhoads, B.L., 1987, Stream power terminology: Professional Geographer, v. 39, p. 189–195, doi: 10.1111/j.0033-0124.1987.00189.x.

Rhoads, B.L., 1995, Stream power: A unifying theme for urban fluvial geomorphology, *in* Herricks, E.E., ed., Stormwater Runoff and Receiving Systems: Impact, Monitoring, and Assessment: Boca Raton, Florida, Lewis Publishers, p. 65–75.

Rhoads, B.L., 2003, Protocols for Geomorphic Characterization of Meander Bends in Illinois: Conservation 2000 Ecosystems Project—Embarras River 001-98, prepared for Illinois Department of Natural Resources by Department of Geography, University of Illinois, Urbana, 142 p.

Rhoads, B.L., and Herricks, E.E., 1996, Naturalization of headwater agricultural streams in Illinois: Challenges and possibilities, *in* Brookes, A., and Shields, D., eds., River Channel Restoration: Chichester, UK, Wiley & Sons, p. 331–367.

Rhoads, B.L., and Urban, M.A., 1997, A human-induced geomorphic change in low-energy agricultural streams: An example from east-central Illinois,

in Wang, S.S.Y., Langendoen, E.J., and Shields, F.D., eds., Management of Landscapes Disturbed by Channel Incision: Oxford, University of Mississippi, p. 968–973.

Rhoads, B.L., Wilson, D., Urban, M., and Herricks, E.E., 1999, Interaction between scientists and nonscientists in community-based watershed management: Emergence of the concept of stream naturalization: Environmental Management, v. 24, p. 297–308, doi: 10.1007/s002679900234.

Rhoads, B.L., Schwartz, J.S., and Porter, S.A., 2003, Stream geomorphology and variability of hydraulic habitat for fish in four Midwestern agricultural streams: Water Resources Research, v. 39, p. 1218, doi: 10.1029/2003WR002294.

Rosgen, D., 2006, Watershed Assessment of River Stability and Sediment Supply (WARSS): Fort Collins, Colorado, Wildland Hydrology, 193 p.

Simon, A., 1989, A model of channel response in disturbed alluvial channels: Earth Surface Processes and Landforms. v. 14, p. 11–26.

Simon, A., Doyle, M., Kondolf, M., Shields, F.D., Jr., Rhoads, B.L., and McPhillips, M., 2007, Critical evaluation of how the Rosgen classification and associated "Natural Channel Design" methods fail to integrate and quantify fluvial processes and channel response: Journal of the American Water Resources Association, v. 43, p. 1117–1131, doi: 10.1111/j.1752-1688.2007.00091.x.

Soong, D.T., Ishii, A.L., Sharpe, J.B., and Avery, C.F., 2004, Estimating Flood-Peak Discharge Magnitudes and Frequencies for Rural Streams in Illinois: U.S. Geological Survey Scientific Investigations Report 2004-5103, 147 p.

Stall, J.B., and Fok, Y., 1968, Hydraulic Geometry of Illinois Streams: Urbana, University of Illinois, Illinois State Water Survey, Water Resources Center Research Report 15, 52 p.

Swales, S., 1988, Fish populations of a small lowland channelized river in England subject to long-term river maintenance and management works: Regulated Rivers: Research and Management, v. 2, p. 493–506, doi: 10.1002/rrr.3450020403.

Urban, M.A., and Rhoads, B.L., 2003, Catastrophic human-induced change in stream-channel planform and geometry in an agricultural watershed, Illinois, USA: Annals of the Association of American Geographers, v. 93, p. 783–796, doi: 10.1111/j.1467-8306.2003.09304001.x.

Wolf, P.R., and DeWitt, B.A., 2000, Elements of Photogrammetry with Applications in GIS: New York, McGraw-Hill, 608 p.

MANUSCRIPT ACCEPTED BY THE SOCIETY 15 SEPTEMBER 2008

The Geological Society of America
Special Paper 451
2009

Geomorphic evolution of the Le Sueur River, Minnesota, USA, and implications for current sediment loading

Karen B. Gran

Department of Geological Sciences, University of Minnesota, Duluth, 1114 Kirby Dr., Duluth, Minnesota, 55812, USA

Patrick Belmont

National Center for Earth-surface Dynamics, St. Anthony Falls Lab, 2 Third Ave. SE, Minneapolis, Minnesota 55414, USA

Stephanie S. Day

National Center for Earth-surface Dynamics, St. Anthony Falls Lab, 2 Third Ave. SE, Minneapolis, Minnesota 55414, USA, and Department of Geology and Geophysics, University of Minnesota, Twin Cities, 310 Pillsbury Dr. SE, Minneapolis, Minnesota 55455, USA

Carrie Jennings

Department of Geology and Geophysics, University of Minnesota, Twin Cities, 310 Pillsbury Dr. SE, Minneapolis, Minnesota 55455, USA, and Minnesota Geological Survey, 2642 University Ave. W, St. Paul, Minnesota 55114, USA

Andrea Johnson

Department of Geological Sciences, University of Minnesota, Duluth, 1114 Kirby Dr., Duluth, Minnesota, 55812, USA

Lesley Perg

National Center for Earth-surface Dynamics, St. Anthony Falls Lab, 2 Third Ave. SE, Minneapolis, Minnesota 55414, USA, and Department of Geology and Geophysics, University of Minnesota, Twin Cities, 310 Pillsbury Dr. SE, Minneapolis, Minnesota 55455, USA

Peter R. Wilcock

National Center for Earth-surface Dynamics, St. Anthony Falls Lab, 2 Third Ave. SE, Minneapolis, Minnesota 55414, USA, and Department of Geography and Environmental Engineering, Johns Hopkins University, 3400 North Charles St., Ames Hall 313, Baltimore, Maryland, 21218, USA

ABSTRACT

There is clear evidence that the Minnesota River is the major sediment source for Lake Pepin and that the Le Sueur River is a major source to the Minnesota River. Turbidity levels are high enough to require management actions. We take advantage of the well-constrained Holocene history of the Le Sueur basin and use a combination of remote sensing, field, and stream gauge observations to constrain the contributions of different sediment sources to the Le Sueur River. Understanding the type, location, and magnitude of sediment sources is essential for unraveling the Holocene

Gran, K.B., Belmont, P., Day, S.S., Jennings, C., Johnson, A., Perg, L., and Wilcock, P.R., 2009, Geomorphic evolution of the Le Sueur River, Minnesota, USA, and implications for current sediment loading, *in* James, L.A., Rathburn, S.L., and Whittecar, G.R., eds., Management and Restoration of Fluvial Systems with Broad Historical Changes and Human Impacts: Geological Society of America Special Paper 451, p. 119–130, doi: 10.1130/2009.2451(08). For permission to copy, contact editing@geosociety.org. ©2009 The Geological Society of America. All rights reserved.

development of the basin as well as for guiding management decisions about investments to reduce sediment loads.

Rapid base-level fall at the outlet of the Le Sueur River 11,500 yr B.P. triggered up to 70 m of channel incision at the mouth. Slope-area analyses of river longitudinal profiles show that knickpoints have migrated 30–35 km upstream on all three major branches of the river, eroding $1.2–2.6 \times 10^9$ Mg of sediment from the lower valleys in the process. The knick zones separate the basin into an upper watershed, receiving sediment primarily from uplands and streambanks, and a lower, incised zone, which receives additional sediment from high bluffs and ravines. Stream gauges installed above and below knick zones show dramatic increases in sediment loading above that expected from increases in drainage area, indicating substantial inputs from bluffs and ravines.

INTRODUCTION

The Minnesota River drains 43,400 km² of south-central Minnesota (Fig. 1), a landscape dominated by agricultural land use. The Minnesota River carries a high suspended sediment load, leading to the listing of multiple reaches as impaired for turbidity under Section 303d of the Clean Water Act. Analyses of sediment cores from Lake Pepin, a naturally dammed lake on the mainstem Mississippi River, serving as the primary sediment sink for the Minnesota, St. Croix, and upper Mississippi River systems, indicate that sediment loads into Lake Pepin have increased tenfold since the onset of European settlement in the mid-1800s, from a background of ~75,000 Mg yr⁻¹ to ~900,000 Mg yr⁻¹ (Engstrom et al., 2008). Of this sediment load, the vast majority (85%–90%) comes from the Minnesota River (Kelley and Nater, 2000).

To help restore clean water and improve ecosystem functionality in the Minnesota River and Lake Pepin, a large-scale effort is under way to lower sediment loading to the system. This involves targeting the dominant sources of sediment to the system, which are poorly constrained. Our research focuses on establishing an integrated sediment budget in one of the major tributaries of the Minnesota River, the Le Sueur River, in an effort to better define the source locations and transport processes for sediment entering the Minnesota River. Once source locations are well defined, best management practices can be targeted toward reducing the sediment load coming from these areas.

The first phase of our sediment budget involves bracketing the range of sediment volumes that have been eroded through time to compare current sediment loading with historic and Holocene average rates. Recent changes in both land use and hydrology in

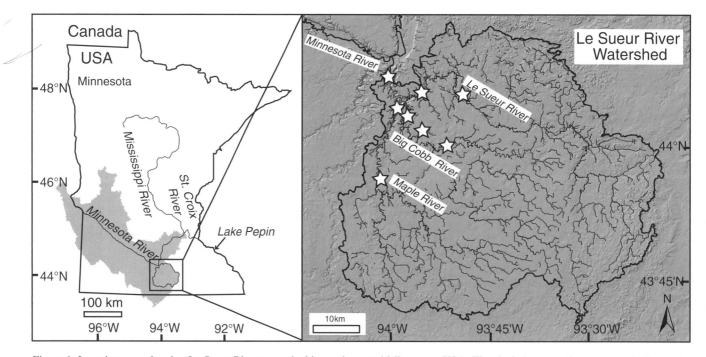

Figure 1. Location map showing Le Sueur River watershed in south-central Minnesota, USA. The shaded area on the state map indicates the extent of the Minnesota River basin. Stars on the inset watershed map on the right indicate locations of gauging stations.

the system may be exacerbating erosion in certain parts of the landscape, resulting in the observed increase in sediment loading to Lake Pepin in the past 170 yr. The next phase involves setting bounds on the relative magnitude and proportion of sediment coming from each primary sediment source to determine which sources are currently important contributors of sediment to the Le Sueur River.

BACKGROUND

The Le Sueur River drains north and west to the Minnesota River in south-central Minnesota (Fig. 1). It covers 2880 km² of primarily agricultural land use (87%), the vast majority of which is in row crops (>90%) (Minnesota Pollution Control Agency [MPCA] et al., 2007). There are no major urban areas, although the municipality of Mankato is expanding into the northern part of the watershed. The Le Sueur River has three main branches: the Maple River, the Big Cobb River, and the mainstem Le Sueur. The three branches come together within a span of 3 km, ~10 km upstream of the Le Sueur confluence with the Blue Earth River. The Blue Earth flows into the Minnesota River 5 km downstream from the junction with the Le Sueur River.

Modern sediment-gauging efforts indicate that ~24%–30% of the total suspended solids (TSS) entering the Minnesota River come from the Le Sueur River, making it a primary contributor to the mainstem Minnesota and Lake Pepin (MPCA et al., 2007). This is a disproportionate sediment contribution relative to the Le Sueur watershed area, which constitutes a mere 7% of the Minnesota River basin. From 2000 to 2006, TSS measured at the mouth of the Le Sueur River ranged from 0.9 to 5.8 × 10⁵ Mg yr⁻¹ (mean = 2.9 × 10⁵ Mg yr⁻¹) (MPCA et al., 2007; MPCA, P. Baskfield, 2007, personal commun.) (Table 1). Annual flow-weighted mean concentrations of TSS from 2000 to 2006 ranged from 245 to 918 mg L⁻¹ (mean = 420 mg L⁻¹) (MPCA et al., 2007; MPCA, P. Baskfield, 2007, personal commun.). Target values set by the MPCA in this region are 58–66 mg L⁻¹ (McCollor and Heiskary, 1993).

The lower reaches of the Le Sueur, Maple, and Big Cobb Rivers are currently incising. Knickpoints are migrating upstream along major tributaries, leading to high relief in the lower, incised portion of the watershed. At the mouth of the Le Sueur, the channel is incised 70 m in a valley up to 800 m wide. High bluffs border many of the outer bends along the channel, and steep ravines snake into the uplands. This is in stark contrast to the low-gradient to flat uplands, which occupy most of the watershed area.

The basin is underlain by tills, glacial outwash, and ice-walled lake plains with a thin mantle of glaciolacustrine silts and clays covering 65% of the upland surface. The river is currently incising through the layered Pleistocene tills and the underlying Ordovician dolostone bedrock. Bedrock outcrops have been observed along the channel in patches within 15 km of the mouth.

The high relief in the lower Le Sueur River Valley is the result of knickpoint migration through the basin. These knickpoints originated from a sharp drop in base level on the mainstem Minnesota River during the catastrophic draining of glacial Lake Agassiz. As the Laurentide ice sheet retreated from the Midcontinent at the end of the last glaciation, meltwater from the wasting ice was impounded by a low moraine dam in western Minnesota and formed glacial Lake Agassiz. It eventually covered much of western Minnesota, eastern North Dakota, Manitoba, and western Ontario (Upham, 1890, 1895; Matsch, 1972). The only outlet for much of this time was to the south through glacial River Warren, the valley now occupied by the Minnesota River. River Warren incised older tills and saprolite, and in places exposed resistant rock in the valley floor (Matsch, 1983), creating a valley that was 45 m deep at its mouth and 70 m deep near Mankato, 300 km downstream.

The initial incision was ca. 11,500 radiocarbon yr B.P. (rcbp) (Clayton and Moran, 1982; Matsch, 1983). The valley was occupied until ~10,900 rcbp. Two other outlets were used between 10,900 and 10,300 (Thorleifson, 1996) and between 10,000 and 9600 rcbp (Lowell et al., 2005) during which time the southern outlet was not used. River Warren was reoccupied after 9600 rcbp and finally lost glacial lake discharge by 8200 rcbp. Preexisting tributaries such as the Blue Earth and Le Sueur Rivers were low-gradient streams of glacial-meltwater origin that were stranded above the master stream when the initial incision occurred 11,500 rcbp. Knickpoint migration continues today, with bedrock waterfalls within 5–10 km of the confluence on several major tributaries. In the Le Sueur River the record of incision following glacial River Warren is manifested in >400 terrace surfaces spread throughout the lower basin. Knickpoints are expressed as slope discontinuities evident on all three major branches of the river, and they have propagated approximately the same distance upstream on each branch.

The glaciolacustrine deposits blanketing much of the Le Sueur River watershed were deposited in glacial Lake Minnesota, which drained shortly before the initial carving of the Minnesota River valley. These deposits are composed of highly erodible silts and clays. Given the fine-grained, erodible soils of the Le Sueur

	2000	2001	2002	2003	2004	2005	2006[§]	Mean
TSS* (Mg)	5.8 × 10⁵	4.2 × 10⁵	1.1 × 10⁵	8.6 × 10⁴	4.1 × 10⁵	2.7 × 10⁵	1.5 × 10⁵[§]	2.9 × 10⁵
FWMC[†] (mg/L)	918	355	318	245	475	356	270[§]	420

TABLE 1. TSS LOADS IN LE SUEUR RIVER, 2000–2006

Note: 2000–2005 data from the Minnesota Pollution Control Agency (MPCA et al., 2007).
*TSS—total suspended solids.
[†]FWMC—flow-weighted mean concentration.
[§]2006 data from MPCA (P. Baskfield, 2007, personal commun.), preliminary.

River watershed and the high relief in the basin, the watershed is primed to have high suspended-sediment loads relative to other watersheds in the basin, and it is susceptible to erosion driven by changes to the landscape following the arrival of settlers of European descent in the mid-1800s.

The presettlement landscape of the Le Sueur River was dominated by prairie vegetation that covered two-thirds of the basin, with hardwoods in the river valleys and the northeastern corner of the watershed. Wet prairie and open lakes occupied at least 15% (Marschner, 1974), and possibly as much as one-third, of the watershed area (Minnesota Department of Natural Resources, 2007). Two major changes to the landscape have occurred in the past 200 yr: conversion of original prairie to agriculture, and alterations to the basin hydrology. Land cover in the basin is now primarily row crops (currently 87% cropland; MPCA et al., 2007), with lakes and wetlands covering only 3% of the watershed area. Hydrologic alterations include draining wetlands, connecting previously closed basins to the drainage network, ditching small tributaries, and tiling agricultural fields to ensure rapid drainage of surface, vadose, and, in some places, groundwater. The hydrologic alterations are both pervasive and dynamic. Nearly all farm fields have artificial drainage, and the depth, density, and capacity of drainage have generally increased over time (Water Resources Center, 2000). Little documentation exists for these progressive hydrologic changes. Superimposed on these direct changes to the hydrologic system are indirect changes from climate change in the last ~50 yr, including state-wide increases in mean annual precipitation, to number of days with precipitation and number of intense rainfall events per year (Novotny and Stefan, 2007). These changes are, in turn, superimposed on the template of the geomorphically evolving, incised channel network that was initiated by deep, rapid incision in the Minnesota River Valley.

METHODS

This research effort focused on sediment loading to the Le Sueur River over multiple temporal and spatial scales, with the goal of identifying sources, fluxes, and sinks in the evolution of the drainage system and its response to human alteration. Most of the work on the volume of Holocene erosion was done through analyses of digital topography, including high-resolution topography acquired through LiDAR (light detection and ranging) in Blue Earth County. This data set covers ~30% of the total watershed area, including all of the area below the major knickpoints. Holocene erosion volumes are compared with 2000–2006 sediment loads measured at stream gauges as a comparison of current rates versus background rates. Both of these erosion measures are compared with the signal of deposition at Lake Pepin over the past 400 yr from Engstrom et al. (2008).

Sediment sources to the Le Sueur River include upland-derived sediment, high bluffs, terraces, and ravines. Major sediment sources are shown in Figure 2. The primary sediment sources above the knick zone include upland-derived sediment and sediment eroded from streambanks owing to lateral migration of channels. Normally, streambanks are not a net source of sediment because the sediment eroded is balanced by deposition on flood-plains. However, because the river is migrating into terraces and high bluffs, erosion from these features can lead to net sediment contributions to the channel from stream migration. Most of the terraces are below the major knick zone, but there are smaller terraces throughout the basin, remnants of the passage of the upper knickpoint through the system. Through and below the major knick zones, ravines and bluffs have become important sediment contributors. Information on total sediment flux was derived from paired gauging stations above and below the knick zones on major tributaries. Analyses of historical air photos from 1938 to 2003 help constrain channel migration patterns and dynamics. These data combine to determine which sediment sources are significant components of the modern sediment budget.

LiDAR Analyses

We extracted river longitudinal profiles from 30 m SRTM (Shuttle Radar Topography Mission) data obtained from the U.S. Geological Survey and analyzed the relationship between local channel gradient and contributing drainage area (see Wobus et al., 2006) along the entire river profile using the Stream Profiler utility (www.geomorphtools.org) with a 3-m contour, a 1-km smoothing window, and an empirically derived reference concavity of 0.45 (Fig. 3). Slope-area analyses were conducted on each of the three mainstem channels to find major slope discontinuities (see Fig. 3B). In a graded system, the slope-area relationship should increase monotonically throughout the entire fluvial portion of the watershed. The sharp discontinuities evident in the slope-area plot highlight the locations of knickpoints.

We estimated the mass of sediment that has been excavated over the past 11,500 yr from the incised, lower reaches of all three branches of the Le Sueur River. To calculate the missing mass, we hand-digitized polygons delineating the incised portion of the river valleys using the 3-m resolution aerial LiDAR digital elevation model (DEM) (Fig. 4). Precision in this process was enhanced by overlaying the DEM with a semitransparent hill shade and using a multiband color scheme for the DEM, which we manipulated to depict most effectively small differences in the elevation range of interest. The valley walls are generally strikingly clear and easy to trace using this technique. Valley polygons were split into 3-km-long reaches. We then converted each of those polygons to grids, attributing a paleosurface elevation value to each cell in the grid. The mass removed was determined by subtracting the current topography from the paleosurface.

To generate minimum and maximum estimates of the mass of excavated sediment, we used two different paleosurface elevations. Our maximum estimate assumed that the watershed was initially a planar glacial lake bed with a paleosurface elevation of 327 m above sea level for all valley polygons, consistent with the average elevation of the surrounding, low-gradient uplands in this area. Our minimum estimate assumed a different paleosurface elevation for each 3-km valley reach consistent with the elevation of the highest terraces mapped in that reach. These elevations are the highest levels that we know were occupied by the river in the past 11,500 yr.

Using the same approach, we hand-digitized all 95 ravines (considering only those with a planar area of an incised valley >0.5 km²) and calculated the mass of material that has been excavated by ravines as a result of ravine incision and elongation only. The paleosurface elevation of each ravine was determined using the average of 10 upland-surface elevations surrounding the ravine.

Volumes of sediment removed were converted into mass using a bulk density of 1.8 Mg m⁻³ (Thoma et al., 2005). To

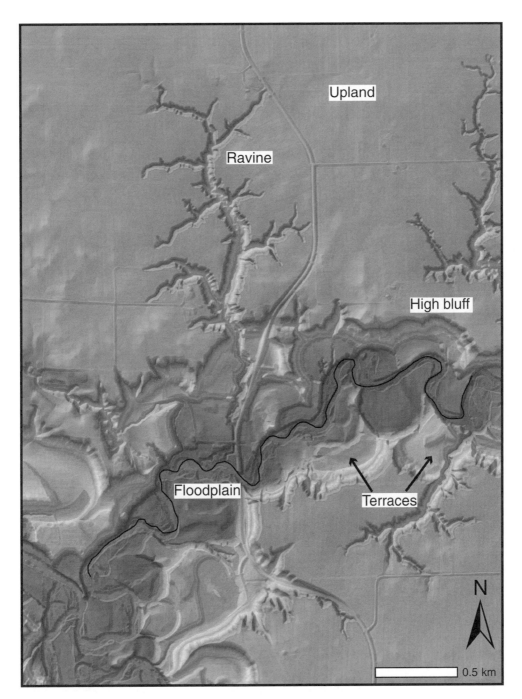

Figure 2. Primary sediment sources in the Le Sueur River watershed include uplands, ravines, high bluffs, and terraces. Shown here is a merged LiDAR (light detection and ranging) digital elevation model (DEM) and a slope map of the lower Le Sueur River with different source areas labeled. Relief is ~70 m from river valley to uplands.

compare with TSS measurements, we assumed that only the silt and clay fractions (65% of the total mass) move downstream as suspended load. This mass could then be compared with the inorganic fraction of TSS from modern gauging efforts.

We mapped fluvial terrace surfaces from the 3 m aerial LiDAR DEM, using a semitransparent hill shade to enhance visual precision (Fig. 5). The criterion used to delineate terrace surfaces was visual observation of undissected, planar (<1 m of relief) surfaces within the incised river valley that are >2 m above the river water-surface elevation from the LiDAR data set. This relief criterion excluded floodplain surfaces where active deposition is still occurring.

Historic Rates of Channel Migration

Aerial photographs from 1938 and 2003 were used to constrain short-term river migration rates. The 1938 photos were georeferenced in ArcGIS. At least seven stable control points were selected and matched in each photo, fit with a second-order polynomial function, and rectified after a total root mean square error (rmse) <0.5 was achieved. Channel banks were digitized by hand in ArcGIS. In cases where vegetation obscured the channel edge, the bank was estimated assuming a width consistent with adjacent up-downstream reaches. To calculate channel migration rates, we used a planform statistics tool described in Lauer and Parker (2005) (available at http://www.nced.umn.edu/Stream _Restoration_Toolbox.html). This tool maps the center line of the channel based on the user-defined right and left banks. The program then compares the center line of the 1938 channel with the 2003 channel center line using a best-fit Bezier curve. The overall georeferencing error was ±4.5 m, although individual images varied around this average.

To estimate the potential net contribution of sediment eroded through lateral migration, bank heights were calculated

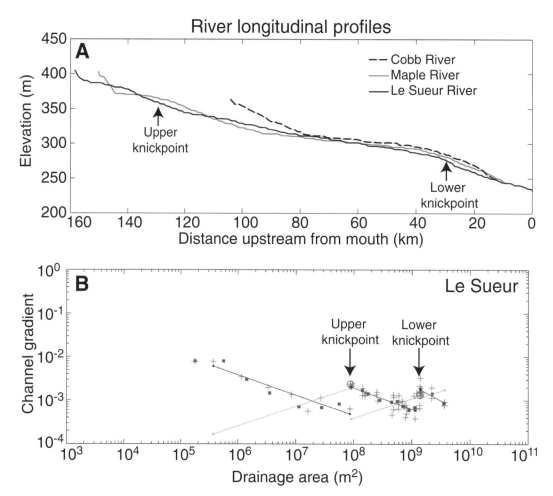

Figure 3. (A) Longitudinal elevation profiles of the Le Sueur River and its two primary tributaries, the Cobb and Maple Rivers, extracted from a 30 m DEM (digital elevation model). The locations of the two knickpoints delineated on the Le Sueur River branch using the slope-area analysis in plot B are shown. (B) Analysis of local channel gradient and contributing drainage area of the Le Sueur River longitudinal profile, after smoothing with a 1-km moving window and sampling every 3 m drop in elevation. The discontinuities in the slope-area relationship indicate the locations of two knickpoints. Both data sets were extracted using the stream profiler tool available at geomorphtools.org.

along a profile line adjacent to the top of the banks in 2003. Bank elevations were averaged every 100 m, and reach-average channel elevations were subtracted to get bank heights. Since channels both erode and deposit on their floodplains, resulting in no net gain or loss of sediment, we removed areas with elevations at or below the floodplain elevation, leaving only banks in terraces and bluffs. This methodology gives a measure of the potential net flux of sediment into the channel from channel migration into these higher surfaces. Floodplain heights were measured off the LiDAR DEM at 25 different sites along the mainstem Le Sueur River. The average floodplain height was 1.8 m ±0.5 m in the lower 25 km and 1.0 ±0.1 m from 25 to 75 km upstream. We measured volumes of sediment potentially entrained from terraces and bluffs along the lower 73.6 km of the mainstem Le Sueur River and then extrapolated to the rest of the mainstem Le Sueur, Maple, and Big Cobb Rivers, a total of 410 river km, to get a measure of the potential net volume of sediment that would be eroded into the channel from lateral migration into terraces and bluffs. These volumes were converted to mass using a bulk density of 1.8 Mg m^{-3}, and to potential suspended sediment load assuming a silt-clay content of 65% of the total sample.

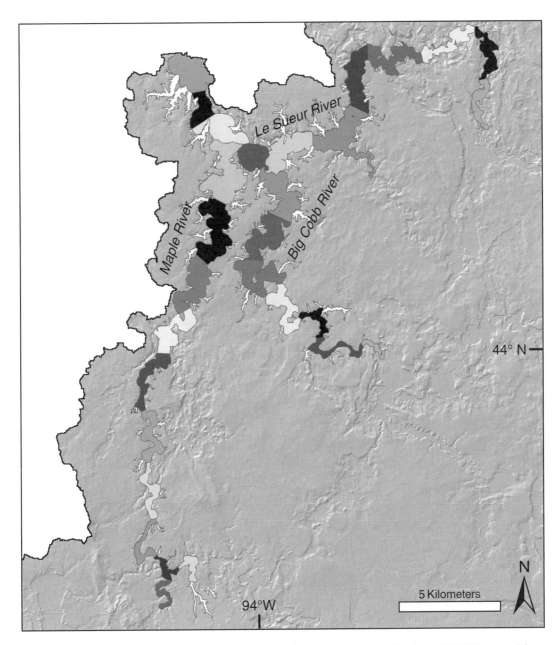

Figure 4. Valley and ravine polygons used to determine sediment mass excavated in the past 11,500 yr, overlain on the LiDAR DEM (light detection and ranging digital elevation model).

Gauging Data

Modern sediment fluxes were calculated through continuous-flow gauging at nine stations in the Le Sueur River watershed by the MPCA (Fig. 1; Table 2). Approximately 30–40 grab samples were collected and processed by the MPCA throughout the year at each of these gauging stations and analyzed for TSS. Individual samples were converted into flow-weighted mean sediment concentrations by agency staff using the U.S. Army Corps of Engineers' FLUX program. Data from 2000 to 2005 were reported in MPCA et al. (2007). Data from 2006 come from the MPCA (P. Baskfield, 2007, personal commun.) and include preliminary data from gauges in their first year of operation.

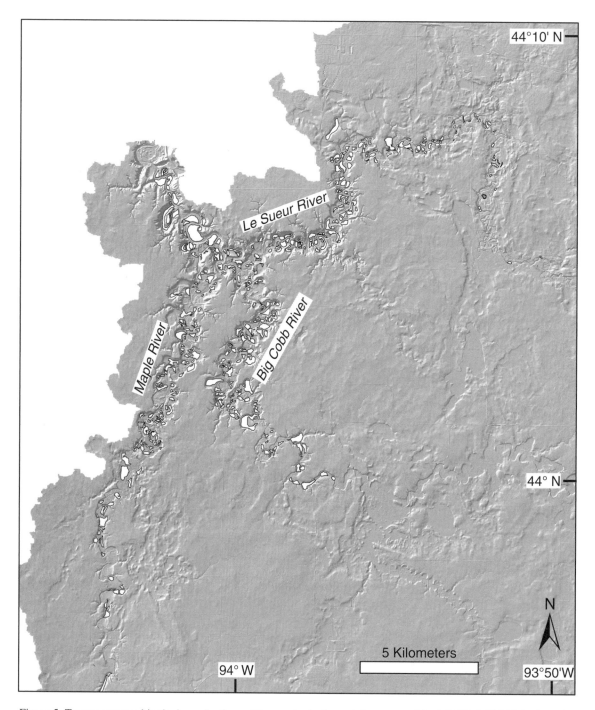

Figure 5. Terraces mapped in the lower Le Sueur River watershed, overlain on top of the LiDAR DEM (light detection and ranging digital elevation model). Only terraces >2 m above the channel were mapped, to exclude active floodplains.

TABLE 2. GAUGING STATIONS IN THE LE SUEUR RIVER WATERSHED

Station	Location	Years of operation*	Drainage area (km²)
LS1	Le Sueur R. at Red Jacket, BE County Rd. 66	1939–	2880
LS2	Le Sueur R., BE County Rd. 90	2006–	1210
LS3	Le Sueur R. at St. Clair, BE County Rd. 28	2007–	870
LC	Little Cobb R., BE County Rd. 16	1996–	336
BC	Big Cobb R., BE County Rd. 90	2006–	737
LM	Lower Maple R., BE County Rd. 35	2003–	878
UM	Upper Maple R., BE County Rd. 18	2006–	780
BD[†]	Beauford Ditch, Minnesota Highway 22	1999–	18

*As of 2008 these stations are currently in operation.
[†]BD site was a former U.S. Geological Survey gauging site in operation from 1959 to 1985.

To compare modern TSS loads with volumetric estimates of sediment removed over the Holocene, we removed the estimated organic fraction of the TSS. Samples were also analyzed for total suspended volatile solids (TSVS). Using TSVS as a proxy for the organic content of TSS, estimates of the organic content of TSS samples from the Le Sueur River in 1996 ranged from 16% to 34% (Water Resources Center, 2000). We adjusted the average TSS load from 2000 to 2006 by this amount to compare inorganic fractions only.

RESULTS

Until glacial River Warren incised and widened the ancestral Minnesota River Valley, the Le Sueur River watershed contained a series of low-gradient, ice-marginal meltwater channels and a relatively flat glacial lake bed masking former channels. Most of the current river-valley topography formed in the time since 11,500 yr B.P. Terraces in the lower valley record the history of incision (Fig. 5). On all three branches, knickpoints have migrated 30–35 river km upstream from the confluence with the Blue Earth River (Fig. 3), an average knickpoint migration rate of 3.0–3.5 m yr^{-1} over the past 11,500 yr. A second knickpoint is seen between 120 and 140 river km upstream on all three branches, indicating an average upstream migration rate of 10.9–12.6 m yr^{-1}. These exceptionally high migration rates speak to the poor strength of the underlying till and glaciolacustrine sediments at the surface. The elevation drop associated with the upper knickpoint appears to be relatively minor. Most of the relief in the basin is related to migration of the lower knickpoint.

The mass of sediment evacuated from incision since the initial base-level drop was used to determine an average yield per year (Table 3), broken down by sediment removed from the major river-valley corridor versus sediment removed by ravines still present along the valley walls for each of the three major channels in the Le Sueur River watershed. Sediment removed from the valley was probably removed through a combination of lateral erosion into bluffs and streambanks, erosion by ravines no longer present because they were consumed by lateral valley erosion, and vertical channel incision.

The amount of sediment excavated probably varied through time as the channel incised and the network expanded. Some studies of newly forming drainages have shown high rates of sediment evacuation early, diminishing through time (Parker, 1977; Hancock and Willgoose, 2002). Other studies have found the opposite, with lower rates of erosion initially, increasing until the drainage network was fully established (Hasbargen and Paola, 2000). The Le Sueur River is still very much in transition. It is in the early stages of channel incision and knickpoint migration, but in the latter stages of drainage development, particularly following anthropogenic alterations to the drainage network. Other fluctuations in the sediment load probably occurred during the well-documented mid-Holocene dry period, ca. 5–8 ka B.P. (Grimm, 1983; Webb et al., 1984; Baker et al., 1992; Webb et al., 1993; Geiss et al., 2003), which intermittently slowed sediment contributions from the Minnesota River to Lake Pepin (Kelley

TABLE 3. MASS EXCAVATION FROM VALLEYS AND RAVINES

	Valley excavation (minimum estimate)		Valley excavation (maximum estimate)		Ravine excavation	
	Mass (Mg)	Flux* (Mg yr^{-1})	Mass (Mg)	Flux* (Mg yr^{-1})	Mass (Mg)	Flux* (Mg yr^{-1})
Maple	2.6 x 10⁸	2.3 x 10⁴	6.4 x 10⁸	5.6 x 10⁴	4.0 x 10⁷	3.5 x 10³
Cobb	1.6 x 10⁸	1.4 x 10⁴	4.3 x 10⁸	3.7 x 10⁴	4.2 x 10⁷	3.7 x 10³
Le Sueur	5.9 x 10⁸	5.2 x 10⁴	1.3 x 10⁹	1.2 x 10⁵	1.4 x 10⁸	1.2 x 10⁴
Total	1.0 x 10⁹	8.8 x 10⁴	2.4 x 10⁹	2.1 x 10⁵	2.2 x 10⁸	1.9 x 10⁴

*Fluxes are average rates over the past 11,500 yr.

at al., 2006). Averaging over all of the variability during the last 11,500 yr results in the average sediment export from the incised portion of the Le Sueur River Valley and ravines as $1.1–2.3 \times 10^5$ Mg yr^{-1}, equivalent to a suspended load (silt and clay fractions only) of $0.7–1.5 \times 10^5$ Mg yr^{-1}. The average annual suspended sediment load was probably higher, given the contribution of fine sand to the suspended load during peak-flow events.

Modern sediment fluxes at the mouth of the Le Sueur River measured from 2000 to 2006 are listed in Table 1. The annual TSS flux for these seven years ranged from 0.86 to 5.8×10^5 Mg yr^{-1}, with an average of 2.9×10^5 Mg yr^{-1}. The inorganic fraction (66%–84% of TSS) was therefore $\sim$1.9–2.4 $\times 10^5$ Mg yr^{-1} on average from 2000 to 2006. These values are 1.3–3.4 times higher than the Holocene average rate, considering only silt and clay fractions.

Spatial variations in sediment loading become apparent when we compare the 2006 results from gauges positioned above and below the major knickpoints on two of the main branches (Table 4). On the Maple River the drainage area increases very little from the upper gauge to the lower gauge (a 13% increase), but the TSS load increases by a factor of 2.8. From the gauge on the Little Cobb River to the gauge farther downstream on the Big Cobb River, the drainage area increases by a factor of 2.2, but TSS increases by an order of magnitude. Processes on the uplands do not change markedly from the upper watershed to the lower watershed. The primary difference is that the lower watershed includes contributions from bluffs and ravines. If we assume that upland sediment yields do not change appreciably from upstream to downstream, we can use the yield at the upper basin as a measure of upland erosion. These yields are 9.8 Mg km^{-2} on the Maple and 11.2 Mg km^{-2} on the Big Cobb. Applying these yields to the drainage areas at the lower gauges, we end up with a mass of sediment that cannot be accounted for by upland erosion and get a measure of the potential importance of ravine and bluff erosion. On the Maple River the excess sediment amounts to 14,000 Mg or 61% of the total sediment load. On the Big Cobb the excess sediment is 25,000 Mg or 74% of the total sediment load. The role of bluff and ravine erosion compared with the total sediment budget in the Le Sueur River watershed is substantial and must be accounted for in the sediment budget.

To determine the relative importance of streambank erosion from lateral migration, we measured the potential volume of sediment that would be removed from lateral migration into high bluffs and terraces using average lateral migration rates from aerial photographs. Along the Le Sueur mainstem, channels moved an average of 0.2 m yr^{-1} between 1938 and 2003, with much of the movement concentrated on mobile bends. Given the current channel configuration and near bank elevations, this migration would lead to an average of 130 Mg river km^{-1} yr^{-1} of material entering the channel from lateral migration into terraces and high bluffs. If this rate is applied on all three mainstem rivers, the potential net sediment flux to the channel is $\sim$4.4 $\times 10^4$ Mg yr^{-1}, or 2.7×10^4 Mg yr^{-1} of silt and clay, should migration rates continue at the same pace.

DISCUSSION

The Le Sueur River currently has a very high suspended-sediment load. TSS loads measured on the Le Sueur River are an order of magnitude higher than current standards set by the MPCA (MPCA et al., 2007). Sedimentation records from Lake Pepin indicate that deposition rates are an order of magnitude higher than presettlement deposition rates (Engstrom et al., 2008), and by extrapolation we might assume that the Le Sueur River had an order of magnitude increase in erosion rates over presettlement background rates as well. However, when comparing sediment volumes removed in the Le Sueur River, averaged over the past 11,500 yr, with gauging records from 2000 to 2006 at the mouth of the Le Sueur River, the increase appears more modest: an increase of 1.3–3.4 times over the Holocene average background rate rather than a tenfold increase.

The major modern sources of sediment to the mainstem channels include ravines eroding through incision, elongation, and mass wasting; bluffs eroding through mass wasting as a result of fluvial undercutting and sapping; upland erosion on agricultural fields (particularly in spring prior to closure of the row-crop canopy); and streambank erosion above and beyond the volume involved in floodplain exchange. The Le Sueur River has been involved in two major changes to the landscape that have affected erosion from these sources: conversion of original prairie and forests to agriculture, and alterations to the basin hydrology that have increased overall peak flows (Novotny and Stefan, 2007).

Clearing and continued use of land for agriculture probably only affected erosion from upland sources directly. Changes in basin hydrology and climate, which led to higher discharges, could have increased erosion from streambanks and bluffs through channel widening and potentially higher rates of lateral channel migration. An increase in discharge in the large ravines could have increased erosion significantly. These landscape features have high channel and side slopes and are particularly sensitive

	Maple		Cobb	
	Upper	Lower	Upper	Lower
Drainage area (km^2)	780	878	336	737
TSS[†] (Mg yr^{-1})	7.9×10^3	2.2×10^4	4.0×10^3	3.3×10^4
TSS[†] yield (Mg km^{-2})	9.9	25.4	11.8	45.4

TABLE 4. TSS DATA FROM PAIRED GAUGES IN 2006*

*Data from MPCA (P. Baskfield, 2007, personal commun.), preliminary.
[†]TSS—total suspended solids.

portions of the landscape. In many cases, drainage-tile outlets empty directly into ravines, increasing peak flows dramatically. Observations from the field indicate that headcuts in ravines are highly active, particularly where ravine tips are eroding into glaciolacustrine sediments. Field observations during storm flows in ravines have found water running clear in low-intensity storms and very muddy in high-intensity storms, possibly indicating a threshold response in sediment flux from ravines, once overland flow is generated.

Paired gauges on the mainstem channels give us some insight into the relative importance of bluff and ravine erosion versus upland erosion. Gauges installed on the upper and lower Maple River and on the Big Cobb and Little Cobb Rivers provide a basis for estimating sediment contributions from bluff and ravine erosion. The upper gauge receives sediment primarily from upland fields, smaller tributaries and ditches, and streambank erosion into low terrace surfaces. The lower gauge contains additional sediment derived from ravines and erosion of high bluffs. The observed increase in TSS, above and beyond that expected from an increase in drainage area or discharge, indicates that bluffs and ravines are playing a significant role as sediment sources to the lower reaches. If the TSS yield from the watershed measured at the upper gauge is applied to the increase in watershed area above the lower gauge, the remaining TSS load provides an estimate of the contribution from ravines, banks, and bluffs. For the Maple and Cobb Rivers in 2006, 61%–74% of the sediment was potentially derived from these non-upland sources. Previous studies in the neighboring Blue Earth River have estimated that bank and bluff erosion alone account for 23%–56% of TSS load (Thoma et al., 2005) and 31%–44% according to Sekely et al. (2002). Ongoing work by S. Schottler and D. Engstrom (2008, personal commun.) indicates that >75% of the suspended sediment at the mouth of the Le Sueur River may be derived from non-field sources, including ravines, bluffs, terraces, and stored floodplain sediments.

Assessments of stream-migration rates on the mainstem Le Sueur River, coupled with bank and floodplain elevations, indicate that stream migration on the three major branches of the Le Sueur River could potentially contribute 2.7×10^4 Mg yr^{-1} of suspended sediment as a net source to the channel not balanced by floodplain deposition. This volume is 11%–14% of the average TSS load at the mouth of the Le Sueur River. Because the channel is incised, and channel migration occurs into these high surfaces, not just into floodplains, a significant mass of sediment can be contributed to the channel above and beyond the amount deposited on the floodplain.

CONCLUSIONS

The Le Sueur River has a well-constrained geomorphic history that can be used to understand the current sediment dynamics of the system. A major knickpoint migrating through the Le Sueur River network divides the watershed into two main regions: above the knick zone, where the watershed is dominated by low-

gradient agricultural uplands composed of glaciolacustrine and till deposits, and below the knick zone, where high bluffs and steep-sided ravines are added to the system. Gauging efforts indicate a significant rise in sediment load as rivers move through the lower reaches of the channel, below the knick zone, highlighting the importance of bluffs and ravines as sediment sources in the lower watershed. In addition, channel-migration studies indicate that streambank erosion from channel migration may contribute a significant volume of sediment to the overall TSS load that is not lost to floodplain deposition owing to the presence of high terraces and bluffs along the channel edge.

Sediment loads are high in the Le Sueur River, an order of magnitude higher than MPCA target values. Records from Lake Pepin indicate an order of magnitude increase in deposition, a rise that should be mirrored in the Le Sueur River, a major contributor of sediment to the Minnesota River and ultimately to Lake Pepin. However, calculations of sediment removed from the valley since base-level fall 11,500 yr B.P. indicate that modern sediment loads are only 1.3–3.4 times higher than the average load over the past 11,500 yr, even when grain-size variations and organic content are accounted for. This Holocene average rate assumes a linear progression of erosion through time, and the history of valley incision and erosion is more complicated than this. Efforts are ongoing to determine terrace ages in the lower Le Sueur River Valley to better constrain the history and evolution of incision and thus of sediment flux from the basin. Unraveling terrace histories will help resource management by better constraining presettlement sediment yields as well as by shedding light on the pattern and style of landscape evolution in an incising system.

ACKNOWLEDGMENTS

This work was funded by the Minnesota Pollution Control Agency with funds from the Minnesota Clean Water Legacy Act. Additional support came from the STC program of the National Science Foundation via the National Center for Earth-surface Dynamics under agreement no. EAR-0120914. We thank the Minnesota Pollution Control Agency staff for providing us with preliminary 2006 gauging data. We appreciate the comments of two anonymous reviewers. We are grateful for resources from the Minnesota Supercomputing Institute.

REFERENCES

Baker, R.G., Maher, L.J., Chumbley, C.A., and Van Zant, K.L., 1992, Patterns of Holocene environmental change in the Midwestern United States: Quaternary Research, v. 37, p. 379–389, doi: 10.1016/0033-5894(92)90074-S.

Clayton, L., and Moran, S.R., 1982, Chronology of late-Wisconsinan glaciation in middle North America: Quaternary Science Reviews, v. 1, p. 55–82, doi: 10.1016/0277-3791(82)90019-1.

Engstrom, D.R., Almendinger, J.E., and Wolin, J.A., 2000, Historical changes in sediment and phosphorus loading to the Upper Mississippi River: Mass-balance reconstructions from the sediments of Lake Pepin: Journal of Paleolimnology, 26 p., doi: 10.1007/s10933-008-9292-5.

Geiss, C.E., Umbanhowar, C.E., Camil, P., and Banerjee, S.K., 2003, Sediment magnetic properties reveal Holocene climate change along the Minnesota prairie-forest ecotone: Journal of Paleolimnology, v. 30, p. 151–166, doi: 10.1023/A:1025574100319.

Grimm, E., 1983, Chronology and dynamics of vegetation change in the prairie-woodland region of southern Minnesota, USA: New Phytology, v. 93, p. 311–350, doi: 10.1111/j.1469-8137.1983.tb03434.x.

Hancock, G.R., and Willgoose, G.R., 2002, The use of a landscape simulator in the validation of the SIBERIA landscape evolution model: Transient landforms: Earth Surface Processes and Landforms, v. 27, p. 1321–1334, doi: 10.1002/esp.414.

Hasbargen, L.E., and Paola, C., 2000, Landscape instability in an experimental drainage basin: Geology, v. 28, p. 1067–1070, doi: 10.1130/0091-7613 (2000)28<1067:LIIAED>2.0.CO;2.

Kelley, D.W., and Nater, E.A., 2000, Historical sediment flux from three watersheds into Lake Pepin, Minnesota, USA: Journal of Environmental Quality, v. 29, p. 561–568.

Kelley, D.W., Brachfeld, S.A., Nater, E.A., and Wright, H.E., Jr., 2006, Sources of sediment in Lake Pepin on the Upper Mississippi River in response to Holocene climatic changes: Journal of Paleolimnology, v. 35, p. 193–206, doi: 10.1007/s10933-005-8686-x.

Lauer, J.W., and Parker, G., 2005, Net transfer of sediment from floodplain to channel on three southern US rivers: Paper presented at ASCE World Water and Environmental Resources Congress, Anchorage, Alaska, 15–19 May 2005.

Lowell, T.V., Fisher, T.G., and Comer, G.C., 2005, Testing the Lake Agassiz meltwater trigger for the Younger Dryas: Eos (Transactions, American Geophysical Union), v. 86, p. 365–373.

Marschner, F.J., 1974, The original vegetation of Minnesota, a map compiled in 1930 by F.J. Marschner under the direction of M.L. Heinselman of the U.S. Forest Service: St. Paul, Minnesota, Cartography Laboratory of the Department of Geography, University of Minnesota.

Matsch, C.L., 1972, Quaternary geology of southwestern Minnesota, *in* Sims, P.K., and Morey, G.B., eds., Geology of Minnesota: A Centennial Volume: St. Paul, Minnesota Geological Survey, p. 548–560.

Matsch, C.L., 1983, River Warren, the southern outlet of Lake Agassiz, *in* Teller, J.T., and Clayton, L., eds., Glacial Lake Agassiz: Geological Association of Canada Special Paper 26, p. 232–244.

Minnesota Department of Natural Resources, 2007, Native Plant Communities and Rare Species of the Minnesota River Valley Counties: St. Paul, Minnesota Department of Natural Resources, Minnesota County Biological Survey Biological Report 89.

McCollor, S., and Heiskary, S., 1993, Selected water quality characteristics of minimally impacted streams from Minnesota's seven ecoregions: St. Paul, Addendum to descriptive characteristics of the seven ecoregions in Minnesota, 18 p.

Minnesota Pollution Control Agency (MPCA), Minnesota Department of Agriculture, Minnesota State University, Mankato Water Resources Center, and Metropolitan Council Environmental Services, 2007, State of the Minnesota River: Summary of Surface Water Quality Monitoring, 2000–2005: St. Paul, 20 p.

Novotny, E.V., and Stefan, H.G., 2007, Stream flow in Minnesota: Indicator of climate change: Journal of Hydrology, v. 334, p. 319–333, doi: 10.1016/j.jhydrol.2006.10.011.

Parker, R.S., 1977, Experimental study of drainage basin evolution and its hydrologic implications [Ph.D. thesis]: Fort Collins, Colorado State University, 331 p.

Sekely, A.C., Mulla, D.J., and Bauer, D.W., 2002, Streambank slumping and its contribution to the phosphorus and suspended sediment loads of the Blue Earth River, Minnesota: Journal of Soil and Water Conservation, v. 57, p. 243–250.

Thoma, D.P., Gupta, S.C., Bauer, M.E., and Kirchoff, C.E., 2005, Airborne laser scanning for riverbank erosion assessment: Remote Sensing of Environment, v. 95, p. 493–501, doi: 10.1016/j.rse.2005.01.012.

Thorleifson, L.H., 1996, Review of Lake Agassiz history, *in* Teller, J.T., Thorleifson, L.H., Matile, G., and Brisbin, W.C., 1996, Sedimentology, Geomorphology and History of the Central Lake Agassiz Basin: Geological Association of Canada/Mineralogical Association of Canada Annual Meeting, Winnipeg, Manitoba, 27–29 May 1996, Field Trip Guidebook B2, p. 55–84.

Upham, W., 1890, Report of exploration of the glacial Lake Agassiz in Manitoba: Geological Survey of Canada Annual Report, 1888–89, pt. E, 156 p.

Upham, W., 1895, The Glacial Lake Agassiz: U.S. Geological Survey Monograph 25, 658 p.

Water Resources Center, Minnesota State University, Mankato, 2000, Le Sueur River Major Watershed Diagnostic Report: Le Sueur River Basin Implementation Framework, MPCA Clean Water Partnership Project no. 951-1-194-07, 162 p.

Webb, T., III, Cushing, E.J., and Wright, H.E., Jr., 1984, Holocene changes in the vegetation of the Midwest, *in* Wright, H.E., Jr., ed., Late-Quaternary Environments of the United States, Vol. 2, The Holocene: Minneapolis, University of Minnesota Press, p. 142–165.

Webb, T., III, Ruddiman, W.F., Street-Perrott, F.A., Markgraf, V., Kutzbach, J.E., Bartlein, P.J., Wright, H.E., Jr., and Prell, W.L., 1993, Climatic changes during the past 18,000 years: Regional syntheses, mechanisms, and causes, *in* Wright, H.E., Jr., Kutzbach, J.E., Webb, T., III, Ruddiman, W.F., Street-Perrott, F.A., and Bartlein, P.J., eds., Global Climates since the Last Glacial Maximum: Minneapolis, University of Minnesota Press, p. 514–535.

Wobus, C., Whipple, K.X., Kirby, E., Snyder, N., Johnson, J., Spyropolou, K., Crosby, B., and Sheehan, D., 2006, Tectonics from topography: Procedures, promise, and pitfalls, *in* Willett, S.D., Hovius, N., Brandon, M.T., and Fisher, D.M., eds., Tectonics, Climate and Landscape Evolution: Geological Society of America Special Paper 398, p. 55–74.

MANUSCRIPT ACCEPTED BY THE SOCIETY 15 SEPTEMBER 2008

The Geological Society of America
Special Paper 451
2009

Vanishing riverscapes: A review of historical channel change on the western Great Plains

Ellen Wohl
Dena Egenhoff
Department of Geosciences, Colorado State University, Fort Collins, Colorado 80523-1482, USA

Kelly Larkin
Arapaho-Roosevelt National Forest and Pawnee National Grassland, Sulphur Range District, P.O. Box 10, Granby, Colorado 80446, USA

ABSTRACT

The South Platte and Republican River basins provide examples of historical channel changes on the western Great Plains. Flow regulation and diversion caused substantial channel narrowing and vegetation encroachment along larger, perennial rivers that head in the Rocky Mountains. Intensive groundwater pumping has reduced the volume and longitudinal connectivity of refuge pools along smaller intermittent or ephemeral channels that head on the plains. A case study from the Pawnee National Grassland of Colorado illustrates the dynamics of intermittent streams, as well as measures that can be taken to protect and restore refuge pools along these streams. The implications of channel change, and the need to protect and rehabilitate rivers, are less widely recognized for smaller rivers of the western Great Plains than for the larger, perennial rivers. Our objectives in this chapter are to provide a regional context for understanding changes in smaller plains rivers during the past century by reviewing the diversity of channel types and historical changes in the western Great Plains, and to briefly explore the dynamics of smaller plains rivers and the challenges to preserving these riverscapes.

INTRODUCTION

Increasing recognition of human-induced alterations in river ecosystems led to a dramatic rise in attempts to rehabilitate rivers during the last decades of the twentieth century. Rehabilitation measures vary in method from intensive engineering of channel form to modification of dam operation or land uses adjacent to the river channel (Kondolf, 1996; Bernhardt et al., 2005; Wohl et al., 2005), and in scope from short segments of

a few hundred meters of a stream channel to major rivers such as the Kissimmee, Colorado, and Mississippi (Toth et al., 1993; Gloss et al., 2005; O'Donnell and Galat, 2008). Rehabilitation projects have begun on some of the larger rivers of the western Great Plains, including the Missouri and the Platte (Graf et al., 2005; Adams et al., 2007). Smaller rivers of the western Great Plains have received less attention in terms of rehabilitation than smaller rivers in other regions of the United States, despite the fact that the shortgrass prairie of the western Great

Wohl, E., Egenhoff, D., and Larkin, K., 2009, Vanishing riverscapes: A review of historical channel change on the western Great Plains, *in* James, L.A., Rathburn, S.L., and Whittecar, G.R., eds., Management and Restoration of Fluvial Systems with Broad Historical Changes and Human Impacts: Geological Society of America Special Paper 451, p. 131–142, doi: 10.1130/2009.2451(09). For permission to copy, contact editing@geosociety.org. ©2009 The Geological Society of America. All rights reserved.

Plains is one of the most endangered ecosystems in the country (Manning, 1995).

This chapter briefly reviews the types of rivers present in the western Great Plains and the historical land uses that have altered these rivers, focusing on parts of the South Platte and Republican Rivers. We then use a case study of ephemeral streams on the Pawnee National Grassland in northeastern Colorado to illustrate the challenges of understanding and rehabilitating the ecosystems of smaller river systems in the western Great Plains. Our intent is to call attention to the importance of smaller, ephemeral and intermittent channels on the western Great Plains. These channels, which are more likely to be overlooked by those concerned with river protection, are an integral part of the riverscape of the western Great Plains. Fausch et al. (2002) introduced the term *riverscape* to emphasize the importance of viewing a river not as disjunct reaches but as an entire spatially heterogeneous ecosystem. Recent research compilations emphasize the importance of perennial headwater channels in the flow of water, sediment, nutrients, and organisms through riverscapes (Nadeau and Rains, 2007), but in drylands ephemeral and intermittent headwater channels can be equally important.

RIVERS OF THE WESTERN GREAT PLAINS

The western Great Plains here refers to the portion of the United States from the 100th meridian west to the base of the Rocky Mountains or, in the south, the Basin and Range Province (Osterkamp et al., 1987). (We include all of the historical prairie lands, from the tallgrass prairie of Illinois to the shortgrass prairie along the eastern edge of the Rockies, within the Great Plains [Covich et al., 1997; Savage, 2004].) Shortgrass prairie vegetation of bunchgrasses, shrubs, and cacti dominate the semiarid western Great Plains (Savage, 2004). Much of the flat or gently rolling terrain is covered by fluvial and eolian sediments of Quaternary age (Osterkamp et al., 1987; Madole, 1994, 1995). These sediments are underlain by Mesozoic and Cenozoic sedimentary rocks deposited in shallow-marine and terrestrial environments, with the Rockies as the primary source area (Madole, 1995).

Rivers of the western Great Plains are of three basic types. The larger rivers originate in the Rockies and flow eastward toward the Missouri-Mississippi system. These rivers are perennial or in some cases intermittent at greater distances from the mountains. Peak flows are supplied by snowmelt from the Rockies, supplemented at lower elevations by groundwater recharge and rainfall runoff. Rivers draining the Rocky Mountains discharge >70% of their annual water budget during 2 to 3 months of snowmelt and have instantaneous discharges 10 to 100 times the mean low flow (Hauer et al., 1997). The primary larger rivers of the western plains, from south to north, are the Canadian, Arkansas, South Platte, North Platte, Niobrara, Cheyenne, Little Missouri, Yellowstone, Missouri, and Milk. Of these rivers, only the Yellowstone remains relatively unaffected by flow regulation and land uses within or adjacent to the river corridor. The Cimarron, Smokey Hill, and Republican are

exceptions in that they are large rivers that head on the plains, rather than in the mountains.

Smaller rivers that head on the plains can be intermittent systems fed by groundwater seeps or springs, or ephemeral channels that depend entirely on surface runoff from the adjacent plains. Many of the smaller rivers, which are tributary to the larger, perennial rivers, or end in playas, have also been substantially altered by land use patterns including pumping of groundwater, irrigated agriculture, road development, and grazing (Fausch and Bestgen, 1997; Falke and Gido, 2006; Ficke, 2006).

This chapter focuses on channels in parts of the South Platte and Republican catchments in eastern Colorado. Changes in the hydrologic regime and channel characteristics of these two catchments reflect changes occurring in other river systems of the western plains (Nadler and Schumm, 1981; Fausch and Bestgen, 1997; Strange et al., 1999; Peters and Schainost, 2005).

Prior to ca. 1860 the larger streams of the western Great Plains were braided, with relatively straight, shallow channels 1–2 km wide and perennial or intermittent flow (Williams, 1978). Historic descriptions of the South Platte, the Platte, and the Arkansas emphasized the character of these rivers with descriptive phrases such as "too thick to drink but too thin to plow" and "a mile wide and an inch deep." Photographs from the 1860s to early 1900s depict channels so wide that it is sometimes difficult to detect the opposite bank, and banks largely bare of woody vegetation (Williams, 1978). Flow was highly seasonal, but even the large snowmelt peaks apparently did not go overbank (Eschner et al., 1983). These seasonal peaks were sufficient to rapidly erode the banks, causing the channel instability characteristic of braided rivers, and limiting the establishment of woody riparian vegetation. Rivers of the western plains have more fluctuating conditions of flow, temperature, and nutrients, as well as relatively simple habitat, in comparison with the more diverse and stable headwater mountain streams or with streams of the wetter eastern Great Plains. These conditions limited the diversity of fish species in rivers of the western plains but also led to the evolution of several endemic species with sensory and reproductive adaptations to turbidity and widely fluctuating flow. These adaptations include barbels and tactile sense organs that reduce the fish's dependence on vision; smaller, thicker scales resistant to abrasion; a metabolism tolerant of high temperatures and low levels of dissolved oxygen; and buoyant eggs that float downstream to suitable habitats, even as the embryos inside develop and hatch in as little as 24 h into precocious larvae capable of swimming soon after hatching (Matthews, 1987; Fausch and Bestgen, 1997).

Intermittent streams had longitudinally continuous flow each spring, but by summer flow was limited to disconnected pools maintained by groundwater. Ephemeral streams might be incised arroyos or shallow, swale-shaped channels, but were characterized by extremely flashy hydrographs when summer convective storms created peak flows that commonly lasted less than an hour. Fish living in these smaller streams developed strategies to compress their reproduction and growth into short periods of high flow that occurred unpredictably, maximize their mobility between suitable habitats that remained physically isolated for much of the time as a result of lack of flow, and survive physiologically stressful periods of high temperature and low dissolved-oxygen levels (Matthews, 1987; Fausch and Bestgen, 1997).

Although many of the intermittent and ephemeral streams were integrated into drainage networks that fed larger, perennial streams, some ended in playas. Playas of the western plains were widely scattered and typically small; the great majority covered <12 ha (Batt, 1996). These small, shallow, ephemeral lakes nonetheless formed a vital part of the riverscapes of the western plains. An estimated 25,000 playas spread from eastern Colorado and western Nebraska south to western Texas and Oklahoma. Only 10% to 20% of the playas contained water in an average year, but they supported invertebrates and plants adapted to long periods of dryness, as well as more than a million ducks, geese, cranes, and shorebirds that stopped to feed and rest in playas during their spring and fall migrations (Batt, 1996; Nickens, 2006).

CONSUMPTIVE WATER USE AND CHANNEL CHANGES

Changes in land and water use altered river characteristics across the western Great Plains as people of European descent began to settle the region ca. 1860. The first settlers quickly constructed small ditches to divert water from the larger rivers and irrigate crops growing on floodplains. By the 1870s, larger canals were being built to irrigate terraces, and reservoirs were constructed to store snowmelt runoff (Eschner et al., 1983).

The establishment of prior appropriation as the rule governing water usage in Colorado facilitated these changes. Prior appropriation—often paraphrased as "first in time, first in right"—guarantees that the earliest legal claimants to water rights maintain priority over any subsequent claimants. Prior appropriation also facilitates commercial transfer of water rights through purchase, and physical transfer through diversion. More than one example in the history of the western United States indicates that during years of greater than average flow it was possible to allocate more water to consumptive uses than normally exists in the river (Hundley, 1975; Stockton and Jacoby, 1976). The earliest record of overappropriation on the western Great Plains in Colorado comes from the Cache la Poudre River, a tributary of the South Platte, in 1876 (Eschner et al., 1983). Faced with potential water shortages, the rapidly growing agricultural communities at the eastern base of the Rockies began to divert water from the western slope.

Transbasin water diversions, particularly from the Colorado River, and groundwater pumping were used to supplement surface-water supplies on the plains starting in the 1890s and 1880s, respectively (Eschner et al., 1983). Transbasin diversions in the South Platte basin culminated with completion of the Colorado–Big Thompson Project in 1953, in which water is diverted across the Continental Divide from the Colorado River into the Big Thompson River, a tributary of the South Platte. Out-of-basin sources now account for nearly a quarter of the South Platte's total flow (Strange et al., 1999).

The net effect of diversions and storage on flow regime along the larger rivers was a decrease in peak flows, an increase in base flows, and a transition to more perennial flow farther away from the mountain front. Water tables rose locally as a result of infiltration from irrigated fields and more consistent streamflow. These changes facilitated the establishment of dense riparian forests of cottonwood and willow trees (Johnson, 1994) that stabilized channel banks and led to substantial reductions in channel width. Documented changes in channel width include sites on the South Platte (535 m wide in 1867; 80 m wide in 1952), the Arkansas (350 m wide in 1892; 34 m wide in 1977) (Nadler and Schumm, 1981), the North Platte (1280 m wide in 1865; 150 m wide in 1965), and the Platte (1405 m wide in 1865; 90 m wide in 1965) (Williams, 1978). Most of the larger rivers on the western Great Plains now have single-thread channels or an anastomosing planform.

Changes in flow along the smaller, intermittent and ephemeral rivers are more likely to reflect changes in the water table associated with groundwater pumping and agricultural irrigation. Although flood irrigation of crop fields can raise the water table locally, the most common effect of irrigation has been declining water tables because pumping rates exceed recharge. Much of the western Great Plains is underlain by the Ogallala aquifer, a heterogeneous sequence of clays, silts, sands, and gravels that extends beneath 372,000 km^2 of the plains (Gutentag et al., 1984). Declines in the water table in the Ogallala have been particularly extensive in the middle and southern portions of the western Great Plains (Gutentag et al., 1984). The Ogallala has dropped more than 8 m, for example, across ~5200 km^2 of eastern Colorado. In comparison with the extensive literature of historic channel changes induced by flow regulation on the larger rivers, few studies have documented the effects of groundwater declines on flow in smaller rivers. One of the better known case studies is that of the Arikaree River, an eastern Colorado tributary of the Republican River.

Although the Arikaree River drains 4,480 km^2, most streamflow is derived from the underlying Ogalalla aquifer. Areas contributing groundwater to the stream lie mostly within 5–10 km of the channel. The Ogalalla aquifer as a whole has been described as being more like an egg crate than a bathtub, which implies that groundwater recharge and pumping from local areas can strongly influence local streamflow. High-capacity groundwater pumping in the region of the Arikaree drainage began during the mid-1960s, and farmers in the surrounding county now pump almost 370,000,000 m^3 (300,000 acre-feet) of groundwater annually (Durnford et al., 2007). Mean annual discharge on the Arikaree declined dramatically starting in the mid-1960s (Durnford et al., 2007). The river historically had long, dry segments from mid-late summer to the following spring, but the existence of pools that retained water throughout the year provided critical habitat for fish such as the brassy minnow (*Hybognathus hankinsoni*), which was once widely distributed in northeastern Colorado but is now almost entirely restricted to 10 km of the Arikaree River (Scheurer et al., 2003). Groundwater modeling of 10 fish refuge pools indicates that pool depths reflect long-term trends associated with groundwater pumping, with shorter term fluctuations caused by precipitation and riparian evapotranspiration (Durnford et al., 2007). Along perennial segments of the river, flow drops rapidly once the irrigation season starts, and does not resume until about three weeks after pumping ceases in the autumn (Fardal, 2003).

The highly restricted range of the brassy minnow reflects the situation for many native fishes of the western Great Plains (Propst and Carlson, 1986; Peters and Schainost, 2005). Six of 38 native plains fish species in Colorado are known to have been lost since the first fish collections were made in the late nineteenth century, and an additional 13 species are listed by the state as endangered, threatened, or of special concern; in other words, half of the native plains fish species have either declined or gone extinct in eastern Colorado (Fausch and Bestgen, 1997). These fish are incredibly resilient, able to withstand unusually low levels of dissolved oxygen and high water temperatures, and possess unique strategies for surviving and reproducing in this harsh environment. Many of the fish grow to a maximum total length of <10 cm, probably because of the small size of potential habitats in many plains streams. Their small size, however, means that structures such as irrigation intakes, dams, and road or railroad culverts that create vertical barriers only a few centimeters high effectively preclude fish passage, fragment habitat, and restrict the ranging and migration behavior of plains fish that evolved to migrate in search of spawning, foraging, and refuge habitats. Ficke (2006) documented more than a hundred such structures in one 1,375 km² tributary basin of the 59,930 km² South Platte River basin.

A CASE STUDY: STREAMS OF THE PAWNEE NATIONAL GRASSLAND

It is within this context of historically changing riverscapes and declining and threatened populations of native aquatic species that we present a preliminary examination of potential controls on refuge pools. We use the term *refuge pools* to refer to depressions along stream channels that retain water throughout the year. Research along the Arikaree suggests that these features are highly vulnerable to groundwater pumping, but the western Great Plains are also in the midst of a relatively severe drought that began in 1999 and is presumably also lowering water tables. As a means of evaluating the relative influence of local consumptive water use versus regional climatic controls on water levels in refuge pools, we examined pools along channels tributary to the South Platte River in the Pawnee National Grassland, which lies ~100 km north of the Arikaree River basin. Unlike the situation in the Arikaree River basin, there is no center-pivot irrigation in the Pawnee study area.

Our primary objective was to conduct a preliminary examination of potential regional- and local-scale controls on the location and dynamics of refuge pools on the Pawnee National Grassland. Dynamics refers primarily to fluctuations in water volume through time, and to a lesser extent, fluctuations in fish populations. Regional-scale controls include interannual variations in precipitation and position of the pools with respect to a prominent bedrock escarpment known as the Chalk Bluffs. (Because these bluffs are the most prominent bedrock exposure and topographic high point at the Grassland, we reasoned that increasing downstream distance might correlate with increasing depth of alluvium and thus decreasing runoff and surface flow in this region of limited precipitation.) Local-scale controls include drainage area, topography, lithology, depth to bedrock, and surrounding land use. The examination is preliminary because we have no data on subsurface flow paths, which are likely to influence the location and volume of the refuge pools. A secondary objective was to compare the dynamics of refuge pools on the Pawnee National Grassland to those along the Arikaree River, where center-pivot irrigation and intensive pumping of groundwater have been shown to strongly influence flow from springs that supply the intermittent river. The absence of center-pivot irrigation at the Pawnee sites provides an opportunity to evaluate the relative influence on flow along intermittent streams of regional drought, which has affected both the Arikaree and Pawnee sites since 1999, and groundwater withdrawal. An improved understanding of controls on the location and dynamics of refuge pools at the Pawnee Grassland can be used to develop more effective programs for conserving native plains fishes.

Field Area

The Pawnee National Grassland represents conditions common across large parts of the western Great Plains in terms of geologic, climatic, and land-use history. Covering 79,876 ha, the Grassland lies in northeastern Colorado between the South Platte River and the Wyoming state line (Fig. 1). The elevation decreases from 1935 m in the northwest to 1310 m in the southeast.

The Grassland lies within the Colorado Piedmont where it borders the High Plains to the east (Trimble, 1993; Madole, 1995). The High Plains, differentiated as a portion of the western Great Plains with minimal fluvial incision (Osterkamp et al., 1987), were formed during the Late Cretaceous–early Tertiary Laramide uplift of the Rockies. Silts, sands, and gravels carried eastward from the mountains were deposited across an extensive fluvial surface, forming a vast ramp tilting down to the east. The Fox Hills Sandstone and the Laramie Formation preserve Cretaceous sedimentation (Scott, 1978). Three main Paleogene and Neogene sedimentation cycles are preserved in the Oligocene White River Group (including the Brule and Chadron Formations), the Miocene Arikaree Formation, and the Pliocene Ogallala Formation. These Cretaceous, Paleogene, and Neogene sediments have undergone minimal subsequent erosion except in places such as the Colorado Piedmont. Streams tributary to the South Platte River have eroded progressively headward into an escarpment known as the Chalk Bluffs, which parallels the Colorado-Wyoming border. In the process, these tributaries have captured eastward-flowing channels. The Chalk Bluffs are capped by Miocene sandstones and conglomerates that are more resistant to erosion than the underlying White River Group. The White River Group includes fluvial and eolian sandstones, siltstones, and shales. Most of these sediments are soft, densely fractured, and readily erodible (Trimble, 1993). Deeply incised ephemeral channels and badland topography commonly form where rocks of the White River Group are exposed or close to the surface.

In general, groundwater slopes toward the south to southeast, following the drainage network of the South Platte River. The water table varies throughout the Grassland as a result of differences in permeability and thickness of the water-bearing material or as a result of additions (isolated recharge areas associated with summer thunderstorms) or withdrawals of water. Specific water-bearing formations in the Grassland are the Cretaceous Fox Hills Sandstone and the Laramie Formation, the Paleogene White River Group, and the Neogene Arikaree and Ogallala Formations. The Cretaceous strata consist of interbedded sandstone, siltstone, and claystone units deposited in shallow-marine to nonmarine environments. Both the Cretaceous Fox Hills Sandstone and Laramie Formation yield moderate supplies of water to wells in the area and are under sufficient hydrostatic pressure to cause artesian wells (Babcock and Bjorklund, 1956). The Paleogene White River Group consists of interbedded sandstone and mudstone units. Within the Brule Formation, impermeable siltstones with fractures and joints lead to potential irrigation groundwater sources (Babcock and Bjorklund,

1956). The Neogene Arikaree Formation consists exclusively of sandstones, whereas the overlying Ogallala Formation shows a complete suite of grain sizes from conglomerates through sand- and siltstones to shales. In both units, water-bearing beds are relatively thin and yield water for stock and domestic uses in the area (Babcock and Bjorklund, 1956).

Soils in the Pawnee National Grassland are diverse, but are predominantly well-drained, shallow to deep loams, clay loams, and sandy loams of depths <<1 m (Crabb, 1981; NRCS, 2008). Fluvial and eolian processes, along with underlying lithology, create substantial spatial variations in soils despite the relatively subdued topography of the region. Patches of exposed gravel and cobbles and barren siltstone badlands alternate with sandy soils along stream terraces and finer-textured soils in swales. Playas and riparian areas commonly have alkaline soils.

The area of the Pawnee National Grassland has a highland continental climate. Westerly winds dominate throughout much of the year. Most of the moisture that these winds carry inland from the Pacific Ocean is lost as air masses cross the Rocky Mountains, creating a rain shadow that keeps the western Great Plains semiarid. Annual precipitation averages 30–38 cm across the region. Cold, polar air masses travel southward into the region during autumn and winter, creating extremely low temperatures of −29 to −34 °C; the average winter temperature is −2 °C (Crabb, 1981). Warm, moist air traveling inland from the Gulf of Mexico reaches the area during spring and summer. The heaviest rainfalls occur during spring, when air masses from the Pacific, the Arctic, and the Gulf of Mexico collide over the western plains. Seventy to eighty percent of the annual precipitation falls between April and August (Badaracco, 1971). Although an average of 100 cm of snow falls in northeastern Colorado, desiccating winds create high rates of sublimation, and relatively little of the snow actually melts and infiltrates except on the leeward sides of hills and around shrubs (Hazlett, 1998). Summer temperatures on the Grassland can exceed 38 °C; the average summer temperature is 21 °C (Crabb, 1981; WRCC, 2008). Precipitation during summer falls from localized convective storms that create flash floods. Relative humidity is typically low throughout the year (Badaracco, 1971).

Severe weather in the form of tornadoes, hailstorms, blizzards, and droughts are a regular part of the climate of the western Great Plains. Droughts, in particular, strongly influence regional vegetation and stream characteristics. A 400 yr climatic record from tree rings in western Nebraska indicates an average period of only 20.6 yr between droughts that persist for 5 yr or more; on average, droughts persist for 12.8 yr (Weakly, 1943).

The Grassland lies within the central shortgrass prairie ecoregion (The Nature Conservancy, 1997), also known as the shortgrass steppe. All of the available soil moisture is transpired before the end of the growing season, and less than half of the ground surface is covered by vegetation (Hazlett, 1998). Dominant plant species include blue grama grass (*Bouteloua gracilis*), buffalo grass (*Buchloe dactyloides*), threeawn grass (*Aristida pupurea*), fringed sage (*Artemisia frigida*), rabbitbrush

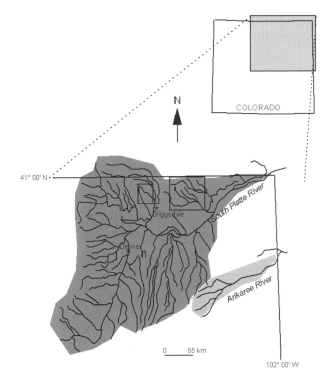

Figure 1. Location map of the South Platte basin (darker shading), Arikaree River basin (lighter shading), the two main units of the Pawnee National Grassland (squares near Briggsdale), and Briggsdale. Inset shows location of the detailed map within the State of Colorado.

(*Chrysothamnus nauseosus*), snakeweed (*Gutierrezia sarothrae*), ring muhly (*Muhlenbergia torreyi*), prickly pear cactus (*Opuntia polyacantha*), western wheatgrass (*Pascopyron smithii*), scurf pea (*Psoralidium tenuiflorum*), and scarlet globemallow (*Sphaeralcea coccinea*) (Hazlett, 1998). Sand sage (*Artemisia filifolia*) and soapweed (*Yucca glauca*) are common on sandy soils, several species of aquatic plants are present in seasonal wetlands, and cottonwood trees (*Populus deltoides*) and sandbar willow (*Salix exigua*) occur along some riparian corridors (Hazlett, 1998).

The Pawnee National Grassland was established after the 1930s Dust Bowl in response to severe soil erosion from agricultural lands. An estimated 60% of the grassland in Weld County, which includes the Grassland, had been plowed by 1930 (Hazlett, 1998), mostly for dryland agriculture. At present, the area within the Grassland is a mosaic of lands owned by the federal government, the state government, and private individuals. Although some dryland cropping occurs, the most widespread land use is grazing of domestic cattle.

Channels and Riparian Zones

Stream channels on the Pawnee National Grassland are intermittent or ephemeral. All of the channels drain south-southeast to the South Platte River. The degree of incision along individual channels is highly longitudinally variable. Many channels begin downstream of broad, shallow, unchannelized grassy swales that have low (<1 m), arcuate scarps spaced irregularly downstream (Fig. 2). These characteristics, along with the presence of small pipes in channel cutbanks, suggest that subsurface piping strongly influences the surface expression of channels. The channelized portion of a network commonly shows indications of past incision, although the contemporary channel may now take the form of a grassy swale with a relatively broad, shallow, active channel (Fig. 3). Active headcuts and short (50–300 m) segments of deeply incised channel occur at irregular intervals downstream. Incised channel segments commonly begin at amphitheater-shaped headcuts and increase only slightly in width downstream, suggesting that piping exerts an important control on the location of headcuts and actively incising segments. Although little is known of the history of channel incision in the area, coring of junipers (*Juniperus scopulorum*) growing within stabilized incised channels suggests that incision occurred prior to 115–200 yr ago (Badaracco, 1971).

Ephemeral channels flow briefly, primarily during spring and summer in response to snowmelt and rainfall. Intermittent channels are supplied by groundwater recharge from shallow, perched aquifers. Most of the Grassland is underlain by the Ogallala Formation, and the Brule member of the White River Group also serves as an

Figure 2. Upstream view of a collapse feature along South Pawnee Creek on the Pawnee National Grassland. Photograph taken in October, when the channel is dry but for refuge pools (upstream edge of pool in lower right corner of photo). Notice the unchannelized swale upstream.

aquifer in some areas. Wells pumped by windmills and for residential use commonly tap into these units at depths >45 m. Artesian springs that feed intermittent channels may be supplied by these deeper units, but may also be supplied by shallower, perched aquifers formed in Quaternary fluvial and eolian sediments where less porous and permeable bedrock rises to within a few meters of the surface along drainages. Many of these springs are identified and named on 1:24,000-scale topographic maps, suggesting that they are persistent features. Observations by residents and Forest Service employees indicate that some of these artesian springs commonly go dry during the later summer and autumn, whereas others typically persist throughout the year.

The only other form of surface water that persists throughout the year along the network of ephemeral channels occurs in depressions along the channels that appear to be piping-collapse features (Fig. 2). These depressions create pools that support resident populations of several native plains fishes, including plains topminnow (*Fundulus sciadicus*), plains killifish (*Fundulus zebrinus*), green sunfish (*Lepomis cyanellus*), fathead minnow (*Pimephales promelas*), Iowa darter (*Etheostoma exile*), northern creek chub (*Semotilus atromaculatus*), black bullhead (*Ameiurus melas*), and white sucker (*Catostomus commersoni*), as well as frogs, turtles, salamanders, and aquatic insects. Although the depressions appear to be collapse features, scour and fill resulting from flash floods during summer thunderstorms probably also modify the depressions.

Methods

Biologists with the Colorado Division of Wildlife and the U.S. Department of Agriculture Forest Service began monitoring the physical characteristics and organisms present in a series of refuge pools in the Pawnee National Grassland in 1988. Measurements have continued to the present but have been carried out by different individuals and have not consistently included the same parameters each year. Our first task therefore was to assemble the data collected from a variety of records kept at different agency offices. From these data we chose a subset of 13 refuge pools for which we could compile the most information (Fig. 4; Table 1). Because all of the stream channels containing refuge pools are ungauged, and the annual surveys were not referenced to benchmarks, we cannot evaluate the effects that scour and fill during brief, infrequent flash floods might have had on pool location or geometry.

Our analyses of pool locations were designed to evaluate whether average pool volume correlated with the physical

Figure 3. Downstream view of a now mostly stabilized incised channel network on the Pawnee National Grassland. Note the grassy bottom of the channel at the lower left of the photo and the presence of scattered juniper trees along the channel network; vegetation indicates contemporary stability of much of the incised valley bottom.

characteristics of the drainage area, elevation, relief, or mapped rock unit or soil unit. Although we interpret the refuge pools as piping-collapse features (on the basis of longitudinally discontinuous, arcuate scarps associated with pools) with volumes that predominantly reflect subsurface flow and erosion and the location of the local water table, we wanted to determine whether pool volume might be predictable on the basis of the characteristics listed above. We conducted multiple regression analyses (ANOVA) using average pool volume and average number of fish caught during annual surveys, respectively, as response variables.

In order to evaluate regional controls on pool dynamics, we compared pool volume to annual precipitation at the closest precipitation gauge (Briggsdale, Colorado; Fig. 1). This also provided a means of evaluating our assumption that the pools predominantly reflect subsurface processes rather than surface runoff. Finally, we visited 11 mapped springs in the vicinity of the refuge pools during November 2007 to determine whether the ongoing drought had caused any of these springs to go dry.

Results and Discussion

One of the most striking characteristics of the refuge pools surveyed on the Pawnee National Grassland is the extreme inter-

annual variability in pool volume and the number of fish caught, as reflected in the large standard deviations in these numbers (Table 1). Some of the larger pools have even gone dry for a year or two at a time during the two decades of discontinuous monitoring.

Pool volume has little correlation with annual precipitation (Fig. 5), although this is not surprising given the high spatial variability in precipitation from the summer convective storms that produce much of the surface runoff in the region. Annual precipitation at Briggsdale varied from 20 to 39 cm over the short period of 2000–2007. It is likely that interannual variability was just as high across the study area, and annual totals varied between sites. Our visits to mapped springs during the dry season of the year also indicate that the continuing regional drought has not caused the springs to cease flowing. Ten of the 11 springs were flowing steadily in November 2007, and nearby residents who have lived in the area for three generations said that the dry spring has always flowed only briefly during springtime. Six of the 11 springs are underlain by the Ogallala Formation, the primary regional aquifer; the remaining sites are underlain by the White River Formation. The refuge pools, in contrast, are mostly underlain by other formations (Table 1) that do not form aquifers as effectively. Although the continued activity of springs does not definitively indicate that the regional drought is not the primary

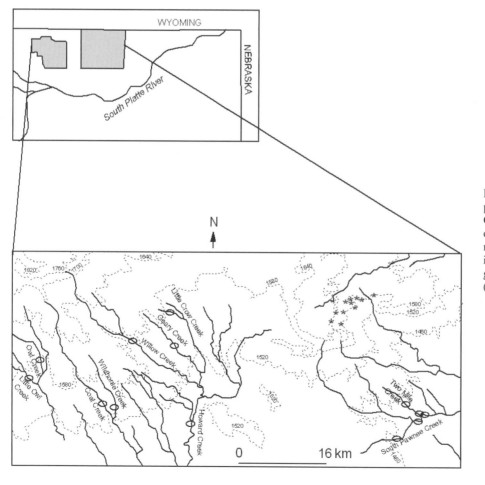

Figure 4. Location map of the refuge pools and springs at the Pawnee National Grassland. Inset map shows the two units of the Grassland (gray shading); detailed map shows the primary ephemeral and intermittent channels (solid lines), topographic contours (dashed lines), springs (asterisks), and refuge pools (ellipses).

TABLE 1. CHARACTERISTICS OF REFUGE POOLS ON THE PAWNEE NATIONAL GRASSLAND, 1993–2007

Site	Drainage area (km²)	Elevation (m)	Relief (m)	Bedrock geology	Pool volume (m³)		Number of fish caught		Years of data collection
					Avg.	Std. dev.	Avg.	Std. dev.	
Coal Creek	106	1523	206	Laramie Fm	272	204	74	63	1993, 1999–2002
Geary Creek	201	1526	85	Laramie Fm	59	40	2	4	1993, 2001
Howard Creek	10	1532	70	Laramie Fm	353	185	295	321	1993, 1999–2007
Tributary to Little Crow Creek	2.8	1559	52	White River Group	228	185	148	144	1993, 1998–2001
Little Owl Creek	86	1556	304	Laramie Fm	132	0	66	66	1993, 1998–2001
Owl Creek	212	1578	346	Laramie Fm	540	283	245	230	1993, 1998–2005
South Pawnee Creek Box	290	1398	137	Pierre Shale	978	705	160	201	1998–2002
South Pawnee Fiscus	11	1404	131	Pierre Shale	184	117	88	147	1998–2006
South Pawnee Kibben	24	1438	97	Fox Hills Ss	421	273	255	312	1999–2007
South Pawnee Simmons	33	1406	129	White River	693	332	266	304	1998–2007
Two Mile Creek	3	1401	21	Alluvium	135	100	8	9	1998–2002
Wildhorse Creek	47	1517	140	Laramie Fm	301	256	18	16	1999–2002
Willow Creek	94	1550	228	Laramie Fm	743	546	193	176	1998–2007

Note: Cretaceous Laramie Formation is interbedded sandstone, siltstone and claystone units; Oligocene White River Group is interbedded sandstone and mudstone units; Cretaceous Pierre Shale is marine shale; Cretaceous Fox Hills Sandstone is shallow-marine sandstone; Pleistocene alluvium is coarse sand and gravel and lenses of silt, clay, cobbles, and boulders.

mechanism causing some of the refuge pools to go dry during certain years, it suggests that local controls may be exerting more influence on pool dynamics.

The multiple regression analyses did not produce a statistically significant model for the response variables of average pool volume and average number of fish caught in each pool. This indicates either that the sample size is too small to provide insight into the complexity of interacting controls on pool and fish characteristics or that the potential control variables analyzed in the test are not the best predictors of pool and fish characteristics.

The implication of these analyses is that the average volume and interannual variability in volume in refuge pools on the Pawnee National Grassland reflect local, site-specific controls rather than predictable criteria such as a minimum threshold of drainage area or relief. The numbers and diversity of fish present in a refuge pool partly reflect the size of that pool, as indicated by correlations between pool volume and average number of fish caught, and between standard deviation in pool volume and standard deviation in number of fish caught, respectively, that are significant at $\alpha = 0.05$. Fish abundance and diversity in a refuge pool also partly reflect the site-specific history of flow magnitude and duration, which control longitudinal connectivity between refuge pools and may influence pool geometry through scour and fill.

Summarizing the results of fish surveys on the western Great Plains of Colorado, Kehmeier and VanBuren (1990) noted that all fish species found in refuge pools were widely scattered and that the biggest limiting factor appeared to be the lack of water; even if fish could consistently reach a pool during higher flows of springtime, biologists interpreted the variability between annual samples to indicate that refuge pools go dry or undergo die-offs as a result of freezing or lack of dissolved oxygen. Observations at the Pawnee National Grassland sites of complete drying of some pools that had been present for several years and then were present again in subsequent years support this interpretation.

Concerned about the status of several endemic plains fish species, the Colorado Division of Wildlife has in the past actively stocked some of the refuge pools on the Pawnee National Grassland, only to have these pools subsequently go dry. The lack of correlation between pool location and dynamics and regional-scale controls suggests that the best strategy for maintaining endemic fish populations may be to concentrate on those pools that annual samples indicate have consistently large volume. Such pools can be targeted for protection by restricting consumptive water use or drilling for oil and gas in the vicinity, and by limiting construction of structures such as road culverts that could limit longitudinal connectivity in the drainage system during periods of high flow. Owl Creek, Willow Creek, and South Pawnee Creek, which have numerous large refuge pools that are only a few river kilometers apart, are particularly good candidates for this type of targeted protection.

The refuge pools at the Pawnee National Grassland sites also provide an interesting contrast to those along the Arikaree River. Measurements of pool dynamics throughout the spring, summer, and autumn indicate that seasonal groundwater pumping along the Arikaree reduces local water tables and volume of refuge pools, with a very short lag time between the start and cessation of pumping and the response of pool volumes. Pools at the Pawnee Grassland are not subject to local water withdrawals and drawdowns but still exhibit tremendous interannual variability in volume and ability to support aquatic life. Although we were not able to statistically demonstrate the controls on this variability, further examination of subsurface parameters that influence the water table locally might improve the ability to predict which pools most reliably contain sufficient water to support fish populations.

PROTECTING AND RESTORING RIVERSCAPES OF THE WESTERN PLAINS

The Great Plains as a whole is an exceptionally endangered ecosystem. An estimated 1% of grasslands with native plant communities remain across the spectrum of tallgrass prairie in the eastern plains, mixed-grass prairie in the central plains, and shortgrass prairie in the western plains (Manning, 1995). Alterations of plant

communities, soils, and topography have resulted primarily from agricultural land use, and to a lesser extent from transportation corridors and urbanization. Plains rivers of varying size have also been substantially altered during the past 150–200 yr. Channelization, flow regulation, levees, and increased sediment yields are the most important land-use changes to alter rivers in the eastern plains, whereas groundwater pumping and flow regulation have created the greatest effect on rivers of the western plains.

Several studies have documented the historical metamorphosis of channel form and function along larger rivers of the western Great Plains that originate in the Rocky Mountains (Williams, 1978; Nadler and Schumm, 1981; Eschner et al., 1983; Johnson, 1994), as well as the effects of this metamorphosis on native fishes, migratory birds, and other species of plants and animals (Propst and Carlson, 1986; Graf et al., 2005). Public awareness of the negative aspects of these historical changes has led to efforts to restore some of the form and function present along these rivers prior to 1850. These efforts range from national-scale studies and coordinated programs (e.g., Graf et al., 2005) to groups of local stakeholders who organize public information

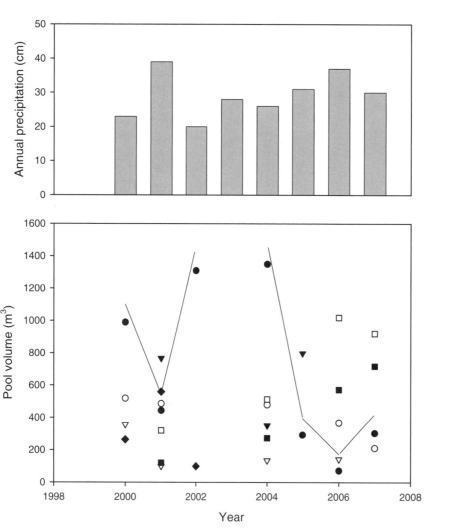

Figure 5. Plots of interannual variations in pool volume and annual precipitation at Briggsdale, Colorado, for 2000–2007. Each symbol in the lower plot represents a different pool. The symbols for the Willow Creek refuge pool are connected to illustrate more clearly interannual variability; the gap represents the absence of a sample in 2003.

fora and commission studies and restoration projects (e.g., Big Thompson Watershed Forum, Annual South Platte Forum).

Public awareness of analogous historical changes along smaller, intermittent and ephemeral rivers of the western plains is much lower, perhaps in part because of fewer and more recent scientific studies of these changes and their effects on biotic communities, and perhaps in part because many people do not think of ephemeral or intermittent channels as supporting riverine ecosystems. Loss of refuge pools and longitudinal connectivity along these smaller channels is likely to have the greatest impact on aquatic communities, although riparian grazing may create an equally significant impact on riparian communities. Loss of pools and longitudinal connectivity may reflect changes in the rainfall-runoff regime as a result of land use, but fluctuations in regional and local, perched water tables are likely to be the most important control at many sites, including the Arikaree River catchment and Pawnee National Grassland sites discussed in this paper. Understanding the relative importance of variables that influence fluctuations in water tables thus becomes critical for effectively managing populations of native plants and animals that are at risk because of loss of riparian and aquatic habitat along ephemeral and intermittent streams.

Research to date on smaller rivers of the western plains has been undertaken primarily by fish biologists who, as Labbe and Fausch (2000) note, ". . . typically assumed that abundance within habitats was primarily controlled by local environmental factors and that, once established, most populations would persist indefinitely" (p. 1774). Research by Fausch and others suggests that ecosystem-scale processes exert an important control by creating a context within which smaller-scale physical and biotic processes influence the distribution and abundance of plains fishes. Consequently, effective conservation of plains biodiversity requires a landscape-scale approach that considers the controls on movement of fishes between isolated habitat refugia.

Labbe and Fausch's (2000) study of the distribution of Arkansas darters (*Etheostoma cragini*) in two pools in small, headwater subwatersheds within the 8412-km² watershed of Big Sandy Creek in southeastern Colorado provides an example of how processes operating at different scales interact to influence fish populations. Darters persisted in the deeper pools that were most permanent during summer droughts, dying only when the pools dried out. Flow variation among seasons and years controlled habitat connectivity and thus dispersal, reproduction, and distribution and age composition of darters. Juvenile darters, for example, were more abundant and hatched earlier and grew faster in the warmer downstream pool that can freeze during winter and have harsh, variable thermal regimes during summer. Older fish dominated populations in the spring-fed pool upstream. Adult darters were more mobile, dispersing out of the upstream pool in early spring and returning upstream before the onset of summer drying. Large summer floods along the two channels scoured new spring-fed pools that provided darter refugia, and filled other pools, continually altering the distribution, abundance, and quality of habitat available to darters. Labbe and Fausch (2000) con-

sequently concluded that "To be effective, recovery efforts for species inhabiting variable environments must consider multiple scales, from landscape-level processes that create and maintain refugia to fine-scale factors that regulate the abundance and persistence of local populations" (p. 1774).

The case study summarized here examines the relative importance of regional- and local-scale controls on the dynamics of refuge pools at the Pawnee National Grassland. Unlike previously studied field areas on the plains of Colorado, scour and fill during flash floods (Labbe and Fausch, 2000) and intensive groundwater pumping (Durnford et al., 2007) do not appear to be the most significant influences on longitudinal connectivity and water-level fluctuations in refuge pools at the Pawnee sites. Instead, nonhuman, local-scale controls dominate connectivity and pool volume through their influence on local water tables. Our results imply that protecting and restoring riverscapes and ecological communities in the Pawnee drainages require identifying the most consistently suitable refuge pools and then limiting patterns of land use that could affect either water tables or longitudinal stream connectivity in these drainages. This is likely to be easier to implement than restoration strategies in catchments such as the Arikaree River, where the existence of irrigated agriculture implies that refuge pools can be most effectively protected if consumptive water use on adjacent lands is reduced or eliminated. The recognition that many endemic, endangered fish species of the western Great Plains depend on refuge pools, and that adjacent land uses can alter the ability of these pools to sustain fish populations, can guide efforts to manage scarce water resources in the region.

ACKNOWLEDGMENTS

We thank Rich Madole and an anonymous reviewer for constructive comments on an earlier version of this paper.

REFERENCES CITED

Adams, D., Hughes, M., and Sundstrom, G., 2007, Riparian forest restoration initiative project proposed for the North and South Platte Rivers: Colorado Water, v. 25, p. 26–29.

Babcock, H.M., and Bjorklund, L.J., 1956, Ground-Water Geology of Parts of Laramie and Albany Counties, Wyoming, and Weld County, Colorado: U.S. Geological Survey Water-Supply Paper 1367, 61 p.

Badaracco, R.J., 1971, An interpretive resource analysis of Pawnee Buttes, Colorado [Ph.D. thesis]: Fort Collins, Colorado State University, 341 p.

Batt, B.D.J., 1996, Prairie ecology–prairie wetlands, *in* Samson, F.B., and Knopf, F.L., eds., Prairie Conservation: Preserving North America's Most Endangered Ecosystem: Washington, D.C., Island Press, p. 77–88.

Bernhardt, E.S., Palmer, M.A., Allan, J.D., Alexander, G., Barnas, K., Brooks, S., Carr, J., Clayton, S., Dahm, C., Follstad-Shah, J., Galat, D., Gloss, S., Goodwin, P., Hart, D., Hassett, B., Jenkinson, R., Katz, S., Kondolf, G.M., Lake, P.S., Lave, R., Meyer, J.L., O'Donnell, T.K., Pagano, L., Powell, B., and Sudduth, E., 2005, Synthesizing U.S. river restoration efforts: Science, v. 308, p. 636–637, doi: 10.1126/science.1109769.

Big Thompson Watershed Forum, 2008, http://www.btwatershed.org/.

Covich, A.P., Fritz, S.C., Lamb, P.J., Marzolf, R.D., Matthews, W.J., Poiani, K.A., Prepas, E.E., Richman, M.B., and Winter, T.C., 1997, Potential effects of climate change on aquatic ecosystems of the Great Plains of North America: Hydrological Processes, v. 11, p. 993–1021, doi: 10.1002/(SICI)1099-1085(19970630)11:8<993::AID-HYP515>3.0.CO;2-N.

Crabb, J.A., 1981, Soil Survey of Weld County, Colorado, Northern Part: U.S. Department of Agriculture Soil Conservation Service and Forest Service in cooperation with Colorado Agricultural Experiment Station, 1 p.

Durnford, D., Squires, A., Falke, J., Fausch, K., Oad, R., and Riley, L., 2007, Agricultural and water management alternatives to sustain a vulnerable aquatic ecosystem on the eastern High Plains of Colorado: Fort Collins, Colorado Water: Newsletter of the Water Center of Colorado State University, p. 14–19.

Eschner, T.R., Hadley, R.F., and Crowley, K.D., 1983, Hydrologic and Morphologic Changes in Channels of the Platte River Basin in Colorado, Wyoming, and Nebraska: A Historical Perspective: U.S. Geological Survey Professional Paper 1277-A, 39 p.

Falke, J.A., and Gido, K.B., 2006, Spatial effects of reservoirs on fish assemblages in Great Plains streams in Kansas, USA: River Research and Applications, v. 22, p. 55–68, doi: 10.1002/rra.889.

Fardal, L.L., 2003, Effects of groundwater pumping for irrigation to stream properties of the Arikaree River on the Colorado plains [M.S. thesis]: Fort Collins, Colorado State University, 71 p.

Fausch, K.D., and Bestgen, K.R., 1997, Ecology of fishes indigenous to the central and southwestern Great Plains, in Knopf, F.L., and Samson, F.B., eds., Ecology and Conservation of Great Plains Vertebrates: New York, Springer-Verlag, p. 131–166.

Fausch, K.D., and Bramblett, R.G., 1991, Disturbance and fish communities in intermittent tributaries of a western Great Plains river: Copeia, v. 1991, p. 659–674.

Fausch, K.D., Torgersen, C.E., Baxter, C.V., and Li, H.W., 2002, Landscapes to riverscapes: Bridging the gap between research and conservation of stream fishes: Bioscience, v. 52, p. 483–498, doi: 10.1641/0006-3568 (2002)052[0483:LTRBTG]2.0.CO;2.

Ficke, A.D., 2006, Fish barriers and small plains fishes: Fishway design recommendations and the impact of existing instream structures [M.S. thesis]: Fort Collins, Colorado State University, 104 p.

Gloss, S.P., Lovich, J.E., and Melis, T.S., eds., 2005, The State of the Colorado River Ecosystem in Grand Canyon: U.S. Geological Survey Circular 1282, 220 p.

Graf, W.L., Barzen, J.A., Cuthbert, F., Doremus, H., Harrington, L.M.B., Herricks, E.E., Jacobs, K.L., Johnson, W.C., Lupi, F., Murphy, D.D., Palmer, R.N., Peters, E.J., Shen, H.W., and Thompson, J.A., 2005, Endangered and Threatened Species of the Platte River: Washington, D.C., National Academies Press, 299 p.

Gutentag, E.D., Heimes, F.J., Krothe, N.C., Luckey, R.R., and Weeks, J.B., 1984, Geohydrology of the High Plains Aquifer in Parts of Colorado, Kansas, Nebraska, New Mexico, Oklahoma, South Dakota, Texas, and Wyoming: U.S. Geological Survey Professional Paper 1400-B, 63 p.

Hauer, F.R., Baron, J.S., Campbell, D.H., Fausch, K.D., Hostetler, S.W., Leavesley, G.H., Leavitt, P.R., McKnight, D.M., and Stanford, J.A., 1997, Assessment of climate change and freshwater ecosystems of the Rocky Mountains, USA and Canada: Hydrological Processes, v. 11, p. 903–924, doi: 10.1002/(SICI)1099-1085(19970630)11:8<903:AID-HYP511>3.0.CO;2-7.

Hazlett, D.L., 1998, Vascular Plant Species of the Pawnee National Grassland: Fort Collins, Colorado, U.S. Department of Agriculture Forest Service, Rocky Mountain Research Station, General Technical Report RMRS-GTR-17, 26 p.

Hundley, N., 1975, Water and the West: The Colorado River Compact and the Politics of Water in the American West: Los Angeles, University of California Press, 417 p.

Johnson, W.C., 1994, Woodland expansion in the Platte River, Nebraska: Patterns and causes: Ecological Management, v. 64, p. 45–84, doi: 10.2307/2937055.

Kehmeier, K., and VanBuren, R., 1990, Plains fisheries investigations: Fort Collins, Colorado Division of Wildlife Northeast Region Aquatic, unpublished report, 34 p.

Kondolf, G.M., 1996, A cross section of stream channel restoration: Journal of Soil and Water Conservation, v. 51, p. 119–125.

Labbe, T.R., and Fausch, K.D., 2000, Dynamics of intermittent stream habitat regulate persistence of a threatened fish at multiple scales: Ecological Applications, v. 10, p. 1774–1791, doi: 10.1890/1051-0761(2000)010[1774:DOISHR]2.0.CO;2.

Madole, R.F., 1994, Stratigraphic evidence of desertification in the west-central Great Plains within the past 1000 yr: Geology, v. 22, p. 483–486, doi: 10.1130/0091-7613(1994)022<0483:SEODIT>2.3.CO;2.

Madole, R.F., 1995, Spatial and temporal patterns of late Quaternary eolian deposition, eastern Colorado, USA: Quaternary Science Reviews, v. 14, p. 155–177, doi: 10.1016/0277-3791(95)00005-A.

Manning, R., 1995, Grassland: The History, Biology, Politics, and Promise of the American Prairie: New York, Viking, 306 p.

Matthews, W.J., 1987, Physicochemical tolerance and selectivity of stream fishes as related to their geographic ranges and local distributions, in Matthews, W.J., and Hein, D.C., eds., Community and Evolutionary Ecology of North American Stream Fishes: Norman, University of Oklahoma Press, p. 111–120.

Nadeau, T.-L., and Rains, M.C., 2007, Hydrological connectivity of headwaters to downstream waters: Introduction to the featured collection: Journal of the American Water Resources Association, v. 43, p. 1–4.

Nadler, C.T., and Schumm, S.A., 1981, Metamorphosis of South Platte & Arkansas rivers, eastern Colorado: Physical Geography, v. 2, p. 95–115.

Nature Conservancy, The, 1997, Archipelagos of Hope: Arlington, Virginia, Guidelines for Ecoregion-Based Conservation, 84 p.

Nickens, T.E., 2006, Here today, gone tomorrow: Audubon, v. 108, p. 42–47.

NRCS (Natural Resources Conservation Service) online, 2008: http://oil-gas.state.co.us/infosys/Maps/LoadMap.cfm.

O'Donnell, T.K., and Galat, D.L., 2008, Evaluating success criteria and project monitoring in river enhancement within an adaptive management framework: Environmental Management, v. 41, p. 90–105, doi: 10.1007/s00267-007-9010-5.

Osterkamp, W.R., Fenton, M.M., Gustavson, T.C., Hadley, R.F., Holliday, V.T., Morrison, R.B., and Toy, T.J., 1987, Great Plains, in Graf, W.L., ed., Geomorphic Systems of North America: Boulder, Colorado, Geological Society of America, Geology of North America Centennial Special Volume 2, p. 163–210.

Peters, E.J., and Schainost, S., 2005, Historical changes in fish distribution and abundance in the Platte River in Nebraska: American Fisheries Society Symposium, v. 45, p. 239–248.

Propst, D.L., and Carlson, C.A., 1986, The distribution and status of warmwater fishes in the Platte River drainage, Colorado: Southwestern Naturalist, v. 31, p. 149–167, doi: 10.2307/3670555.

Savage, C., 2004, Prairie: A Natural History: Vancouver, Canada, Greystone Books, 308 p.

Scheurer, J.A., Fausch, K.D., and Bestgen, K.R., 2003, Multiscale processes regulate brassy minnow persistence in a Great Plains river: Transactions of the American Fisheries Society, v. 132, p. 840–855, doi: 10.1577/T02-037.

Scott, G.R., 1978, Map Showing Geology, Structure, and Oil and Gas Fields in the Sterling 1° × 2° Quadrangle, Colorado, Nebraska, and Kansas: U.S. Geological Survey Miscellaneous Investigations Series Map I-1092, scale 1:250,000, 1 sheet.

South Platte Forum, 2008: http://www.southplatteforum.org/.

Stockton, C.W., and Jacoby, C.G., 1976, Long-Term Surface-Water Supply and Streamflow Trends in the Upper Colorado River Basin: Tucson, Arizona, Lake Powell Research Project Bulletin 18, 79 p.

Strange, E.M., Fausch, K.D., and Covich, A.P., 1999, Sustaining ecosystem services in human-dominated watersheds: Biohydrology and ecosystem processes in the South Platte River basin: Environmental Management, v. 24, p. 39–54, doi: 10.1007/s002679900213.

Toth, L.A., Obeysekera, J.T.B., Perkins, W.A., and Loftin, M.K., 1993, Flow regulation and restoration of Florida's Kissimmee River: Regulated Rivers: Research and Management, v. 8, p. 155–166, doi: 10.1002/rrr.3450080118.

Trimble, D.E., 1993, The Geologic History of the Great Plains: U.S. Geological Survey Bulletin 1493, 54 p.

Weakly, H.E., 1943, A tree-ring record of precipitation in western Nebraska: Journal of Forestry, v. 41, p. 816–819.

Williams, G.P., 1978. The Case of the Shrinking Channels—The North Platte and Platte Rivers in Nebraska: U.S. Geological Survey Circular 781, 48 p.

Wohl, E., Angermeier, P.L., Bledsoe, B., Kondolf, G.M., MacDonnell, L., Merritt, D.M., Palmer, M.A., Poff, N.L., and Tarboton, D., 2005, River restoration: Water Resources Research, v. 41, W10301, 12 p.

WRCC (Western Regional Climate Center), 2008, Historical climate information: http://www.wrcc.dri.edu/CLIMATEDATA.html.

Manuscript Accepted by the Society 15 September 2008

The Geological Society of America
Special Paper 451
2009

Characterizing environmental flows for maintenance of river ecosystems: North Fork Cache la Poudre River, Colorado

Sara L. Rathburn*
Department of Geosciences, Colorado State University, Fort Collins, Colorado 80523, USA

David M. Merritt
U.S. Forest Service, NRRC, 2150 Centre Ave., Bldg. A, Suite 368, Fort Collins, Colorado 80526, USA

Ellen E. Wohl
Department of Geosciences, Colorado State University, Fort Collins, Colorado 80523, USA

John S. Sanderson
The Nature Conservancy, 117 E. Mountain Ave., Fort Collins, Colorado 80521, USA

Heather A.L. Knight
The Nature Conservancy, 1235 Cherokee Park Rd., Livermore, Colorado 80536, USA

ABSTRACT

Streamflow on the North Fork Cache La Poudre River, a tributary of the South Platte River in north-central Colorado, has been modified by impoundments for a century. A proposed expansion of the largest reservoir on the North Fork, Halligan Reservoir, presents an opportunity to modify dam operation to achieve environmental flows that sustain the river ecosystem while augmenting municipal water supplies. Over the past century, decreases in flood-related disturbances have resulted in reduced bed scouring through sediment transport and significant shifts in community composition and population structure of the dominant woody species present along the North Fork. We propose a four-step method to characterize environmental flows that maintain sediment mobility and riparian vegetation composition and structure. Our environmental flow standards explicitly address the fundamental role of sediment in creating and maintaining riparian habitat. Environmental flows to transport bedload are lower magnitude, higher frequency events (2 yr recurrence interval) that serve many in-channel functions, whereas environmental flows directed at riparian vegetation respond over longer time scales to high magnitude, lower frequency events (10 yr and 25 yr floods). Field evidence suggests the need for a 10 yr flood to saturate overbank areas and exclude xeric species near the channel. Managed 25 yr floods serve

*rathburn@cnr.colostate.edu

Rathburn, S.L., Merritt, D.M., Wohl, E.E., Sanderson, J.S., and Knight, H.A.L., 2009, Characterizing environmental flows for maintenance of river ecosystems: North Fork Cache la Poudre River, Colorado, *in* James, L.A., Rathburn, S.L., and Whittecar, G.R., eds., Management and Restoration of Fluvial Systems with Broad Historical Changes and Human Impacts: Geological Society of America Special Paper 451, p. 143–157, doi: 10.1130/2009.2451(10). For permission to copy, contact editing@geosociety.org. ©2009 The Geological Society of America. All rights reserved.

as a target flow for generating canopy gaps, creating regenerative habitat, enhancing biogeochemical processes, maintaining habitat heterogeneity, and possibly disrupting the coarse bed-surface layer and scouring pools to maintain fish overwinter habitat within the North Fork. Where field evidence is lacking, selection of target flows can be guided by daily discharge exceedence values.

INTRODUCTION

Investigators have recognized for decades that dams alter the timing and amount of water and sediment delivery in rivers and cause the degradation of downstream riverine ecosystems (Collier et al., 1996; Williams and Wolman, 1984; Graf, 2002; Postel and Richter, 2003; Richter and Thomas, 2007). There is now general scientific agreement about the fundamental ecological needs of regulated rivers, recognizing that the flow of water is central to the maintenance of fluvial systems and their biota (Poff et al., 1997; Postel and Richter, 2003; Arthington et al., 2006). Following a theme summarized by Postel and Richter (2003), a new course of research has emerged that focuses on understanding the natural variations in a river's flow regime in relation to the associated ecosystem (Junk et al., 1989; Arthington and Pusey, 1993; Arthington et al., 2006; Poff et al., 1997; Sparks et al., 1990; King et al., 2003). Diversion and storage of water for agricultural, industrial, and municipal use is in many cases necessary and desirable, yet societies increasingly express a simultaneous desire to protect the environmental and social benefits that healthy rivers provide. The challenge facing scientists is to identify the environmental flows necessary to maintain a healthy river ecosystem. For the purposes of this paper, an *environmental flow* is one that is intended to create and maintain the natural function of a river ecosystem while still accommodating some human use of river water. *Natural function* is defined in terms of specific, quantifiable ecosystem components such as pool-riffle sequences or riparian vegetation composition. Magnitude, frequency, timing, duration, rate of change, and sequences of discharge are commonly important components of an environmental flow.

Despite the large number of published studies linking flow alteration to multiple aspects of ecosystem function (see Tharme, 2003, for 207 different environmental-flow methods used in 44 different countries), and the advanced conceptual understanding of the multifaceted flow regimes needed to maintain river ecosystems (e.g., Arthington et al., 2006), there are still relatively few reports that integrate flow needs of multiple ecosystem components (e.g., Clipperton et al., 2003) in order to provide a quantitative basis for requesting environmental flows over a period of multiple years. To our knowledge, this extensive body of literature on environmental flows also does not include any approaches that incorporate sediment transport into development of environmental-flow standards. We currently have a unique opportunity on the regulated North Fork Cache la Poudre River ("North Fork") in north-central Colorado (Fig. 1) to work with water users during the expansion of a water-supply system (U.S. Army Corps of Engineers, 2006) to identify the characteristics

of flow components (Richter et al., 1996) necessary to maintain conservation targets supported by the river. We use process-based field data on sediment transport, characteristics of riparian vegetation, and an analysis of natural versus altered flows to identify environmental flows that can be expected to maintain abiotic and biotic processes that will achieve conservation management targets identified for the North Fork. Development of these environmental flows for river ecosystem maintenance is occurring simultaneously with the permitting of enlarged Halligan and Seaman Dams, the largest impoundments on the North Fork (Fig. 1). The permitting process provides a timely union of field studies of sediment transport and riparian vegetation, and engineering dam designs that can supply the environmental flows, based on management targets, to the downstream environment. This chapter outlines the methodology we used to characterize environmental flows for the North Fork. Although the specific details are unique to this case study, the approach and methods described in this paper can also be applied to other managed rivers.

The overall goal of this research is to identify environmental flows necessary for maintenance of riparian and aquatic ecosystem health by integrating data on sediment transport, riparian vegetation, and river discharge for the North Fork Cache la Poudre River. Environmental flows were developed using a four-step process: (I) identify the conservation targets and other ecosystem components to be maintained, (II) describe conceptually the flow components necessary to maintain these targets, (III) use existing data to quantify the flow components, and (IV) integrate flow components into a series of hydrographs that can guide the actions of dam managers (Fig. 2). Steps I and II were completed through a process led by The Nature Conservancy of Colorado, which manages a nature preserve on the North Fork; the results are only briefly described herein. To address step III, we (i) use sediment transport data to identify the magnitude of flows needed for bedload transport and channel maintenance, (ii) use riparian vegetation data to identify the magnitude of flows that generate overbank flooding, and (iii) analyze reconstructed hydrologic (flow) data to estimate the recurrence intervals of flow magnitudes identified in (i) and (ii). Finally, to address step IV, we integrate the flow components and quantities identified in step III to develop environmental flow hydrographs that are being used during the project-planning process and can be used in the future during project implementation to guide day-to-day reservoir management.

In this paper we focus primarily on applying steps II–IV to the sediment component of environmental flows, largely because it is more straightforward to quantify critical shear stress to mobilize bedload and the bed substrate than it is to quantify the flow

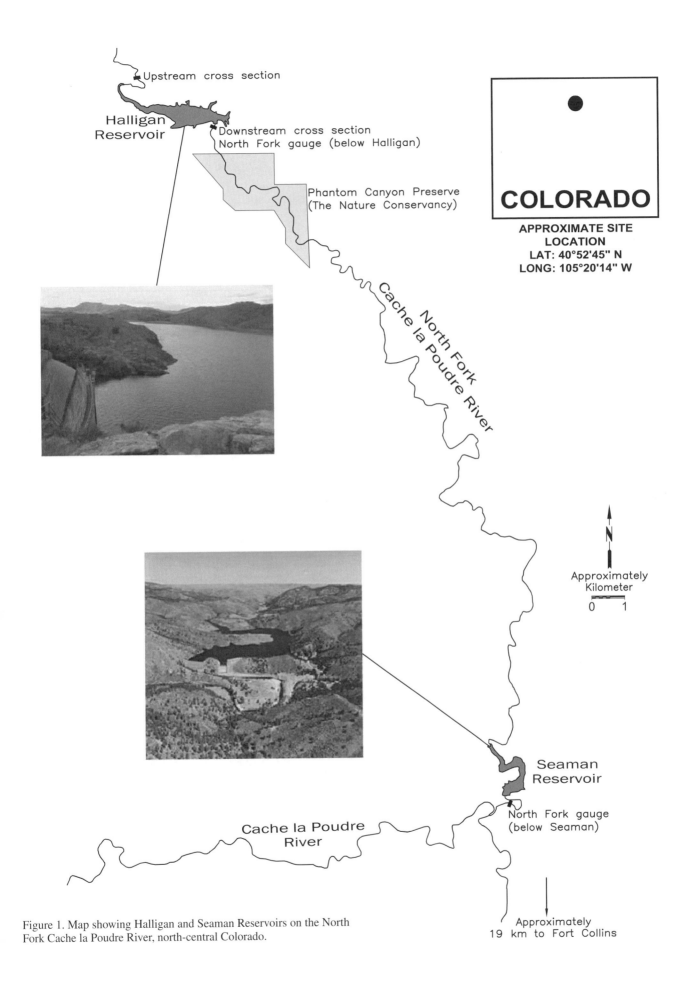

Figure 1. Map showing Halligan and Seaman Reservoirs on the North Fork Cache la Poudre River, north-central Colorado.

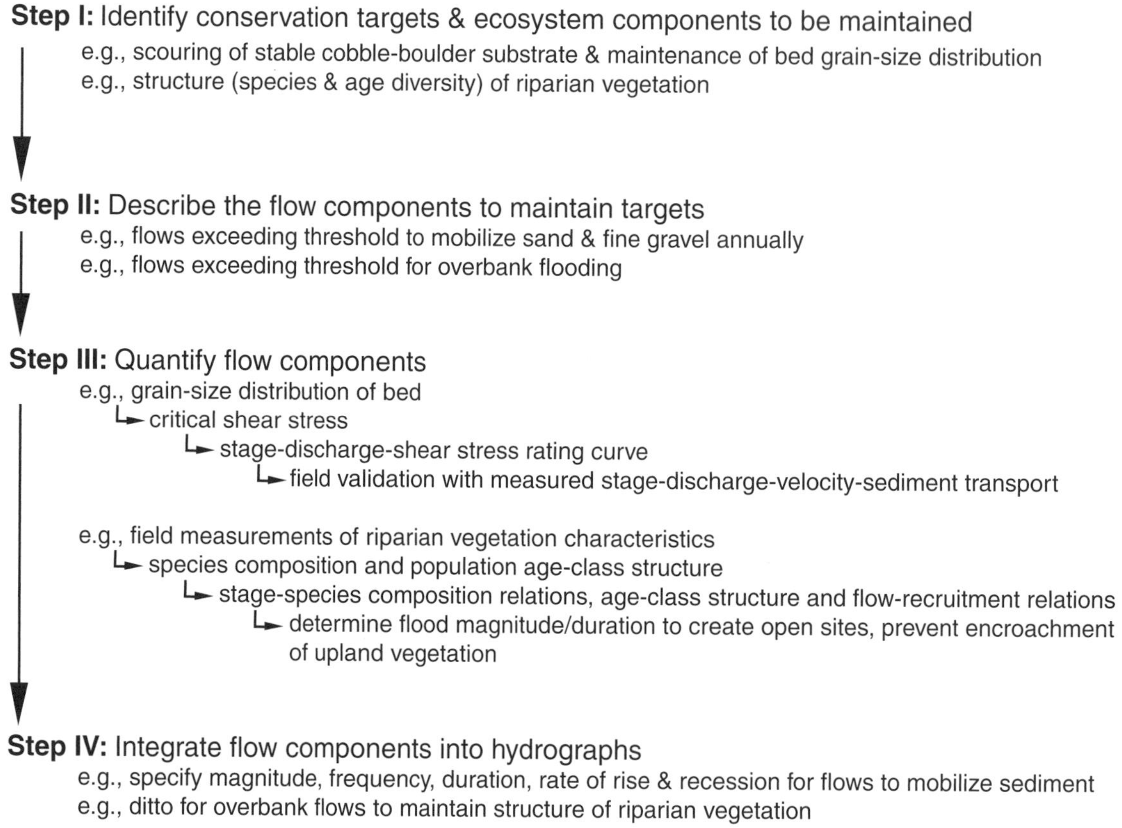

Step I: Identify conservation targets & ecosystem components to be maintained
  e.g., scouring of stable cobble-boulder substrate & maintenance of bed grain-size distribution
  e.g., structure (species & age diversity) of riparian vegetation

Step II: Describe the flow components to maintain targets
  e.g., flows exceeding threshold to mobilize sand & fine gravel annually
  e.g., flows exceeding threshold for overbank flooding

Step III: Quantify flow components
  e.g., grain-size distribution of bed
    ↳ critical shear stress
      ↳ stage-discharge-shear stress rating curve
        ↳ field validation with measured stage-discharge-velocity-sediment transport

  e.g., field measurements of riparian vegetation characteristics
    ↳ species composition and population age-class structure
      ↳ stage-species composition relations, age-class structure and flow-recruitment relations
        ↳ determine flood magnitude/duration to create open sites, prevent encroachment
         of upland vegetation

Step IV: Integrate flow components into hydrographs
  e.g., specify magnitude, frequency, duration, rate of rise & recession for flows to mobilize sediment
  e.g., ditto for overbank flows to maintain structure of riparian vegetation

Figure 2. Idealized four-step approach used to characterize environmental flows. Whereas steps I–IV are more generalized, the two examples under each step are specific to the North Fork Cache la Poudre River and the flow components that maintain sediment transport and riparian vegetation structure. For example, under step I, if scouring of the bed to maintain a bed grain-size distribution is a conservation target, then environmental flows that exceed the threshold to mobilize sand and fine gravel annually can be characterized by following steps II–IV. Likewise, if a conservation target is maintenance of riparian vegetation structure (step I, second example), then steps II–IV provide an approach to characterize flows that exceed the threshold for overbank flooding.

magnitude necessary to create canopy gaps by removing riparian vegetation. Our environmental-flow quantification for vegetation focuses on overbank flows that maintain riparian vegetation structure by saturating overbank areas.

STUDY SITE

The North Fork Cache la Poudre River is tributary to the mainstem Cache la Poudre River (Fig. 1), which flows through the city of Fort Collins and joins the South Platte River on the eastern plains of Colorado. A regulated river over the past century, the North Fork contains three in-channel storage reservoirs and multiple diversions. The two largest dams, Halligan and Seaman (Fig. 1), are owned and operated by the cities of Fort Collins and Greeley, respectively. Halligan ponds up to 7.9×10^6 m^3 of water and was constructed in 1910–1911; Seaman Dam ponds up to 6.2×10^6 m^3 and was constructed in 1941.

Immediately downstream from Halligan Dam is The Nature Conservancy (TNC) Phantom Canyon Preserve, occu-pying 680 ha, including ~7 km of North Fork River corridor (Fig. 1), one of the last roadless river canyons in the Colorado Front Range. A major TNC goal for the Phantom Canyon Preserve is to conserve the unique riparian and aquatic ecosystems and their associated biodiversity (Knight, 1997). To this end, numerous research projects have been completed within Phantom Canyon to understand the key ecological processes that restore and/or maintain the riverine ecosystem (e.g., Rathburn and Wohl, 2003; Merritt and Wohl, 2006). The research reported herein focuses specifically on characterizing environmental flows from Halligan Dam to ensure maintenance of aquatic and riparian health within the North Fork Poudre River canyons.

Watershed Setting

The North Fork drainage basin above Halligan Reservoir begins at an elevation of 3200 m above mean sea level and contains a total contributing area of ~904 km^2. The flow regime along the North Fork is strongly snowmelt driven, where discharge peaks in late May to early June (average ~9 m³/s under both natural and altered or regulated conditions) (Fig. 3). However, some of the largest flows on record occurred because of late summer thunderstorms (Follansbee and Sawyer, 1948). Base flow occurs throughout the autumn and winter (average ~1 m³/s under natural conditions; 0.5 m³/s under altered conditions) (Fig. 3). No perennial tributaries enter the canyon segment downstream from Halligan Reservoir; hence tributary inflow does not control the location of riffles as in other bedrock channels, nor does tributary inflow significantly augment discharge within the river. Peak daily flows during spring (snowmelt runoff) range from <3 m³/s during drought years, with an overall average flow of 15 m³/s. Instantaneous peaks during summer (convective thunderstorms) can exceed 200 m³/s (Merritt, 2002). Even with Halligan Reservoir in place, morphological bankfull flow below the dam still occurs with near-natural timing, magnitude, and frequency during wetter years (Merritt, 2002), because the reservoir typically fills in high-runoff years, at which point water flows freely over the dam until reservoir levels drop again.

The channel of the North Fork is bedrock-controlled, with a well-developed pool-riffle sequence along a coarse layer of cobbles and boulders (Wohl and Legleiter, 2003) (Fig. 4). Bed slope varies from ~0.011 m/m to 0.04 m/m in some steep-gradient riffle locations. Coarse materials in the cobble- to boulder-size class constitute the bed of riffles within the North Fork system both upstream and downstream from Halligan Dam. Bedrock is exposed in pool thalwegs, with limited sand along the margins of pools. Sources of sand and gravel for the North Fork are limited in the absence of flows that substantially erode the banks or mobilize the coarse subsurface bed layer (Wohl and Cenderelli, 2000).

Two outlet valves at the base of Halligan Dam can release up to ~4 m³/s. When the reservoir exceeds the crest height of the dam each snowmelt season, water also spills over the dam.

Sediment up to gravel size that has accumulated upstream from the dam can also be released with water flow through the outlet valves. Because of the very limited lateral inputs of sand and gravel within Phantom Canyon downstream from the dam during most years, and the normally stable streambed surface of cobbles and boulders, sediment that is passed through the reservoir is an important component of the sediment budget in the canyon. Occasional large sediment releases from the dam, such as that in 1996, when an estimated 7000 m³ was released (Wohl and Cenderelli, 2000; Rathburn and Wohl, 2003), also occur.

Suspended sediment transport is minimal except during snowmelt runoff, so the North Fork typically has low turbidity. Invertebrate organisms are mostly benthic and are dominantly Ephemeroptera and scrapers, collectors, and gatherers (Zuellig et al., 2002). Primary attached macrophytes are bryophytes such as mosses and lichens, with few floating or rooted angiosperms (Ward, 1992).

There is a well-developed but narrow riparian zone both upstream and downstream from Halligan Dam (Fig. 5), containing typical vegetation of the foothills and lower montane physiographic region. Vegetation in the canyon of the North Fork is dominated by *Cercocarpus montanus* (mountain mahogany) and *Sabina scopulorum* (western juniper) shrublands on south-facing slopes and *Pseudotsuga menziesii* (Douglas fir) forests on north-facing slopes. The riparian corridor is locally dominated by

Figure 4. North Fork Cache la Poudre River downstream from Halligan Reservoir, showing the coarse surface bed layer and the narrow riparian zone. View is looking upstream to Halligan Dam, the light gray feature in the upper right of photo.

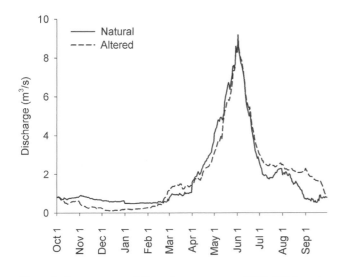

Figure 3. Average natural flows for water years 1987–2006 on the North Fork Cache la Poudre River. Natural flows were modeled to correct for the effects of Halligan Dam.

Betula fontinalis (river birch), *Alnus incana* (alder), *Padus virginiana* (chokecherry), and several *Salix* (willow) species (Merritt and Wohl, 2006). Once the North Fork exits the bedrock canyon, it flows through a broad, low-gradient alluvial reach before entering Seaman Reservoir.

Flow Regime

In-channel low flows dominate the annual hydrograph on the North Fork both upstream and downstream from Halligan Dam. The semiarid nature of the basin translates to ~8 months of base-flow conditions before the onset of snowmelt, so the low-flow level imposes a fundamental constraint on the river's aquatic community.

High flows, up to morphological bankfull, occur along the North Fork during normal spring snowmelt, in April–June, especially during wet years. High flows provide important functions for the maintenance of aquatic and riparian habitats in riverine ecosystems. High flows may provide phenological cues to aquatic and riparian organisms, such as the emergence of aquatic insects, spawning, the timing of flowering, and seed dispersal (Ward, 1992; Braatne et al., 1996). In-channel transport of sand and gravel as bedload sediment scours the channel substrate upstream from the dam, removing algae and aquatic macrophytes from the channel bed, and removing interstitial fine sediments that limit fish spawning. In addition, higher flows may recruit and transport wood downstream (Wohl and Goode, 2008).

Natural overbank floods on the North Fork occur during less frequent high snowmelt runoff, and as a result of intense, localized summer convective thunderstorms. High-magnitude, low-frequency floods influence the geometry of channels with erosionally resistant boundaries by shaping width, depth, and the physical complexity of aquatic habitats (Baker, 1988; Tinkler and Wohl, 1998; Wohl, 2000). Natural floods provide sediment and fine particulate organic matter to the floodplains, give organisms

access to nutrient-rich areas, mechanically remove senescent woody riparian vegetation and create open sites for colonization, induce important biogeochemical cycling of nutrients, and maintain river geometry and ecosystem complexity such as undercut banks (Postel and Richter, 2003). Sediment deposition on the floodplain also creates new germination sites for vegetation and facilitates the formation and maintenance of productive vegetation that may enhance bank stability (Scott et al., 1996). Floods cue fish to spawn, and trigger certain insects to begin a new phase of their life cycle (Allen, 1995). Also important is the natural flood recession from the floodplain, where floodwaters return to the mainstem at a rate that facilitates fine sediment deposition on the floodplain and in lateral channel areas, prevents stranding of fish, and ensures survival of some riparian plants.

METHODS

Development of environmental flows for the North Fork was completed following the four-step process (Fig. 2) modified from the frameworks presented by Postel and Richter (2003), Arthington et al. (2006), and Richter et al. (2006). In step I, a list of aquatic and riparian conservation targets for the North Fork was developed (Table 1) when TNC purchased the Phantom Canyon Preserve (Knight, 1997). In step II, a TNC-sponsored scientific workshop was held in 2005 to describe key conceptual relationships of conservation targets to flow components (Table 1). In step III, data on (i) bedload transport, (ii) riparian vegetation, and (iii) reconstructed natural flows occurring prior to systematic stream gauging were used to quantify the magnitude of flow components necessary to maintain these conceptual relationships. In step IV, quantified flow components were synthesized into hydrographs for dry, average, and wet years that are being used during the design phase to analyze project operations and are expected to be used after project implementation to guide day-to-day flow management. Data collection and analysis for this paper were focused on steps III and IV (Fig. 2).

Sediment Transport, Reservoir Loading, and Bed Mobility

Data on sediment transport derive from a 4 yr sediment budget that was completed for Halligan Reservoir, utilizing a bathymetric comparison and sediment-loading measurements (Telesto Solutions, Inc., 2003; Rathburn, 2006). Four field seasons of water and sediment data were collected from 2002 through 2005 at two measurement cross sections upstream and downstream from Halligan Reservoir (Fig. 1) to quantify sediment influx and outflow. The field data include measurements of discharge and suspended load and bedload transport over several years that ranged from among the driest on record to slightly above average. Water discharge at the upstream cross section was measured using a Marsh-McBirney one-dimensional velocity meter (instrument sampling error is ±0.02 m/s and ±2% of the reading). Velocity readings were taken at specified intervals along the cross section, and the measurements were used to calculate discharge. Depth-integrated suspended sediment samples were collected at regular intervals

Figure 5. North Fork Cache la Poudre River upstream from Halligan Reservoir, showing bedrock control and narrow riparian zone. View is looking upstream.

TABLE 1. CONSERVATION TARGETS AND ASSOCIATED ENVIRONMENTAL FLOWS, NORTH FORK CACHE LA POUDRE RIVER

Target	Environmental-flow characteristics
Fish, including hybrid cutthroat trout, longnose dace, fathead minnow, Johnny darter, and Iowa darter	Floods and high flows mobilize bed material to scour bed and remove aquatic vegetation (vascular plants and algae), and maintain channel width, depth, and complexity (e.g., undercut banks, coarse woody debris, off-channel pools). Moderate and low flows govern total available habitat and minimum wetted area/habitat, provide connectivity during driest periods, provide over-wintering habitat, and affect temperature and oxygen content.
Aquatic macroinvertebrates	Floods and high flows maintain channel width and complexity (e.g., undercut banks, coarse woody debris, off-channel pools), which are linked to habitat and species diversity, impact channel and sediment characteristics; clear interstitial sediment and open up habitat. Moderate and low flows govern total available habitat and minimum wetted area/habitat; less total habitat results in lower total abundance and productivity.
Riparian/wetland plants and plant associations dominated by narrowleaf cottonwood, skunkbush, river birch, chokecherry, alder, blue spruce, and willows	Floods and high flows scour banks, removing vegetation and sediment (during rising limb and peak), but also deposit sediment and propagules (e.g., seeds and live branches) during descending limb, provide surfaces for recruitment of riparian species (e.g., willow, cottonwood, and birch), and affect distribution of riparian vegetation by creating anoxic conditions and affecting nutrient cycling. Moderate and low flows maintain alluvial groundwater levels and soil moisture.
Preble's meadow jumping mouse	Floods and high flows maintain structure and composition of riparian habitat.

along the upstream measurement cross section using a DH-48 sampler. Bedload was collected with a 75-mm Helley-Smith bed-load sampler over a 2-min sampling interval along the same stations at which suspended sediment was collected. Cross-section widths vary from 14 m to 20 m, downstream and upstream from Halligan Reservoir, respectively, with at least 10 stations sampled for velocity and sediment transport during each field outing.

Water discharge data at the downstream cross section were obtained from the U.S. Geological Survey gauging station below Halligan Reservoir (no. 06751150; Fig. 1). Suspended sediment samples were collected at the downstream cross section prior to the last flow above a winter baseflow release at the end of the water-supply season, usually in September, which included a 6-day sampling effort in 2002, a 3-day sampling period in 2003, a 1-day sampling in 2004, and a 10-day period using an automatic ISCO sampler in 2005. Bedload samples were not collected at the downstream cross section because coarse sediment is not discharged from the reservoir during fall drawdown.

Both suspended and bedload sediment samples were transported to the laboratory and filtered through a 1.5-mm glass fiber filter. The sediment and filter were then placed into a drying tin that was oven dried overnight at 105 °C. After drying, the weighing tin and filter membrane were weighed. Both sediment load quantities were converted to units of total mass per time using methods described by the U.S. Geological Survey (USGS) (1999).

A bathymetric survey of the top-of-sediment surface in Halligan Reservoir was conducted in June 2003 and was compared with historical reservoir surveys on record with the Colorado State Engineer's Office. A 1941 reservoir survey contained adequate, accurate benchmarks and was of a resolution useful for comparison with the 2003 bottom survey. This allowed for quantification of 62 yr of net reservoir sedimentation in Halligan Reservoir.

The delta surface was cored during low flow, when the sediment was exposed, using a 1.5-m-long clear plastic tube. Only the fine-grained surface sediment to a depth of 0.7 m was collected because of the inability to sample the coarser sands and gravel with an open-ended tube. Field measurements of the coarser fraction of the delta sediments were made along the bank cut through the delta, showing abundant gravel-sized grus. A hydrometer analysis was completed on the finer fraction of delta sediment retained in the plastic core.

Pebble counts were completed for the upstream and downstream cross sections through representative riffles and nearby pools. The d_{50} and d_{84} of each pebble count were obtained to evaluate hypothetical scenarios of incipient motion using an equation developed by Komar (1987) for mixed-bed grain sizes. Komar's approach bases critical shear stress associated with particle entrainment on the grain diameter of the largest grain expected to be entrained (d_{84}) relative to the deposit as a whole, in this case represented by the d_{50}.

Riparian Woodland Characterization

Riparian vegetation methods are outlined in detail in Merritt (2002) and in Merritt and Wohl (2006) in an analysis of the relationship between reconstructed historical flows and riparian vegetation both upstream and downstream from Halligan Reservoir. Vegetation surveys were conducted upstream and downstream from this reservoir during the 1997 field season (Merritt, 2002; Merritt and Wohl, 2006). Vegetation was sampled in 178 systematically located plots by choosing a random location at the upstream end of the intended study segment and then placing vegetation sampling sites at 0.5 km intervals (75 upstream and 103 downstream from Halligan Reservoir) along the North Fork. Plots at each site were established along transects placed perpendicular to the channel and spaced to represent each distinct geomorphic surface from the channel to the edge of the riparian zone. Sampling plots were rectangular 1 m^2 for sampling herbaceous vegetation and 4 m² for sampling shrub and tree species. The percentage of cover for all vascular plant species present was recorded in each plot. For the current study we calculated average frequency (percentage of plots in which species are present) and cover of three key riparian woodland species, *Alnus incana* (alder), *Betula fontinalis* (river birch), and *Sabina scopulorum* (western juniper), for the reaches upstream and downstream from Halligan Reservoir, using the survey data. Frequency and cover of willow (*S. amygdaloides*, *S. bebbiana*, *S. drummondiana*, *S. exigua*, *S. lucida* subsp. *caudata*, and *S. lucida* subsp. *lasiandra*) were also measured and consolidated (sum of cover) as *Salix* spp. Upstream to downstream comparisons of all other plant species sampled and plot species richness are summarized here and treated in detail in Merritt and Wohl (2006).

In addition, population studies were undertaken to determine the age-class distributions of the three important woodland species within the riparian zone of the North Fork upstream and downstream from the reservoir. The largest stem diameter was measured from each individual of the three study species along a 3-km reach upstream from Halligan Reservoir and a 7-km reach downstream from the reservoir. Diameter-age relationships were developed by aging a range of size classes of each species by counting annual growth rings from increment cores, wedges, and stem cross sections taken from individuals. Power functions were fitted to the age-diameter data and the relations used to predict the age of all measured individuals. Upstream and downstream age-class distributions were fitted separately with three-parameter Gaussian functions for each species. Upstream and downstream Gaussian curves were formally compared, using the extra sums of squares (ESS) principle (Bates and Watts, 1988).

Hydrologic Analysis

Using U.S. Geological Survey (USGS) gauging-station data and historic diversion and reservoir storage records from the North Fork basin, Merritt (2002) characterized the flow regime downstream from Halligan Reservoir. These regulated flows were statistically contrasted with natural flows developed from gauge records and field evidence for upstream of the reservoir. Quantification of natural flows provides an estimate of what discharge would be downstream from Halligan Reservoir in the absence of Halligan Dam.

Natural (unaltered) and historic (altered) flows were analyzed using daily-flow data for water years 1987–2006. Gauging-station data downstream from the reservoir provide regulated flow conditions. A gauge was installed below Halligan Dam in 1998 (USGS gauge no. 06751500), and continuous records of historic (altered) flows are available starting with that year. Altered flows were reconstructed for water years 1987–1998, and natural flows were reconstructed for 1987–2006. Flows were reconstructed with data from (1) USGS gauge no. 06751490, North Fork Cache La Poudre River at Livermore, Colorado (~16 km downstream from the dam); (2) Colorado Decision Support Systems (CDSS) records of storage and releases at Halligan Reservoir, used to cal-

culate change (Δ) in reservoir storage; and (3) CDSS records of diversions at the North Poudre Irrigation Company (NPIC) Canal (~10 km downstream from the dam). The NPIC canal is the only diversion from the river in this reach.

For water years 1987–1998, natural and historical mean daily flows were estimated using a mass-balance approach in which gauge records were adjusted to account for diversions, reservoir storage, and reservoir releases as:

Historical flow = Livermore gauge flow + North Poudre Canal headgate diversions
and
Natural flow = historical flow + Δ reservoir storage

Reconstructed flows downstream from Halligan Reservoir were summarized and compared with measured post-dam flows using Indicators of Hydrologic Alteration (IHA) software (Richter et al., 1996). IHA is designed to evaluate changes in important components of natural flows in comparison with regulated flows, including monthly water conditions, magnitude and duration of annual extreme flows, timing of annual extremes, frequency and duration of high and low pulses, and rate of change in discharge. The summary statistics provided as output are directed at understanding changes and trends in biologically important hydrologic processes along the North Fork resulting from Halligan Dam and associated flow diversions.

IHA output was also used to identify year types and flow-exceedence values. Wet, average, and dry years were defined as the upper, middle, and lower third of maximum annual one-day flow under natural conditions. We modeled our classification after similarly arbitrary but useful groupings that allow for straightforward discussion of management goals while maintaining some semblance of among-year variability (e.g., Muth et al., 2000). Within each year type, the 75th and 25th exceedence values for daily flow were identified for each month. These values were used in step IV to set daily-flow targets between floods.

In addition to the analysis of mean daily flows, natural flood frequency and magnitude were assessed using available literature, cultural records, field evidence of paleoflooding, and regional hydrologic data. Field evidence included, for example, a debris jam dated to a 1976 flood of sufficient magnitude to uproot, transport, and deposit *Betula fontinalis* as a pile on the floodplain. For the regional hydrologic analysis, 10 unregulated but climatically and geologically similar streams were selected within the South Platte River basin for development of relationships between watershed area and floods of various recurrence intervals. Peak discharges of 1, 10, 25, 50, 75, and 100 yr recurrence-interval flows were estimated by fitting Pearson Type III distributions to the log-transformed instantaneous annual maximum flows from USGS gauge records for each year of record (USGS, 1981). From these relationships, the magnitude of each recurrence interval flood was estimated for the North Fork. The flood stages for each of these recurrence interval floods were related to the elevation of various plant communities through rating curves developed in the field and through hydraulic modeling.

Integrating Flow Components into Hydrographs

To analyze options for water-system operation and to guide future flow management, key flow component criteria were synthesized into daily hydrographs of environmental flows for the stream reach immediately downstream of Halligan Reservoir (Figs. 1, 4). Quantification of flows based on sediment transport and riparian vegetation was used to set the peak magnitudes during wet years. Because morphological bankfull and flood conditions occur during a relatively small part of the hydrograph, daily flow targets outside these conditions were bounded by the 75th and 25th percentile exceedence values for, respectively, minimum and maximum monthly flows, except in conditions where inflows to Halligan Reservoir are outside these bounds. These lower and upper bounds were chosen as reasonable initial targets for monthly flows in the absence of more thorough ecological understanding (Richter et al., 1997), with the expectation that they will be implemented in an adaptive management context and may be adjusted over time.

RESULTS

Sediment Transport

Four years of field measurements of sediment transport into and out of Halligan Reservoir captured wet, average, and dry years of discharge and sediment. Overall, suspended sediment made up ~95% of the total sediment load, indicating that it is an important component of the abiotic system. Suspended sediment quantities at the upstream cross section spanned four

orders of magnitude, with a strongly correlated ($r^2 = 0.93$; $P < 0.0001$) regression equation defining the suspended sediment rating curve (Fig. 6). This fine sediment is transported downstream to Halligan Reservoir, with intermittent storage disrupting the transport because of localized low velocity near obstructions such as large boulders, channel-margin areas, and, more importantly, beaver dams along the channel. Episodic transport of this suspended sediment occurs when high flows cause a breach in the beaver dams, as was observed in the field during summer 2003.

The onset of bedload transport of the finer (sand) fraction of bed sediment occurred at a threshold discharge of 0.6 m³/s, which moved sediment on top of the coarser clasts of the bed. Quantities of bed load spanned four orders of magnitude, and the bedload sediment rating curve shows less correlation ($r^2 = 0.56$; $P < 0.0001$) between discharge and bed load than the suspended sediment rating curve (Fig. 7). A second bedload transport threshold is identified at ~9 m³/s, based on field evidence of sustained bedload transport (gravel) during sampling in 2003, a wet year based on 20 yr of record. This sustained bedload transport did not break up the coarse surface layer of cobbles and boulders. In addition, the flood frequency analysis indicates that 9 m³/s corresponds with a 2 yr recurrence interval flood under natural conditions, a management flow that satisfies conservation targets within Phantom Canyon for in-channel processes of limiting filamentous algae and macrophyte growth in the channel, and mobilizing interstitial bed sediment.

Comparison of the 2003 reservoir bottom topography with historical contour maps indicates that the total amount of water storage lost to sediment over a 62 yr operational history of Halligan Reservoir is ~11% of the total active storage within the reservoir, or ~407,000 m³ (6565 m³/yr). The areas of greatest

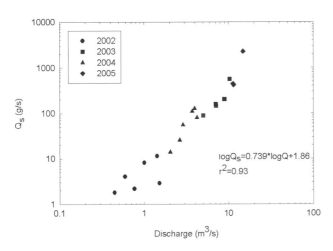

Figure 6. Suspended sediment transport along the upstream measurement cross section of the North Fork Cache la Poudre River. Transport of the finest fraction of sediment occurs over a range of discharges, even during dry years (average flow <1.1 m³/s) such as 2002. Q_S is suspended sediment of discharge.

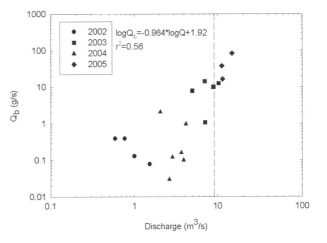

Figure 7. Bedload transport along the upstream measurement cross section of the North Fork Cache la Poudre River. Threshold value, indicated by dashed line, of ~9 m³/s is determined from field evidence of sustained sediment transport during a wet year (average flow ≥2.3 m³/s), which corresponds to a 2 yr recurrence interval from flood frequency analysis. Q_b is bedload discharge.

sedimentation include the delta at the head of the reservoir (up to 3.6 m thick), as exposed in cutbanks of the North Fork during periods of low water level in the reservoir, and immediately adjacent to the dam (maximum thickness, 4 m). Sediment transfer to the reservoir occurs most prominently during wet years, when sustained high flows transport sediment downstream to Halligan Reservoir in much greater quantities than can be released during fall drawdown. Conversely, during dry years, much lower discharges in upstream reaches transport smaller quantities of sediment to the reservoir such that the volume of inflowing sediment more closely equals sediment quantities that can be released from the dam.

Based on sediment analyses, the dominant grain size of surface delta sediments is 0.53 mm, or coarse silt size. Calculations of trapping efficiency over the length of the reservoir indicate that 99% of the d_{50} of surface delta sediment is trapped in Halligan Reservoir. These fine sediments are prone to movement via fetch along the west-east orientation of the reservoir, transporting the fines toward the dam and the outlet valve at the base of the dam. As mentioned, only ~11% of the total reservoir storage has been lost to sedimentation, but transport of fines toward the dam will continue to be problematic for reservoir operations and headgate inspections (Rathburn and Wohl, 2001, 2003).

The d_{50} and d_{84} for riffle-bed material downstream from Halligan Dam are 12 cm and 32 cm, small cobble and small boulder sizes, respectively. Critical shear stress for incipient motion of the d_{84} within a riffle bed downstream for Halligan Dam is 130 Pa, using an incipient motion equation from Komar (1987). In comparison, average boundary shear stress using shear velocity (Julien, 1995) at the downstream cross section for a natural 25 yr flow ranges from ~70 to 80 Pa. This range of boundary shear stress was obtained by extrapolating bankfull depth estimates from the rating curve upward by 10% and 25%, a reasonable range of increased depth of the 25 yr flood. Extrapolating the rating curve to a 25 yr flood allows a first-order approximation of the mobilization potential of the coarse surface layer downstream from Halligan Dam, which would have substantial effects on the channel configuration and associated riparian vegetation and aquatic organisms. In steeper riffles, where slopes are commonly 0.02–0.04 m/m, the boundary shear stress is calculated at 133 Pa, which is sufficient to mobilize the coarsest clasts in the bed layer in downstream reaches below Halligan Dam. It is important to note, however, that a large amount of uncertainty is associated with these estimates of incipient motion using boundary shear stress compared with critical motion calculations. Uncertainty results primarily from unmeasured depths of flow during a large, infrequent event like the natural 25 yr flood, with a discharge of ~212 m³/s, and also from the very high bed roughness and extreme turbulence observed even under morphological bankfull conditions. Under these circumstances the extreme fluctuations in boundary shear stress probably exert more influence on entrainment of coarse bed particles in the surface layer than average hydraulic forces.

Riparian Vegetation

Although there are slight differences in plant species richness upstream (120 species) compared with downstream (123 species) from Halligan dam, there is slightly higher average plot-level species richness upstream from Halligan dam (7.9 species/plot) compared with downstream (7.3 species/plot; t = 1.0; P = 0.03 [t test]; Merritt and Wohl, 2006). An important difference in vegetation upstream compared with downstream from Halligan Dam on the North Fork is the higher abundance of wetland–lake margin species such as *Persicaria amphibia* (water smartweed), *Carex emoryi* (sedge), *Veronica anagallis-aquatica* (speedwell), and *Mentha arvensis* (fieldmint) within the annually flooded areas downstream from the dam. These wetland–lake margin species are distributed immediately adjacent to the stream at elevations below mean annual water level and provide an indication of a relatively stable water table. Downstream from Halligan Dam the riparian zone has narrowed, with more terrestrial species (intolerant of flooding) growing nearer the channel (Merritt and Wohl, 2006). The frequency of *Salix* is significantly lower downstream (14%) from Halligan Reservoir compared with upstream (80%; Fig. 8).

Age-class distributions of three woodland species upstream and downstream from Halligan Reservoir indicate that alder has a wider age-class distribution downstream compared with upstream locations (Fig. 9). The age-class distributions were significantly different upstream and downstream from the dam (P < 0.05 [ESS F test]). This suggests that alder populations are doing well under both regulated and unregulated conditions but have broader age-class distributions under regulated conditions (Fig. 9). The frequency of alder is also higher downstream compared with upstream, and it appears that alder occupies areas that may formerly have been dominated by willow species. Willow

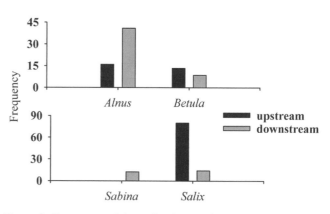

Figure 8. Frequency of three riparian species along reaches upstream and downstream from Halligan Reservoir. Frequency is the number of plots in which the species was present divided by the total number of plots sampled along the reach. In all, 75 plots were sampled upstream from Halligan Reservoir, and 103 downstream. Differences were significant (chi-square contingency tests; P < 0.05) in all cases except for *Betula*.

likely declined downstream from the dam as a result of reduced physical disturbance and associated opportunities for colonization and establishment.

There is lower frequency of river birch downstream from the dam and better representation of older individuals (P < 0.05; ESS F test; Fig. 10). Dendrochronology of wood debris piles upstream from the dam indicates that shallow-rooted birch were uprooted during high flows associated with flooding in 1976, and may have undergone such removal and transport at flows of 235 m³/s, a discharge that is approximately equivalent to the natural 25 yr recurrence interval flood. The frequency of such flooding and the frequency of uprooting have declined downstream from the dam, allowing older individuals to persist downstream from the dam and making the recruitment of river birch an uncommon

event (Fig. 10). These decadent stands are less structurally complex and form monocultures in some places.

Juniper populations differ upstream and downstream from the reservoir (P < 0.05; ESS F test; Fig. 11). Mostly older (dating to the 1930s) individuals occur upstream from the reservoir, and many young individuals (ranging in age from 5 to 40 yr old) are present downstream from the reservoir. This indicates that terrestrialization of the riparian zone is occurring downstream, probably because of a lack of prolonged flooding and fluvial disturbance that would have served to exclude juniper. Juniper grow immediately adjacent to the stream channel along regulated reaches, which is unusual for a xeric (flood-intolerant) woodland plant. Ten-year recurrence interval flows are of sufficient magnitude to fully saturate near-channel substrates and, if of sufficient

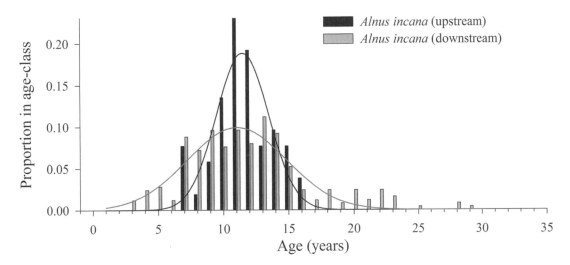

Figure 9. Age-class distribution of alder upstream and downstream from Halligan Reservoir.

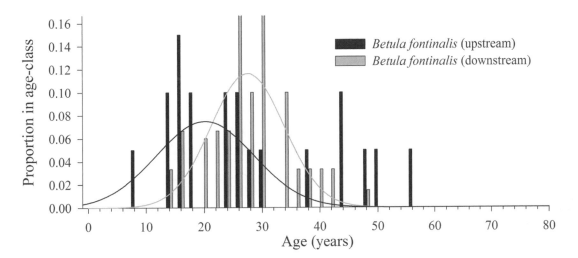

Figure 10. Age-class distribution of birch upstream and downstream from Halligan Reservoir.

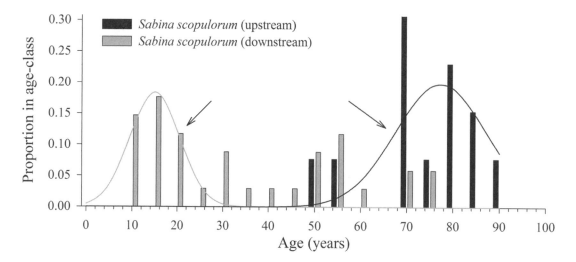

Figure 11. Age-class distribution of juniper upstream and downstream from Halligan Reservoir. Arrows highlight the divergence of upstream to downstream populations of juniper.

duration, will serve to exclude terrestrial vegetation from persisting near the channel.

Analysis of Natural Daily Flow

Discharge under natural conditions did not differ substantially from altered conditions at high flows but did differ at low flows (Fig. 12). Average annual discharge did not change significantly between natural (2.12 m³/s) and altered (2.1 m³/s) conditions (two-tailed t test; P = 0.9190). Peak flow (mean of the maximum daily average flow for each year) under altered conditions was 6% lower than under natural conditions (16.7 m³/s versus 17.8 m³/s, respectively), but this difference was not signifi-

cant (two-tailed t test; P = 0.8809). The average date of the peak was 21 May for natural conditions in comparison with 25 May for altered conditions. Winter (October–February) flows were reduced 42% under altered conditions when compared with natural conditions (mean of 0.40 m³/s versus 0.69 m³/s, respectively; two-tailed t test; P = 0.0001).

Based on the analysis of daily discharge data, the magnitude of the 2 yr recurrence interval flood, ~9 m³/s, did not differ between altered and natural conditions. The 20 yr flow reconstruction was insufficiently long to estimate 10 yr and 25 yr recurrence interval floods, so these magnitudes were estimated for natural conditions using regional relations as 145 m³/s for the 10 yr flood and 212 m³/s for the 25 yr recurrence interval flood.

Integrating Flow Components into Environmental-Flow Hydrographs

Daily hydrographs, synthesized using data from sediment, riparian vegetation, and hydrologic records, indicate that high flows can be reduced from altered levels experienced since Halligan Reservoir was built, and that low (base) flows will have to increase in order to achieve environmental-flow guidelines (Figs. 13, 14). Flow values based on sediment data indicate that the target value for peak flows during wet years should be 9 m³/s (Fig. 13), a discharge that coincides with the threshold for bedload transport that will clean the bed of fine sediment and scour in-channel vegetation such as filamentous algae. Hydraulic modeling indicates that a flood of 145 m³/s (the magnitude of a natural 10 yr recurrence interval flood) would be necessary to inundate floodplain soils and create anoxic conditions for a sufficient duration to exclude upland vegetation. Flow values based on riparian vegetation and regional flood analysis indicate that a discharge near 212 m³/s (the magnitude of a natural 25 yr recurrence interval flood) is necessary to scour riparian areas near the

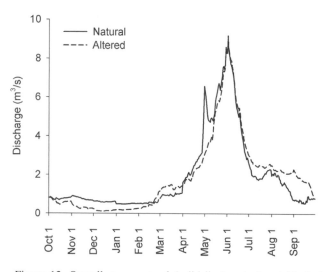

Figure 12. Overall mean natural (solid line) and altered (dashed line) hydrographs for the North Fork Cache la Poudre River. Values are mean daily discharge for water years 1987–2006.

channel, to uproot woody vegetation, and to facilitate recruitment of woodland species. Both the 145 m³/s and the 212 m³/s floods would be superimposed on the wet-year hydrograph. The substantial parts of the environmental-flow hydrographs that are not flood based were determined on the basis of 75th percentile exceedence values for the lower limits (shown in Figs. 13, 14) and 25th percentile exceedence values for the upper limits (not shown). The natural timing of such floods is in late May–early June when associated with snowmelt or in late summer if caused by convective precipitation (Follansbee and Sawyer, 1948).

DISCUSSION AND CONCLUSIONS

Relationships between flow and sediment transport and riparian vegetation form a crucial starting point for identifying environmental flows on regulated fluvial systems. Because sediment deposits form the substrate for riparian communities within riverine environments, sediment is a key, yet a commonly overlooked, component of ecological systems and must be considered in developing environmental-flow standards. To date, literature on environmental flows has not incorporated the role of sediment in maintaining ecosystem health. This study provides the first attempt to explicitly address the importance of sediment in producing sites for regeneration and nutrient-rich riparian habitat by mobilizing and depositing fine-grained sediment. Although this is a relatively simple approach, by focusing on a few conservation targets we utilize existing data to develop environmental flows directed at mobilizing bed sediment and maintaining the riparian vegetation community, two foundational components of riverine ecosystems.

The need for environmental flows on the North Fork Cache la Poudre River is clear, given the lack of bedload transport downstream from the dam and the shifts in community composition and changes in age-class distributions of riparian vegetation upstream versus downstream from Halligan Dam, particularly

with the prospect of a greater than sixfold increase in the size of the reservoir, which could further impact flood flows. The existing data on sediment transport, riparian vegetation, and hydrologic analyses, along with the current permitting processes, make for fertile ground in which not only to identify environmental flows but also to inform engineering designs of a future enlarged dam that can be applied to new dam specifications for accommodating various flows to meet specific conservation targets. In the case of the North Fork, the current permit review by the U.S. Army Corps of Engineers represents a real situation in which environmental flows will be requested if the enlarged dam is constructed.

In general, sediment transport drives many in-channel ecological functions and responds on time scales shorter than the 2 yr magnitude flow to more frequent events, and to larger recurrence interval flows where bedload sediment is mobilized and sustained and where the bed substrate may be disrupted. Riparian vegetation is linked to out-of-channel flood processes and responds on longer time scales to less frequent flow (extreme and low flows). Extant riparian vegetation is maintained (water stress avoided) by the maintenance of baseflow, whereas recruitment of disturbance-adapted species is linked to less-frequent flood-related processes. Community composition and population structure of riparian vegetation respond on longer time scales to extreme high and low flows. Although riparian vegetation responds to a full range of historic flows, maintenance of the magnitude, frequency, and duration of the 2, 10, and 25 yr recurrence interval flows will provide for the maintenance, regeneration, and heterogeneity in plant communities and populations of individual species.

A flood with a magnitude of 9 m³/s (the 2 yr recurrence interval flood under natural conditions), corresponding to the mean annual snowmelt peak of a wet year, would serve many short-term needs within the channel by scouring the bed through bedload transport. These low-magnitude, high-frequency flows would be sufficient to transport sediment released from the reservoir, mobilize sediment within the bed interstices, scour the bed to remove algae and aquatic plants and maintain pool depths, and

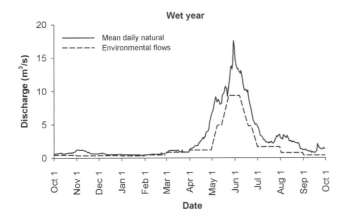

Figure 13. Typical wet-year hydrograph for the North Fork Cache la Poudre River for natural and environmental flows. Peak environmental flow is ~9 m³/s (318 ft³/s), which corresponds to the 2 yr flow.

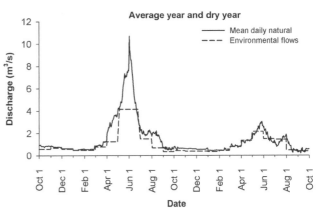

Figure 14. Typical average-year and dry-year hydrographs for the North Fork Cache la Poudre River for natural and environmental flows. Peak environmental flow is ~4.2 m³/s (141 ft³/s).

redistribute sediment onto the floodplain. The 2 yr flow is important in regularly recharging shallow alluvial water tables, moistening the soil profile, and supporting extant vegetation (Workman and Serrano, 1999).

A 145 m³/s flood (corresponding to the magnitude of the 10 yr flood under natural conditions) is necessary to inundate floodplain soils and create anoxic conditions for a sufficient duration to exclude upland vegetation. Maintenance of the frequency and magnitude of the 10 yr recurrence interval flow will facilitate deposition of fine-grained mineral sediment on floodplain surfaces and decomposition of organic material on the floodplain, enhance biochemical processes, and prevent encroachment of upland vegetation on the channel.

Reduction in flood-related disturbances has resulted in significant shifts in the population structure of the dominant woody species present along the North Fork, including reduction in disturbance-tolerant species and overall terrestrialization of downstream reaches. There is a management need along the North Fork for a large flood to physically disrupt the floodplain and remove senescent vegetation. A 212 m³/s flood (corresponding to the magnitude of the natural 25 yr flood)—a high-magnitude, low-frequency event—would likely mechanically remove patches of riparian vegetation and bank sediment, help to maintain channel complexity, redistribute nutrients overbank, and provide germination sites for riparian vegetation. Because many disturbance-adapted species are poor competitors for space, recruitment events such as large floods are key to maintaining such species in the system and preventing dominance by a few competitive species (Karrenberg et al., 2002). In addition to influencing species composition through providing opportunities for disturbance-adapted species, rare, high-magnitude floods also maintain structural heterogeneity in the vegetation through influencing age-class structure of woodland species. Structural heterogeneity is important for wildlife in that it provides a range of cover types that accommodate a wide variety of species (Ellis et al., 1997).

In addition, a 212 m³/s flood provides an upper level at which to assess sediment transport during infrequent events. Based on a first-order approximation, it is likely that the coarse bed layer within the North Fork would be disrupted locally in steep-gradient riffles by this very large flood. With the bed destabilized at riffles, entrainment of the largest grain sizes present would probably occur along the length of the North Fork through Phantom Canyon, possibly scouring pools to maintain pool depth for fish overwinter habitat. Disruption of the coarse surface bed layer would undoubtedly provide sufficient scour potential to uproot riparian vegetation within the canyon without the need for artificially removing or weakening vegetation prior to a managed flood.

As is the case with the North Fork, most environmental flow standards are developed on a site-by-site basis. Because of the time, energy, and resources required to explore hydrologic history of sites, to determine characteristics of flow alteration, to document effects of alteration of biotic and abiotic processes, and to understand hydrologic-life-history relations of species, developing flow standards for many streams may be impractical or impossible. Transferability of environmental flow standards from one particular site to another site would be difficult without some framework to guide scientists and water managers. There has been a recent recognition of the potential value of developing regional standards for setting ecological limits of hydrologic alteration (Arthington et al., 2006). ELOHA (Ecological Limits of Hydrologic Alteration) is a framework for developing flow standards that incorporate the general relationships between biota and stream hydrology and can be transferred beyond the site (Poff et al., 2009). The basic premise behind ELOHA is that morphologically similar streams within a particular hydroclimatic region or ecoregion may have similar biota and similar ecological flow requirements. If relationships between flow and measurable attributes of riparian biota and channel characteristics are determined for a system (or a number of systems within a region), then such information should be transferable to rivers for which such intensive data are unavailable. Quantitative linkages between streamflow attributes and biota such as those presented in this paper could inform such regional frameworks.

Although the conservation targets in this study focus on sediment transport and riparian vegetation, numerous other conservation objectives will simultaneously be met by the environmental flows developed for the North Fork below Halligan Dam (Table 1). In this way, managed flows will consider multiple ecosystem components in order to capture system processes and biological community interactions that are essential for creating and maintaining conditions for conservation targets. The four-step process used to characterize environmental flows for the North Fork is broadly applicable to other regions in which scientists seek to quantify environmental flows to improve the ecological health in regulated fluvial systems.

ACKNOWLEDGMENTS

We are grateful for the thorough, insightful reviews by Greg Pasternack and an anonymous reviewer. Funding for this research was provided by two grants to S. Rathburn and Telesto Solutions, Inc., from North Poudre Irrigation Company; by support from The Nature Conservancy to D. Merritt through Rodney Johnson and Katherine Ordway Grants; and through U.S. National Science Foundation grant EAR-9725384 to E. Wohl and D. Merritt. We thank Steve Smith of North Poudre Irrigation Company for his financial and logistical support, Jim Finley and Kurt Stauder for field support, especially during high flows, and Ben Whitman and Kevin Pilgrim for summer field assistance, and Stacy Tyler for assistance with Figure 1.

REFERENCES CITED

Allen, J.D., 1995, Stream Ecology: Structure and Function of Running Waters: London, Chapman and Hall, 388 p.

Arthington, A.H., and Pusey, B.J., 1993, Instream-flow management in Australia: Methods, deficiencies and future directions: Australian Biologist, v. 6, p. 52–60.

Arthington, A.H., Bunn, S.E., Poff, N.L., and Naiman, R.J., 2006, The challenge of providing environmental flow rules to sustain river ecosystems:

Ecological Applications, v. 16, p. 1311–1318, doi: 10.1890/1051-0761 (2006)016[1311:TCOPEF]2.0.CO;2.

Baker, V.R., 1988, Flood erosion, *in* Baker, V.R., Kochel, R.C., and Patton, P.C., eds., Flood Geomorphology: New York, Wiley & Sons, p. 81–95.

Bates, D.M., and Watts, D.G., 1988, Nonlinear Regression Analysis and Its Applications: New York, Wiley & Sons, 365 p.

Braatne, J.H., Rood, S.B., and Heilman, P.E., 1996, Life history, ecology, and conservation of riparian cottonwoods in North America, *in* Stettler, R.F., Bradshaw, H.D., Heilman, P.E., and Hinckley, T.M., eds., Biology of *Populus* and Its Implications for Management and Conservation: Ottawa, Canada, NRC Research Press, p. 57–85.

Clipperton, G.K., Koning, C.W., Locke, A.G., Mahoney, J.M., and Quazi, B., 2003, Instream flow needs determination for the South Saskatchewan River Basin, Alberta, Canada: Calgary, Alberta Environment and Sustainable Resource Development (Pub. no. T/719), 271 p.: http://www3.gov.ab.ca/env/water/regions/ssrb/IFN_reports.asp.

Collier, M., Webb, R.H., and Schmidt, J.C., 1996, Dams and Rivers: A Primer on the Downstream Effects of Dams: U.S. Geological Survey Circular 1126, 94 p.

Ellis, L.M., Crawford, C., and Molles, M.C., 1997, Rodent communities in native and exotic riparian vegetation in the middle Rio Grande Valley of Central New Mexico: Southwestern Naturalist, v. 42, p. 13–19.

Follansbee, R., and Sawyer, L.R., 1948, Floods in Colorado: U.S. Geological Survey Water Supply Paper 997, 151 p.

Graf, W.L., 2002, Dam Removal Research: Status and Prospects: Washington, D.C., The H. John Heinz III Center for Science, Economics and the Environment, 151 p.

Julien, P.Y., 1995, Erosion and Sedimentation: New York, Cambridge University Press, 280 p.

Junk, W.J., Bayley, P.B., and Sparks, R.E., 1989, The flood pulse concept in river-floodplain systems: Proceedings of the International Large River Symposium, v. 106, p. 110–127.

Karrenberg, S., Edwards, P.J., and Kollmann, J., 2002, The life history of Salicaceae living in the active zone of floodplains: Freshwater Biology, v. 47, p. 733–748, doi: 10.1046/j.1365-2427.2002.00894.x.

King, J.M., Brown, C.A., and Sabet, H., 2003, A scenario-based holistic approach to environmental flow assessments for rivers: River Research and Applications, v. 19, p. 619–640, doi: 10.1002/rra.709.

Knight, H., 1997, Goals and objectives for Phantom Canyon Preserve Management Plan: Internal document, The Colorado Program of The Nature Conservancy.

Komar, P.D., 1987, Selective gravel entrainment and the empirical evaluation of flow competence: Sedimentology, v. 34, p. 1165–1176, doi: 10.1111/j.1365-3091.1987.tb00599.x.

Merritt, D.M., 2002, Maintenance of riparian woodlands along mountain stream channels: Role of historic disturbance and hydrologic variability: Final report submitted to The Nature Conservancy, Phantom Canyon Preserve, 43 p.

Merritt, D.M., and Wohl, E.E., 2006, Plant dispersal along rivers fragmented by dams: River Research and Applications, v. 22, p. 1–26, doi: 10.1002/rra.890.

Muth, R.T., Crist, L.W., LaGory, K.E., Hayse, J.W., Bestgen, K.R., Ryan, T.P., Lyons, J.K., and Valdez, R.A., 2000, Flow and temperature recommendations for endangered fishes in the Green River downstream of Flaming Gorge Dam: Lakewood, Colorado, Final Report, Project FG-53, Upper Colorado Endangered Fish Recovery Program.

Poff, N.L., Allan, J.D., Bain, M.B., Karr, J.R., Prestegaard, K.L., Richter, B.D., Sparks, R.E., and Stromberg, J.C., 1997, The Natural Flow Regime: A paradigm for river conservation and restoration: Bioscience, v. 47, p. 769–784, doi: 10.2307/1313099.

Poff, N.L., Richter, B., Arthington, A.H., Bunn, S.E., Naiman, R.J., Kendy, E., Acreman, M., Apse, C., Bledsoe, B.P., Freeman, M., Henriksen, J., Jacobson, R.B., Kennen, J., Merritt, D.M., O'Keeffe, J., Olden, J., Rogers, K., Tharme, R.E., and Warner, A., 2009, Ecological Limits of Hydrologic Alteration (ELOHA): A new framework for developing regional environmental flow standards (in press): Freshwater Biology.

Postel, S., and Richter, B., 2003, Rivers for Life: Managing Water for People and Nature: Washington, D.C., Island Press, 253 p.

Rathburn, S.L., 2006, Halligan Reservoir sediment budget 2002–2005: Progress Report submitted to City of Fort Collins, Colorado, 14 p.

Rathburn, S.L., and Wohl, E.E., 2001, One-dimensional sediment transport modeling of pool recovery along a mountain channel after a reservoir sediment release: Regulated Rivers: Research and Management, v. 17, p. 251–273, doi: 10.1002/rrr.617.

Rathburn, S.L., and Wohl, E.E., 2003, Predicting fine sediment dynamics along a pool-riffle mountain channel: Geomorphology, v. 55, p. 111–124, doi: 10.1016/S0169-555X(03)00135-1.

Richter, B.D., and Thomas, G.A., 2007, Restoring environmental flows by modifying dam operations: Ecology and Society, v. 12, p. 12: http://www.ecologyandsociety.org/vol12/iss1/art12/.

Richter, B.D., Baumgartner, J.V., Powell, J., and Braun, D.P., 1996, A method for assessing hydrologic alteration within ecosystems: Conservation Biology, v. 10, p. 1163–1174, doi: 10.1046/j.1523-1739.1996.10041163.x.

Richter, B.D., Baumgartner, J.V., Wigington, R., and Braun, D.P., 1997, How much water does a river need?: Freshwater Biology, v. 37, p. 231–249, doi: 10.1046/j.1365-2427.1997.00153.x.

Richter, B.D., Warner, A.T., Meyer, J.L., and Lutz, K., 2006, A collaborative and adaptive process for developing environmental flow recommendations: River Research and Applications, v. 22, p. 297–318, doi: 10.1002/rra.892.

Scott, M.L., Friedman, J.M., and Auble, G.T., 1996, Fluvial process and the establishment of bottomland trees: Geomorphology, v. 14, p. 327–339, doi: 10.1016/0169-555X(95)00046-8.

Sparks, R.E., Bayley, P.B., Kohler, S.L., and Osborne, L.L., 1990, Disturbance and recovery of large floodplain rivers: Environmental Management, v. 14, p. 699–709, doi: 10.1007/BF02394719.

Telesto Solutions, Inc., 2003, Halligan Reservoir sediment budget 2002 and 2003: Colorado, Technical report presented to North Poudre Irrigation Company, 20 p.

Tharme, R.E., 2003, A global perspective on environmental flow assessment: Emerging trends in the development and application of environmental flow methodologies for rivers: River Research and Application, v. 19, p. 397–441, doi: 10.1002/rra.736.

Tinkler, K., and Wohl, E., 1998, A primer on bedrock channels, *in* Tinkler, K.J., and Wohl, E.E., eds., Rivers over Rock: Fluvial Processes in Bedrock Channels: Washington, D.C., American Geophysical Union Press, p. 1–18.

U.S. Army Corp of Engineers, 2006, Final Scoping Report for Halligan Seaman Water Management Project Environmental Impact Statement, Omaha District: Cheyenne, Wyoming, Regulatory Office: http://greeleyspace.com/files/43/seaman/HSWMP_Final_Scoping_Report.pdf.

U.S. Geological Survey, 1981, Guidelines for Determining Flood Flow Frequency: Bulletin 17B, Hydrology Subcommittee, 194 p.

U.S. Geological Survey, 1999, Field Methods for Measurement of Fluvial Sediment: Techniques in Water Resources Investigations, Book 3, Applied Hydraulics, ch. C2, 89 p.

Ward, J.V., 1992, A mountain river, *in* Calow, P., and Petts, G.E., eds., The Rivers Handbook: Oxford, UK, Blackwell Scientific Publications, p. 493–510.

Williams, G.P., and Wolman, M.G., 1984, Downstream Effects of Dams on Alluvial Rivers: U.S. Geological Survey Professional Paper 1286, 83 p.

Wohl, E., 2000, Mountain Rivers: Washington, D.C., American Geophysical Union Press, 320 p.

Wohl, E.E., and Cenderelli, D.A., 2000, Sediment deposition and transport patterns following a reservoir sediment release: Water Resources Research, v. 36, p. 319–333, doi: 10.1029/1999WR900272.

Wohl, E., and Goode, J.R., 2008, Wood dynamics in headwater streams of the Colorado Rocky Mountains: Water Resources Research, v. 44, W09429, doi: 10.1029/2007WR006522.

Wohl, E., and Legleiter, C.J., 2003, Controls on pool characteristics along a resistant-boundary channel: Journal of Geology, v. 111, p. 103–114, doi: 10.1086/344667.

Workman, S.R., and Serrano, S.E., 1999, Recharge to alluvial aquifers from overbank flow and excess infiltration: Journal of the American Water Resources Association, v. 35, p. 425–432, doi: 10.1111/j.1752-1688.1999.tb03600.x.

Zuellig, R.E., Kondratieff, B.C., and Rhodes, H.A., 2002, Benthos recovery after an episodic sediment release in a Colorado Rocky Mountain river: Western North American Naturalist, v. 62, p. 59–72.

Manuscript Accepted by the Society 15 September 2008

The Geological Society of America
Special Paper 451
2009

Testing the linear relationship between peak annual river discharge and drainage area using long-term USGS river gauging records

Joshua C. Galster*

Department of Earth and Environmental Studies, Montclair State University, 1 Normal Ave., Montclair, New Jersey 07043, USA

ABSTRACT

River discharge is the fundamental process that operates in a fluvial system. The increase in discharge and drainage area downstream is intuitive, but data sets that describe this increase within individual watersheds are not common. The scaling of discharge and drainage area can be described as $Q = kA^c$, where Q is river discharge, A is drainage area, and k and c are scaling constants. The variable k is not often illustrative of watershed processes, but the constant c represents the rate at which discharge (Q) increases downstream when compared to drainage area (A). This study compiles the annual peak discharge records of rivers from U.S. Geological Survey (USGS) gauges to determine the rate (c) at which discharge and drainage increase downstream. The peak annual discharge records were selected to represent a variety of watersheds spanning multiple climatic and geographic settings as well as to illustrate the effects of anthropogenic land-use change and river-management practices over the length of the records. It is often assumed that the scaling between discharge and drainage area is linear ($c \sim 1$), and 16 of these rivers exhibit this behavior over the length of their record. However, most of the rivers studied show nonlinear behavior and/or secular trends in their c values. Eleven rivers have peak annual discharge scaling values (c) of <1, three have c values substantially larger than 1, and ten exhibit secular changes in c over part or all of their records. These nonlinear and changing c values can be attributed to both natural and anthropogenic causes, such as dams, urbanization, and other land-use changes. These c values indicate the need for caution before assuming that discharge and drainage area are linearly related.

INTRODUCTION

Discharge of water is the fundamental process operating in watersheds. Discharges erode, transport, and deposit sediment both inside and outside of the active channel and are responsible for establishing and maintaining the longitudinal profile of a river. River discharge is used by biologic systems as transport routes (i.e., anadromous fish) and is essential in providing fluvial aquatic habitats. Discharge is also a critical resource for humans and is used for hydropower, irrigation, drinking water, industrial activity, and waste disposal. Peak annual discharges are effective agents in shaping channel morphology and transporting sediment, and are the focus of this paper.

*galsterj@mail.montclair.edu

Galster, J.C., 2009, Testing the linear relationship between peak annual river discharge and drainage area using long-term USGS river gauging records, *in* James, L.A., Rathburn, S.L., and Whittecar, G.R., eds., Management and Restoration of Fluvial Systems with Broad Historical Changes and Human Impacts: Geological Society of America Special Paper 451, p. 159–171, doi: 10.1130/2009.2451(11). For permission to copy, contact editing@geosociety.org. ©2009 The Geological Society of America. All rights reserved.

River discharge is intimately connected to its drainage basin, the source area for the flow. The drainage area is often used as a proxy for discharge in fluvial studies, as it is intuitive that river discharge and drainage area would grow linearly together downstream: if the drainage area doubles, the discharge should also double. This assumption is valid if the rate of discharge generated per unit area of drainage basin is spatially constant. However, the amount of discharge generated per unit of drainage area is affected by variables such as slope, precipitation intensity and amount, surface permeability, and vegetation, which may vary spatially in a complex manner. The general relationship between discharge and drainage area can be empirically cast as:

$$Q = kA^c, \qquad (1)$$

where Q is river discharge (m^3/s), k is a constant, A is upstream drainage area (km^2), and c is the scaling power relating A and Q. In this study Q represents the peak annual discharge (based on water year) at each gauging station in a watershed. Discharge (Q) can range from low-flow value up through a 100 yr flood event (Q100). The peak annual discharge was chosen because of its availability but also for its approximation to bankfull discharge for many rivers. However, it is recognized that the peak annual discharges recorded at any gauge will include a range of magnitudes, including the possibility of extreme events. The value of c for each river is a critical measure of the rate of increase in discharge with increasing area downstream. The value of k has not been shown to be particularly useful (e.g., Galster et al., 2006) for explaining discharges across broad spatial areas, although it is necessary for calculating discharge at a specific site as per equation 1. The units of k vary depending on the units of Q and A, and are determined by a particular watershed's hydrologic setting.

A c value of 1 or nearly 1 represents a linear relation between discharge and drainage area, and is caused by different areas of a drainage basin that contribute runoff at equal rates. This situation is more likely to occur in areas with spatially constant hydrologic conditions (Dunne and Leopold, 1978; Galster, 2007). A river with c values <1 represents a situation in which the upstream areas of the watershed generate more discharge per unit area than downstream areas. The opposite holds true in rivers where c is >1: the downstream areas generate proportionately more runoff than the upstream areas.

Most analyses of the scaling relationship between drainage area and discharge have focused on regional data that compile discharges from multiple rivers. This method has been employed for flood events (O'Connor and Costa, 2004; Solyom and Tucker, 2004) and for bankfull discharges (e.g., Cinotto, 2003; Dudley, 2004). However, the grouping of multiple rivers, even from the same physiographic province, may disguise the variability of the scaling factors of individual rivers and smooth out any outliers. Analyzing the scaling of discharges within one watershed is rarer (Goodrich et al., 1997; Gupta and Waymire, 1998; Ogden and Dawdy, 2003; Galster et al., 2006; Galster, 2007), but it is proposed here that this individualized approach is more valid than

grouping different rivers together. Galster (2007) analyzed five rivers without major dams on their mainstems (John Day River, Oregon; Salmon River, Idaho; Yellowstone River, Wyoming–Montana; Wabash River, Indiana; Greenbrier River, West Virginia) and found that whereas many of these rivers had scaling relationships close to linear ($c \sim 1$), the Yellowstone River had a c value closer to 0.5. The Yellowstone also exhibited a secular decrease in its c values over the length of its record, an indication of a possible climatic signal. Additionally, Galster et al. (2006) demonstrated that rivers with drainage basins with urbanized land concentrated in the downstream areas can have c values as high as 1.8.

A linear relationship between discharge and drainage area is advantageous for various river and watershed applications. If this linear relationship is valid, then drainage area can be used directly as a proxy for discharge in modeling applications of longitudinal profiles and landscape evolution (e.g., Kooi and Beaumont, 1994; Tucker and Slingerland, 1997; Whipple, 2004; Bishop et al., 2005). It is mathematically possible for drainage area to be substituted for discharge when their relationship is nonlinear, although critical values of the equations, such as the stream power erosion equation, would change. The exponents of the stream power equation (kA^mS^n, where A is drainage area, S is channel gradient, and k, m, and n are all constants) would change if discharge and drainage area are not linearly related. The substitution of discharge with drainage area is advantageous, as drainage area can be quickly determined from digital elevation models (DEMs), while discharge measurements are comparatively time intensive. River-management and stream-restoration professions also use drainage area as a proxy for discharge when relating channel geometries such as width or depth to upstream drainage. For rivers, of course, it is not the drainage area that directly shapes channel morphology, but discharge.

This study was done to expand on the previous work examining river discharge and drainage area by presenting a large data set showing the c values of 40 rivers, most of them in the eastern United States (see Fig. 1). The goal is to test the validity of the assumption regarding the linear relationship (i.e., $c \sim 1$) between discharge and drainage area for a group of rivers with significant differences in their hydrologic, climatic, and physiographic settings. In this paper *peak annual discharge* refers to the maximum discharge recorded during one year's time, whereas discharge refers to the general properties and processes of water flowing in a river, with generalized units of volume/time.

METHODS

Rivers were included in this analysis if they met a few simple criteria. First, the length of peak annual discharge records available for download had to exceed 30 yr. Second, there needed to be at least three gauging stations operating on the river in order to perform the linear regression. Last, the rivers were mostly restricted to rivers proximate to the Appalachian Mountains, with a few obvious exceptions (e.g., Kansas, Arkansas, Platte Rivers; Fig. 2). This was done to constrain the data-set size as well as

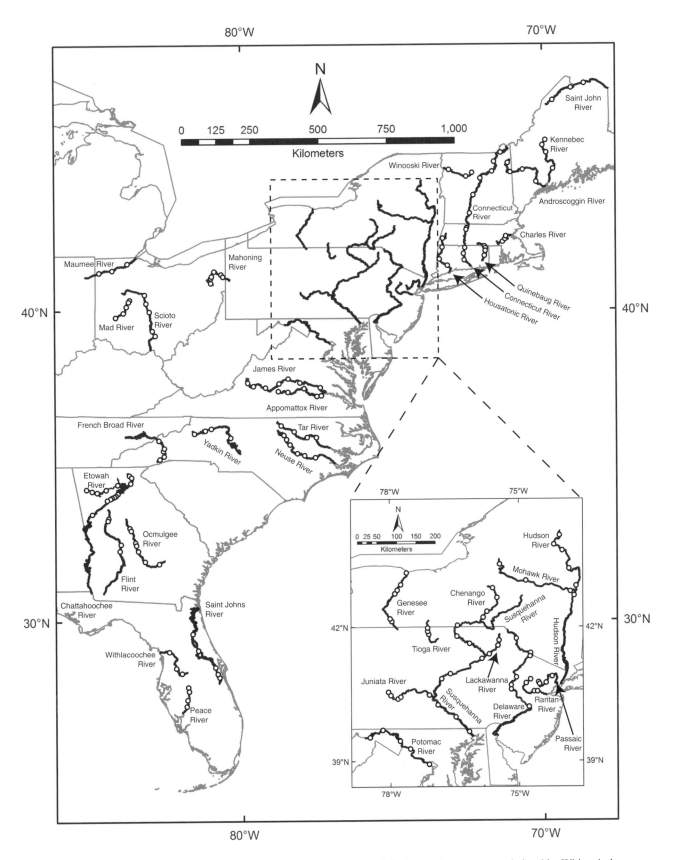

Figure 1. Location map of 37 of the rivers studied for their peak annual discharge–drainage area relationship. White circles represent gauging stations used for analysis; where two stations overlap the downstream station is on top. Inset map displays rivers of the upper Mid-Atlantic Region.

to limit the variability of the hydrologic variables presented by these rivers and their watersheds. However, it is recognized that these rivers encompass a range of climatic, precipitation, lithologic, land-use, and river-management regimes. This multitude of watershed variables is unavoidable in a data set of this size, but it is also not completely undesirable. If the results of the analysis are similar in spite of this range of variables, then they may sug-

gest the existence of shared hydrologic processes acting across many of these watersheds.

The instantaneous annual peak discharges for these rivers were obtained from the U.S. Geological Survey (USGS). These data are available for downloading from the USGS National Water Information System. The English units of the data were converted to SI units (cubic feet per second to cubic meters per second), as

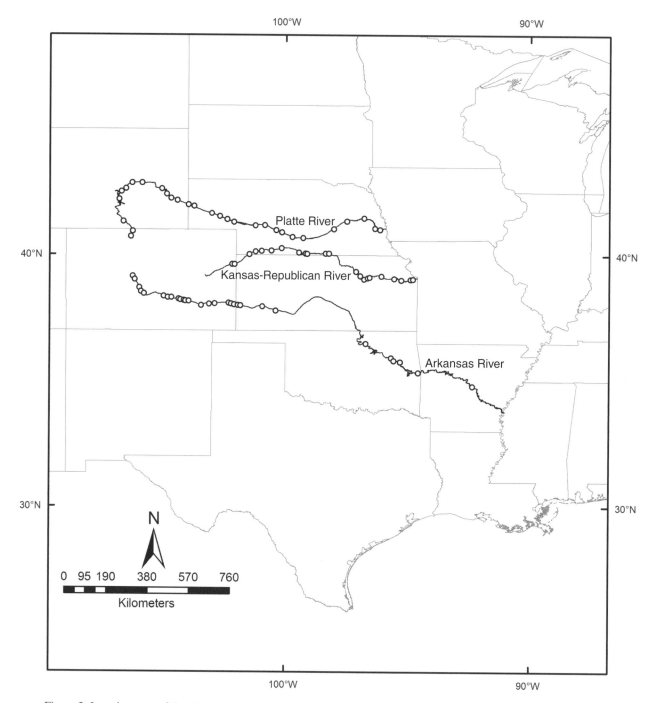

Figure 2. Location map of the Platte, Kansas-Republican, and Arkansas Rivers. White circles represent gauging stations used for analysis; where two stations overlap the downstream station is on top.

were the upstream drainage area (square miles to square kilometers) associated with each gauging station. Some annual peak discharge values are noted as being "estimates" by the USGS, and the accuracy of these large discharges is unknown. The gauging stations typically covered at least an order of magnitude of change downstream in drainage areas, with many rivers having two or three orders of magnitude (hundreds of square kilometers to 100,000 km²) of drainage area. The drainage area of the farthest downstream gauge that measured peak annual discharge and was included in this analysis is listed in Table 1. The length of record for each river is dependent on having the minimum three gauging stations for linear regression. The number of gauging stations listed for each river (Tables 1, 2) is the total number analyzed and may not represent the number used in determining every annual c value. It is common for gauging stations to have become active or inactive during the period analyzed.

TABLE 1. DRAINAGE BASIN CHARACTERISTICS AND c VALUES

Name	State	Drainage area* (km²)	Length of record analyzed	Number of gauging stations	Average c
$c \sim 1$					
Winooski	Vermont	2704	1927–2003	3	1.16 ± 0.03
Raritan	New Jersey	2033	1903–2003	4	1.01 ± 0.03
Mohawk	New York	8936	1929–2003	3	1.00 ± 0.04
Housatonic	Connecticut	3999	1924–2003	4	0.99 ± 0.06
Lackawanna	Pennsylvania	860	1959–2004	3	0.98 ± 0.07
Withlacoochee	Florida	5491	1932–2004	3	0.97 ± 0.13
Quinebaug	Connecticut	1847	1932–2003	4	0.92 ± 0.05
Scioto	Ohio	13,289	1921–2002	5	0.88 ± 0.04
Maumee	Ohio	16,395	1925–1982	3	0.87 ± 0.03
Saint Johns	Florida	7951	1941–2004	5	0.87 ± 0.18
Saint John	Maine	15,317	1951–2003	3	0.83 ± 0.03
Mad	Ohio	1645	1926–2002	5	0.75 ± 0.04
Juniata	Pennsylvania	8686	1936–2003	5	0.74 ± 0.03
Potomac	Maryland–Virginia	29,940	1924–2003	5	0.72 ± 0.05
Yadkin	North Carolina	5905	1940–2003	4	0.70 ± 0.05
Flint	Georgia	7511	1913–2002	4	0.69 ± 0.06
$c > 1$					
Androscoggin	Maine	8451	1914–2003	4	1.64 ± 0.09
Peace	Florida	3541	1940–2003	4	1.60 ± 0.10
Kennebec	Maine	10,951	1908–1982	4	1.50 ± 0.10
$c < 1$					
Mahoning	Ohio	2779	1931–2002	6	0.65 ± 0.05
Delaware	New Jersey–Pennsylvania	17,560	1906–2004	7	0.60 ± 0.05
French Broad	North Carolina	3450	1928–2004	5	0.49 ± 0.04
Chattahoochee	Georgia	6294	1919–2004	10	0.44 ± 0.05
Appomattox	Virginia	3481	1927–2004	5	0.40 ± 0.07
Charles	Massachusetts–Connecticut	650	1960–1998	3	0.39 ± 0.15
Tar	North Carolina	5654	1940–2004	4	0.39 ± 0.05
Neuse	North Carolina	6972	1919–2004	6	0.36 ± 0.06
Platte	Nebraska	218,078	1901–2005	29	0.34 ± 0.04
James	Virginia	17,503	1925–2002	7	0.29 ± 0.08
Ocmulgee	Georgia	13,416	1909–2002	7	0.04 ± 0.08
Secular changes in c					
Kansas	Kansas	155,213	1902–2005	22	1.23 ± 0.12
Chenango	New York	3841	1938–2003	4	0.84 ± 0.03
Susquehanna	Pennsylvania	70,189	1893–2004	9	0.81 ± 0.02
Hudson	New York	20,953	1917–2003	6	0.77 ± 0.03
Connecticut	Massachusetts–Connecticut	25,019	1912–2003	11	0.69 ± 0.05
Passaic	New Jersey	1974	1904–2003	4	0.67 ± 0.05
Etowah	Georgia	4711	1919–1995	5	0.54 ± 0.06
Arkansas	Oklahoma–Arkansas	382,691	1901–2005	29	0.52 ± 0.06
Genesee	New York	6390	1909–2003	6	0.37 ± 0.06
Tioga	Pennsylvania	1155	1975–2004	3	0.04 ± 0.21

*The drainage area of the farthest downstream gauge, not necessarily the total drainage area of the river.

TABLE 2. GAUGING STATION IDENTIFICATION NUMBERS BY RIVER

River	Gauging stations
_c ~ 1_	
Winooski	04285500*; 04286000*; 04290500*
Raritan	01396500; 01397000; 01400500; 01403060
Mohawk	01336000*; 01347000*; 01357500*
Housatonic	01197500*; 01199000*; 01200500*; 01205500*
Lackawanna	01534300*; 01534500*; 01536000*
Withlacoochee	02310947; 02312000*; 02313000; 02319000
Quinebaug	01124000*; 01124151*; 01125500*; 01127000*
Scioto	03219500; 03221000*; 03227500*; 03231500*; 03234500*
Maumee	03328000; 03328500; 03360000*; 04183500; 04192500; 04193500
Saint Johns	02232000; 02232400; 02232500*; 02236000; 02244040
Saint John	01010000; 01010500; 01014000
Mad	03266500; 03267000; 03267900; 03269500; 03270000*
Juniata	01556500; 01558000; 01559000; 01563500*; 01567000
Potomac	01610000; 01613000; 01618000; 01638500; 01646500
Yadkin	02111000; 02112000; 02112250*; 02112000*
Flint	02344500; 02346180; 02347500; 02349500
_c > 1_	
Androscoggin	01053500*; 01054000*; 01054500*; 01059000*
Peace	02294650; 02294898; 02295637; 02296750
Kennebec	01041000*; 01042500*; 01046500*; 01048500*
_c < 1_	
Mahoning	03086500; 03090500*; 03091500*; 03094000*; 03098000*; 03099500*
Delaware	01427510*; 01434000*; 01438500*; 01446500*; 01446700*; 01457500; 01463500
French Broad	03439000; 03443000; 03448000; 03451500; 03453500
Chattahoochee	02330450*; 02331000; 02331600; 02334500*; 02335000; 02335450*; 02335990*; 02336000*; 02337170*; 02338000*
Appomattox	02038800; 02039500; 02041500; 02040000; 02041650
Charles	01103500*; 01104500*; 01104200*
Tar	02081500; 02081747; 02082000; 02083500
Neuse	02087000; 02087190; 02087500; 02087570; 02089000; 02089500
Platte	06613000*; 06620000*; 06627000*; 06630000*; 06636000*; 06642000*; 06645000*; 06646800*; 06652000*; 06652800*; 06657000*; 06656000*; 06674500*; 06679500*; 06684500*; 06686000*; 06687500*; 06693000*; 06691000*; 06686500*; 06766000*; 06768000*; 06766500*; 06770500*; 06770000*; 06774000*; 06796000*; 06805500*; 06801000*
James	02016500; 02019500; 02025500; 02026000; 02029000; 02035000; 02037500
Ocmulgee	02210500*; 02212500; 02213000; 02213700; 02215000; 02215260; 02215500
Secular changes in _c_	
Kansas	06824500*; 06825000; 06826500*; 06828500*; 06829500*; 06857100*; 06837000*; 06843500*; 06844500*; 06849500*; 06850500; 06853000*; 06853500*; 06856600*; 06857000*; 06879100*; 06879500; 06887500*; 06889000*; 06891000*; 06892350*; 06892500
Chenango	01503980; 01505000; 01507000; 01512500*
Susquehanna	01541000; 01541200*; 01541303*; 01542500*; 01545500; 01515000; 01551500; 01553500*; 01536500; 01531500; 01533400; 01540500; 01554000; 01570500; 01576000; 01578310*
Hudson	01312000; 01314000; 01315500*; 01318500*; 01335500; 01358000*
Connecticut	01129200*; 01129500*; 01131500*; 01138500*; 01144500*; 01154500*; 01167000*; 01170500*; 01184000*; 01190070; 01193000*
Passaic	01378690; 01379000; 01379500; 01389500*
Etowah	02389000; 02392000; 02394670; 02395000*; 02396000
Arkansas	07081200*; 07086000*; 07091200*; 07091500*; 07093700*; 07094500*; 07096000*; 07097000*; 07099400*; 07099500*; 07109500*; 07117000*; 07119700*; 07123000*; 07124000*; 07130500*; 07133000*; 07134180*; 07135500*; 07137500*; 07138000*; 07139000*; 07139500*; 07152500; 07164500; 07165570*; 07194500*; 07263500*; 07246500*
Genesee	04221000; 04221500; 04223000; 04227500*; 04228500*; 04232000*
Tioga	01516350; 01518700*; 01518000

*These stations are designated as being impacted by dams and/or diversions.

A linear regression analysis of the logarithm of peak annual discharge and drainage area was completed in SPSS (version 13.0) for each water year (1 October through 30 September) for every river that had a minimum of three gauging stations for the linear regression. Unlike previous methods (Galster, 2007), each peak annual discharge value was used. Galster (2007) only examined peak discharges that occurred within the same 30-day window in order to restrict analysis to discharges from the same event. This approach, while grouping discharges by hydrologic events, ignores localized peak annual discharges that may be geomorphically important. In order to more fully encapsulate the spectrum of annual peak discharges in a drainage basin, this filtered approach of Galster (2007), while still valid, was not used.

The result of the linear regression analysis of the logarithms of peak discharges for a given water year (Q) and the logarithms of drainage area (A) provides the c value in equation 1. The intercept of the regression is the k value (equation 1), which is determined by the units of discharge and drainage area. The units chosen do not affect c, the slope of the regression analysis and the focus of this paper. The 95% confidence interval of the regression is the expression of error, and was calculated as twice the standard error of the regression value. For Table 1 the error is the 95% confidence interval of the calculated mean annual c values of each river, and the error bars in Figures 3–9 represent the 95% confidence interval.

RESULTS

The average c values for the peak annual discharges of the 40 rivers are presented in Table 1. The rivers are divided into four categories: (1) rivers whose average c values are ~1 ($0.75 < c < 1.25$) (Fig. 3), (2) rivers with c values >1.25 (Fig. 4), (3) rivers that have c values <0.75 (Fig. 5), and (4) those rivers that have a secular trend to their c values over all or part of the length of their record (Figs. 6–9). These delineations, while somewhat arbitrary, are helpful in grouping rivers with similar relationships between discharge and drainage areas.

The group of rivers that have average c values for their peak annual discharges of approximately 1 is the largest of these four groups. However, this group does not comprise a majority of the rivers studied, with only 16 out of 40 having c values close to 1. These rivers range in size from the Lackawanna in Pennsylvania (860 km²) to the Potomac (29,940 km²). The rivers with c values >1 is the smallest of the four groups, with only three rivers (Table 1). The other two groups ($c < 1$ and c secular change) comprise ~10 rivers each.

DISCUSSION

c ~1

The 16 rivers in this study that have c values close to 1 (Table 1) have linear relationships between their peak annual discharges and their drainage areas (Fig. 3). In spite of a wide range

in hydrologic variables such as drainage-basin size (~1000 to ~30,000 km²), climatic ranges (i.e., Vermont to Florida), glaciated (Maine) versus unglaciated (South Carolina) terrains, vegetation, potential for frozen ground and/or snowmelt to contribute to peak annual discharges, and bedrock lithologies, it is remarkable that all of these rivers have c values near 1 (Table 1; Fig. 3). Although it would most likely be false to assume that the actual mechanics of discharge generation is identical (for the reasons stated above) among different drainage basins, the net result of these processes produces linear relationships between drainage-basin area and peak annual discharges. This set of rivers suggests that the linear relationship between drainage area and peak annual discharge is an appropriate first-order approximation for hydrologic applications and replicates similar studies for undammed rivers (Galster, 2007), semiarid rivers (Goodrich et al., 1997), and very small (~20 km²) drainage areas (Ogden and Dawdy, 2003).

$c > 1$

This assumption of linearity between peak annual discharge and drainage area should be applied with caution, as most

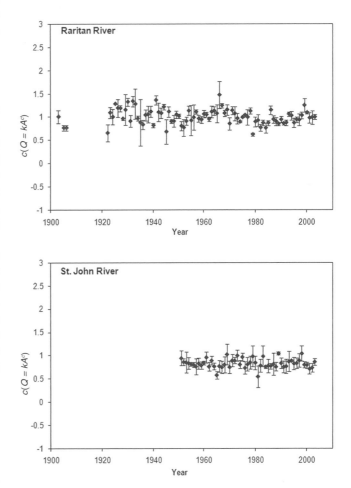

Figure 3. Two of the 16 rivers (Raritan and St. John; Table 1) that have almost constant c values approximating 1.

(24 out of 40) of the rivers analyzed here exhibited either a value of c different than 1 or whose values changed secularly with respect to time. The Androscoggin and Kennebec Rivers in Maine and the Peace River in Florida all have c values significantly >1 (Fig. 4). In these three watersheds, processes must be operating to decrease the generation of discharge in upstream areas or increase discharge production in downstream areas. Either or both of these changes would produce steeper regression values and thus higher c values. Although there are many differences in the hydrologic settings of these two rivers, they do share one commonality: the presence of relatively large lakes in their headwaters. The Androscoggin (Mooselookmeguntic), Kennebec (Moosehead), and Peace (Hancock) all have headwaters originating in lakes that should attenuate peak annual discharges in the headwaters. The lakes should act as natural buffers, lengthening the time period of the peak annual discharges and attenuating their magnitude. Lakes are also an indication of a poorly established fluvial network, and this hydrologically disconnected landscape would produce lower peak annual discharges (Gupta and Waymire, 1998). This decrease in peak annual discharge proportional to area at small drainage areas would serve to increase the slope of the regression line (c) through a river's annual peak discharges. However, this is not to suggest that all rivers with lakes in the headwaters of their drainage areas have high c values. The Withlacoochee and Saint Johns Rivers in Florida originate in lakes-wetlands, but at least in the case of the Saint Johns River numerous lakes are along the river length, which would attenuate the peak annual discharges along the entire river length. It should also be noted that the three rivers with c values >1 are somewhat unique in that c values this large have previously been observed in rivers with large downstream increases in impervious surfaces (Galster et al., 2006).

$c < 1$

Eleven rivers have c values <1 (Table 1; Fig. 5). These rivers are characterized by hydrologic processes that cause relative increases in upstream discharge or relative decreases in downstream discharge generation. These changes decrease the slope of the regression and result in smaller increases in peak annual discharges with increasing drainage area downstream. Factors such as changes in slope, evapotranspiration, vegetation, and snowmelt may contribute to more discharge being generated per unit drainage area in upstream regions than downstream (Galster, 2007). However, as long as the c values are positive, the absolute magnitude of discharges will increase downstream, although the drainage area will increase at a faster rate than discharge. The extreme example from this group of such behavior is the Ocmulgee River in Georgia, which has a long-term average c value of 0.04 ± 0.08. The peak annual discharges in this river do not statistically increase downstream ($c \sim 0$), a situation that is counterintuitive to our standard model of fluvial systems in humid or subhumid regions. In the case of the Ocmulgee this unusual discharge regime is most likely created by Lake Jackson, a large (~ 18 km^2) reservoir near the headwaters of the Ocmulgee. This reservoir, constructed in 1911, is primarily used for the generation of hydroelectric power (National Inventory of Dams). The reservoir may create artificially high discharges at these smaller drainage areas by releasing stored water and generating higher discharges than would normally be created only from runoff.

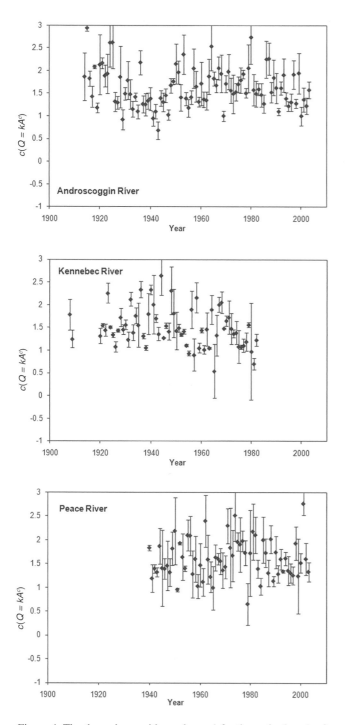

Figure 4. The three rivers with c values >1 for the entire length of their record: Androscoggin, Kennebec, and Peace.

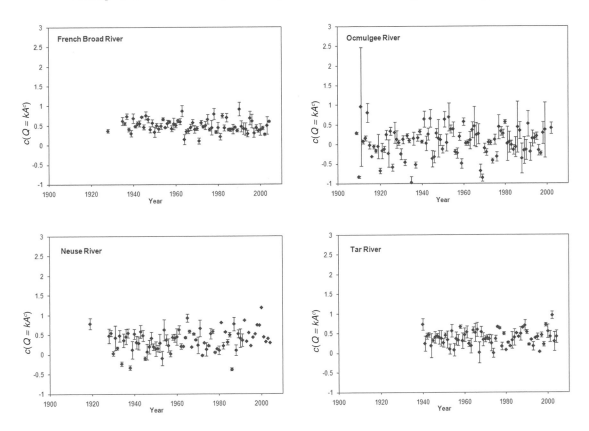

Figure 5. Four rivers representative of the group characterized by *c* values <1. The French Broad (North Carolina), Ocmulgee (Georgia), Neuse (North Carolina), and Tar (North Carolina) are all either in the Piedmont or Atlantic Coastal Plain physiographic region or in both (Fig. 1).

It should also be noted that many of the studied rivers from the Piedmont and Atlantic Coastal regions had *c* values <1. The Delaware (Pennsylvania–New Jersey), Appomattox (Virginia), Tar (North Carolina), Neuse (North Carolina), James (Virginia), and Ocmulgee (Georgia) Rivers all flow across one or both of these regions. There are exceptions to this pattern (e.g., the Saint Johns in Florida), but it is remarkable that these two physiographic regions appear to produce rivers with low (<1) *c* values. This may be a result of the low slopes in the downstream Coastal Plain areas that would generate proportionately less discharge per unit drainage area than the steeper, high-elevation headwaters, although further testing would be needed to validate this hypothesis.

Secular Changes in *c* over Time

The last group of rivers exhibits secular changes in *c* values over time. These rivers have *c* values of varying magnitudes, but each river exhibits secular patterns of increasing or decreasing *c* values over part or all of its record. The Genesee (New York), Hudson (New York), and Connecticut (Massachusetts-Connecticut) rivers exhibited increasing *c* values from ~1910 to 1930 (Fig. 6).

Although the timing is similar, the magnitude of the increase in *c* (Genesee, 0.9; Hudson, 0.5; Connecticut, 0.6) varies among these rivers, as do the trends after this initial increase. Why? Dam construction in upland areas and urbanization in downstream areas may have contributed to this trend, although this is speculation. The *c* values for the Hudson and Connecticut stabilized after ~1940, although the values for the Genesee River fluctuate more. Part of the fluctuation in *c* values for the Genesee may be attributed to dam construction, but there are also large dams on the Connecticut. The Genesee's downstream regions also have some karst areas, where proportionately more discharge may be naturally diverted to groundwater and would also explain some of the low *c* values. Downstream karst regions would act to decrease *c*, as the downstream areas would generate proportionately less discharge than other regions of the watershed.

In contrast to these three rivers is the trend of the *c* values for the Susquehanna River. There the *c* values monotonically increase over the length of the record, beginning at ~0.6 and increasing to almost 1.0 (Fig. 7). A *c* value of 1 has been documented before for the Susquehanna (Slingerland et al., 1994), but not the trend. This trend suggests that a process (processes) is operating at the watershed scale to systematically increase the

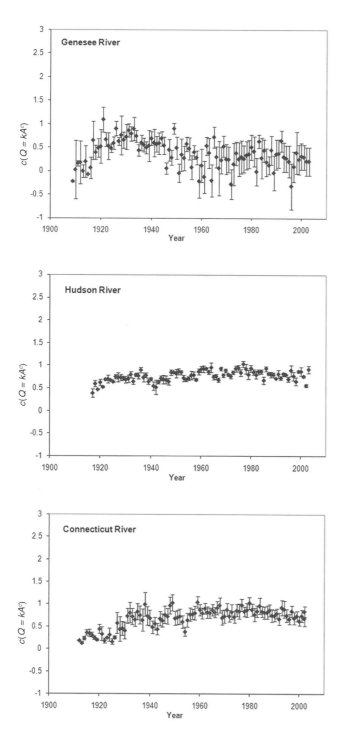

Figure 6. Three rivers with increasing *c* values over the beginning (Genesee and Connecticut) or entire (Hudson) length of their discharge records.

downstream discharge contributions and/or decrease upstream discharges. Although similar, the observed trends in the Susquehanna basin are not coincident with those of the Hudson and Connecticut basins. Similar processes (e.g., land-use change and dam construction) also may be driving the trends in the Susquehanna basin, although further study of all three watersheds is needed to determine the cause. If an external forcing such as climate change was the driving factor, then a similar trend should be observed in nearby rivers such as the Hudson, Mohawk, and Delaware.

The *c* values for the Chenango and Tioga Rivers, headwater tributaries of the Susquehanna, suggest, at the minimum, upstream changes that occur as the rate of discharge increases (Fig. 7). The *c* values for the Chenango River decrease from ~1.1 to 0.7 over its peak annual discharge record from ~1940 to the present. A similar trend occurs for the Tioga River, although its record begins in the late 1970s. If the *c* values for peak annual discharge are decreasing in the Chenango, Tioga, and other Susquehanna headwater tributaries, then this may produce the overall increasing trend in *c* values observed for the mainstem

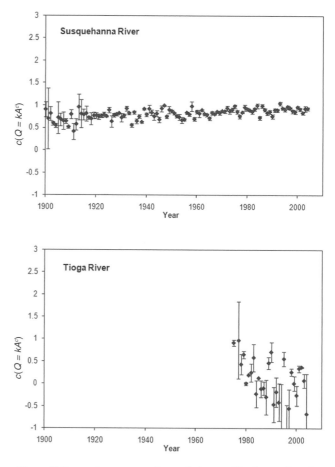

Figure 7. Increasing monotonic trend observed in the *c* values for the Susquehanna River may be caused by decreasing *c* values in headwater tributaries. Data from both the Chenango and Tioga Rivers exhibit decreases in *c* values.

of the Susquehanna. A decrease in the c value at small drainage areas would cause an increase in the c value for the overall watershed. Factors such as land-use change and river management may be affecting these smaller watersheds and driving changes in the larger Susquehanna drainage basin. The Tioga River, for example, had a large dam (Hammond) completed in 1979 for flood control and storm-water management (National Inventory of Dams). These dams would decrease the magnitude of the larger discharges (Magilligan and Nislow, 2005; Graf, 2006), including the peak annual discharges presented here.

The Susquehanna also has more variability in its discharges at the beginning of its record (before ~1910), as seen by the greater error bars for the early c values (Fig. 7). Although there are differences in the timing for each river system, this pattern of increased variability early in the peak annual discharge record is seen in other rivers as well (e.g., the Arkansas). For the Susquehanna River, several of the largest dams were constructed between 1900 and 1930 (National Inventory of Dams). As river discharge is managed for human purposes (e.g., flood control, hydropower, irrigation), it is not surprising to see a decrease in the variability of the downstream discharge increase. The use of dams for flood control would decrease the peak annual discharges at these downstream sections of the river (i.e., large drainage areas) and would result in smaller c values for the river post-dam.

The Passaic River (New Jersey) and Etowah River (Georgia) exhibit comparable trends in their c values (Fig. 8). Both rivers have a decrease in c values over the length of their record and have larger 95% confidence intervals in more recent scaling values. The Etowah River had large dams completed on it relatively recently (1965 and 1986), and a change in river-discharge management may explain the shift in c values. Land-use change in the form of urban sprawl has been cited as a major issue for the Etowah drainage basin (The Nature Conservancy, 2005), and an increase in impervious areas associated with development may change the spatial characteristics of discharge generation. The dams on the Passaic River were completed mostly during the gap in peak annual discharge records (~1910–1940) and would not explain the observed shift in c values. More detailed analysis of these watersheds may reveal changes in other hydrologic conditions that would have caused the observed shift in c values.

Finally, the Kansas and Arkansas Rivers also exhibit interesting behavior in their long-term c values (Fig. 9). The Kansas River analyzed here includes the Republican River, but hydrologically they can be considered one fluvial system operating along a continuous mainstem channel. The downstream half of the mainstem is free of large reservoirs that would impound and attenuate the peak annual discharges, whereas there are large reservoirs on several of the tributaries (e.g., Clinton, Perry, Tuttle Creek) and in the upstream region of the drainage basin (Fig. 2; Table 2). The increasing trend of c values from the 1930s (~0.5) to the present (~1.9) is caused by the reduction of peak annual discharges at the smaller drainage areas. As an example, the peak annual discharge below the Harlan County Dam (Nebraska) in 2000 was only 6.4 m³/s. This extremely low discharge is in spite of the Har-

lan County Dam having >35,000 km² of drainage area upstream. Another gauging station at Stratton, Nebraska, had a peak discharge of 4.8 m³/s and a drainage area of almost 9,600 km². From the Stratton gauge to the Harlan County gauge the river increases in drainage area almost fourfold, and yet the annual peak discharge only increased by one-third. These peak annual discharges that barely increase downstream because of human river management are typical for the 1990s and 2000s in these river systems. These depressed peak annual discharges in upstream areas produce a much higher value for c for the larger watersheds downstream, as the slope of the regression increases.

The Arkansas River c values also demonstrate the imprint of human river management. A series of large flood-control and navigation dams were constructed during the 1960s on the mainstem of the Arkansas River (Table 2). This corresponds exactly to the shift in c values from an average of ~0.8 to 0.3. The lower c values represent the decrease in annual peak discharges between these time periods. The three gauging stations farthest downstream (Ralston, Oklahoma; Tulsa, Oklahoma; Dardanelle,

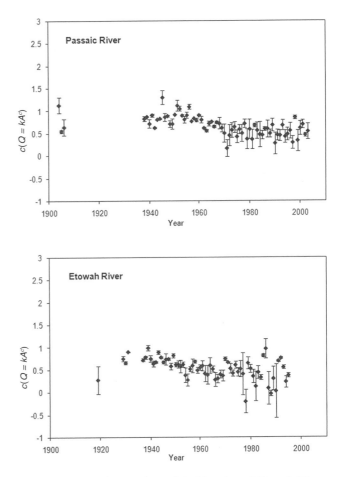

Figure 8. Decreasing c values of the Passaic and Etowah Rivers. What is forcing the changes observed in these two watersheds is not clear, although land-use change may be a factor, especially in the Etowah drainage basin.

Arkansas), with records from both the 1940s and 1980s, show a 39%–48% decrease in the average annual peak discharge between the two decades.

CONCLUSIONS

The rivers presented here suggest that the linear relationship between peak annual discharge and drainage area may be an appropriate initial assumption for many rivers. The rivers with c values approximating 1 exist in a variety of hydrologic, physiographic, and climatic settings, and the group of rivers with average c values near 1 is the most numerous of the four groups presented here. The assumption of a linear relationship between peak annual river discharge and drainage area may be appropriate until proven otherwise for general fluvial applications. The assumption of linearity should not be blindly applied, however. A majority of the studied rivers (24 out of 40) either had c values that differed substantially from 1 or had secular trends or abrupt shifts in their c values or both. These rivers also

encompass the same geographic range as the rivers with c values approximating 1, suggesting that few generalizations are to be made on the discharge-drainage area relationship on the basis of geographic location.

The observed range in the scaling relationships between peak annual discharge and drainage area has many implications. The conclusion that human river management has affected river discharge is certainly not new, but in casting the effects in terms of c a quantitative tool is provided that may improve our spatial understanding of these impacts. These impacts include direct changes through the human use of rivers (e.g., irrigation, drinking-water supplies, hydropower), biologic changes (e.g., high discharges can be important for maintaining a particular channel morphology critical for aquatic habitats), and geologic changes (e.g., sediment transport and channel maintenance). For long-term geologic models of landscape evolution, the linear replacement of peak annual discharge by drainage area may be reasonable if done with caution. This data set suggests the need for added caution in applying that assumption in the hydrologic (i.e., large lakes in the headwaters) or physiographic (i.e., Atlantic Coastal Plain) examples where nonlinear c values appear to be more common.

The calculation of c values should be in addition to the comparison of discrete changes in discharges at one point. Thus c values can provide insight into basin-wide changes that affect discharges, and should augment more direct methods. Further analysis of mean annual discharges and expanding the data set to include more climatic, hydrologic, and tectonic settings also should be done.

ACKNOWLEDGMENTS

The insightful reviews by Peter Cinnotto and an anonymous reviewer improved this manuscript.

REFERENCES CITED

Bishop, P., Hoey, T.B., Jansen, J.D., and Artza, I.L., 2005, Knickpoint recession rate and catchment area: The case of uplifted rivers in eastern Scotland: Earth Surface Processes and Landforms, v. 30, p. 767–778, doi: 10.1002/esp.1191.

Cinotto, P.J., 2003, Development of Regional Curves of Bankfull-Channel Geometry and Discharge for Streams in the Nonurban, Piedmont Physiographic Province, Pennsylvania and Maryland: U.S. Geological Survey Water-Resources Investigations Report 03-4014, 27 p.

Dudley, R.W., 2004, Hydraulic-Geometry Relations for Rivers in Coastal and Central Maine: U.S. Geological Survey Scientific Investigations Report 2004-5042, 37 p.

Dunne, T., and Leopold, L.B., 1978, Water in Environmental Planning: New York, W.H. Freeman, 818 p.

Galster, J.C., 2007, Natural and anthropogenic influences on the scaling of discharge with drainage area for multiple watersheds: Geosphere, v. 3, p. 260–271, doi: 10.1130/GES00065.1.

Galster, J.C., Pazzaglia, F.J., Hargreaves, B.R., Morris, D.P., Peters, S.C., and Weisman, R.N., 2006, Land use effects on watershed hydrology: The scaling of discharge with drainage area: Geology, v. 34, p. 713–716, doi: 10.1130/G22633.1.

Goodrich, D.C., Lane, L.J., Shillito, R.M., Miller, S.N., Syed, K.H., and Woolhiser, D.A., 1997, Linearity of basin response as a function of scale in a

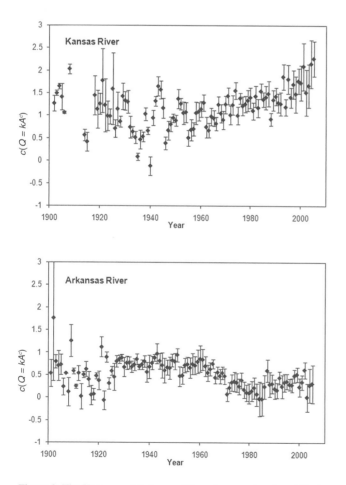

Figure 9. The Kansas and Arkansas Rivers have contrasting shifts in their c values despite similar settings (Fig. 2). These changes both may be driven by dam construction and human river management, but in either upstream (Kansas) or downstream (Arkansas) regions.

semiarid watershed: Water Resources Research, v. 33, p. 2951–2965, doi: 10.1029/97WR01422.

Graf, W.L., 2006, Downstream hydrologic and geomorphic effects of large dams on American rivers: Geomorphology, v. 79, p. 336–360, doi: 10.1016/j.geomorph.2006.06.022.

Gupta, V.K., and Waymire, E.C., 1998, Spatial variability and scale invariance in hydrologic regionalization, *in* Sposito, G., ed., Scale Dependence and Scale Invariance in Hydrology: Cambridge, UK, Cambridge University Press, p. 88–135.

Kooi, H., and Beaumont, C., 1994, Escarpment evolution on high-elevation rifted margins; insights derived from a surface process model that combines diffusion, advection, and reaction: Journal of Geophysical Research, v. 99, p. 12,191–12,209, doi: 10.1029/94JB00047.

Magilligan, F.J., and Nislow, K.H., 2005, Changes in hydrologic regime by dams: Geomorphology, v. 71, p. 61–78, doi: 10.1016/j.geomorph.2004.08.017.

Nature Conservancy, The, 2005, The Upper Etowah River Watershed: Atlanta, The Nature Conservancy in Georgia, 2 p.

O'Connor, J., and Costa, J.E., 2004, Spatial distribution of the largest rainfall-runoff floods from basins between 2.6 and 26,000 km^2 in the United States and Puerto Rico: Water Resources Research, v. 40, W01107, doi: 10.1029/2003WR002247.

Ogden, F.L., and Dawdy, D.R., 2003, Peak discharge scaling in a small hortonian watershed: Journal of Hydrologic Engineering, v. 8, p. 64–73, doi: 10.1061/(ASCE)1084-0699(2003)8:2(64).

Slingerland, R., Harbaugh, J.W., and Furlong, K.P., 1994, Simulating Clastic Sedimentary Basins: Englewood Cliffs, New Jersey, Prentice Hall, 220 p.

Solyom, P.B., and Tucker, G.E., 2004, Effect of limited storm duration on landscape evolution, drainage basin geometry, and hydrograph shapes: Journal of Geophysical Research, v. 109, p. F03012, doi: 10.1029/2003JF000032.

Tucker, G.E., and Slingerland, R., 1997, Drainage basin responses to climate change: Water Resources Research, v. 33, p. 2031–2047, doi: 10.1029/97WR00409.

U.S. Geological Survey National Water Information System: http://nwis.waterdata.usgs.gov/usa/nwis/peak.

Whipple, K.X., 2004, Bedrock rivers and the geomorphology of active orogens: Annual Review of Earth and Planetary Sciences, v. 32, p. 151–185.

MANUSCRIPT ACCEPTED BY THE SOCIETY 15 SEPTEMBER 2008

The Geological Society of America
Special Paper 451
2009

Geomorphic changes resulting from floods in reconfigured gravel-bed river channels in Colorado, USA

John G. Elliott
Joseph P. Capesius
U.S. Geological Survey, Box 25046, MS 415, Denver Federal Center, Lakewood, Colorado 80225, USA

ABSTRACT

Geomorphic changes in reconfigured reaches of three Colorado rivers in response to floods in 2005 provide a benchmark for "restoration" assessment. Sediment-entrainment potential is expressed as the ratio of the shear stress from the 2 yr, 5 yr, 10 yr, and 2005 floods to the critical shear stress for sediment. Some observed response was explained by the excess of flood shear stress relative to the resisting force of the sediment. Bed-load entrainment in the Uncompahgre River and the North Fork Gunnison River, during 4 and 6 yr floods respectively, resulted in streambed scour, streambed deposition, lateral-bar accretion, and channel migration at various locations. Some constructed boulder and log structures failed because of high rates of bank erosion or bed-material deposition. The Lake Fork showed little or no net change after the 2005 flood; however, this channel had not conveyed floods greater than the 2.5 yr flood since reconfiguration.

Channel slope and the 2 yr flood, a surrogate for bankfull discharge, from all three reconfigured reaches plotted above the Leopold and Wolman channel-pattern threshold in the "braided channel" region, indicating that braiding, rather than a single-thread meandering channel, and midchannel bar formation may be the natural tendency of these gravel-bed reaches. When plotted against a total stream-power and median-sediment-size threshold for the 2 yr flood, however, the Lake Fork plotted in the "single-thread channel" region, the North Fork Gunnison plotted in the "multiple-thread" region, and the Uncompahgre River plotted on the threshold. All three rivers plotted in the multiple-thread region for floods of 5 yr recurrence or greater.

INTRODUCTION

Channel reconfiguration, or "restoration," to mitigate a variety of riverine conditions has become a widespread practice in the Western United States. Reasons cited for channel reconfiguration include restoration to more "natural" or historical conditions, improved water conveyance in flood-prone areas, mitigation of

unstable streambed and streambanks, increasing sediment transport, and enhancement of riparian habitat or recreation. Many private entities and resource-management agencies have reconfigured stream and river channels by using designs based on different geomorphic philosophies and classification schemes (Mosley, 1982; Miall, 1985; Montgomery and Buffington, 1993; Whiting and Bradley, 1993; Rosgen, 1996; Federal Interagency Stream

Elliott, J.G., and Capesius, J.P., 2009, Geomorphic changes resulting from floods in reconfigured gravel-bed river channels in Colorado, USA, *in* James, L.A., Rathburn, S.L., and Whittecar, G.R., eds., Management and Restoration of Fluvial Systems with Broad Historical Changes and Human Impacts: Geological Society of America Special Paper 451, p. 173–198, doi: 10.1130/2009.2451(12). For permission to copy, contact editing@geosociety.org. ©2009 The Geological Society of America. All rights reserved.

Restoration Working Group, 2001). Many kilometers of stream and river channels in Colorado and other regions have been reconfigured; however, geomorphic response to, and the effectiveness of, these modifications over a period of time have not been assessed in a consistent manner (Kondolf and Micheli, 1995; Kondolf, 1998).

Many river channel reaches "restored" by using the "natural channel design" criteria (Rosgen, 1996) exhibit unanticipated or undesirable geomorphic changes after the conveyance of greater than "bankfull" floods (Kochel et al., 2005). These include continued lateral erosion and meander-bend migration, entrainment and dislodging of boulder and log "habitat-improvement" and flow-directing structures, and sedimentation near and on these structures. Problems originating from the use of a natural channel design procedure in river restoration, or reconfiguration, generally tend to be related to the procedure's reliance on (1) assuming that the reconfigured channel function (water and sediment conveyance, aquatic habitat, etc.) will follow its imposed reconfigured form; (2) the use of fixed-location boulder, log, and rip-rap structures in a dynamic river channel; (3) strict correlation of channel form (width, depth, meander wavelength, etc.) with a single discharge value (the "bankfull discharge") commonly estimated from a "reference reach" assumed to have characteristics similar to the desired reconfigured channel; (4) failure to account for natural variability in channel morphology over time; (5) failure to account for the imbalance in driving and resisting forces or sediment supply and transport capacity; or (6) design focus only on average channel conditions at the reach scale (Juracek and Fitzpatrick, 2003; Smith and Prestegaard, 2005; Simon et al., 2007).

Judging the success or failure of various restoration methods is not within the scope of this paper, that being determined by the objectives and standards established by the designers and stewards of each project. However, the geomorphic changes of monitored, reconfigured reaches in response to flood discharges of known magnitude and recurrence probability provide benchmarks against which individual project performance can be assessed and are the subject of this paper. Monitoring and performance assessment are essential, though often overlooked or underfunded, components of "river restoration" projects. A monitoring program based on consistently collected data, in a representative location, conducted for a hydrologically appropriate duration, provides critical information to management groups and regulatory agencies on which project success or failure can be judged (Johnson and Brown, 2001; Roper et al., 2002). Performance assessment of monitored reconfigured channels that have adjusted to flows in excess of bankfull discharge, or the equivalent, can provide information on the hydraulic conditions associated with channel adjustment, as well as input for mitigation and design modification (Smith and Prestegaard, 2005).

THE RECONFIGURED-CHANNEL MONITORING AND ASSESSMENT PROGRAM

Long-term monitoring and geomorphic analysis of reconfigured channels can reveal how and why a particular reconfiguration design in a particular geomorphic setting may have remained functional or failed. If a channel modification fails under specified project design criteria, post-event analysis can identify the dominant processes by which failure occurred. These processes could include bank erosion, high sediment-transport rates, streambed deposition or incision, floodplain deposition or scour, and loss of riparian vegetation through root scour, soil-moisture deficit, or prolonged submergence. Conversely, long-term monitoring and periodic analysis can identify geomorphic characteristics of reconfigured channels that have remained stable, in quasi-equilibrium, or functional over a wide range of hydrologic events. Site-specific, post-project analysis provides information about a reconfigured channel reach and enables interested parties to assess whether the reconfiguration has resulted in persistent qualities deemed acceptable to land managers and the public. This type of analysis also is useful in problem mitigation and future design modification.

The U.S. Geological Survey (USGS) is engaged in a program designed to monitor and evaluate selected river reaches that have undergone reconfiguration—the Reconfigured-Channel Monitoring and Assessment Program (RCMAP) (Elliott and Parker, 1999). The RCMAP includes multiple surveys, photographs, and sediment data for monitored, reconfigured reaches of several western Colorado rivers. Periodically, data from these sites are evaluated and analyzed to assess geomorphic responses to hydrologic conditions and events. The RCMAP database includes reconfigured reaches that represent a range of geomorphic, sedimentologic, and hydrologic stream types. Data and photographs from these sites periodically are updated on the USGS RCMAP Website.

RCMAP monitoring activities are ongoing and consist primarily of replicate measurements and photographs of channel characteristics and geomorphic and hydrologic evaluations of the river reach. The measurements are made with field methods familiar to most geomorphologists (Dunne and Leopold, 1978; Harrelson et al., 1994; Kondolf and Micheli, 1995; Fitzpatrick et al., 1998; Smelser and Schmidt, 1998). Monitored reach layout and measurements are tailored to a specific reach and entail topographic surveys of the channel cross section and longitudinal profile; measurement of sediment-size characteristics of the streambed, banks, alluvial bars, and terraces (Wolman, 1954); and oblique photography from monumented locations through the reach. Geomorphic evaluations are based on existing topographic maps or digital elevation models (DEMs), aerial photographs, and on-site observations and measurements. Hydrologic evaluations are based on peak-flow frequency and streamflow-duration analyses of discharge recorded at nearby streamflow-gauging stations.

Data are collected over a monitored reach of at least several channel widths in length from reconfigured channels and, if present, from an adjoining unaltered control reach. A set of measurements is made prior to reconfiguration, if possible, and during the first year after reconfiguration before the first substantial streamflow. These measurements are replicated in subsequent years to evaluate channel change in the reconfigured reach; the time interval between replicate measurements is determined partly by the hydrologic history at the monitored reach. Monitoring strategy and data-collection methods are described in greater detail in Elliott and Parker (1999) and on the USGS RCMAP Website "Monitoring Methods" link.

The objectives of the RCMAP are to (1) develop uniform and versatile monitoring methods for reconfigured channel reaches and apply these methods to selected reaches, (2) create and maintain a database consisting of numerous monumented stream reaches, and (3) revisit these reaches periodically and assess regional and temporal trends in the geomorphic response of the stream to the imposed channel modifications and subsequent streamflow. In this paper we (1) evaluate the potential changes of the reconfigured channels in response to three hypothetical flood discharges of constant recurrence period, the 2, 5, and 10 yr floods, and (2) evaluate the observed geomorphic responses of three monitored reaches to the 2005 peak discharges.

METHOD OF ANALYSIS

The three monitored sites are located in the vicinity of USGS streamflow-gauging stations that have been operated for a minimum of 48 yr, recording instantaneous and daily discharge (U.S. Geological Survey Real-Time Water Data Website). Flood recurrence intervals, the reciprocal of the probability that a specific discharge will be equaled or exceeded in any given year, were determined according to methods prescribed by the U.S. Interagency Advisory Committee on Water Data (1982) (USIACWD).

Many reconfigured channel geomorphic variables estimated by using the natural channel design method are scaled in relation to idealized bankfull channel dimensions (Rosgen, 1996). The associated bankfull discharge, the discharge assumed to be most influential in creating and maintaining alluvial-channel dimensions and hence the bankfull channel scale and proportion, often is unknown, difficult to define, and may be irrelevant in disturbed or degraded rivers (Juracek and Fitzpatrick, 2003). To avoid dependence on the bankfull discharge, and yet to provide some reference against which the 2005 flood peaks can be compared, the 2 yr recurrence interval (RI) flood was used as a surrogate for bankfull discharge in this paper. The 2 yr flood (Q_2) can be determined objectively for gauging-station records of sufficient length by using the USIACWD (1982) methods (Flynn et al., 2006), and Q_2 was found to be a better estimator of the bankfull discharge than was drainage basin area (Wilkerson, 2008). The 5 yr (Q_5) and 10 yr (Q_{10}) floods also were determined by this method and, along with the Q_2, were used as reference discharges for site-to-site comparisons. High-water marks (usually organic flotsam and occasionally fine-grained slack-water sediment) were surveyed during the post-flood topographic surveys to estimate the peak-discharge water-surface elevation at many points in the monitored reaches. The resulting peak water-surface profile in each monitored reach was associated with the 2005 peak discharge recorded at the nearest streamflow-gauging station.

The one-dimensional water-surface profiles model HEC-RAS was used to estimate water-surface elevations, water-surface slopes, flow depths, and hydraulic conditions for the Q_2, Q_5, and Q_{10}, and for the 2005 peak discharge in each monitored reach (HEC-RAS Website). The model used surveyed, pre-flood channel cross sections and was verified by comparison of the computed peak-discharge water-surface elevation with surveyed high-water marks associated with the 2005 discharges.

The hydraulic models were calibrated by varying the Manning's n roughness coefficient until the calculated water-surface elevations matched the surveyed 2005 peak discharge water-surface elevations as closely as possible. Computational errors were minimized and the accuracy of the models was improved by inserting interpolated cross sections to balance velocity heads and water-surface elevations in some reaches. Hydraulic output from the modeling runs included water-surface elevations, energy gradients, water-surface slopes, and channel-average boundary shear stresses at the cross sections.

Lateral and downstream variations in cross-section morphology, flow depth, bed form and particle drag, and variations in energy gradient with discharge result in a wide range of boundary shear stresses nonuniformly distributed across the channel (Graf, 1971). Consequently, this nonuniformity produces variable hydraulic conditions for sediment entrainment, sorting, and deposition at different locations on the streambed (Smith and Prestegaard, 2005). In addition to channel average shear stresses computed with the HEC-RAS model, cross-channel boundary shear stresses also were estimated for the Q_2, Q_5, Q_{10}, and 2005 peak flood discharges.

The cross-channel boundary shear stress in this study was approximated by the relation between boundary shear stress, hydraulic radius, and energy gradient given by the duBoys equation (Chow, 1959):

$$\tau_o = \gamma R S, \tag{1}$$

where τ_o is the cross-section mean boundary shear stress (N/m^2), γ is the specific weight of water (9807 N/m^3), R is the hydraulic radius (m), and S is the energy gradient (m/m) for a specific discharge. In this analysis, flow depth, D, was substituted for R, and the water-surface slope computed with HEC-RAS was substituted for the energy gradient.

Point depths along each monitored cross section were substituted for the cross-section mean flow depth in equation 1 to estimate boundary shear stress at specific points across the channel in order to examine the relative effects of different reference discharges and the 2005 floods at specific locations on the channel boundary and other inundated surfaces (streambed, banks, alluvial bars, low terraces). Except for low-flow conditions, monitored cross sections in this study did not have a trapezoidal shape. However, all reconfigured channels initially had single-thread channels at less than flood discharges, and all had widths at least 20 times mean-flow depth. Streamflow in the study reaches was assumed to be steady; there were no significant local inflows to, or withdrawals from, the monitored reaches. Streamflow was nonuniform where boulder structures ("J-hooks," "cross-vanes," etc.) altered the flow path, but most monitored cross sections used in the HEC-RAS model were not influenced by these structures, and uniform flow was assumed. Infiltration losses were assumed to be insignificant, although this could not be confirmed.

Channel instability in reconfigured river reaches is associated with entrainment of the sediment composing the streambed, streambanks, and alluvial bars. Sediment entrainment in alluvial channels is partly a function of the boundary shear stress acting on sediment particles resting on or in the streambed. The critical shear stress, the shear stress at which movement of sediment begins, has been related to sediment-size characteristics (Shields, 1936; Lane, 1955; Fahnestock, 1963; Milhous, 1982; Carling, 1983; Komar, 1987; Wiberg and Smith, 1987; Wilcock and Southard, 1988; Wilcock, 1992). The boundary shear stresses associated with reference discharges and the 2005 floods were compared with the critical shear stresses for sediment in the channel to evaluate the sediment-entrainment potential of each discharge (Elliott and Hammack, 1999, 2000).

The Shields (1936) equation was used to estimate the critical shear stress (τ_c) for entrainment of the streambed median sediment size, or d_{50}:

$$\tau_c = \tau^*_c \, (\gamma_s - \gamma) \, d_{50}, \qquad (2)$$

where τ_c is the critical shear stress (N/m²); τ^*_c is the dimensionless critical shear stress, or Shields parameter; γ is the specific weight of water (9807 N/m³); γ_s is the specific weight of sediment (here assumed to be 2.65 times the specific weight of water); and d_{50} is the median sediment-particle size (m). Use of equation 2 requires an estimated or calculated dimensionless critical shear stress, or Shields parameter, τ^*_c, a value that varies with particle size, sorting, subsurface particle size, and bed-material structure (Meyer-Peter and Muller, 1948; Neill, 1968; Parker et al., 1982; Andrews, 1983; Komar, 1987; Powell and Ashworth, 1995).

Geomorphic and sedimentologic changes attributed to the 1995 Gunnison River flood were quantified by Elliott and Hammack (2000) and were used to estimate τ^*_c and sediment-entrainment thresholds for gravel and cobble surfaces in an alluvial reach of the Black Canyon of the Gunnison (Elliott and Hammack, 1999). Most τ^*_c values fell between 0.028 and 0.046, with a tendency for lower values to be associated with increasing surface particle size. These values were in general agreement with those of Andrews' τ^*_{ci} (1983) and Komar's θ_{ti} (1987) if one assumes that the surface d_{50} is ~1.5–3 times the subsurface d_{50} (Parker et al., 1982). A Shields parameter value of 0.030, at the conservative end of the range, was used for subsequent critical shear stress (τ_c), and sediment entrainment estimates in the Gunnison River by Elliott and Hammack (1999, 2000). Similarly, a value of 0.030 was used in the following analyses in this paper.

The use of a conservative value for the Shields parameter (0.030), rather than a larger value (for example, 0.045), results in a smaller τ_c and, consequently, an entrainment ratio of unity

at a smaller discharge. When assessing the potential for channel instability from sediment entrainment, estimates based on a conservative value of the Shields parameter result in a greater safety factor.

The relative differences between boundary shear stress and the critical shear stress for sediment entrainment at specific locations and over a range of reference discharges were used to assess whether observed channel geometry changes in the monitored reaches resulted from an imbalance between the driving forces (flood shear stress) and resisting forces (sediment critical shear stress) (Elliott and Hammack, 1999). Sediment-entrainment potential at each cross section associated with the Q_2, Q_5, Q_{10}, and 2005 flood discharges was expressed as the ratio of the mean boundary shear stress (τ_o) to the critical shear stress for the median sediment size at the cross section (τ_c). The τ_o/τ_c ratio (or sediment-entrainment ratio) integrates several geomorphic and sediment variables (flow depth, energy gradient or water-surface slope, median sediment-particle size, critical shear stress) and is applicable over a wide range of variable values. When calculated for specific discharges at several consecutive cross sections in a river reach, the τ_o/τ_c ratio facilitated site-to-site comparison of entrainment potential and provided a method for evaluating the relative effects of observed or hypothetical flood discharges (Elliott and Hammack, 2000).

The critical shear stress associated with sediment entrainment (equation 2) is, at best, a minimum estimate of the critical discharge at which sediment moves and hydraulically induced channel adjustments begin, because only a small area of the entire surface or a few particles of the d_{50} size might be entrained by the critical discharge (Lisle et al., 1993; Milhous, 1982). Wilcock and McArdell (1993) observed that complete mobilization of all streambed particles in a size fraction, such as d_{50}, occurred at roughly twice the shear stress necessary for incipient motion of individual particles in that size fraction. In this analysis, it was assumed that partial sediment mobilization was possible at a cross section or on a specific channel-boundary surface (streambed, banks, alluvial bar) when the sediment-entrainment ratio, τ_o/τ_c, was 1.0 or greater. Widespread sediment mobilization (bed material transport or erosion) was assumed when τ_o/τ_c was 2.0 or greater.

MONITORED RECONFIGURED REACHES

Reconfigured reaches on three rivers in Colorado, the Uncompahgre River at Ridgway, the North Fork Gunnison River at Hotchkiss, and the Lake Fork at Gateview (Fig. 1) have been monitored for several years and were revisited after the 2005 peak runoff. The geomorphic response of each, and probable cause, is the subject of this paper.

The Uncompahgre River conveys discharge originating in the northern San Juan Mountains of southwestern Colorado, is dominated by a snowmelt hydrograph, and has a channel composed of coarse bed material (Table 1). Near Ridgway and upstream from the reconfigured reach, the river has a braided channel with an unstable streambed and banks and a shallow flow depth at most discharges. Alluvial gravel mining upstream and in the lower part of the study reach has contributed to channel instability. The monitored reach begins at the State Highway 62 bridge in Ridgway, Ouray County, Colorado, and extends ~1040 m downstream (north) (Fig. 2). Streamflow-gauging station 09146200, Uncompahgre River near Ridgway, Colorado, is ~2.9 km (1.8 river miles) downstream from the lower end of the monitored reach. The streambed in the monitored reach is composed of gravel with a reach-average median sediment-particle size (d_{50}) of 25 mm (Table A1 in the Appendix at the end of this paper).

The reconfiguration objectives of the Uncompahgre River project reach were to confine a braided channel into a single-thread channel, create stable floodplain areas, and restore the disturbance from gravel mining in the lower study reach. Other objectives were to stabilize streambanks to facilitate a greenbelt riparian zone, a recreational trail, and wetland areas; stabilize the streambed near the Highway 62 bridge; provide whitewater recreation; create off-channel, backwater aquatic habitat; and allow bed-material transport (C. Philips, Riverbend Engineering, October 2003, oral commun.). Reconfiguration was performed in phases between October 2003 and July 2004 by decreasing the width/depth ratio and increasing sinuosity through channel excavation and grading of bed material. Boulder and log bank-stabilization and grade-control structures were installed, as were several aligned-boulder structures designed to direct streamflow away from banks, structures known as groins, cross vanes, and J-hooks (Rosgen, 1996). The boulders, up to 1 m or larger in diameter, were imported and originally were not part of the local streambed and bank material. Riparian trees and shrubs were planted along banks, bars, and the adjoining floodplain (Fig. 3). USGS monitoring of the Uncompahgre River reconfigured reach began in October 2003, and measurements were made in October

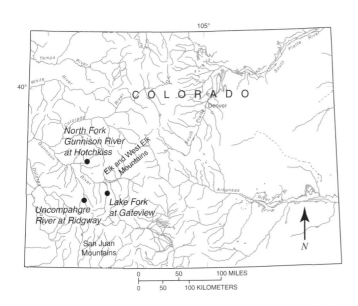

Figure 1. Map of reconfigured-channel monitoring assessment sites in western Colorado.

TABLE 1. CHARACTERISTICS OF RECONFIGURED CHANNEL MONITORED REACHES

Drainage area (km²)	Reach elevation above NAVD 88 (m)	Reach length (m)	Reach mean gradient (m/m)	Reach mean sediment size (mm)	Reach sediment size range (mm)	Mean annual precipitation (mm)	2-yr flood discharge (m³/s)	5-yr flood discharge (m³/s)	10-yr flood discharge (m³/s)	2005 peak discharge (m³/s)	2005 peak discharge recurrence (yr)
Uncompahgre River at Ridgway, Colorado. Reconfigured October 2003 to July 2004*											
386	2124	1040	0.0040	25	16 to 48	704	32.4	43.4	50.0	39.4	4
North Fork Gunnison River at Hotchkiss, Colorado. Reconfigured winter and spring 2000†											
2210	1621	1880	0.0056	70	13 to 132	686	82.2	118	144	123	6
Lake Fork at Gateview, Colorado. Reconfigured late 1997§											
865	2387	600	0.0062	91	57 to 128	721	46.7	60.4	68.5	48.7	2.4

Note: Sediment particle sizes exclude structural boulders placed in the channel or banks. Vertical coordinate information is referenced to the North American Vertical Datum of 1983 (NAVD 88).
*Discharges from USGS streamflow-gauging station 09146200, Uncompahgre River at Ridgway, Colorado.
†North Fork Gunnison River discharges estimated with the Vaill (2000) Northwest Colorado regional regression equations.
§Discharges from USGS streamflow-gauging station 09124500, Lake Fork at Gateview, Colorado.

2003, July 2004, and July 2005. Additional sediment measurements were made in September 2007.

The North Fork Gunnison River drains headwaters in the Elk and West Elk Mountains of west-central Colorado. The North Fork Gunnison hydrograph is dominated by snowmelt, and the river has a channel composed of coarse bed material (Table 1). The river channel near Hotchkiss was unstable and prone to flooding owing to a history of in-channel gravel mining, riparian vegetation eradication, artificial sinuosity reduction, and large bedload discharges (J.P. Crane, North Fork River Improvement Association, April 1997, oral commun.; U.S. Army Corps of Engineers, 1980). The 1880-m-long monitored reach begins ~100 m upstream (east) from the State Highway 92 bridge (cross section 3) in Hotchkiss, Delta County, Colorado, and extends ~250 m downstream from the County Road 3400 bridge (cross section 14) (Fig. 4).

Discharge is recorded at three USGS streamflow-gauging stations near the study reach (Crowfoot et al., 2003). Station 09135950, North Fork Gunnison River below Leroux Creek near Hotchkiss, Colorado (drainage area 2390 km²), is ~1.6 km downstream (southwest) from Hotchkiss but operates only seasonally. Station 09134100, North Fork Gunnison River below Paonia, Colorado (drainage area 1920 km²), is ~10 km upstream (northeast) from Hotchkiss but has operated only since 2000. Station 09132500, North Fork Gunnison River near Somerset, Colorado (drainage area 1360 km²), is ~27 km upstream (northeast) from Hotchkiss and has operated since 1933. The streambed in the monitored reach is composed of large gravel and cobbles with a reach-average d_{50} of 70 mm (Table A2 in the Appendix).

The reconfiguration objectives of the North Fork Gunnison River project reach were to confine a braided channel into a single-thread channel with lower sinuosity to facilitate bed-material transport and stabilize streambanks to protect an irrigation canal and headgate. Other objectives were to stabilize the streambed near the Highway 92 bridge, create stable floodplain

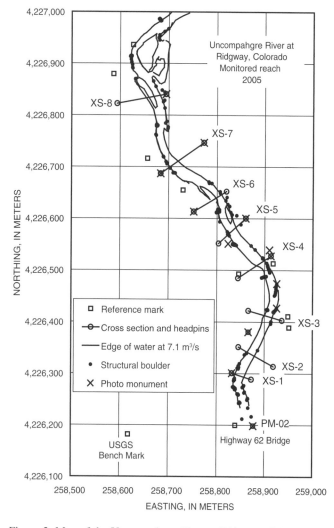

Figure 2. Map of the Uncompahgre River at Ridgway, Colorado, reconfigured channel monitored reach, showing cross sections, reference marks, and photo monuments. Flow to north. XS—cross section.

Figure 3. Uncompahgre River at Ridgway, looking downstream from photo monument PM-02: (A) 5 April 2002, 4.0 m³/s, before reconfiguration; (B) 13 July 2004, 5.1 m³/s, after reconfiguration.

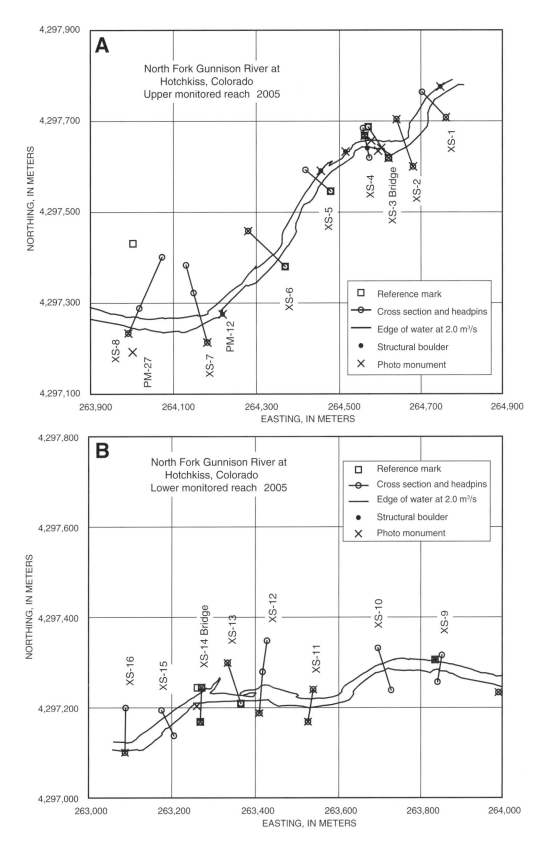

Figure 4. Map of North Fork Gunnison River at Hotchkiss, Colorado; reconfigured channel monitored reach showing cross sections, reference marks, and photo monuments: (A) upper reach; (B) lower reach. Flow to west. **XS**—cross section.

areas, create off-channel, backwater aquatic habitat, and provide whitewater recreation (J.P. Crane, North Fork River Improvement Association, April 1997, oral commun.).

Reconfiguration was performed in the winter and spring of 2000 by decreasing the width/depth ratio and decreasing sinuosity through channel excavation and grading of bed material. Former channel bends were converted into backwater areas where the sinuosity was decreased by the new channel alignment. Boulder bank–stabilization riprap was imported from off site and installed at a few high-priority areas (near the irrigation canal and headgate), and several aligned-boulder structures (groins and J-hooks) were constructed to direct streamflow away from banks and into the midchannel area. Riparian shrubs were planted along banks, on constructed bars, and on the adjoining regraded floodplain (Fig. 5). A short subreach, including cross sections 8 and 9 (Fig. 4), was not reconfigured. USGS monitoring of the North Fork Gunnison reconfigured reach began in March 2000, with replicate surveys and measurements made in August 2005. Replicate sediment measurements also were made in April 2001.

The Lake Fork drains headwaters in the northern San Juan Mountains of southwestern Colorado, is dominated by a snowmelt hydrograph, and has a channel composed of coarse bed material (Table 1). The river flows through a wide alluvial valley upstream from the reconfigured reach. Aerial photography shows paleochannels indicative of a formerly braided pattern and the results of historical attempts to straighten the channel and laterally confine the floodplain with a levee. The monitored reach is ~600 m long and includes USGS streamflow-gauging station 09124500, Lake Fork at Gateview, Colorado (Fig. 6). The streambed in the monitored reach is composed of cobbles with a reach-average median sediment-particle size (d_{50}) of 91 mm, based on numerous pebble counts (Wolman, 1954) (Table A3 in the Appendix).

The primary reconfiguration objective of the Lake Fork project was to create compensatory fish habitat to replace former habitat inundated by construction of Blue Mesa Reservoir on the Gunnison River, into which the Lake Fork flowed. Other objectives included streambank stabilization and riparian-zone enhancement (A. Hayes, U.S. Bureau of Land Management, February 1999, oral commun.). Before reconfiguration, the project reach had a wide and shallow channel (Fig. 7A). A 3.2-km reach of the Lake Fork was reconfigured in late 1997. The channel width/depth ratio was decreased by excavation of existing bed material, and sinuosity was increased by constructing alternate bars composed of excavated bed material (Fig. 7B). Numerous stabilization and flow-steering structures were constructed of imported boulders, fish-habitat-enhancement boulders were placed in midchannel, and the banks were fenced to prevent livestock access (Elliott and Parker, 1999). A short subreach, including monitored cross sections 3 and 4 and the USGS streamflow gauge (Fig. 6), was not reconfigured. USGS monitoring of the reconfigured reach began in September 1998, approximately 1 yr after reconfiguration; however, the spring 1998 discharge peak was only 35.1 m³/s and did not inundate and affect the composition and form of constructed banks or alternate bars.

Figure 5. North Fork Gunnison River at Hotchkiss, looking upstream from photo monument PM-27, showing the 1999 outline of the former channel before reconfiguration. Photograph date, 17 May 2000; 31.1 m³/s, after reconfiguration.

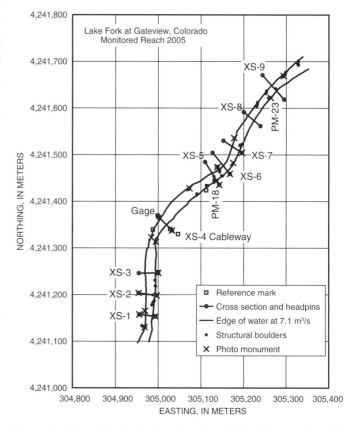

Figure 6. Map of Lake Fork at Gateview, Colorado, reconfigured-channel monitored reach showing cross sections, reference marks, and sediment-measurement sites. Flow to northeast. **XS**—cross section.

Subsequent measurements were made in September 1998, August 2000, and August 2005.

GEOMORPHIC CHANGE AT RECONFIGURED REACHES

Heavy late-winter snowfall in 2005 resulted in greater spring runoff than had been recorded in several years at some of the monitored RCMAP reaches. Consequently, this snowmelt runoff provided the first opportunity since the channels were reconfigured to observe geomorphic change in response to greater than "bankfull" discharge.

Uncompahgre River at Ridgway

The peak snowmelt discharge in 2005 on the Uncompahgre River at Ridgway was 39.4 m^3/s on 25 May (R. Crowfoot, U.S. Geological Survey, June 2006, oral commun.). That discharge, comparable to a 4 yr RI flood, was the largest discharge since the channel was reconfigured in 2004. The 2005 hydrograph showed a strong, diurnal-snowmelt pattern for weeks, with daily instan-

Figure 7. Lake Fork at Gateview, looking downstream from cross section 2: (A) 28 July 1992, 7.6 m^3/s, before reconfiguration; (B) 2 September 1998, 6.5 m^3/s, after reconfiguration.

taneous discharge peaks exceeding 28 m^3/s on seven consecutive days in late May. Subsequent to the replicate channel surveys made in July 2005, a greater annual peak discharge (47.9 m^3/s, approximately an 8 yr RI flood) resulted from a severe monsoonal thunderstorm on 10 August 2005 (U.S. Geological Survey 2005 Water Data Report Website). The geomorphic response of the reconfigured reach to the rainfall-runoff flood peak was not quantified because the flood occurred after the data collection period was concluded at this site.

The reconfigured channel was altered by the May 2005, 4 yr RI flood throughout the monitored reach. Bank erosion and lateral channel migration up to 3.1 m were visible at many places, and streambed scour as great as 0.3 m was detected at many cross sections in the replicate surveys (Fig. 8). Some sediment was deposited in a midchannel bar near the lower end of the monitored reach. Most boulder structures were unmoved by the streamflow but were partly buried by transported and redeposited gravel-size material. Other boulder structures created upstream eddies during high flow that eroded the adjacent banks. Log-bank protection structures that projected at a normal angle into the streamflow were eroded and rotated from their installed orientation (Fig. 9).

Channel cross-section and longitudinal-profile surveys, made before and after the May 2005 flood peak, and surveyed high-water marks created by the 2005 flood, enabled estimation of the flood-peak water-surface profile, flow depths, and boundary shear stresses (τ_o) at various places in the monitored reach. Sediment-size characteristics from pebble counts (Wolman, 1954) made before and after the flood enabled calculation of the critical shear stress for sediment entrainment (τ_c) at each cross section and at various locations within a specific cross section (Table A1). Together, the flood shear stress and critical shear stress for sediment entrainment explain much of the geomorphic response to the 2005 flood.

The reach-average d_{50} was 25 mm in the Uncompahgre River monitored area, but d_{50} ranged from 14 to 48 mm on different geomorphic surfaces at individual cross sections. The critical shear stress for this sediment ranged from 6.8 to 24 N/m^2 (Table A1). Because of the reconfigured channel cross-section geometry and slope, the cross-section-averaged shear stresses generated by the May 2005 4 yr flood exceeded the critical shear stresses at all cross sections.

Sediment entrainment potential at each cross section is shown in Figure 10 as the ratio of shear stress to critical shear stress for the three reference discharges and the 2005 flood. Figure 10 indicates that some sediment probably was entrained by the 2005 flood and could have been entrained by a discharge as common as Q_2 at cross sections 1, 2, 3, and 7. Figure 10 also indicates that much sediment could have been entrained by the Q_2 at the other cross sections.

Some streambed scour and some bank erosion by the May 2005 Uncompahgre River flood can be explained by the relation between the cross-channel shear-stress distribution and the sediment composing the streambed and banks, for example at cross

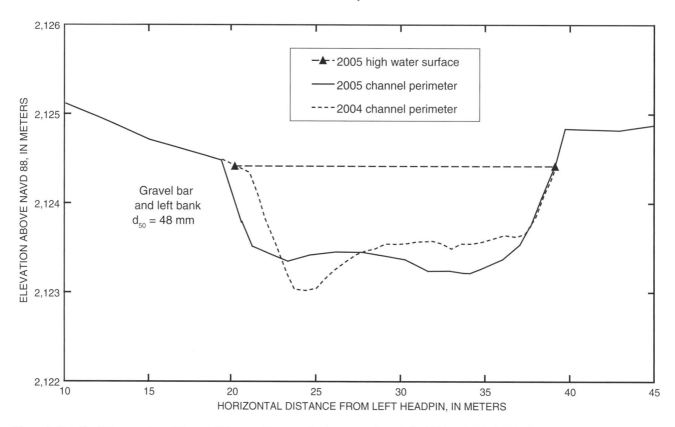

Figure 8. Detail of Uncompahgre River at Ridgway. Cross-section 2 surveys from July 2004 and July 2005, showing streambed scour and deposition and lateral erosion of the left bank by the 2005 flood.

section 8 (Fig. 11). The 2005 flood shear stress and even the Q_2 shear stress were at least twice the τ_c for sediment in the deepest part of the channel at cross section 8. Erosion at cross section 8 was limited to lateral migration of the right bank, a constructed geomorphic feature having a d_{50} of 20–21 mm. A new midchannel gravel bar (d_{50}, 26 mm) formed from material transported

Figure 9. Uncompahgre River at Ridgway, looking downstream from left bank near cross section 5 on 26 May 2005, 24.2 m³/s, one day after the peak discharge.

from upstream by the 2005 flood and deposited as the flow and shear stress decreased below a threshold sufficient to transport the gravel (Fig. 11).

Other cross sections in the Uncompahgre River monitored reach were composed of comparable-sized material and, subjected to similar shear stresses, responded in similar fashion to the 2005 flood. Plots showing the other Uncompahgre River cross sections are presented on the RCMAP Website.

North Fork Gunnison River at Hotchkiss

The peak discharge in 2005 on the Gunnison River in the Hotchkiss monitored reach was estimated by using HEC-RAS because there was no operating streamflow-gauging station nearby at the time of the peak discharge, and because the nearest operating gauging station had an insufficient record length. The Q_2, Q_5, and Q_{10} were estimated using regional discharge equations from Vaill (2000), a drainage area of 2210 km², and mean annual precipitation of 686 mm (Table 1). The water-surface elevation from surveyed high-water marks was compared to the Q_2, Q_5, and Q_{10} water-surface elevations computed with HEC-RAS, and a peak discharge of ~123 m³/s with an RI of ~6 yr was estimated for the 2005 peak discharge in the monitored reach. This was the largest discharge since the channel was reconfigured in the winter and spring of 2000. The 2005 hydrograph showed a

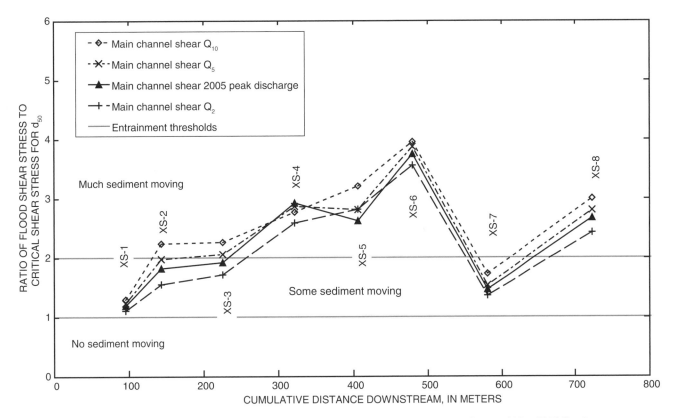

Figure 10. Uncompahgre River sediment-entrainment potential for the 2 yr, 5 yr, 10 yr, and May 2005 floods.

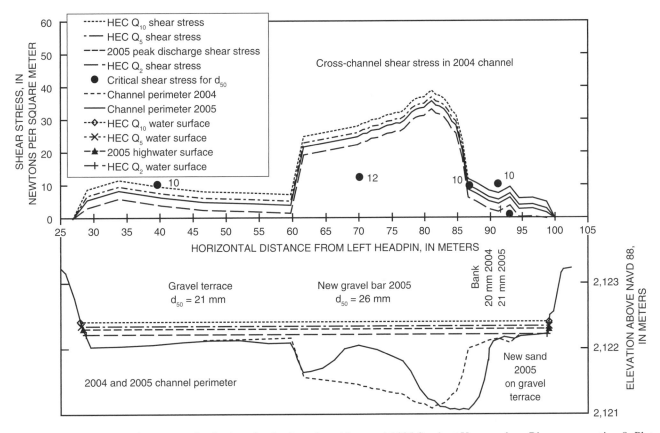

Figure 11. Cross-channel shear-stress distributions for the 2 yr, 5 yr, 10 yr, and 2005 floods at Uncompahgre River cross section 8. Plot shows the critical shear stress for sediment at selected locations and the resulting channel cross section after the 2005 flood.

strong diurnal snowmelt pattern for several weeks from late May through early June.

The 2005 flood altered the reconfigured channel to various degrees throughout the monitored reach. The peak discharge inundated many constructed cobble bars, and the imbricated orientation of large cobbles on these bars was evidence of locally high shear stresses. Bank erosion and lateral channel migration of as much as 25 m were visible in many locations, and streambed scour as great as 1.0 m was detected at many cross sections in the replicate surveys (Fig. 12). Large quantities of coarse sediment were deposited in new and enlarged alternate bars, and some constructed backwater areas were partly filled.

Entrainment and redeposition of large quantities of coarse sediment altered the function of some constructed boulder structures. A large cobble bar formed upstream from one boulder structure downstream from cross section 6 (Fig. 4), filling the upstream pool and causing the channel to shift laterally into an alternate bar constructed in 2000 on the opposite bank (Fig. 13). Another boulder structure at cross section 6, connected to the left bank when constructed in 2000, was isolated in mid-channel when the left bank was laterally eroded 7.5 m and was nearly buried as the right bank aggraded laterally by a comparable distance (Fig. 12).

Channel cross-section and longitudinal-profile surveys and sediment-size measurements, made before and after the 2005 flood, and surveyed high-water marks created by the flood, enabled estimation of the flood-peak water-surface profile, peak-flow depths, and the critical shear stress at various locations in the North Fork Gunnison monitored reach. The reach-average d_{50} was 70 mm in the North Fork Gunnison monitored reach, but d_{50} ranged from 13 to 132 mm on different geomorphic surfaces at individual cross sections. The critical shear stress for this sediment ranged from 6.3 to 64 N/m^2 (Table A2).

Sediment entrainment potential at each North Fork Gunnison cross section is shown as the ratio of flood shear stress to critical shear stress for the three reference discharges in Figure 14. The entrainment ratios indicate that sediment mobility is highly variable from cross section to cross section in the monitored reach for all discharges. Some or much sediment probably was moved by the Q_5 and the 2005 flood (RI ~6 yr) at all cross sections except cross sections 6, 9 (an unaltered area in the middle of the monitored reach), and 12, where the Q_5 shear stress was nearly equal to the sediment critical shear stress.

The relation between the cross-channel shear-stress distribution and the sediment composing the streambed and banks explains some streambed scour and some bank erosion by the 2005 North Fork Gunnison flood. An example is cross section 5, where the

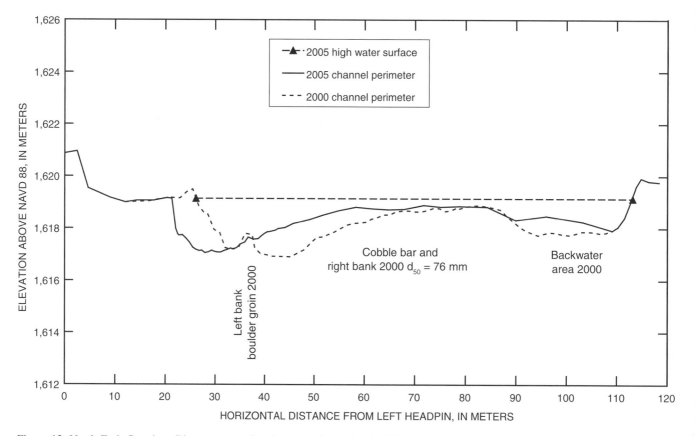

Figure 12. North Fork Gunnison River, cross-section 6 surveys from March 2000 and August 2005, showing streambed scour, alluvial bar deposition, and lateral erosion of the left bank by the 2005 flood.

boundary shear stress associated with Q_2 is comparable to the critical shear stress of sediment (d_{50}, 29 and 55 mm) that composed the left bank in 2000 and 2001 (Fig. 15). Discharges greater than Q_2 and up to the 2005 peak discharge generated sufficient shear stress to scour the left bank and streambed at cross section 5.

Other cross sections in the North Fork Gunnison monitored reach responded in similar fashion to the 2005 flood. Plots showing the other North Fork Gunnison cross sections are presented on the RCMAP Website.

Lake Fork at Gateview

The peak discharge in 2005 on the Lake Fork at Gateview was 48.7 m³/s on 25 May (U.S. Geological Survey 2005 Water Data Report Website). That discharge was comparable to a 2.4 yr RI flood. Snowmelt flood peaks of comparable magnitude occurred on the Lake Fork in 1999 and 2000, with 2.4 and 2.5 yr RI, respectively; however, these peak floods had only a

Figure 13. North Fork Gunnison River at Hotchkiss, looking upstream from photo monument PM-12: (A) 7 October 2001, 2.3 m³/s; boulder structure on left bank downstream from cross section 6; (B) 18 August 2005, 2.0 m³/s; deposition upstream from the boulder structure and lateral channel relocation by the 2005 flood.

minor effect on the channel geometry and the constructed alternate bars at monitored cross sections. Single, imported habitat boulders in at least two locations were displaced a short distance between the 1998 and 2000 surveys, presumably in 1999 or 2000 (see Lake Fork site, view of photo monument PM-23, on the RCMAP Website).

The relatively minor, cumulative changes in the Lake Fork cross sections from 1998 to 2005 are represented by cross section 6 (Fig. 16). The flood peaks between the 1998 and 2000 surveys resulted in minor streambed scour or deposition at some locations as the reconfigured channel adjusted slightly. A habitat boulder installed just upstream from cross section 6 in 1998 moved into the cross-section survey transect and was captured by the 2000 replicate survey. The 2005 flood (2.4 yr RI) had little effect on the channel cross section but was sufficient to move downstream the habitat boulder that had been relocated between 1998 and 2000. The comparative photos of cross section 6 in Figure 17 illustrate the relatively static condition of the right bank and the left, constructed alternate bar between 1998 and 2005. Most of the change above the low-discharge elevation was overbank deposition on the left alternate bar, where vegetation has encroached since 1998 (Fig. 16).

Channel cross-section and longitudinal-profile surveys and sediment-size measurements, made before and after the 2005 flood, and surveyed high-water marks created by the 2005 flood enabled estimation of the flood-peak water-surface profile, peak-flow depths, and critical shear stress at various locations in the Lake Fork monitored reach. The reach-average d_{50} was 91 mm in the Lake Fork monitored reach, but d_{50} ranged from 57 to 128 mm on different geomorphic surfaces at individual cross sections. The critical shear stress for this sediment ranged from 28 to 62 N/m² (Table A3).

The 2005 flood shear stress was comparable to shear stresses generated by similar floods in 1999 and 2000. Sediment-entrainment potential of the 2005 flood at each cross section is shown as the ratio of the cross-section-averaged shear stress to critical shear stress for the three reference discharges and the 2005 flood in Figure 18. The entrainment ratios for Q_2 and the 2005 peak discharge were equal to or slightly greater than unity at cross sections 1 through 4 and 7, indicating the potential for some sediment entrainment at these locations. The entrainment ratio for these discharges approached 2 at cross sections 5, 8, and 9, indicating that much sediment potentially could have moved in 2005.

Examination of the cross-channel shear-stress distribution at cross section 8 is informative of the geomorphic response to the 2005 peak discharge in the Lake Fork monitored reach (Fig. 19). Shear stress associated with the Q_2 and 2005 flood was twice the critical shear stress for sediment on the streambed. Some entrainment of bed material is indicated by the change in streambed topography between the 1998 and 2005 surveys, but there was little net change in streambed elevation or bank configuration. This is a possible indication that the streambed has been mobile, but that the channel geometry has remained stable under the flow regime between 1998 and 2005. However, because this cross

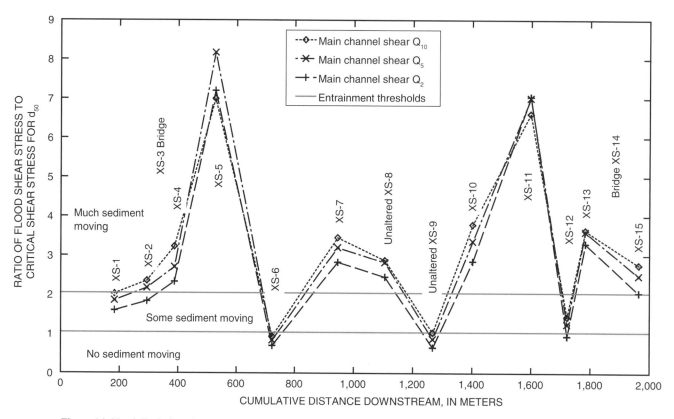

Figure 14. North Fork Gunnison River at Hotchkiss, sediment-entrainment potential for the 2 yr, 5 yr, and 10 yr floods.

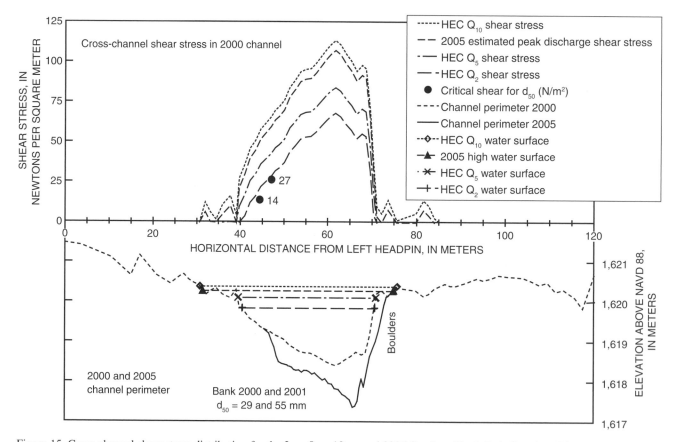

Figure 15. Cross-channel shear-stress distribution for the 2 yr, 5 yr, 10 yr, and 2005 floods at North Fork Gunnison River cross section 5. Plot shows the critical shear stress for sediment at selected locations and the resulting channel cross section after the 2005 flood.

section and the entire monitored reach have not conveyed discharges approaching the Q_5 or Q_{10}, as have the Uncompahgre and North Fork Gunnison Rivers, the channel-stability question has not been resolved for the Lake Fork reconfigured reach.

Other cross sections in the Lake Fork monitored reach were composed of comparable-sized material (Table A3). Although shear stresses for the Q_2, Q_5, Q_{10}, and 2005 peak discharge generally were greater in downstream than in upper cross sections (Fig. 18), all nine Lake Fork monitored cross sections showed little change in cross-section profile as a result of the flood peaks of 1999, 2000, and 2005. Plots showing the other Lake Fork cross sections are presented on the RCMAP Website.

DISCUSSION

The 2005 snowmelt floods at the three monitored reconfigured reaches had different magnitudes and recurrence intervals. The geomorphic response of each reconfigured reach to a flood of known magnitude, however, and recurrence probability and the association of those floods with estimated boundary shear stresses, provide a mechanism for understanding observed change, or lack of change, during the monitoring period.

The cross-section mean boundary shear stress, computed with HEC-RAS, gave a general quantification of the eroding

forces created by each flood. The mean sediment size and the Shields (1936) equation (equation 2) gave a general quantification of the resisting forces of gravel and cobbles composing the channel perimeter. However, nuances of channel geometry (depth) and sediment-size variance across the channel on different geomorphic surfaces require a more detailed look at the balance of eroding and resisting forces in most channels. Therefore, point depths across the channel and the duBoys equation (equation 1) also were used to compute flood shear stress and to assess sediment-entrainment potential.

Sediment entrainment in the monitored reaches during the 2005 floods resulted in a variety of responses at different monumented cross sections. Bed-load transport resulted in streambed scour at some locations and streambed deposition or alluvial-bar accretion at other locations (Figs. 11, 15). The channel geometry (width and depth) changed at some cross sections as a result of bed material redistribution (Fig. 8). Some constructed boulder structures (groins, J-hooks) were buried by laterally accreting bars (Fig. 12). Other boulder structures impeded downstream sediment transport and were buried by sediment deposited on the upstream side of the structure (Fig. 13). Constructed backwater areas also were partly filled by transported sediment from upstream (Fig. 12). Isolated habitat boulders were repositioned by the flood peaks (Figs. 16, 19). Overbank deposition was observed

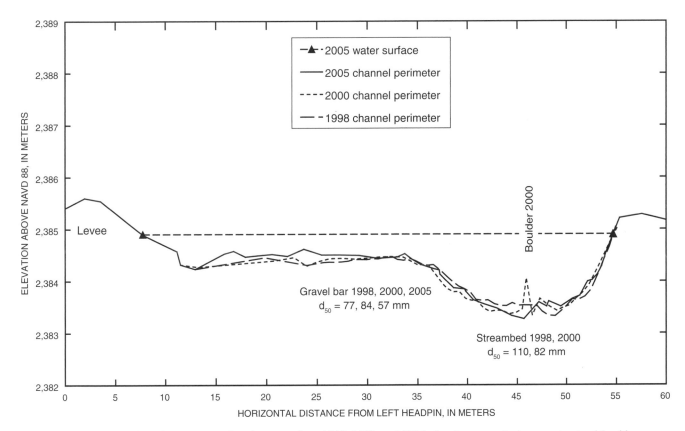

Figure 16. Lake Fork at Gateview, cross-section 6 surveys from 1998, 2000, and 2005, showing streambed scour, structural-boulder movement, and overbank deposition since reconfiguration.

where floodwater transported, then subsequently deposited, sediment on inundated, low-relief bars and terraces (Figs. 11, 16). Many of these changes could be linked to the excess of flood-boundary shear stress relative to the resisting force, or critical shear stress, of the sediment composing the streambed and other alluvial surfaces.

Bank erosion also was observed and was partly explained by the excess of shear stress to critical shear stress of the bank materials. High rates of bank erosion occurred where the bank material, consisting of a wide range of particle sizes, was easily entrainable and where alluvial bar formation or accretion forced streamflow against the opposite bank (Figs. 9, 11, 12). Relocation of the channel position and channel thalweg commonly were associated with zones of greatest bank erosion.

Some alluvial bar formation and enlargement may be due to an imbalance of sediment supply into, and sediment transport through, the monitored reach. Entrainment of the d_{50}-size sediment in one cross section does not guarantee transport of that same size sediment through the next cross section if the flood-generated

Figure 17. Lake Fork at Gateview, looking downstream from photo monument PM-18 at cross section 5: (A) 3 September 1998, 6.2 m³/s; structural boulders and recently constructed alternate bar 5_6_7 on left bank; (B) 9 August 2005, 6.9 m³/s, after three annual peak discharges with 2.4 to 2.5 yr recurrence.

shear stress in the subsequent section falls below the critical shear stress of the sediment transported into it. Such a situation may have existed in the lower monitored reach of the Uncompahgre River, where the mean channel entrainment ratio (τ_o/τ_c) was much greater than 2.0 at cross sections 4, 5, and 6 but dropped to ~1.5 at cross section 7 (Fig. 10). A large gravel bar formed in cross section 8 from sediment transported from upstream as the shear stress decreased below the entrainment threshold when discharge decreased to base-flow conditions (Fig. 11).

Channel-width expansions and contractions are not accounted for in the one-dimensional analysis used in this study, but they have an effect on bed-material entrainment, transport, and deposition through the monitored reaches. Cross section 5 in the North Fork Gunnison monitored reach was narrow and laterally confined by riprap on the right bank. The entire 2005 flood was contained within the 39-m-wide reconfigured channel, and the streambed incised 1.0 m at cross section 5 (Fig. 15). Cross section 6, 195 m downstream, conveyed low discharges (7.9 m³/s) in a single channel, but the 2005 flood overtopped a large, constructed alluvial bar and flowed over a width of 87 m (Fig. 12). Consequently, the entrainment ratio decreased abruptly from cross section 5 to cross section 6 (Fig. 14), and the alluvial bar accreted laterally and the left bank retreated at cross section 6 (Fig. 12).

Reliance on in-channel structures whose desired hydraulic function depends on the structure's orientation relative to a static channel pattern and cross section can lead to unintended consequences when the streambed or banks become mobile (Kochel et al., 2005). Failure of boulder and log structure anchor points by bank erosion (Figs. 9, 12), burial by redeposited sediment (Fig. 13), or removal and relocation of carefully placed, imported boulders (Figs. 16, 19) changes the intended flow path through and around the structures and individual boulders, potentially creating severe erosion in places the structures were designed to protect. This response illustrates the problem of reliance on "fixed-point" flow-steering structures (and riprap) constructed in dynamic channels that periodically transport large volumes of sediment.

Some large habitat boulders (d_{50}, 600–800 mm) in the Lake Fork presumably were repositioned by the 1999, 2000, and 2005 flood peaks. Although the flood shear stresses those years were far less than the critical shear stress for a streambed composed entirely of boulder-sized sediment in this size range, some of these boulders were moved by the relatively low shear stress created by the 2.4 and 2.5 yr RI floods. This is probably due to the protrusion of the habitat boulders into the flow, making them susceptible to selective entrainment, and due as well to the installation of the large boulders on smaller, more entrainable gravel- and cobble-bed material.

The main channel entrainment ratio for the 2005 flood at Lake Fork cross section 8 was 1.9 (Fig. 18), yet there was little net change in the channel at this and other cross sections (Figs. 16, 19), and the channel pattern has remained static since monitoring began in 1998. Some change in sediment size has occurred on constructed alternate bars in the monitored reach; for example, bar 5_6_7 at cross section 6 (Fig. 16) became slightly coarser

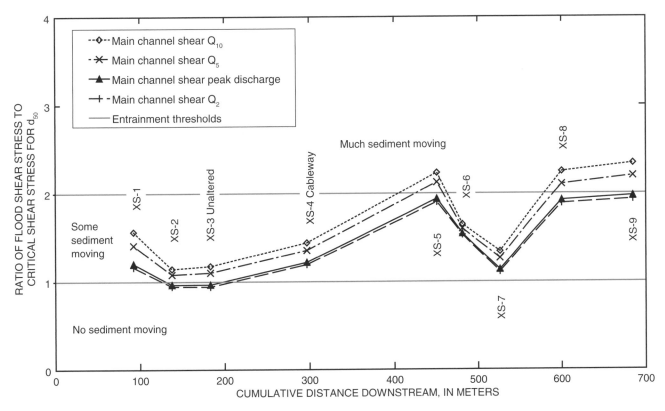

Figure 18. Lake Fork sediment-entrainment potential for the 2 yr, 5 yr, 10 yr, and 2005 floods.

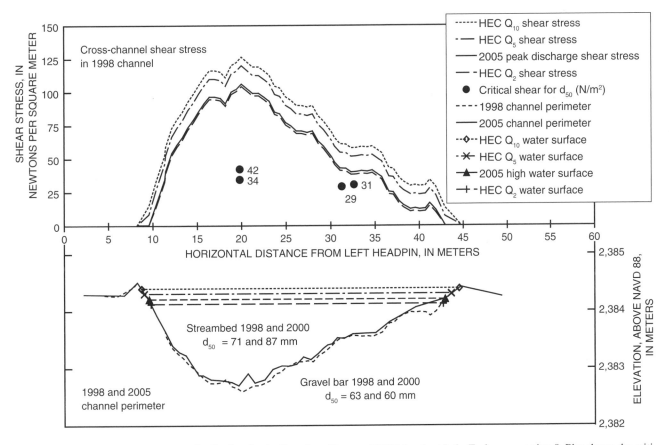

Figure 19. Cross-channel shear-stress distribution for the 2 yr, 5 yr, 10 yr, and 2005 floods at Lake Fork cross section 8. Plot shows the critical shear stress for sediment at selected locations and the resulting channel cross section after the 2005 flood.

after the first inundation, then slightly finer as overbank sediment was deposited on the bar (Table A3) and vegetation became established (Fig. 17).

The absence of net streambed scour, pattern adjustment, or channel-geometry change at Lake Fork cross sections indicates that (1) some sediment did move during the flood, but the net change in channel geometry was negligible; or (2) significant sediment movement and channel change probably will not occur until larger discharges are conveyed by the channel. The main channel entrainment ratios are greater than 2.0 at cross sections 5, 8, and 9 for the Q_5 and Q_{10}, peak discharge conditions that have not occurred in the Lake Fork since it was reconfigured in 1997. It is difficult to assess whether a reconfigured channel such as the Lake Fork, showing little or no change over several years, is in dynamic or steady-state equilibrium if the channel has not conveyed floods much greater than the bankfull discharge, in this study approximated by the 2 yr flood. Without consulting the recent streamflow history at the Lake Fork at Gateview site, one could conclude that the reconfigured channel has withstood 7 yr of streamflow without undesirable adjustment and that this is a sign of success. In fact, however, the system has not yet been tested by large streamflows.

Some reconfigured channels may not be in appropriate geomorphic settings to sustain a static position or a single-thread, meandering channel of imposed geometry and pattern. Leopold and Wolman (1957) defined a threshold line for channel pattern based on channel slope and bankfull discharge that distinguished between meandering streams (single-thread channels with sinuosity greater than 1.5) and braided streams (streams with stable alluvial islands and more than one channel). Natural streams with meandering channels plotted below the threshold line, whereas natural streams that were braided plotted above the threshold line (Fig. 20). The bankfull discharges used by Leopold and Wolman (1957) were from stable, self-formed channels with well-defined bankfull stage. Recently reconfigured channels, such as those studied here, have not developed self-formed banks; rather, the "banks" in reconfigured channels are arbitrarily constructed breaks in riparian topography. Consequently, bankfull discharge in these reaches cannot be determined empirically. In this study, the 2 yr flood (Q_2), a statistically definable discharge in rivers with sufficient streamflow data, was used as a surrogate for the bankfull discharge at the monitored sites.

Channel slope and the Q_2 from three reconfigured river reaches in this analysis were plotted on the channel-pattern threshold plot (Fig. 20). The Q_2 could not be derived statistically from recorded discharge for the North Fork Gunnison River at Hotchkiss monitored site because the closest stream gauge did not have a sufficiently long period of streamflow record. Q_2 was estimated for the North Fork Gunnison using the regional discharge equation derived with streamflow data through water year 1993 by Vaill (2000). Streamflow statistics recomputed with data through 2004 yielded slightly higher values for some of the sites used in the regional analysis; therefore, Q_2 estimates from the Vaill equation could be understated. The plotting position for all three monitored sites in this analysis was above the threshold line, that is, in the "braided channel" region. The implication of this is that all three reconfigured reaches may exist in areas of sufficiently steep channel slope and large Q_2 magnitude where channel braiding and alluvial island or midchannel bar formation, rather than a classical, single-thread meandering channel, is the natural tendency (Vincent and Elliott, 2007).

Data from the three reconfigured channels of this analysis also were plotted against a channel-pattern threshold developed for the relation between median bed-material size (d_{50}) and the total stream power index (discharge times channel slope) (Richards, 1982). All three channels were reconfigured to be single-thread channels, but when the bankfull-discharge surrogate, Q_2, was used to compute the total stream-power index, the Lake Fork plotted below the threshold line in the "single-thread channel" region, the Uncompahgre River plotted on the threshold line, and the North Fork Gunnison plotted above the threshold line in the "multiple-thread channel" region (Fig. 21). The total stream-power index also was computed with Q_5 and Q_{10}, resulting in plotting positions in the multiple-thread channel region for all three reconfigured rivers.

The plotting positions in Figure 21 are supported by post-flood observations at the three sites. Whereas multiple-thread channels did not develop at the Uncompahgre River and the North Fork Gunnison as a result of the 2005 floods (RI, 4 yr and 6 yr, respectively), lateral erosion and mid-channel- and alternate-bar deposition were observed (Figs. 8, 11, 12) and may reflect a tendency for these reaches to evolve into multi-thread channels when conveying floods equal to or greater than the Q_2. By contrast, the Lake Fork showed very little channel geometry or position adjustment to the 2005 and earlier floods of comparable magnitude (RI, 2.4–2.5 yr) (Fig. 16). If channel pattern

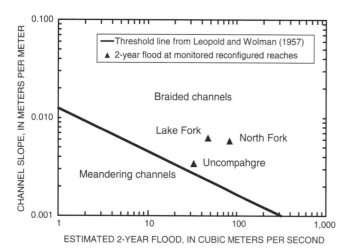

Figure 20. Plot of reconfigured-reach channel slope and 2 yr flood with the Leopold and Wolman (1957) threshold for meandering and braided channel patterns.

adjustment is to occur at the Lake Fork, Figure 21 indicates discharges comparable to a 5 or 10 yr flood may be necessary.

One-dimensional analysis using mean-channel shear or cross-channel shear for a range of reference discharges, and the Shields critical shear stress for sediment composing the channel perimeter, is appropriate and has been used for sediment-mobility assessment on the streambed and on inundated alluvial-bar surfaces (Elliott and Hammack, 1999, 2000). It is less suitable for assessing bank erosion where the banks are steep and composed of more cohesive or rooted material, and bed-form and particle-roughness variables are not quantified in one-dimensional streamflow analysis. The one-dimensional method applies to discrete cross sections but not to the intervening river segments, and downstream variance between cross sections (for example, width expansions and contractions, or changes in channel geometry) is not well accounted for. The one-dimensional analysis of this study, however, does give some idea of the potential for alluvial channels to adjust by sediment entrainment under different streamflow scenarios and, therefore, is considered to be an appropriate tool for assessing reconfigured channel design.

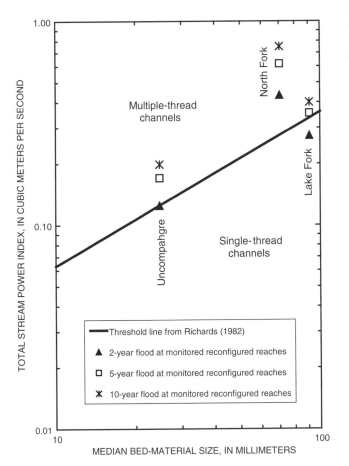

Figure 21. Plot of reconfigured-reach total stream power index for the 2, 5, and 10 yr floods and median bed-material size with the threshold for single-thread and multiple-thread channels.

Sediment erosion, transport, and redeposition in the RCMAP monitored reaches are not necessarily indications of long-term channel instability. Natural channels exhibiting "dynamic equilibrium" (Leopold et al., 1964, p. 266) or "steady-state equilibrium" (Schumm, 1977, p. 98) are not static features. Rather, equilibrium channels maintain a stability in form (cross-section geometry) and local slope (bed elevation) over time while transporting water and sediment, ultimately migrating laterally across the floodplain or valley floor, eroding one bank while aggrading the opposite bank. In the geomorphic distinction between "stable" and "unstable" channels, unstable channels are those that are adjusting their dimension, slope, pattern, and shape rapidly and progressively (Schumm, 1977, p. 132).

For a reconfigured channel to be in a state of dynamic or steady-state equilibrium, the volume of sediment supplied to, entrained and transported through, and redeposited within must be in balance within the entire reach. An assessment of this balance or imbalance is not easily made through an analysis of cross-section geometry and slope change alone, although monitoring and one-dimensional modeling give clues to the existence of disequilibrium. A more sophisticated approach, including computing a sediment budget and using multidimensional-streamflow and sediment-transport models, can give a clearer assessment.

SUMMARY

This paper analyzes the geomorphic changes of three monumented, reconfigured rivers in western Colorado in response to observed floods in 2005. The floods at each monitored reach had different magnitudes and recurrence intervals and, as such, the channel responses are not directly comparable from site to site. Use of a one-dimensional streamflow model to compute hypothetical hydraulic conditions for reference discharges comparable to the 2, 5, and 10 yr recurrence interval floods (Q_2, Q_5, and Q_{10}) does provide a means of quantitatively evaluating the individual responses of these channels to relatively common floods.

Analyses were performed with data collected under the USGS Reconfigured-Channel Monitoring and Assessment Program (RCMAP) at three long-term monitored sites on reconfigured, or "reclaimed" river reaches in Colorado: the Uncompahgre River at Ridgway, the North Fork Gunnison River at Hotchkiss, and the Lake Fork at Gateview. Heavy late-winter snowfall in 2005 resulted in greater spring runoff than had been recorded in several years at these reaches and provided an opportunity to observe the responses of these reconfigured channels to greater than bankfull discharges. Flood-peak discharges and recurrence intervals (RI) were 39.4 m³/s (4 yr RI) at the Uncompahgre River, ~123 m³/s (6 yr RI) at the North Fork Gunnison River, and 48.7 m³/s (2.4 yr RI) at the Lake Fork. Data and photographs from these and other sites periodically are saved on the USGS RCMAP Website.

The geomorphic responses of the monitored reaches to the 2005 floods and to the Q_2, Q_5, and Q_{10} were assessed using the

HEC-RAS, one-dimensional streamflow model. The channel-average shear stress computed with HEC-RAS quantified the eroding forces created by the flood. The mean sediment size and the Shields equation were used to quantify the resisting forces of sediment composing the channel perimeter. Nuances of channel geometry (depth) and sediment-size variance across the channel on different geomorphic surfaces (streambed, banks, alluvial bars, low terraces) implied that a more detailed examination of the balance of eroding and resisting forces is appropriate. Consequently, point depths across the channel also were used to compute flood shear stress and to assess sediment-entrainment potential at specific locations on the channel.

Sediment-entrainment potential at each cross section for the three reference discharges was expressed as the ratio of the flood-generated boundary shear stress to the critical shear stress for the median sediment size at the cross section (τ_o/τ_c). It was assumed that partial (some) sediment mobilization was possible at a cross section or on a specific channel-boundary surface (streambed, banks, alluvial bar) when the sediment-entrainment ratio, τ_o/τ_c, was 1.0 or greater. Widespread (much) sediment mobilization (bed material transport or erosion) was assumed when τ_o/τ_c was 2.0 or greater.

A Shields parameter value of 0.030, at the conservative end of the range, was used for critical shear stress (τ_c) and sediment entrainment estimates. The use of a conservative value for the Shields parameter (0.030), rather than a larger value (for example, 0.045), results in a smaller τ_c and, consequently, an entrainment ratio of unity at a smaller discharge. When assessing the potential for channel instability owing to sediment entrainment, estimates based on a conservative value of the Shields parameter result in a greater safety factor.

Some observed streambed scour, deposition, and bank erosion can be explained by the sediment-entrainment ratio and the excess of flood boundary shear stress relative to the resisting force, or critical shear stress, of the sediment. Bed-load transport in the Uncompahgre River, during a 4 yr flood, and the North Fork Gunnison River, during a 6 yr flood, resulted in streambed scour at some locations, deposition or alluvial-bar accretion in other locations, and channel migration by bank erosion. Constructed boulder or log structures were rendered inoperable at some locations because of high rates of bank erosion, bed-material deposition, or movement of individual boulders and logs.

The monitored cross sections in the Lake Fork reach showed little or no net change over a 7 yr period. It was difficult, however, to assess whether this reconfigured channel was in a state of dynamic equilibrium, or whether the channel was unchanged because it had not conveyed floods much greater than the bank-full discharge, in this study approximated by the 2 yr flood. The largest discharges in the Lake Fork reach during the monitoring period were comparable to the 2.5 yr flood.

Channel slope and the 2 yr flood from the monitored river reaches were compared to a channel slope and bankfull discharge channel-pattern threshold. Data from all three reconfigured reaches included in this study plotted above the threshold line in the "braided channel" region. The implication is that all three reconfigured reaches may be in areas of sufficiently steep channel slope and frequent high discharge where channel braiding and alluvial island or midchannel bar formation, rather than a classical, single-thread meandering channel, is the natural tendency.

Data from the monitored reaches also were compared to a "single-thread channel"–"multiple-thread channel" threshold. Based on plotting positions, the Uncompahgre River and the North Fork Gunnison showed a tendency to evolve toward multiple-thread channel patterns when conveying streamflow as little as the 2 yr flood. The Lake Fork, a river that has not conveyed streamflow greater than the 2.5 yr flood during the monitoring period, appears to maintain a stable, single-thread channel when conveying the 2 yr flood, but could show a tendency to become a multiple-thread channel with the 5 or 10 yr flood.

ACKNOWLEDGMENTS

Conception of the reconfigured-channel monitoring and assessment program originated from onsite observations and many discussions with Randy Parker, USGS, retired, and many other colleagues. Ongoing monitoring and data analysis was done by the U.S. Geological Survey in cooperation with the Colorado River Water Conservation District (CRWCD). Many individuals assisted with data collection over several years. These include Stephen J. Char, Heather S. Eppler, Jonathan B. Evans, Ashley K. Heckman, George P. Ingersoll, Paul J. Kinzel, Pamela Mellone, and Michael R. Stevens, of the USGS. Additional onsite assistance was provided by Ray D. Tenney, CRWCD; Wallace H. Erickson, Division of Reclamation, Mining and Safety, Colorado Department of Natural Resources; and Shawn LaBounty, Paonia, Colorado. The authors wish to thank the project managers who provided restoration design information and to landowners who granted access to monitored sites. The quality of the manuscript has been greatly enhanced by review comments from Andrew Simon, U.S. Department of Agriculture, National Sedimentation Laboratory; and Ray Tenney, CRWCD. All photographs were taken by John G. Elliott, USGS.

APPENDIX: SEDIMENT-SIZE STATISTICS

A1. Table showing sediment-size statistics determined from Wolman pebble counts of sediment at the Uncompahgre River at Ridgway monitored reach. Measurements were made on several geomorphic surfaces in 2003, 2004, 2005, and 2007.

A2. Table showing sediment-size statistics determined from Wolman pebble counts of sediment at the North Fork Gunnison River at Hotchkiss monitored reach. Measurements were made on several geomorphic surfaces in 2000, 2001, and 2005.

A3. Table showing sediment-size statistics determined from Wolman pebble counts of sediment at the Lake Fork at Gateview monitored reach. Measurements were made on several geomorphic surfaces in 1998, 2000, and 2005.

TABLE A1. SEDIMENT-SIZE STATISTICS FROM WOLMAN PEBBLE COUNTS AT THE UNCOMPAHGRE RIVER AT RIDGWAY MONITORED REACH

Measurement location, code, and date	River side	Nearest cross section	Fine fraction d_{16} (mm)	Median size d_{50} (mm)	Coarse fraction d_{84} (mm)	Critical shear for d_{50} (N/m^2)	Remarks
2003 measurements							
Bar.6.03	R	at 6	18	38	55	18	Before reconfiguration.
Bar.7.03	L	at 7	12	19	39	9.2	
Bar.8.03	R	at 8	13	23	39	11	
Mean 2003				27			
2004 measurements							
Bar.4.04	L	at 4	7.0	14	25	6.8	Reconfigured, before 2005 discharge peak.
Bar.6.04	L	at 6	7.8	25	55	12	Channel relocated from R to L. Sample site relocated from L to R.
Bank.7.04	R	at 7	7.8	26	53	13	Channel relocated from L to R. Sample site relocated from R to L.
Bar.8.04	R	bel 8	1.8	20	40	9.7	R gravel bar migrating downstream.
Mean 2004				21			
2005 measurements							
Bar.3.05	L	abv 3	28	48	78	24	Resulting from 2005 discharge peak. Between XS-2 and XS-3.
Bar.4.05	L	abv 4	6.8	20	36	9.7	Sampled from J-hook 23 m upstream to XS-4.
Bar.5.05	R	bel 5	7.0	24	54	12	Sampled 0 to 30 m below XS-5, opposite Splay.5.05 site.
Bar.6.05	L	at 6	0.125	18	35	8.7	Sampled 6 m abv to 36 m below XS-6.
Bar.7.05	R	bel 7	15	31	47	15	Sampled 12 to 73 m below XS-7.
Bar.8.05	R	bel 8	0.125	21	43	10	R bar migrating downstream; 0 to 61 m above waste-water return channel.
Splay.5.05	L	bel 5	8.0	21	41	10	Random sample, 25–30 m upstream from XS-6, ~25 m below XS-5.
Mean 2004				26			
2007 measurements							
Bank.1.07	L	abv 1	6.0	16	41	7.8	Resulting from 2005, 2006, and 2007 discharge peaks. Random sample, L bank below second drop structure.
Bank.2.07	L	abv 2	9.0	30	58	15	L bank below third drop structure, 0.6 m from L edge water.
Bank.3.07	R	abv 3	13	28	57	13	2 linear traverses on sloping R bank between R edge water and terrace.
Bank.7.07	L	at 7	9.0	22	44	11	Linear transect near L edge water at XS-7.
Bar.8.07	L	at 8	13	26	39	12	Linear transect in middle of gravel bar at XS-8.
Mean 2007				24			
Mean of all years				25			

Note: d_{16}—16th percentile; d_{50}—50th percentile; d_{84}—84th percentile; mm—millimeters; m—meters; N/m^2—newtons per square meter; XS—cross section; L—left; R—right; abv—above; bel—below. Critical shear calculated with 0.030 Shields parameter.

TABLE A2. SEDIMENT-SIZE STATISTICS FROM WOLMAN PEBBLE COUNTS AT THE NORTH FORK GUNNISON RIVER AT HOTCHKISS MONITORED REACH

Measurement location, code, and date	River side	Nearest cross section	Fine fraction d_{16} (mm)	Median size d_{50} (mm)	Coarse fraction d_{84} (mm)	Critical shear for d_{50} (N/m²)	Remarks
2000 measurements							
Bank.1.00	R	at 1	23	67	131	33	Reconfigured before 2000 peak discharge. 3 m from R edge water.
Bank.2.00	L	at 2	8.8	37	91	18	3 m from L edge water.
Bank.2.00	R	at 2	11	47	107	23	9 m from R edge water.
Bank.5.00	L	at 5	3.4	29	73	14	4 m from L edge water.
Bank.6.00	R	at 6	43	76	150	37	
Bank.7.00	R	at and abv 7	1.0	26	102	13	1 to 4 m from R edge water.
Bar.8.00	R	at 8	25	74	145	36	Unaltered bar, fining downstream.
Bank.9.00	R	at 9	1.0	85	180	41	Unaltered bar, imbricated (higher on bank than 2001 measurement).
ChanBar.9.00	C	at 9	55	95	147	46	Unaltered midchannel bar.
Bank.11_12.00	L	abv 12	1.0	13	46	6.3	2.4 m from L edge water.
Mean 2000				55			
2001 measurements							
							Resulting from 2000 peak and before 2001 peak discharge.
Bank.1.01	R	at 1	49	90	140	44	2 m from R edge water.
Bank.2.01	L	at 2	20	54	112	26	
Bank.2.01	R	at 2	12	58	130	28	2 traverses.
Bank.5.01	L	at 5	16	55	120	27	1 m from L edge water.
Bank.6.01	R	at 6	32	75	140	36	1.5 m from R edge water.
Bank.7.01	R	at and abv 7	20	65	130	32	1 to 2 m from R edge water.
Bar.8.01	R	at 8	16	60	151	29	1 to 2 m from R edge water, 33 m from R intermediate pin.
Bank.9.01	R	at 9	60	132	210	64	1 to 2 m from R edge water, 13 to 14 m from R intermediate pin.
ChanBar.9.01	C	at 9	45	83	160	40	Unaltered midchannel bar, 29 m from L headpin.
Bank.11_12.00	L	abv 12	33	73	125	35	1 m from L edge water, reworked.
Mean 2001				74			
2005 measurements							
							Resulting from 2005 peak discharge.
Bank_Bar.1.05	L	at 1	42	83	170	40	1 to 3 m from L edge water.
Bank_Bar.2.05	R	at 2	43	113	205	55	10 m from R edge water.
Bank_Bar.6.05	R	at 6	52	90	191	44	~5 m from R edge water from field-note sketch.

(continued)

TABLE A2. SEDIMENT-SIZE STATISTICS FROM WOLMAN PEBBLE COUNTS AT THE NORTH FORK GUNNISON RIVER AT HOTCHKISS MONITORED REACH (continued)

Measurement location, code, and date	River side	Nearest cross section	Fine fraction d_{16} (mm)	Median size d_{50} (mm)	Coarse fraction d_{84} (mm)	Critical shear for d_{50} (N/m^2)	Remarks
2005 measurements (continued)							
Bank_Bar.7.05	L	abv 7	43	115	196	56	4 m from L edge water on new bar above photo monument PM-12 groin.
Bar.10.05	L	at 10	41	95	165	46	1 to 5 m from L edge water, little lateral size variation on bar.
Bar.11.05	R	at 11	21	51	147	25	3 to 5 m from R edge water.
Bar.13.05	R	at 13	23	72	146	35	4 m from R edge water.
Bar.14.05	L	abv 15	30	55	126	27	4 m from L edge water.
Mean 2005				84			
Mean of all years				70			

Note: d_{16}—16th percentile; d_{50}—50th percentile; d_{84}—84th percentile; mm—millimeters; m—meters; N/m^2—newtons per square meter; XS—cross section; L—left; R—right; C—center; abv—above. Critical shear calculated with 0.030 Shields parameter.

TABLE A3. SEDIMENT-SIZE STATISTICS FROM WOLMAN PEBBLE COUNTS AT THE LAKE FORK AT GATEVIEW MONITORED REACH

Measurement location, code, and date	River side	Nearest cross section	Fine fraction d_{16} (mm)	Median size d_{50} (mm)	Coarse fraction d_{84} (mm)	Critical shear for d_{50} (N/m^2)	Remarks
1998 measurements							Reconfigured after 1998 peak discharge.
XS.2.98	XS	2	53	128	263	62	Bankfull to bankfull. Structural boulder excluded.
XS.3.98	XS	3	50	110	190	53	Unaltered section. Bankfull to bankfull.
XS.5.98	XS	5	40	97	147	47	Traverse bar and channel. Structural boulder excluded.
XS.6.98	XS	6	42	110	198	54	Traverse bar and channel. Structural boulder excluded.
XS.9.98	XS	9	33	71	185	34	Traverse bar and channel. Structural boulders excluded.
Bar.1_2.98	L	1 and 2	31	92	190	45	2 to 3 m from L edge water.
Bar.5_6_7.98	L	5, 6, and 7	38	77	145	37	2 to 3 m from L edge water.
Bar.8_9.98	R	8 and 9	22	63	137	31	2 to 3 m from R edge water.
Mean 1998				94			
2000 measurements							Resulting from 1999 and 2000 peak discharge.
XS.2.00	XS	2	23	117	240	57	Bankfull to bankfull. Structural boulder excluded.
XS.3.00	XS	3	34	97	160	47	Unaltered section. Bankfull to bankfull.
XS.5.00	XS	5	27	95	152	46	Traverse bar and channel. Structural boulder excluded.
XS.6.00	XS	6	11	82	200	40	Traverse bar and channel. Structural boulder excluded.
XS.9.00	XS	9	28	87	250	42	Traverse bar and channel. Structural boulders excluded.
Bar.1_2.00	L	1 and 2	33	117	202	57	2 to 3 m from L edge water.
Bar.5_6_7.00	L	5, 6, and 7	39	84	150	41	2 to 3 m from L edge water.
Bar.8_9.00	R	8 and 9	28	60	136	29	2 to 3 m from R edge water.
Mean 2000				92			
2005 measurements							Resulting from 2005 peak discharge.
XS.3.05	XS	3	42	96	167	46	Unaltered section. Bank to bank.
XS.9.05	XS	9	20	88	186	43	Traverse bar and channel. Structural boulders excluded.
Bar.1_2.05	L	1 and 2	27	92	201	45	1 m from L edge water.
Bar.5_6_7.05	L	5, 6, and 7	13	57	125	28	~1 m from L edge water.
Bar.8_9.05	R	8 and 9	26	88	190	42	
Mean 2005				84			
Mean of all years				91			

Note: d_{16}—16th percentile; d_{50}—50th percentile; d_{84}—84th percentile; mm—millimeters; m—meters; N/m^2—newtons per square meter; XS—cross section; L—left; R—right. Critical shear calculated with 0.030 Shields parameter.

REFERENCES CITED

Andrews, E.D., 1983, Entrainment of gravel from naturally sorted riverbed material: Geological Society of America Bulletin, v. 94, p. 1225–1231, doi: 10.1130/0016-7606(1983)94<1225:EOGFNS>2.0.CO;2.

Carling, P.A., 1983, Threshold of coarse sediment transport in broad and narrow natural streams: Earth Surface Processes, v. 8, p. 1–18, doi: 10.1002/esp.3290080102.

Chow, V.T., 1959, Open-Channel Hydraulics: New York, McGraw-Hill, 680 p.

Crowfoot, R.M., Boulger, R.W., and O'Neill, G.B., 2003, Water resources data, Colorado, water year 2003, v. 2, Colorado River Basin: U.S. Geological Survey Water-Data Report CO-03-2, 575 p.

Dunne, T., and Leopold, L.B., 1978, Water in Environmental Planning: San Francisco, W.H. Freeman, 818 p.

Elliott, J.G., and Hammack, L.A., 1999, Geomorphic and sedimentologic characteristics of alluvial reaches in the Black Canyon of the Gunnison National Monument, Colorado: U.S. Geological Survey Water-Resources Investigations Report 99-4082, 67 p.

Elliott, J.G., and Hammack, L.A., 2000, Entrainment of riparian gravel and cobbles in an alluvial reach of a regulated canyon river: Regulated Rivers: Research and Management, v. 16, p. 37–50, doi: 10.1002/(SICI)1099-1646(200001/02)16:1<37::AID-RRR564>3.0.CO;2-V.

Elliott, J.G., and Parker, R.S., 1999, Reconfigured-channel monitoring and assessment program: U.S. Geological Survey Water-Resources Investigations Report 99-4111, 6 p.

Fahnestock, R.K., 1963, Morphology and hydrology of a glacial stream—White River, Mount Rainier, Washington: U.S. Geological Survey Professional Paper 442-A, p. 1–70.

Federal Interagency Stream Restoration Working Group, 2001, Stream corridor restoration—Principles, processes, and practices: Washington, D.C., Government Printing Office, variously paginated.

Fitzpatrick, F.A., Waite, I.R., D'Arconte, P.J., Meador, M.R., Maupin, M.A., and Gurtz, M.E., 1998, Revised methods for characterizing stream habitat in the National Water-Quality Assessment Program: U.S. Geological Survey Water-Resources Investigations Report 98-4052, 67 p.

Flynn, K.M., Kirby, W.H., and Hummel, P.R., 2006, User's manual for program PeakFQ annual flood-frequency analysis using Bulletin 17B guidelines: U.S. Geological Survey, Techniques and Methods, Book 4, ch. B4, 42 p.

Graf, W.H., 1971, Hydraulics of Sediment Transport: New York, McGraw-Hill, 513 p.

Harrelson, C.C., Rawlins, C.L., and Potyondy, J.P., 1994, Stream channel reference sites—An illustrated guide to field technique: U.S. Department of Agriculture, Forest Service General Technical Report RM-245, 61 p.

HEC-RAS, http://www.hec.usace.army.mil/software/hec-ras/ (accessed 5 January 2009).

Johnson, P.A., and Brown, E.R., 2001, Incorporating uncertainty in the design of stream channel modifications: Journal of the American Water Resources Association, v. 37, p. 1225–1236, doi: 10.1111/j.1752-1688.2001.tb03634.x.

Juracek, K.E., and Fitzpatrick, F.A., 2003, Limitations and implications of stream classification: Journal of the American Water Resources Association, v. 39, p. 659–670, doi: 10.1111/j.1752-1688.2003.tb03683.x.

Kochel, R.C., Miller, J.R., Lord, M., and Martin, T., 2005, Geomorphic problems with in-stream structures using natural channel design strategy for stream restoration projects in North Carolina: Geological Society of America Abstracts with Programs, v. 37, no. 7, p. 329.

Komar, P.D., 1987, Selective gravel entrainment and the empirical evaluation of flow competence: Sedimentology, v. 34, p. 1165–1176, doi: 10.1111/j.1365-3091.1987.tb00599.x.

Kondolf, G.M., 1998, Lessons learned from river restoration projects in California: Aquatic Conservation: Marine & Freshwater Ecosystems, v. 8, p. 39–52, doi: 10.1002/(SICI)1099-0755(199801/02)8:1<39::AID-AQC250>3.0.CO;2-9.

Kondolf, G.M., and Micheli, E.R., 1995, Evaluating stream restoration projects: New York: Environmental Management, v. 19, p. 1–15.

Lane, E.W., 1955, Design of stable channels: Transactions, American Society of Civil Engineers, v. 120, p. 1234–1279.

Leopold, L.B., and Wolman, M.G., 1957, River channel patterns—Braided, meandering and straight: U.S. Geological Survey Professional Paper 282-B, p. 39–84.

Leopold, L.B., Wolman, M.G., and Miller, J.P., 1964, Fluvial processes in geomorphology: San Francisco, W.H. Freeman, 522 p.

Lisle, T.E., Iseya, F., and Ikeda, H., 1993, Response of a channel with alternate bars to a decrease in supply of mixed-size bed load—A flume experiment: Water Resources Research, v. 29, p. 3623–3629, doi: 10.1029/93WR01673.

Meyer-Peter, E., and Muller, R., 1948, Formulas for bedload transport: Proceedings of the International Association of Hydraulic Research, 2nd Meeting, Stockholm, 1948, p. 39–64.

Miall, A.D., 1985, Architectural-element analysis—A new method of facies analysis applied to fluvial deposits: Earth-Science Reviews, v. 22, p. 261–308, doi: 10.1016/0012-8252(85)90001-7.

Milhous, R.T., 1982, Effect of sediment transport and flow regulation on the ecology of gravel-bed rivers, *in* Hey, R.D., Bathhurst, J.C., and Thorne, C.R., eds., Gravel-Bed Rivers: Chichester, UK, Wiley & Sons, p. 819–842.

Montgomery, D.R., and Buffington, J.M., 1993, Channel classification, prediction of channel response, and assessment of channel condition: Report TFW-SH10-93-002, prepared for the SHAMW committee of the Washington State Timber/Fish/Wildlife Agreement, 84 p. plus figs.

Mosley, M.P., 1982, A procedure for characterising river channels: Christchurch, New Zealand, Christchurch Water and Soil Science Centre, Ministry of Works and Development, Water and Soil Miscellaneous Publications 32, 67 p.

Neill, C.R., 1968, A Re-Examination of the beginning of movement for coarse granular bed materials: Wallingford, UK, Hydraulics Research Station, Report INT 68, 37 p.

Parker, G., Klingman, P.C., and McLean, D.G., 1982, Bedload and size distribution in paved gravel-bed streams: American Society of Civil Engineers, Journal of the Hydraulics Division, v. 108, HY4, p. 544–571.

Powell, D.M., and Ashworth, P.J., 1995, Spatial pattern of flow competence and bed load transport in a divided gravel bed river: Water Resources Research, v. 31, p. 741–752, doi: 10.1029/94WR02273.

Richards, K., 1982, Rivers—Form and Process in Alluvial Channels: London, Methuen, 358 p.

Roper, B.B., Kershner, J.L., Archer, E., Henderson, R., and Bouwes, N., 2002, An evaluation of physical stream habitat attributes used to monitor streams: Journal of the American Water Resources Association, v. 38, p. 1637–1646, doi: 10.1111/j.1752-1688.2002.tb04370.x.

Rosgen, D.L., 1996, Applied river morphology: Pagosa Springs, Colorado, Wildland Hydrology, various pagination.

Schumm, S.A., 1977, The Fluvial System: New York, Wiley & Sons, 338 p.

Shields, A., 1936, Application of similarity principles and turbulence research to bedload movement, *translated from* Anwendung der Aehnlichkeitsmechanik und der Turbulenzforschung auf die Geschiebewegung: Mitteilung Preussischen Versuchanstalt für Wasserbau und Schiffbau, Berlin, No. 26, by W.P. Ott and J.C. van Uchelen: Pasadena, California Institute of Technology Hydrodynamics Report 167, 43 p.

Simon, A., Doyle, M., Kondolf, M., Shields, F.D., Jr., Rhodes, B., and McPhillips, M., 2007, Critical evaluation of how the Rosgen classification and associated "natural channel design" methods fail to integrate and quantify fluvial processes and channel response: Journal of the American Water Resources Association, v. 43, p. 1117–1131, doi: 10.1111/j.1752-1688.2007.00091.x.

Smelser, M.G., and Schmidt, J.C., 1998, An assessment methodology for determining historical changes in mountain streams: U.S. Department of Agriculture, Forest Service General Technical Report GTR-6, 29 p.

Smith, S.M., and Prestegaard, K.L., 2005, Hydraulic performance of a morphology-based stream channel design: Water Resources Research, v. 41, W11413, doi: 10.1029/2004WR003926, 17 p.

U.S. Army Corps of Engineers, 1980, Flood Hazard Information—North Fork Gunnison River, Hotchkiss to Somerset, Delta and Gunnison Counties, Colorado: U.S. Army Corps of Engineers, Sacramento District, variously paginated.

U.S. Geological Survey Real-Time Water Data, http://waterdata.usgs.gov/co/nwis/rt (accessed 5 January 2009).

U.S. Geological Survey Reconfigured-Channel Monitoring and Assessment Program (RCMAP): http://co.water.usgs.gov/projects/rcmap/ (accessed 5 January 2009).

U.S. Geological Survey Reconfigured-Channel Monitoring and Assessment Program (RCMAP): http://co.water.usgs.gov/projects/rcmap/monitormethods.html (accessed 5 January 2009).

U.S. Geological Survey 2005 Water Data Report, http://wdr.water.usgs.gov/wy2005/search.jsp (accessed 5 January 2009).

U.S. Interagency Advisory Committee on Water Data (USIACWD), 1982, Guidelines for determining flood-flow frequency, Bulletin 17B of the

Hydrology Subcommittee: Reston, Virginia, U.S. Geological Survey, Office of Water Data Coordination, 183 p.

Vaill, J.E., 2000, Analysis of the magnitude and frequency of floods in Colorado: U.S. Geological Survey Water-Resources Investigations Report 99-4190, version 3, 35 p.

Vincent, K.R., and Elliott, J.G., 2007, Response of the upper Animas River downstream from Eureka to discharge of mill tailings, ch. E22, *in* Church, S.E., von Guerard, P.B., and Finger, S.E., eds., 2007, Integrated Investigations of Environmental Effects of Historical Mining in the Animas River Watershed, San Juan County, Colorado: U.S. Geological Survey Professional Paper 1651, 1096 p. plus CD-ROM.

Whiting, P.J., and Bradley, J.B., 1993, A process-based classification system for headwater streams: Earth Surface Processes and Landforms, v. 18, p. 603–612, doi: 10.1002/esp.3290180704.

Wiberg, P.L., and Smith, J.D., 1987, Calculations of the critical shear stress for motion of uniform and heterogeneous sediments: Water Resources Research, v. 23, p. 1471–1480, doi: 10.1029/WR023i008p01471.

Wilcock, P.R., 1992, Flow competence—A criticism of a classic concept: Earth Surface Processes and Landforms, v. 17, p. 289–298, doi: 10.1002/esp.3290170307.

Wilcock, P.R., and McArdell, B.W., 1993, Surface-based fractional transport rates–Mobilization thresholds and partial transport of a sand-gravel sediment: Water Resources Research, v. 29, p. 1297–1312, doi: 10.1029/92WR02748.

Wilcock, P.R., and Southard, J.B., 1988, Experimental study of incipient motion in mixed-size sediment: Water Resources Research, v. 24, p. 1137–1151, doi: 10.1029/WR024i007p01137.

Wilkerson, G.V., 2008, Improving bankfull discharge prediction using 2-year recurrence-period discharge: Journal of the American Water Resources Association, v. 44, no. 1, p. 243–258.

Wolman, M.G., 1954, A method of sampling coarse river-bed material: Eos (Transactions, American Geophysical Union), v. 35, p. 951–956.

MANUSCRIPT ACCEPTED BY THE SOCIETY 15 SEPTEMBER 2008

The Geological Society of America
Special Paper 451
2009

Assessing geomorphological and ecological responses in restored step-pool systems

Anne Chin
Department of Geography, University of Oregon, Eugene, Oregon 97403, USA

Alison H. Purcell
Department of Environmental and Natural Resource Sciences, Humboldt State University, Arcata, California 95521, USA

Jennifer W.Y. Quan
Vincent H. Resh
Department of Environmental Science, Policy and Management, University of California, Berkeley, California 94720, USA

ABSTRACT

Although step-pools are increasingly used in stream restoration to stabilize steep channels, few studies have examined artificially manipulated step-pool systems after restoration. Whereas monitoring efforts have emphasized morphological change within restored systems, knowledge of the ecological potential for restoration using step-pool sequences is particularly incomplete. Baxter Creek (El Cerrito, Contra Costa County) and Codornices Creek (Berkeley, Alameda County) in California provide two unique cases of restored step-pool systems with which to assess post-restoration responses. Since restoration was completed in 1996 and 2003, respectively, Baxter Creek and Codornices Creek have achieved geomorphic stability, characterized by maximum flow resistance and minor change in channel cross sections. The integrity of the restored step-pool channels has been maintained through storms that have exceeded the 14–20+ year recurrence interval. Comparison of the types and characteristics of benthic macroinvertebrates in the restored reaches with unrestored sites upstream and downstream, as well as with a reference channel (Wildcat Creek, Contra Costa County), indicates that restoration has effectively created ecological environments consistent with the overall watershed settings within Baxter Creek and Codornices Creek. Biological metrics used to represent ecological conditions indicate that Wildcat Creek, the reference site, had a healthier condition, which was reflected in a higher percentage of sensitive taxa (e.g., Ephemeroptera, Plecoptera, Trichoptera or EPT) and a lower percentage of tolerant taxa (e.g., oligochaetes and midge larvae). No significant differences were found between the restored reaches in Baxter Creek and Codornices Creek, and those upstream and downstream of the restored

Chin, A., Purcell, A.H., Quan, J.W.Y., and Resh, V.H., 2009, Assessing geomorphological and ecological responses in restored step-pool systems, *in* James, L.A., Rathburn, S.L., and Whittecar, G.R., eds., Management and Restoration of Fluvial Systems with Broad Historical Changes and Human Impacts: Geological Society of America Special Paper 451, p. 199–214, doi: 10.1130/2009.2451(13). For permission to copy, contact editing@geosociety.org. ©2009 The Geological Society of America. All rights reserved.

sites. Comparison of the biological metrics among habitat types (steps, pools, riffles) within each stream and across watersheds indicates a tendency toward higher biological quality (characterized by a higher percentage of sensitive organisms) in steps compared with pools. These findings suggest the ecological potential of stream restoration using step-pools, because step clasts may offer habitats for higher percentages of sensitive and specialized organisms.

INTRODUCTION

River restoration continues to gain momentum as the range of anthropogenic impacts on streams and watersheds is increasingly recognized (e.g., James and Marcus, 2006), and as the public becomes more aware of the accompanying loss of ecosystem goods and services (Bernhardt et al., 2007). Yet, despite expenditures of more than one billion dollars annually to restore our nation's rivers (Bernhardt et al. 2005), comparatively little effort has been placed on understanding the successes and failures of restoration projects (e.g., Kondolf and Micheli, 1995; Bernhardt et al., 2005, 2007; Palmer et al., 2007). The lack of systematic evaluations of completed restoration projects has limited our lessons learned for adaptive management (Downs and Kondolf, 2002; Kondolf et al., 2007) and hindered feedback to theory development. As synthesis efforts have sharpened our focus toward a restoration science that is process based (Wohl et al., 2005; Bernhardt et al., 2005, 2007), an increased understanding of the responses within restored river systems becomes exceedingly important.

The restoration of stream channels using step-pool sequences has especially accelerated in recent years (Chin et al., 2009). Step-pools are gravel bedforms commonly found in steep river channels that typically exceed a ~3%–5% slope. Steps comprising cobbles and boulders alternate with finer sediments in pools to form a rhythmic, staircaselike longitudinal profile. The repetitive arrangement of steps and pools induces energy dissipation in the tumbling flow (Peterson and Mohanty, 1960) that otherwise would cause excessive erosion and channel degradation in high-gradient environments. Until recently, little was known about step-pool sequences compared with pools and riffles associated with meandering rivers in lowland areas (Chin, 1989). Intensified research over the past two decades has produced significant advances in theory for step-pool systems (Chin and Wohl, 2005; Church and Zimmermann, 2007), so that restoration using step-pools is now possible and increasingly common (Chin et al., 2009). Such applications have occurred concomitantly with an increasing need to restore incising channels brought on by hydrologic alterations associated with human-induced changes to the landscape (e.g., urbanization; James and Marcus, 2006); these include greater magnitudes and intensities of runoff and reduced sediment supplies in built areas. Impacts to step-pool channels are also more frequent where urbanization increasingly encroaches upon mountain fronts in response to population growth (e.g., Chin and Gregory, 2001). The potential habitat-enhancement benefits provided by step-pools (Scheuerlein, 1999), as well as the need to restore culverts to enable fish passage (e.g., Maxwell

et al., 2001), further make step-pools an increasingly valuable and promising approach in stream restoration and streambed stabilization (Lenzi, 2002).

Despite progress in constructing realistic step-pool sequences that meet grade control and habitat improvement purposes (Chin et al., 2009), these cases have not been studied in detail following restoration. Limited information exists as to how artificially manipulated step-pool systems function, especially in the context of the watershed. The few instances that have reported monitoring for reconstructed step-pool sequences have emphasized morphological changes within the restored reaches (Lenzi and Comiti, 2003; Chin et al., 2009). Our understanding is particularly incomplete with regard to the ecological potential for restoration using step-pool sequences (Scheuerlein, 1999; Comiti et al., 2009), and how step-pools might contribute to the overall ecological improvements within the watershed.

In this article we examine the geomorphological and ecological responses in two cases of stream restoration using step-pool sequences in the San Francisco East Bay Area of northern California (Fig. 1). First, we outline the background to the restoration projects of Baxter Creek and Codornices Creek and report the morphological adjustments in the step-pool systems following restoration. We assess the present morphology in the context of natural channels in similar settings. Next, a field study is outlined that investigates the ecological characteristics of the restored step-pool channels. We test the hypothesis that, although step-pools provide a primary function of grade control in restoration, the restored step-pool reaches would also show improved ecological functioning. Presumably, enhanced ecological conditions would result from the multiple habitats that are created by the step-pool sequences (e.g., Townsend and Hildrew, 1994), in addition to the lessened erosion (e.g., Wood and Armitage, 1997). Thus, we also test the hypothesis that ecological characteristics would vary among habitats within step-pool sequences in the restored channels. Our study represents a first step in exploring the ecological significance of step-pool sequences in steep channels. Our results provide insight into how restored step-pool systems function in the context of the larger watershed, as well as feedback for restoration design and theory development.

RESTORATION AND CHANNEL ADJUSTMENTS

Baxter Creek

Baxter Creek drains 7.5 km² (0.7 km² upstream of restoration site) of an urban watershed through the city of El Cerrito,

California (Contra Costa County; 37°56'07"N, 122°19'00"W, 60 meters above sea level [m a.s.l.]) (Fig. 1). Similar to many urban creeks in the San Francisco Bay area, parts of Baxter Creek are underground culverts en route to San Francisco Bay. Culverts had been placed in these creeks since the 1940s to address concerns related to flood control. In 1996 a 70 m reach of Baxter Creek was opened or "daylighted" in an effort to renovate storm drains in the area. Rather than investing in costly maintenance and repair, the City of El Cerrito decided that reconstructing a natural creek channel through Poinsett Park would be more economically feasible (Owens-Viani, 1997). Purcell et al. (2002) provide additional context for the restoration.

Baxter Creek lies within a Mediterranean climate characterized by dry, warm summers and cool, wet winters with little freezing (Gasith and Resh, 1999). The creek has perennial flow that generally follows rainfall patterns in the winter with a continuous baseflow throughout the summer. Low flow is augmented by springs and urban sources, such as irrigation and landscape watering (Owens-Viani, 2004). The Baxter Creek catchment lies along the Hayward fault; the geology includes serpentine matrix mélange in the upper watershed. Holocene alluvial-fan and fluvial deposits constitute the sediments in the lower catchment (Graymer, 2000). Land use within the watershed is characterized by parks and a golf course in the upper catchment, with urban, residential, and commercial areas giving way to industrial zones in the lower areas. The restored reach of Baxter Creek lies within a residential setting.

The design of the restored channel dimensions for this ungauged creek utilized regional hydraulic geometry relationships based on drainage area (A.L. Riley, 2000, 2004, personal commun.). These relations yielded a design width of ~2 m and a depth of ~0.3 m for this channel reach. These dimensions were intended to accommodate a 10 yr flood (Owens-Viani, 1997). Characteristics of the region, including a steep 10% valley slope, also provided guidelines for selecting the channel sinuosity and slope. Additionally, native tree species, including willow (*Salix* sp.), alder (*Alnus* sp.), big leaf maple (*Acer macrophyllum*), and California dogwood (*Cornus californica*), were planted into channel banks to provide stabilization.

The channel was constructed using step-pool morphology to accommodate the steep slope (~10%), although little published information on step-pools was available at that time to guide channel design. Using salvaged rocks from the excavation, five step structures were built to span the 70-m channel reach (Figs. 2A, 2B). This spacing corresponded to an average step length of 14 m, or ~7 channel widths.

Because equilibrium step-pool geometry requires a closer spacing, however, as shown by more recent research, natural flows redistributed much of the rock material into more closely spaced steps. Movement of the step clasts began during the winter flows of 1997 (Chin et al., 2009). By 2005, 20 well-developed step-pool sequences were documented (Fig. 2C; Fig. 3). These bedforms were characterized by an average step length L of 2.9 m and an average step height H of 0.28 m (as defined by Abrahams et al., 1995) for a slope S of 9.0% for the surveyed reach in 2005. The mean step particle size was 261 mm (defined as the average of the five largest rocks (b-axis) composing each step; Chin, 1999).

Analysis of the morphological relations of the 2005 channel gives insight into the postrestoration adjustment processes. Whereas the initial spacing between steps was too far apart, the average step length in 2005 corresponded to 1.6 channel widths (for a measured average active width of 1.8 m). This spacing matches the modes exhibited by many natural step-pool sequences (e.g., Billi et al., 1998; Chin, 1999). The ratio of average step height to average step particle size of 1.1 is also consistent with those reported for natural step-pool sequences (Chartrand and Whiting, 2000) in similar environments (Chin, 1999). Examination of length and height relations relative to slope further yielded an average $(H/L)/S = 1.1$. This step-pool geometry fits within the range of $1 \leq (H/L)/S \leq 2$ that Abrahams et al. (1995) have suggested maximizes flow resistance. Thus, because the mixture of rocks was sufficiently sized relative to slope and the flow regime, natural adjustments occurred through a self-organization process toward a morphology that reflects apparent stability in the system (Chin and Phillips, 2007). In the years since restoration, the creek had undergone storms with recurrence intervals >14 yr (Boucher, 2006). The integrity of the channel cross sections has also been maintained (Fig. 4).

Codornices Creek

The Codornices Creek catchment (total catchment area, 7.4 km²; 1.5 km² upstream of restoration site) begins its

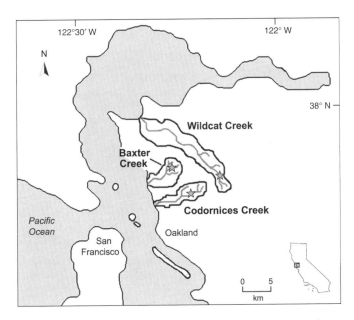

Figure 1. Restored reaches in Baxter Creek (37°56'07" N, 122°19'00" W) and Codornices Creek (37°53'03" N, 122°16'01" W); Wildcat Creek is reference site (37°53'08" N, 122°13'52" W). Stars indicate sampling sites.

headwaters in the Berkeley Hills (Alameda County; 37°53′03″N, 122°16′01″W, 97 m a.s.l.), flows through the city of Berkeley, and empties into San Francisco Bay (Fig. 1). The watershed also lies within the Mediterranean climatic regime and exhibits similar land uses as those in the Baxter Creek watershed. Codornices Creek similarly alternates between open and closed (underground) channels en route to San Francisco Bay. The creek generally flows year-round. The geology of the catchment includes alluvium deposits from the Holocene and Pleistocene (Graymer, 2000). Older alluvial fans and fluvial deposits exhibit stronger soil-profile development and a greater degree of dissection. They are overlain by more permeable Holocene deposits on the lower parts of the alluvial plain. Stream channels are incised into vertically varied layers of sandy clay and sandy silt (Graymer, 2000; Clearwater Hydrology, 2002). A large, active landslide occupies an area north and east of the project site that includes the north bank. This creeping slide mass contributes to channel-bank insta-

bility and provides one source of sediment into the study channel (Clearwater Hydrology, 2002).

The project site is a 36-m section of Codornices Creek that was deeply incising below an outlet from a culvert (Fig. 5A). The incision was probably caused by installation of another culvert downstream that had displaced the channel thalweg (Clearwater Hydrology, 2002). The channel instability within this reach triggered multiple slump failures along the incised banks. The overwidened channel cross sections with nearly vertical banks were also vulnerable to local failures during high flows. Additionally, although Codornices Creek supplies minimal spawning and rearing habitat for Central California Coast steelhead (*Oncorhynchus myskiss*), significant barriers to fish passage existed because of large drops in elevation at several locations along the creek. These included the incised area below the outlet from the culvert into the project reach that resulted in a waterfall and a deep plunge pool (Figs. 5A, 6). Downstream of the plunge pool the

Figure 2. Baxter Creek. (A) During construction, 1996; photograph by A.L. Riley. Note size of step clasts relative to individuals in photograph. (B) Following construction, 1996; photograph by A.L. Riley. (C) Part of the same view of Baxter Creek as in Figure 2B, taken in March 2005 by A. Chin.

channel transitioned from a pool-riffle morphology into a long, continuous riffle (Fig. 5B) within a reach with a ~3.5% slope. Bed sediments ranged from medium to coarse sands to large cobbles (Clearwater Hydrology, 2002).

The use permit issued by the City of Berkeley called for a restoration plan that included the principal objectives of bed and bank stabilization to reduce bank erosion and downstream sedimentation, improved fish passage and anadromous fish habitat, and the establishment of a healthy riparian corridor (Clearwater Hydrology, 2002). To guide channel design, the 2 yr and 100 yr discharges were computed using flood-frequency equations for the San Francisco Bay region and a mean annual precipitation of 24.5 in. (Rantz, 1971). The 2 yr discharge yielded geomorphic parameters for the bankfull channel, whereas the 100 yr flow provided guidelines for determining the height of the bank revetment work. Bank-stabilization efforts included a revetment made of native material, such as boulders, logs, rootwads, and alluvial backfill. Riparian plantings included willow, dogwood, and cottonwood (*Populus* sp.) that extended from the edge of the creek to the upper terraces (Clearwater Hydrology, 2002, 2003).

The slope of the project reach from the outlet of the culvert to the downstream end was 7.5%, requiring step-pool morphol-

ogy for the channel bed. A series of cascades, comprising boulder and log weirs, was planned, with intervening pools targeted as resting areas for fish. Some of these boulders were anchored by rebar; others were allowed to move. An important design consideration required the minimum depth of each pool to be set at 0.6 m to allow for fish passage, meeting the standards of the National Marine Fisheries Service (NMFS, 2000). These considerations resulted in design step lengths ranging from 2.7 to 3.4 m for the 10 steps total (Clearwater Hydrology, 2002, 2003). This step-pool configuration was also intended to permit energy dissipation through the steep channel reach.

Since completion of the project in the summer of 2003 (Fig. 5C), several large floods in the winter have tested the integrity of the restored channel of Codornices Creek. These floods were generated by storms with estimated recurrence intervals of 10 yr in December 2004 and 2006, 25 yr in February 2004, and 10–20+ years in December 2005 (Clearwater Hydrology, 2006; Fig. 5D). The floods caused localized erosion and slump failures along banks, but the step-pool structures remained largely intact. Clearwater Hydrology (2006) showed the detailed year-to-year changes in cross section and longitudinal profile. The main morphological adjustments in the channel bed occurred at the upstream end of the reach, where movement of boulders resulted in the loss of one step-pool series and created a run (Clearwater Hydrology, 2006; Fig. 6). As might be expected, minor shifting and settling of rock material has also fine-tuned the staircase-like structure into the present morphology.

In 2007, measurements of the step-pool sequences in the restored channel reach yielded an average step length L of 3.4 m and an average step height H of 0.57 m (definitions of Abrahams et al., 1995) for a surveyed reach of 34 m with a slope S of 7.8% (Fig. 6). Similar to the adjusted step-pool spacing in Baxter Creek, the step length of the restored reach of Codornices Creek corresponds to an average spacing of 1.5 channel widths (for a measured average active width of 2.2 m). The ratio of average step height to average step particle size (517 mm; definition

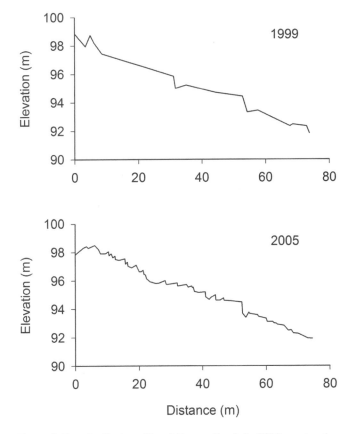

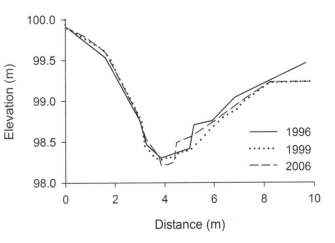

Figure 3. Longitudinal profile of Baxter Creek in 2005, contrasting with that in 1999, showing the few initial large steps (after Chin et al., 2009). Vertical exaggeration is 4.5.

Figure 4. Cross sections surveyed in 1996, 1999, and 2006; Baxter Creek (after Chin et al., 2009). Vertical exaggeration is 3.2.

of Chin, 1999) of 1.1 also matched that reported for Baxter Creek and other natural streams (Chartrand and Whiting, 2000; Chin, 1999). Analysis of geometric relations further yielded a (H/L)/S ratio of 2.2 for the 2007 surveyed profile. This value falls slightly outside of the ideal 1–2 range as described by Abrahams et al. (1995). Ratios exceeding 2 reflect deep pools and exaggerated reverse-gradient step treads (Fig. 6) and are commonly reported for natural streams (e.g., Chartrand and Whiting, 2000; Zimmermann and Church, 2001).

The restored reach of Codornices Creek has remained passable by fish, especially at moderate to high flows (Clearwater Hydrology, 2006). Although many of the pools have lost depth because of sediment deposition, most of the pools remain >0.5 m deep at higher flows. An additional issue common for artificial step-pools is the "sealing" of the steps (Morris and

Moses, 1998; Chin et al., 2009), where settling of gravel in the interstitial spaces between boulders is expected to prevent seepage of flow through the steps. For the constructed channel reach in Codornices Creek, several steps are passing less than the targeted threshold of 80% of flow over their crests at low flows (Clearwater Hydrology, 2006). Nevertheless, this characteristic is not considered critical to the future ecological performance of the step-pool channel for fish.

ECOLOGICAL RESPONSES

Conceptual Approach

In order to assess the ecological conditions present in the restored step-pool channel reaches in Baxter Creek and

Figure 5. Codornices Creek. (A) Before restoration (2002), showing the culvert outlet (top left of photo) into the open creek and plunge pool below. (B) Segment of the reach downstream of plunge pool, 2002, before restoration. (C) Part of the restored reach at low flow, April 2007. Channel width is ~2.2 m. (D) Restored reach during flood, December 2005. Culvert outlet is the same as that shown in Figure 5A. (Photographs 5A, 5B, and 5D by Clearwater Hydrology; photograph 5C by A. Chin.)

Codornices Creek, we used benthic macroinvertebrates as indicators of water quality and biological conditions (Resh et al., 1996). Members of this diverse and ecologically important group occur in almost every stream environment and are sensitive to physical and chemical perturbations. Analysis of macroinvertebrate assemblages has successfully detected changes in ecological conditions following disturbances related to streamflow, habitat, and water quality (e.g., Paul and Meyer, 2001; Walsh et al., 2005). In addition, studies comparing several regions within the United States have found predictable relationships between watershed disturbances and macroinvertebrate composition (e.g., McMahon and Cuffney, 2000; Barbour et al., 2006).

To characterize the ecological functioning of the restored step-pool channels, we compared the presence and types of macroinvertebrates found within the restored sites with those in neighboring and reference sites (Fig. 1). To assess the extent to which the restored sites were characteristic of the biotic communities within those watersheds, we compared biological samples in the restored channels with those in step-pool reaches upstream and downstream of those sites. We also selected a reference site (Wildcat Creek) with natural step-pool sequences and minimal disturbance to determine the extent to which the restored step-pool channels in Baxter Creek and Codornices Creek have approached the ecological conditions of a pristine stream. Additionally, to test for variations in ecological characteristics among habitats, we compared samples according to the habitats present within study reaches.

Wildcat Creek

The catchment of the reference Wildcat Creek (27.5 km² total catchment area, 0.5 km² upstream of sampling site) begins its headwaters in Tilden Regional Park in Berkeley, flows northwest through the city of Richmond, and flows out into San Pablo Bay (37°53'08"N, 122°13'52"W, 365 m a.s.l) (Fig. 1). In contrast to the urban watersheds of Baxter Creek and Codornices Creek, Wildcat Creek consists primarily of parkland in the upper catchment with minimal disturbance. Although urban and industrial land uses are also found in the lower watershed, we conducted all biological sampling near the pristine headwaters of the mainstem of the creek. The mainstem flows year-round, although many of the small tributaries are dry in the summer. The geology of the Wildcat Creek catchment includes the Franciscan Formation in the upper area and Holocene alluvial deposits in the lower watershed (Graymer, 2000).

Wildcat Creek is an appropriate reference stream for this study in terms of its channel and watershed characteristics (Fig. 7). The sampled reach (31 m) exhibits a slope of 7.6% and an average width of 1.7 m. The sizes of the step clasts average 249 mm (definition of Chin, 1999) and are comparable to those in the study channels. Although the Wildcat Creek sampling site is located at a higher elevation (365 m a.s.l.) than the Baxter Creek (60 m a.s.l.) and Codornices Creek (97 m a.s.l.) sites, several other localized environmental factors were selected to be similar

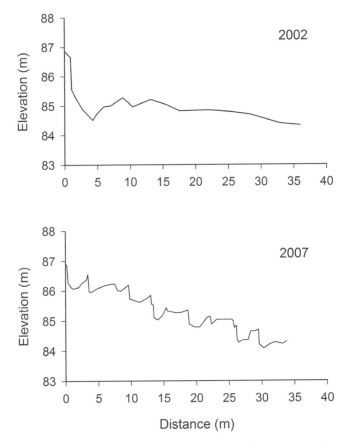

Figure 6. Longitudinal profile of Codornices Creek before restoration in 2002 (data from Clearwater Hydrology), contrasting with that in April 2007 (as surveyed by authors); vertical exaggeration is 4.5. Note that movement of boulders has created a run near station (distance) 5 m by 2007.

Figure 7. Natural step-pools in Wildcat Creek at low flow. Channel is ~1.7 m wide. (Photograph by A.H. Purcell.)

at each site for comparison purposes (e.g., the area of upstream watershed, channel width and depth, substrate size, slope, riparian cover). Also set within a Mediterranean climate (Gasith and Resh, 1999), Wildcat Creek exhibits a similar flashy flow regime as in Baxter Creek and Codornices Creek, characterized by high flows in winter and low flows in summer. In addition, the character of the step-pool channels of Wildcat Creek, Baxter Creek, and Codornices Creek is similar to those studied in the Santa Monica Mountains of southern California (e.g., Chin, 1999) in terms of climate and geologic setting, flow regime, size, slope, and grain size, including the mobility of the step clasts (Chin, 1998). Results from this study, therefore, can be discussed in a broader context for possible generalizations.

Field Sampling

Field sampling took place in May 2007 and proceeded systematically from downstream to upstream in each of the study reaches. The sample reaches were each ~30 m long; the restored reaches in Baxter Creek and Codornices Creek were separated from upstream and downstream counterparts by at least 200 m. Three habitat types (i.e., step, pool, and riffle) were sampled within each study reach, and three replicates were collected from each habitat type. Samples from steps were further distinguished as taken from two microhabitats: the surface ("step surface") or from within the interlocking boulders and cobbles ("step inside") to test for variations among microhabitats. Altogether, 28 samples were obtained from Baxter Creek (10 steps, 9 pools, and 9 riffles), 32 samples from Codornices Creek (18 steps, 8 pools, and 6 riffles), and 9 samples from Wildcat Creek (6 steps and 3 pools, with no riffles present). Uneven sample sizes reflect the availability of habitats within the study reaches.

Standard methods in stream ecology provided the protocols for field sampling (Hauer and Resh, 2006; Barbour et al., 1999). A 500-micron D-frame kick net was used to collect the biological samples by vigorously disturbing the upstream substrate for 1 min time periods. Each sampling area was ~0.19 m². The step samples required a flexible collection device to fit the multidimensional surfaces of the steps. Thus, a flexible frame net was constructed by attaching rubber tubing around the mouth of the 500-micron mesh net. Samples from the step surface were collected by rubbing the face of the step to dislodge the organisms, while holding the flexible frame net directly downstream. Next, samples from the inside of steps were taken by loosening the step clasts that could be moved and disturbing the finer substrate beneath those rocks. All rocks were put back into their original positions following sample collection.

The samples were composited and preserved in the field with 95% ethanol and placed into plastic bags, after removal of large organic (leaves and twigs) and inorganic material. If the collection contained large amounts of inorganic material (rocks and fine sediment), the samples were elutriated from the inorganic materials by swirling the collection in a pan and pouring the remains through a 500-micron sieve. The remaining inorganic material was examined for organisms with high specific gravity, such as case-making Trichoptera (caddisflies) and gastropods.

Laboratory and Analytic Procedures

In the laboratory, sorting and identification of the field samples followed standard taxonomic identification methods (e.g., Merritt et al., 2008). Organisms were identified primarily to the family level. Individuals from the groups Gastropoda and Crustacea were identified to their respective classes. Individual organisms were identified, counted, separated by taxa, and placed into glass vials filled with 75% ethanol.

Several common biological metrics provided indication of the types of organisms found in each of the sites. These metrics often indicate the ecological condition and environmental quality at stream sites (Rosenberg and Resh, 1993; Merritt et al., 2008). The metrics included number of individuals, taxa richness, percentage of EPT individuals (organisms from the orders Ephemeroptera, Plecoptera, and Trichoptera, which are generally sensitive to pollution), percentage of sensitive EPT individuals (percentage of EPT individuals excluding the families Baetidae and Hydropsychidae, which are considered tolerant to pollution), percentage of Oligochaeta individuals (organisms generally regarded as tolerant to adverse environmental conditions), and percentage of Chironomidae individuals (also generally regarded as tolerant). Additional indices were calculated to reflect the environmental quality at the study sites, including (1) Shannon's Diversity Index (H′), which is commonly used to characterize species diversity and includes evenness of the taxa present; and (2) an urban index composed of macroinvertebrate groups that shows a predictable decline to increased levels of urbanization (Purcell, 2007). Table 1 lists the metrics and indices analyzed, their definitions, and expected response to disturbance.

One-way analysis of variance (ANOVA) procedures provided tests for differences in the biological metrics and indices among stream reaches and habitat types. First, the metrics and indices were compared within watersheds (among restored and unrestored step-pool reaches in Baxter Creek and Codornices Creek) and between watersheds (among Baxter Creek, Codornices Creek, and Wildcat Creek). These tests were conducted to reveal the biological functioning of the restored step-pool channels compared with neighboring reaches in their respective watersheds, as well as to the reference site. Second, the metrics and indices were compared for differences among habitats. These differences indicated variations in ecological characteristics within steps and pools and gave insight into the ecological potential of stream restoration using step-pool sequences. The SAS statistical package (JMP 5.1.2) provided the software for the analyses (SAS Institute, 2004). The significance level (α) was 0.017 after applying the Bonferroni correction for comparison among multiple sites.

TABLE 1. DESCRIPTION OF BIOLOGICAL METRICS CALCULATED AT EACH STREAM SITE AND THEIR EXPECTED RESPONSE TO DISTURBANCE

Metric	Description	Expected response to disturbance
Total number of individuals	Total count of the number of individual organisms in each sample	Increase or decrease
Taxa richness	Total number of taxa in each sample	Decrease
% EPT individuals	Percentage of individuals in the insect orders Ephemeroptera, Plecoptera, and Trichoptera, generally sensitive to pollution	Decrease
EPT richness	Number of taxa in the insect orders Ephemeroptera, Plecoptera, and Trichoptera, which are generally sensitive to pollution	Decrease
% sensitive EPT individuals	Percentage of individuals in the EPT orders excluding the families Hydropsychidae and Baetidae, which are generally tolerant of pollution	Decrease
% Oligochaeta individuals	Percentage of individuals in the class Oligochaeta (worms), which are tolerant to pollution	Increase
% Chrionomidae individuals	Percentage of individuals in the family Chironomidae (midge flies), which are tolerant to pollution	Increase
Evenness	Relative abundance or proportion of individuals among the species	Decrease
% clingers	Percentage of individuals with behavioral or morphological adaptations for clinging to surfaces in stream riffles	Decrease
Clinger richness	Number of taxa with behavioral or morphological adaptations for clinging to surfaces in stream riffles	Decrease
% shredders	Percentage of individuals within the functional feeding group that consumes coarse organic matter	Decrease
Shredder richness	Number of taxa within the functional feeding group that consumes coarse organic matter	Decrease
Shannon Diversity (H')	Index used to measure diversity in an assemblage by incorporating evenness and abundance	Decrease
Urban index	Index composed of macroinvertebrate groups (% EPT, % clingers, % shredders) that exhibit a predictable decline to increased levels of urbanization (developed by Purcell, 2007)	Decrease

Note: Based on predictions in Merritt et al. (2008). EPT—Ephemeroptera, Plecoptera, and Trichoptera.

Results

Site Comparisons

Analysis of the biological samples indicates that the study reaches in Baxter Creek and Codornices Creek were dominated by organisms in groups considered to be tolerant to perturbations in stream quality, whereas more sensitive taxa were found in Wildcat Creek (Table 2). The tolerant groups found included aquatic segmented worms (Oligochaeta), flatworms (Turbellaria), snails (Hydrobiidae, Physidae, and Lymnaeidae), a tolerant family of mayflies (Baetidae), midge larvae (Chironomidae), black fly larvae (Simuliidae), damselflies (Coenagrionidae), and tolerant families of caddisflies (Hydroptilidae and Hydropsychidae). Baxter Creek contained these tolerant taxa in particularly substantial numbers. Although some of the same tolerant taxa were also present in Wildcat Creek, a range of organisms in the general EPT grouping, considered sensitive (e.g., Rosenberg et al., 2008), were also found there. These include the more sensitive families of mayflies (Heptageniidae and Leptophlebiidae), stoneflies (Chloroperlidae and Nemouridae), and caddisflies (Rhyacophilidae and Odontoceridae). These results suggest a healthier biological condition in Wildcat Creek compared with Baxter Creek and Codornices Creek. The differences in ecological character among the three study watersheds are statistically significant ($p < .017$) in all metrics except the total number of individuals and percentage of oligochaetes (Table 3).

Although the presence of the tolerant taxa within the restored step-pool reaches of Baxter Creek and Codornices Creek suggests

poorer biological conditions compared with those of Wildcat Creek, similar groups of organisms were also found in the reaches upstream and downstream of the restored segments (Table 2). Results of one-way ANOVA tests conducted within each watershed revealed that none of the metrics for the restored reaches were significantly different from the unrestored upstream and downstream sites (Table 4). These findings, therefore, suggest that the organisms present in the restored step-pool channel reaches are characteristic of those in their respective watershed settings.

Variations among Habitats

For analyzing variations among habitats, the results described above suggested that an appropriate refinement to the analytical procedures could be used. First, because no significant differences were detected among study reaches within Baxter Creek and Codornices Creek, the data for the restored sites were combined with those from the unrestored upstream and downstream reaches for analysis according to habitats. Second, given that the three study watersheds are significantly different in ecological character, the data for habitats were explored separately within each watershed. These data were then combined for the three watersheds to examine overall trends in variations among habitats.

A comparison of the ecological metrics within each study watershed found no significant differences among habitats for Baxter Creek and Wildcat Creek, whereas several important differences were recorded for Codornices Creek (Table 5). The differences in Codornices Creek include a significantly higher percentage of oligochaetes, a tolerant group, in pools (Fig. 8)

TABLE 2. COMMON TAXA FOUND AT SAMPLING REACHES

Macroinvertebrate taxa		Baxter Creek			Codornices Creek			Wildcat Creek
General group (common name)	Taxa	DS	RS	US	DS	RS	US	Reference
Tolerant taxa								
Annelida (segmented worm)	Oligochaeta	X	X	X	X	X	X	X
Platyhelmenthes (flatworm)	Turbellaria	X	X	X	X	-	X	
Ephemeroptera (mayfly)	Baetidae	-	-	X	X	X	X	X
Diptera (midge fly)	Chironomidae	X	X	X	X	X	X	X
Diptera (black fly)	Simuliidae	X	X	X	X	X	X	X
Odonata (damselfly)	Coenagrionidae	X	X	X	X	X	X	
Gastropoda (snail)	Hydrobiidae	X	X	X	-	X	X	-
Gastropoda (snail)	Lymnaeidae	X	X	X	-	-	X	-
Gastropoda (snail)	Physidae	-	X	X	-	-	-	
Trichoptera (caddisfly)	Hydroptilidae	-		X	-	-	-	
Trichoptera (caddisfly)	Hydropsychidae	X	-	-	-	-	X	X
Arachnida (mite)	Acari	-	-	-	-	-	X	X
Sensitive taxa								
Ephemeroptera (mayfly)	Heptageniidae							X
Ephemeroptera (mayfly)	Leptophlebiidae							X
Plecoptera (stonefly)	Chloroperlidae							X
Plecoptera (stonefly)	Nemouridae				X	X	X	X
Trichoptera (caddisfly)	Rhyacophilidae				-			X
Trichoptera (caddisfly)	Odontoceridae							X

Key: DS—downstream site; RS—restored site; US—upstream site; X—taxa present in >1% of sample; hyphen (-)—taxa present in <1% of sample; blank entry—no taxa present in sample.

TABLE 3. RESULTS OF ANOVA TESTS AMONG WATERSHEDS, COMPARING BAXTER CREEK, CODORNICES CREEK, AND WILDCAT CREEK

Metrics	*p* value	Comments
Total number of individuals	.1643	
Taxa richness	**.0108**	Wildcat Creek higher than Baxter Creek
% Oligochaeta	.0822	
% Chironomidae	**<.0001**	Wildcat Creek lower than Baxter Creek and Codornices Creek
% EPT	**<.0001**	All sites different (Baxter Creek < Codornices Creek < Wildcat Creek)
% sensitive EPT	**<.0001**	Wildcat Creek higher than Baxter Creek and Codornices Creek
EPT richness	**<.0001**	All sites different (Baxter Creek < Codornices Creek < Wildcat Creek)
Shannon Diversity (H')	**.0028**	Wildcat Creek higher than Baxter Creek and Codornices Creek
Evenness	**.011**	Wildcat Creek higher than Codornices Creek
% clingers	**<.0001**	Wildcat Creek higher than Baxter Creek and Codornices Creek
Clinger richness	**<.0001**	Wildcat Creek higher than Baxter Creek and Codornices Creek
% shredders	**<.0001**	All sites different (Baxter Creek < Codornices Creek < Wildcat Creek)
Shredder richness	**<.0001**	All sites different (Baxter Creek < Codornices Creek < Wildcat Creek)
Urban index	**<.0001**	All sites different (Baxter Creek < Codornices Creek < Wildcat Creek)

Note: A *p* value <.017 indicates a significant difference between at least two of the three watersheds. Comments describe the specific differences. Values in bold indicate significance. ANOVA—analysis of variance; EPT—Ephemeroptera, Plecoptera, Trichoptera.

TABLE 4. RESULTS OF ANOVA TESTS CONDUCTED WITHIN EACH WATERSHED, COMPARING RESTORED REACHES WITH UNRESTORED SITES UPSTREAM AND DOWNSTREAM

Metrics	Baxter Creek	Comments	Codornices Creek	Comments
Total number of individuals	0.078		0.599	
Taxa richness	0.056		**0.004**	US > RS
% Oligochaeta	0.179		0.111	
% Chironomidae	0.749		0.074	
EPT	0.028		0.046	
% sensitive EPT	0.131		**0.006**	DS > US
EPT richness	0.121		0.821	
Shannon Diversity (H')	0.090		**<0.0001**	US > RS, DS
Evenness	0.386		0.039	
% clingers	**0.015**	RS > DS	0.342	
Clinger richness	0.106		0.206	
% shredders	0.833		0.004	DS > US, RS
Shredder richness	0.818		0.049	
Urban index	0.075		0.691	

Note: Bold indicates significant *p* value < .017.
Key: DS—downstream site; RS—restored site; US—upstream site; > —significantly greater than. ANOVA—analysis of variance.

TABLE 5. RESULTS OF ANOVA TESTS CONDUCTED WITHIN EACH WATERSHED, COMPARING MICROHABITAT TYPES

Metrics	Baxter Creek	Codornices Creek	CC comments	Wildcat Creek
Total number of individuals	0.105	0.077		0.226
Taxa richness	0.347	0.055		0.038
% Oligochaeta	0.037	**0.008**	Pool > SS, SI & R	0.273
% Chironomidae	0.400	0.027		0.216
% EPT	0.459	**0.017**	Pool < SS, SI	0.987
% sensitive EPT	0.492	**0.016**	Pool < SS, SI	0.388
EPT richness	0.248	0.103		0.445
Shannon Diversity (H')	0.846	0.060		0.198
Evenness	0.344	**0.002**	Pool < SS, SI & R	0.264
% clingers	0.068	**0.000**	Pool < SS, SI & R	0.623
Clinger richness	0.174	0.604		0.037
% shredders	0.763	0.030		0.019
Shredder richness	0.920	0.839		0.196
Urban index	0.041	**0.000**	Pool < SS, SI & R	0.352

Note: Bold indicates significant *p* value < .017.
Key: SS—step surface; SI—step inside; R—riffle; > —significantly greater than; < —significantly less than; CC—comments for Codornices Creek. ANOVA—analysis of variance.

compared with step habitats. The percentage of EPT (representing sensitive taxa) and the percentage of sensitive EPT organisms were also significantly greater in steps (Figs. 9, 10). Additionally, pools exhibited significantly less evenness, a lower percentage of clingers, and a lower urban index value compared with other habitats (Table 5). Because the urban index was developed to measure stream health in urban catchments (Purcell, 2007), a higher value in the index for step surfaces indicates that higher proportions of organisms sensitive to urbanization were found there, compared with pools. Taken together, these results suggest higher biological quality in step habitats compared with pools along Codornices Creek.

Several trends also emerged when the three study watersheds were analyzed together for variations among habitats (Table 6). First, pools showed a higher percentage of Oligochaeta than other

habitats. Second, the surfaces of steps had higher percentages of EPT than riffles or pools. Third, steps (surfaces or insides) also had higher percentages of clingers, shredders, and urban index scores than pools. Because higher values of these metrics indicate high biological quality (Table 1), these results also suggest an association between step habitats and good ecological conditions.

DISCUSSION

Geomorphological Considerations

In summary, analysis of the artificially manipulated step-pool channels of Baxter Creek and Codornices Creek suggests the following insights for restoration. First, as one of the early documented applications of step-pools in stream restoration (Chin et al., 2009), Baxter Creek demonstrated how natural flows are capable of reorganizing the artificial step-pool sequences, given appropriate particle sizes for the flow regime and channel slope. This rearrangement has produced a step-pool morphology consistent with those of natural channels (e.g., Chin, 1999) and includes a (H/L)/S ratio of 1.1 that has been suggested to offer maximum flow resistance (Abrahams et. al., 1995). The adjustment process is likely analogous to those in natural channels (Madej, 2001; Chin and Phillips, 2007) where the destruction of step-pool sequences during floods and the subsequent reorganization have been documented. In the Rio Cordon of Italy (Lenzi, 2001), for example, the ratio of (H/L)/S changed from 1.3 to 0.79 immediately after a large flood, then increased progressively following a series of smaller events to the pre-flood ratio of 1.33. For stream restoration, the example of Baxter Creek suggests the possibility of allowing natural fluvial processes to do some of the work of determining the ultimate equilibrium step-pool geometry. Attention to proper particle sizes may be appropriate using this approach (Chin et al., 2009).

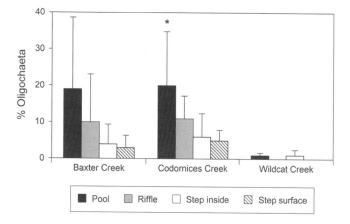

Figure 8. Percentage of Oligochaeta (tolerant taxa) within microhabitats in each study creek. No riffle habitats were available to sample at the Wildcat Creek site. Asterisk (*) indicates a significant ($p < .05$) difference.

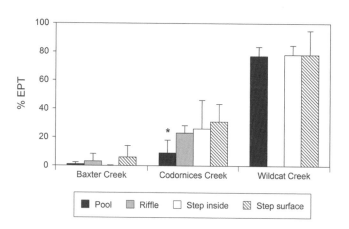

Figure 9. Percentage of EPT (sensitive taxa) within microhabitats in each study creek. No riffle habitats were available to sample at the Wildcat Creek site. Asterisk (*) indicates a significant ($p < .05$) difference.

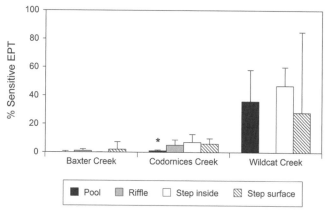

Figure 10. Percentage of sensitive EPT within microhabitats in each study creek. Sensitive EPT consists of EPT excluding the families Baetidae and Hydropsychidae, considered tolerant to pollution. No riffle habitats were available to sample at the Wildcat Creek site. Asterisk (*) indicates a significant ($p < .05$) difference.

TABLE 6. RESULTS OF ANOVA TESTS CONDUCTED WITH COMBINED
WATERSHED DATA, COMPARING MICROHABITAT TYPES

Metrics	*p* value	Comments
Total number of individuals	.117	
Taxa richness	.023	
% Oligochaeta	**.002**	Pool > SS, SI
% Chironomidae	.564	
% EPT	.044	(Wilcoxon *p* = 0.0169) SS > R, pool
% sensitive EPT	.208	
EPT richness	.112	
Shannon Diversity (H')	.545	
Evenness	.047	
% clingers	**.001**	Pool < SS, SI
Clinger richness	.347	
% shredders	**.012**	Pool < SS
Shredder richness	.836	
Urban index	**.004**	Pool < SS, SI

Note: Bold indicates significant *p* value < .017.
Key: SS—step surface; SI—step inside; R—riffle; > —significantly greater than; < —significantly less than. ANOVA—analysis of variance.

For Codornices Creek, restoration in 2003 had the benefit of more recent research on step-pool systems. A channel design approximating equilibrium conditions for step-pool sequences is reflected in the minor adjustments that have occurred since restoration. The stability of the channel reach is aided by key step particles that are anchored in place, as well as step particles in the high end of the range of sizes for comparable channels, including Wildcat Creek and those studied in the Santa Monica Mountains of southern California (e.g., Chin, 1999). Large step particle sizes are consistent with large heights (Chin, 1999; Chartrand and Whiting, 2000) that produce a (H/L)/S ratio of 2.2 for the restored reach, reflecting deep pools and reverse-gradient step treads. The stability of the restored channel reach is further enhanced by the monitoring program that is in place as part of the permitting process (W.B. Vandivere, 2007, personal commun.). Thus, soil along banks removed by localized erosion during floods is replaced (Clearwater Hydrology, 2006), preventing progressive scouring around steps that has been reported in some cases without monitoring programs (Chin et al., 2009).

The cases of Baxter Creek and Codornices Creek illustrate some of the fundamental and philosophical issues identified for restoration of step-pool streams (Chin et al., 2009). These include the question of how much to design step-pool sequences in restoration. On the one hand, allowing the creek to do some of the work (Baxter Creek) is advantageous and effective if the specific project permits some degree of reorganization in the channel. The recent restoration of a tributary of Dry Canyon Creek on the property of the Mountains Restoration Trust in Calabasas, California, for example, utilized this somewhat experimental approach (Chin et al., 2009). In contrast, private ownership in densely populated settings places a high premium on the stability of restored channels, so that larger-than-expected step-pool sequences are often designed. This situation was demonstrated in the restoration of East Alamo Creek near San Ramon, California, in 2001 (Chin et al., 2009) and is reminiscent of the artificial step-pool channel of Codornices Creek at the stable end of the spectrum. Consideration as to whether to construct pools (and how deep) also includes requirements for fish passage (Codornices Creek), energy dissipation (East Alamo Creek), and cost considerations. Cost was one factor for selecting a step-pool design to enable flows to scour pools naturally in a tributary of Karnowsky Creek in the Coast Ranges of Oregon (Chin et al., 2009). Clearly, a range of options for the design of step-pool sequences is now available for restoration, given the context of the particular case and our current state of understanding of the step-pool morphology in steep channels.

Ecological Processes

Concerning ecological processes, analysis of the restored and unrestored step-pool channels in Baxter Creek, Codornices Creek, and Wildcat Creek produces several general points. First, Baxter Creek and Codornices Creek exhibited generally lower ecological conditions than Wildcat Creek. This finding is not surprising, given that Baxter Creek and Codornices Creek are impacted by urbanization even in the upper watersheds, whereas Wildcat Creek approximates conditions with minimal disturbance. Because the specific geology, geochemistry, mosaic of land uses, and human impacts in the watershed influence ecological characteristics, such as local taxa composition, differences among watersheds are expected and have long been known (e.g., Hynes, 1970).

Second, the restored step-pool channels in Baxter Creek and Codornices Creek showed no significant differences from the unrestored reaches upstream and downstream. One interpretation of this finding is that the aquatic assemblages at the restored channels are at least on a par with adjacent areas within the watershed. This interpretation suggests that restoration of the step-pool channels had effectively created ecological environments consistent with the overall watershed settings. However, the fact that the ecological conditions of the restored reaches were not significantly better than the neighboring unrestored section could be attributed to the limiting factors of highly impacted urban watersheds. Impacts from flashy flows, low dissolved oxygen, and increases in stream temperatures, nutrients, metal, and pesticides could contribute to limits in ecological recovery (Paul and Meyer, 2001). These environmental conditions are particularly prevalent in Baxter Creek, which exhibited the most impacted assemblage of the three catchments examined (Purcell, 2004; A.L. Riley, 2008, personal commun.). Additionally, the lack of longitudinal connectivity created by multiple culverts along the path of the stream may decrease the ability of potential invertebrate colonists to reach the restored sites via flight or drift (Purcell et al., 2002). The urban setting also meant that any accumulation of large wood or coarse particulate organic matter would be removed during maintenance, inhibiting the development of more complex food webs. Thus, the ecological characteristics found in the restored reaches are consistent with those permitted by the environmental conditions within the urban watersheds.

In addition, despite overall conditions, the findings of this study suggest variations in faunal occurrences among habitats, especially between steps and pools. In particular, the biotic assemblages within Codornices Creek showed a tendency toward higher biological quality in steps compared with pool habitats. This is reflected in higher percentages of EPT and sensitive EPT, and higher evenness, a higher percentage of clingers, and a higher urban index value for step habitats compared with pools. Although Baxter Creek and Wildcat Creek did not exhibit the same variations among habitats as those in Codornices Creek, the lack of statistical differences may be attributed to the low sample size in Wildcat Creek, and to the highly impacted urban setting of Baxter Creek. The analysis of all three watersheds together further supports the point that step habitats may create high-quality ecological environments.

The variations in macroinvertebrates found between step and pool habitats are compatible with the findings that oxygen availability (e.g., Chambers et al., 2006), streamflow intensity (e.g., Lorenz et al., 2004), and amount of fine sediment (e.g., Kaller and Hartman, 2004) can affect the distribution of benthic organisms. Taxa such as EPT individuals have specialized behavioral, physiological, and life history characteristics (Poff and Ward, 1990) that often require high levels of dissolved oxygen. Other organisms, such as oligochaetes or midges, are adapted to depositional habitats with low velocities (Brinkhurst and Gelder, 2001), such as pools; they can tolerate less oxygen and withstand smothering from sediments (Angradi, 1999). Because dissolved-oxygen contents are higher in areas of rapid water flow, and because sensitive taxa, such as EPT individuals, require high levels of dissolved oxygen in order to survive, sensitive organisms might be expected to inhabit rocky step microhabitats. Despite high levels of dissolved oxygen, however, step-pool systems can be harsh environments for stream biota in general because of the high flow velocities and great turbulence, so that organisms may have difficulties attaching to the bed substrate (Scheuerlein, 1999). Therefore, the faunal composition of step-pool habitats probably will comprise a few highly specialized organisms that are adapted to colonizing these unique ecosystems.

For stream restoration, these findings raise the issue of whether a continuous riffle-step, low-gradient cascade, or simply coarse riprap, may have served as a better channel design, given that sensitive organisms would probably inhabit rocky step microhabitats. From a purely ecological standpoint, our results indeed suggest this case. Potential ecological benefits, however, must be balanced against the geomorphological requirements of a step-pool morphology, given the high gradients (~8%–10%). As demonstrated in Baxter Creek and elsewhere (e.g., Lenzi, 2001; Chin and Phillips, 2007), a continuous riffle-step or coarse riprap may reorganize into step-pool sequences by natural flows over time, if the appropriate particle sizes are in place. Thus, the ultimate selection of an appropriate channel design depends on the purpose of the restoration project and probably requires consideration of both geomorphological and ecological processes.

CONCLUSION

In conclusion, Baxter Creek and Codornices Creek provide two examples of artificial step-pool systems from which to learn valuable insights. As the need to restore river channels with step-pool sequences increases, the lessons provided by completed projects become exceedingly important. The restored reaches of Baxter Creek and Codornices Creek have been tested by storms exceeding the 14–20+ year recurrence interval. These cases demonstrate the range of responses within such systems, where geomorphic stability can be achieved through natural adjustment processes (Baxter Creek; Chin and Phillips, 2007), or in the initial design and post-construction maintenance program (Codornices Creek). Although the primary purpose of using step-pools in stream restoration is often grade control and streambed stabilization, results from Baxter Creek and Codornices Creek also suggest the potential ecological significance of step-pool sequences in such efforts. Further research should reveal more completely the ecological processes associated with step-pool systems. Artificially manipulated step-pool channels provide opportune laboratories with potential to reveal the geomorphologic and ecologic complexities of natural systems.

ACKNOWLEDGMENTS

We thank Ann Riley (Waterways Restoration Institute) for generously providing background information and data for Baxter Creek, including the photographs taken in 1996 (Figs. 2A, 2B) and the 1996 and 1999 cross sections and longitudinal profiles (Figs. 3, 4). We also thank William Vandivere (Clearwater Hydrology) for providing detailed design plans and monitoring data for the restoration of Codornices Creek, including the longitudinal profile of the pre-restoration study reach (Fig. 6), as well as the photographs of the creek taken in 2002 and 2005 (Figs. 5A, 5B, 5D). We are grateful, additionally, to the Congregation Beth El Temple for granting permission to conduct physical and biological surveys in Codornices Creek. Shannah Anderson, Kate Huxster, and Rune Steoresund assisted with surveys in Baxter Creek; Margaret Groff helped with identifying the biological samples in the laboratory. Laura Laurencio produced Figure 1; David Laurencio provided assistance with manuscript preparation. Ellen Wohl and an anonymous reviewer offered helpful comments that greatly improved the final paper. This study was supported in part by the U.S. National Science Foundation (BCS 0620543).

REFERENCES CITED

Abrahams, A.D., Li, G., and Atkinson, J.F., 1995, Step-pool streams: Adjustment to maximum flow resistance: Water Resources Research, v. 31, p. 2593–2602, doi: 10.1029/95WR01957.

Angradi, T.R., 1999, Fine sediment and macroinvertebrate assemblages in Appalachian streams: A field experiment with biomonitoring applications: Journal of the North American Benthological Society, v. 18, p. 49–66, doi: 10.2307/1468008.

Barbour, M.T., Gerritsen, J., Snyder, B.D., and Stribling, J.B., 1999, Rapid Bioassessment Protocols for Use in Streams and Wadeable Rivers: Periphyton, Benthic Macroinvertebrates and Fish (2nd edition): Washington, D.C., U.S. Environmental Protection Agency, Office of Water, EPA/841-B-99-002, 339 p.

Barbour, M.T., Paul, M.J., Bressler, D.W., Purcell, A.H., Resh, V.H., and Rankin, E., 2006, Bioassessment: A tool for managing aquatic life uses for urban streams: WERF Research Digest #01-WSM-3, 58 p.

Bernhardt, E.S., Palmer, M.A., Allan, J.D., Alexander, G., Barnas, K., Brooks, S., Carr, J., Clayton, S., Dahm, C., Follstad-Shah, J., Galat, D., Gloss, S., Goodwin, P., Hart, D., Hassett, B., Jenkinson, R., Katz, S., Kondolf, G.M., Lake, P.S., Lave, R., Meyer, J.L., O'Donnell, T.K., Pagano, L., Powell, B., and Sudduth, E., 2005, Synthesizing U.S. river restoration efforts: Science, v. 308, p. 636–637, doi: 10.1126/science.1109769.

Bernhardt, E.S., Sudduth, E.B., Palmer, M.A., Allan, J.D., Meyer, J.L., Alexander, G., Follastad-Shah, J., Hassett, B., Jenkinson, R., Lave, R., Rumps, J., and Pagano, L., 2007, Restoring rivers one reach at a time: Results from a survey of U.S. river restoration practitioners: Restoration Ecology, v. 15, p. 482–493, doi: 10.1111/j.1526-100X.2007.00244.x.

Billi, P., D'Agostino, V., Lenzi, M.A., and Marchi, L., 1998, Bedload, slope and channel processes in a high-altitude torrent, *in* Klingemann, P.C., Beschta, R.L., Komar, P.D., and Bradley, J.B., eds., Gravel-Bed Rivers in the Environment: Highlands Ranch, Colorado, Water Resources Publications, p. 15–38.

Boucher, M., 2006, Report on the December 31, 2005 Storm Update: Contra Costa [County, California] Flood Control and Water Conservation District, 31 January 2006.

Brinkhurst, R.O., and Gelder, S.R., 2001, Annelida: Oligochaeta, including Branchiobdellidae, *in* Thorp, J.H., and Covich, A.P., eds., Ecology and Classification of North American Freshwater Invertebrates: San Diego, Academic Press, p. 431–504.

Chambers, P.A., Culp, J.M., Glozier, N.E., Cash, K.J., Wrona, F.J., and Noton, L., 2006, Northern rivers ecosystem initiative: Nutrients and dissolved oxygen—Issues and impacts: Environmental Monitoring and Assessment, v. 113, p. 117–141, doi: 10.1007/s10661-005-9099-z.

Chartrand, S.M., and Whiting, P.J., 2000, Alluvial architecture in headwater streams with special emphasis on step-pool topography: Earth Surface Processes and Landforms, v. 25, p. 583–600.

Chin, A., 1989, Step-pools in stream channels: Progress in Physical Geography, v. 13, p. 391–408, doi: 10.1177/030913338901300304.

Chin, A., 1998, On the stability of step-pool mountain streams: Journal of Geology, v. 106, p. 59–69.

Chin, A., 1999, The morphologic structure of step-pools in mountain streams: Geomorphology, v. 27, p. 191–204, doi: 10.1016/S0169-555X(98)00083-X.

Chin, A., and Gregory, K.J., 2001, Urbanization and adjustment of ephemeral stream channels: Annals of the Association of American Geographers, v. 91, p. 595–608, doi: 10.1111/0004-5608.00260.

Chin, A., and Phillips, J.D., 2007, The self-organization of step-pools in mountain streams: Geomorphology, v. 83, p. 346–358, doi: 10.1016/j.geomorph.2006.02.021.

Chin, A., and Wohl, E., 2005, Toward a theory for step-pools in stream channels: Progress in Physical Geography, v. 29, p. 275–296, doi: 10.1191/0309133305pp449ra.

Chin, A., Anderson, S., Collison, A., Ellis-Sugai, E., Haltiner, J.P., Hogervorst, J.B., Kondolf, G.M., O'Hirok, L.S., Purcell, A.H., Riley, A.L., and Wohl, E., 2009, Linking theory and practice for restoration of step-pool streams: Environmental Management, doi: 10.1007/s00267-008-9171-x (in press).

Church, M., and Zimmermann, A., 2007, Form and stability of step-pool channels: Research progress: Water Resources Research, v. 43, p. W03415, doi: 10.1029/2006WR005037.

Clearwater Hydrology, 2002, Engineering hydrologic design for channel stabilization and habitat restoration on Codornices Creek, 1301 Oxford Street, Berkeley, California: Prepared for Congregation Beth El, Berkeley, California, 24 June 2002.

Clearwater Hydrology, 2003, Mitigation and monitoring plan for the Codornices Creek (Beth El) bank stabilization and fisheries restoration project, 1301 Oxford Street, Berkeley, California: Memorandum to Regional Water Quality Control Board—San Francisco Bay Region, 22, 2003.

Clearwater Hydrology, 2006, Codornices Creek restoration (RWQCB Site 02-01-C0630): Hydrologic and geomorphic monitoring: Year 3 Annual Report, 8 p. + appendix.

Comiti, F., Mao, L., Lenzi, M.A., and Siligardi, M., 2009, Artificial steps to stabilize moutain rivers: A post-project ecological assessment: River Research and Applications, v. 24, p. 1–21, doi: 10.1002/rra.1234.

Downs, P.W., and Kondolf, G.M., 2002, Post-project appraisals in adaptive management of river channel restoration: Environmental Management, v. 29, p. 477–496, doi: 10.1007/s00267-001-0035-X.

Gasith, A., and Resh, V.H., 1999, Streams in Mediterranean climate regions: Abiotic influences and biotic responses to predictable seasonal events: Annual Review of Ecology and Systematics, v. 30, p. 51–81, doi: 10.1146/annurev.ecolsys.30.1.51.

Graymer, R.W., 2000, Geologic map and map database of the Oakland Metropolitan Area, Alameda, Contra Costa, and San Francisco Counties, California: Department of the Interior and U.S. Geological Survey pamphlet to accompany Miscellaneous Field Studies Map MF-2342, 31 p.: geopubs.wr.usgs.gov (accessed 12 July 2007).

Hauer, F.R., and Resh, V.H., 2006, Chapter 16: Macroinvertebrates, *in* Hauer, F.R., and Lamberti, G.A., eds., Methods in Stream Ecology: San Diego, California, Academic Press, p. 339–370.

Hynes, H.B., 1970, The Ecology of Running Waters: Toronto, University of Toronto Press, 555 p.

James, L.A., and Marcus, W.A., 2006, The Human Role in Changing Fluvial Systems: Proceedings of the Binghamton Symposium on Geomorphology, 37th: Amsterdam, Elsevier, 506 p.

Kaller, M.D., and Hartman, K.J., 2004, Evidence of a threshold level of fine sediment accumulation for altering benthic macroinvertebrate communities: Hydrobiologia, v. 518, p. 95–104, doi: 10.1023/B:HYDR.0000025059.82197.35.

Kondolf, G.M., and Micheli, E.R., 1995, Evaluating stream restoration projects: Environmental Management, v. 19, p. 1–15, doi: 10.1007/BF02471999.

Kondolf, G.M., Anderson, S., Lave, R., Pagano, L., Merenlender, A., and Bernhardt, E.S., 2007, Two decades of river restoration in California: What can we learn?: Restoration Ecology, v. 15, p. 516–523, doi: 10.1111/j.1526-100X.2007.00247.x.

Lenzi, M.A., 2001, Step-pool evolution in the Rio Cordon, northeastern Italy: Earth Surface Processes and Landforms, v. 26, p. 991–1008, doi: 10.1002/esp.239.

Lenzi, M.A., 2002, Stream bed stabilization using boulder check dams that mimic step-pool morphology features in northern Italy: Geomorphology, v. 45, p. 243–260, doi: 10.1016/S0169-555X(01)00157-X.

Lenzi, M.A., and Comiti, F., 2003, Local scouring and morphological adjustments in steep channels with check-dam sequences: Geomorphology, v. 55, p. 97–109, doi: 10.1016/S0169-555X(03)00134-X.

Lorenz, A., Hering, D., Feld, C.K., and Rolauffs, P., 2004, A new method for assessing the impact of hydromorphological degradation on the macroinvertebrate fauna of five German stream types: Hydrobiologia, v. 516, p. 107–127, doi: 10.1023/B:HYDR.0000025261.79761.b3.

Madej, M.A., 2001, Development of channel organization and roughness following sediment pulses in single-thread, gravel bed rivers: Water Resources Research, v. 37, p. 2259–2272, doi: 10.1029/2001WR000229.

Maxwell, A.R., Papanicolaou, A.N., Hotchkiss, R.H., Barber, M.E., and Schafer, J., 2001, Step-Pool Morphology in High-Gradient Countersunk Culverts: Transportation Research Record 1743, Paper no. 01-2304: Washington, D.C., National Academy of Sciences, p. 380–390.

McMahon, G., and Cuffney, T.F., 2000, Quantifying urban intensity in drainage basins for assessing stream ecological conditions: Journal of the American Water Resources Association, v. 36, p. 1247–1261, doi: 10.1111/j.1752-1688.2000.tb05724.x.

Merritt, R.W., Cummins, K.W., and Berg, M.B., 2008, An Introduction to the Aquatic Insects of North America (4th edition): Dubuque, Iowa, Kendall/Hunt, 1158 p.

Morris, S., and Moses, T., 1998, Channel and streambank stabilization in a steep colluvial valley, Lake Oswego, Oregon, *in* Winning Solutions for Risky Problems: Steamboat Springs, Colorado, International Erosion Control Association, Proceedings of Conference, 29th, Reno, Nevada, p. 367–371.

National Marine Fisheries Service (NMFS), 2000, Guidelines for salmonid passage at stream crossings, 16 May: NMFS, Southwest Region; 12 p.: http://www.fws.gov/midwest/fisheries/streamcrossings/Reference.htm (accessed 26 January 2009).

Owens-Viani, L., 1997, Daylighting a creek: Urban Ecologist, v. 1, p. 9.

Owens-Viani, L., 2004, The Baxter Creek Watershed: A Cultural and Natural History: Richmond, California, The Watershed Project, 11 p.

Palmer, M., Allan, J.D., Meyer, J., and Bernhardt, E.S., 2007, River restoration in the twenty-first century: Data and experiential knowledge to inform future efforts: Restoration Ecology, v. 15, p. 472–481, doi: 10.1111/j.1526-100X.2007.00243.x.

Paul, M.J., and Meyer, J.L., 2001, Streams in the urban landscape: Annual Review of Ecology and Systematics, v. 32, p. 333–365, doi: 10.1146/annurev.ecolsys.32.081501.114040.

Peterson, D.F., and Mohanty, P.K., 1960, Flume studies of flow in steep rough channels: Proceedings of the American Society of Civil Engineers, Journal of the Hydraulics Division, v. 86, p. 55–70.

Poff, N.L., and Ward, J.V., 1990, Physical habitat template of lotic systems: Recovery in the context of historical pattern of spatiotemporal heterogeneity: Environmental Management, v. 14, p. 629–645, doi: 10.1007/BF02394714.

Purcell, A.H., 2004, A Long-Term Post-Project Evaluation of an Urban Stream Restoration Project (Baxter Creek, El Cerrito, California): Berkeley, University of California, Berkeley River Restoration Symposium, 31 p.

Purcell, A.H., 2007, Benthic macroinvertebrates and ecological assessments: Examining the biological potential of urban stream restoration in the San Francisco Bay area [Ph.D. thesis]: Berkeley, University of California, Berkeley, Department of Environmental Science, Policy, and Management, 233 p.

Purcell, A.H., Friedrich, C., and Resh, V.H., 2002, An assessment of a small urban stream restoration project in northern California: Restoration Ecology, v. 10, p. 685–694, doi: 10.1046/j.1526-100X.2002.01049.x.

Rantz, S.E., 1971, Suggested criteria for hydrologic design of storm-drainage facilities in the San Francisco Bay Region, California: Menlo Park, California, U.S. Geological Survey Open-File Report, November, 69 p.

Resh, V.H., Myers, M.J., and Hannaford, M.J., 1996, Macroinvertebrates as biotic indicators of environmental quality, *in* Hauer, F.R., and Lamberti, G.A., eds., Methods in Stream Ecology: San Diego, Academic Press, p. 647–665.

Rosenberg, D.M., and Resh, V.H., eds., 1993, Freshwater Biomonitoring and Benthic Macroinvertebrates: New York, Chapman & Hall, 504 p.

Rosenberg, D.M., Resh, V.H., and King, R.S., 2008, Use of aquatic insects in biomonitoring, *in* Merritt, R.W., Cummins, K.W., and Berg, M.B., eds., An Introduction to the Aquatic Insects of North America (4th edition): Dubuque, Iowa, Kendall/Hunt, p. 87–97.

SAS Institute, 2004, JMP: The Statistical Discovery Software, version 5.1.2.

Scheuerlein, H., 1999, Morphological dynamics of step-pool systems in mountain streams and their importance for riparian ecosystems, *in* Jayawardena, A.W., Lee, J.H., and Wang, Z.Y., eds., River Sedimentation: Theory and Applications: Rotterdam, A.A. Balkema, p. 205–210.

Townsend, C.R., and Hildrew, A.G., 1994, Species traits in relation to a habitat templet for river systems: Freshwater Biology, v. 31, p. 265–275, doi: 10.1111/j.1365-2427.1994.tb01740.x.

Walsh, C.J., Fletcher, T.D., and Ladson, A.R., 2005, Stream restoration in urban catchments through redesigning stormwater systems: Looking to the catchment to save the stream: Journal of the North American Benthological Society, v. 24, p. 690–705.

Wohl, E., Angermeier, P.L., Bledsoe, B., Kondolf, G.M., MacDonnell, L., Merritt, D.M., Palmer, M.A., Poff, N.L., and Tarboton, D., 2005, River restoration: Water Resources Research, v. 41, p. W10301, doi: 10.1029/2005WR003985, doi: 10.1029/2005WR003985.

Wood, P.J., and Armitage, P.D., 1997, Biological effects of fine sediment in the lotic environment: Environmental Management, v. 21, p. 203–217, doi: 10.1007/s002679900019.

Zimmermann, A., and Church, M., 2001, Channel morphology, gradient stresses and bed profiles during flood in a step-pool channel: Geomorphology, v. 40, p. 311–327, doi: 10.1016/S0169-555X(01)00057-5.

MANUSCRIPT ACCEPTED BY THE SOCIETY 15 SEPTEMBER 2008

The Geological Society of America
Special Paper 451
2009

River restoration strategies in channelized, low-gradient landscapes of West Tennessee, USA

Douglas P. Smith*
Division of Science and Environmental Policy, California State University, Monterey Bay, Seaside, California 93955, USA

Timothy H. Diehl
U.S. Geological Survey, 640 Grassmere Park Drive, Suite 100, Nashville, Tennessee 37211, USA

Leslie A. Turrini-Smith
Earth Sciences, Monterey Peninsula College, Monterey, California 93940, USA

Jason Maas-Baldwin
Zachary Croyle
Division of Science and Environmental Policy, California State University, Monterey Bay, Seaside, California 93955, USA

ABSTRACT

West Tennessee has a complex history of watershed disturbance, including agricultural erosion, channelization, accelerated valley sedimentation, and the removal and reestablishment of beaver. Watershed management has evolved from floodplain drainage via pervasive channelization to include local drainage canal maintenance and local river restoration. Many unmaintained canals are undergoing excessive aggradation and complex channel evolution driven by upland erosion and low valley gradient.

The locus of aggradation in fully occluded canals (valley plugs) moves up-valley as sediment continues to accumulate in the backwater behind the plug. Valley plugs that cause canal avulsion can lead to redevelopment of meandering channels in less disturbed areas of the floodplain, in a process of passive self-restoration. Some valley plugs have brought restored floodplain function, reoccupation of extant historic river channels, and formation of a "sediment shadow" that protects downstream reaches from excess sedimentation. Despite the presence of numerous opportunities, there is presently no mechanism for including valley plugs in mitigation projects.

In 1997 a survey of 14 reference reach cross sections documented relations between drainage area and bankfull geometry of relatively unmodified streams in West Tennessee. Reassessment of seven of those sites in 2007 showed that one had

**douglas_smith@csumb.edu

Smith, D.P., Diehl, T.H., Turrini-Smith, L.A., Maas-Baldwin, J., and Croyle, Z., 2009, River restoration strategies in channelized, low-gradient landscapes of West Tennessee, USA, *in* James, L.A., Rathburn, S.L., and Whittecar, G.R., eds., Management and Restoration of Fluvial Systems with Broad Historical Changes and Human Impacts: Geological Society of America Special Paper 451, p. 215–229, doi: 10.1130/2009.2451(14). For permission to copy, contact editing@geosociety

been dammed by beaver and that two sites could not be analyzed further because of significant vertical or lateral instability. In contrast to other regions of North America, the results suggest that stream channels in this region flood more frequently than once each year, and can remain out of banks for several weeks each year.

INTRODUCTION

West Tennessee, between the Tennessee River divide and the Mississippi River, provides a field laboratory for understanding the post-disturbance evolution of low-gradient drainage systems. Five major regional watersheds contribute flow to the Mississippi River: the Wolf, Hatchie, Loosahatchie, Forked Deer, and Obion Rivers (Fig. 1). Historical watershed disturbance in this region includes beaver removal, deforestation, pervasive channelization, levee construction, and wetland drainage (Wolfe, 1994; Diehl,

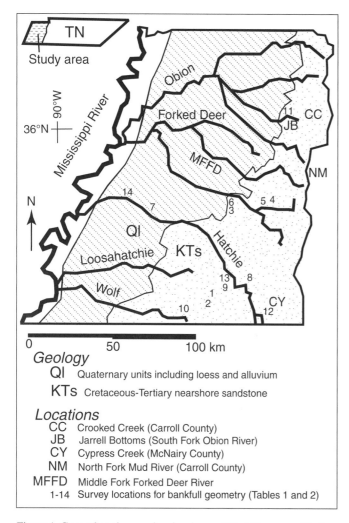

Figure 1. General geology and major rivers of West Tennessee. Eastern boundary of sandstone deposits is approximate location of Tennessee River divide. Cretaceous and Tertiary units include the Midway Group and Claiborne and Wilcox Formations. Geological contacts drawn after Greene and Wolfe (2000) and Hardeman (1966).

2000; Johnson, 2007). Within the context of steep, erodible sandy uplands, these activities have combined to generate gullies and sheetflow with attendant locally high sand loads and complex channel-valley responses, including the formation and growth of valley plugs (Happ et al., 1940; Diehl, 1994; Shields et al., 2000). This region is one of the most hydraulically altered landscapes in North America with hundreds of kilometers of drainage canals excavated in the last century to support agricultural and urban development of the low-gradient floodplains (e.g., Johnson, 2007). Channelization (*sensu* Brookes, 1988) in West Tennessee has not ended, but in the mid-1990s, watershed management goals became more complex with the addition of river and wetland restoration as competing elements of officially recognized management plans (e.g., GIWC, 1994; TN, 1994).

Human disturbance of this region, beginning with fur trapping in the late 1600s, set in motion what is essentially a long-term, large-scale experiment in fluvial landscape evolution. An understanding of the pre-EuroAmerican settlement conditions of West Tennessee is paramount for those involved in developing watershed policy here, and for those engaged in local or regional restoration projects. Just as important to future management is an understanding of the geometry and dynamics of extant relatively unmodified stream-floodplain systems in the region. The existing institutional paradigm of restoring only single-thread channels in this region may be flawed if "natural" (i.e., "presettlement") conditions are the goal of restoration.

Geologic Setting

West Tennessee lies in the Coastal Plain geomorphic province of the Mississippi Embayment (Miller, 1974). The surface stratigraphy includes three main units (Fig. 1): (1) westward-dipping, poorly consolidated Upper Cretaceous and lower Tertiary sandy, pericoastal deposits exposed in the uplands; (2) Quaternary loess that forms thick deposits in the west and pinches out eastward; and (3) Quaternary alluvium in the valley bottoms (Miller et al., 1966; Miller, 1974). The regional physiography can be generalized as dissected rolling hills in the east that give way to low-gradient rivers in broad-floored valleys in the west. The westernmost edge of West Tennessee includes the floodplain and bounding bluffs of the Mississippi River. Digital elevation analysis shows that the landscape gradient rapidly decreases from 0.10 in the headwater streams to 0.0007 between the eastern uplands and the bounding bluffs of the Mississippi floodplain. Although West Tennessee lies in a mid-plate setting, neotectonic warping along the New Madrid Fault zone and Reelfoot Rift has produced pervasive basin asymmetry within the Mississippi Embayment (Cox et al., 2001; Garrote et al., 2006; Csontos et al., 2008) and may play a subtle role in reducing fluvial gradients in West Tennessee by eastward tilting of basement rocks.

Historical Watershed Disturbance

West Tennessee has a complex history of human disturbance. Lacking natural predators, beaver were no doubt ubiquitous in this region ca. 1700 (Nairne, 1988). West Tennessee valleys with drainage areas perhaps as large as 160 km² would have been pervasively dammed, ponded, and locally aggrading. Each dam would have inundated large areas of the valley floor, as they do in areas without beaver management today (Houston et al., 1995). Fur trapping after 1700 greatly reduced beaver abundance (Grabau, 2007, personal commun.). By the Chickasaw Cession of 1816, the streams may have still been adjusting to the loss of beaver. Without beaver dams to control grade, streams probably incised and developed knickpoints that cut headward, possibly extending drainage networks farther into erodible upland soils (Grabau, 2007). Crockett (1834) depicts the main branches of the Obion River as debris-choked and subject to prolonged valley-wide flooding, supporting the idea that accelerated upland erosion was active at that time.

Early economic development of West Tennessee included logging and agriculture on steep, sandy hillslopes. By the mid-1800s, upland erosion from agriculture was contributing to sediment deposition over formerly fertile bottomland (Hilgard, 1860). Widespread channelization in the 1900s was a response to the effects of this upland agricultural erosion (Ashley, 1910; Morgan and McCrory, 1910). Institutional efforts to drain the landscape and to relieve flooding through channelization and levees began in 1909 with the formation of "levee and drainage districts":

… the County Court of any county in this State is hereby vested with the jurisdiction, power, and authority at any regular, special, or adjourned session to establish a drainage district or districts, and to locate and establish levees, and cause to be constructed, as hereinafter provided, any levee, ditch, drain, or watercourse, or to straighten, widen, deepen, or change any natural watercourse in such county, or provide for the same being done whenever the same will be of public utility or conducive to the public health or welfare and as hereby provided. (Private Acts, 2004, p. 24)

Most of the region was channelized by such districts, except for the largest rivers. Pervasive channelization of the drainage networks had the effect of increasing sediment yield to downstream reaches through post-channelization channel adjustment, as has happened more recently (e.g., Simon and Robbins, 1987; Simon, 1989a, 1989b, 1994). In response, the Federal Flood Control Act of 1948 was passed to improve flood control and drainage on 360 km of the West Tennessee tributaries to the Mississippi River (e.g., USCA, 2007) in an effort called the West Tennessee Tributaries Project (WTTP). Large-scale dredging peaked in Tennessee in the 1960s, when the U.S. Army Corps of Engineers (USACE) channelized the largest reaches of the Obion and Forked Deer Rivers. In 1959 the Obion–Forked Deer Basin Authority (OFDBA) was formed to maintain the flood capacity of the planned WTTP canals and all preexisting canals in the region (Private Acts, 2007).

In response to post-1970 federal environmental laws, the language of West Tennessee watershed management policy gradually shifted to include wetland restoration and preservation in addition to drainage. A federal court halted WTTP channelization because of an inadequate environmental impact report (TN, 1994; USACE, 1996; USCA, 2007), and the USACE agreed to purchase 12,950 ha of mitigation lands to compensate for the negative impacts of channelization (TN, 1994). Since that time, both permitted and nonpermitted dredging and lower-impact efforts (IAFWA, 1983) have been used to keep the canals functioning for flood control. By the 1990s, State environmental policy language clearly expressed the value of wetlands and acknowledged the ecological value of natural streams (GIWC, 1994). The mission of the OFDBA changed in 1996 from flood control through channelization to restoration of natural flood conveyance, and it was renamed the West Tennessee River Basin Authority (WTRBA) (USCA, 2007). The nascent WTRBA was empowered with the authority to "restore where practicable, in a self-sustaining manner, natural stream and floodplain dynamics and associated environmental and economic benefits" (USCA, 2007). The most recent watershed activities include a mixture of canal maintenance, canal decommissioning, and channel restoration. A range of river and wetland restoration designs, philosophies, and technologies are in use.

Current Problems in Stream Restoration in West Tennessee

A clear intent to improve environmental conditions and habitat in West Tennessee streams has been publicly documented (GIWC, 1994; TN, 1994; USCA, 2007; TSMP, 2007). Several key issues, however, constrain the potential for successful, long-term stream restoration. A realistic set of regional strategies, goals, and success criteria has not yet been agreed upon in the regulatory or resource-management communities (e.g., TDEC, 2004; Johnson, 2007; Paine, 2007). Reference reaches used to design or assess restoration projects are rare. Mitigation goals typically focus on reach-scale restoration (e.g., TSMP, 2007) rather than ecosystem-scale management or regional conservation. Excess sediment, large woody debris, and beaver activity continue to pose significant threats to restored stream reaches. The potential role of valley plugs and avulsion in restoration-conservation efforts has not been fully explored (Smith and Diehl, 2002).

In this paper we present a summary of bankfull geometry of relatively unmodified streams; give examples of restoration in West Tennessee, including unintentional large-scale self-restoration and intentional reach-scale restoration; and provide a discussion of research needs to improve restoration success and sustainability.

METHODS

The descriptions and conclusions presented in this paper are based on analysis of published and unpublished data. Data include U.S. Geological Survey (USGS) topographic maps, geologic maps, high-resolution aerial photography, digital elevation models, repeated cross-sectional surveys, and reconnaissance surveys by foot and small craft of disturbed, recovering, restored, and relatively unmodified fluvial systems in West Tennessee. The field and laboratory data, not all presented here, were collected in numerous visits to the region between 1996 and 2007. Partial data sets and results have been presented in various conference proceedings (e.g., Smith and Diehl, 2000, 2002), technical reports commissioned by the U.S. Environmental Protection Agency (e.g., Smith and Turrini-Smith, 1999a, 1999b), Tennessee Department of Environment (e.g., Smith and Rosgen, 1998; Smith, 1999) and nongovernmental organizations interested in natural resource protection (e.g., Smith, 2007).

Bankfull Geometry of Unmodified Channels

In 1997 we surveyed the bankfull geometry of 14 rivers in West Tennessee to evaluate and guide stream assessment and restoration efforts. Survey data are presented in Smith and Turrini-Smith (1999a, 1999b). An initial list of potential survey sites was generated from published ecoregion reference sites (e.g., Arnwine et al., 2000), map and aerial photographic analysis, and previous field experience. Sites were then eliminated if the watershed or local reach was significantly modified, as determined by site visit or map analysis. From the remaining sites, a single cross section was surveyed within a straight reach of channel, provided there were no obvious geomorphic signs of chronic bank erosion, aggradation, or degradation. Surveys were conducted where bankfull indicators were locally present, the channel geometry was not complicated by excess woody debris, and the morphology appeared typical of the reach. The cross-section surveys generally included 50–75 survey points tied to at least one, but usually two, benchmarks, except for Cypress Creek at Howell-Buntin Road, where no benchmarks were placed. The surveys typically include the bankfull channel, the natural levee system, and a significant width of floodplain on at least one side of the channel. The dominant particle size (e.g., silt-clay, sand, gravel) was recorded. A boat with an electronic or physical depth finder was used for surveying unwadable rivers.

Bankfull geometry was chosen to represent the stage at which the water would flow to the adjacent valley bottom, or, in the case of Harris Creek, the incipient floodplain. Bankfull elevation was selected either at the clear break in slope between channel and floodplain or at the elevation of the backswamp beyond natural levees. Seven of the surveyed sites were revisited and visually assessed in September 2007.

Our scope and methods biased us toward sites with single-thread channels within a few minutes' walk or boat ride from access roads. In no case was bankfull geometry chosen from an existing analysis of flood-recurrence interval, eliminating one potential source of bias in geomorphic analysis. Except in the case of Harris Creek, which is an incised stream, the sites were typically in aggrading valley bottoms.

Valley Plug Evolution in Low-Gradient Valleys

Our description of valley plug evolution as one mode of canal failure, and the consequent processes of passive self-restoration, stem from several sources, including extant literature, aerial photography, USGS topographic maps (1:24,000 scale), and fieldwork. Happ et al. (1940) provided a detailed examination of the physical processes in low-gradient canals of the region. Our ideas on this topic evolved from numerous field trips to the region, including various combinations of surveys, small-craft traverses, foot traverses, and both fixed-wing and helicopter reconnaissance flights. Aerial photographs used to analyze valley plug evolution include Tennessee Department of Transportation (TDOT) black-and-white photographs from various years between 1979 and 2003, and at various scales ranging between 1:40,000 and 1:24,000, and digital imagery from TDOT at various resolutions. We also used digital black-and-white images of various scales downloaded from the USGS orthoquad series (USGS, 2008). The schematic maps of valley plugs presented in this paper were created by combining our field observations with feature tracings from recent digital black-and-white aerial photographs.

Review of Restoration Strategies

Descriptions of intentional restoration projects have been gathered through site visits, review of web-based literature (TSMP, 2007), and participation in design reviews (e.g., Smith and Rosgen, 1998) and project designs.

GEOMETRY OF RELATIVELY UNMODIFED CHANNELS

Ideally, naturally formed alluvial streams that have fully adjusted their geometry to existing watershed conditions would be selected as reference reaches for research, assessment, and restoration design (Leopold and Maddock, 1953; Emmett, 1975; Dunne and Leopold, 1978; Hey, 2006; Rosgen, 2006). Unfortunately, pervasive watershed alteration and channelization have left no fully natural streams in West Tennessee. The Hatchie and Wolf Rivers have long unchannelized reaches, but both streams are affected by excess sediment from a great number of channelized tributaries (Diehl, 1994, 2000). The bankfull geometry of 14 relatively unmodified streams is provided in Tables 1 and 2. These sites include several unchannelized reaches and one river that has reestablished an unconfined, sinuous channel following canal avulsion. Each of the stream channels, except for Harris Creek, which is moderately entrenched, is situated within a broad, frequently flooded valley.

TABLE 1. BANKFULL CROSS-SECTIONAL GEOMETRY FOR RELATIVELY UNMODIFIED STREAMS OF WEST TENNESSEE

ID	Name	DA (km²)*	Area (m²)	Width (m)	Depth (m)[†]	Bed material	Channel type[§]
1	Marshall Creek at Van Buren Rd.	15	2	5	0.4	Sand	E5/C5
2	West Fork Spring Creek at Van Buren Rd.	36	10	9	1.1	Sand	E5
3	Cypress Creek at Howell Buntin Rd.	43	7	6	1.2	Mud	E6
4	Spencer Creek at Hammlett Rd.	46	7	9	0.8	Mud	E6
5	Harris Creek above Potts Chapel Rd.	46	11	10	1.1	Sand	E5
6	Cypress Creek at Lower Brownsville Rd.	57	14	11	1.3	Sand-mud	E5/E6
7	Lagoon Creek near Estes Rd.	96	15	10	1.5	Mud	E6
8	Little Hatchie Creek above Powell Chapel Rd.	215	32	18	1.8	Sand	E5
9	Spring Creek at Sain Rd.	300	15	13	1.1	Sand	E5/C5
10	Wolf River at La Grange	510	25	14	1.8	Sand-mud	E5/E6
11	South Fork Obion River at Jarrell Bottoms	770	22	19	1.2	Mud?	C
12	Hatchie River at Pocahontas	2150	96	32	3.0	Mud?	E6
13	Hatchie below Bolivar	3790	119	60	2.0	Sand	C5
14	Hatchie at Rialto	5910	132	40	3.3	Sand	C5

Note: Data from Turrini-Smith et al. (2000). See Figure 1 for general location.
*DA—drainage area for cross section.
[†]Depth—area/width.
[§]Level II stream classification from Rosgen (1994). Streams near the border of two types are given two classes.

TABLE 2. DESCRIPTION OF SITES LISTED IN TABLE 1

ID	Name of site surveyed in 1997	Reconnaissance notes on or before Sept. 2007
1	Marshall Creek at Van Buren Rd.	Ponded by beaver dam before March 2007
2	West Fork Spring Creek at Van Buren Rd.	Not visited
3	Cypress Creek at Howell Buntin Rd.	Low bed load because site is located downstream from valley plug; site appeared stable
4	Spencer Creek at Hammlett Rd.	Not visited
5	Harris Creek above Potts Chapel Rd.	Rapid bank erosion left several centimeters of erosion pins exposed; 9 cm of deposition on benchmarks; bedrock influence
6	Cypress Creek at Lower Brownsville Rd.	5 cm of deposition on benchmarks; wood accumulation dam located upstream from site; located downstream from valley plug
7	Lagoon Creek near Estes Rd.	Not visited
8	Little Hatchie Creek above Powell Chapel Rd.	3 cm of deposition on benchmarks; site appears unchanged
9	Spring Creek at Sain Rd.	3 cm of deposition on benchmarks; cross-section site stable because of cypress knees; site no longer characteristic of reach, which has widened; several tributaries have valley plugs
10	Wolf River at La Grange	3 cm of deposition on benchmarks; site appeared stable; located downstream from valley plug
11	South Fork Obion River at Jarrell Bottoms	Not visited in 2007 (within valley plug system)
12	Hatchie River at Pocahontas	Not visited in 2007 (located below valley plugs)
13	Hatchie below Bolivar	Not visited
14	Hatchie at Rialto	Not visited

Determination of bankfull stage represented our best assessment of the point of incipient flooding of the adjacent broad valley floor or backswamp without prior knowledge of stage recurrence interval. Lowland streams in this region flood the valley floor more frequently than annually, and the larger channels are commonly out of banks for several weeks at a time, so there was little risk of misidentifying a terrace as bankfull elevation. For example, USGS hydrologic data and field surveys indicate that the Hatchie River at Rialto, Tennessee, has a bankfull discharge of ~150 m³/s (Fig. 2). Based upon the most recent 40 yr of record, 200 m³/s is exceeded ~14% of the days in the record, or 50 d/yr on average (Fig. 3). The Log-Pearson type III return period for bankfull discharge at this site is 1.02 yr, but the river floods more frequently than once each year, illustrating the limits of using Log-Pearson type III analysis of annual flood series data to assess return periods of frequent flows (e.g., Dunne and Leopold, 1978). This gauge is representative of other gauges in the region.

In September 2007, 10 yr after the original survey, we revisited 7 of the 14 surveyed sites (Table 2). All seven sites had clear indicators of floodplain inundation, and most had several centimeters of floodplain sediment covering benchmark caps. Of the seven revisited sites, one is now a beaver pond, one has excessive erosion and is bedrock influenced, one is stable only because of the strength of the knee of a local tupelo tree, and four appeared relatively unchanged on the basis of site photos and memory (Table 2). Figures 4 and 5 provide the bankfull geometric plots of the remaining 12 sites, with Harris Creek and Spring Creek removed. Elimination of these two creeks did not significantly change the equations relating drainage geometry to drainage area, and R² values slightly improved.

Hidinger and Morgan (1912) surveyed cross sections on the Hatchie River in comparable locations with this study (Figs. 4, 5). Although we cannot directly compare cross-section sites, we note that the river channel appears to have decreased in depth by a few meters and has lost cross-sectional area over the 85 yr since 1912 (Fig. 4). Widths have been steady over the same period (Fig. 5). Recent shoaling of the Hatchie River was quantified by

Diehl (2000). Alternatively, the Hatchie River may have remained stable for 85 yr, given that the same data differences would have resulted if Hidinger and Morgan (1912) had used the natural levee tops as bankfull, rather than the local points of incipient flooding (sporadic swales eroded through natural levees), in their geometric calculations.

In contrast to unmodified streams, the channelized rivers (drainage canals) of West Tennessee are straight, earthen drainage canals with levees or spoil on one or both sides (Fig. 6). First- and second-order streams typically terminate upstream in the weak sandy bedrock underlying the eastern rolling hills. Gullying and headward extension of the first-order channels in response to channelization, cultivation, and deforestation increases the sand yield to the low gradient trunk streams (Happ et al., 1940; Simon, 1989a; Diehl, 1994). An example of a longitudinal profile of one headwater stream of the Obion River shows headwater gradients ranging from 0.06 to 0.12, but then abruptly flattening to a slope of ~0.0003 (Fig. 7). This break in slope, where sediment-laden headwater streams terminate on a flat floodplain, is a typical place for high sedimentation rates, trunk stream occlusion, and valley plug growth (Happ et al., 1940).

CHANNEL EVOLUTION OF VALLEY PLUGS AND PASSIVE RESTORATION

Happ et al. (1940) coined the term *valley plug* to describe the processes and deposits resulting from an occluded canal or stream channel. The term is widely applicable in West Tennessee, where high sediment and debris yield have led to canal blockages in numerous places in all the major river basins. Valley plugs commonly result from excess sand load where channel flow is impaired. The sand originates in eroded uplands and tributary fans. Flow impairment can be initiated by beavers, large wood accumulations, or poorly drained road and railway crossings. In

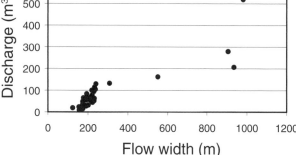

Figure 2. Hydraulic geometry for the Hatchie River at Rialto (U.S. Highway 51 bridge). Abrupt increase in width as discharge rise is indication of incipient flooding at a discharge of ~150 m³/s.

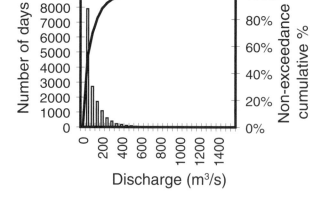

Figure 3. Left scale is number of days of flow in 40 yr of daily average series data at Hatchie River at Rialto stream gauge. Right scale is percentage of non-exceedance cumulative frequency, showing that 150 m³/s is not exceeded on ~86% of the days of record (is exceeded on 14% of the days).

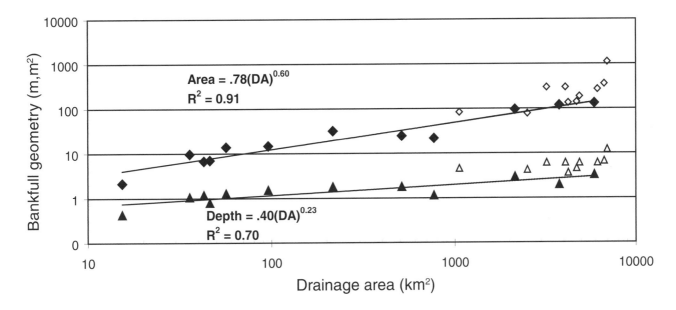

Figure 4. Bankfull cross-sectional area and average depth of select streams and rivers of West Tennessee (Table 1). Data shown by open symbols are from Hidinger and Morgan (1912). DA—drainage area; R^2—coefficient of determination in the power function modeling bankfull geometry from drainage area.

most cases, once the canal is plugged, the valley bottom becomes perennially ponded, killing the bottomland forest and leaving an open marsh environment. The upstream end of the plug can grow upstream through sediment deposition in ponded water. As aggradation continues, the valley bottom may become dry enough to support bottomland hardwood forests.

Many evolutionary pathways are possible in the valley bottom, once a valley plug forms (Happ et al., 1940; Smith and Diehl, 2002). Some of these pathways passively lead to a self-restored river-floodplain system that reoccupies the floodplain adjacent to an occluded canal. We describe two self-restored river reaches below. A theme in these two examples is that a valley plug can effectively decommission a canal and trap excess sediment. Trapping sediment has two effects—aggrading the valley bottom of

swamped valleys to a point where hardwoods can exist, and providing a "sediment shadow" that reduces sand transport and deposition downstream from the plug. The time required for passive self-restoration to occur can vary from nearly instantaneous, where avulsed flow leads directly to an extant relict channel, to decades, where avulsed flow reoccupies a part of the floodplain where no relict pre-channelization channels exist.

Cypress Creek (McNairy County)

Recent aerial photography (TDOT, 1979–2004) showing relict channel features indicates that Cypress Creek (Fig. 8) was once a single-thread, low-gradient (0.0001), sinuous (k = 1.9) stream. The creek probably had a sand bed and a broad (2 km), forested

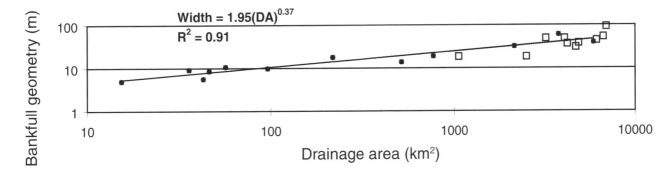

Figure 5. Bankfull cross-sectional width of select streams and rivers of West Tennessee (Table 1). Data shown by open symbols are from Hidinger and Morgan (1912). DA—drainage area; R^2—coefficient of determination in the power function modeling bankfull geometry from drainage area.

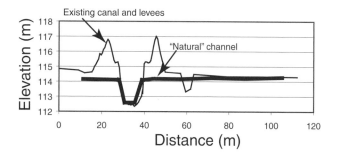

Figure 6. Cross-sectional survey of leveed canal (light line) of Crooked Creek (Carroll County), several hundred meters downstream from State Highway 77 bridge. Heavy line is a trapezoidal superimposition representing the approximate geometry of a natural stream having the same drainage area as indicated by analysis of data in Table 2.

floodplain. Beginning early in the twentieth century, channelization and straightening of Cypress Creek and many of its tributaries allowed agricultural and urban encroachment on the Cypress Creek floodplain. It is likely that accelerated upland erosion and incised tributaries delivered the voluminous sand load and large woody debris that have chronically impaired the Cypress Creek canal. Although the complete history of canal occlusion is not known, local blockages are visible in a 1979 aerial photograph. By 1999 the blockages had grown to form a 2.1-km-long debris jam (38,000 m^3) that forced most of the flow from the canal onto the right floodplain through a well-developed crevasse-splay sys-

tem (Fig. 8). Boat and foot reconnaissance between 1999 and 2003 documented the flow paths shown in Figure 8. After leaving the canal, water flowed ~750 m laterally across the floodplain in numerous distributary channels toward the topographic low of the valley bottom and then turned to flow down the valley axis (Fig. 8). Flow alternately reoccupied reaches with anastamosing small channels and remnant channels of pre-channelized Cypress Creek. Between 1992 and 2003 (Fig. 8) the head of the canal blockage had episodically migrated up-valley at an average rate of 200 m/yr.

Although there has been no human effort to restore this disturbed valley bottom, a new riverine system has naturally evolved to have many of the characteristics of a "restored" river. A key component of the restoration is sediment management. The excess sand is trapped at the head of the system in the crevasse splay (Fig. 8), which provides a sediment shadow for the channel reaches downstream. Some of the fine sediment settles out in relative calm water that ponds as the water turns from lateral to axial flow at the toe of the crevasse splay. The water exiting the 5.6-km-long "self-restored" reach is free of sand and has improved clarity compared with the water entering the reach. The self-restored channel-floodplain system grew to at least 2.5 km in length before nonpermitted dredging cleared the canal and caused abandonment of the crevasse system in 2006.

Jarrell Bottoms (South Fork Obion River)

The South Fork Obion River at Jarrell Bottoms (Figs. 1, 9) historically flowed in a sinuous, single-thread river channel that

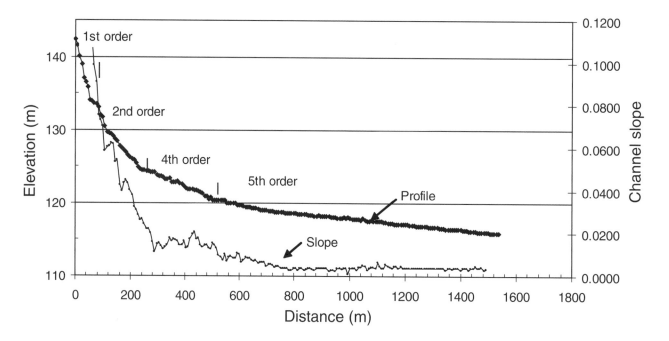

Figure 7. Longitudinal profile and slope of a typical low-order stream system in the Obion River system (Fig. 1). Strahler stream order shown. Data derived from modified-resolution digital elevation model.

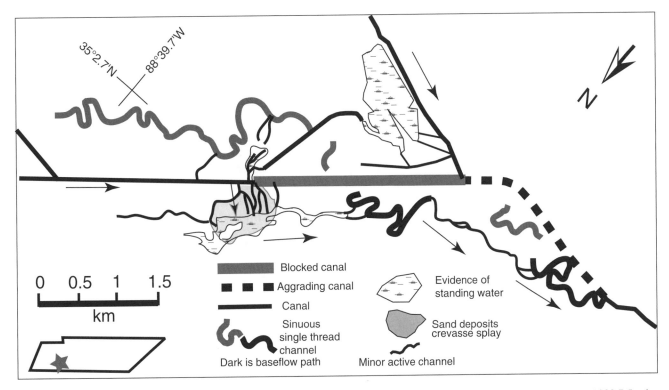

Figure 8. Map of Cypress Creek (McNairy County) as it appeared in a 2003 aerial photograph. Some details derived from a 1983 7.5-min U.S. Geological Survey topographic map and from foot and canoe traverses. Arrows show main water-flow paths at baseflow conditions. See Figure 1 for location.

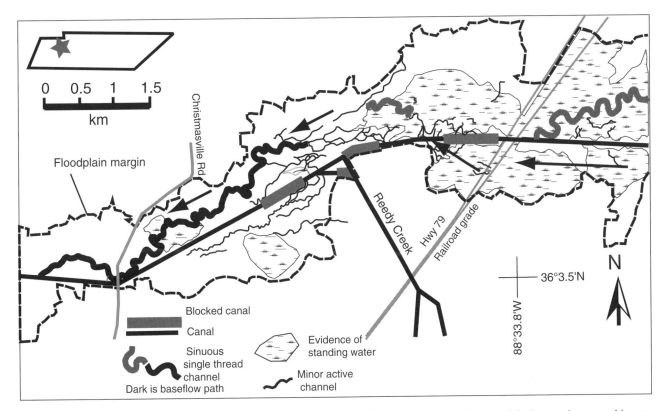

Figure 9. Map of Jarrell Bottoms valley plug system on South Fork Obion River. Details derived from aerial-photo and topographic-map interpretation and canoe traverses. Arrows show main water-flow paths at baseflow conditions. Three blockages on canal are named upper, middle, and lower, from right to left. See Figure 1 for location.

occupied a 1- to 2-km-wide forested floodplain. Channelization and levee construction isolated flow from the natural channel and floodplain. The South Fork Obion River canal is now occluded in three places at Jarrell Bottoms, and flow has been naturally restored to a long reach of pre-channelized river channel (Diehl, 1997; Fig. 9). A reach of that reoccupied channel was selected for a reference reach survey (site 11 of Table 1).

The South Fork Obion River canal was first blocked by excess sediment from Reedy Creek (Fig. 9). The canal avulsed upstream from that blockage, and the canal has remained blocked upstream from Reedy Creek (middle blockage of Fig. 9). A new bypass canal was excavated to reattach the mouth of Reedy Creek to the South Fork Obion River canal at a point farther west than the first (Fig. 9). The original Reedy Creek canal was then re-excavated after the bypass filled in with sediment (Fig. 9). Renewed sediment from Reedy Creek then occluded the South Fork Obion River canal downstream from the mouth of the bypass (lower blockage of Fig. 9). The third occlusion (upper blockage of Fig. 9) formed just downstream from the railroad bridge and adjacent U.S. Highway 79 bridge.

The valley plug system is now 5.8 km long, located between U.S. Highway 79 and Christmasville Road (Fig. 9). Excess sediment entering the system from the South Fork Obion River canal is trapped in a 200-m-long delta downstream from the Highway 79 bridge. Excess sediment from Reedy Creek is filling the South Fork Obion River canal at the head of the lower blockage (Figs. 9, 10) and is forming crevasse-splay deposits downstream from numerous avulsion channels (Figs. 9, 10). Downstream from these sediment shadows the South Fork Obion River occupies a network of anastamosing channels that gradually coalesce into a single-thread, meandering channel in the floodplain north of the mouth of Reedy Creek. The South Fork follows ~4 km of its natural channel from that point to Christmasville Road. Just

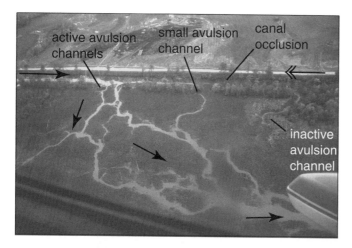

Figure 10. Oblique aerial photograph of part of Jarrell Bottoms, showing avulsion channels upstream from the lower blockage (Fig. 11). View is toward south. Arrows show base-flow water pathways. Double-headed arrow indicates apparent migration direction of upstream end of occlusion. Image width is ~250 m.

downstream from Christmasville Road, most flow reenters the canal through a short cutoff that has formed since 1991. Road crossings strongly influence self-restored systems because they typically have only one or two major openings, sometimes directing restored channel flow back to a canal.

The depth of the reestablished main channel is adequate for small boats, even during summer low flow. Hunters and fishermen maintain a boat trail passable by canoes and johnboats through most of Jarrell Bottoms by cutting small gaps in drift that blocks the dominant channel. In multiple-channel reaches, these gaps concentrate flow in the deepest channel. Boat-trail maintenance is contributing to the reestablishment of a single main channel throughout Jarrell Bottoms.

INTENTIONAL RESTORATION DESIGNS AND PROJECTS

In the 1990s watershed-management policy shifted to include valuing wetland and floodplain restoration (Johnson, 2007). These efforts have included a range of ideas including a 24-km-long dual-channel system, natural channel design using rock and wood structures, and simple augmentation of self-restoration processes. We provide an example of each of these approaches.

Dual-Channel Restoration for Low-Gradient Channels (Middle Fork of Forked Deer River)

The Middle Fork Forked Deer River (Fig. 1) prior to channelization had a sinuous course within a wide floodplain (Fig. 11). Drainage districts dug long, straight canals in the floodplain following the 1909 Drainage Act (Private Acts, 2004). The WTTP included plans for enlarging the Middle Fork Forked Deer canals, but the WTTP dredging was halted before that part of the work began. In 1992, Tennessee requested that the WTTP be reformulated to embody "environmentally sensitive" ways to "reduce flood damage, reduce erosion, restore floodplain integrity, and improve water quality" (TN, 1994). One of several locations where this new approach would be tried was the Middle Fork Forked Deer River canal (Fig. 11).

In response to the reformulated WTTP, the USACE produced a restoration design for 24 km of the Middle Fork Forked Deer River that included a two-part system. One part was a sinuous "bankfull" channel that would generally follow the extant remnant meanders and probable path of the historic river channel (Fig. 11; USACE, 1996; Doeing et al., 1996). This "bankfull" channel was to mimic the natural functions and benefits of the historic channel (USACE, 1996). The second part was an improved canal system in the place of the existing canal (Fig. 11). The two systems would intersect at six places, where 1.1-m-tall concrete weirs would deflect baseflow, up to 8.5 m³/s, into the historic meanders. The canals were proposed to carry floodwater in excess of that diverted to the meandering channels.

Smith and Rosgen (1998) pointed out a number of flaws in the proposed plan. Design problems included an undersized and disproportionate "bankfull channel" (Fig. 12), a large uncertainty about bed load and large woody debris accumulation where flow separation occurs at the 90° channel intersections, and a large, in-canal sediment basin that would require 10 clean-outs per year. Smith and Rosgen (1998) also pointed out that high-stage flow conveyance was impossible in a leveed canal that repeatedly intersects a smaller river that has low banks. The plan was not implemented.

Incised Headwater Channel Restoration (North Fork Mud Creek)

The Tennessee Stream Mitigation Program (TSMP, 2007) is a nonprofit organization created in 2002 to enhance or restore impaired streams. This program has completed several restoration projects in West Tennessee using principles of natural channel design (Rosgen, 2006). This program is the main mitigation program for the Tennessee Department of Transportation, so it will be the chief purveyor of restoration activities in Tennessee into the foreseeable future. We provide a description of North Fork Mud Creek (Fig. 1; Carroll County), as a sample of river-restoration practices employing natural channel design with hard structures for incised headwater channels. Although the project lies a few kilometers east of the Tennessee River divide (Fig. 1), its physical setting and geologic context are identical to headwater streams west of the divide, where our studies have focused.

The North Fork Mud Creek project, completed in December 2006, includes 4.3 km of constructed channel along first- and second-order streams leading to Big Sandy Creek. The preexisting conditions included a deeply incised creek channel with tall, failing banks of weak sandstone (Fig. 13). Restoration techniques on most of the site employed "priority-two" restoration techniques of Rosgen (1997). The restored system is a sinuous, riffle-pool channel with a narrow floodplain bounded by tall terraces (Fig. 14). Rock and log structures are incorporated throughout the project for grade control, hydraulic roughness, and habitat diversity. For example, most straight reaches include cobble and pebble rock riffle constructed of angular limestone. While wood is a common component of local rivers, hard rock such as limestone is unknown in the region. Natural rock riffles are dynamic features constructed by the temporary residence of gravel that is gradually transported downstream and renewed from sources

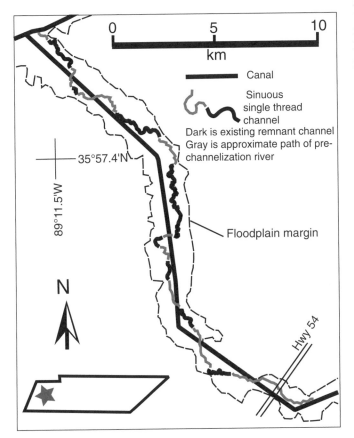

Figure 11. Proposed restoration of 27 km of Middle Fork Forked Deer River. Map based on USACE (1996) data.

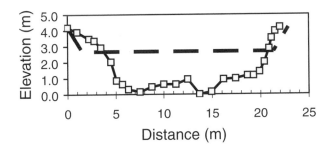

Figure 12. Proposed natural channel design for the Middle Fork Forked Deer River (dashed trapezoid; USACE, 1996) compared with river channel size-scaled from regional studies of bankfull geometry (Smith and Rosgen, 1998; Table 1).

Figure 13. Incised stream typical of North Fork Mud Creek before restoration. Photo site is 30 m downstream from restoration site. Right bank height is ~2.5 m tall (September 2007).

upstream. If the North Fork Mud Creek riffles are also dynamic features, they will eventually disappear through transport or burial by sand, which is the native bed load in the region.

Natural Channel Design for Low-Gradient Channels (Crooked Creek, Carroll County)

The Carroll County Watershed Authority was required to design and construct several kilometers of new sinuous stream channel as mitigation for a new 395 ha reservoir constructed for recreation and improved county tax basis (CCWA, 2000). The mitigation project will decommission several kilometers of functioning Crooked Creek drainage canal, and will redirect flow to a newly excavated sinuous channel within a broad floodplain historically used for corn and other agriculture. The design is complete, and construction will occur over 2 yr, starting in 2008. The new channel of Crooked Creek (Fig. 1) will drain a 72 km² watershed. The chief goal of the new channel is frequent flooding and draining of the broad floodplain in support of new wetlands and bottomland forest that will be cultivated there. In advance of channel design, a new USGS stage gauge was installed just upstream from the site, 12 shallow groundwater-monitoring wells were installed, and the site was surveyed in detail.

The channel size (Fig. 6) and planform were derived from a subset of the regional reference reaches (sites 1, 2, 6, and 8 of Table 1), local historic remnant channels, and one-dimensional hydraulic modeling. The reference sites were selected because they match the conditions of the Crooked Creek setting in several ways: They are sand-transporting streams not located in the sediment shadow of a valley plug; they have bed material of similar size; and they span the appropriate drainage area. Coincidentally, the design channel depth derived from the reference stream data is the deepest that can exist between the vertical constraints imposed by the existing floodplain (channel top) and the grade of

Figure 14. Typical section of newly constructed channel on North Fork Mud Creek, several months after construction during baseflow conditions (September 2007).

the canal (channel bottom) to which the new channel must connect in two places. The only way to achieve a larger channel that maintains the width-to-depth ratio of reference streams would be to import an enormous volume of sediment to raise the floodplain or to construct continuous levees, which would counter the goal of floodplain function. The last 25% of new channel will be less deep than the rest because the landscape drops in elevation as compared with the canal where the new channel must connect. We anticipate floodplain aggradation along the entire site, especially in the last 25% of the project.

Reach-scale restoration efforts may be problematic if excess sand is entering the system from disturbed drainage basins. Although sediment transport was not directly measured in the canal upstream from the project area, helicopter, field, and canoe reconnaissance, and aerial photographic evidence, suggest that the Crooked Creek watershed is not a chronic source of excess sediment. Independent evidence for relatively low perennial sediment yield is that the drainage canal, which was constructed in 1915, has required no re-dredging (David Salyers, West Tennessee River Basin Authority, 2007, personal commun.). Thus, the canal is one geometric solution that is in steady-state equilibrium. The design channel has roughly the same geometry as the canal, if the canal levees were removed (Fig. 6). Bed-load transport modeling (Ackers and White, 1973) of well-sorted 0.29 mm sand confirms that the design channel capacity will be similar to the canal capacity in flows up to bankfull. Gauge analysis shows that bankfull conditions will be exceeded several times each year. Such conditions will lead to floodplain aggradation, which is beneficial, given the low relative elevation of the valley bottom. However, frequent sand deposition on the valley floor may pose a challenge to young trees planted during restoration. Monitoring will determine if valley-bottom aggradation should precede forest replanting.

It has been stated that hard structures are used in stream design to give riparian vegetation a chance to become established as the primary protection from bank erosion. A unique aspect of the Crooked Creek project is that flows will not be introduced to the channel for at least 1 yr after construction. Densely planted riparian woody species and grasses will have a year or more to mature into bank-stabilizing thickets before flow is fully avulsed from the canal. Large woody debris will be gradually recruited from upstream and stream-side sources.

Ditching and Levee Breaching for Low-Gradient Channels (Middle Fork of Forked Deer River at Law Road)

When drainage canals fill and fail to drain the land, farms get flooded, and landowners occasionally attempt to improve drainage. Anecdotal evidence, combined with reconnaissance fieldwork, can sometimes reveal the effects of these landowner projects. When the Middle Fork Forked Deer River drainage canal became occluded by sediment near Law Road, the landowner excavated a small ditch to redirect the flow from the canal to a nearby remnant meander of the historic river channel. This pilot channel enlarged and became the primary base-flow channel. So, with little effort, this landowner inadvertently augmented self-restoration of this river system. The restored reach is >1 km long and is functioning at this writing.

DISCUSSION

West Tennessee has a long history of watershed disturbance, culminating in pervasive channelization commencing in 1909. In keeping with contradictions in wetland policy at the federal level (Votteler and Muir, 1996), the policy juxtaposition of canal maintenance and stream restoration in West Tennessee provides a complex setting for modern watershed managers.

The term *restoration* has many possible working definitions. One definition is the restoration of a site to a preconceived ideal of the fluvial landscape that would be present in the absence of human disturbance (e.g., Wohl and Merritts, 2007). In keeping with that philosophy, Tennessee stream mitigation guidelines require contractors to "return the channel to its most probable natural state, given the individual local constraints of the project location and watershed conditions" (TDEC, 2004). In pre-European West Tennessee, as now, the most probable natural state of much of the landscape is arguably a beaver pond. If restoration of "natural conditions" were the goal for West Tennessee streams, then the practice of beaver eradication would have to cease (e.g., Houston et al., 1995). After a few decades of this ecosystem-based management strategy, the valleys with drainage areas <~160 km^2 might resemble our view of the pre-European regional setting: forested, locally ponded, slowly aggrading valleys. The sediment shadow downstream from beaver populations would reduce sediment impacts on larger single-thread streams that are too big for beaver to dam. In current practice, however, beaver are considered pests and a threat to restoration projects; a beaver pond would be deemed a failed restoration project.

River restoration in West Tennessee ranges from unmanaged canal avulsion to precisely constructed pool-riffle reaches employing imported rock (e.g., North Fork Mud Creek). The immediate results of these activities include canal decommissioning, reestablishing floodplain function and bottomland forest, sediment control (valley plugs), habitat improvement, erosion control (e.g., North Fork Mud Creek), and improved conditions for hunting and fishing. Given the range of "treatments" being applied to the landscape, we can view the region as a site of long-term, large-scale experiments in landscape evolution. The knowledge gained will depend on the quality of the descriptions of the pretreatment conditions, restoration activities, post-restoration monitoring, and the presence of controls for comparison. It is hoped that the results will eventually contribute to sustainable restoration efforts whose cumulative effects will reverse environmental damage. Realizing such benefits, however, will require publication of both successful and failed restoration attempts in a variety of local settings.

Two areas of concern for channel-restoration projects include flood-frequency analysis and excess sediment. The low-gradient valley bottoms of West Tennessee naturally flood more frequently than once per year. If new channel designs are based upon the untested assumption that natural channels typically flood once every 1.5 yr (e.g., TDEC, 2004), the resulting channel will be oversized compared with extant, relatively unmodified streams of West Tennessee. Economic losses will occur if expensively restored channels become occluded by high sediment loads from headwater erosion and upstream canal-bank adjustment (e.g., Simon, 1989a, 1989b), and flow impairment from large wood accumulations and beaver dams. Single-thread river-restoration projects in low-gradient valleys will have a greater chance of success if sited in the sediment shadow of a valley plug.

Challenges remain in local and regional restoration efforts. State-sanctioned stream-mitigation policy (TDEC, 2004), as actualized in the Tennessee Stream Mitigation Program (TSMP, 2007), does not include enhancement or conservation of valley-plug systems or augmentation of self-restoration conditions associated with extant historic meanders. Thus, a number of large-scale, potentially high-impact and low-cost restoration opportunities are receiving little attention. Because remnant historic channels pose opportunities for low-effort, low-risk restoration, there is a need for more detailed channel-evolution models for avulsed canals (e.g., Happ et al., 1940). A practical approach would be to observe how rivers are naturally recovering, and to accelerate those processes using appropriate scales of technology (handsaws, track-hoe, explosive charges, etc.). Policies that encourage the augmentation of natural stream recovery may offer the lowest cost, lowest risk restoration opportunities available, because natural processes can do much of the work and maintenance. The best opportunities will be found where a canal is partially or completely occluded by sediment or woody debris, and assisted avulsion would result in the flow reoccupying historic channels (e.g., Figs. 8 and 9 and Middle Fork Forked Deer River at Law Road). Challenges with this approach include fixing the position of the avulsion channel in cases where upstream migration (e.g., Fig. 10) is undesirable, and sediment and large wood are a threat to the avulsion channel (e.g., Cypress Creek, McNairy County).

ACKNOWLEDGMENTS

We greatly appreciate the critical reviews and comments of William Wolfe (U.S. Geological Survey, Nashville) and Faith Fitzpatrick (U.S. Geological Survey, Wisconsin Water Science Center). We thank anonymous reviewer 3 for editorial comments. Warren Grabau was a leading scholar in the interplay of humanity and the landscape in this region; we gratefully acknowledge his input on those topics. Warren Grabau passed away on 8 December 2008. We thank Joey Woodard and Rob Bailey (Tennessee Stream Mitigation Program) for in-depth discussion, restoration-site access, and restoration-design parameters. Fieldwork to collect reference stream geometry was funded by the U.S. Environmental Protection Agency.

REFERENCES CITED

Ackers, P., and White, W.R., 1973, Sediment transport: New approach and analysis: American Society of Civil Engineers, Journal of the Hydraulics Division, v. 99, p. 2041–2060.

Arnwine, D.H., Broach, J.I., Cartwright, L.K., and Denton, G.M., 2000, Tennessee Ecoregion Project, 1994–1999: Nashville, Tennessee Department of Environment, Division of Water Pollution Control, 158 p.: http://www.state.tn.us/environment/wpc/publications/Eco region%20report%20for%20web.pdf (accessed 15 January 2008).

Ashley, G.H., 1910, Drainage problems in Tennessee: Tennessee Geological Survey Bulletin, v. 3-A, p. 5–15.

Brookes, A., 1988, Channelized Rivers: Perspectives for Environmental Management: New York, Wiley & Sons, 326 p.

CCWA (Carroll County Watershed Authority), 2000, Supporting documents for the proposed Carroll County Lake: Section 404, Army Corps of Engineers permit application, Office of the Memphis District Engineer, 4 sections, 6 attachments, 10 exhibits, various page numbers.

Cox, R.T., Van Arsdale, R.B., Harris, J.B., and Larsen, D., 2001, Neotectonics of the southeastern Reelfoot rift zone margin, central United States, and implications for regional strain accommodation: Geology, v. 29, p. 419–422, doi: 10.1130/0091-7613(2001)029<0419:NOTSRR>2.0.CO;2.

Crockett, D., 1834, A narrative of the life of David Crockett of the state of Tennessee: Philadelphia, E. L. Carey and A. Hart: http://ia331319.us.archive.org/3/items/narrativeoflifeo00crocrich/narrativeoflifeo00crocrich_djvu.txt (accessed 13 May 2008).

Csontos, R., Van Arsdale, R., Cox, R., and Waldron, B., 2008, Reelfoot rift and its impact on Quaternary deformation in the central Mississippi River valley: Geosphere, v. 4, p. 145–158, doi: 10.1130/GES00107.1.

Diehl, T.H., 1994, Causes and effects of valley plugs in West Tennessee, *in* Sale, M.J., and Wadlington, R.O., eds., Proceedings of Extended Abstracts, Symposium on Responses to Changing Multiple-Use Demands; New Directions for Water Resources Planning and Management: Nashville, American Water Resources Association, p. 97–100: http://tn.water.usgs.gov/pubs/plug_7b.html (accessed 27 January 2008).

Diehl, T.H., 1997, Channel evolution in Jarrell Bottoms, Tennessee, *in* Gangaware, T., LeQuire, E., Perry, K., and Cordy, T., eds., Proceedings, Extended Abstracts from Seventh Tennessee Water Resources Symposium: Nashville, American Water Resources Association, Tennessee Section, p. 267–268.

Diehl, T.H., 2000, Shoals and Valley Plugs in the Hatchie River Watershed: U.S. Geological Survey Water-Resources Investigations Report 00-4279, 8 p.

Doeing, B.J., Gaines, R.A., and Thomas, W.A., 1996, Restoration of abandoned meanders on the Middle Fork Forked Deer River, Tennessee: American Society of Civil Engineers, Proceedings, North American Water and Environment Congress & Destructive Water Conference, p. 3375–3380.

Dunne, T., and Leopold, L.B., 1978, Water in Environmental Planning: New York, W.H. Freeman, 818 p.

Emmett, W.W., 1975, The channels and waters of the upper Salmon River Area, Idaho: U.S. Geological Survey Professional Paper 870-A, p. 1–116 and i–viii.

Garrote, J., Cox, R.T., Swann, C., and Ellis, M., 2006, Tectonic geomorphology of the southeastern Mississippi Embayment in northern Mississippi, USA: Geological Society of America Bulletin, v. 118, p. 1160–1170, doi: 10.1130/B25721.1.

GIWC (Governor's Interagency Wetlands Committee), 1994, Tennessee Wetlands Conservation Strategy Report by Governor's Interagency Wetlands Committee: Nashville, Tennessee State Planning Office, no. 315133, 66 p.

Greene, D.C., and Wolfe, W.J., 2000, Superfund GIS—Geology of Tennessee [map, scale 1:250,000]: Nashville, U.S. Geological Survey: http://water.usgs.gov/GIS/metadata/usgswrd/XML/geo250k.xml (accessed 28 January 2008).

Happ, S.S., Rittenhouse, G., and Dobson, G.C., 1940, Some Principles of Accelerated Stream and Valley Sedimentation: Washington, D.C., U.S. Department of Agriculture, Technical Bulletin 695, 134 p.

Hardeman, W.D., 1966, Geologic Map of Tennessee: Tennessee Department of Environment and Conservation, Division of Geology, scale 1:250,000, 4 sheets.

Hey, R.D., 2006, Fluvial geomorphic methodology for natural stable channel design: Journal of the American Water Resources Association, v. 42, p. 357–374, doi: 10.1111/j.1752-1688.2006.tb03843.x.

Hidinger, L.L., and Morgan, A.E., 1912, Drainage problems of Wolf, Hatchie and South Fork of Forked Deer Rivers in West Tennessee, *in* The Resources of Tennessee: Tennessee Geological Survey, v. 2, p. 231–249.

Hilgard, E.W., 1860, Report on the Geology and Agriculture of the State of Mississippi: Jackson, E. Barksdale, State Printer, State of Mississippi, 391 p.

Houston, A.E., Pelton, M.R., and Henry, R., 1995, Beaver immigration into a control area: Southern Journal of Applied Forestry, v. 19, p. 127–130.

IAFWA, 1983, "SORG"—Stream Obstruction Removal Guidelines by the Stream Renovation Guidelines Committee of the Wildlife Society and American Fisheries Society: International Association of Fish and Wildlife Agencies, 8 p.

Johnson, J.W., 2007, Rivers under Siege: The Troubled Saga of West Tennessee's Wetlands: Knoxville, University of Tennessee Press, 239 p.

Leopold, L.B., and Maddock, T.M., Jr., 1953, The hydraulic geometry of stream channels and some physiographic implications: U.S. Geological Survey Professional Paper 252, p. 1–57.

Miller, R.A., 1974, The Geologic History of Tennessee: Tennessee Division of Geology, Bulletin 74, 63 p.

Miller, R.A., Hardeman, W.D., and Fullerton, D.S., 1966, Geologic Map of Tennessee, West Sheet: Tennessee Division of Geology, scale 1:250,000, 1 sheet.

Morgan, A.E., and McCrory, S.H., 1910, Preliminary report upon the drainage of the lands overflowed by the North and Middle Forks of the Forked Deer River and the Rutherford Fork of the Obion River in Gibson County, Tennessee: Tennessee State Geological Survey Bulletin, v. 3-B, p. 16–43.

Nairne, T., 1988, Nairne's Muskhogean Journals: The 1708 Expedition to the Mississippi River. Edited, with an introduction, by Alexander Moore: Jackson, University Press of Mississippi, 108 p.

Paine, A., 2007, Levee divides state agencies, TWRA dams up swamp despite regulators, denial: Nashville, The Tennessean Newspaper: http://www.tennessean.com/apps/pbcs.dll/article?AID=/20071110/NEWS0201/711100355 (accessed 26 January 2008).

Private Acts, 2004, Private Acts of Fayetteville County (revised edition), Tennessee County Technical Assistance Service: Nashville, University of Tennessee Institute for Public Service, 153 p.: http://www.ctas.utk.edu/public/CTASpriv.nsf/PrivateActs/96E5CB0DD39CFDF986256F950054A8ED/$FILE/FAYETTE+CO+-+2004+-+Updated+2006.pdf (accessed 26 January 2008).

Private Acts, 2007, Private Acts of Chester County (revised edition), Tennessee County Technical Assistance Service: Nashville, University of Tennessee Institute for Public Service, 153 p.: http://www.ctas.utk.edu/public/CTASprivnsf/PrivateActs/8F42DBBCF0FD0D4D862567760051B1A1/$FILE/CHESTER+CO+-+2007.pdf (accessed 26 January 2008).

Rosgen, D.L., 1994, A classification of natural rivers: CATENA, v. 22, p. 169–199, doi: 10.1016/0341-8162(94)90001-9.

Rosgen, D.L., 1997, A geomorphological approach to restoration of incised rivers, *in* Wang, S.S.Y., Langendoen, E.J., and Shields, F.D., Jr., eds., Proceedings of the Conference on Management of Landscapes Disturbed by Channel Incision: Oxford, University of Mississippi, p. 3–22.

Rosgen, D.L., 2006, Natural channel design using geomorphic principles: Proceedings, Federal Interagency Sedimentation Conference, 8th, Reno, Nevada, USA, p. 394–401.

Shields, F.D., Jr., Knight, S.S., and Cooper, C.M., 2000, Cyclic perturbation of lowland river channels and ecological response: Regulated Rivers: Research and Management, v. 16, p. 307–325, doi: 10.1002/1099-1646(200007/08)16:4<307::AID-RRR582>3.0.CO;2-2.

Simon, A., 1989a, The discharge of sediment in channelized alluvial streams: Water Resources Bulletin, v. 25, p. 1177–1188.

Simon, A., 1989b, A model of channel response in disturbed alluvial channels: Earth Surface Processes and Landforms, v. 14, p. 11–26, doi: 10.1002/esp.3290140103.

Simon, A., 1994, Gradation, Process and Channel Evolution in Modified West Tennessee Streams: Process, Response, and Form: U.S. Geological Survey Professional Paper 1470, 84 p.

Simon, A., and Robbins, C.H., 1987, Man-induced gradient adjustments of the South Fork Forked Deer River, West Tennessee: Environmental Geology and Water Sciences, v. 9, p. 109–118, doi: 10.1007/BF02449942.

Smith, D.P., 1999, Post-Channelization Stream Management of Cypress Creek, McNairy County: A Model for Watershed Management in Low-Gradient Rivers of West Tennessee: Tennessee Department of Environment and Conservation, West Tennessee River Basin Authority, 33 p.

Smith, D.P., 2007, Re-evaluation of proposed Canadian National Railroad Hatchie River Bridge modification, Rialto, TN—Tennessee Aquatic Resources Alteration permit Application NRS 96.667: Report prepared for the Tennessee Chapter of The Nature Conservancy, January 29, 2007, 14 p.

Smith, D.P., and Diehl, T.H., 2000, An example of river self-restoration?: Cypress Creek, McNairy County, TN: Proceedings, Annual Tennessee Water Resources Symposium, 10th, Nashville, p. 1C-13–1C-17.

Smith, D.P., and Diehl, T.H., 2002, Complex channel evolution in West Tennessee and northern Mississippi: Geological Society of America Abstracts with Programs, v. 34, no. 6, p. 104.

Smith, D.P., and Rosgen, D.L., 1998, Recommendations for river restoration and watershed management in West Tennessee: Technical report submitted to the Tennessee Environmental Policy Office, Tennessee Department of Environment and Conservation, 21 p.

Smith, D.P., and Turrini-Smith, L.A., 1999a, Western Tennessee fluvial geomorphic regional curves: U.S. Environmental Protection Agency, Water Management Division, Region IV, 41 p.

Smith, D.P., and Turrini-Smith, L.A., 1999b, Cross-sectional and planform geometry of selected, unmodified, low gradient rivers of western Tennessee: U.S. Environmental Protection Agency, Wetlands Section of Region IV, 7 p.

TDEC (Tennessee Department of Environment and Conservation Division of Water Pollution Control), Natural Resources Section, 2004, Stream Mitigation Guidelines for the State of Tennessee, 25 p.: http://www.tennessee.gov/environment/wpc/publications/StreamMitigationGuidelines.pdf (accessed 26 January 2008).

TDOT (Tennessee Department of Transportation), 1979–2004, Miscellaneous large-format black-and-white digital aerial photographs, various resolutions, photographed between 1979 and 2004: Tennessee Department of Transportation, Aeronautics Division, 607 Hangar Lane, Building 4219, Nashville, Tennessee 37217.

TN (Tennessee), 1994, Reformulation of the West Tennessee Tributaries Project, report presented to the U.S. Army Corps of Engineers by the State of Tennessee: Nashville, Tennessee State Planning Office, no. 315134, 62 p.

TSMP (Tennessee Stream Mitigation Program), 2007, Tennessee Stream Mitigation Program: http://tsmp.us/TSMP/Home.html (accessed 24 November 2007).

Turrini-Smith, L.A., Smith, D.P., and Diehl, T.H., 2000, Development of western Tennessee fluvial geomorphic regional curves: Proceedings, Annual Tennessee Water Resources Symposium, 10th, Nashville, p. 1C-1–1C-9.

USACE (U.S. Army Corps of Engineers), 1996, West Tennessee tributaries project limited reevaluation report: U.S. Army Corps of Engineers, Memphis District, 46 p. and numerous unlabeled appended sections.

USCA (U.S. Court of Appeal), 2007, National Ecological Foundation, et al. v. Clifford Alexander (Secretary of the Army) et al.: United States Court of Appeal for Sixth Circuit: http://altlaw.org/v1/cases/181269 (accessed 26 January 2008).

USGS (U.S. Geological Survey), 2008, Web-based black-and-white orthoquad server: http://terraserver-usa.com/ (accessed 18 May 2008).

Votteler, T.H., and Muir, T.A., 1996, Wetland protection legislation, *in* Fretwell, J.D., Williams, J.S., and Redman, P.J., eds., National Water Summary on Wetland Resources: U.S. Geological Survey Water Supply Paper 2425: http://water.usgs.gov/nwsum/WSP2425/legislation.html (accessed 18 May 2008).

Wohl, E., and Merritts, D.J., 2007, What is a natural river?: Geography Compass, v. 1, p. 871–900, doi: 10.1111/j.1749-8198.2007.00049.x.

Wolfe, W.J., 1994, Human and natural influences on channel conditions along the Wolf River, West Tennessee, *in* Sale, M.J., and Wadlington, R.O., eds., Proceedings of Extended Abstracts: American Water Resources Association, Symposium on Responses to Changing Multiple-Use Demands; New Directions for Water Resources Planning and Management, Nashville, p. 91–92.

MANUSCRIPT ACCEPTED BY THE SOCIETY 15 SEPTEMBER 2008

Index

Note: Page numbers with "f" and "t" indicate material in figures and tables, respectively.

About the Contributors

This volume resulted from the concerted writing and research efforts of a large group of people. Fifty-four authors and editors contributed to the chapters in this book.

Chiara Audisio is a research assistant at the Institute for Geohydrological Protection of the National Research Council (Torino, Italy). Her research interests include fluvial geomorphology, debris flows, GIS, and applied geomorphology (flood and landslide risk).

Patrick Belmont is a postdoctoral research associate with the National Center for Earth-surface Dynamics at the University of Minnesota. His research integrates geomorphology and aquatic ecology.

Chance J. Bitner is a hydraulic engineer with the U.S. Army Corps of Engineers, Kansas City District. His background is in surface-water hydraulics and sediment transport, with an emphasis on operation and maintenance of the navigation channel and aquatic habitat restoration in the Missouri River.

Dale W. Blevins is a supervisory hydrologist with the U.S. Geological Survey in the Kansas City office of the Missouri Water Science Center. His background is in water quality and surface-water hydrology with an emphasis on large rivers and riparian wetlands.

Joseph P. Capesius graduated with a BA in geography from the University of Northern Iowa (1992) and an MA in geography from the University of Denver in 1996. He has worked for the USGS for 15 years in Indiana, Arizona, and Colorado conducting studies in surface-water hydrology, hydraulics, paleoflood hydrology, fluvial geomorphology, and streamflow statistics. He is currently serving as a supervisory hydrologist of the USGS Austin field unit in Austin, Texas.

Anne Chin is a courtesy professor of geography at the University of Oregon. Her research interests include the energetics of step-pool mountain streams, human impacts on landscape change, and river management and restoration. She is the recipient of the 2004 G.K. Gilbert Award for Excellence in Geomorphological Research from the Association of American Geographers (AAG). In 2006–2007, she served as chair of the Geomorphology Specialty Group of the AAG and director of the Geography and Regional Science Program of the National Science Foundation.

Zachary Croyle is a hydrologist with the U.S. Forest Service. He is also an MS candidate in coastal and watershed science and policy at California State University, Monterey Bay. His thesis research investigates the influence of upland groundwater use on tributary baseflows within the Carmel River watershed in Monterey County, California.

Stephanie S. Day is a graduate student in the geology and geophysics department at the University of Minnesota as well part of the National Center of Earth-surface Dynamics. Her research focuses on the development of ravine systems and the role of bluffs and ravines on sediment loading in the Le Sueur River.

Timothy H. Diehl is a hydrologist in the Tennessee District office of the U.S. Geological Survey. He has research interests in fluvial systems, valley sedimentation, channel meandering, flood hydrology, and woody debris.

Dena Egenhoff is a graduate student in the geosciences department at Colorado State University. Her research focuses on surface-subsurface hydrological linkages at the Pawnee National Grasslands in Colorado.

John G. Elliott graduated with a BS in economics from the University of Missouri, Columbia, (1973) and an MS in geomorphology from Colorado State University (1979). He has been a research hydrologist and geomorphologist with the U.S. Geological Survey Colorado Water Science Center (USGS CWSC) since 1978 where he holds the position of sediment specialist. He has been project leader of the USGS Reconfigured-Channel Monitoring and Assessment Program and numerous other studies. He has conducted research on hillslope erosion and sediment yields in Mancos Shale badlands in western Colorado, studies of river channel stability and sediment transport, debris flows in canyon rivers, and arroyo formation. Other studies have investigated erosion at reclaimed surface mines and in wildland fire areas. He is the author or co-author of over 36 professional reports, journal articles, and book chapters.

Faith A. Fitzpatrick is a research hydrologist with the U.S. Geological Survey, Wisconsin Water Science Center, Middleton, Wisconsin. She has a PhD in geography from the University of Wisconsin, Madison, and 20 years research experience focused on hydrogeomorphic responses of streams to human disturbance and large floods, with emphasis on historical geomorphic processes in the upper Great Lakes and Upper Mississippi River systems. Her research applications include aquatic habitat assessment, dam removal, and restoration evaluation. She is a member of the Geological Society of America, American

Water Resources Association, and the American Society of Civil Engineers. She has written numerous publications for journals and USGS report series and is an associate editor for the *Journal of American Water Resources Association.*

Joshua C. Galster is an assistant professor in surficial hydrology at Montclair State University, Montclair, New Jersey, where he has been since 2007. His interests include fluvial geomorphology, climate change/land-use change and their impacts on watersheds, using historic aerial photographs and GIS to quantify river changes, and other watershed-scale studies.

Subhajit Ghoshal is working on his doctorate at the University of South Carolina. His dissertation is focused on using high-resolution cartographic and topographic data for developing sediment budgets and measuring channel changes in the lower Yuba and Feather Rivers, California. His research applies remote-sensing techniques to fluvial geomorphology.

Karen B. Gran is a fluvial geomorphologist in the geological sciences department at the University of Minnesota, Duluth. Her research interests include fluvial processes and sediment transport, disturbed systems, volcanic geomorphology, and interactions between physical landscapes and ecological systems.

İnci Güneralp is assistant professor of geography at Texas A&M University, where she has been since 2008. She is a fluvial geomorphologist whose research interests include meandering river morphodynamics. She has participated in watershed-scale ecosystem restoration and urban stream naturalization studies.

Cliff R. Hupp was a student of the late John T. Hack at the George Washington University, where he received his doctorate in 1984. He has investigated riparian vegetation ecology in relation to fluvial landforms and processes for 30 years. Additional research includes studies on channel evolution, floodplain processes and forms, sedimentation dynamics, and carbon sequestration in riparian ecosystems in the United States and Western Europe. He has been employed by the U.S. Geological Survey since 1978 where he is research project chief of the Vegetation and Hydrogeomorphology Relations Project. Dr. Hupp is the 1993 recipient of the Ecological Society of America W.C. Cooper Award for outstanding research in physiographic ecology. He received the U.S. Department of Interior Superior Service Award in 2006. He has served on the editorial boards for the Ecological Society of America journals *Ecology* and *Ecological Monographs* since 1999.

Robert B. Jacobson is a research hydrologist with the U.S. Geological Survey, Columbia Environmental Research Center, Columbia, Missouri. His background is in geomorphology and surficial processes, and his research focus is on interdisciplinary approaches to understanding habitat dynamics in large rivers.

L. Allan James is a fluvial geomorphologist with allied interests in flood hydrology, human impacts on river systems, and river management. He is a professor of geography at the University of South Carolina and director of the BioGeomorphology laboratory. He has served as chair of the Geomorphology and Water Resources Specialty Groups (Association of American Geographers) and as a panelist for the Quaternary Geology

and Geomorphology Division of GSA. He is on the editorial boards of *Geomorphology* and *The Southeastern Geographer.*

Carrie Jennings is a glacial geologist at the Minnesota Geological Survey with a background in glaciology and geomorphology and an interest in process. She is interested in how glaciers respond to a variety of forces, how that affects the final sediment record in Minnesota, and how this helps us predict the behavior of modern ice sheets. She is also interested in how the distribution of glacial sediment in Minnesota affects the distribution and quality of resources including surface and ground water.

Andrea Johnson is a graduate student in the geological sciences department at the University of Minnesota, Duluth. Her research focuses on floodplain and terrace history in incising systems.

Heather A.L. Knight has been a project director for The Nature Conservancy in northern Colorado since 1994. Heather's specialty is community-based conservation and working with diverse human communities, both public and private, to find creative solutions to conservation challenges.

James C. Knox is Evjue-Bascom Professor-at-Large at the University of Wisconsin, Madison, and research associate of the Wisconsin Geological and Natural History Survey. His teaching and research interests emphasize fluvial geomorphology and Quaternary geomorphology, especially in the context of how natural and human-related environmental changes impact floods, erosion, sedimentation, river morphology, and landscape evolution. His current research is focused on floods and fluvial history of the upper Mississippi River. He received the Mel Marcus Distinguished Career Award from the Geomorphology Specialty Group of the Association of American Geographers (AAG) in 2001, the Easterbook Distinguished Scientist Award from the Quaternary Geology and Geomorphology Division of the Geological Society of America in 2006, and the Presidential Achievement Award from the AAG in 2007.

Kelly Larkin is a fishery biologist with the Arapaho-Roosevelt National Forest in Colorado. She has BS and MS degrees in natural resource management from Colorado State University.

Jason Maas-Baldwin received his master's degree from the Division of Science and Environmental Policy at California State University, Monterey Bay. His thesis research was a project for the California Department of Water Resources attempting to quantify the success of urban stream restoration projects in Central California. In the past, he has led fundraising efforts to conserve important Pacific slope watersheds in northern Costa Rica. He hopes to continue conducting riverine systems research and promoting community watershed awareness.

Mary Ann Madej is a research geologist with the U.S. Geological Survey Western Ecological Research Center, and project leader of the Redwood Field Station in Arcata, California. She has a PhD in geosciences from Oregon State University. May Ann's interests cover a range of geomorphic topics: slope stability analysis, stream temperature monitoring and modeling, and assessing the effectiveness of watershed restoration